'... a textbook exam[ple...] public figure and a fascina[ting...] of not ju[...]'
Herald Sun

'*Jonestown* is a sad, often empathetic, portrait of a successful but deeply flawed individual.'
Bridget Griffen-Foley, *Sydney Morning Herald*

'The aim of *Jonestown* is to take Jones seriously as a person and as a broadcaster, so as to begin a serious debate about the nexus between politics and the media in Australia ... [it] is an important contribution to that debate.'
Matthew Ricketson, *The Age*

'*Jonestown* is a fascinating account of a man who, by rights, should not play such a prominent role in NSW and turns the spotlight on those who wrongly thought they could use him when all the while he was using them.'
Sun Herald

'Masters' account of the abuse of political power is startling.'
Mike Carlton, *Sydney Morning Herald*

'Chris Masters has done extensive research and the result is a compelling story of the rise and rise of Alan Jones.'
Newcastle Herald

'... an extraordinarily well-written, well-researched biography.'
Illawarra Mercury

CHRIS MASTERS
JONES TOWN

THE POWER AND THE MYTH OF ALAN JONES

ALLEN&UNWIN

First published in 2006
This paperback edition published in 2007

Copyright © Chris Masters 2006

All rights reserved. No part of this book may be reproduced or transmitted in any form or by any means, electronic or mechanical, including photocopying, recording or by any information storage and retrieval system, without prior permission in writing from the publisher. The *Australian Copyright Act 1968* (the Act) allows a maximum of one chapter or 10 per cent of this book, whichever is the greater, to be photocopied by any educational institution for its educational purposes provided that the educational institution (or body that administers it) has given a remuneration notice to Copyright Agency Limited (CAL) under the Act.

Allen & Unwin
83 Alexander Street
Crows Nest NSW 2065 Australia
Phone: (61 2) 8425 0100
Fax: (61 2) 9906 2218
E-mail: info@allenandunwin.com
Web: www.allenandunwin.com

National Library of Australia
Cataloguing-in-Publication entry:

Masters, Chris, 1948– .
Jonestown: the power and the myth of Alan Jones.

Includes index.
ISBN 978 1 74175 156 7 (hb).
ISBN 978 1 74175 320 2 (pb).

1. Jones, Alan, 1943–. 2. Radio broadcasters – New South Wales – Sydney – Biography. 3. Rugby football coaches – Australia – Biography. 4. Speechwriters – Australia – Biography. I. Title.

791.443

Set in 10 on 12.5pt Sabon
Printed by McPherson's Printing Group

10 9 8 7 6 5 4 3 2 1

To my father Charlie (1914–1988)

Teaching us still

CONTENTS

Reporting on Alan ix

PART 1   THE MAGIC
1   Son of the Earth 3
2   'Big Al' 21
3   The Birthday Boy 35
4   Riding in Cars with Boys 47
5   Among Kings 68
6   Citizen Jones 100
7   Wearing the Green and Gold 133
8   My Team 157
9   Watershed 185

PART 2   THE MYTH
10   From Pedagogue to Demagogue 209
11   Dictators and Tigers 229
12   Runs on the Board 254
13   The Godfather 270
14   Pick and Stick 302
15   A Veritable Tsunami 338
16   Money for Nothing 380
17   The Emperor's New Clothes 401
18   The Misinformation Revolution 441

Afterword: The Cringe Factor 459
Endnotes 470
Acknowledgements 504
Index 507

REPORTING ON ALAN

I STILL THINK OF THE UNOFFICIAL 'swearing in' of prospective New South Wales Police Minister Michael Costa at Alan Jones' home in November 2001 as dumbfounding. New South Wales Premier Bob Carr must have known it was stupid. Carr had scant respect for Jones, and Carr's advisors had even less respect for the broadcaster's advisors, also assembled.

Successive administrations in New South Wales had learned to treat policing as an unexploded bomb, so for Carr to surrender reason and bargain with a sensitive portfolio says a lot about the power of Alan Jones. The episode is even more remarkable when you consider the timing and Jones' reputation. The preceding year Australian Broadcasting Authority findings had seriously challenged Jones' honesty and integrity.

The episode raises important questions. What does it say about my own industry that a man succeeds despite—or even because of—dishonesty? And what does it say about the rest of us who allow him so much power? In November 2001, with a future *Four Corners* program in mind, I began asking questions about Alan Jones. Within days his own question bounced back to me through the canyons of Sydney: 'Does he think I'm a cunt?'

Above the din of Australia's largest city the tattle lifts and settles. The rules of all jungles require reliable intelligence on the disposition of the enemy. In Jonestown Alan has constructed his own world, where particular attention is paid to understanding boundaries between allies and enemies. When he asked 'Does he think I'm a cunt?' he wanted to know where I stood.

At the time I knew he had been a teacher, a political speechwriter and rugby coach before becoming a famous broadcaster. I had heard some of the whispers that had been circulating for decades about his ongoing bachelor status. But before 2001 I had no particular interest in Alan Jones, which makes the last few years of intensive investigation surprising, even to me.

From the start, listening to his radio program, I understood there was a lot worth learning. Alan Jones breaches many conventions about what works on radio. He does not run away from 'feel bad' subjects, championing causes such as care for the disabled and respect for victims of mental illness. While the national attention span ever narrows, Alan runs uninterrupted interviews in prime time for 15 minutes and more. In Australia's largest radio market he has dominated ratings for 15 years. His power, whether real or perceived, has all manner of princes and premiers bowing before him.

The more telephone calls I made the more his power intrigued and worried me. While I was not going to waste concern on quivering politicians, it seemed unhealthy for ordinary people, even his friends, to be so frightened of Alan. As they routinely sought permission before speaking to me, I saw that Jones was not just powerful, but controlling. And this was even more disturbing. Whereas I accept that people commonly feel discomfort about lack of control over their reputation, a world where reputations are controlled is far more frightening.

Two weeks after the notorious 'swearing in' of Michael Costa, I sat down with Alan Jones at the same address. My brother Roy had brokered the meeting at Jones' request. The two former football coaches were well acquainted. Indeed, Roy was one to pass on Jones' crudely expressed query about what I thought of him. The Alan Jones I sat down with on 30 November 2001 was courteous and composed. Conversation proceeded as through quicksand, his composure slipping just once, shifted by a short circuit spark of anger when I tried to make a point about police reform. Alan is not used to disagreement. The meeting trailed away and I slumped off, even more bothered.

My next engagement that day was a Friends of the ABC Christmas party. I am sure part of my unease stemmed from my sense that I was about to be drafted into a kind of Left versus Right, commercial versus public, culture war. When I mentioned at the gathering that I had just spoken to Alan Jones there was a rasp of scoffing, which brought no comfort. The ABC is supposed to exist for all Australians. The idea that my friends are Alan's enemies would be worrying if it were true.

I view the new ideological boundaries, like Jones' politics, as more complicated—indeed, all over the place. I came to understand that the politicians who most appeased him were from the New South Wales Labor Party and that while his strongest political allies are certainly Liberal, his strongest political enemies are also Liberal.

There was already too much ground to cover when I put my *Four Corners* television profile of Jones to air in 2002. In 20 years of making such programs I have never encountered a more diverse reaction. Viewers said they loved the program and loved Jones: 'a great insight into a great Australian'. They hated the program and hated Jones: 'Jonestown cowered before the biggest bully of them all'. They hated Jones and admired the program: 'It was pleasing to see the program expose the Jones myth'. They loved Jones and hated 'Jonestown': 'an appalling character assassination'.

Television has its limits. My own view was that a 45-minute program could never reach far below the surface, so I kept on going, on a marathon postscript that turned into this book. It is bigger than expected because I had not realised what a long life a sleep-deprived Alan has led.

Over time I thought of Alan Jones as leading seven lives—not one of them his own. Read on and you will meet them all. There is the blokey, foul-mouthed ex-football coach; the courtly, non-swearing charmer of older women; the farmer's (miner's/union official's/teacher's) son; the thwarted prime minister; the ombudsman of Struggle Street; the Oxford orator; and the hidden homosexual, forever hunting for love among the twentysomethings.

My investigation will go too far for some, particularly Alan Jones, but I could not avoid the elephant in the room. I am not alone in observing that Alan Jones appears to be homosexual. I can't see why homosexuality should be shameful, and I don't see why it is easier to smirk about it than speak about it. The masking of his apparent homosexuality is a defining feature of the Jones persona.

Jones' apparent self-belief that, on the one hand, he is damaged and, on the other hand, special goes a long way to explaining an unusual personality. It informs consistently curious behaviour, his private self frequently intruding on the public self. Alan Jones' impassioned attacks on some and defence of others often appear to have some grounding in perceived or real emotional connections to some of the parties. There are plenty of examples of Alan using his power to get closer to the young heterosexual males he appears to favour. There are also examples in his teaching, coaching and broadcasting of personal attitudes influencing public behaviour—for example, his lifelong habit of playing favourites. While I accept Alan Jones has a similar right to privacy as the rest of us, I came to the view that there is nothing honourable about his concealment of his sexuality. The lie that Alan Jones maintains is, I am sure, more for the sake of preserving a dishonest power base than it is about protecting personal privacy.

This book also challenges the notion that Jones is a prime protector of the interests of his self-proclaimed 'Struggle Street'. In doing so it goes beyond a profile of a flawed human to a study of a flawed industry that has come to thrive in this new political landscape.

Alan Jones is a key player in the ongoing debate about whose interests are being served by the waning 'elitist' media. The success of Jones and other populist commentators is often seen as evidence that this 'quality' media, unwilling to waste skills on the unworthy, has been wrong-footed by an audience moving in its own direction.

Alan Jones' power base rises from a neglected constituency that politicians are keen to capture and Jones is seen to control. His wealth has also grown as a result of a keenness on the part of major corporations to buy some of that influence and market share.

My own research found little that is honourable in the way Alan Jones and his controllers exercise influence. What I came to see was politicians and corporations courting Jones because of his lack of scruples, and his audience for its vulnerability to propaganda.

Close examination of Alan Jones' attitude to giving his audience the facts, be it about Telstra, Optus, Labor or Liberal, reveals a fraud at work. There is a wealth of evidence to show Jones lies, flatters, dissembles and excludes. While he does work determinedly for his Struggle Street audience, by underpinning his power base they also work effectively for him.

Alan Jones has his own explanation for his running war with journalists such as myself. My explanation for the enmity is his disrespect for the neutrality of information—and his hypocrisy. Jones' emptiness, his fundamental lack of beliefs, means that, oddly, he can be both gullible and convincing. Whatever the idea, and however much it might contradict what he argued yesterday, Alan sounds like he believes.

I had only two face-to-face meetings with Jones. There was also some written communication, as I set about establishing a working arrangement. Alan Jones' employer, John Singleton, intervened, offering help. In the course of conversation he explained it would have been worth it to him to pay $100 000 for a recently completed biography of himself not to be written. A figure of $300 000 was mentioned as what might be paid for a biography undertaken with Jones' cooperation. I asked whether that would mean Alan assuming editorial control. John

Singleton said that that was something to sort out between Jones and myself. It was never sorted.

Before completing the final draft I telephoned and emailed Alan Jones, offering to discuss the contents of the book. His lawyer replied to my publisher, stating: 'As the book is now complete and about to be published this disingenuous offer by Mr Masters, obviously acting on legal advice, is a futile attempt to set up a legal defence for any material in the book defamatory of our client'. The initiative was my own and not as asserted a product of legal advice.

So this was written at a distance, missing, it is fair to say, some of the Alan in close-up that others can find likeable. Alan Jones' cooperation would obviously have led to a different book, although I am not convinced a necessarily more reliable one. Like the rest of us, Alan is no unassailable authority on his past. And I doubt that Alan was ever one for dialogue anyway. His radio career is like an extension of a lifelong monologue. For over three years I listened and learned as much and possibly more than would have emerged from a series of personal interviews. It could even be that he is at his most personal on air. One reason for his success is his way of treating his audience like family.

After those years of listening I can't count getting to know Alan as a cherished experience. In a way I felt sadder every day. Alan Jones admits the failure of his private life. What he does not admit is that the on air button is like a self-medicating device that separates him from the pain of his personal affairs. It is as if his morning radio show has become a means of functioning. I also felt sad for his family/audience. They will be the last to agree they deserve better.

As it turned out Alan Jones was not interviewed for this book. If an agreement had been brokered, I would have interviewed him. Even then I am not confident my questions could have reached behind his many masks, laid out alongside the silk ties and handkerchiefs. But a bonanza of correspondence did help me reach further. As Jones watchers know, Alan generates a lot of mail. Wading through it seemed at times like an interview with the inner selves. The correspondence, dealt with in a later chapter, is revealing of Alan Jones' endeavours as both broadcaster and activist. Again, the letters do not tell all but are revealing nonetheless.

In the end a study of what has made Alan Jones successful and powerful is worth it, for allies and enemies alike. What the big picture reveals is a recurring pattern of behaviour that should help answer a recurring question about Alan: is he worth the price?

Alan Jones is often said to be complex and chameleon-like. What I find most interesting is his way of forcing others to show their colours. Believe him and you are touched by the magic. Disbelieve him and you recoil from the myth.

PART 1
THE MAGIC

CHAPTER 1
SON OF THE EARTH

ALAN JONES IS AN ANGRY MAN. The rages explode without warning like terrorist bombs. There are many moments when he detonates in sudden fury before production staff, hotel receptionists, chauffeurs and airport clerks. Seething and manic, it is as if competing personalities join forces, egging each other on. Jones the motivator inspires himself to greater fury.

The rages are sometimes caught on tape when an interview displeases. A slow burn erupts into uncontrolled wrath: 'You are scumbag guttersnipe stuff ... what a joke ... just a moment, you are in my office'. Up and down from his chair, pacing, pouting, glasses on and glasses off, discharging the inner fury. 'Just shut up for a moment and listen. I'm half minded to grab you and ram you against the wall. You absolute scumbag ...'[1] When friends are caught in the middle or on the sidelines, they stare mute and aghast, wondering how this anger builds. After witnessing withering attacks some vow to forever keep their distance.

When Alan Jones loses members of his loyal audience it can be for a similar reason. They tire of the harping. Between 5.30 and 10.00 am, as the sun rises over Sydney and the airport noise curfew lifts, Alan shrills, whines and roars like the arriving aircraft, venting his irritation, agitation and anger at all who continue to so wilfully disappoint. 'The Primary Industry Minister John Anderson is still suffering from a serious kick in the head. Some cow must have got onto him.'[2] 'It is clear Police Commissioner Peter Ryan is no longer capable of doing his job.'[3] 'Carl Scully's political career is vanishing in front of him. He has only himself to blame.'[4] 'That Amanda Vanstone could not run a pigsty.'[5]

Australia's loudest voice in commercial radio is rich, famous and at war with his own life. His anger reaches beyond the common story of a man unfulfilled by personal fortune. He was cheated well before he began to accumulate all that material wealth. Alan Jones' anger goes back to the beginning.

Alan Jones was born on 13 April, while World War II raged. The year of his birth, dealt with in a later chapter, remains a mystery even to friends. His place of birth is better known. The multimillionaire broadcaster anchors his battler's credentials on a humble start at Acland, in southeast Queensland. Two hours west of Brisbane, Acland sees few tourists. Heading north along the Warrego Highway from Toowoomba to Dalby, drivers who blink would miss the turnoff to the tiny coalmining town. South of the town, on sparser pastures that begin to rise as the Darling Downs meet the Great Dividing Range, the Jones' family farm is even harder to find.

Sold up in 1968, nothing is left but rotting stumps to mark home and hearth for Charlie and Elizabeth Jones and their three children, Robert, Alan and Colleen. A neighbour, Max Kuhl, recalls a small cottage of no more than four rooms, with a hipped roof that gave it the look of a backwater schoolhouse. The bath, he says, was a little iron tub that was filled using buckets. In the 1940s running water and town electricity had not found their way onto the farms the locals knew as 'starvation blocks'.

Alan himself says, 'Everything comes from those formative years',[6] and certainly this unusual person does have an unusual and fractured past. Yarning on air with interviewer Michael Parkinson, Jones was quick to point out they were both the progeny of miners.[7] When he addressed a CFMEU rally in 2003 he proudly informed members his dad was a union official. To his audience and many of his bushie mates he is ever eager to explain that his extraordinary work ethic comes from his start as the son of a farmer. And it is all true enough: Alan Jones' free-ranging identity does have natural grounding. While he makes a practice of dressing the facts to suit the circumstance, his portrait of a tough beginning is accurate. Indeed, he may not know half the tears and torment leached into the foundations of his being.

The Acland farm was acquired by Alan's grandfather, John Thomas Jones, on Australia Day 1905. There were three blocks totalling 312 acres, with prospects for expansion given that John Jones had already married an influential neighbour's daughter. Twenty-three-year-old Mary Anne Brady, a fellow Catholic, became Mary Anne Jones on 3 May 1904 at nearby Jondaryan. Her parents, Charles and Margaret Brady, farmed the more substantial 'Erin Vale', opposite the Sugarloaf coalmine and almost adjoining the Jones holding. The Bradys, according to the all-powerful CS Abernethy, manager of the Bank of Australasia at nearby Oakey, were 'old and well known residents, upright of good character and hardworking'.[8]

Alan's father, Charles Thomas Jones, was born on 21 April 1906. Within the next seven years John and Mary had produced four more children: John Reginald, Clarence Joseph, Mary Elizabeth and Vincent. Another daughter appears to have died at birth. Acland public school records have Alan's dad starting his education in 1913 at nearby Lagoon Creek at the age of seven years and three months. His oldest son, Robert Jones, believed his father was orphaned at about this age. Alan Jones has also said his dad was an orphan: 'He had no money, no parents and no education. That's a reasonable trifecta isn't it.'[9]

A clue to a different fate for Grandad Jones emerges in a land transaction record of 30 July 1913: 'The Curator of Insanity is authorised to sell the within land belonging to the Estate of John Thomas Jones a person of unsound mind'.[10] It turns out John Jones did not die in 1913 although he did, in a sense, cease to exist. On 30 May that year John Jones was committed to an asylum for the insane in Toowoomba as patient number 147.

Two months later Mr Justice Chubb of the Queensland Supreme Court ordered the Curator of Insanity to sell up the three blocks of land as well as one plough, a dray, six cows and four horses.

The true story might have been lost forever but for records in the Queensland State Archive. From among them, like a page torn from Dickens, emerged the following tale. It began in the early months of 1913 when the local Acland police officer arrested Jack Jones, as he was better known, after he had threatened the life of a range of people, including his wife. Later, in a poignant letter to the Curator of Insanity, Mary Anne Jones gave an account of a tormented marriage. She said that following their wedding eight years earlier, she noticed her husband becoming 'strange in his actions'. The letter went on to describe his behaviour as having deteriorated to the point of it being 'almost unbearable': 'His nights were quite sleepless, he would wander about outside and imagine he was fighting policemen and different people and could see all kinds of images and animals and would come in and threaten and frighten myself and the children'.[11]

The letter also spoke about how her husband had allowed the farm to run down: 'For the last 3 years he has been most incapable of managing, making extraordinary bad deals in horses, cattle and sheep, untill [sic] his property is mortgaged to its full extent, up to date over £580 to the Bank of Australasia, Oakey'.

For what would appear these days to be a manageable illness, possibly schizophrenia, Jack Jones was given a life sentence. He was locked away in the Willowburn Asylum at Toowoomba, better known by the locals as 'The Nuthouse'. One month after his incarceration, patient 147 was described by the medical superintendent as 'able bodied and industrious but liable to breakdown under conditions of special stress'. In the opinion of the consulting doctor, Jack Jones would never recover. The presumption that Jones was incurably insane might have been influenced by the circumstance of a brother who, according to further correspondence, had been an inmate at Willowburn for the preceding ten years or more.[12]

After Jones was deemed insane, the Curator of Insanity assumed title and prepared to auction the farm. In the *Dalby Herald* of 23 August 1913 a headline spared no feelings, describing for sale: 'THE PROPERTY OF JOHN THOMAS JONES—(PATIENT)'. The 312 acres were said to be a good farm with improvements consisting of a new four-roomed weatherboard 'house lined and ceiled; Dairy, Yards, Cow Bails, Piggery, Barn', etc. Included were tanks, troughing and a good bore. CS Abernethy, manager of the Oakey bank that was owed £585/8/6, was anxious for a swift settlement as the paddocks were being overtaken by prickly pear.

The bank manager hoped for £1200 but the highest offer was only £685. Despite his insistence that he would not bid—the Bradys had been accused by a presumably paranoid Jones of 'in his bad turns ... endeavouring to steal his property'[13]—Charles Brady bought the farm for £1000, borrowing to do so. The plan was to have his sons take over for the sake of Mary Anne, who was thought to be 'entirely unfit to manage the place'.[14] Their widowed sister, who had four children and one on the way was, in her own words, in a 'helpless condition'.[15] The condition further deteriorated.

A year later Charles Brady paid out the bank and his son Charles Brady Junior took over the title. In that same year Mrs Margaret Brady became the guardian of newborn Vincent Jones. According to local memory, Mary Anne Jones then moved into Acland and her children were farmed out, mostly to the care of the Bradys. Five years later, on 12 September 1919, she died of acute appendicitis at the St Denis Hospital in Toowoomba.[16]

Alan Jones' dad, Charlie, was the oldest of five surviving children. Acland old-timers fondly remember Charlie, Clarrie and Vince as 'ordinary men who liked life'. Clarrie moved on to Brisbane and Vince to Toowoomba, where he would go into business with Charles Brady's brother, Jack, sinking dams in western Queensland. John Jones junior also moved to Toowoomba. Jack Brady's son, Gary, described him as 'a man of immense kindness and gentlemanly nature', and a regular churchgoer with 'never a bad word passed about others'.[17]

The only living daughter, Mary Elizabeth, lived with Charles and Margaret Brady, leaving Acland at the age of 24 to marry a farmer and settle at Roma. Alan's Aunt May, as she was better known, believed both parents died when she was young.

Alan Jones believes his grandmother died while giving birth to his father.[18] It is an odd belief considering the living presence of uncles and an aunt younger than his dad. That Grandad died when their dad was seven, though also untrue, does seem to have been accepted by Alan and his siblings. It's possible Charlie knew better: at the age of seven he was old enough to notice. His mother's account of the nightmare did speak of the children being frightened.

In small rural communities gossip dies hard, the whispers trailing people like mongrel dogs. Tolerance was not a feature of Australian provincial life at this time. Children with physical disabilities were put away. Homosexuals left town or learned to suppress their feelings. Children born out of wedlock endured lifelong shame. The stigma of mental illness unquestionably and unfairly left its mark on the Jones family. In Charlie's later years the pride he took in an honest and respectable reputation might suggest an awareness that there was a history to live down. Alan Jones' own championing of the cause of care for sufferers of mental illness is also noteworthy.

When the Willowburn Asylum wrote to the Bradys in 1927 to ask about relatives of John Thomas Jones, they were told little was known of his family. The medical superintendent duly wrote into the file of patient number 147: 'nothing is known of the whereabouts of relatives. It is many years since patient's relatives have communicated.'[19] His oldest son, Charlie Jones, was then living on the Brady property where he was soon to meet his future wife, 21-year-old Elizabeth Belford, who, on 1 June 1928, was appointed to the one-teacher school at nearby Sabine.

The rural gentry of the northern Darling Downs was more tolerant, if only marginally, of outsiders than they were of the mentally ill. Social apartheid separated the miners and the farmers, the Catholics and the Protestants, but generally, the racial profile was homogenous, families being drawn singularly from Europe and principally from Britain. The local Aboriginal tribe, the Jaoweir people, had long been moved on from the sickly yellow grasslands of the northern Downs.

The arrival of a newcomer, a forthright, opinionated woman travelling alone in her own small car, did turn heads, not all of them approving. Accommodation being scarce, Miss Belford was put up on the Brady farm, within walking distance of the school. Her signature can still be seen on the Sabine school attendance records. She was 'Beth' of the shining red hair and proud, bold nature that Alan inherited.

According to her son Robert, his mother's confidence bordered on arrogance. While her manner did not win everyone over, a woman of means as well as learning enhanced the community. As the Depression began to bite, the new teacher drew a reliable annual salary plus allowances of £195. In the class-conscious Darling Downs the Belfords also pulled a bit of rank. The extended clan located south of Toowoomba had larger properties than the smaller holdings around Acland.

The first Belford to settle on the Downs was Elizabeth's grandfather, James. Having emigrated from Ireland in the 1870s he made it to the Victorian goldfields before the luck ran out. James Belford took away enough gold to buy a small block outside Stanthorpe, just north of the New South Wales border and about 200 kilometres from Acland. A generation later a son, Richard Belford, married Elizabeth Osbaldeston, expanding the holding to over 1000 acres. Richard and Elizabeth were expansive in other ways, too, producing twelve children—four boys and eight girls. Two daughters inherited their mother's name. The first Elizabeth died in 1894 at the age of two. The second Elizabeth was the ninth-born.

Smart and proud, Elizabeth the second was placed in an Anglican girls' boarding school at Stanthorpe. Grandfather James Belford, to the chagrin of some of the family, doted on her and sister Freda, paying the St Catherine's boarding fees. According to Freda it was here that Lizzie, or Girlie as the family knew her, became Beth, to distinguish her from Sister Elizabeth, one of the teachers.

Freda says Elizabeth's first job was at the Sheahan pharmacy in Stanthorpe where, according to the family, she was asked to leave because she was not a Catholic. Then, in 1926, at the age of 20, she was appointed to the position of governess with a well-to-do family, the Maudsleys, at Goomeri, north of Kingaroy, where she is said to have improved her sense of culture. Freda's son Les Thompson, who is close to Alan in age, remembers the Victorian ways of the Belford women. When walking the Stanthorpe streets they would cross the road to avoid passing too close to the hotels.

In 1927 Elizabeth acquired her next job and an annual salary of £100 as an assistant teacher at Stanthorpe Public School. The following year she was promoted to the head teacher position at Sabine, a whistlestop away from Acland, the Bradys and Charlie Jones. Beth and Charlie began to be seen together partnering each other at local dances and in mixed doubles tennis competitions. Acland locals remember her as short and robust alongside a stooped Charlie, who appeared even smaller.

It turned out to be an interrupted courtship. In her four years at Sabine the mood turned increasingly against her. Beth was keen to continue teaching but by August 1932 she could find nowhere to stay. The local parents' committee ganged up, refusing to provide accommodation but making it clear they would do so for a different female teacher. The secretary of the Sabine school committee, William Harth, wrote to Queensland's Department of Public Instruction: 'There has arrisen [sic] recently a tendancy [sic] for all the committeemen and parents to be opposed to Miss Belford and for her interests and the school in general I would recommend a transfer at the Department's earliest convenience'.[20]

Effectively, the committee gave Beth the boot. While precise details are lost it is clear she had divided the community. As would be the case with her famous son, there were strong supporters among those she taught. Her son Robert remembers former students enthusing about her brilliance; his mum was a strong character who would tell her kids they could do anything.

But most of the parents saw little virtue in ideas that could not be put to use on the farm. The parents' committee made staying on impossible by offering Beth a room at the Acland Hotel, an address they knew was entirely unfit for a single woman. So before the 1932 school year ended, Beth took another job as assistant teacher at the Milford State School, back on the border. On 22 May 1933 she moved on again, teaching at the Blind and Deaf School in Brisbane, where she rose to the position of head teacher. Education Department records show her as a paid-up union member who by 1936 was earning an annual wage plus allowances of £255.

Giving up a secure and well-paid profession, most particularly at a time of economic crisis, was asking a lot. But there was something in the Downs that tugged like a magnet and on 12 July 1936 Beth Belford's resignation as a teacher became effective. The day before at St Luke's Anglican church in Toowoomba she had married Charles, the Education Department's rule of the day obliging her to give up a cherished occupation. The cherished income was lost, too, with responsibility for earning a wage falling substantially on her husband.

Social engineering of the time generated an absurd scenario, forcing an educated woman into a role she was not trained for. According to sister Freda, before coming to Acland Beth had never been near a cow or a kitchen stove. She was a good learner though. The new Mrs Jones first set up house in a shack on a neighbouring farm owned by the Chicken family. The plan was to buy back the farm lost to her husband's father 23 years earlier.

Three years later and one year after the birth of their first child, Robert Charles, they partially succeeded. On 21 December 1939, 154 acres of the Jones' farm, having been Brady property since 1913, became the Jones' farm again, albeit with help from the bank. This land constituted one of the three blocks that had formed Charlie Jones' father's original 312 acres. After Beth's cousin, Bill Belford, took over management of the Bank of New

South Wales at nearby Oakey, the mortgage was transferred to his bank.

According to Robert Jones and his Aunt Freda, Beth took on the running of the farm. 'You could not get a stronger woman than Beth', says neighbour Max Kuhl. She got up, did the milking, carted the water, fired up the stove, prepared the breakfast and got the kids off to school. Max recalls his own mother saying that Beth Jones, who 'never wore makeup or saw a hairdresser', went without a lot.

The smaller the farm, the harder it is to make a go of. When these tiny soldier-settler blocks were assigned, a cruel burden was heaped on future generations of farmers who would struggle, often hopelessly, for sustainability. Locals estimate that even then you needed at least 500 acres. The Jones 154 acres were carved from unpropitious low scrub country. There was little room to collect and store water. The configuration of the roads meant there was no shared fencing. Max Kuhl said it was, unluckily, also on a claypan, which meant barely five acres was up to growing feed.

Over the years Alan Jones has spoken of coming from a mixed dairy and wheat farm, which surprised locals, who have no memory of fields of rippling wheat. According to Alan: 'You played a role in the team. I mean, I'd be harvesting all night, driving the tractor into the early hours of the morning with the lights on and if the lights went off, I'd keep driving.'[21]

Robert Jones says they ran a herd of dairy cows, which did call for unremitting labour. While other kids took holidays the Jones kids, when at home, were up as early as half past three, in the cold and dark, herding around 30 jersey cows. There were pigs, too, with the temerity to regard themselves as family, invading the home along with the odd snake that had to be shooed from the beds. There was wood to cut and water to cart, but even then Alan saw purpose beyond the drudgery. 'I was always proud as a little kid that my father could rely on me. I'd be there, I'd go the distance ... I think I always felt there were things to be done ... and I suppose I was never satisfied with what I had done.'[22]

For all the hard labour there was good food to eat, fellowship and conversation, literature and music, and the trappings of refinement and ritual that persist into Alan's present-day routines. No matter what the workload, his mother would stop to prepare morning and afternoon tea. Cousin Les Thompson says his favourite aunt, Beth, became renowned for what she conjured from the wood-fired stove.

Alan Jones' own family portrait has his dad turning to mining in the 1950s to pay for the kids' secondary education. This is unlikely to be true as there is evidence to show that Charles and his brothers were already working in the mines. One neighbour, Col Viethar, thought the Jones boys had gone into coalmining straight out of school.

In the early 1940s mining was a reserved occupation so this and his age probably explain how Charlie missed World War II. He was employed not at Acland, but first at the Sugarloaf mine, and later at the nearby Woolooroo colliery, about a mile down the road and opposite the Brady farm. Alan also often speaks of his father being racked with arthritis, stretched out in pain on the kitchen table, a legacy of those long shifts shovelling coal in waist-deep water—although a local doctor thought Charlie Jones' stooped gait might also have been a consequence of mild polio.

In time he must have been liberated from the backbreaking work in the mines as he was later remembered as working in the office. His son Robert says his dad's natural aptitude for maths showed up when he figured out the company payroll in his head. There is no doubt about his union credentials. Records show a Charles Jones as a coal industry union delegate in 1945, well before Alan went to high school. His brother Clarrie was also an official at a different mine. There are those who recall the Jones brothers as being an irritant to their employers, with Charlie said to have his men out at the drop of a helmet.

Alan tells a different story: 'My father always had difficulties with the union movement. You see he left the farm to go and work in a mine in the 1950s when everyone was walking off their farms.' When asked in the same interview how his family voted, he said: 'I suppose they voted for the National Party. But I mean they voted for the local member. You know you met him at the pig and calf sales. It wasn't a political sort of thing.'[23] Conversely, according to his brother, the family's politics were 'Labor, Labor, Labor'. Robert Jones said Charlie's hero was another unpretentious and self-educated Australian, Labor Prime Minister Ben Chifley. He remembers copies of *The Worker* in the home.

The confusion about the genesis of Alan Jones' politics extends to a signature issue, drought relief. Alan acknowledges his 'Watering Australia' campaign as home-grown. 'My old man used to say, you'd think it would rain, wouldn't you, ten times a day.' He has spoken of being infected by his father's worry but calmed to a degree by the steadying words of his mother, who saw that the best way to deal with a problem was to work rather than worry. He has spoken about how drought takes your mind prisoner: 'you can never escape the legacy that it scorches upon your consciousness'.[24]

Whether, indeed, his mind was taken is one thing, but it is difficult to see drought as the culprit. The subtropical Darling Downs are not notably drought-prone. The average annual rainfall at the Acland Post Office between 1912 and 1993 was a decent 690 millimetres, an average that was maintained during Alan's time on the farm. In common with most of rural Australia, there are peaks and troughs. According to the Brisbane Bureau of Meteorology's monthly records, the 1950s, the period he identifies as having suffered 'the most awful drought', experienced higher than average rainfall. It is true that in 1957 the Acland rain gauge measured a low 375 millimetres, but a year earlier it had climbed to a bountiful 1035.2 millimetres.

While Jones effortlessly reconstructs the past to suit his present, his parents did the reverse. They were some of those magnificently selfless people who direct profit to their children ahead of themselves. While becoming a wife had stopped Beth Jones working as a teacher, becoming a mother gave her a new start. The Jones kids developed a reputation for being brainy;

peers were jealous of the assumed advantage gained from their teacher mum.

The children were first enrolled at Acland Primary. Robert Jones says they would ride their horse between home and school, coaxing the former showjumper over the fences; not all the kids managed to stay aboard. The horse would be left with a neighbour, Mrs Williams, until the bell sounded, after which they wolfed down a piece of cake and galloped for home. But when Beth Jones found herself at odds with the teaching methods of principal Ken McPherson, the children adopted a new routine. They would ride to the Sugarloaf siding and hop the Cooyar railmotor to a preferred school about 15 kilometres south at Oakey. The railway schedule was such that they arrived at least half an hour after the 9.30 am start, which meant an escape from the morning ritual of saluting the flag and the monotonous repetition of times tables.

Alan can be seen in the 1950 school photo, which means he had started at Oakey by Grade 3. The general recollection is that Alan either topped or came second in class exams. Former student David Stannard is one of many to say the seating order was arranged according to exam results, and 'Alan never had to shift his books'. Those at the top of the class were allowed to sit at the back of the room. Here, Alan alternated with the other top student, Helen Shrapnel. Classmates remember a kind of natural pairing. Helen and Alan became soul mates, frequently locked in conversation and once performing a duet at a school concert. Years later a young male friend of Jones' said Alan told him Helen (now deceased) was the only girl he had ever loved.

Classmate Margaret Weise says Alan was 'more gentlemanly and refined, articulate and polite to the teachers'. Her friend Joan Robertson said Alan preferred 'the more genteel side of life', remembering him arriving immaculately turned out in starched shorts, a neatly creased shirt, polished shoes and clean socks. The Jones kids were outfitted by a travelling provedore, Norm Hanna, who would sell clothing from the back of his truck.[25] With the help of the courteous Mr Hanna, Beth Jones found another way to defy poverty in the presentation of her children. Accordingly, he copped it from the other boys. Skinny little Alan—who walked as he talked, unhesitatingly, legs working like scissors, head held high—was shielded from the taunts by his mum's pride and a growing fund of self-confidence.

From his arrival at Oakey the boys called him 'Pansy', a nickname that stuck through his primary years. One of the boys said his dumbstruck reaction, decades later, was 'Fair dinkum?', when he learned that Jones had been appointed coach of the Wallabies. The Oakey boys and girls never saw Alan take an interest in rough and tumble sports.

The between class intervals of play lunch and big lunch presented difficulties for Alan to find separation from his barefoot tormentors. The school kept the boys and girls apart, the girls playing hopscotch and vigoro as the boys hunkered down over marbles. After school there was little opportunity to make friends as Alan usually had to rush for the railmotor home. When he did stay back there was sanctuary in the company of a male friend who was also a target of the bullies. Rodney Rush was something of a Dick Smith character, in love with crystal sets and model planes. When Alan had to wait for a later train he would shelter in Rodney's house, his senses overtaken for a time by the smell of balsawood and glue and the static of Rodney's chatter.

While Alan is not remembered as joining in the winter football matches, he could hold his own in summer, when cricket was played. But the best way to confront the sniping was on the school tennis court, where Alan first showed his capacity for high achievement.

Robert Jones said he and his younger brother would practise for hours, banging a tennis ball against the milking shed. Alan says an important turning point in his life was the acquisition of a tennis racquet. At the age of ten or eleven he came up with a plan: 'I am going to ask my father whether he will buy me a racquet, which was a very precocious thing to do. And I remember fully expecting him to say look, where do you think money comes from, do you think it grows on trees? And he was delighted when I asked, and he bought me a second-hand racquet, and we had a tennis court, and we sort of played on this and that was a factor in me becoming a player of some merit.'[26]

Alan's parents ended up doing a lot of miles in their black Ford Prefect to a patchwork of clay and ant bed courts spread across southeast Queensland. It was a pattern already established, as tennis was part of the social routine of the Downs. The nearby Kuhl family staged mixed doubles competitions on their homemade court; Beth Jones is remembered as a 'solid hitter with her own technique'. But Alan's genuine affection for sport more clearly comes from his father. Charlie and his brothers played soccer, the miners' code. Charlie was also an excellent cyclist, holding a record for the fastest time between Toowoomba and Brisbane. Uncle Vince was also a champion athlete and record holder for the 100 yards dash.

Just as clearly, Alan's love of the arts comes from his mum. His later students remember him frequently bursting into song and telling them how he used to practise in the back paddocks. With enthusiasm and feeling, Alan Jones told the ABC's Caroline Jones in a 1987 radio interview that Beth would play the piano and they would sing in the evenings (although sister Freda has no memory of a piano or of Beth ever having learned to play).

Church was one Sunday routine that appeared to bypass the Jones family. Perhaps the circumstances of their mixed marriage had soured Charlie and Beth. On Charlie's side, the Brady family were staunch Catholics, while some Belfords were known to never again speak to family members who married Catholics. If anything Alan kept to his mother's faith. He was later known to take regular communion at an Anglican church in Brisbane, but later still developed a reputation for perceived anti-Christian attitudes.

In her ABC interview Caroline Jones asked Alan whether he was a Christian. 'Well I was asked that when I went to primary school and I didn't know how to answer it because I didn't know enough.' Jones went on to say that he felt the judgement was more for others to make, so he had worked out a standard reply on the basis of advice he said came from his headmaster: 'I say to them that I am trying and God willing one day I will make it' (though on 2GB on 17 May 2005, he attributed this advice to his mother).

In the Jones household Sunday was a day for games and talking and sitting around the radio. It was also Beth's day. According to journalist David Leser, 'Every Sunday evening for half an hour as she read to him or they listened to opera on the radio, young Alan would brush her long, titian hair. It was their cherished weekly ritual.'[27]

The other half of the weekend was more for dad. And again, radio helped form a bond. Charlie Jones was known to sneak a bet with the local Oakey SP bookie. The excitement of listening in and willing his selections home had far-reaching effects on his equally enthusiastic middle child. Now with interests in as many as fifty racehorses, Alan has named one Stromberg Carlson, in homage to their bakelite radio. On his own show he explained that 'living so far west', it was his family's only form of entertainment.[28]

Alan's listeners have come to know Charlie Jones well. Hardly a week goes by without Alan referring with affection to his 'old man', a confirmed alter ego. It works well. Of the many Jones personas, Charlie is the most likeable. Around Acland he is remembered as a doer and a dreamer, with 'funny ways', a little Chaplinesque perhaps, with his straw hat, baggy pants and arthritic gait. And, like his son, he was full of homilies: 'If you are going to be a mechanic make sure you're the foreman'. 'You can't sell a Holden by rubbishing a Mercedes.' 'There are more ways of killing a cat than choking it with butter.' Alan has spoken amusingly about his father, cross at some indiscretion, saying to him: 'The next time I take you on a picnic you'll stay at home'.

Beth's cousin Barnie Belford puts it well. He said men with charm often turn out to be con men. In Charlie's case the opposite was true. Charlie was a great charmer and he was honest. Another neighbour, Ken Gordon, confirms that Charlie's old world courtesy and honesty defined him: 'Charlie was the type of bloke who, if you agreed to buy a heifer for five bob and someone later offered him more, he would forgo the extra profit and stick to the original deal'. When Tom Phillips bought the Jones farm in 1968, the vendor, obviously proud of his reputation as an honest man, told Tom that if anyone came looking for Charlie Jones saying money was owed, Tom should pay him and Charlie would settle up later. Tom says in the almost 40 intervening years no such person turned up.

In contrast to regular evocations of his old man, Alan speaks only occasionally of his mum. Maybe this is one subject where words fail him, or are unnecessary. Alan's tribute to his mother is part and parcel of him, it is visceral, personified in the man from birth. He is Alan Belford Jones. He honours her, too, by taking her maiden name for his company, Belford Productions.

I am not the first to see brother Robert as more like his unpretentious bushie dad, Robert Charles Jones, inheriting his dad's nature as well as his name. Alan is closer to his adored mother, who he nominates as the most influential person in his life. 'She was loving, scholastic and embodied everything that was good in people.'[29] 'She was smart, but she didn't ever imagine it was going to be easy.'[30] He told journalist Janise Beaumont that some of the credit for his own philosophies goes to his mother. 'We're all an amalgam of many ideas but she used to talk to me about these things in a Victorian and civilised way.' Jones said he took his mother for granted until he read in *King Lear* about the pain of having a thankless child.[31] When journalist Gerard Henderson asked about his family Alan said of his father: 'He just went along. He never had too many views about anything.' Henderson: 'The strong influence was your mother?' Jones: 'Totally, totally'.[32]

But in Alan's language, at least, there are traces of his father. 'Holy Nelly', 'God strike me', he says, and it is easy to picture them listening to the races on the crackling radio as dad rolled his smokes. A famous Alan party trick is a rendition of past Melbourne Cup calls. He is able to reel off verbatim races first heard in the electric atmosphere of that small family home over 50 years ago.

Listening in on air, I sometimes wonder whether the neighbourly spirit of the Downs has also found its way into the airwaves that reach Sydney's meaner streets. I have heard Alan talking to a distressed former Ansett employee whose husband was unable to find work. 'Well, let's get him a job then', said Alan, who wants his words to make a difference, and with the woman's baby crying in the background you hear him going to work on something other than broadcasting. The woman says: 'Thank you, Alan'. Alan says: 'You are most welcome', and I somehow hear Charlie. But when a talkback caller contemplating a wager asks for a tip and receives instead a gentle lecture—'Now don't you waste your money on gambling'—it is Beth I hear.

The alchemy in Jones' past has conjured a kind of magic that enables him to transform his personality in an instant. He is ashamed, he is proud. He is Mum, he is Dad. He is cultured, earthy, privileged and poor. 'When my mother and father bought a bunch of grapes we thought we were rich.'[33] While he proclaims a sparse, no pocket money, no Christmas present childhood, the picture of humble circumstances is relative. Others looking at the Joneses arriving at a school fete saw a tidily turned out family who could afford the toffee apples. Alan also talks of a home with fine china, a piano and tennis court, which does not suggest privation.

This magical ability to transform the past could also be turned on the future. Through a range of careers, Jones would have followers seeking his miracle touch. Within the Jones repertoire there would be subtle magic that changed the lives even of non-believers. There would be explosive magic that could make or break careers. Whether it is good or evil magic depends on where the spell falls.

CHAPTER 2
'BIG AL'

On 6 December 1952, what Alan Jones has described as Australia's only inland tornado flattened Acland. Jones has told his listeners how his dad warned him to let the dogs loose as the swirling wind tunnel approached, lifting a farm tank off its stand as it struck. Alan said he was 'about five or six' at the time.[1]

Alan Jones was a bit like that tornado, impossible to contain down home on the Acland farm. Most of Alan's classmates at Oakey Public finished school in what was known as Scholarship year, at about the age of fourteen. Waiting for them at the school gate was a pause before marriage, maybe a job at the farm or mine, an apron and boning knife at the abattoir or, for those who could wear a clean shirt and count, perhaps the bank. Further education was an option only for the privileged few.

Alan Jones completed Scholarship at Oakey in 1954 before taking this next step. He told Gerard Henderson: 'We went to boarding school and everyone thought we were silvertails. But if you didn't go to boarding school there was no school to go to. We were just too removed from anywhere.'[2]

Queensland had only 20 state high schools in the early 1950s, the nearest being 50 kilometres south at Toowoomba. It is Alan's mum who is said to have pushed for the kids to go instead to a private boarding school, which to many in Acland might have been as remote a prospect as going to the moon. Beth Jones would have had a strong, if ironic, belief in education as a liberator from poverty. According to cousin George Belford, she was adamant her kids go to a 'proper' school.

Toowoomba sits comfortably in the saddle of the Great Dividing Range. Queensland's largest inland city, with its oak trees, rose gardens and grand country mansions, is still an important education centre. The choice for the Jones boys was where some Belfords sent their boys, Toowoomba Grammar School, which was able to advertise itself as 'One of the Nine Great Public Schools of Queensland'.

In Toowoomba there were also known relatives who could ease some of the pain of lonely weekends. Robert and his younger brother would roll up on their pushbikes at cousin Merle Ball's home for Sunday lunch. Merle often tucked homemade biscuits and chocolate cake into their bags, to be smuggled back to the dormitory. Brisbane solicitor Bill Stubbs' most enduring memory of Toowoomba Grammar is the 'absolutely shocking, gaolable food'. The yearning for a decent meal was a strong enough force to overcome the boarders' low regard for dayboys, whose parents might invite them home. In later years Alan became known for his regular visits to the homes of generous mothers.

Alan Belford Jones is proud of his time at Toowoomba Grammar, honouring it as another defining period. Here, Jones grappled with a hurricane swirl of pressures to be successful and accepted. With instructions from his mother to become involved and belong, a slight, effeminate Alan was soon projected into one of the toughest boarding schools in the land. At Grammar, cadets and rugby were as much as compulsory. The school, jostling with the raw-boned sons of Queensland graziers, even gave prizes for manliness. As in many such boarding schools acute maleness merged with the conventional confusion of adolescence to form an environment that, paradoxically, scorned and sustained homosexuality. Throughout Alan's high school years and beyond, the often traumatic spectacle of the various

Joneses trying to get on with one another is all too obvious. Over the next four years a curious metamorphosis of a very gay male in a very straight jacket occurred. His high school years also turned the boy into the bully.

Older brother Robert was the first to arrive, in 1953. He was a bike ride across town from Willowburn Asylum where Grandfather Jones had spent the last 40 years. Unbeknown to the Jones boys this melancholy chapter in their family history concluded on 3 July that year, when John Thomas Jones died of a cerebral haemorrhage, arteriosclerosis and senility. His death certificate notes that the passing was witnessed by two trainees, and that patient number 147/13 was buried as an 'Indigent'.

For Robert it was a bitter first night away. The school had its own *Lord of the Flies* initiations. Newcomers—or 'squirts', as they were called—were subjected to the 'crow-peck': a thump with a knuckle on the middle of the skull. The more malevolent boys employed a brutal variation, which brought the knee up under the chin as the fist whacked the head. Solicitor Les Thompson, a Jones cousin, joked about adding ten per cent to the bills of old boys for the crow-pecks they gave him. Alan would later comment: 'Bullying is mongrel behaviour. It's awful stuff and we've all had it.'[3] In 1955, two years after Robert, Alan Jones arrived at Toowoomba Grammar as one of 156 boarders. He later told columnist Miranda Devine that he was ten at the time.[4] One of his first impressions was the shock of the stink from the kitchen. Alan remembers something resembling sausages being slopped before him: 'I never saw anything like it call itself food'.[5]

In the same intake was Rodney Rush, a fellow victim of the bullies back at Oakey. Rush recalls Alan's new nickname, drawn from a popular song of the day, 'The Jones Boy', as being an improvement at least on the pansy jeer that had stuck through primary school. Like Alan, Rodney was again a sitting duck for the squirt bashing, both of them being slight. Rush says neither of them could fight back: 'You just took it, or did your best to avoid it'. Jim Priebe, who also caught the railmotor south, and who started Grammar the previous year, felt a duty to protect kids from his district. Priebe thought Alan was targeted because 'if you didn't play football you got heaps, and he didn't play football'.

A constant trial for the squirts was running a gauntlet through the large dormitory to and from the bathroom. The bigger boys would swing at trembling victims with spiked shoes and cricket bats. The squirts were used to clean sandshoes, make the beds and warm the lavatory seats for older boys. Les Thompson says he still carries a mental image of younger boys standing at the sink crying as they washed their tormentors' jockstraps and football socks.

There are mixed feelings about the bullying. Jim Priebe remembers the school's reputation in those days for boarders shooting through, and former students refusing to send their own kids there. But he also feels that if you could handle it, you were equipped for life. Rodney Rush, who at term break would limp home a mess of scratches and bruises, is still angry at the way the school staff tolerated the ritual bastardisation.

Robert Jones, older and more physically robust than Alan, thought he did not handle the bullying as well as his younger brother. Jim Priebe agrees. Alan's cockiness and the sting of his tongue partly compensated for a lack of brute strength. Jones might also have received some protection from the man he counts as the next most influential figure after his mother. The headmaster for most of Alan's time at Grammar, Len 'Pud' Heenan, was, like many of his colleagues, an ex-serviceman. There is a telling account of the former RAAF instructor's dynamic teaching style in the school's official history. When Heenan asked a question in class he would not accept 'I don't know' for an answer. 'Don't say I don't know, say purple cow, say anything but don't say I don't know, sir.' So in answer to a question the boys would often say 'purple cow, sir'. Heenan would reply, 'No, boy, sit down', and the lesson would proceed.[6]

Heenan became an influential model for Alan Jones' later teaching career. 'A remarkable teacher. I am an unapologetic Heenan supporter. He brought rigour and discipline and scholarship and expectations to the school.'[7] As would later be the case with Alan, there are polarised views about Heenan. Some saw the headmaster as a civilising force who attempted to turn back the culture of bastardisation and fulfil the role of father figure to boarders such as Jones. Others thought he played favourites with the smart and gifted. Indeed, a few thought Heenan, who coached Jones in tennis, treated his star player like a pet. This counterview has Heenan as a tyrant in his treatment of those who did not fit his vision of meritocracy. Alan's cousin Les Thompson remembers him 'belting the shit out of some of the kids', going berserk with the cane to a point where he wondered whether the headmaster was losing his mind. A high proportion of teachers, fresh from the war, seemed to hold to a parade ground view that the occasional thrashing might break a few but would turn the majority into men.

The school's deputy principal, Edgar 'Bluey' White, a Shakespeare and Milton scholar and a New Guinea veteran, did not warm to Jones as much as Heenan did. Bluey's son, Brian White, and Alan Jones developed an instant rivalry. One of Brian's early memories is of a precocious Jones standing at the front of the class writing on the blackboard, exclaiming: 'I could be a teacher'. Young Brian thought him 'not a pleasant sort of bloke'.

However, White was also one of many to acknowledge that the show-off up the front did have something to show off. Alan has always loved words, particularly those spoken by himself. Rodney Rush marvelled at what he saw as freakish intelligence: 'Jings, he would remember whole texts, word for word'. Bill Taylor, later a federal member for the local seat of Groom, thought the younger Jones 'had a mind like a razor'. But while the mind raced the fingers fumbled. Rush was relieved to see Jones struggling when more technical skills were called for. A confessed technophobe, Alan has also spoken about how he could not wait to get out of chemistry classes, having learned the theory by heart but never grasping the practical requirements.[8]

The first major test of Jones' increasingly remarked upon intelligence was the Queensland Junior Public Examination in his second high school year. Surprisingly, his best subject was not English. His 1956 results saw a B in English, an A in French, a C in Geography, a C in Maths A, a B in Maths B, an A in Bookkeeping and a C in Chemistry. Charlie expected better. Robert says their dad anticipated results at least in the 80s, and was not above getting out the strap if the report cards were disappointing.

In Alan's time fees for tuition and board alone rose to around £80 a term for a three term year. In 1959, sister Colleen, the youngest Jones, was sent to board at St Margaret's Anglican Girls School in Brisbane, a sister institution to St Catherine's at Stanthorpe where Mum had been educated. Over ten years three lots of school fees was a struggle. The fortnightly wage at the mine averaged £30, and on the farm it was a battle to do better than break even. Alan says he does not know to this day how his parents could have afforded the fees. An answer seems to lie in a National Bank of Australasia mortgage taken out on the farm on 8 January 1952, before Robert started at Grammar. It was finally discharged on 18 April 1968.

The worry of keeping the bank off his back and maintaining the fees might at times have got to Charlie. Neighbours remember him fidgeting, always on edge, biting his fingernails to the point of bleeding. The Jones kids, like most kids, would not have understood the extent of their parents' sacrifices. Their ingrate middle child has joked about constantly arguing with his dad, who would respond: 'There you go again,' he'd say, 'I give you an education and you use it against me'.[9]

But according to Alan, ingratitude did not stretch to shame. While he saw the contrast between other parents and the way his mum and dad turned out, while he saw the flasher cars dropping off other kids, he never felt unequal. One reason was the great Australian leveller, sport. Toowoomba Grammar School is a member of the Greater Public Schools, or GPS. This century-old association is a clique of mostly private schools whose annual sporting competitions draw large crowds and high kudos. While rugby was the big game at Grammar and in the GPS, and in his earlier years Jones still kept to the sidelines, he began to make a name for himself and the school with another winter sport, tennis. By his third year at Grammar, Alan Jones was ranked as 'the outstanding singles player in the GPS schools'.[10]

With the help of disciplined coaching from Len Heenan, Jones' game accelerated. He began beating older players around Oakey six-love, six-love. His slight, agile frame and strong dairy farmer's wrists helped him take out the local schoolboys' championships. Charlie and Beth were proud. One of Jones' tennis partners fondly recalls them 'sitting faithful and silent' in hats and long sleeves, beneath the harsh Queensland sun. Charlie could be seen willing his son to victory. The sharp-eyed also noticed Alan turning up to play on a Sunday wearing the same outfit he had worn on Saturday, scrubbed clean in the meantime by his indefatigable mum.

While his parents' loyal and constrained support won respect, their son was not so applauded. John Corfe, another former Oakey boy also enrolled at Grammar, was not thrilled when the younger Jones stripped him of a local trophy. Another to be beaten by a cocksure Alan, Andy Gordon, was unimpressed at Jones' snorting and feet stamping: 'I have no qualms in calling him a bad sport'.

John Corfe believed Alan Jones' improvement was a result of prodigious training. Later Jones seemed to favour athletes who, similarly, worked at rather than won talent as a natural inheritance. If a sporting creed was developing it was to refuse to accept there were natural limits to ability. This attitude came from his mother, who would impress upon her children the notion that they could do anything.

Beyond her occasional weekend visits to Toowoomba, Alan could rely upon a letter a week from his mother. She maintained the flow of correspondence all her life. The letters influenced her son's later behaviour and attitudes. Alan Jones, possibly Australia's most prolific letter writer, scribbles in the manner of his mum, in what he describes as the James Joyce 'stream of consciousness' style. The technique is also evident in his broadcasting. Jones' 'tell them the time and not the make of the watch' approach to storytelling also seems to have been derived from Mum.

Alan told Caroline Jones that another of life's lessons emerged from further motherly advice. 'My mother said look, they are going to ask you to be in things. She said always say yes and ask what it is later. And I just kept putting my hand up you see, it was the debating team, or it was a play or it was rugby or it was whatever. And I did it and I remember once one of the housemasters came in and said there was a concert at the Town Hall and would anyone like to go. I put my hand up. There was a black soprano singing whom no one had ever heard of doing a concert tour of Australia. Her name was Leontine Price who became one of the great coloratura sopranos and I saw her at the Toowoomba Town Hall at thirteen.'[11]

Beth Jones seemed to want her children to embrace the multitude of opportunities she had largely been denied. Her son obeyed, developing a lifelong compulsion to fill every minute. At Grammar he wrote cricket reviews for the school magazine. He took on singing, acting and public speaking roles in school theatre. He won prizes for talks on 'British Birds and Their Way of Living' and, no doubt inspired by his dad, 'A Tour Through a Coalmine'. Alan Jones must owe some of his extensive confidence as a public speaker to his many turns at the rostrum in Grammar's Old Hall. He became secretary of the debating society, winning again for arguing in the affirmative that 'Shakespeare is More Enjoyed in the Reading than in the Stage Presentation'.

The influence was not always positive. Jones still treats adversarial interviews as if they are debates. He has never been able to transform the debater's approach, constantly trying to win points instead of seeking answers to questions. In his editorials, too, there is a hint of the debater's gift for using language to triumph over logic.

When I asked Toowoomba Grammar old boys to share memories of school days, what seemed to stick in their minds was the horrible food, the bullies, the inter-dorm raids and the annual football grudge match against Downlands College. When they remembered Alan Jones they remembered his stage performances. Jones' acting in a series of plays won commendation. One performance was described in the school magazine as 'valiant'. His best performance, in *The Winslow Boy*, was written up in the *Toowoomba Chronicle* and described as 'convincing'.

Although never blessed with a mellifluous voice, Alan's forthright personality burned bright. What also worked, and makes him so remembered, was his talent for putting on a skirt. In *Socrates* he played the flute girl, Euthenoe, 'with a creditable feminine air'. In *Charlie's Aunt* he was Donna Lucia d'Alvadorez. A picture of Jones and the cast in costume can be seen in the 1956 school magazine. In *The Winslow Boy* he played Catherine. 'It was really a difficult play for boys, particularly in the female roles; Alan Jones is to be congratulated ...'[12]

In general former students did not see Jones' aptitude for playing women as a sign that he was gay. As Bill Stubbs put it, there was no big deal about Alan taking on the role of Catherine—it was, after all, a boys' school, and somebody had to play the girl. In the 1950s the idea of homosexuality was not prominent on the radar of teenagers, although one ex-student did think Alan had an eye for some of the black New Guinea boys who began enrolling at this time.

Although most of those spoken to later came to respect Jones and take pride in having a shared school experience, his competitiveness and self-promotion did not make him entirely popular. To some he was 'arrogant', to others 'an arsehole'.

One who thought Alan Jones was 'well liked' was also liked by Jones. Greg Colborne, a 193-centimetre tall fast bowler from Quilpie, made enough of an impression for Jones to refer to his cricketing team mate when, years later, he spoke to Caroline Jones of the importance of 'laughter and the love of friends'. Telling her about the sad failure of males to express innocent love for one another, he explained how he later regretted not telling 'Coley' what he'd meant to him. 'You weren't meant to say, Coley you've just been fantastic to me, without you I couldn't have survived. You didn't do that. As I got older I thought I have never seen Coley since, and it was 20 years before I saw him. And I thought I am never going to allow that to happen again. If someone matters to me I am going to say it.'[13]

As Alan advanced through puberty he remained weedy but began to develop a wiry athleticism. His quick eyes and hands also served him well on the cricket oval where he was marked up as a chatterbox wicketkeeper and middle order batsman. Alan made it into the First XI in his final year, but it was not a great year, the Firsts winning just two of seven matches. But Alan Jones was evidently good enough to be described in an election dossier 20 years later as a 'former interstate schoolboy cricketer'.[14]

In athletics he did better still, at further expense to his popularity. Middle distance running remains a passion. Alan can quote world record times from memory. In the 1950s the big deal was the mile. To win, he had to beat the school's best runner, his rival Brian White. Another good trainer, White held the school's best time of 4 minutes and 51 seconds. Toowoomba Grammar had a system that allowed winners to be challenged, which is what Jones did, a touch pompously according to White. What White did not know was that his challenger tried to conspire to have fellow boarders run as well and box White in. But Jones' tactic fell on uncooperative ears: the boarders kept out of the dayboy's way. Brian White remembers the episode well, years later recalling: 'I beat him—soundly'.

Alan Jones is then said to have more sportingly admitted that Brian White was the better athlete—over the mile at least. But on 22 April 1958, Alan's sheer tenacity turned the tables in the school's annual cross-country race. One hundred and seventy-five boys sloshed through a teeming rainstorm with a determined Jones in front. He beat the previous record by 59 seconds. Brian White finished third. As his brother Robert said, 'Alan might have looked like a wimp, but underneath he was as tough as steel'.

Although Robert has maintained a lifelong pride in Alan's achievements, they don't appear to have been kindred spirits and have not kept in close contact. Beyond the boundaries of loyalty and family, friends detected an unexplained distance. Robert was gone from the school and Alan not yet in his final year when Jones the younger won his colours, the treasured blazer earned for his first sport, tennis. Toowoomba Grammar tied with Brisbane's Church of England Grammar School for the GPS tennis premiership. Alan Jones went through the season undefeated.[15]

While this helped Alan Jones' status in the school, it still did not quite make him a sporting hero. To be worshipped at Toowoomba Grammar and in the GPS system, a boy was expected to bleed into a rugby jersey. When rugby later made him famous, the question of whether he ever skinned his knees and tore his cartilages for the sake of the game became one of the first asked about Alan. It was one he seemed largely to avoid. When hospitalised in 1991 he did say the back ailment that laid him low was the result of an old rugby injury. Inquiries I made about his rugby pedigree to fellow students and even to Robert met with an insistence that Alan was better known for not playing the game. Rodney Rush remembers Alan among the fellow outcasts standing on the sidelines when Grammar played Downlands.

But despite not being remembered, even by team mates, Jones did play. Indeed, he did well enough in his final year to make it into the school's Second XV. His speed won him a place on the wing, a creditable achievement for a latecomer. According to the school magazine in 1958, the Seconds 'tried hard', but no wins were recorded.

Alan's limited playing time placed no limit on his confidence in his own opinion about how the game should be played, though. 'I played a lot of schoolboy sport, but I suppose the perception was I was better at tennis than anything else. But I played rugby at school and always thought the coaches were dreadful and I had lots of arguments and they once said famously, who's coaching the team? And I said well if I was I think we'd win more games—that got me an early shower.'[16]

The rugby jersey also helped him into leadership positions in the school. In 1958 Alan Jones became a prefect and captain of

Stephens House. His cousin, Les Thompson, says the prefects as much as ran the school. As the headmaster's report for 1958 puts it: 'A. Jones the chief boarder prefect has been a tower of strength in the house and often single-handedly has promoted discipline there'.[17] According to his fellow students Jones liked to identify with the tougher boys. Harry Barlow, who went on to win the 1959 prize for manliness, says Alan 'liked to be one of the boys'. A fellow boarder says Jones' nickname switched to 'Big Al', because 'we thought him a bit big for his boots'.

There are also those who thought Alan might have expected higher honours. The coveted head prefect position went to rival Brian White, whose father had taken over the running of the school when Alan Jones' mentor Pud Heenan suffered a heart attack. Young Brian was also awarded a school prize that literally had Jones' name on it. The Belford Prize, awarded along Rhodes Scholar lines to distinguished all-rounders, had been bestowed by Ted Belford, a first cousin of Alan's mother.

There was some grumbling about Jones being a victim of favouritism, ironic considering his later reputation for playing favourites. The experience might also have given his finely tuned sense of injustice and self-righteousness an early workout. Brian White began to hear that his fellow prefect, Alan Jones, was undermining his authority. White understood the complaints of nepotism, but believed the staff rather than his father had made the decision. So Brian White had it out with his disloyal fellow prefect and managed the rare feat of silencing Alan Jones.

The Toowoomba Grammar School motto is *Fidelis in Omnibus*—'Faithful in all things'. Many of Jones' fellow students count school loyalty as a strong and enduring influence. Bill Stubbs laughs out loud when he remembers a bunch of boys sneaking out to buy sausages to overcome the suffering inflicted by a heartless kitchen. Caught by the housemaster, Stubbs was commanded to give up his co-offenders. When he refused he was told: 'I'm proud of you, son', and the penalty was reduced. The school motto is close to Jones' own 'pick and stick' philosophy. Alan Jones went on to proclaim loyalty as a prime personal virtue. But there were already hints that Alan had egocentric notions about what constitutes loyalty.

Jones took away from the school another philosophy, which he attributes to Headmaster Heenan: 'I think I got from him the notion that the most important thing in life is not doing something—I mean we can all kick footballs and broadcast—but being someone. It is important to be someone.'[18] Len Heenan does sound like a Jones man, but I wonder whether the reverse would still be true. On Speech Day 1957 Heenan said: 'The great challenge to modern youth is to maintain a sense of proportion. Basic virtues do not change. Those who have the advantages of a good home background, a moral training and a religious upbringing rarely lose their heads.'[19] Another big question about Jones in later life revolves around his command of these virtues of balance and proportion.

Alan Jones completed his Senior Public Examination at Toowoomba Grammar in 1958. His results are not of the standard he came to expect of his own bright students. Jones got Bs in English, French and Maths 1, and Cs in Maths 2, Chemistry and Bookkeeping. The problem might have been reconciling study with that motherly entreaty to volunteer for everything. Young Alan had spread himself thin. In a later interview he said the workload took a lot out of him: 'I was very young when I was in my final year at school and because I was in everything I was very tired'.[20]

In 1986 Alan Jones, then an international rugby coach, made a triumphant return to his old school as guest speaker. He also made a $250 000 non-conditional 'leadership gift' to the school.[21] This surprised Rodney Rush, who remembered Alan Jones being bullied. In contrast Rush, who was never able to forgive the school for its tolerance of the bullying, told me: 'I don't associate with the old boys. It affected my life.'

While it might have done so differently, I am sure the same goes for Alan. Jones' self-portrait of his formative years is of a tough battler from western Queensland. He also insinuates into the picture a hint of frenetic boy genius. While this self-image does not bear too close a scrutiny, Jones had won a hard-fought battle. The skinny child derided by the tough boys in his primary school days was now able to identify with his old enemy.

'Hello, champion ... mate, I'm good ... you're a madman ... you're a star.' On air these days Alan is often heard engaged in blokey banter. When he yarns with Mark Waugh about the trots, when he called Kerry Packer to complain about the placement of a casino gaming table or when he lectures John Howard about the delivery of rural subsidies, it is more than apparent that Alan is one of the big boys.

CHAPTER 3
THE BIRTHDAY BOY

'I'VE WORKED HARD ALL MY LIFE, and I've never taken a cent from the government.'[1] One of Alan Jones' first students, the writer Tony Maniaty, has noticed over the years that when discussing his past, Alan Jones seems to have forgotten his time in public education, where he got his start.

When Alan Jones graduated from high school in 1958, career opportunities were limited. Older brother Robert liked the idea of studying medicine but family finances were not up to covering the university fees. Charlie Jones was said to be keen for Alan to go to agricultural college, but again, money as well as marks narrowed the choices.

Instead, Robert and Alan followed an identical career path to Brisbane's Kelvin Grove Teachers' College. In 1959 Alan agreed to a deal with the Queensland government whereby, in return for around £13 a fortnight, he would do one year's study for a primary teaching certificate, and then spend a minimum of three years working in the state school system.

Teaching did not seem an unhappy choice. All the Jones kids inherited their mother's talent for instruction. Lindsay Jones (no relation), in the same student teacher intake as Alan Jones, saw from the start a potential GPS headmaster. Alan was not the sort to go unnoticed. Lindsay remembers Alan would 'volunteer for everything', jumping on stage to act as master of ceremonies at the dance haunt, Cloudland, and not the least shy about bursting into song.

The larger stage fuelled his need for admiration. His new income also enhanced the trappings. Alan has always liked to dress well. Not that it always worked. As he headed for Cloudland in a tight-fitting shiny suit and narrow tie, one observer thought he looked like an 'English spiv'. To another he was a 'dandy'. Robert Jones saw his brother as 'debonair'. At the time Alan, with his short haircut, wing-nut ears, angry eyes and hairless face, appeared more boy than man. The youthful look held into early adulthood. On later occasions, whenever he started a new job there was a presumption that Alan Jones was younger than his peers.

This leads to another big, but not easily answered, question about Alan: in what year was he born? As he aged he seemed to get younger. According to a sheaf of newspaper cuttings, in 1985 he was forty-two, making his birth year 1943. In 1989 he was forty-five, making the birth year 1944. In 1992 he was forty-seven, making it 1945. The most common birth date used, as given in *Who's Who*, is 13 April 1943. If this is correct, then when he started at teachers' college in 1959, Alan Jones was just fifteen.

Some who are close to Alan remain curious. When friends propose birthday celebrations in landmark years, the birthday boy, a touch uncharacteristically, prefers to avoid the fuss. People who knew him from this earlier time, such as fellow students and tennis partners, commonly suspect he was born earlier than 1943, a suspicion supported by further research. School records show him starting at Acland Primary in 1946, when he would have been just three, which seems extraordinary, even for Alan. A 16 March 1957 Brisbane *Courier Mail* report about a tennis coaching camp refers to him as fifteen at the time, and therefore born in 1941. Family members say three cousins were born in 1941, one of them, Keith Belford, just two days after Alan.

So his rightful birth date appears to be 13 April 1941, meaning that when he started teachers' college Alan Jones was about the same age as his peers. One advantage of being seen to be younger than normal was that it made his talent seem more remarkable. Later it would also make friendships with younger males seem less remarkable.

Turning eighteen in 1959, Alan was approaching a crossroads that would not only direct him towards a career, but would also fix in his mind what sort of man he wanted to be. At the time, if this remarkable young man was to make an impression on the world, the likely place to do it was the tennis court. Australians, you might even say Queenslanders, were taking centre court in world tennis. Roy Emerson from Kingaroy, another son of a dairy farmer and Wimbledon champion of 1959, became a prolific grand slam titleholder. According to Alan Jones and others the 'Rockhampton Rocket', Rod Laver, ranks as the all-time best, and Ken Fletcher, a Wimbledon doubles winner through the 1960s, remained a Jones mate until his death.

A key contributor to Australia's golden era in tennis was the legendary coach Harry Hopman. Hopman was then hosting tennis camps around Australia, which brought together promising juniors and lifted the standard of competition. In his final year at Toowoomba Grammar, Alan Jones made the Brisbane squad. Hopman seems to be another to have had a profound impact on Alan as well as on the game. The pioneer super-coach introduced professional standards of training and technique, and his annual camps were well known for their bootcamp-like discipline and rigour. Nev Hay, who sweated alongside Alan on the Milton courts, told me he 'could hardly walk afterwards'.

Alan was also helped by a small sponsorship, at first from Spalding, and later from Slazenger. The sponsors provided gear, racquet maintenance, entry fees and transport assistance. The helping hand probably further influenced Alan's benevolence and advocacy in securing sponsorship for rising athletes.

Alan's competitive streak was again noticed but in this elevated company it was no longer seen as negative and unsportsmanlike. Nev Hay says this was the pre McEnroe period when 'there was no swearing, except under your breath'. Alan Jones' competitors saw a player who used his brains, was very fast, had a good serve and forehand, and played a clever and slightly unorthodox game. One amused competitor thought he played a 'minimalist, efficient game, devoid of flourish, nothing at all like his oratory'. A fellow racqueteer, Betty Vievers, befriended a 'dynamic, hard hitting, risk taking player, not a Mr Consistency but a player who went for it'.[2]

Alan's closest tennis mate, Madonna Schacht, who went on to become one of Australia's top players, saw 'a natural sportsman and exceptional player', who was more interesting for other reasons: 'Frankly, I was in awe of him'.[3] Aged 14 when they first met, Madonna says they would share milkshakes 'while his conversations ranged on a never-ending continuum'. She became very keen on this young boy who seemed an expert on anything. Alan was known even then for reading newspapers from end to end. While others gossiped, flirted or read comics between sets, Alan was engrossed in study or the news of the day.

Madonna assumed Alan was a Labor sympathiser but not a mindless devotee. His views were not readily categorised, although Alan was consistent in his position on the proclaimed plight of rural communities. Alan Jones was also known for his support of a hometown politician, Jack Duggan, the representative for Toowoomba North, who was the only member of the Vince Gair Cabinet to stay loyal to the ALP after the bitter split of 1957. Lindsay Jones, later state secretary of the ALP, still sees Alan as 'a political accident'. While they went separate ways politically, Lindsay recalls an echo of his fellow student teacher declaring that 'The only thing people have to sell is their labour'. When he took up his first teaching job in 1960, Alan Jones maintained an interest in politics. Students say that in classroom discussions he would sometimes express an ambition to become prime minister.

His first school was Ironside Primary, a prized post. The state school near the Brisbane River has done a sterling job for Australia. The painter Lloyd Rees is listed among its past pupils, along with a host of other high achievers, conspicuously in the arts. Down still unpaved roads, boys and girls from a skinnier generation than today made their way from tidy high-block homes to the school in the smiling hills of St Lucia, their uniforms washed in new electric machines and pegged to rotary clotheslines, where they dried in no time flat.

Like the kids, Australia was growing, postwar reconstruction now delivering prosperity. According to a fellow teacher, Graham Shipstone, well-motivated pupils from families with regular incomes made teaching a pleasure: 'In those days teachers did all the talking and the kids did all the listening'. For a public school, Ironside was well appointed. A swimming pool was two years old when Alan arrived. Facilities were better than usual as the school was set up to accommodate trainee teachers. It was also conveniently close to the University of Queensland where Alan continued his own education as a part time Bachelor of Arts student.

As I discovered talking to former Ironside students, if you were in Mr Jones' class, you were not going to forget him. One Ironsider still values Jones introducing Australian poetry to the class despite, as he recalls, opposition to home-grown culture from the school establishment.

What the students most commonly recollect, though, is how frightened they were of Mr Jones. Tony Maniaty says his teacher was perpetually angry, hurling chalk and disciplining boys by smacking them on the backside with a wooden ruler: Jones was 'the most intimidating teacher I had'. Theatre and film director Mark Gould thought Jones 'an incredibly good teacher', but 'scary'. Gould says Jones had a nice side but 'I remember being afraid to go to school'.

Another Ironside student, one who became a teacher himself, says he often wonders about Jones' teaching methods: 'You got it right in a Jones' class but mostly because you were frightened of him'. He would go home at lunchtime to get the answer to a maths problem. When he returned better prepared, there was Jones in his mohair jumper, 'tough and angry, standing at the front of a class with a stick, slapping boys who got a date wrong, keeping you in until you got it right'. Motivation was derived from fear and a repeated negative message: 'We were told endlessly that we would end up sweeping gutters if we did not do well'. A surly Jones up the front of the class could swing around, hurl a duster and hit a kid on the head with slip field accuracy.

At that time this behaviour was not unusual. Alan Jones was hardly the only teacher with a temper and a duster. Teachers will admit, not always openly, that a common technique to guarantee obedience from a class was to pick out one boy and terrorise the life out of him. Banishment was to become a trademark. Throughout and beyond his teaching career Jones was constantly banishing offenders. His inclination to form a court where those inside could do no wrong and those outside could do no right became a habit he would never break.

One disapproving Ironside mother said Alan Jones was well known then for playing favourites. She said he would ingratiate himself with the influential parents and favour particular boys. And she made no bones about whom he favoured: 'Appearance came into it. He liked a boy who was intelligent and nice looking.'

Others thought his favourites were not always the brightest and most talented. Paul Deuble, an Ironsider given tennis coaching by Jones, thought 'he liked the top athletes and the bottom-rung performers'; he enjoyed helping the gifted excel and the not so gifted improve. One of his Ironside students has a striking memory of Jones bringing one of the struggling boys to a front desk, forging an agreement that they would both work on improving his grades, and doing just that. The story is important because it is an early example of a great many contradictory observations. A mother upset at the treatment of the same boy complained to Jones and was told: 'But he's got no brains'.[4]

Another student thought the favoured boys were closer to Mr Jones than his fellow teachers. Alan would stay in to share lunch with his 'best' boy, forgoing the conviviality of the staffroom. Again, recurrent behaviour is evident in these visible demonstrations of favouritism. Whether it was intended or not, for the next 30 years students and athletes sent by Jones on personal errands were perceived by others as being involved in a special, personal relationship.

One incident stuck in the mind of a former student because of its curious nature. Suffering a head cold, Jones sent a boy to the corner shop for a box of tissues. When the boy returned with pink tissues (which had been introduced into the Australian marketplace in 1959) Jones was infuriated by the choice of colour.

As he approached manhood there was perhaps growing sensitivity about perceived glimpses of a feminine side. Mark Gould thought Alan Jones was different. 'He wore a tennis hat in a girlish way. He sat like a woman, lowering himself to the ground as if wearing a skirt. He had feminine movements, but also a brutal masculinity.' Mark's older brother, Warwick Gould, Professor of English at the University of London, saw 'A symphony in powder blue: the first person I ever saw who wore pleatless hipster trousers with vertical pockets at the front. He obviously spent more on clothes than anyone else in his peer group.'[5]

While Jones probably knew by now that he was homosexual, he represented himself as conventionally heterosexual. As a ladies' man he was convincing too, to some male colleagues and many women, who found his good manners enchanting. Madonna Schacht was commonly considered to be his girlfriend. Some still believe the pair were once engaged, and even married. Tennis mate Betty Vievers was convinced he only had eyes for Madonna. Years later, when Alan said something to her along the lines of, 'Betty, I did not realise you were such a good sort', she replied, 'Alan, you never looked'.

Madonna, a glamorous, high-profile tennis player, says they were very close, but never to a point where they planned a life together. 'We never dated in the sense that young couples did. There was not much money available on teachers' salaries at that time. It wasn't a physical relationship but the relationship was significant, emotionally, in that for the many years that I was seeing a lot of Alan I was not involved with anybody else.'[6]

Now a teacher herself, Madonna saw Colleen Jones, Alan's sister, who began boarding in Brisbane when Alan commenced teachers' college, as one of the few women to have a central role in Alan's life. 'After his mother the closest person to him was his sister Colleen. She was indeed as beautiful as Alan had described. Deep blue-green eyes, flawless complexion and dark curly hair. These two women were the apple of Alan's eye and he loved both of them with a passion he was not to share with any other woman.'[7]

The protection of a fragile identity can call for skilful lies. At this time Jones liked to be seen with glamorous women, such as Miss Queensland contenders. High-profile and unattainable women are popular with masking homosexuals. Being photographed with glamorous women, and being seen to be close to women who are otherwise claimed, is one effective mask.

The relationship with Madonna Schacht was a solid indicator that Jones was not up to a conventional heterosexual partnership. Jones told others he wanted to propose to Madonna. He has long suggested to others that he and Madonna were in an intimate relationship, but while the friendship was genuine, and Madonna wished for a sexual relationship, they never became lovers.

Another group of women was devoted to Alan—indeed, they now underpin his fan base. Alan has always had a way with older women. Beyond an undoubted genuine affection for women closer to his mum's age, flirting was safe and easy. It may also have helped him get closer to their sons. In my view this was the closeness that more likely mattered, although I am not suggesting closeness meant intimacy. I have never seen in Alan Jones' behaviour indicators of a sexual interest in children. Nor would it be fair to say his relationships with women were essentially insincere.

Keeping company was certainly important. Flatting at St Lucia with a tennis mate who was soon to be married, Jones did not seem to like being alone at night. Fellow teachers got a strong sense that he was lonely. But while he wore out some welcome mats, others were just as assuredly being laid out, particularly by the mums.

The Vollers were one of many Brisbane families to tuck him under their wing. In response to Alan Jones' coaching, Geoff Voller became a promising batsman. His tennis game also improved, as did his grades. When his mother, Opal Voller, learned Geoff's teacher was getting by on a boiled egg diet, she invited the young man home. The Vollers were charmed as well as impressed, and Alan was soon a regular guest. Opal says they were happy times. Alan was thoughtful company, bringing her gifts of fine music. Soprano Elizabeth Schwarzkopf was a favourite, but according to Alan only Renate Tebaldi could reach the high notes in *Aida*.

Opal Voller was one who appreciated Jones' old-fashioned courtesy, but she says it was difficult pinning him down. According to Opal, Alan avoided the constriction of routine, preferring an informal, nothing fancy, country town form of socialising. What Opal might not have realised is just how many invitations Alan began to receive as he got to know more parents. Families started competing for the privilege of hosting the young teacher to a plate piled high with roast meat, potatoes, peas and gravy. Alan just might have been weighing the options.

At the Voller household, Jones made enough of an impression for his birthday to be remembered. 'June thirty,' Opal quotes with confidence, although when 30 June wheeled around again, Jones was confused by renewed plans to honour the birthday boy. Upon arrival at these homes Alan, it appears, developed a trick of announcing that it was his birthday. Some time later his attention-seeking ploy aroused questions and discussion among a growing band of mothers. Patricia Trewin, the mother of a later Jones favourite, says she got onto him when she told a group of mothers that they had celebrated the young teacher's birthday, to be greeted by a chorus of 'But he had his birthday at our place last month'. Pat Trewin thought none the less of Alan Jones, presuming he was lonely and missing the devotion of home.

Not all the mothers were won over, nor were all his colleagues at Ironside. Graham Shipstone heard enough as they drove to and from school to recognise Alan Jones as contemptuous of the ability of his fellow teachers. For all that 'he never struck me as being as intelligent as he thought he was'. Jones had not hit it off with Headmaster JL Murray. According to Mark Gould, 'Legs' Murray was a 'weird and scary, but soft and gentle man, who hated Jones with a passion'.

Through the Alan Jones story lies a vein of Jones' moments in which, like a tidal wave bearing down on a reef, the depth of Alan's feelings overwhelms his judgement. At Ironside, the Jones' moment occurred within the hallowed environment of the exam hall. Students had gathered in one large and hushed auditorium. The practice was for the headmaster to stand before the sea of anxious faces and boom out the questions. Teachers such as Alan Jones stood to the side and were meant to calculate their class averages as the exam proceeded. They were further required to stay quiet, never an Alan forte.

In those days headmasters expected unconditional respect, which for younger teachers was not always easy. Graham Shipstone thought some of Murray's questions past their use-by date. Old favourites were dredged up regardless of their relevance: for example, Tasmania's tin-mining industry clung to the curriculum even after the fields had closed down. After one such question Jones broke the silence with an unheard-of objection. Murray, outraged by the public insubordination, called for an inspectorial inquiry.

Alan Jones was reprimanded and transferred to Kelvin Grove State School, for him an unhappy development. Shipstone remembers Alan pleading for reinstatement. After leaving him out in the cold for about three weeks, Murray relented. Jones' teaching career, barely started, was already under a cloud. With his university studies a long way from complete, his options were limited.

With some of the Ironside mothers he talked over what he should do. A future in tennis must have been considered. Alan

Jones won a half-blue at the University of Queensland in 1961. In occasional newspaper articles he is said to have played in the Wimbledon qualifying rounds in 1961. His agent's press release later stated: 'As a youngster he was a member of the Australian Junior Davis Cup squad under the guidance of the legendary Harry Hopman'.[8]

Alan Jones has never needed to overstate his achievements on the tennis court. Even so, inaccurate claims have been made, perhaps not directly by Jones. There is no record of him playing in the Wimbledon qualifying rounds. Putting himself in the Davis Cup squad seems another stretch of the truth. Alan was not at the top of the Queensland juniors, let alone the Australian juniors. He knew how to hit a ball but not to the standard of a Davis Cup junior such as John Newcombe.

Alan's competitors saw him as good rather than great, with a second serve and backhand shaky enough to be exploited by a keen-eyed opponent. More than one believes he would have succeeded more readily as a coach. Madonna Schacht thought 'He appeared to enjoy talking about and analysing the game just as much as playing. An exclusive career in tennis would not have challenged his intellectual powers.'[9]

Another Queensland junior, Nev Hay, saw an impediment beyond both the limits and reach of Jones' talents. You needed money to try out on the international circuit. An overseas trip cost over £500. Alan Jones later told interviewer Clive James that in his day 'either you made the Davis Cup or you retired'.[10]

In 1962 Alan turned twenty-one. He had reached the crossroads. The matrix of influences that formed the man was in place. His uncommon personality seemed to settle on two central pillars, both within a narrow population percentile. The repression of his sexual identity seemed to freeze his emotional development and limit his emotional intelligence. In addition, this masking merged with a definable personality disorder. When I see or listen to Alan the word 'narcissist' does come to mind. Although I am not qualified to make a professional diagnosis, and am not aware that any such formal diagnosis has been made,

Alan Jones exhibits a range of symptoms consistent with narcissistic personality disorder, a condition that often presents in early adulthood and is found in less than one per cent of the population. His sense of self-importance, need for admiration, lack of empathy, the presumption that he is special, his vanity and arrogance, all conform to the textbook profile.[11]

Alan now set a course for the future, fixed on success rather than happiness. Too much of the boiling energy in Alan was negative. But there were other influences, many of them positive. A degree of genuine hardship made him strive. His charm, maybe some of his dreams, his dedication to the simple answer and whatever is left of the commonplace Alan came from his dad. His can-do confidence, capacity for industry and determination never to waste potential came more from Mum. Also from Mum came the formula for overachievement. By now Alan Jones had learned well how to go far. The critical lesson he missed was how to avoid going too far.

CHAPTER 4
RIDING IN CARS WITH BOYS

IN 1963 THE MENZIES COALITION Government ruled Australia. The Nicklin Coalition Government ruled Queensland. A little known Kingaroy politician, Johannes Bjelke-Petersen, became its new Minister for Works and Housing. In 1963 Alan Jones also moved upwards.

Brisbane Grammar School, on top of Spring Hill, is in the dress circle above the city centre and the Brisbane River, snaking down from the bush and Alan's past. Considering his slender primary teaching qualification, it was quite a move when he was taken on as an English and French teacher at Brisbane's oldest secondary school for boys.

Brisbane Grammar, another in the Greater Public Schools network, had a character that was not built on prestige alone. A Grammar boy had just topped the state in the Senior Public exams.[1] He was one of 1000 students in the school's Oxford and Cambridge blue colours. There were four times as many on the waiting list. The fees at non-denominational Grammar were reasonable. Parked alongside the Mercedes Benzes on sports days was the odd Holden. Even so, in Brisbane, if you belong at Brisbane Grammar, you belong.

At least one recent account has Jones as 19 when he started at Grammar.[2] Although he was about to turn 22, staff and students at the time considered him still a teenager. One student, born eight years after Jones, reckoned he was 'not much older'.

The talent most responsible for delivering the juvenescent Jones to Grammar was probably tennis. Brisbane Grammar had an excellent tennis pedigree. Roy Emerson was an old boy. And with Queensland still building secondary education, properly qualified teachers, particularly French teachers, were as rare as truffles. Furthermore, boarding schools are always on the lookout for busy bodies such as Jones. Single young men who could attend to athletics training, tennis, the choir and see a herd of rambunctious boys off to bed well after the married teachers had gone home were invaluable.

In turn, one of the many advantages for Alan Jones was the opportunity to make his name as a coach. At this time, when sport was still essentially amateur, the school campus was one of the few places you could coach and make a living. The famous Australian swimming coach, Lawrie Laurence, had also come through Kelvin Grove Teachers' College at about the same time.

Alan's own fame as a sports coach is also directly connected to education. But he had to take classes too. In his job interview with Headmaster Harry Newell, Alan Jones evidently impressed. A story later relayed to his friend Madonna Schacht is telling. After Newell gave Jones a tour of the school library he asked for Jones' opinion. Alan asked whether it carried a copy of FR Leavis's *The Great Tradition*. Leavis was a literary academic then in fashion for views that Alan seemed to embrace. Leavis argued that there was only one interpretation of a text—the right interpretation. In his view, the only great English writers were Jane Austen, George Eliot, Henry James and Joseph Conrad. Alan, who looks on indecisiveness as a sign of weakness, had a soul mate in Leavis. The headmaster was impressed and gave Jones the job. Newell, 198 centimetres tall and also a former RAAF instructor and man's man, might have seemed to Jones like another Len Heenan, his mentor back at Toowoomba Grammar.

Alan was off to a good start, as at Ironside and many workplaces to follow, attracting a Jean Brodie-like cell of followers. In the boarding house environment, Assistant House Master Alan Jones was soon like a tomcat pissing pheromones. His new authority meant he could indulge his habit of marking boundaries. There was more freedom to surround himself with 'special' people. But it was a dangerous exercise. Selecting in meant selecting out; the Jones' power base arose from the bones of sacrifice as well as success. His own survival relied on making himself indispensable, so that the sacrifices might be excused. Up on Spring Hill, an important, recurring operating principle was first revealed. In order to have his bad behaviour absolved, Alan would hold his community in debt.

His first major success was, predictably, on the tennis court, where Jones applied some of the Harry Hopman rigour to the Grammar training program. During the season there would be three two-hour sessions a week, with plenty of overtime, and he was prepared to continue training programs beyond school commitments, even during holidays. He would place two players at the net with the opposing baseline player 'working his guts out', as one described it. The coach identified weaknesses and attacked them. In his first year at Grammar, Jones' tennis team went through the season undefeated, taking out the GPS premiership.

Drew Hutton, as convenor of the Queensland Greens, would decades later become a political enemy, but back then, as champion GPS hurdler and a member of the tennis team, the lean, well-muscled athlete was one of the chosen. Hutton thought Jones' energy set him apart. 'He was intelligent but I wouldn't call him a skilful coach. There was not a lot of skills development but there was an enormous amount of energy and motivation.' Hutton appreciated Jones' dedication, which his coach expected to be reciprocated. When young Drew arrived for a 5 am training session, Alan would be waiting.

Although Drew Hutton was later to question the virtues of being one of the chosen, many other student athletes saw nothing wrong with striving to be the best. John Covacevich, an elite Grammar athlete, formed a strong bond with his teacher.

The way another, Ian Whittle, saw it, 'if you didn't have a go, he didn't respect you'.

Paul Deuble, one of a group of Ironside boys to go on to Grammar, made it onto the tennis and athletics teams. Nicknamed 'Miss Australia' by Jones because of his long and shapely legs, Deuble thought his coach stood head and shoulders above others. He remembers that the track and field training was as intense as the tennis. A series of sprints, a walk, a spew and more sprints, with occasional relief when Jones kneeled and fiddled with a transistor radio to catch up with race results.

Some fellow teachers were critical of Jones' keenness to work with those who would excel, leaving other teachers to attend to the two-left-feeters. As one said, at this stage Alan wasn't one to 'wait for results'. The other worry that emerged in Jones' first year was to do with his fascination with the better-looking boys. By now he had his first car, a second-hand Volkswagen. His use of the car to ferry favourites about became, for all his time at Grammar, a common routine and a focus of concern.

In his first year, one glamorous middle distance runner, a dayboy, was favoured with lifts to his suburban Chelmer home. Alan Jones' intense interpersonal exchanges in the little Volkswagen could go on for hours. In this case, the ferry service stopped when the boy's father came out and tersely ordered his son inside. Mark Gould, another former Ironsider, came to understand that, with Alan Jones, 'there were dispensations for beauty'. Gould, who began boarding at Grammar in 1964, remembers feeling his heart sink when he saw who was to be his new housemaster.

Familiar with the moods and manners of the school boarding house, Alan Jones was able to play the Lord Protector with a fierceness denied him five years earlier as a mere chief boarder prefect. There were Brisbane Grammar boarders who hated him so much they wanted him dead. While the plotting never progressed beyond dark murmurs, a few did inflict their loathing on the Volkswagen, borrowing half a pound of sugar from the housekeeper and pouring it into the petrol tank.

As always there were loyalists, too, many with equally strong, positive opinions of Jones. Ian Whittle says his love of fine music developed after Alan Jones introduced him to the joys of Liszt and Beethoven. Students could hear the music when the assistant housemaster was at home. He became a keen fan of John Cargher's *Singers of Renown*, which the ABC began broadcasting in 1966.

Alan Jones' accommodation, if not monastic, was modest. He had a lounge chair borrowed from the Voller family. A bed, a sink, a record player and a radio were expressions of the Calvinist Alan. The rest of his personality was found in his closet which, according to some of the boys, was bursting with Carnaby Street clothing. Alan Jones worked on a cultured exterior. One visitor remembers him describing himself as 'a scholar, a sportsman and a gentleman'.

The sounds coming from the room at the top of the stairs were not music to all. The student athletes favoured by Alan Jones noisily kept him company into the night. When a training or study program caused them to miss a boarding house meal, Jones would buy rounds of large hamburgers. David Izatt, a senior boarder not embraced into the inner circle, remembers the anointed giggling and feasting in the master's room.

Another sound to strike fear into the hearts of the boarders, the juniors in particular, was the swish of the cane. The shower room, close to Jones' room, doubled as a punishment centre. Alan Jones gained an odd kind of respect for his accuracy with the cane. Four cuts each in the same spot got him the nickname 'Blood on Four Strokes Jones'. Errant boys would return gingerly to class. Gould is one who remembers the underpants sticking to his bloodstained bum.

At the age of fifty-two, Mark Gould recalled with pride the solidarity of the boys, who, after lights out one evening, refused to give up a malefactor after he had farted or in some other way disturbed the peace, provoking laughter and causing the lights to flash on and an angry Jones to appear. When the boys kept their silence Jones marched them into the shower room and ordered them to drop their pants. Each boy got four cuts across the bottom. Even then, Gould says, he sensed Jones' behaviour was linked to self-loathing. Also upstairs in that junior dormitory was Malcolm Farr, later to become the Sydney *Daily Telegraph*'s chief political reporter. Farr remembers a separate incident when Jones, patrolling the showers, 'thrashed' him with three cuts for flicking water from his toothbrush.

After morning inspection and before breakfast, Alan Jones would supervise the communal showers with flexed cane. With 60 boarders and only limited showerheads, the boys would have to share the water back to back, a practice known as 'having a bum'. Jones is remembered as one of the teachers who would hang around the communal showers, watching the boys. Another boarder, Richard Bryan, thought Jones 'creepy and evil'. He recalls Jones presenting his favourites with gifts. Bryan says he avoided going to Jones' room.

As perverse as some of this may seem today, many of the boys who spent long hours with Jones, including some who were not fans, state with conviction that they did not witness what they considered impropriety. Phil Enright, who went on to play in the rugby Firsts, is one to say there were other teachers who were guilty of sexual abuse, so it is not as if the issue was unknown to them. He also says that even in the areas of physical and emotional abuse, there were teachers worse than Jones. This says a lot about the very different standard of what was considered tolerable in the 1960s.

Forty years later, when I asked about his manhandling of boys, there was still plenty of anger. One former Brisbane Grammar student wrote: 'I was his pupil in French for three years ... Almost every period I was subjected to physical assaults as a result of infringements such as mispronouncing words. He would take hold of my tie and shirt collar and violently pull me towards him. At each change of direction he forcibly slapped me on the face ... I always assumed him to be mad. I also assumed that I was the example to subdue the rest of the group.'

Drew Hutton witnessed occasional brutality. 'I was embarrassed and angry often at the way he would treat other boys. He would deliberately pick on kids, for no apparent reason. I can remember him knocking to the ground a kid on the oval once because he didn't get the baton properly while practising for a relay team. And he would belittle kids who were on the outer. He had an extraordinary ability to say things that were really cutting.'[3]

The corollary of the narcissism, which helped form his handsome court, was repugnance for outsiders whose appearance was not to his standard. One boy who had suffered an ugly face burn that left a permanent scar was another tormented. He has never forgotten getting back an English essay with Jones' words: 'Are you a moron?' scrawled in the margin.

A 1964 dayboy, Graeme Twine, sensed that, because he was introverted and not a rugby player, Jones took an instant dislike to him, subjecting him to 'humiliating and degrading treatment'. Jones would wonder out loud how the 14 year old had made it into the superior English class. 'He would go red in the face and walk right up beside you in the classroom and literally scream at you within inches of your face.' Graeme Twine left the school in 1965, partly because of Alan Jones: 'I was emotionally and physically abused by him and I am sure that if the same type of thing occurred today he would find himself before a court'.[4]

Malcolm Farr was another to keep his distance, later reflecting that he was lucky he did not excel at sport, if being owned by Jones was a consequence. Another Grammar student to make a name as a journalist, Andrew Olle, was also cautious about Alan Jones, but one of many to acknowledge his teacher could teach.[5]

In Alan Jones' second year at Grammar, Headmaster Harry Newell retired to be replaced by yet another former air force officer, Max Howell, an import from Camberwell Grammar in Victoria. According to Howell, Newell's parting advice on the question of Jones was to 'get rid of him'. But Alan Jones' ability as a teacher, coach and general organiser made this difficult. His tennis team had won its second successive GPS premiership. He was helped to a degree by the arrival of a quiet boy from the Gold Coast, Geoff Masters, a future Wimbledon winner then being privately coached by Trevor Fancutt.

Jones was also showing his skills on the cricket pitch and athletes such as Deuble and Whittle promised good results at forthcoming GPS meets. Indeed, Jones' third year, 1965, proved to be important for the discovery of Grammar's most successful middle distance runner of this period. Phil Byth was an easy winner of the Under 15 880. Unknown to Jones before the event, Byth had worked out his own training program, which meant trying to keep up with the older runners. The goal fixed in his young mind was breaking the school's mile record, which had stood since 1956. It began to look like he could do it. Byth soon got the whole school talking, and not just about his athletic potential. The son of a judge, he was from a high achieving family; intelligent, athletic and with Hollywood looks, he became Jones' most favourite Brisbane favourite. Young Phil was soon awarded the milkshakes and lifts home routine, the journeys extending into long discussions about life well after the Volkswagen's engine clattered to a halt.

If Alan Jones sensed that with some teachers and parents he was overstepping the mark, it made no difference. And it would be wrong to say the experiences were discomforting for all the boys. Mark Gould counted sharing a ride in the mobile classroom as among the good times, when Jones was generous and interesting. The hard part for Jones was saying goodbye.

Years later, in her *Search for Meaning* radio program, Caroline Jones asked a good question. She wanted to know the importance to Alan of time out for peace, reflection and meditation. In his answer Alan Jones acknowledged the value of solitude, showing off a touch by calling to mind that 'lovely little essay' by Virginia Woolf, *A Room of One's Own*.[6] Sceptical listeners might have wondered what a polemic on feminism had to do with meditation, just as I have wondered whether, in truth, Alan Jones did all he could to avoid reflection. He seemed to feel keenly the emptiness of a silent room, needing a state of exhaustion in order to get to sleep in the long hours before dawn. After evening university classes and mucking about with his special boys, he would throw himself into preparing lessons. When the boys wondered how he did it, Alan Jones would tell them Winston Churchill got by on four hours' sleep and that, like the former British prime minister, his mind was too busy for conventional sleep patterns.

Madonna Schacht noticed this further development of his prodigious work ethic. 'There was a fierceness about his aspirations, a desperate quality in that he drove himself to the point of exhaustion. In the sixties, when he was relatively poor, he used to stay up all night correcting French examination papers, only to earn a pittance. These were papers sent to him by the Board of External Studies. It was possible for teachers to earn a bit of extra cash during the Christmas holidays in this way. He willed himself to stay awake.'[7]

After a settling-in period, the early part of the evening was more often filled with social engagements. Directly beyond the inner circle of special boys there was a constantly revolving satellite of hospitable parents with whom Jones continued to celebrate his galaxy of birthdays. There were formal school functions too, and invitations from colleagues. Madonna Schacht was often beside him. 'This was the true Alan. On these occasions he was most himself, at ease with his audience and glowing in the admiration and interest he so easily aroused.'[8]

When the head of the English department, Russell Cowie, invited Jones home, he and Mrs Cowie discovered the young teacher could be 'totally charming'. But by now Cowie, who was senior housemaster as well, was also aware of Jones' lesser qualities. The new headmaster was at least as sceptical. Max Howell did not take to Jones' ceaseless monologue. He noticed Jones was more effusive in his praise of the students of influential families, soon developing a reputation for hobnobbing with the well-to-do. At this time Jones also appeared to dress up his own past, talking of coming from a wheat farm out Dalby way.

While Alan Jones' successes and charisma helped him gain acceptance, there was only one way he could become indispensable. As at Toowoomba Grammar, it sometimes seemed as though the only victories that mattered were those on the rugby field. In the GPS, rugby is like a dominant religion. When a winning team filed back into the dining hall after a big victory, the entire hall would go quiet. St Joseph's Nudgee College, with more than 30 GPS rugby premiership wins, seemed to really believe rugby was the game played in heaven. The Catholic college was known for having supporters who would kneel with their priest and pray as the goal kicker prepared his run-up.

Despite its comparatively modest record of just three GPS rugby premierships, Grammar also counted itself a rugby school. The game was in the very soil of the place; its lower oval having been leased by the Queensland Rugby Union meant the grounds bore the prints of Wallabies, Lions and Springboks.

By the mid 1960s, prospects of imminent success improved commensurate with the successes of junior teams. Russell Cowie, who had played senior rugby in New Zealand, was bringing some good young players through. In 1965 Cowie's First XV had Grammar's best season since 1959. But a light forward pack and a stalking curse of bad luck told in the final breath of a deciding match, won by Nudgee.

Many years later a magazine profile of Alan Jones referred to this period. 'Far younger than any other teacher and possessed of pulsating intelligence and that freakish energy, he quickly established himself as an educator and sports master without peer. He taught the school how to compete. He coached swimming. He took rugby out of the doldrums.'[9] The comment rankled with some. If, indeed, rugby was rising out of the doldrums, Cowie deserved credit. The school had earlier embarked on a development program, touring south to gain experience, while the Ladies' Auxiliary purchased a scrum machine to beef up training at home. The program seemed to be working, with a few of the junior teams going through preceding seasons undefeated.

Alan Jones had charge of one of the junior teams, the 16As. With a little experience from Toowoomba Grammar to call on, advice from Grammar old boys, such as the 1958 GPS winning captain Alex Evans, and a very large coaching manual, he was turning his acute mind to the minutiae of the game. He also forged a strong relationship with his captain, Andrew Jenkins. The Under 16As won eleven out of thirteen games, finishing runners-up. Soon after Jones was promoted to take over the Firsts. Russell Cowie later explained that, as senior housemaster, he had a lot on his plate.

When the next season came around some of the players Alan Jones inherited began to whisper to their former coach: 'Sir, he is using your moves'. Under Cowie, the team had developed a series of moves coded using the names of popular cigarette brands, such as Peter Stuyvesant and Benson and Hedges. Not that Jones was without his own repertoire. Indeed, he had very particular skills. Andrew Jenkins, who stepped up to captain the senior team, thought Alan Jones merged and concentrated his substantial gifts not just as a motivator but also as a student, an analyst and communicator. While Jones had much to learn about rugby, when it came to explaining what he wanted, he had few peers.

The fullback recruited in that year, Ross Parry, was a beneficiary. A convert from Australian Rules who was slow to warm to rugby, Parry knew how to kick a ball but was less sure about what to do when he received it. After training, Jones would hand him foolscap pages of notes complete with a range of options detailing what to do in various circumstances. When the whistle blew to start a game, Parry found himself recalling the notes and thinking, as the ball sailed towards him, 'Should I take option one, two, three or four?' 'It was very governed. You did what you were told, and he was merciless if you did not follow instructions.'

Alan Jones also adapted some of the Harry Hopman approach, insisting on rigour and discipline. The coach expected total dedication, and no excuses. A favourite Jones' expression was: 'The only thing that will stop training is an earthquake'.

Of all his boys, the First XV players were the most special. The training ground became another Shakespearean theatre full of sound and fury. The players were not there for fun. Jones' passions could get away from him. He did not seem to have a means of turning down his temper. Even his special boys found the tirades that inspired could also intimidate and bewilder. But non-players got it worse. The vitriol Alan Jones reserved for the frail and uncoordinated was withering. They were disparaged as 'Aunty Fannies' and worse. Excised was any trace of the empathy that might have been expected in someone similarly scorned a decade earlier.

Jones' bullying would probably have been overlooked—after all, tyrannical coaches are often forgiven, indeed, lauded, when they win. For Alan Jones to win a GPS rugby premiership in his maiden year would have made him heroic as well as unsackable. And he almost did it. But for another of those Jones' moments, Alan might have earned his legend status earlier. At the beginning of 1966 the team had toured south, building momentum by the time the Brisbane GPS competition began. The ultimate winner would be the team to have accumulated the most points at season's end. Brisbane Grammar went well enough to be a premiership contender with one game to go. If they could beat more favoured Nudgee College there was a chance of finishing at the top of the ladder.

At the game's end Grammar was one kick away from glory. As the final whistle sounded, Brisbane crossed for an intercept try, giving the kicker an easy shot from in front. Victory seemed a fait accompli, as earlier in the game Ross Parry dropped them over from both sidelines. What happened next has been talked about constantly in the intervening 40 years. Stunned spectators saw Ross Parry hand the ball to captain Andrew Jenkins. Parry felt his heart rate rise as he saw Jenkins take the ball, he thought too far back. The captain hesitated, kicked, and above the roar from the crowd the angels might have been heard cheering—for the Catholic boys.

Jenkins' kick just missed. Nudgee was delirious. A member of their large cheer squad, Sean Dorney—later the ABC's Pacific correspondent and captain of the New Guinea Rugby League team—was one of many to assume the lucky win was a consequence of the Grammar captain's misplaced quest for glory. Andrew Jenkins' account of the game in the school magazine suggests as much: 'Now, should Parry take a drop-kick from the position or should I place-kick it? I decided upon the latter.' The captain blamed himself and congratulated his coach: 'I extend a sincere thank you on behalf of the team for the sacrifices on behalf of football in the school.'[10] Now a plastic surgeon, Andrew Jenkins sees it as ironic that he should be scarred for life by this small moment. For years afterwards people have stopped him to ask: 'Are you the bloke who missed that kick?'

But Jenkins should not have shouldered all the blame. There are more than a few witnesses who remember that Jones moment, when the coach ran to the sideline and yelled his instruction. Along with others Ross Parry, now a Brisbane dentist, heard Jones' unmistakable voice telling him to 'give the ball to Andrew'. Jenkins agrees. He and Parry both thought Jones had calculated a place kick from in front as the safer option. Max Howell had a different take. Watching from close by, the headmaster interpreted the intervention as classic Jones. By handing the moment of glory to a perceived favourite, he thought his headstrong teacher helped snatch defeat from the jaws of victory.

Alan Jones had three more opportunities to capture the GPS shield, but while maintaining a competitive side, he never again came as close to rugby glory at Brisbane Grammar. The football years were turbulent, and without victory to assuage the pain, the costs of handling Alan seemed higher. With every passing year Jones' favouritism increasingly intruded on rational judgement. Too often selections appeared to be based on who was in with the coach rather than who was playing well. And Jones' obsessive attention to his boys also got in the way of the running of the school.

By 1967, Russell Cowie was fed up. Boarders began to see their housemaster and his assistant arguing loudly. There were several run-ins when Jones failed to turn up for rostered duties, sending a prefect instead. The assistant master would advance the excuse that he was working his guts out for the school, but that did not help Cowie, who felt Jones failed to discriminate between school and boarding house duties, which had to be met.

That same year Jones was sacked as assistant housemaster. He carried on teaching and coaching, living for a time, it seems, off campus in the very first home of his own. This first acquisition in what is now a grand property portfolio was a fenceless housing commission-style property in South Pine Road Everton Park, one of Brisbane's northern suburbs. Madonna Schacht says, 'He was proud of his investment, a three bedroom brick and tile house which was rented'.[11] Jones must have also lived for a period in the house; some of the boys remember post-match parties there and occasional visits after training.

At about this time Beth Jones experienced the recurrence of an illness that had shadowed her for years. Her sister Freda says that while Beth was leaning over the stove at home in Acland, she suffered a giddy spell and was hospitalised.

Charlie and Beth, at the age of 60, no doubt exhausted after years of battling to make a go of the tiny farm, and perhaps a bit lonely, decided to sell their home of 30 years. Alan persuaded his parents to come to Brisbane so his mother could be close to medical help.[12] He had a hand in seeing his parents into their first Brisbane home. In 1968 his parents moved to another tiny cottage, in Hale Street, Margate, a beachside suburb within easier reach of their three children.

According to Madonna Schacht, at this time Alan Jones rarely spoke of his father. 'He definitely was closer to his mother, and spoke of her often. He genuinely felt great sorrow that her life on the farm had been harsh and difficult, her considerable talents and intellect wasted. He spoke as though her life could have been different had she the chance to pursue a career. When he spoke of his mother, his eyes would mist over.'[13]

Mum had reason to be proud of Alan's prestigious teaching post and, by now, the letters after his name. Following six years of study, on 28 April 1967 Alan Jones received his Bachelor of Arts degree. An AEd (Qld) qualification (Certificate of Education), a component of the arts degree, was included in his curriculum vitae. There is no record of him completing a Diploma of Education, begun earlier.

His sports-mad dad had reason to be proud too. Alan's tennis teams remained unbeatable. His athletes continued to do well, although there were concerns Jones might have been overtraining them and, for that matter, overstretching himself.

Towards the end of his time at Brisbane Grammar, Alan Jones took over the coaching of a star athlete from rival Nudgee College. Roy Rankin went on to become Australia's top junior middle distance runner, so good that he broke a national record by an unheard-of two seconds. At this stage Rankin seemed destined for the Commonwealth or Olympic Games. Two decades later Alan Jones was still proud: 'Coaching is about helping young people believe in themselves. Coaching Roy Rankin to national junior athletics titles 20 years ago is among my happiest memories in sport.'[14] In Rankin's own retrospective, Jones was a major and positive influence. 'He was the type of person who made you believe in yourself.' But Rankin's career was to falter due to injury. Now a coach himself, Rankin came to see his young physique was not ready for Jones' intensive coaching style, and injury was as much as inevitable.

The story with Jones' Brisbane Grammar star, Phil Byth, was similar. At the 1968 GPS championships, Queensland's best schoolboy middle distance runner suffered stomach strain. This did not stop him winning his races, but the coveted mile record remained unbroken.

Phil Byth also broke a growingly oppressive relationship with Alan Jones. The young athlete tired of the extensive training. 'The pressure of dealing with Jones had taken the fun out of it. I was not ready to be owned.' After training he would go through the milkshake and lift home routine, finding himself parked under a tree, listening to Jones until well past midnight. His parents became more concerned when Jones turned up while they were holidaying at Fingal, south of the border, during the

Christmas break. They thought it odd that Jones would literally go so far to coach their son. Young Phil Byth thought that it was because Jones did not have anything else to do.

Jones' closeness also generated problems with Byth's peers, who would snigger at the sight of the teacher walking with his arm draped over the shoulder of his protégé. In his final school year Byth, then something of an angry young man, snapped. He was sick of Jones and told him so. There was a noisy public quarrel.

As is his way, Alan moved on. A boys' school has plenty to choose from. Another star athlete, the good-looking and speedy Steve Trewin, went through a similar estrangement after a similar courtship. During a pre-season rugby tour to New Zealand, Trewin was treated as if he were Jones' date, invited to special dinners and the movies. Fellow players resented the favouritism, taking it out on Trewin when they ran onto the field. Back in Brisbane there was the same parking and talking routine. Young Steve remembers sitting in the cramped Volkswagen, listening to Jones going on about Shakespeare, smelling his own sweat and his mum's cooking, and wanting to get inside, 'to have a shower and have my tea'.

While appreciative of Jones' efforts towards enlightening him, the experiences became claustrophobic. Steve Trewin thought that his keenness to break free of Alan Jones' clutches caused his teacher to get, as he puts it, 'thingy'. One of Jones' pet boys in 1968, Trewin was dropped to the Seconds in 1969. Admirably sanguine then and now, Steve refused to be bothered by the pique: 'If anything it was a relief to have him out of my life'.

Despite his contributions to the school, by the end of the decade Jones' credit was running out. Max Howell, who had wanted to get rid of him for a while, says he counselled Jones constantly, but to no obvious effect. 'I don't know that he listened as well as he talked. I think one had dialogue with him but I don't think he listened all that much.'

There were now other Brisbane families asking questions about Jones. As one put it, the jury was out on the question of whether he was 'a genius or a madman'. Paul Deuble says that one Sunday night his old man thought they had seen a bit too much of his loquacious teacher and sent Jones packing. One concerned parent asked Max Howell what would keep an adult teacher talking with a boy in his car until three in the morning. According to Howell, when he spoke to Jones about this particular incident, his sports master was unrepentant, saying he had been with the boy but had done nothing wrong.

While there was an obvious and enduring suspicion that Jones was being sexually predatory, again, no evidence of physical impropriety had emerged. Phil Byth said Jones had never touched him, but for all that he still felt abused. Byth was too young to discern complex motives and understand his own vulnerability. He would later come to a view that Jones was homosexual and taking advantage of Byth's immaturity, interposing a fantasy relationship. The angry young man became even angrier at the general failure to manage Jones: 'He was too strong for the school and most parents to deal with.'

For Howell, it was a difficult management issue. Jones worked hard, and was an achiever. In his seven years at the school there were seven tennis premierships. The school magazine reported the run of 57 successive victories as possibly unequalled in GPS sporting history. His achievements and his fervent support base could not be ignored. Nor was there a critical incident that could clearly justify dismissal. But for all that, Max Howell thought the school would be better off without him. As he saw it the problem was that Jones was manipulative, domineering and controlling. Howell felt adolescent boys needed room to move, and Jones was giving them no space.

After a decade of teaching, a strong sense of moral responsibility was not an obvious Jones' attribute. Nor did he seem to understand an obligation to extend a duty of care to all. Alan was not one of those teachers to adopt the medico's maxim: first you do no harm.

By the end of the decade Alan Jones was looking for another job. A career in politics might have beckoned—the Brisbane Grammar period had improved his connections, but not to the point where Queensland's ruling cliques would have given him the nod. Nor was Alan seen busily working his way through one of the party machines. When the other university students joined the anti-Vietnam marches, according to Madonna Schacht, 'Alan was strangely absent'.[15] Alan Jones is not remembered for activism in turbulent political times.

In 1968 Kingaroy politician Joh Bjelke-Petersen became premier of Queensland, retaining his police minister's post and presiding over a corrupt domain. Beyond the active support of his court of cronies, he passively assisted the criminal community. A Royal Commission into police corruption five years earlier failed to do more than reconstruct the old order. The former system, which allowed a percentage of Charlie Jones' bets with the SP bookmaker in Oakey to reach the police commissioner, metastasised as 'the Joke'. By 1968 a more sophisticated arrangement saw graft from prostitution and drug trafficking, as well as illegal gambling filter up.

In addition to protecting organised criminals, Queensland police also bashed street marchers, hippies and homosexuals. In Bjelke-Petersen's Queensland, homosexuals who braved the beats at Albert Park, the Botanic Gardens and New Farm were not just belted, but charged if they were caught. For the entire 19 years of the Bjelke-Petersen term, homosexuality remained illegal. As Joh once famously put it, 'You are not supposed to put the oil where you put the water'. Alan Jones became one of his biggest supporters.

Not yet ready for politics, rugby might have seemed a more suitable occupational choice, but here, too, opportunities were remote. Jones was a millennium away from a serious rugby job, but he had made a start. Indeed, his term at Brisbane Grammar introduced him to the man many rugby followers came to consider his secret weapon. In 1969 Alex Evans was made director of physical education at Brisbane Grammar. Evans was also a lethal weapon. The Iron Man front rower is still known for his toughness, in all playing sixty-four games for his state.

Since Alan Jones' first year at Grammar Alex Evans had been coming back to help muscle up the forwards. In time he and Jones formed a bond, Alan providing the mercurial vision and energy, Alex contributing the practical and metaphysical. A later Brisbane Grammar coach, Brian Short, calls it a meeting of different minds, 'but a meeting of minds nonetheless'. Short, who went on to coach Grammar to that prized premiership in 1972, acknowledges the Jones–Evans contribution. He believes they lit fires in the place, changing the culture to a point where players were inspired and began to believe they could win. The Brisbane period probably did much the same for Jones. The autodidact had made some valuable mistakes. The experience would later help him adjust to a more measured approach to team building and skills development. These credentials were of interest to another school with a proud reputation, one that had faded a touch after a lean run on the playing fields.

Alan Jones knew well the famous King's School in Sydney. His tennis and rugby teams had played and beaten King's on earlier tours. He was offered a job as English master, Jones saying his teaching rather than his coaching won him the appointment.[16] Some new colleagues presumed otherwise, seeing his arts degree as an underqualification. While Max Howell thought the new school had not thoroughly investigated Alan Jones' past—not the recollection of King's Headmaster Canon Stanley Kurrle—he was happy to see Jones move on. He felt Brisbane had become too small.

So Alan moved south, though he did not completely leave his home state behind. The Queensland vernacular lingered to the present: 'He is a good fellow, eh?' He would later acquire substantial property in southeastern Queensland, using his getaways as retreats for himself and his friends. A strong Queensland network was maintained. Over subsequent decades Alan Jones became a regular passenger in the front row of northbound aircraft, returning many times for reunions and too many funerals. At one service for a former athlete, John Covacevich, Alan Jones described the occasion as the saddest day in his life. There were also funerals for a range of his Brisbane 'mothers'.

Brian Short, a coaching successor and later Brisbane Grammar deputy head, believes Jones' legacy was largely positive: 'You can't measure the inspiration or count the number of students who were changed, sometimes in a magnificent way'. Short said some boys were even motivated by Jones to become teachers.

Alan Jones' teacher mother would certainly miss him, and she kept up her correspondence. Sister Colleen, another teacher, also kept in touch. With Robert, communication was more strained. Extremely proud of his brother's achievements, Robert later tired of trying to make appointments to see Alan.

Although they did not get engaged, marry or become lovers—as many presumed they did—Madonna Schacht stayed close. She would soon find new cause to value their friendship.

Phil Byth was happy to sever all ties. He still feels his entanglement with Jones soured his school years. Having moved on to manage a surgery wing in Newcastle, Dr Byth was able to disprove an implied suggestion that Jones was necessary to his protégé's success. Normally a gentle spirit, he becomes angry again at the mention of Jones' name. Phil Byth says he could not get far enough away from his former Svengali.

Mark Gould, a theatre and film director, later used Jones as a model for his stage direction of the vicious, manic, camp teacher in the play *Boy's Own Macbeth*, which he recalls Jones attended.

It is hard to imagine that all that fury, all that energy, came without a sense of destiny. Those demons tugging at Alan Jones had to be taking him somewhere. But Alan says there was no grand plan. 'I think everyone imagines I have got some great calendar of achievement and that when I was 21 I envisaged that one day I would be doing these things. It never entered my head that I would ever work for a prime minister, I was never interested in coaching Australia. As for being a broadcaster and talking to hundreds of thousands of people, that never entered my head. I was always happy with what I was doing.'[17]

In all I think Max Howell was right. Brisbane was too small for Alan Jones. Australia's third largest city had not shed its country town temperament. Cronyism and corruption were tolerated, but only to the point where they became visible enough to be offensive. Like the politician he later championed, Sir Joh Bjelke-Petersen, Alan Jones was eager to surrender principle in pursuit of simple-minded and self-serving notions of progress. It would not last for Joh. It would not have lasted for Alan.

CHAPTER 5
AMONG KINGS

IT MIGHT HAVE BEEN AN OMEN. Jones' new headmaster, Reverend Stanley Kurrle, remembers well the arrival of his new English master. 'It was quite dramatic. He was late. When I somewhat jokingly asked him why, he said that a wheel had fallen off his car coming south.'[1]

It was classic Alan to carry on, eyes fixed forward, irrespective of the warning signals. The mishap with the car behind him, Jones soon settled in. It was also classic Alan to feel at home within an elite environment. Australia's oldest independent school, The King's School at Parramatta, was founded in 1831 for 'the benefit of the Children of the Upper Classes of Society in the Colony'.[2]

One hundred and forty years later Australia's squattocracy, as well as Asian royalty, continue to send their sons to King's, another in the Greater Public School network. But much had changed. Parramatta, once a seat of government and boasting the colony's earliest completed street, was ditched by Sydney's shifting heart. The river port was now out among the fibro and brick veneer of the western suburbs, home to many of the immigrant gangs that Alan Jones would later rail against on radio.

In the 1960s, before Jones arrived, the Anglican private school moved from George Street to higher and safer ground, resettling on 300 acres at North Parramatta. While newer GPS schools boasted more prestigious addresses, King's proclaimed its seniority with a uniform that still turns heads. Like extras in a period drama waiting to be called, King's students could be seen at Parramatta bus stops in colonial grey piped tunics and red-blazed slouch hats. The fancy-dress outfit helped maintain a tradition favoured by local Parramatta thugs, then known quaintly as 'lurkies': bashing King's boys at their front gate.

Of the 903 boys enrolled in the senior school in 1970, 580 were boarders. The majority, from well-to-do country families, were not always pushovers. King's was not first of all a home for snobs. A little of Parramatta, more of the bush and the intermittent prod of Anglican liberalism gave King's some conscience and a character of its own.

A character clash, inevitable from the beginning, makes Jones' years at the Parramatta school one of the most talked about episodes of a crowded life. His time at the school is important because it delivered him influential connections that remained useful. It was important also because he entered an environment that was taken but not fooled. There were plenty of students and teachers at King's who saw through Alan and, in the end, managed to apply a kind of accountability not often seen since.

Former student Walter Ingham recalls a vivid first encounter: 'He turned up in class, quite a young man, wearing a pair of purple snakeskin boots. We all teased him and he took it with good humour.'[3] Again, Jones was presumed to be younger than the twenty-nine he would turn in his first term. Contemporary accounts put him at twenty-five.[4] Many of the boys, conditioned to Mr Chips-like masters, were impressed. There was a joke at King's that some staff knew 'The Rime of the Ancient Mariner' by heart because they were around at the time.

Right in the middle of Australia's largest city, the King's campus retained a scent of the bush. Divided by a creek, gum trees buffering the noise of Pennant Hills Road, with a scattering of boarding houses looking like displaced country motels, the King's campus in the early 1970s was a microcosm of a wider social revolution. King's was undertaking a serious blood transfusion. The gene pool of sons of old boys ever diminished and younger teachers continued to arrive, many reflecting a broader mood for change. Alan Jones continued to be seen as a leftie in tune with Labor's 'It's Time' campaign, which would soon tip the federal Coalition from office.

Jones was first accommodated on campus in bachelors' quarters known affectionately as 'Honeymoon Cottage'. Jones shared with two others, Tony Johnstone and the Reverend Brian Porter, the latter of whom was close enough to Alan 'for him to give me some frank critiques of my own work'. The brash Queenslander was generally, but not always, well received. 'I can remember the first time I saw him in the school shop and was given to wonder about his Queensland enunciation.' 'Gis a pineapple', a different colleague sniped.

Another commonly recalled first impression was shared by a wider audience. On the first Saturday of the school year King's held its Commemoration Day. Parents were invited along to inspect the school, meet the teachers and observe emerging talent. Everyone remembers Commemoration Day 1970, according to one of the minglers: 'The whole school was flabbergasted'. Resplendent in flared trousers and orange cravat Alan, unannounced, got to his feet and belted out a number from the West End musical *Pickwick*, 'If I Ruled the World'. His choice of song still amuses: 'His prayer, you might say', murmured one of those who would later clash with Jones. The aspiring tenor, who takes his singing seriously, was devastated when a few of the staff burst out laughing. The King's community had not waited long to experience their first Jones moment.

Winning over this lot was going to take more than a song. While his English master's post gave him seniority, at King's, as in all royal households, status was more a factor of lineage. What mattered most was what house you belonged to. The boarding houses were like fiefdoms, with boarding house masters commanding total loyalty, and order proscribed by elected senior boys, the Hitler Youth-like monitors. There was a tribal character to the arrangement. An old boy's son would often be assigned to his dad's boarding house, so over time, boarders from certain classes and districts formed alliances and bred rivalries.

The house with the most prestige was Baker. Among its fellows was a large cousinage of Whites. Pioneer pastoralist Arthur White (The King's School 1880–84), from 'Belltrees' near Scone, bequeathed a fortune to the school. The occupants of the other original White properties, 'Havilah' near Mudgee and 'Bando' near Gunnedah, continued to send six generations to King's. Antony or 'Anto' White, a 'Belltrees' descendant, would become another famous Jones favourite.[5]

In those days being selected into a particular house was as important as being selected into the school. Status derived from the pedigree of the boarders, the number of monitors and top athletes in residence and, perhaps most of all, the force of personality of resident housemasters. By 1970, after three years at King's, Roderick West, the Baker housemaster, already claimed a loyal following. Alan Jones seemed to size Rod West up in the way a contender observes an anointed champion. The now retired Trinity Grammar principal was one of the few who could rival Jones in his sway with the boys. The charismatic classics master developed, as he puts it, a love/hate relationship with the new English master—his colleagues agree although, with raised eyebrows, suggest that the love must have come later.

Spectators noted Alan Jones appeared to undermine Rod West by poaching some of his disciples. He united with Baker House when casting actors for his production of *The Winslow Boy*, in the House Drama Festival; Jones directed the play he had starred in as Catherine in his high school days. As assistant housemaster of Hake, Jones was on one of the lesser tiers of royalty at King's. Made up largely of leftovers, shaken out after the school restructured the house system in the 1960s, Hake was looked down upon. But Alan was not one to be constrained by antiquated custom and accepted wisdom. In the face of mounting annoyance, he recruited disciples from wherever he pleased.

It was difficult to pigeonhole Alan into a particular clique—as ever, he was his own clique. Canon Kurrle thought Jones more a traditionalist: 'He probably supported the conservative side of The King's School, you know, the behaviour, the uniform, our short haircuts and the yes sir, no sir, please sir, side of the school at that time. He certainly supported the monitorial system, which, at the school in those days, gave a lot of authority to the senior boys.'[6] Others, including Roderick West, saw him as part of a king tide of change. Jones and West, opposed on some fronts, were united in a quest with other younger masters to end some of King's bastardisation rituals.

The specialty was 'socking', the belting of boys with a sandshoe, which, cosh-like, were sometimes loaded with weights such as torch batteries. Another master, Peter Spencer, is still pained by the forlorn spectacle that greeted him outside the dayboy monitor's study of victims queuing up for a socking. Spencer was so appalled he was driven to steal the sandshoe.

Rod West is proud that his house was the first to banish the practice, but it took him four terms to achieve this, against entrenched opposition from older masters, such as Harry Read, a Saddam Hussein of the boarding houses who headed up the Macarthur fiefdom. Of all the King's houses Macarthur was the most traditional and the most resistant to change. In its constituency of bush kids, many from Queensland, there were shades of Toowoomba Grammar. Its tough reputation was also a reflection of Read, who, like Jones, seemed to be regarded equally as either despotic or brilliant.

In the 1970s, the last of Read's four decades at the school, the iron-fisted rule was broken. It came about in part through opposition from younger teachers, and a scandal that made the *Sunday Telegraph*. On 27 August 1972, sharing space on the front page alongside a photograph of Prime Minister William McMahon's wife Sonia modelling maternity clothes, a story ran about a boy being 'blackballed' (boot polish applied to the testicles) and 'dyked' (head pushed into a flushing lavatory bowl).

It was a common enough episode but the public airing of the scandal demanded consequences. John Sharp, house captain at the time and later a federal minister, accepted some responsibility and was demoted. Harry Read was conveniently one step removed, having sanctioned senior boys to take care of disciplinary matters. As it turned out, Alan Jones became a friend of both the victim and John Sharp, who was considered by some of the teachers to have received a raw deal.

The older masters were soon surrendering their rituals and their place in the school. Perhaps talent does come in waves, because the cohort replacing them still appears exceptional. Six of the staff in Alan Jones' time became headmasters of independent schools.

Looking back, Jones sees his own reputation at King's as similarly based on improving the quality of education. 'I got the job because even then I had reasonable success in the things I'd done ... The Headmaster wanted to lift the academic standards, so I was immediately separated from any sporting responsibilities in order to try to lift the standard of English teaching and English results.'[7]

King's records, however, show otherwise. In his first year, far from being separated from sporting responsibilities, Alan Jones was up to his armpits in them. As at Brisbane Grammar, he continued to coach tennis and athletics, with immediate success. Walter Ingham, one of three sons from the famous poultry family enrolled at King's, gives a telling account of the Jones miracle touch. Standing beside the training track with his teacher, Ingham says young Winton Kurrle approached them, saying something to the effect that, as the headmaster's son, 'no one likes me, and do you think you could teach me to run?' Walter Ingham remembers Jones sent Kurrle around the track to have a look. He asked Walter what he thought. 'He can't run. He's hopeless,' said Walter. 'You're wrong,' said Jones. 'I bet you that kid will win the 800 metres at the GPS competition. And you know why? Because he has commitment.' Young Kurrle went on to prove Jones correct.[8]

At his first Sydney GPS athletics carnival, King's senior team finished fifth. But the juniors, many of whom were coached by Jones, finished on top, generating a frisson of anticipation throughout the school community. Alan Jones' high-pressure training regime produced success but, as at Brisbane, there was fallout. Seventeen-year-old Angus Roberts, another runner and the school's best athlete, went through a gruelling routine, but the 1500 metres record holder did not compete at the GPS finals, nor did he finish his schooling at King's.

The beginning of the end for Roberts was a preliminary event that saw the young athlete spiked. Distressed and bleeding, he stopped to attend a wound that would subsequently need 12 stitches. When Jones dismissed his lament as 'histrionics', Robert's father was upset. When Alan pushed Angus to resume a demanding training program before his father considered the convalescence complete, Roberts senior drove to Jones' cottage to have it out. Confronting an unrepentant and belligerent Jones, Lyle Roberts was moved to threaten: 'If you don't shut up I'm going to drop you'. Alan Jones backed off then, but when the training regime resumed unchanged, the fed-up father returned and removed his son in the middle of the night. Angus Roberts never returned, and when he became a father, he sent his sons to Shore rather than King's.

As one promising athletics career was cut short, others proceeded apace. King's success with its juniors was also showing up on the rugby field. While the school had an excellent rowing squad, as ever it was rugby that mattered, and a GPS premiership trophy had not been sighted at King's since 1960.

While Alan Jones appears to disagree, others at King's see 1970 as the beginning of his long-term plan to capture the prized trophy. In that year the Under 14s had the greatest depth of talent. A later unbeatable combination was drawn in the main from this squad. At this time Jones coached the 13As, which included his captain, Antony White, and a bullocky young prop, Will Abram, who became another mainstay. Alan Jones might have hinted at a plan when he suggested 'They may in future years be a force to be reckoned with'.[9]

As at Brisbane, training was not optional. Alan Jones' squads hit out four times a week and were expected to do sprint and weight training in their own time. Will Abram remembers that 'The training sessions were basically harder than the games. If you trained hard and you were disciplined about picking up your mistakes, and you pushed to the limit, when it came to the game it was easy.'[10]

Andy Simkin, a dynamo halfback who did not do so well under Jones, noticed the coach's hand–eye coordination served him better on the tennis court and cricket pitch. 'When the ball went his way we could see he could not catch or kick. The only time he would demonstrate something was when we practised line-outs. He would wheel the ball in the old-fashioned style and was furious with anyone who could not throw it straight. It seemed to be his only skill.'

The Brisbane experience was repeated—families were split on Jones. Andy's older brother, Chris, saw his coach as remarkable. He remembers Jones blowing the whistle to stop a movement during training to point out how the players were out of position. Chris Simkin thought Jones' orchestrations of play akin to that of a stage director positioning his actors.

In the classroom there were also contrasting reactions. Dugald Anthony, son of then Country Party Leader Doug Anthony and now a Coca-Cola executive, thought it a privilege to be in Jones' English class: 'An unforgettable mix of menace and wonder. You were with him or you were not.'[11] Rod West's son Michael, now a journalist with the *Australian*, also enthused: 'The way he would bring poetry alive for those country boys was a marvel. They were hanging on his words.'

The future state Liberal politician Michael Photios counts meeting Jones as the first time he faced charisma. 'He didn't teach a class, he commanded a class. He brought alive texts that frankly we weren't otherwise interested in. His teaching was all about theatre and he was the actor.'[12]

Charles Milne, now a housemaster at Eton College, is well positioned to judge his former English master. 'In school I would characterise Alan's teaching style as dynamic, informed, hugely encouraging. The dynamism, which characterises his life, operated in the classroom very effectively, and he had a captive audience of boys who had by and large been drilled in a pretty uninspirational way by many teachers at King's. The best teachers are often not the most intellectual: motivating the students and giving them insights is what works most effectively for the majority, and Alan excelled at that.'[13]

His brother, Peter Milne, was a beneficiary. 'I can still remember a word he used, "ratiocinate" ... Worked up in a class he would let fly without taking a breath,' and from this breathless moment came a spittle of information never forgotten: 'It means,' says Peter, 'to reason'.

Top silk Bret Walker saw Alan Jones as a 'jet of oxygen', but not so influential in his academic success. Another Sydney barrister taught by Jones thought he drilled his English students as if there were prescribed answers, but 'more often than not it worked'.

Yet another gifted King's student had this to say: 'He was an appalling English master. Anti-intellectual, derisory of those who read literature.' Some fellow educators saw Alan Jones as more teacher than scholar. Visitors to his study noticed an absence of books—perhaps understandable considering the little time he had to read. Serious English students, sensing superficiality, took to studying purchased crib notes for his classes. One who noticed Jones teaching from the same notes was later castigated. The story of Jones humiliating a boy for using the same cheat sheets as his teacher soon did the rounds among the growing assembly of interested outsiders.

The polarisation around Jones is never clearer than in responses to his teaching. While the shunned remain suspicious and disrespectful, the anointed enthuse. Even fellow teachers were impressed with the effort he took to help the favoured. Anto White, a struggling English student, was given taped study notes Jones prepared in his own time. Chris Simkin, in a different English class, once asked Jones for help with *Wuthering Heights*. The classic Bronte tale, one well known and loved by Jones but not by Simkin's class, was given an outing in an extracurricular Saturday session. After three hours the boys, formerly bored stupid, were passionate Bronte fans. Simkin, still bearing a trace of that enthusiasm in his voice, says Alan Jones has a gift for giving vision to the words.

As at Brisbane, Alan Jones' peculiar and contradictory behaviour with boys became a murmuring point. The old story of Jones seeking to surround himself with handsome courtiers persisted. He continued to be cruel and abusive to those less attractive to the eye. Henry Fiander received similar treatment to that dished out to Graeme Twine back in Brisbane.

Bespectacled and unathletic, young Toby Fiander, as he was known, took refuge in reading. Considering his interest, he expected to enjoy and excel in English. In Alan Jones' classes, however, 'I would give what was my considered view about whatever point we were discussing and then it would be ridiculed in a fairly aggressive way and that went on systematically for almost all the time that I was in the class and I developed quite a dislike for English'.[14] Fiander said he ended up fearing Jones' classes and being turned off both English and King's.

Another student, Richard Collins, whom Toby Fiander remembers standing up for him in class, says he was another who did not respond to Alan Jones: 'I did better in other subjects with less charismatic teachers'. The personal attacks went on year after year. A student from the following year remembers the words Alan Jones used to attack a classmate: 'You are an amorphous lump of jelly'.

Murmurs about Jones soon reached his colleagues, among whom there were growing reservations. As in Brisbane, the person at the wellspring of discontent was largely unfussed. From the start, back at Ironside, Alan Jones figured the hothouse of staffroom politics was not for him. One King's colleague recalled that, in all his time, he saw Jones in the staff dining room only once or twice.

Alan Jones was again scornful of colleagues who went home to families and partners, for their lesser capacity for work: he called them 'the 3 o'clock rockets'. Alan prided himself that he never gave students homework, ensuring all they needed to learn took place in class—a claim that is commonly disputed by students and teachers who say he not only gave homework, but took forever to mark it.

The same tension that had seen Alan Jones shunted from the boarding house at Brisbane also arose at King's. Meals had to be taken by 6 pm, the kitchen closing at five past six. By then hot water was also running out, so students being coached or tutored by Jones were frequently missing meals and hot showers. Housemasters, whose students were like extended family, looked at Alan as a disruptive usurper. Jones' answer to the hunger pangs, at least, was to hop in the little orange Renault that had replaced his Volkswagen and race up to the Kentucky Fried Chicken outlet with two of the boys. An impressed Stanley Kurrle says: 'He would fill up the car with chicken and take it back to feed the boys. This would happen at least once a week and he never asked for a cent back from the school.'[15]

Some teachers felt Jones received dispensation from above because of a rapport with the headmaster's wife. Lorna Kurrle, pretty and shy, was known to perform with Alan at King's musical soirees. Other staff members saw that Alan Jones was the only one among them who could enter the Kurrle kitchen and make himself a sandwich. The story is at odds with Stanley Kurrle's own account. While impressed by Jones' strengths as a teacher and coach, he did not count the English master as a friend.

But, as in Brisbane, there were plenty who were smitten. The bright young teacher became a regular guest of the Whites, not just at country properties such as 'Belltrees', but at their Terrigal holiday homes. Jones later spoke of helping Judy White write the family history, *The Whites of Belltrees*.

Alan Jones was, in turn, captivated, sometimes appearing as an irrational, impassioned and possessive protector of the White boys. One successful student and athlete carries to this day a memory of being summoned to Jones' quarters late at night after Jones learned the boy had criticised one of the Whites. A tirade followed, with Jones pointing out that White was a much better person than his critic, and ending threateningly: 'Good luck in your life; you're going to need it'.[16]

There were plenty of other invitations to country estates. The polo-playing companion of the British royal family, Sinclair Hill, also had a son at King's. Noel Hill became another of Jones' top rugby players. The Binnaway graziers, the Renshaws, with two athletic sons at King's in Jones' time, were counted in the Jones circle. According to housemate Brian Porter, 'He was a bit of a snob. A Queensland redneck of humble origins coming to King's, he knew whom to cultivate. He accepted the invitations to the big properties.'

A strong bond also formed with the Milne family, closer to home at Dural, during a winter term break. Fellow teacher Peter Yeend, walking through a near-deserted campus, found Jones alone and ill in his flat. Yeend remembers Jones telling him later: 'I could have died here'. When Yeend brought his plight to the notice of the Milnes, they bundled him in a blanket and took him home.

Charles Milne tells a story familiar to many who have spent an evening with Jones, of their dinner guest talking till he dropped. 'I do remember clearly Alan's exhaustion, his falling asleep after dinner in an armchair, and my mother pinning a note on his recumbent figure telling him where the spare room was'.[17] Charles's father, John Milne, recalled Jones' impetuosity: 'One time he wanted to buy a house at Terrigal and he persuaded us to drive up and take a look—at midnight, a bit dark for a proper inspection'. As with others, the bond held, Alan Jones seeking opportunities to repay the generosity in later life. John Milne said simply of his wife Enid, who passed away in 2003: 'She loved Alan'.

While there were notable exceptions, Alan Jones was generally more popular with the mothers. Not only were the Simkin brothers split on Alan, but so too were their parents. Their North Shore home was one of many to welcome Alan, who became a regular for Sunday barbecues. Marie Simkin was another mother who liked to make an extra effort if Alan was coming. On one occasion, while she was busily preparing in the kitchen, youngest son Mark smashed a mirror, cutting himself. Mark approached his mother, who brushed him off, telling him to look after himself as she was busy preparing a meal for Mr Jones. When Dad came home soon after he found Mark had severed an artery. The ABC correspondent still bears the scar, an emblem of a family joke about how Mum almost let him bleed to death because Alan Jones was coming to dinner.

At school the collateral damage accompanying the steady rise of Alan was, at this stage, bearable. By his second year at King's, Jones was again on track to making himself indispensable. In 1971 he was made master in charge of athletics, with Bret Walker, in his subsenior year, deputising as athletics captain. Walker is in no doubt that, on the athletics field, Jones was exceptional: 'Schools athletics was not so developed in those days. [Jones] was a strong motivator, convincing you that success would be good for you. He also exposed you to unbelievably tough training. And he would constantly review the results. He would be tough on those who had natural talent but just coasted. And he would not just select the elites. The plodders did well too, so there was a depth of athletic achievement.'

Alan Jones' deputy clearly picked up some of the skills. When Winton Kurrle won the GPS Under 13 800 metres he credited Walker with assisting him to victory, by counselling him on running tactics: 'The other runners were bigger but they were not told what to do. Good thinking as well as good running won the race.' The Open 400 metres went to Walker himself. Younger brother Scott took the Under 15 100 metres, the long jump and, remarkably for a 14 year old, the Under 17 800 metres.

An incident immediately following the running of the race is another Jones moment that is still talked about. The referee, citing interference, wanted the race rerun. Young Walker was prepared to run again, but Jones dug his heels in. He clashed noisily with an unflinching referee, the coach refusing to let

Walker run. Later, writing of the episode in the school magazine, Alan Jones stepped into the third person to explain: 'Mr Jones [would not allow him to start] because of the excessive demands that this would have made on a 14-year-old boy'.[18] Fellow teachers, well aware of the demands Alan Jones placed on his athletes, saw it more as a case of grandstanding at the expense of valuable competition points.

But again, there was steady improvement in both athletics and rugby. Alan Jones moved up to coach the 15As and 15Bs. Scott Walker was their leading try scorer. Training was ramped up. Holidays, which continued to be empty spaces for Alan, were now filled with pre-season tours and football camps. When he asked his rugby squad to stay on during a mid-term break, the old complaints resurfaced. Parents were keen to see their kids, and for many of the boys, a boarding house dormitory was the last place they wanted to be during a holiday.

In term time, too, some extracurricular activities selected by Alan Jones raised eyebrows among parents and teachers, but they didn't always cause the boys to complain. Day boy Simon Dodshon said that busting out of the boarding house for excursions to *The Rocky Horror Picture Show* and the visiting Senegalese dancers was 'like a breath of fresh air'.

The recurring pattern of Jones spending every waking minute with boys again became an issue, with a much-discussed incident at Honeymoon Cottage bringing the concern into focus. Alan Jones' housemate, Brian Porter, was well aware of the housemasters' mounting concern about Jones keeping boys up until 3 or 4 am when they were supposed to be back in their dormitories and in bed by 10.30 pm. 'Alan wanted loyalty to himself which undermined the boys' loyalty to the housemasters. Alan was upbraided about it but he said he did not give a damn. Being a coach and mentor to the boys was more important.'

On one such evening the other tenant of Honeymoon Cottage, Tony Johnstone, became annoyed when the noise from Alan Jones' room kept him awake. According to Brian Porter, 'At about 3 am Tony knocked on Alan's door and made a polite complaint about the noise, asking him to talk more quietly. Alan got stuck into Tony for daring to interrupt his coaching session. Tony became ruffled and socked him. There was a scuffle. Alan screamed and ran to Rod West. [Jones] did have the capacity to enrage, but he was not up to a physical fight. I thought the way he ran off screaming was rather cowardly.'

Rod West has only a hazy memory of this much-discussed moment which may have fused with other similar incidents: 'I can remember Porter talking in a very proper way about the fisticuffs'. But the person in the centre of the ring, Tony Johnstone, or 'Juicy' as the boys knew him, insists there is a significant flaw in the story. Johnstone, who won an Oxford Blue for boxing, remembers having words with Jones but is sure he did not hit him.[19]

In 1972 Jones moved from Honeymoon Cottage to Broughton House, one of the older and more respected houses. Disquiet about Jones' appointment to assistant housemaster being tantamount to putting the fox among the chickens was met with the tongue in cheek observation from one of the staff members that 'he was not attracted to Broughton boys'.

Here he improved his friendship with the housemaster and his wife, Peter and Brenda Spencer. With some 80 boys to care for, the Spencers put in long days, which sometimes extended into the next when Jones dropped in for a late-night chat. Alan Jones was quartered in a downstairs flat, which again was regularly visited by his 'bum boys', as they were now known to some brooding critics. But again, there was no clear evidence of physical impropriety.

In the meantime, achievements mounted. The junior athletes topped the GPS points table once more. King's athletes, one of them Scott Walker, broke three GPS records. His brother Bret, perhaps a victim of overtraining, fell back in the field due to 'restricting injury'.[20]

Nineteen seventy-two was also the year of Jones' most cited academic success, which again seemed to rest significantly on a Walker. The school captain and dux, Bret Walker, was an outstanding student who did very well in English. It was later reported that, of the 32 000 New South Wales students who sat for the English Higher School Certificate exam that year, 'Three of the top ten places in the state were filled from Jones' classes'.[21] It is a remarkable claim, one that has entered Alan Jones' folklore. But it is not a claim made by Bret Walker or the school, nor can it be verified by the New South Wales Board of Studies. As is the way with Alan, from real achievements mythology grows.

On the rugby field there was further steady improvement. Alan Jones moved up with his squad, expanding his role to group coach of the 16 Division. The 16As toured, taking Alan Jones to Brisbane Grammar where King's defeated his old school's Second XV. In Sydney there was another win at a Wallabies curtain-raiser. As group coach, Alan Jones had an expanded talent pool of 30 players. The sense of competition was heightened by something more than the honour of making the top team. There was excitement, too, about what was to come.

In April 1972 an announcement was made that a squad of thirty would be selected to tour England and the US between November and January. The Grand Tour, as it was known, had one central mission, one to stir the blood of the much-snubbed colonials. The King's School Parramatta was to take on The King's School Canterbury, in a match to commemorate a centenary of rugby. Jones was designated coach. His power as a selector was accordingly accentuated, as was the commonplace squabbling over favouritism. Eleven of Alan Jones' Under 16s made it into what accordingly became a youthful senior side.

The designated tour manager and a principal organiser was Ian Humphreys. Another of those strikingly astute masters to share the campus with Jones, Humphreys was a King's old boy with an MA from Oxford. Returning to the fields and spires of his own student days would be a cherished pilgrimage for Ian Jessel Humphreys.

Like Jones, Humphreys was a bachelor with a keen eye for the game of rugby. In 1972 he had taken a touring team to New Zealand and in the Sydney GPS competition coached the Second

XV, which was beaten only once. Although weedy and ill-matched to the physical demands of the game when he played in his youth, Humphreys loved rugby in the way a hungry man loves food. There all similarities with Jones ended. The economics teacher was more the character, while the English teacher was more the personality. Shrewd and droll, Humphreys could upstage with a glance. In his mid forties, bald and bespectacled, the man known to the boys as 'Chrome Dome' also had his followers.

Rod West is one of many to say Ian Humphreys was not a hater. West remembers Humphreys offering a defence of Jones: 'If you put a tiger in the tank be prepared for some scratches'. But for all that, it was clear that he and the younger Jones would not be ideal travelling companions, so Canon Kurrle thought it wise to come along: 'I knew there would be trouble'.

On Sunday 19 November the party set off from Sydney on a Boeing 707, stopping over at Singapore where a training session was undertaken in sweltering heat on the lawns of the Singapore Cricket Club. They then kangaroo-hopped to London to arrive before a distinguished welcoming committee. London would become a favourite Jones haunt, but it is unclear whether this was his first trip—in later years he would tell friends that in his youth he hitchhiked through Europe and was picked up by the famous French singer Charles Trenet, then known as 'The Singing Madman'; Alan said the pair of them performed boisterous duets as they wheeled through the south of France.

In addition to the rugby, a range of social functions was scheduled, presumably more for the sake of the adult contingent of masters and parents. According to the headmaster, Alan largely avoided them. 'In the end I asked him where he was disappearing to because his absence had been noted. Turns out that after every match he would get two boys to gather up all the football socks, shorts and jerseys and find the nearest laundromat.'[22]

As ever, Alan Jones' attention was fixed on the boys and, to the chagrin of some, on his favourite boys, as usual. A new favourite had emerged in another good-looking young man, Christopher

Benness, a talented lock forward. Chris and his mate Chris Simkin would accompany Jones to the laundromat, as well as to historic sites and the theatre, where they saw *Applause*, featuring Lauren Bacall. In this different environment Chris Simkin got to know and like Jones more. He says the contact was at all times innocent. But that did not stop anxiety breeding, particularly among fathers, who, given the nature of the tour, were more than usually in evidence. Some of these fathers might have had memories of predatory teachers from their own school days. More than one wife of ex-boarding school boys has been known to wonder about the origin of her husband's habit of sleeping with his hands crossed over his genitals.

One of Alan Jones' footballers, Peter Gemell, is another who says his mother was close to Jones but not his father: 'A lot of fathers did not like him because of his influences on their sons'. The fathers saw Jones accepting boys into a space that teachers normally kept quarantined. The boys might be asked to buy toiletries for Jones and talk about relationships, as well as sharing secrets and a personal, rather than physical, intimacy. As in Brisbane, though, there was no evidence of sexual impropriety. Sending a boy to buy his toothpaste did not cross a line that clearly distinguishes between proper and improper behaviour. Jones, characteristically indifferent to censure, continued to mark his own boundaries. John Polain, a member of the touring party not in the inner circle, noticed that 'He would lavish praise on the favourites. Lonely boys away from home could find this seductive.' Roy Buckland, the team goal kicker, thought that whether they were in the inner or outer circles, most of the boys appreciated Jones as 'one of the few who treated us as adults'.

In the early round of matches, played in drizzle and mud, King's lost two games and won two games. The main focus was the big match against the Canterbury King's. Finding their feet and their form, the squad trained nearly every day, Alan Jones' eloquence bemusing British spectators as Headmaster Kurrle discovered. 'He certainly opened the eyes of the English onlookers with his flow of language. I don't mean bad language. He would train whenever he could. Those boys were very fit and won almost all their games. Tactfully, we did not win the game against King's Canterbury.'[23] When the final whistle blew on 11 December 1972, the Parramatta boys shuffled disconsolately from the field having suffered a 19–9 loss. The defeat produced more disappointment than was ever formally admitted.

Within the touring Australian squad was a belief that they could easily win. Excuses offered up later, like ashes in the mouth, referred to the youth of the team, the heavy schedule and the eager competition. A view that Jones had blown it was left unsaid. Instead, Ian Humphreys, writing for the school magazine, complimented Alan Jones as 'Coach Extraordinary, endowed with the energy of three normal people, equally at home encouraging his men through the pouring rain, swapping after dinner speeches with distinguished headmasters, being the life and soul of the post-match entertainment, or handling temperamental washing-machines in the local Laundromat.'[24]

Two years later, a perspicacious, unpublished valedictory on Jones, written by Humphreys, said what he really thought:[25]

> There was no happy mean with Alan; everything was all black and white, no grey. A boy was either brilliant, brilliant or a lazy no-hoper. This led to charges of favouritism when he promoted some boys beyond what others considered to be their merits, and of victimisation when he turned his wrath against others. It undoubtedly led him to some questionable selections. So confident was he in his own infallible method, he tended in my opinion at least, to overrate the importance of having players who knew thoroughly his techniques and patterns of play, while underrating natural ability and strength. Who else could have looked forward to a particular match for 6 months, planned moves and tactics for every situation, studied every possible angle ... and finally selected a team which gave him no chance whatever?

Ian Humphreys would also puzzle over how Alan Jones could think no lasting animosity would result from him publicly accusing an international referee of incompetence and the president of the Schools' Rugby Union of corruption.

The squad returned to Australia in January 1973 having won ten of its seventeen matches and, best of all, gaining invaluable match experience. This was particularly evident with his younger senior players. Alan Jones continued to move up with his squad, now coaching the First and Second XVs. The latter, more youthful team would go through the entire 1973 season undefeated. Many of these seasoned players were available for selection the following year.

The rising optimism was, however, shadowed by alarm about the fury in Jones and its effect on the boys. His rages, bursting like napalm in the schoolyard, had been leaving colleagues breathless since his Ironside days. One unsettling spectacle helped prompt Deputy Headmaster Tommy Cuff to move on. Cuff had seen a boy on the JS White Oval being torn to shreds by Jones for what appeared to be an insignificant misdemeanour. A well-respected master, Cuff left The King's School at the end of 1973 to become Headmaster at the Blue Mountains Grammar School.

The rages in Alan Jones seemed as hard to control as they were to fathom. There may be many explanations but perhaps the strain of maintaining a complicated pretence was, at times, too much. Jones' emotional attachment to the boys could not give way to unambiguous physical expression. The curious romantic dance he undertook seemed to exhaust both himself and his unwitting partners. When they got the steps wrong, or were in the wrong place at the wrong time, Alan would let go with terrifying blasts of compressed anger. Brian Porter believes 'There were a couple of boys who were brought to the edge of a nervous breakdown by Alan'.

If Jones' repression of his sexuality was connected to self-loathing, his expression of contempt was not exclusively directed inward. One group to be targeted by a seemingly homophobic

Jones was men who were openly homosexual. As one former student saw it, Jones' manipulative ways and need for power were related to inner control: 'He hates himself because of his apparent homosexuality. So he behaves in a self-justifying way.' A King's boy and aspiring poet who later died of an AIDS-related illness, Anthony Coppock was one who loathed Alan Jones and sought his approval. On his deathbed Coppock, a gregarious homosexual, lamented his treatment at the hands 'of that cunt Jones'.

Although Alan Jones disputes the proposition, another group who appeared to be targeted were Christians. Deputy Prime Minister John Anderson, never an Alan Jones' boy, is remembered as one subjected to the familiar public tirades. A shy Christian boy, Anderson needed help rather than humiliation. As a 14 year old he had been a party to a cruel accident, striking a cricket ball that killed his sister. Coping with boarding school in the circumstance was hard enough, but even worse for a victim of emotional abuse. Perhaps there is a clue that suggests an underlying Jones' strategy, however misguided. His fellow teachers saw him attacking boys he presumed to be weak. They thought his way was to strip them down before building them back up. Perhaps Alan felt it had worked for him back at Toowoomba Grammar.

These attacks on the godly were, understandably, to cause difficulties in a Christian school. Reverend Kurrle said he understood that Alan Jones was without Christian conviction. The only discussion they had on the subject was to reach an agreement that Jones would not put anything in the way of the school's Christian stance. Reverend Brian Porter, who used Alan Jones as a sounding board when he was preparing sermons, saw no evidence of subversion. Porter remembers Jones appearing in chapel from time to time. Classics Master Rod West says it best: 'Jones was opposed to anyone who had a Christian interest. God was too much of a competitor.' Jones was not openly subversive; the challenge was more a case of dealing with an alternative force that also called for submission.

Another Christian to have been similarly brutalised reflected: 'Alan Jones had a real hatred of Christians. No question about it. He would have a go at a couple of us. I did first level English and we studied Hopkins. Alan did not understand Hopkins, who wrote from a Christian perspective ... He would pick on us whenever he could.'

A committed Christian and sometime Jones' footballer, John Polain was another singled out in class. Polain now observes mildly that he thought Jones not the right type to teach children. 'You copped it if you did not do certain things. He would scream at you for fifteen minutes. It did not seem to me to be a great educational tactic. He was talented but an egomaniac. He seemed to be driven by a need for more power and control.'

Jones' wrath was not just directed at the boys. Walking across campus one day a fellow teacher came upon Alan Jones laying into one of the housemasters, the mild-mannered Reverend Walter Newmarch. Alan was not holding back: 'You are nothing of a schoolteacher. You can't coach sport. The boys despise you ... you are hopeless ...', and so on. When the colleague, a friend of Jones', counselled him about the unnecessary savagery of his words, Jones looked at him protesting, 'But it's true'.

By 1973 Alan's impassioned support of some and lack of empathy for others became too great an issue to be ignored. There was deepening anxiety about continued late-night excursions to Jones' room. One master, according to colleagues, became obsessed with worry. He is alleged to have done some ogling of his own, climbing a tree to try to get a better view of what was going on in Jones' room.

Chris Simkin was in a good position to know. He was often in the room with Alan Jones until late at night. 'I was in there for hours. The door was never locked.' Simkin says they used to watch the *Ernie Sigley Show* on television. Scott Walker, another constant visitor, had a varied experience. Like Phil Byth at Brisbane Grammar, Walker began to feel violated. 'If you had muscle strain he would insist on strapping your legs. He would take you into the shower and tell you to take your clothes off. I was shattered with awkwardness. It was weird and uncomfortable and seemed voyeuristic.'

Housemate Brian Porter says: 'I never saw a breach of fiduciary duty. I never saw evidence of predatory behaviour. But he was manipulative and voyeuristic. He would love watching athletes on television and film. He saw the beauty of the human form in full flight. He loved the strength, the freshness and the vitality of boys.'

Disquiet about Jones' attachment to some boys grew during a term break when one of the masters found at least one letter, written by Alan Jones to a boy, that had been left behind in a classroom desk. In it Alan spoke of thinking about the boy late at night, expressing his love. While love letters to boys were hardly appropriate, neither were they regarded as smoking gun evidence of misbehaviour. At the time Jones was receiving, it is said, a letter a week from his own mother. The innocent explanation was that Jones' correspondence, like Beth Jones' letters, were Byronesque exhortations of love and inspiration. Jones has spoken of his belief that males should not feel ashamed of expressing love for one another. 'You mean so much to me', one boy remembers him saying when Jones drove him home.[26] The English teacher often made a feature of his sensitivity, telling boys he was too affected by human suffering to teach history.

Nevertheless the discovery of the correspondence was one more reason to be shot of Jones. The core of concern was the same as it had been at Brisbane Grammar. The way some saw it, Jones' power over the boys verged on the immoral. The force of Jones' motivation was limiting rather than liberating. At its worst it was enslavement. As Phil Byth at Brisbane Grammar learned the hard way: 'Ultimately, you realised it was all about him'.

Boarding school boys, in particular, starved of love and sometimes having troubled relationships with their own fathers, need additional protection. So the majority of the housemasters penned a letter of their own. Addressed to Headmaster Kurrle, the letter spoke emphatically of concern about Jones' influence and control over some boys, describing it as 'bad, very bad'. To these masters Jones had become a baleful presence, to one an Alcibiades, a charismatic and devious peddler of loyalty.

The question of when, even whether, the letter actually arrived on Stanley Kurrle's desk is disputed or lost to memory. Kurrle is unsure about the letter, well remembered by others, including one who refused to sign it. Peter Spencer, who also lived in Broughton House, defended Jones and was not alone in seeing his colleague as subject to victimisation and jealousy. Part of Spencer's support for Jones stemmed from a recognition that the law and understood values of the day lagged behind social reality. Jones' suspected homosexuality, in Spencer's view, did not necessarily make him a predator.

It was complex and vexing, for Jones, too. Indeed, it must have been awful for him. Coming out is difficult even now, but in the 1960s and 1970s it was closer to impossible. Homosexuality was illegal in New South Wales and, in particular, Queensland, which was one of the slowest states to embrace homosexual law reform. Confessed homosexuals were still treated as mentally ill. So Jones had continued reason to conceal a central feature of his being. In doing so he gave the school some comfort that he was not in breach of Australia's 'no poofter' code. At King's, Jones seemed to enjoy engaging in sexual banter with his students, giving them reason to presume he was a 'pants man'.

The impression was heightened when, through 1973 and 1974, King's appointed its first female teacher. Inge Bishop, or 'Boobs', as the boys called her, had winning looks as well as winning ways. Inge and Alan began to be seen together. Now Inge Carpenter, his fellow English and French teacher was flattered by the attention, and became keen on Alan, even though Spencer warned her she might be wasting her time. According to Inge, 'There followed a period of more and more flattery and he started asking me out. He would send boys around with notes saying—Will you go with me to the Opera? I started to go with Alan to the Opera and the Rugby. It was always to public events. At the end of the evening he would give me a peck on the cheek and say goodnight.'[27]

Inge was not Alan's only presumed girlfriend. The Queenslander had maintained his friendship with Madonna Schacht, who cut an impressive figure when she visited Alan and stayed on campus. Alan did nothing to contest the belief that Madonna and he were lovers. Brian Porter recalled Jones talking about their mythical broken engagement. But by 1973 Madonna was coping with a broken marriage and confronting the worst ordeal of her life. On 19 July her estranged husband, Dr Rudolph Weber, abducted their two-year-old son from Brisbane and fled to Europe. As Madonna explained, 'My grief was catastrophic. The only way I could recover my child was to follow father and son and do battle through European courts.'[28] Five days later a sobbing Madonna was on a plane in determined pursuit.

Alan Jones' role in helping his distressed friend is another of the often-repeated legends from King's. Later, a comprehensive and astute newspaper profile by journalist David Leser reported Jones as being 'at the centre of a dramatic operation to retrieve the child of a woman he had been close to in Queensland, and had once almost married ... With the child's mother, Jones hatched a daring mission. According to well placed sources, he tracked down the village where the child was being kept, flew there and within five or six days had reclaimed the boy, slipped across the border into Switzerland and returned to Sydney.'[29]

While Alan Jones did seek leave to rush to Austria, borrowed money to do so, and proved to be a great help to a friend in need, the story is another to have undergone favourable adjustments. In fact, the dramatic rescue appears to have taken place 12 months after Jones' visit. Back in Australia he did help lobby for political and financial support. Madonna's good friend provided valuable assistance, but the part about him personally engaging in a derring-do rescue mission does not appear to be true. The timing was all wrong for a start: in mid July 1974 when the child was being rescued, Alan Jones was in the middle of a key mission of his own, securing the long-awaited GPS rugby premiership. A week before the final game was played against Riverview on 27 July, the Firsts, led by Anto White, took an unbeatable lead.

Alan Jones' preparation of his First XV had by now reached the immaculate. The spindly 13 year olds of 1970 were now superbly fit young adults who had learned to work together with orchestral precision. Some of the players who had come through the junior ranks with Alan Jones barely knew what losing felt like. Rod West could not help but admire him: 'His influence was almost hypnotic. I will never forget the Saturdays. The boys would arrive about 11 am. There would be some exercises and maybe a barbecue with a few girlfriends in attendance. The boys would then go off to a private session with Alan. Just before the main match he would lead them across from the school. It was like El Caballo Blanco. They were totally hypnotised, and would go out to demolish all before them.'[30]

There are always narks lurking around the rucks of sporting debate, with criticism this time settling on Jones' adoption of the negative rugby he had condemned in years past. Critics noted the Jones game plan was built on his favourite fly half's kicking game. The formula for victory was simple and allegedly unerring: when the ball left the scrum, Anto White would follow Alan Jones' instruction to 'put it in the box'. Andy Simkin, the halfback displaced by Peter Gemell, says the tactic was perfected in training. Simkin felt Jones 'wanted Antony to be the hero', and when the kick was well executed Jones would enthuse about the moment as 'the equivalent of a rugby orgasm'.

The King's First XV of 1974 was never beaten in the GPS season, although they did play one drawn match against Scots. While there were many excellent footballers, it was recognised even then that the team was better than the sum of its parts, its most important member never taking the field. The player often said to be the best, halfback Peter Gemell, said, 'I don't think the King's First XV was as good as some of the others. It's just that Alan had the capacity to lift the whole team's performance in such a way as to make them winners.'

Around the JS White Oval at season's end, the criticisms did not count. Jones had delivered the long-awaited premiership. The school basked in the glory, old boys booked private rooms for celebratory dinners and Alan Jones' worst enemies, swallowing their words, cheered along with the rest.

Ian Humphreys, a Jones' doubter, put it this way: 'I can safely say that Alan Jones commanded more superlatives than any other coach I have known; best analyst of the game, most knowledgeable exponent of tactics and finer points generally, the keenest eyesight to pick out the all important detail, the most imaginative [deviser] of back line moves, the most energetic driver both of his teams and himself, when the sun had long since set on the White Oval or the rain was pouring down on some dank muddy field in Scotland or New Zealand'.[31]

In track and field in 1974 there was improvement rather than triumph. One promising athlete, David McClelland, was another to fall out with Alan Jones, giving King's and his coach a miss and heading for Barker. Others, such as Cholmondeley 'Chum' Darvall, did well, Darvall giving credit to Jones' modern approach to training. With Jones' continued assistance Darvall went on to compete in the Commonwealth Games. Athletics captain Peter Harvey, who had his own argument with Jones about being asked to do too much, believes Jones extended the horizon of all the young athletes. The results and elevation in self-respect, in his view, put the entire school in further credit.

In his final year Scott Walker was feeling the same stultifying warm front that had overwhelmed his Brisbane predecessor, Phil Byth. During a GPS race the preceding year, Walker collapsed. The burden of training and studying and dealing with Alan had become too much. His relationship with Jones worsened when Scott became serious about a girl. Jones was splenetic, accusing his protégé of wasting his time and his talent. A jealous Jones kept up the sniping, pressuring Scott to advance his athletics training, imposing the same 'excessive demands' he had earlier opposed. Walker said some of the unhappiest moments of his entire life were when Jones openly ridiculed him on the football field. 'We do not have a team, we have fourteen players plus one', Alan spat, glaring at Scott.

The storm finally broke in the unlikely firmament of an English literature class. A disagreement over one of the characters in *Emma* turned nasty. Walker saw the Mr Knightly character as complicated and contradictory, arguing the point with his teacher, who insisted Jane Austen's leading man was a paragon of virtue. By now Walker had come to suspect that Jones was nervous about people who respected subtlety of thinking. He wondered whether his teacher had even read *Emma*.

An offended Jones railed at Walker. The student retaliated with words not found in an Austen text. 'Get fucked,' he told Jones, not for the first time. Walker was sent to the headmaster and did not return to Jones' class. The rift spilled over into his family. This time it was the mother who opposed Jones. Mrs Walker was also sick of him. But it was too late for Scott to change schools so he stayed on at King's.

After the incident Jones gave Walker zero out of fifty for a trial English exam citing poor handwriting, an astonishing result considering Walker was the school's outstanding English student who later finished eighth in the state. The result meant he missed The King's School Club Prize, an award particularly coveted by Walker as it had previously gone to both his older brothers. If this was Jones' revenge, it was cruel and small-minded.

For all that had been achieved on the sporting field, 1974 was the end of the road for Jones at King's. In his later valedictory, Ian Humphreys said: 'Yet his career was by no means one long triumph and what is worse many came to feel that his successes were not worth the price'.[32] By the end of 1974 discontent about Alan Jones had spread beyond the housemasters to parents and members of the school council. Jones' supporters saw difficulties over conspicuous target John Polain, stemming from Jones' failure to pick the boy in the top rugby team. In contrast, Polain's supporters saw Jones' attacks as manic and cruel. One recalls Jones telling other boys that Polain had such a yellow streak that boys sitting behind him should be able to see it. Some of this might have been communicated to Polain's father, who, in 1975, became president of the Old Boys' Union.

Another influential parent, Sydney solicitor David Lane, the head of the Fathers' Committee at King's, had more cause for concern. Lane had five sons at King's. More than one had had trouble with Jones. Robert Lane was another to transfer to Barker College following a Jones' screaming session at a school regatta. The word was getting around. Sir George Halliday, appointed to the position of School Secretary in 1975, was also lined up against Jones now. By the end of the first term in 1975 Stanley Kurrle was persuaded.

'As sudden as a road death' is how one of those eloquent King's teachers described Jones' departure. Stanley Kurrle, now retired for many years and conscious of ongoing speculation about the reasons for Alan Jones' departure, explained that tension had risen to such a point that it seemed only a matter of time before a parent or parents brought a lawsuit against Jones and the school. 'My concern was for him. He was a highly able, terribly energetic schoolmaster and I could see him hurting himself. We talked it over and I said I think it is in your interests that you should look elsewhere. I think he came to see that.'[33]

Alan Jones was on campus when he received a message that the headmaster wanted to speak with him. A 'shell-shocked' Jones returned an hour later to explain, 'I've been sacked'. When asked why, Jones said that, essentially, he did not know but that Kurrle had mentioned 'mounting criticism', explaining that he should resign or he would have to be dismissed.

As it was a term break there were only a few teachers around. Peter Fay, a new English teacher hired by Alan Jones, was one of a rearguard of teachers who attempted to rally support to fight the termination. They found plenty of allies among students, ex-students and parents. Letters from former students, such as Bret Walker, began to arrive in Kurrle's office, protesting about the school's ingratitude. Offers of financial and legal support came from well-connected families, and a plan was soon hatched to mount a legal challenge.

Alan Jones, Peter Fay and their friend Inge Bishop saw more of one another as they coordinated the fightback. The Whites were one of the many families to help with accommodation. On one trip to one of the properties, Inge Bishop seized the opportunity to settle once and for all the question of whether Alan could become a romantic partner. Upon their arrival the host pointed to the guest quarters, explaining they could sort the sleeping arrangements out themselves. Inge took the intiative, claiming a double room for herself and Alan. But, she says, Alan said he had a headache. 'Nothing happened and there were extreme opportunities.'

It was useful at least to have the grip broken on a puzzling relationship. She was left bemused and a touch annoyed that Jones might have benefited from being seen with her for the sake of calming the odd anxious father. The annoyance turned to anger a few years later when one of the boys told her Alan had boasted to him about their 'wonderful sex life'.

Alan Jones' world at King's was crumbling. The final collapse occurred at the Whites' holiday home in Terrigal, where, over the telephone, Jones was persuaded by the school to forgo the fight and resign, or face the sack. A resignation letter was drafted and Reverend Kurrle set out with a colleague and lawyer, Harold 'Bud' Abbott, arriving at Terrigal mid evening. As it turned out, Alan Jones and Peter Fay were at the time consulting with Jones' own lawyer back in Sydney. As usual there are variations in the accounts of what followed. Inge Bishop, another house guest, remembers meeting Kurrle and Abbott and advising them that Jones had not yet returned. So Kurrle went off to wait at his own holiday house at nearby Forresters Beach. By the time they returned and the two parties came together it was close to midnight. An awkward moment was made worse when the headmaster slipped and fell hard on the darkened steps. There was forced politeness. Lighter than air conversation hovered precariously above the sound of the sea. Jones signed the letter. Kurrle put his hand out but it was refused.

In his later radio career, Alan Jones would rate the bureaucrat as a prime enemy. His enmity may have grown from times like this when he saw himself as a victim of a closed club-like mentality that was an enemy of the individualist. In Jones' view small-minded bureaucrats looked upon individualists such as himself as a threat to their own rigid existence.

When the term resumed a note, dated 5 May 1975, was posted on the bulletin board, declaring without further explanation: 'Alan Jones has resigned from the staff and will not be returning to school next term'. Later in the year the school magazine published a formal valediction by Senior History Master, Jonathan Persse, which appeared to share the view that Alan Jones had been extinguished by lesser lights. Persse described Alan as like a comet; hard to ignore: '... one might feel its gleam to be a baleful interruption and a threat to one orderly routine'. He spoke admiringly of success in the English classes and on the sports field, and of Alan's inspirational presence and demand for loyalty. 'This approach, calling for a very high degree of dedication, had its disadvantages in a community of the nature of a boarding school, where all staff and boys are subject to an ever-shifting battery of pressures and Alan undoubtedly was looked on askance by certain members of staff, who either were of a different educational philosophy, or who failed to understand his passions and his dreams, or who genuinely disliked his dynamic and sometimes abrasive manner.'[34]

Jonathan Persse's valediction challenged a decision, which for Stanley Kurrle had been difficult but probably unavoidable. Alan Jones was now 34 years old, clearly too far on to change bad habits. Despite warnings that go back to his time at Brisbane Grammar, he had not learned to moderate his behaviour. There was a continuing failure to exercise restraint in his blind support, or unrelenting condemnation, of individual boys. In his unwillingness to draw back there are strong indications of a deep unhappiness with himself. Having denied who he was to himself he could not be himself. He had instead stuck to his ways, refining a routine of not just denying unhealthy behaviour, but proclaiming it as virtuous.

Alan Jones later described the episode as a devastating blow that was difficult to put behind him. It would have been hard.

He had been teaching for 15 years. A setback like this meant that furthering his teaching career was questionable, and if there had been plans to become a GPS headmaster, they were surely shot to bits. But it was even worse than this. Jones had lost a career and a kingdom. He had been around boarding houses for 20 years. For the best part of two decades fine young men surrounded him and fought for his favour. It is hard to think of another environment in which Alan Jones could pick and choose compliant subjects to captivate, control and excite.

What was revealed to those perceptive masters at King's was Jones' hold on his charges serving a deep need in himself. What they saw was a virus in search of a host. So what new kingdom could be found, where Alan Belford Jones might live his many lives through others?

CHAPTER 6
CITIZEN JONES

'THE ONLY THING YOU GET IN life without hard work is failure.'[1] This favourite Jones' quote, attributed to his mother, was not borne out by his King's School experience. Alan Jones had worked hard and he had failed. In the next period of his life, which saw four failed attempts to enter parliament and exile back to a small country town, there was also a lot of hard work.

Ironically, the failures were important, indeed crucial to his making. Both the King's experience and his excursion into politics gave him contacts and know-how that would last a lifetime. The setback at King's marked the beginning of a period when Alan Jones accelerated his struggle to be somebody. The shift in direction also forced him to raise his sights as a rugby coach. But Alan's narcissism precludes discussion of failure and admission of wrongdoing. Furthermore, a failure to clear the air stimulated suspicion. As he left King's the dust of rumour rose high. It has yet to settle.

In the wide King's diaspora they still argue about Alan. Some family members are split, refusing to talk to one another for years. They recall macroscopic circumstances in microscopic detail. There is acute sensitivity. There are strong views either way. For many boys the mentorship was beneficial. While a few puzzle about a higher purpose, the simple pursuit of excellence has its virtues. As Peter Milne (class of 1972), quoting another Jones' maxim, puts it: 'If you want to grow roses make sure they are the best and biggest roses in the street'. The Jones touch soothes and stimulates. The Jones touch burns like a branding iron.

The wounded came to favour a strategy familiar to victims of later broadcasting tirades. They stayed out of his way. They got on with living, after being excoriated by a man who did not know how to get on with his life.

It was hard for the parents, too. Time and again supporters found they were defending Mr Hyde against Dr Jekyll, having seen nothing of the malevolent Jones. And there is guilt shared by those who did see, but who, like the prison camp guard, lowered their eyes for the sake of favour. The defenders of Alan Jones become excited and anxious. Raw nerves are touched. Parents have a duty to shield their children from the robbers of innocence. Mothers in particular often leapt a barrier of faith when they gave their love and trust to Alan.

Different people have differing accounts of the reckoning that is said to have followed the physical deterioration and mental stress Jones must have experienced on his departure from King's. Certainly, it was an unusual time in his life, one when he needed help. In the photographs from this period he looks his true age. After five years at King's—with a frenetic schedule but little exercise—he had lost the whippet frame, the hair was shaggier and the hipster trousers now had a paunch to contend with.

It may be that some people's memories have morphed, but a consistent belief is that after he left King's he landed in Parramatta Hospital for a month. While he was ostensibly there for the treatment of a physical condition, a belief persisted that he had suffered a nervous breakdown. According to Peter Milne, it was a simple matter of a 'flat battery'.

The obvious step for Jones to take when he recovered was into politics. Parents and students, marvelling at his fluency, saw him as a natural. While Jones himself eschews the idea of teachers pushing a political line, students and colleagues at King's largely took him to be a leftie. A number of people remembered him telling students he voted Labor in 1972,[2] rallying students to listen to Gough Whitlam and expressing his poor opinion of Liberal opponent William McMahon.

Alan Jones' ideas and philosophies have long formed more around a mix of personal connections than personal experience. Jones jumps around so much that understanding his core beliefs has always been difficult. As a teaching colleague put it, 'Alan always believes what he says because he has no existing underlying philosophies to challenge new beliefs'.

Jones appears to be one of many Australians who changed their opinion of Gough Whitlam between 1972 and 1975. In Alan's case the shift seems more an outcome of new allegiances than new ideologies. King's provided Jones with the sort of contacts and patronage that were missing back in Brisbane, although they came from the other side of politics. So a course was set, the Jones compass swinging wildly before settling on the National Country Party and Canberra.

Dugald Anthony does not remember helping Alan towards Canberra, but Doug Anthony, the National Country Party leader, says Dugald was instrumental. Dugald's father was also impressed by Jones, seeing him as a shining light that might help them out of the shadowlands of Opposition.

An opponent of head office interference in preselections, Alan Jones was signed in to the Country Party on 11 August 1975 and he was given a job as research director; he found accommodation in the outer suburb of Torrens. The job was a front for the main mission of winning the federal seat of Eden Monaro. Stretching between the Australian Capital Territory and Bega, on the coast of New South Wales, this electorate figured nowhere in Alan Jones' past. The usual condition of having to wait twelve months before becoming eligible to stand was waived. There is no record of Alan Jones attending federal electorate council meetings other than the preselection meeting of 27 September 1975.

With the support of Federal Chairman Ralph Hunt and Leader Doug Anthony, Alan Jones was considered a shoo-in.

Anthony and his wife approved, inviting Jones to dinner, and noticing that 'he loved to hold the floor'. When vetting Jones' speeches, his new boss could also see a naivety that would need to be overcome.

But there was another problem, unbeknown to Anthony at the time. When the preselection ballot was undertaken Jones finished back in the field, despite the head office endorsement. What the King's giveth, it seems, the King's also taketh away. Doug Anthony explained: 'The King's School clique were involved with the Country Party. Jones had divided King's. The students were for him but the Old Boys were against him. I knew nothing about it until it was too late. They blackballed him.'

Doug Anthony remembers the setback as a big disappointment for Alan Jones, who for a time stayed on in Canberra. Jones has spoken about being there for 11 November, history having generously delivered him a box seat. The deputy leader's office was next to the front door of Parliament House. When Governor-General John Kerr famously sacked Gough Whitlam, Jones was there as protestors gathered outside. While Coalition members watched from the upstairs windows, Alan Jones could not help but smile at the very 'Aussie' approach to confronting a national crisis: '"Jump, jump", yelled the crowd'.[3]

The conservatives, with whom Alan Jones was now aligned, regained power. The Liberal Country Party Coalition under Malcolm Fraser easily won the subsequent election. It was not, however, a win for Jones, whose participatory role in the affairs of the nation would have to wait. At this stage, it was apparent that, to win such a role, he needed to further improve his credentials. In the meantime, he also needed to make a living.

Will Abram says the next career move came as a result of a telephone call from Judy White. Abram and Anto White had both been coached by Jones at King's. If there was a group of King's parents well disposed toward Jones, it was more likely to be found among the rugger buggers: the alignment of King's and conservative politics also embraced rugby. Australian rugby has a chain of command and lines of communication that intersect, in particular, with the Liberal Party. They teach them well in those private schools how to survive the rucks and mauls of public debate.

Getting Jonesy back into his life would be good for young Abram, who had a firm career goal of his own. Having left King's in 1975, after a less successful rugby season, Will had returned to the farm and dreamed of running on for the Wallabies. Judy White asked Bill's father, Victor Abram, whether there might be a job for Alan.

Victor Abram, another King's old boy, was only too pleased. Around the central north of New South Wales, 'Geoff'—or 'Abe', as he was better known—was something of a mini mogul. Beyond the farming, horse breeding, and running a regional airline and a busy medical practice, Dr Abram also championed local rugby. The dynamic doctor was one of those forthright and physical Australians Alan Jones is not alone in admiring, a heroic figure to some. Adrian Harrison, the local tyre merchant, says of the doctor: 'Many a victim of a tractor or shooting accident owe their life to his skill and initiative as a medico'. Although intending to sell his airline, Abram could see Jones fitting in to his interests in both business and sport.

When the profiles are written and the Jones' curriculum vitae trotted out, the Quirindi period—like Ironside—is rarely mentioned. Living in a caravan at 'Rockleigh', the Abrams' property 12 kilometres from town, seems a comedown for the man who would be prime minister, but according to Will Abram, Alan Jones did not complain: 'He handled it well because he's a strong fella and it's the next step. There's no point in crying over spilt milk and I think that was his attitude.'[4]

If in his past Alan Jones had taken the direct route south from Acland, about halfway to Sydney along the New England Highway he would have passed the turnoff to Quirindi, the 'Gateway to the North West', where there was rich soil and third and fourth generation wealth. Quirindi was also the home base of Skyways, which ran a twice-daily service between the region and Sydney. Although Alan Jones had no business or aviation experience, Geoff Abram, knowing him to be a hard worker, made him general manager.

Alan Jones' newly formed Canberra connections were helpful in lobbying for better linkages and patronage. He was made president of the Northern Committee of the Airport Users Association and did the speaking circuit rounds, pushing to get Gunnedah residents to better support the service.[5]

Typically, Alan got stuck into a work routine that started with taking Will through his sprint training before heading to the office, which was next to Abram's surgery. Jones was fortunate in that the mechanics of running the airline were largely in the hands of Abram's secretary, Pauline Henry. Vivacious and versatile, the thirty-something widowed mother worked at the medical practice and Skyways, even piloting the aircraft.

Pauline Henry and Alan Jones often travelled together on company business. Townsfolk began to presume they were a couple. At local dances Pauline and Alan were conspicuous. As Pauline Henry explained: 'Alan and I were about the same age. I liked to jive. He could jive so we danced together.' It was no doubt of help to Alan. Gaining acceptance in small communities such as Quirindi can take forever, and gaining acceptance as a homosexual man, a bit longer. Although not everyone took to Alan, his charm was effective. He continued to visit the big properties, where it was noticed that he took time to talk to the housekeepers. As to the supposed relationship with Pauline Henry, it followed a similar course to the one with Inge Bishop. In all their time together Alan never made a move on Pauline.

Pauline Henry also helped out behind the scenes with the rugby team Geoff Abram supported. Having won three premierships in the 1960s, the Quirindi Lions were going through a fallow period, many of the players from the successful era having retired. By 1976, they were struggling to put a strong side on the paddock. In a sense, the cycle of fortune on the field followed the cycle of fortune on the land—as soon as they found a good leaper in the line-outs, he would hop in his ute and migrate, like the ibis, to a fencing job a thousand paddocks away.

Geoff Abram had good connections to the Sydney rugby scene, which meant his reputation for staging rescue missions was already established. Abram was known for flying in ring-in players from Sydney's most successful club, Randwick. Locals still remember the time the international scrum-half, Ken Catchpole, turned out to play for little Quirindi.

On 7 June 1976, with the season underway, Alan Jones took over as first grade coach. In doing so at least three of the successful King's team of 1974 were reunited—Alan Jones, Will Abram and Noel Hill. The Hill dynasty owned a number of properties, among them 'Willow Tree', outside Quirindi. Alan Jones was a big fan of Sinclair Hill's son, describing him in the team notes of 1974 as 'a beautifully balanced athlete with quick hands'.[6] So Noel Hill would often fly in for the Thursday night training sessions. Before Alan Jones arrived it was hard enough getting players to turn up. Now the training sessions brought spectators as well. Club President John Benham wished he had jotted down some of Jones' sayings. 'Son, run hard—if you practise running slowly long enough, you'll become good at it.' Doug Gowing, another official, recalling word for word the same expression, still smiles at the image of the strain on the faces of players being lectured about commitment by Alan Jones when all they wanted was to head to the clubhouse for a beer.

Noel Hill said Jones made an instant difference. 'We were getting flogged 50–nil until Jonesy came. After he came we might not have won but we didn't get flogged 50–nil anymore.' His centre partner, Mal Pursehouse, agrees. Pursehouse had planned to hang up his boots, but the arrival of the new coach brought on a change of heart.

When Quirindi was going well the football ground became like a picnic race meeting with locals securing parking the night before. Under Alan Jones the crowds started to come back. But there was unrest, too. A bit of grumbling began to circulate around Will Abram and a suspicion that Alan Jones wanted him to take over the captaincy. Players used to turning up for the fun of it had lesser patience for Jones' hectoring.

Over the years Alan's troubles with players often formed around the halves. He is not the only coach to have the problem. The halves largely control on-field manoeuvres, so much of the pressure of Jones' coaching style fell on them. In Quirindi he resurrected the King's tactic of 'kicking it into the box'. If a player decided to run the ball instead, he risked Alan's wrath.

Halfback Stuart Bell had already had a run-in with Alan Jones during training. It soon got worse. Turning up to play against archrival Moree, Bell threaded through a bigger than usual crowd to find his name missing from the program. Fuming, he walked from the ground, refusing to play under Alan Jones again. The ring-in replacement was another former King's footballer, one who knew how it felt to be dropped by Alan Jones. Andy Simkin remembers the call: 'He said to fly up and he would refund the airfare. He still hasn't paid me.'

It turned out to be a losing trip in more ways than one. Quirindi fans watched a disaster unfolding. Andy Simkin did not know the calls and some team mates, unhappy with the selection, appeared to underperform. Quirindi lost and failed to make the play-offs.

Despite the disappointment, the team had shown improvement and Will Abram's mission to play for the Wallabies advanced a touch. Meanwhile, Stuart Bell switched to Rugby League before later returning to Rugby Union and representative selection. Among the disaffected there was discomfort about the way Alan Jones ogled the boys and played favourites. The sight of the elite few turning up fresh after a short hop in the Abrams' plane was not a thrill to players who had risen at dawn for a long drive.

Alan Jones the divider had found an ally, his friendship with Geoff Abram accentuating an existing split. Abram was known at the football games, not always affectionately, for being heard all over the ground. Standing beside an equally forthright Jones, toes over the line, they were an impossible duo to ignore. So noisy was the commentary during a Tamworth game, the referee blew his whistle, stopped the game and ordered them to retreat from the sideline.

They were both known for their fiery tempers and, equally, for good deeds. Pauline Henry recalls Alan Jones taking a caring approach to young Aboriginal athletes, helping with their training. She also remembers Jones' care for his own mother. While Alan was at Quirindi, Beth Jones' condition worsened. Alan had to drop everything, borrow some cash and rush to Brisbane.

Alan Jones coached until the end of the 1976 season, approaching another important turning point. On 14 October the Quirindi Rugby Club formally thanked him for his 'wonderful contribution', regretting that he 'would not be able to continue'.[7] By then he had also thrown in his Skyways job, which was a relief for some of the pilots, who had come to detest him. Oxford, the oldest English-speaking university in the world, had beckoned to Jones, although the exact nature of the beckoning is unclear. Newspaper reports have claimed alternatively that Alan Jones undertook four terms of postgraduate study in politics,[8] that he had won a scholarship[9] and that he was a Rhodes scholar.[10] All appear to be untrue.

As far as I could ascertain, Alan Jones enrolled, as a fee-paying student, for a Special Diploma in Educational Studies, a one-year non-degree course. Education students are fairly regarded as full members of the university, but for many, the Oxford Department of Education is a back-door route to Oxford status.[11]

The cost of the course alone—around £1000—was steep enough, but it appears Alan Jones may have found a benefactor. John Roberts, a founder of Pioneer Cement and another wealthy King's parent who had two sons at the school in Alan Jones' time, was also a believer and supporter. There was some talk in the Roberts family that their dad might have chipped in.

So, in October 1976, Alan Jones moved from dusty roads to dreaming spires when he became a resident of Worcester, one of Oxford's 39 colleges, set amidst 26 acres of gardens and shady walkways, with library, chapel and fifteenth century cottages. Alan Jones was thrilled. The sabbatical was wanted as well as needed. He later spoke of the joy of hiring a Mini Minor and driving to the end of England. For friends and family he produced newsletters telling of visits to international rugby matches and the London theatre district. He saw *Romeo and Juliet*, *Wild Oats*, and Opera Society productions of *Joan of Arc* and *Othello*. He also lined up for *Playboy of the Western World*, *Mame* and *The Rocky Horror Show*.[12]

College life was also stimulating. He told Caroline Jones:[13]

> For 50 p [pence] you went to Vanessa Redgrave. You heard Yevgeny Yevtushenko reading his poetry. You went to see Edward Heath conduct the London Symphony Orchestra with Anneliese Rothenberger and you know it was just endless. Harold Wilson I debated against at the Oxford Union and I thought if my mother could see me now. This is unbelievable and that was a collective influence. Teaches you humility. You know this great opportunity to allow education to express itself as it ought to. That the whole values, virtues, knowledge and examples of past civilisations are here for you if you want it. It's all there. You can take as much. It is up to you. You'll be a winner or a loser according to how much of this you can take and make sure it's got plenty of breadth, I used to say. And so we did the whole town over which was wonderful.

Older than most other students, Alan Jones became an intriguing figure to some fellow Australians at Oxford. One recalls him boasting: 'I am unlike anyone else here. I am living two lives in one. I have already achieved more than anyone I know who is my age, and now I am starting over again.' If he intended to impress, it did not work. A few fellow students got the feeling that he was disappointed with his past and had come to Oxford in an effort to reinvent himself.

There was no confusion about his sporting endeavours. Alan Jones picked up a blue for tennis.[14] As a rugby coach he made more of a name. Fellow Aussies saw Jones spending a lot of his time with and becoming a favourite of many of the young English players. One student can still picture him in the rugby sheds: 'He got the boys going. He had the gift of the gab. He seemed to love adoration.'

Worcester was too small to be a strong competitor in the 'Cuppers' matches played against other Oxford colleges, but in Jones' time it had one of its best years. Interviewed later by Cambridge graduate Clive James, he told the story of how his status on campus rose in accordance with the team's fortunes: 'No one spoke to me and they thought I was a bit of a fool, but then we won the first round match and they did not expect us to win any, and I went to breakfast the next morning [and] the Dons sort of looked at me and nodded. Then we won the second round and they nodded and said, "Morning". Then we won the third round and they nodded and said, "Morning, Mr Jones". Then they won the next round and they said, "Morning, Alan". The week that we got to the final they crossed the street and asked, "Do you think we will win?"'[15]

The Iffley Road ground was the venue for the big match against University College. At some cost, no doubt, to Alan Jones' breakfast conversations, little Worcester lost. But Jones did well and would be invited to coach again.

In the same interview with Clive James he spoke, as he often does, of participating in the Oxford Union debates. Beyond debating Harold Wilson he has told of taking on the most famous unionist of his day, Arthur Scargill—like Jones' dad, a coalminers' representative—in a debate of the topic 'That Terrorists Should Be Hanged'.[16]

There is no record of Alan Jones debating Harold Wilson. Neither is there a listing in the order papers of him debating Arthur Scargill. It is possible, however, that he spoke from the floor after the speakers had left, an opportunity given to everyone in attendance. Neither Clive James nor Alan Jones could recall the other, although they were supposedly on opposite sides of another debate, 'That All Art Is Elitist'.

While his time in England seems to have given release to an even more flamboyant Alan, at Oxford he maintained the façade of heterosexuality. A fellow student says he spoke of ongoing hurt after being jilted by a woman back in Australia. There must have been some compensation in that his Oxford year produced his most famous 'girlfriend'.

Alan Jones often speaks of Benazir Bhutto. He is proud of his friendship with the future Pakistani prime minister, telling friends that he played tennis with her, chauffeured her in her racy yellow MG, and more. Media reports also refer to the strength of their relationship. The *Sydney Morning Herald* reported: 'During the year Jones got to know Benazir Bhutto, daughter of the ill-fated President Bhutto. He helped her in her successful campaign to become President of the Oxford Union. They were he says "very, very close".'[17]

'We were very, very close', Alan told *New Idea*. 'We shared an ambition of becoming Prime Ministers one day. We had a lot of fun together going to the theatre, eating hamburgers and travelling to Europe. I remember she used to get me to organize votes for her Oxford Union. And I used to try to teach her to play tennis, but she was hopeless.'[18]

To Caroline Jones: 'I was very close at University in England to Benazir Bhutto. I mean she is just a beautiful person, Benazir, and a dear friend. Someone whom I'll always love, Benazir, and I was with her in London, when her father won the election, I remember him ringing her at the Randolph Hotel in Oxford, we were having breakfast.'[19]

Victoria Schofield is close to Benazir Bhutto, having written a biography of her father and maintaining a friendship beyond their shared time at university. She also remembers Alan as one of many friends but 'from my own knowledge not one of her closest'. She does recall Benazir, herself and Alan Jones having tea and 'not breakfast' at the Randolph Hotel. Of Alan Jones she says: 'He was also a very kind man—interested and concerned about other people. We kept in touch for a couple of years after Oxford but then lost contact. When Benazir was Prime Minister from 1988–90, he wrote to her and I responded on her behalf.'[20]

When later asked about Alan Jones by reporter George Negus, Benazir Bhutto said she had always assumed her university peer would go into politics. Much to Negus's surprise, however, she thought Alan Jones was pro Labor and trade unions. 'Alan Jones a right-winger?' exclaimed a surprised Bhutto. 'At university he was a pinko.'[21]

Alan Jones finished at Oxford in July 1977. He was awarded a Special Diploma in Educational Studies, which classified him as a postgraduate student and, indeed, an Oxford graduate. He is understandably proud of the Oxford period, which does get a mention on air. A later election dossier also records that while there he was 'a member of a British Government Delegation to EEC and NATO where he delivered a paper on Education and the Future'.[22]

So what to do with the Oxon credential? The additional education qualification might have signalled a return to teaching. Instead, when he reappeared in Australia it was back in Quirindi, with a different plan in mind. When, in May 1977, Geoff Abram caught up with Alan Jones on a visit to England, Jones expressed a desire to return to his old job. The country town again became a launching pad, this time for a more concentrated bid for a parliamentary seat. It saw Alan Jones move neither to the left nor back to the rural right. Alan Jones became a Liberal. His King's backer, John Roberts, with plenty of connections at the big end of town, is understood to have helped once more.

In the late 1970s, the New South Wales Liberals were eager for new blood. After the Askin/Lewis Government was ousted by Neville Wran in 1976, there was fear that a moribund party machine and a front bench of yesterday's men might again consign them to permanent opposition. New methods of preselection were being devised with an eye to energy and talent and not just the party faithful. Bruce McDonald was such a candidate. In 1976 he rolled a former minister from a safe seat in order to enter the party. McDonald then rose to deputy leadership in just two years. He remains a Jones' enthusiast, taking credit for drafting him into the Liberals.

Oxford also helped Jones—now in a flat in Quirindi township and back at Skyways—start a new career that would bring more success and fame and at the same time help raise his profile. Between November 1977 and February 1978, Alan Jones worked at his first media job, writing a weekly column, 'The Way I See It', for the Quirindi *Advocate*. Locals remember picking through his lengthy pieces, baffled and entertained in equal proportions.

As would become apparent in more mainstream columns later, Alan Jones does not work as well in print. Stripped of the passionate presentation and seamless fluency, weaknesses and contradictions more readily surface. His enthusiasm for storytelling works better when he extemporises, his thoughts surging in even and rapid freestyle. Alan Jones' ability to simplify and clarify, so evident in the classroom and on air, goes missing on the page. In print his words are muddled, rambling and in serious need of an editor.

The columns also confirm a suspicion shared by some of his students, that Alan Jones is less interested in improving our intelligence than in showing off his own. 'Collectivist societies provide those at the top with incomparable opportunities for dominating the masses because in that kind of society power is more centralised than anywhere else and more authority is given to those in charge.'[23]

The new Global Citizen Alan brought the world to Quirindi, writing of post-Watergate isolationism, unemployment in West Germany and the evolution of Marxism into democratic socialism. He wrote about attitudes to work, sensing a loss of enthusiasm among Australians. He complained about the media's interpretation of profit as a dirty word and, in doing so, had a dig at a later employer. 'The media ought to know, when it comes to making money, the media knock us all into a cocked hat. Witness the residue profits that Kerry Packer has to throw around not withstanding the virtue of his contribution to sport.'[24]

Remarkably, his Christmas message spoke of the dangers of oratory: 'Man is able to tame and has tamed all other creatures—wild animals and birds, reptiles and fish. But no man has ever been able to tame the tongue. It is evil and uncontrollable, full of deadly poison.'[25]

He wrote of yearning for December in London and then the following week of how Sydney revolted him. 'Not far from the Town Hall lies the Entertainment Centre. The thought of it nearly makes me choke. Inside, midst garish signs, blazing lights, and endless smelly queues of people ranging from the half dressed to the nearly undressed; from the totally unclean to the getting that way, are seven cinemas. The foyer is thronging with people.' Jones could not wait to get back: 'I had spent a day in Sydney. Compared to that Quirindi offered untold treasures. May she not change her ways as Sydney has.'[26]

As usual he does better with sport, but again a full stop is hard to find. 'To a nation bred on world wide sporting success of the fifties; saturated by the smell of Olympic victory in 1956; spoilt by the dedication of Harry Hopman producing Wimbledon champion after champion; excited by the victories of Richie Benaud's cricket teams and fattened on those of his successors; a chastened, humbled and sometimes sulky Australia will now have us believe that winning does not matter; achievement like wealth has become a dirty word.'[27]

The columns also reveal that despite Benazir Bhutto's assumption of leftist leanings, Alan Jones was coming out as a free marketeer. He wrote of the education industry as a public racket, and promoted privatisation and modern liberalism.

Contesting a Liberal seat meant that, despite his contempt for the big smoke and his love of simple country town ways, he was going to have to make a further sacrifice. He would again have to give up Skyways and rugby, despite being reappointed coach of the Lions in November 1977.

In Alan Jones' absence the team had finished at the bottom in both grades. Jones is sometimes blamed for an even worse season in 1978, which saw Quirindi forfeit the competition before it was over. One game played against Moree led to a record loss, with over 100 points scored against Quirindi. The scorer, Doug Gowing, has a strong memory of this game from hell because an ABC reporter interviewed him about the result. Doug says he has been subsequently reminded many times of his response to the effect that 'The Quirindi players were more interested in chasing girls than a football'.[28]

Years later the result was dredged up and used against Alan Jones in newspaper commentary about his coaching record, unfairly as it happens. By the time of the big loss Jones had also tossed in the coaching job in order to join a more important contest.

According to *Who's Who*, Alan Jones' first political post was as senior advisor to Opposition Leader John Mason in 1977. This can't be correct as Mason did not become Opposition Leader until the latter months of 1978. There is also a record of Alan Jones working as a researcher for RJ Birney MP. But Alan Jones had his eyes on more than a back room job. In March 1978, the state seat of Earlwood became vacant when Sir Eric Willis announced that in June he would retire from parliament. There were 12 nominations for preselection. One of them, Alan Belford Jones, was listed as a company manager from Warrawee.

The Warrawee address was that of his sponsors, John and Muriel Roberts, at whose home Jones stayed from time to time. Alan's age was given as thirty-four. Again, two years had gone missing. There was more fudging in a range of publicity. Jones was reported as having contested qualifying rounds at Wimbledon in 1961. One newspaper article stated: 'He holds degrees in arts and education from the University of Queensland and in political science from Oxford University'. Another said: 'He completed a post graduate degree in politics at Oxford University 18 months ago'.[29]

Journalists continued to get these important details wrong. Back in Quirindi the *Advocate* reported: 'Mr Jones is well known in the district and has an impressive educational record ... at Oxford he obtained his degree in Political Sociology, and he was second in his class of 65 students'.[30] The report went on to say Jones had represented Queensland playing tennis and had won an Oxford blue for Rugby Union.

Alan Jones' new credentials probably helped, but Liberal Leader Peter Coleman felt it was more his 'astonishing' skills as a speaker that swung him the preselection on 22 April. According to Coleman, Jones 'wiped the floor' with his competitors. With a by-election three months off, there was a lot to do. Although Earlwood was the childhood home of future Prime Minister John Howard, and had been held for 28 years by Sir Eric Willis, who was State Premier in 1975, it was not a blue ribbon sinecure. The inner west seat with its Greek fish cafes and corner pubs, and its proximity to Sydney's major airport and container terminals, had a Labor look about it.

Labor Premier Neville Wran nominated a local solicitor, Ken Gabb, to oppose Alan Jones. Gabb, a somewhat colourless figure, further helped the Liberals enter the contest as favourites. Despite the fudging there is no doubt its candidate had a lot going for him. Alan Jones was well rounded. He was well educated and knowledgeable, he was a genuine political enthusiast and he had an encyclopaedic knowledge of sport, which included an earthy love of the track. Best of all, he had the gift of oratory. Former student Dugald Anthony was an awestruck spectator: 'I did visit him when he ran for Earlwood and listened to a powerful speech, all off the cuff'.

The day after his preselection, Alan Jones began campaigning. Posters declared, shock jock-like: 'I'm not so concerned with prisoners' comfort—I want the community safer for all of us'. The Liberal candidate was described on his posters as an educated, energetic and sincere man who believed in free enterprise, freedom of the individual and less government interference. Jones promoted the value of struggle and, in contrast to an earlier view, voiced concern about the price of labour: 'Today one man's [wage] increase is another man's job'. The campaign photographs of the time show him looking younger and healthier than did the earlier King's School pictures. Oxford must have been good for Alan.

He moved to Earlwood, confident enough to purchase, with the help of King's backers, a flat at 97 Homer Street, near the electoral office. Campaign manager Graham Grimm, who supported Alan Jones' preselection, saw his confidence rewarded as well, as Alan routinely worked until midnight. But Grimm did have a rearguard action to fight. One of the failed candidates, John Spicer, was heard complaining about the Liberals having elected someone of dubious reputation. Spicer had picked up what was, in all likelihood, no more than King's School gossip. Grimm investigated and put the grumbles down to 'sour grapes'.

Of comfort to the Liberal Party machine, therefore, was the sight of former King's personnel coming out to assist Alan. Remarkably, the man who sacked Jones, Canon Kurrle, was one such supporter. Unbeknown to Kurrle, his presence came as a relief to the campaign team, now able to more confidently dismiss the whispers. This unfamiliar Earlwood territory was soon filled with friendly faces. As well as mates from King's, Alan enlisted supporters from Quirindi.

Alan Jones, a political neophyte, brought his own campaigning style to bear on Earlwood. There were some complaints among Liberals about his inability to take advice. And there was amusement on the other side. Labor campaign director Jim Pearce noticed nonplussed locals crossing the street to avoid ever-eager Alan. Pearce also recalls Jones being harassed by a Gay Liberation candidate, Peter Blazey, who proudly campaigned under the motto 'Put a Poofter in Parliament'.

As the big ballot day approached, so did the next famous Jones moment. Unbeknown to his party, Alan Jones had hatched a secret plan to win over Earlwood's Greek population. For ten days he secretly undertook dancing lessons from a local, Nancy Caruana. On the night of 11 July, locals gathered at the Earlwood–Bardwell Park RSL Club for a large pre-election function. Media reports record that when Alan Jones appeared on stage wearing Greek national dress and kicking up his feet, the audience was flabbergasted.[31]

They were not the only ones glancing nervously at the sight of Alan in a skirt. One powerful Liberal in the audience heard 'the lead balloons landing all over the room'. Peter Coleman worried that the sight of his candidate in a dress would fuel rumours about Alan Jones' sexuality. John Hannaford, a later attorney-general, said, 'everyone was squirming and we knew there was no way we were going to win'.

There was more bad news. On the same day the local newspaper, the *St George and Sutherland Leader*, editorialised in favour of Labor, not mentioning the Liberals: 'A round-up of views within the Earlwood electorate shows that the people have a high regard for the Premier Neville Wran and are prepared on Saturday to give him a vote of confidence'.[32] The newspaper was partly owned by Kerry Packer, who personally delivered the editorial, written by a member of Wran's staff.[33] At this stage Alan Jones' favourite Australian was not being helpful. Having been assisted by Wran in an important move to secure World Series Cricket at the Sydney Cricket Ground, the Packer press was in uncharacteristic support of Labor. Peter Coleman is still of the view that the behaviour of the Packer press amounted to 'dishonourable conduct'.

On Saturday 15 July, the by-election was held with Labor the clear winner. Having campaigned awkwardly for Alan Jones, Canon Stanley Kurrle said he could not be entirely disappointed, because the victor was 'one of us'. Lay preacher Ken Gabb gave thanks to God and Neville. Gabb felt he owed much of his success to the power of his own leader, still in a honeymoon period after the 'Wranslide'.

Alan Jones' immature campaigning, particularly the Greek costume episode, was telling. Later in his media career Jones survived many episodes of chronic misjudgement, a feat not so easy in the less forgiving world of politics. As in his media career, he took no blame. To the surprise of the cheering Labor camp, Alan Jones turned up at their celebrations, and was good enough to congratulate them. According to Jim Pearce, Alan Jones also 'canned the Liberals, and got more applause in the process'.[34]

Disappointed supporters ringing from Quirindi to commiserate say they listened to a recorded message from Jones to the effect of: 'I have taken a few days off to contemplate the mystifying judgement of the electorate'. There are subsequent references to Alan Jones having only lost narrowly—for example, 'by some 700 votes',[35] or in a 'cliffhanger'[36]—when in fact the Liberal vote had 'tumbled by 12.5%'.[37]

The disaster soon spread. An encouraged Neville Wran called for a general election to be staged two months later. While some Liberals had vowed never to allow Alan Jones to run again, the narrow timeframe permitted little choice. Jones lost again and so did the Liberals. More seats went, including that of their leader. Peter Coleman expressed publicly at the time that he had been consigned 'down the gurgle hole of history'.[38]

Following the loss Alan Jones moved to Macquarie Street to work as a speechwriter for the newly elevated leader, John Mason. This brought Jones closer to Mason's deputy, Bruce McDonald, the Kirribilli member who had pushed Jones' cause in Earlwood. North Sydney, Kirribilli's federal equivalent, would soon fall vacant. The private school, rugby demographic seemed more suited to Jones. While the Earlwood experience had soured some Liberals, particularly the moderates, Alan Jones still had supporters who persuaded him to have another go.

In many respects North Sydney proved an even more influential experience than Earlwood in the shaping of Jones' political ego. Preselections are often nasty. This one would leave a bitter aftertaste. At the time one Liberal faction was building such a reputation for brutal tactics they were dubbed the 'Uglies' by their enemies.

Slovenian-born Lyenko Urbanchich led a right wing faction known for attacking the more 'liberal' Liberals. A minute from one of their meetings records their attitude to a new senator: 'Election of C.J. Puplick was a disaster and he must now be ridiculed and discredited'.[39] In response to the influence of the Urbanchich right, a group of smaller 'l' Liberals had formed a loose alliance. Among them were Ted Pickering, John Hannaford and Peter Collins. A fellow moderate, Peter Solomon, was the favoured candidate for the North Sydney seat. Solomon's strongest competitors were Jim Cameron, Terry Metherell and Alan Jones.

Curiously, Jones would later speak to friends about becoming a victim of a dirty tricks campaign allegedly undertaken by the

Uglies. Rumours about the circumstances of his departure from King's began to circulate again. A strange episode occurred at a North Parramatta house he had formerly shared with a King's teacher, Peter Fay. There was an attempt to steal a filing cabinet Alan Jones had left in storage. There were also unsubstantiated stories that 'disgusting material' was found. Alan Jones sent a friend, one of his former students, to recover his possessions.

If such a dirty tricks campaign was underway it is unlikely to have been instigated by the Uglies as the Uglies were behind Jones. Michael Darby, a member of the faction who later worked for Alan Jones, confirmed their support. Jones had also expressed to others a confidence that, with Lyenko Urbanchich behind him, the seat was his. However, before the ballot a public controversy emerged over Urbanchich's alleged links to the Nazi Party in Slovenia during World War II. Urbanchich was subsequently removed from the selection committee, with a member of the state executive, John Hannaford, drafted in as a last minute replacement.

The preselection took place on 15 September 1979. When an elimination ballot reduced the candidates to four, Peter Solomon finished on top with 19 votes, with Alan Jones running third on ten votes. However, had Urbanchich stayed on the panel and supported Jones it is arguable that Jones could have at best tied the vote. Jones has long believed he was cheated, blaming John Hannaford. Hannaford, in a better position to know, thought Alan Jones was short of the numbers. Lyenko Urbanchich is another doubter. While supportive of Jones he says he could 'in no way have guaranteed him the seat'.

But the Uglies were not finished. Another controversy soon broke. Claims made by Peter Solomon on his preselection dossier about his military record were found to be false. Solomon was disendorsed and a new ballot scheduled for 29 March 1980. Alan Jones does not appear to have stood for the second round. As to why, there are varying reports. Some say he was sick of the infighting and had by then moved on to better things. Others say there were fears that Peter Solomon's removal brought concern to the surface about some of Alan Jones' claims. One senior

Liberal remembers: 'Jones gained a reputation for being less than straight with the truth. His background details weren't quite correct. He didn't give accurate information to the Liberal Party. He wasn't all that he claimed to be ... He claimed to have a Masters from Oxford which was not true.'

Yale graduate John Spender QC, an Alan Jones' mate who went on to become shadow minister for foreign affairs and an ambassador to France, ended up with the seat Jones felt should have been his. Alan Jones went back to writing speeches for John Mason and coaching rugby.

In 1979 Jones again connected with some of his former King's School footballers. Players who have trouble giving up an addiction to mud rolling after they leave school sometimes find their way into the sub-district competition. The 'Subbies' serviced the interests of players who were not up to, or did not want, the intensity of first division rugby.

Richard Weekes (class of 1978) was one who stayed in touch. When Weekes moved to Sydney University Jones continued to help him with his cricket and rugby. He says Jones, through his connections, put together an exceptional old boys' team, some of whom had played in the famous 1974 side. The standards lifted as soon as Alan Jones came on board. Weekes was used to coaches whose game plan was to get the ball and put it over the line, but he had never seen a coach so forensically deconstruct a game, identify weaknesses and figure out a program to remedy them. The King's Old Boys went through the 1979 season undefeated, taking the Grand Final 3–0.

When asked later about his greatest achievement in rugby Jones said it was less the results at the end of the season as the development of the fine young men in his care. One picture to find its way into honoured company in his home gallery was of the humble Old Boys team. Alan Jones was proud when players found success beyond rugby. Speaking of them he remarked, 'they're all merchant bankers now'.[40]

After 18 months of political combat, Alan Jones had needed a win. Still living in Earlwood and working in Macquarie Street, he watched his Old Boys moving on to careers while he marked time. But behind the scenes Alan was being noticed. An early *Sydney Morning Herald* profile says his 'voluptuous prose' became a talking point. 'Jones readily admits responsibility for the interminable speeches with which John Mason regularly glazed the eyes of the parliamentary press gallery. He boasts of once having written a 56-page reply to the budget. Press gallery members at the time remember Mason's staff keeping up a busy shuffle between their office and the gallery, distributing the final pages while Mason was still on his feet delivering the speech. I was two pages ahead of him, Jones says.'[41]

From what I can tell it was while working for Mason in 1979 that Jones got one of those life-changing calls. More like a summons, it came from a fellow Oxford graduate, Prime Minister Malcolm Fraser. Alan Jones' voice, when describing it to Caroline Jones nearly a decade later, still carried a note of excitement: 'I suppose when Malcolm Fraser asked me to join his staff just out of the blue, I rang up and he said, "I want to see you". Gosh when the Prime Minister calls you don't say no. So down I went and he said I want you here on Wednesday. There was no debate about whether you were the right person or not. He'd made up his mind; he must have talked to somebody about me. We'd never really spoken before. And down I went and I was there on the Monday and I learned a lot from him about hard work and how to get results.'[42]

Jones has said he was interviewed on a Wednesday and was writing speeches for Fraser on the following Monday.[43] He found a flat in the Roy Grounds apartments in Empire Circuit, a short walk from Parliament House. It was a mighty move for Alan, as it is for most people allowed free and regular access to the control tower of the nation. While backbench work might have better suited the eager advocate, working for a prime minister can feel more important than working for the electorate. The unelected workers at the centre of the pond can have more to do with the running of the country than many a backbencher swimming in the ripples at the edge.

Alan was rightly proud when he told his dad, living up in Margate, of the elevation. 'This was all a bit daunting for him and he said, how much are they going to pay you? I said $39 000 or something and he said I want you to remember, son, that's three salaries.'⁴⁴ A likeable feature of Alan is his modest appreciation of the simple pleasures. Alan Jones has become exceptionally rich because of a passion for what he does rather than a passion for wealth. The $39 000 income, handsome by the standard of the time, was not as important as the opportunity presented.

Harry M Miller, who was later to become his agent, was at his unrestrained best describing the work in Jones' biographical notes: 'This was one of the most powerful and influential appointments in the nation and it took Alan Jones, being a member of the PM's think tank, to practically every corner of the globe and, in particular, to famous landmarks like the White House and Buckingham Palace'.⁴⁵ *Who's Who* defines his term in the national capital from 1978 to 1981, having him working for Fraser when he was working for John Mason. More than a few colleagues from this era feel the period was shorter and the senior advisor description a familiar exaggeration.

Alan Jones joined a team of speechwriters, which did put him in the inner sanctum. Press secretary David Barnett found Alan Jones engaging and fun to have around. Another colleague, one of the many to prefer anonymity, agrees, describing Alan as 'a funny bugger, personable, surprisingly easy to get along with and at that time considerate'. When Jones put in long hours, telephoning colleagues as required at inconvenient times of the day, he had a list of the names of the wives, to help soften the impact. David Barnett saw ability as well. 'Alan was one of those people who could both speak and write very well. Many of us can be good at one or the other. Alan was good at both.'⁴⁶ Barnett came to wonder whether the interest Jones took in what the newspapers reported of the speeches was the start of an interest in a media career.

The work was exacting and demanding. Dennis White, another writer, recalls: 'You would have to be on the same wavelength as the PM or else it wouldn't have worked. Fraser was a very daunting person.'[47] Alan Jones agrees: 'He was a marvellous taskmaster. There was no room for sentiment in a way, in seeking [to serve] the nation. If you were tired and you were sick and the job had to be done then you did it. He didn't sort of say well you better go home and have a rest. He was unfailingly studious about detail. I wrote speeches but he never gave them if he didn't read every word that was written and change and change and this would mean 2 o'clock in the morning.'[48]

Alan Jones' early speeches, of the rousing rally-cry variety, went over well enough. His new boss was appreciative and thoughtful. Robert Jones was impressed by the Prime Minister's kindness to his younger brother: 'At one stage Dad was pretty sick. Fraser handed Alan an envelope and said there's a ticket to Brisbane. There's a car out front waiting to take you to the airport and there will be a car to meet you in Brisbane. Go away for a couple of days and spend it with your dad.' Robert says that, on another occasion at Number 10 Downing Street in London, the telephone rang and Fraser turned to Alan, saying, 'It's for you'. The Prime Minister had arranged for a call to be made to Charlie so Alan could keep in touch.[49]

It was not to last. As time went on Jones seemed to have trouble reaching beyond motivational rhetoric. Good speechwriters are also good researchers and in this area Jones was said to flounder. Barnett explained that, quite reasonably, the Prime Minister wanted more 'stew than soufflé' in a speech. 'Malcolm Fraser was not comfortable with sparkling prose. You have got to be able to make a speech sound serious.'

The weaknesses began to show. The more Jones' lucky-dip convictions and poor command of detail became apparent, the more his charm wore thin. One colleague recalls: 'In time we listened less and less to him. He was an object of suspicion with relation to his sexuality. Jones tried to get involved when the major speeches were written, but was kept at arm's length. He was always trying to push Malcolm Fraser to the right.' Alan

Jones saw that the weakness was in Malcolm Fraser. He told Caroline Jones: 'I don't think he was as tough on the political front as we thought he was so opportunities were let slip and all the rest of it, and many people were disappointed by Malcolm'.[50]

He told Gerard Henderson: 'There was a massive mandate to effect change because the reaction to the profligacy of the Whitlam years was profound and the only way the public would manifest that reaction was through the ballot box. I think what Malcolm Fraser learned was the importance of the political office that he had ... The language of the left was very intimidatory and at the end of the day he couldn't marshal the resources to cope with that. The fact that the mandate was there and it wasn't exercised on either expenditure or reform would be disappointing to him as well. I'm sure he would say that. It was certainly disappointing to those of us who were with him.'[51]

Jones opposed Fraser's advocacy of a boycott of the Moscow Olympics. He was also against his support for 'the ethnics'.[52] The October 1980 election is cited as another catalyst for tension. Perhaps feeling some affinity for a fellow battler from the southeast Queensland bush, Alan Jones believed the Fraser Government was underestimating Opposition Leader Bill Hayden. 'I had an immense regard for Hayden's intellect, for his sheer capacity for hard work, for his integrity. He's an Ipswich bloke, a simple fellow, a man I felt that if the public got to know a little better, the problems he'd had as a boy, impoverished upbringing, leaving school early to become a cop so his mother would have more money, great personal tragedy with the death of his child—then the public could identify with him.'[53]

Jones' drift towards the enemy's camp might also have had something to do with his continuing contempt for the Liberal 'wets': '... that was exactly the problem with Malcolm Fraser. The Liberal Party is riven with people who would be better placed in the Labor Party. Many of their front-line people are far, far to the left of Paul Keating and Peter Walsh.'[54] Alan Jones' protest over Hayden, he believed, influenced his party to take the challenge more seriously. 'As it was Hayden ran us to the wire.

He established his reputation as a thinker and as a leader capable of getting views across that were rational and reasoned.'⁵⁵

In fact Fraser easily won the 1980 election and months later Jones was gone from the inner office. The disagreement over Hayden is not remembered. A collective recognition that Alan Jones was finding the speechwriting too difficult is the more likely reason for his departure. In his years with Fraser, according to one colleague, the easy-to-like Jones became easy to hate: 'He had a disorganised body of beliefs. By the time he left he was cordially hated in the PM's department.' David Barnett disagrees: 'For my sake I was sorry when he went. He livened the place up.'

It is telling of Jones' time with the Prime Minister that he is best remembered for a line he did not write. 'Life wasn't meant to be easy', the phrase that became Fraser's signature saying, has entered folklore as having been penned by Alan Jones, another example of the force field of legend overwhelming truth. In fact Fraser first uttered the words at a Deakin lecture in July 1971. Perhaps Alan's own signature saying could have been 'the truth matters less than what people believe'. By the time he left Fraser there were still plenty who believed in Alan, enough to ensure that life was getting easier.⁵⁶

Alan Jones was headhunted by a powerful industry body, the New South Wales Employers' Federation, becoming its executive director in April 1981. In some respects it was a good match. Australia's largest industrial relations secretariat needed a good spruiker and a willing advocate. There was a union persona in his past to draw upon. In that the Employers' Federation was famous for opposing wage rises and public holidays, it did seem to suit Alan down to the ground.

At the same time as Alan Jones was brought into the gloomy Sydney offices, another bright spark, Garry Brack, Manager of Industrial Relations, arrived. Brack says the lights soon burned until midnight. He liked Alan Jones' capacity to work and his ability to articulate issues. With Jones, the Employers' Federation was more on the front foot. There were many public speaking engagements and 'Jones involved the media to a level never seen before'. It was a heady era for industrial relations and the Employers' Federation needed a better profile to suit the moment. The big issue of the time was superannuation. Jones said he enjoyed entering the fray, explaining: 'there were tremendous conflicts between union and its power'.[57]

Alan Jones also got a new company car, a shiny Holden which, in its first weeks, fell victim to a clueless Sydney taxi driver while Garry Brack was giving it a run. The new position also brought a pay rise, enabling Jones to gain a proper toehold in the Sydney property market.

Alan Jones describes himself as a person without acquisitive interests. 'I mean you can only live in one house, sleep in one bed and drive one car. I don't have any desire to own 15 houses, two beach homes and 10 cars. It makes life too complicated.'[58] When it comes to horses and real estate he may have changed his mind. There is perhaps something in the Jones' family history, a bare, atavistic longing for sustainable acreage, that has compelled him to acquire what is now a very large property portfolio. To this point Alan had invested in a modest house in Brisbane and the flat in Earlwood. While some insist he also spoke of owning a holiday house in Terrigal, it is more likely this was one made available by the White family.

On 8 May 1981, a terrace in Rose Street, Chippendale became a permanent home, perhaps the first real home he had experienced since leaving Acland in the 1950s. Describing himself on the transfer deed as 'Senior Advisor to the Prime Minister', Alan Jones bought the terrace for $87 500. The 'Chippo' address surprised some. Inner urban, semi-industrial grot was not then so fashionable. But Alan Jones knew the area, just across from Sydney University, as some of his former King's students flatted there. The Rose Street terrace was closer, too, to some of Sydney's gay beats. Although Jones was not known to be a client, across the road was an occasional hang-out for male prostitutes.

Gay connections were difficult for Alan. Having spent so much time in boys' schools and out of Sydney, and clinging as he did to a heterosexual world, there were relatively few opportunities for finding willing male partners. Alan seemed to be of the homosexual cohort that preferred discreet and anonymous partners. This period between school and rugby careers appears to be the only one in which Alan Jones is remembered attending some of Sydney's gay bathhouses.

The Chippendale base also put him within five minutes of his office in Haymarket, the trade union quarter so loved by Chinatown restaurateurs. The job also helped with connections, Jones finding himself across the table from union men like Simon Crean. It also put him close to the engine room of the New South Wales Labor Party, another source of knowledge and contacts, valuable in a city that thrives on influence peddling.

Alan Jones' own plans for a seat were suspended for a time, but he stayed close to the political scrum. Indeed, in doing so he made one of his most lasting and important connections. In 1981, Ross Turnbull put his name forward as a prospective Liberal candidate for the seat of Wentworth. Turnbull, a former Wallaby, is another of those gruff, masculine Australians Jones admires. As stand-in manager for a rugby tour to New Zealand in 1978, 'Mad Dog' Turnbull is reputed to have told the Australian forwards, after the backs were dismissed: 'Look, these Phantom comic swappers and Mintie eaters, these blond headed flyweights are one thing, and we will need them after the hard work is done. But the real stuff has got to be done right here by you blokes.'[59]

The Newcastle solicitor and newly appointed member of the Liberal Party Executive took a liking to Jones, after a short session on the tennis court. Big Ross, who saw himself as a 'hack' player, noticed he did a lot better when Alan was his doubles partner. Jones showed the hefty rugby player a few tricks, making him think, 'if this bloke can teach me to play tennis he can do the same to others with rugby'.

Alan Jones is remembered as being present as an observer barracking for Turnbull when the Wentworth preselection panel sat. Another Turnbull, the unrelated Malcolm, then company

In the early 1950s, Alan Jones (bottom left) endured bullying and the nickname 'Pansy' at Oakey Public School. (Private collection)

Robert Jones (left), a fellow Toowoomba Grammar School boarder, would come to see little of his famous younger brother. (ABC Document Archives)

A determined trainer through his high school years, Alan built himself into a competitive athlete winning his school's 1958 cross-country event in record time. (ABC Document Archives)

In his first teaching job at Ironside Public School, Alan Jones was a 'scary' figure and, according to one student, the 'toughest teacher I ever had'. (Private collection)

Although they were never lovers, international tennis player Madonna Schacht was Alan Jones' best-known girlfriend. (Newspix)

Alan (right) with tennis mate John Decker. As a young adult his sense of self-importance and need to be admired became more apparent. (ABC Document Archives)

An excellent tennis player, Alan Jones coached Brisbane Grammar teams to record victories. Standing at far left is future Wimbledon champion, Geoff Masters. Sitting between them is former favourite, Drew Hutton. (ABC Document Archives)

Phil Byth, an easy winner of the 1965 GPS Under-15 880-yards, came to see Alan Jones' coaching and mentorship as claustrophobic. (Private collection)

Although not as well credentialed as a player, Alan Jones preferred coaching rugby to coaching tennis and athletics. Steve Trewin (bottom left), a member of Brisbane Grammar's 1968 First XV, was out of favour by 1969. (Private collection)

Alan Jones, third from right at rear, encountered many disbelievers among his King's School teaching peers. Ian Humphreys, the author of the perceptive Jones valediction, is third from the right in the front row. Front and centre is the headmaster who asked for Jones' resignation, Canon Stanley Kurrle. (Private collection)

Even The King's School disbelievers cheered when Alan Jones delivered the long awaited GPS rugby premiership in 1974. Captain Antony White sits to the left of Alan Jones. Will Abram stands to the right in the middle row. Scott Walker is in the middle row on the far right. (Private collection)

Future Pakistan Prime Minister, Benazir Bhutto, was a friend at Oxford University. Alan Jones would say they were 'very, very close'. (AAP/AFP)

During his period of exile at Quirindi in country New South Wales, Alan Jones (second from right) managed a small airline and advanced his passion for horse racing. Here he joins the presentation of the Skyways Airline Cup at the Quirindi Races. (Courtesy *Quirindi Advocate*)

secretary for Kerry Packer's Consolidated Press Holdings, was also a competitor. According to one Liberal present, Alan Jones noisily disparaged this rival as 'a Kerry Packer stooge', and Packer as 'a media bully'. As it turned out, neither Turnbull was successful, the vote instead going to Peter Coleman, thereby rescuing him from that 'gurgle hole of history'.

Alan Jones later proved a friend indeed for Ross Turnbull, but at this stage Jones was the more in need. When the former Newcastle Wanderer became chairman of the New South Wales Rugby Union, Jones found a powerful ally. On 23 November 1981, Alan Jones was elected, curiously as a country representative, to the Executive Committee of the New South Wales Rugby Union. He began to manage representative teams, which gave him access to the locker rooms and brought him into the purview of others with influence.

He wanted more, but a senior coaching job was harder to crack. In October, Alan Jones had nominated for coach of Sydney University, but breaking into the 'club' was beyond even Jones' persuasive powers. Alan had not worn out his cartilages or bled into a jersey week in and week out. The assembled 'students' remember an enthusiastic and concise presentation. The air still electric with Jones' rhetoric, he was seen from the room, one committeeman commenting: 'That bloke is full of piss and wind. Who's next?'

In 1982 things got both decidedly better and decidedly worse. Still putting in full days and sometimes nights at the Employers' Federation, Jones' need to fill every minute persisted. He hated it when the Chippendale terrace emptied of young friends and the black dog slunk into the room. When an old Brisbane tennis partner, Geoff Voller, dropped in, he said he had never seen Alan looking so depressed.

With his now permanent Sydney base there was more time and opportunity to devote to sport. He continued to help with track and field training, and returned to coaching the King's Old Boys. After the success of 1979, the team had won again in 1980, but was beaten in the semi-finals in 1981. The 1982 season started poorly. Players sensed greater tension and frustration. Alan Jones wanted higher standards than are generally expected in subdistrict football. King's lost its first three games.

Another reason for Jones' gloom was his mother's poor health. The early months of 1982 were particularly bleak. Beth had not been able to communicate from her Redcliffe nursing home for years. Every day Charlie continued to make his way to her bedside. When Brisbane-based Robert visited, bringing her a bunch of bananas, he remembers watching in pain as she ate the lot. For Alan, visiting was more difficult. But in a sense, the loss of her faculties had already taken her from him. It was hard for Alan, too, to watch his once vibrant mother settle into a semipermanent foetal position.

When she died on 20 May 1982, according to Alan, 75-year-old Beth had never taken a holiday. 'She had an abscess on the vaginal wall and it burst and de-oxidised the brain. She wasn't a vegetable but today we would call it Alzheimer's. She died an awful death; it was the manner of her death that made her suffering profound. All the things she enjoyed most, like reading, drama on television and music on the radio, were denied to her in the end.'[60]

The experience influenced his position on mercy killing. 'I have great difficulty with issues that are very personal—euthanasia for example. I'm not too sure that we should be ramming down people's throats what they should and should not do. If push came to shove I don't sit on the fence. I'd have to be for it. I wouldn't want someone to suffer like my mother suffered.'[61]

But Alan's powers of recovery are substantial. He threw himself back into work and sport. The King's Old Boys needed a shake-up. He got on the telephone and persuaded players who would rather go skiing to turn out. Although it was not as happy a season, as it progressed Alan Jones again pulled the team together and again they took the premiership.

Those future merchant bankers could see then that Jones was better than district football. They were not the only ones. In

1982 Alan Jones also toured New Zealand as manager of a good New South Wales side, coached by Peter Crittle. Up against some strong provincial teams, the force of Jones' personality marked him as more than someone who counted the players on and off the bus. Confronting groundskeepers, arguing with hoteliers, Alan was unusual. A colleague from this time says: 'He did not speak like a normal rugby person. He was at pains to describe and was enamoured of the physique of players. It wasn't till later that the penny dropped.'

The Australian coach, Bob Dwyer, saw Alan Jones then as having a bright future as a manager. But Dwyer was soon to see the flaw in his observation—Jones did more than manage. Some of the players on that tour credit him with helping break down an inferiority complex that often dogged Australians playing in New Zealand. The 1982 New South Wales side returned undefeated.

Alan Jones was now forty. He had a good job but it was hard to imagine it was where he wanted to be. His dad still worried that he had not yet found a good woman, as he himself had done. And Beth was now gone. 'She never knew that I worked for the Prime Minister or went to Oxford University or coached the Australian side. It was a sad thing, very sad.'[62]

At the time Alan Jones was nowhere near coaching the Australian side, but he was on the right track to meeting his mum's expectations. Oxford helped him change direction and the Fraser experience was of powerful and lasting influence. Alan Jones learned something of how the country is run. There are trace elements still in the effrontery now heard on air. Alan Jones, PM-like, gives his signature endorsements—'That's a good answer.'[63] 'You have answered all those questions without notes which is excellent.' 'Good on you, Pauline'[64]—or puts his lessers on notice: 'What the hell's going on, Carl? ... You'll have to crack the whip ... get on the front foot.'[65]

A further legacy emerges from his tendency to carry grudges. By now it was increasingly obvious that Alan Jones needed enemies to help him know himself. Although a Liberal he became a Liberal hater, despising the moderates he blamed for thwarting his career. Ted Pickering, a later police minister, would have a tough time. A second-round North Sydney candidate, Peter Collins, would be blacklisted. John Hannaford, who did vote against Jones, was neither forgotten nor forgiven. There would be many more. 'I think I threaten people. There are people in the Liberal Party who feel they're good enough as they are, and they don't need me. It doesn't have the capacity to embrace successful people. Malcolm Fraser sat on the backbench for years.'[66]

What Citizen Alan needed was an arena in which accomplishment could be measured more simply. There was a lot in Alan Jones' peculiar conditioning and development that suited elite sport. Obsessive self-sacrifice and determination to give all were entrenched characteristics. After decades of hard work, Alan Jones was about to see that promised success.

CHAPTER 7
WEARING THE GREEN AND GOLD

'YOU'VE WORN THE GREEN AND GOLD and that makes you special', Alan Jones is fond of saying.[1] Winning the national colours is a proud achievement for any Australian. Alan Jones' Wallabies came to notice their coach's fastidious fondness for his green and gold tracksuit. The uniform formalised Jones' belief that he was indeed special. Between 1982 and 1984 Alan Jones went from coaching subdistrict rugby to controlling the national team, a bit like jumping from a go-cart into a Formula One racing car. So how did he do it?

The answer is in the intervening year. In 1983, Alan Jones seized an opportunity to prove his special talents, winning the Sydney rugby premiership in his first year as a senior coach. It was a brilliant year, the first in a period that gave Alan Jones an undeniable and deserved place in history. Despite being scorned for his scant playing credentials, Alan Jones had spent 20 years improving his understanding of the game. Like swimming coach Don Talbot and athletics coach Percy Cerutty, Alan Jones was another to show you don't have to be a top athlete to be a top coach. As is often the case, there was luck, too. Perhaps it is serendipity that brings good athletes together, or perhaps, like a pearl, excellence is formed organically, in its own time. And again, it might be that a catalyst, an agent of change, is needed to bring out the best.

In the early 1980s, the Australian national rugby team was talented but underperforming. The same was true of one of the Sydney clubs, Manly, which, despite bragging of 13 representative footballers, had not won a premiership since 1950. The northern beachside club had fallen at the Grand Final in 1981 and stumbled again after winning the minor premiership in 1982.

Rob Lane, the team coach, had formed a competitive side with an exceptional forward pack, but what continued to be missing was a winning culture. At Manly, like Sydney University, the notion of appointing a blow-in to fix the problem was sacrilege. Manly had never appointed an outsider. As the big Manly captain and international Steve Williams put it: 'The Eastern Hill mafia would not accept you unless you came to your first Manly match in a pram'.

But at the end of 1982 Jones' name was put forward, with the strongest push again coming from King's School connections. Ross Reynolds (class of 1976), a New South Wales back rower, knew Jones as an athletics coach, and Tony McGeoch (class of 1974), another New South Wales representative, had been the fullback in Jones' winning King's team. McGeoch felt 'the club needed someone like Alan Jones. We had the talent, but not the achievement.'[2]

In 1982, while managing the New South Wales team, Alan Jones became reacquainted with some of these players and made known his wish to coach. When the Manly squad headed for the United States in October for an end of season tour Ross Reynolds, in particular, pressed Jones' case to the Manly club president. Reynolds was so confident he told Peter Bradstreet, 'If we get him we will win'.

When he returned Bradstreet invited Jones to lunch; Alan told his young backers he would neither hedge nor beg: 'Look, if they're interested they can talk to me ... and I straight away told them what I had been saying for the last 20 years ... you're failing because the system, the structures are wrong, the methodology is wrong'.[3]

Concerned about Alan Jones' lack of senior experience, Peter Bradstreet was attentive but cautious. 'What got through to me was his psychological approach, which was superior to his rugby knowledge.' Although Jones thought he had talked his way out of a job, the opposite was the case. Club officials were taken with the pitch, and the majority of the club soon were too. When the 1983 season began the entire squad gathered for a breakfast. Accompanied by the scent of sausages carried on the warm coastal winds, Alan Jones spoke for 45 minutes, with never a stumble or hesitation. Veteran clubman Bob Kirkwood said, 'It was like a machine gun'.

Alan Jones was taking on a lot, not just coaching the firsts, but acting as club coach as well. James Black, who would be his most famous favourite at Manly, was struck by Jones' phenomenal memory: 'He knew the name of every first grader and every fifth grader'.

Jones was welcomed into the northern beachside community as well, making good friends that helped maintain a kinship with Manly. The club vice president, local solicitor and Liberal Party organiser Ian 'Macca' McDonald, would continue to get loyal support from Alan Jones well after his gaoling for fraud. Naturally enough, he also found a support base among other local Liberals. Not long gone from Canberra, he was happy to share his insider's knowledge. One young friend recalls him confident that pretender Bob Hawke would not roll Opposition Leader Bill Hayden. But come March 1983 he got it right. When asked how Malcolm Fraser would go against Bob Hawke in the federal election, Alan Jones predicted his former boss had 'not a chance'.

The Employers' Federation was generous, too, in allowing Jones time to attend to his Manly commitments. Garry Brack never saw Alan Jones let football get in the way. Players saw their coach arriving, sometimes in a white chauffeur-driven Holden Statesman, and changing out of his suit after a speaking engagement or a new round of industrial negotiations. Rugby was then an amateur game, which meant Alan Jones would receive no payment. It was a substantial commitment. The 6.30 Tuesday and Thursday night Curl Park training sessions would increase in frequency and intensity as the year progressed.

The players soon saw that Alan Jones was more than talk. A new second rower Jones lured from Sydney University, Peter FitzSimons, became close before later exile from what he called the JIC, the Jones Inner Circle. FitzSimons, however, still thinks of Jones as the best coach he had in any sport. 'Australian rugby up to that early part of the 1980s, it's going a bit too far to say it was a collection of people who just liked to run into each other, but it certainly wasn't a science ... I remember being a little shocked when I first came across the concept of tackle counts.'[4]

Peter FitzSimons was another surprised upon arriving at training to receive two or three foolscap pages of detailed observations and instructions. Alan Jones was one of the first to use video cameras to dissect performance in detail. If he saw a vulnerability to being beaten on the outside, he would adjust the angle of defence. If he saw a weakness passing to the left, he would re-educate his players in basic human movement.

Peter Bradstreet was amazed, watching Jones take command of these huge men. 'He had them in the palm of his hand. He was able to convince them to listen and do what he wanted them to do.' James Black felt the improvement. Instincts formerly dormant were suddenly found when the need arose. 'Some people say practice makes perfect but Jones would say perfect practice makes perfect'.

The results came quickly. On 4 June 1983, the Manly Blues walked over their neighbour, Warringah, 41–6. Peter FitzSimons took the best and fairest award. The club felt an immediate lift in confidence.

They also felt the additional aches and pains, Alan Jones as ever lifting the physical intensity of training. And like Jones' earlier teams, Manly felt the shock of new standards of discipline. When Tony 'Squeak' McGeoch was delayed by the drawbridge at the Spit and arrived late through an early morning fog, he met a force 10 Jones gale: 'You have got to clear your hip pocket of excuses'. McGeoch, well used to Jones, handled his coach better than most. 'He was forever testing people. He knew that in the heat of battle there are no excuses. He was getting us ready and it was a mistake to bite back.'

Peter FitzSimons, staring down at an enraged Jones, could not help it when he copped a serve. The blood raced to his head and the massive fists began to clench. 'Alan, don't ever speak to me like that. I'll walk. I don't play rugby to be spoken to like that. Not now, not ever.' But Jones, on tiptoes, held his ground, forcing FitzSimons to bow. FitzSimons says Jones 'brought his mouth close to my ear and sort of curled it around and said do you want to take me on, Fitzsy, do you want to take me on?'[5]

In this steamy locker room environment, Jones' law came into its own. A condition of the Jones relationship, that he must dominate, was fair enough with experienced athletes who expected the coach to be boss. One of Jones' consistent beliefs, that players should be unapologetic in pursuit of victory, also suited. Manly, a perpetual runner-up, warmed to the feel of winning. Captain Steve Williams saw his players happy to buy in to the success. Tony McGeoch also found it infectious: 'When a team is successful you don't talk about what is bad'. Generally it was an unusually harmonious year for Alan Jones, although there was a dip halfway through the season when the Blues lost two in a row. Peter FitzSimons can still picture Alan Jones after a loss to St George, his head in his hands, lamenting, 'I'll be a laughing stock'.[6]

While the essential strength in the team was in the forwards pack, there were problems too. FitzSimons, one of the players least inclined to follow Jones' instructions, instead grabbing the ball and taking his chances, was on occasions offside with team mates as well as with Jones. Like others before him FitzSimons was conscious that Jones was interested in talent, 'but he prized more highly those who were prepared to follow an established game plan'.[7]

Alan Jones, not at his best coaching forwards, had a remedy. He got on the phone to his Brisbane mate, Alex Evans, and asked for help. Soon Evans began to fly to Sydney for specialist coaching sessions. Ten years later, coaches routinely called upon sprint trainers, weight trainers, kicking coaches, physiotherapists, nutritionists, psychologists and more. But back then assistants were rare. President Peter Bradstreet has no memory of Alan Jones asking for additional expenses. He presumed Jones made the arrangements and covered Evans' costs.

Steve Williams and the others in the pack found their performance lifting in the line-outs and scrums. It was not just a matter of improving their grunt, but also of integrating the strengths and multiskilling the team. Evans and Jones threw out old notions of forwards working like shunting engines while the backs stood off searching the crowd for a pretty girl. They wanted continuous motion from backs who could push and forwards who could pass. Manly recovered its momentum. After the two losses in June, the Blues won their next five matches.

The real test was to be Randwick. Like the New Zealand All Blacks, the famous Greens had an intimidating reputation. Their coach was the Australian coach, Bob Dwyer. Their captain was the Australian captain, Mark Ella, the game's most famous player. There was more, not just two extra Ellas, but a nucleus of internationals who for five straight years had helped Randwick to the Shute Shield.

In the final game of the second round the Manly Blues and Randwick Greens played a 20–all draw. When Mark Ella rescued his team after Manly led 14–4 at half-time, he helped set up an exciting final series that saw the teams meet again in the Grand Final.

After a tough 1982, Jones was enjoying his better fortune. He became well known at some of the harbourside dining establishments, where he would haul out his trick of ghost-calling the Melbourne Cup. The improved income from the Employers' Federation also helped cultivate a taste for the good life. Boxes of Penfolds Grange addressed to Mr Jones were delivered to the club and often generously shared with selected players who dined until late at night at Chippendale. 'We never put our hand in our pocket', says one who thought Jones was 'a different bloke' then.

While Alan Jones' gifts were well received, a few cracks were showing. Predictably, the largest resulted from his habit of picking favourites. The elegant inside centre James Black, who easily held his place in the team, took the brunt. Jones gave his full attention to the shy bank teller, spending a lot of time on more than his football. Black found the mentorship beneficial, his confidence improving on and off the field. 'Jones had an enormous influence on my life. I was naturally reserved. It was the way I was brought up, but in rugby aggression is required.'

Alan Jones' bachelor status, a matter of indifference to schoolboy footballers, was more of a talking point among adult men. The players would wonder out loud. Their coach was not seen with women, but neither was he explicit in his relationship with men. Like the adolescents before them, young men who spent hours with Alan reported that Jones never made an obvious advance. Some players thought he must have been asexual. Others remained suspicious that something was being hidden.

But when he turned up at the footy ground wearing a pink sweater, and when he gave someone that adoring look, word was bound to spread. Occasionally it found its way into the barrackers' chant. If a Jones favourite fumbled a kick or missed a tackle, a cry might go up: 'Pull him off, Alan', and a titter would ripple through the crowd. Alan Jones seemed not to hear. Players who took a lot of sledging on field blocked it out, like James Black: 'If you let it affect you it will affect you'.

As Grand Final day approached, Randwick, the minor premiers, was favoured to win. But there was more at stake than the Shute Shield. To Jones, the contest was about subjugation as well as victory. The Manly coach was sniping for Bob Dwyer's job as Australia's coach. The 347 grade game veteran player turned coach was very different to Jones, and just as quicksilver

Randwick was vulnerable to the more disciplined Manly play, there was a weakness in Dwyer's defence of the Wallabies job. Though ranked as second only to the All Blacks, in July and August his team lost matches they should have won against Argentina and New Zealand.

Before the September Grand Final, Alan Jones spoke with his friend Ross Turnbull, chairman of New South Wales Rugby: 'Well Alan was on the New South Wales Rugby Union and he approached me ... and said he would like to coach Australia, and I was pretty unhappy with the way that the Australian team was performing ... and I said ... so it's pretty simple, mate, if Manly beat Randwick, I will support you as the Australian coach'.[8]

Alan Jones' team was well prepared. On the preceding Monday they had a meeting. On Tuesday they trained hard against a co-opted side. And 'on Wednesday we began our taper off, urging one another of the finality of the days ahead. Thursday night proceeded to plan with a growing confirmation within the team that it was just a matter of time before the Shute Shield hung in the Manly Club ... As the time passed, the team's resolution became total. The job would be done.'[9]

When James Black ran onto the Sydney Sports Ground he sensed 'that something great was going to happen'. Fullback Tony McGeoch also noticed calmness overtake the side, confidence never deserting them even when the scores were close. Captain Steve Williams, who scored Manly's sole try, kept his side to the Jones game plan. 'The ball probably went out the back line no more than four times. The five eighth was instructed to kick, and if he didn't James Black, acting as a second five eighth, used his long raking kick.' The Ellas were rushed and flustered and not allowed to play their natural game.

As the clock ticked towards the final minute, Manly led 12–10, but a potential loss was only a drop-kick away. After the siren sounded, Mark Ella received the ball from a scrum within range of a field goal. He lined up for a left foot kick, well within his ability. Manly players burst forward to unsettle Ella, forcing him to kick with his right boot. The next few seconds might have been the most important in Jones' professional life. A victory on this day opened doors that might never open again. Winning a premiership in your first year is an indicator of brilliance. It is not enough to be almost brilliant.

Mark Ella has spoken wistfully of that fateful moment: 'I probably was selfish. Manly had a good scrum. They wheeled the ball. Come out to me. I had a shot. Missed. Alan Jones got the Wallaby job.'[10] The Randwick and Australian captain was unusually tormented. 'There have been Test matches I've lost where it didn't really bother me too much because I knew at least we had done our best. But after that match I couldn't sleep for weeks. Not for weeks.'[11] Maybe there was intuitive foreboding about Jones, Ella being close to Dwyer. 'Jonesy knew my position. We may have spoken. I don't know whether we made phone calls, but he knew I was supportive of Bob.'[12]

In the stand Peter Bradstreet had one of those moments clubmen live for. Alan Jones standing on the sideline beamed as his players jogged from the field, saving his embrace for James Black. His favourite had made an important game-turning tackle and had kicked two penalties and a conversion. According to Manly half Phillip Cox, 'His boot won us the Grand Final'.

As Alan often says, 'Winners have parties and losers have meetings.'[13] That night the beer flowed freely at the Manly Rugby Club. Phillip Cox was grateful that 'Jones never stopped us from having fun after a game'.[14] Peter Bradstreet tried not to worry about how an amateur club could afford to dispense free beer. James Black still counts the achievement of 'winning a Premiership with your mates' as a highlight of his life. At Manly it had not happened in 33 years. The local mayor organised a street parade. A ball was held in honour of the team at the newly opened Manly Pacific Hotel, a surfside landmark owned by the Kalajzich family.

The story of Manly's win has a postscript that became better remembered than the win itself. The day after the match the rumour began at the front bar of the Steyne Hotel and it continues to circulate in many a back bar to this day. Jones, it was said, had been seen in the back seat of his car in the car park of the clubhouse the night before, kissing and cuddling with James Black. In the way of hot gossip, the story took on a range of permutations.

Alan Jones was now on the wrong side of his capacity for generating legend. The tattle was damaging to his chance of winning the Wallabies job. Angry on behalf of himself and James Black, he was soon in damage control mode. Some Manly players believe he hired a private inquiry agent to identify the source of the gossip. When he learned the tale had reached the ear of fellow coach Peter Fenton, Jones rang him at 6 am, complaining that Fenton should have protested Jones' innocence. Fenton, who worked in the film industry where homosexuality raised few eyebrows, told Jones he did not know him well enough to do that, and he did not care one way or the other if he was gay.

The gossip, as best I can tell, appears baseless. Alan Jones was well known for sitting in cars with boys. As he was sometimes chauffeured, sitting and talking in a back seat would not have been too remarkable. At the post-match ball, he and Black were seen to arrive together, with the tactile Jones' arm draped over Black's shoulder. Some in the club think the story sprang from this moment. Some Manly supporters, bitter about the appointment of an outsider, might have been dirty that history had proved them wrong.

James Black deserves to be better remembered for the 188 points he scored in 1983, a club record. Asked about the episode he acknowledged the story, which he says is an urban myth: 'I have no idea how it started. It did not happen. People make up stories.'

Peter Bradstreet maintained his confidence in Jones, signing him for another season. Knowing Jones was a candidate for national coach, Bradstreet agreed that if successful, he would not be held to Manly. Caucusing became intense. There was energetic—and some thought mischievous—lobbying on both sides. Dwyer's position weakened further when the Wallabies lost a short series in France. His record for 1982 and 1983 was five wins, six losses and a draw. His predecessor, Queensland coach Bob Templeton, was another competitor, but his 1981 team had also come back from Europe with slim pickings.

Alan Jones was said to be openly confident about the numbers, although Ross Turnbull's ability to deliver the New South Wales votes did not assure his mate success. Delegates from different states are allowed a vote and the large Queensland bloc historically opposed the New South Wales choice. To assist with the selection an exam was set by a panel led by Dick Marks. The national coaching director, RJP Marks, had a similar connection to Alan Jones as did Alex Evans, having captained Brisbane Grammar's First XV in 1960 and played for Australia the following year.

The candidates were Evans, Templeton, Dwyer and Jones, who later said of the outcome, 'When the results came out I got 172 out of 180 and I won't say where the others finished but one prominent candidate got about 123. So they were left with no choice, but they then decided not to make the examination public. That was treated as if it didn't exist, so it didn't advance my cause in any way.'[15] The actual vote was much closer. Alan Jones had the support of New South Wales but not his home state. Queensland delegate Lyn Crowley had 'serious reservations about Jones', but also a problem with Bob Dwyer for having previously selected New South Wales fullback Glen Ella over Queenslander Roger Gould. Crowley was undecided until 'in the last few seconds [he] realised [he] could not forgive Dwyer'.[16]

It was another great achievement for Alan. Up in Margate Charlie Jones, polite and smiling, accepted congratulations on behalf of his son. Robert, who had little to do with Alan, suppressed a tear when later speaking of his pride in his brother.[17] Another Queenslander, less well disposed toward Jones, was mortified. *Sydney Morning Herald* journalist Evan Whitton, who had played rugby for Toowoomba Grammar rival Downlands, wrote: 'To say that this decision is a disgrace will seem to many supporters of the game to elaborate the obvious'.[18] Alan Jones added a new enemy to a lengthening list.

Ironically, Alan Jones' media savvy and communication skills were seen as major points in his favour, at a time when a capacity to promote the game was increasing in importance. People like Dick Marks were there to help overcome Alan Jones' perceived practical weaknesses.

The man who would controversially become his new captain, Andrew Slack, did not see too many: 'He was very different to what we experienced before. He thought outside the square. He was very thorough and he really knew the game. Don't believe that bullshit about how he was just a motivator ... He removed himself from the old rugby culture and tried to make rules about behaviour and drinking.'

Taking the captaincy from Mark Ella and giving it to Andrew Slack made Alan Jones' appointment even more controversial. Though not famous for training, Ella was a rugby god, so naturally gifted when he ran onto the field that, as Evan Whitton put it, 'the game plan was Ella'.

At the end of his career Mark Ella would speak caustically of Alan Jones, but at this stage, in his easygoing way, there was no tossing of boots or slamming of locker doors. For years, though, Jones took a lot of heat over the sacking, despite the initiative having come from selectors Bob Templeton and John Bain. As Jones later explained, 'look, it wasn't my decision ... there was strong feeling against my other two colleagues about Mark's lack of discipline'.[19] John Bain confirms Alan Jones' account, but does not place the same emphasis on concern about Ella's attitude to discipline: 'Mark would have been fine for one Test, but taking all into consideration we felt that Slacky was the better captain for a longer tour'.

As at Manly, Jones was lucky the talent was there to begin with. When the best-ever sides are picked his squad figures prominently. In the Jones line-up there would be 'the Tiger Woods of Rugby', as he dubbed Mark Ella, and 'the Don Bradman of Rugby', as he dubbed David Campese. And they were just two, although there were some in his own squad who thought the earlier Wallabies even stronger.

What Alan Jones did well was apply his fresh vision to choose a team based on the strategies devised and the skills needed, rather than the conventional method of picking the best performing players and expecting their talents to synchronise. Alan Jones brought in a stocky young halfback, Nick Farr-Jones, who, like his coach, had managed only to make the seconds at high school. He also selected a line-out specialist in Steve 'Skylab' Cutler, to assure possession, and a clever goal kicker in Michael Lynagh, to assure points. Courage must have been required when he read out his maiden team's names in alphabetical order—the first three being from Manly—but Alan Jones was not the first or last to favour familiar players. Indeed, the man he beat, Bob Dwyer, was known for his partiality to Randwick.

Alan Jones had to juggle work commitments for what would be a big touring year. The Employers' Federation was at first reluctant to grant him leave, but when Alan offered to resign, an arrangement was struck whereby, for the longer periods of his absence, he would take leave without pay.[20] Alan Jones remained content to subsidise rugby, which he said was his hobby.

The first trip, a ten-day tour of Fiji, was an ideal orientation exercise. Once off the plane he went into housemaster mode, specifying the standards required. The teacher in Jones was ever present in the coach. Many a parable stuck. A favourite was about the rise of the Gucci empire. One Gucci questions why they would wish to manufacture footwear that few can afford. The other Gucci replies, 'Long after the price is forgotten the quality will remain'. For Nick Farr-Jones the lesson resonated. Jones was saying that long after the pain of training was forgotten the skills and the results would live on.

The training gear was soon soaked by tropical mud and sweat as well as rhetoric. David Campese found coping with the physical conditions easier than the verbal torrents. 'Oh, he was pretty good. I mean I just said to him jokingly, look, can I bring my dictionary along because some of the words, I've got no idea what you are talking about and we had a bit of a laugh. You know, coming from Queanbeyan I had no idea.'[21] Dr Bill Campbell, making his debut, enjoyed what he saw as a more 'cerebral' approach to the game: 'Jones had different strategies to match different teams, which for me made rugby more interesting'. Simon Poidevin, already at a peak of fitness, was refreshed: 'Training sessions were fun because there was a lot of variation going on'.[22]

Two warm-up matches showed that the games would not be a holiday either. Jones saw Fiji as a 'very tough rugby nation. They are the sort of outfit that can knee you in the groin and give you a late tackle but because they smile with their lovely big teeth and pick you up afterwards, everyone says they are good sports.'[23]

On 9 June 1984, in the slosh of Suva, Jones' Wallabies had their first Test win. The 16–3 result was celebrated in the conventional boys-on-the-road manner, stumbling to an amiable conclusion in a room shared by two of the backup players, Peter FitzSimons and Nick Farr-Jones. Close friends and equally messy, a matter of hours later Fitzy and young Nick were the last on the airport bus. The housemaster glared: 'The room you two have been living in is a pigsty, a shambles, a shocker, a disgrace ... it is not good enough when you are representing Australia'.[24] Fitzsy would wait some time before pulling on the gold jersey again. But as he retreated from Jones' inner circle, his handsome young friend began to be invited back to Chippendale more often.

There was little time to muck about. As soon as Alan Jones finished one set of interviews about football, he turned to another set of microphones, arguing the Employers' Federation case for containing Consumer Price Index growth, and challenging the affordability of the Labor Accord. 'The reality is quite separate from the rhetoric of Simon Crean. Just before the last election we had an arrangement reached between the ACTU and the Labor Opposition which virtually told us under the guise of an economic accord what the future economic directions of Australia were going to be.'[25]

Then it was back to questions about football. For the next Test, against New Zealand, there was a lot of interest. In international rugby there was no better outfit to measure your ability against. As Charlie's son put it, 'they were farmers. They were tough people.'[26] But for the July Test in Sydney, the tough farmers could not manage to cross the Australian line. The Wallabies won 16–9. Beyond a problem with goal kicking, they were looking good.

The result was also encouraging for the Sydney team, the core of the Wallabies squad. Coached by Peter Fenton and already having beaten the two touring sides, Scotland and France, Sydney looked a reasonable chance. The first sign that Jones' win-at-all-costs approach could bear a local price emerged when he withdrew the Wallabies who played for Sydney. Citing 'niggling injuries and jadedness',[27] Jones' removal of Sydney's eight test players upset the Kiwis and Fenton, who later wrote: 'The New Zealanders were naturally incensed, and admitted to the Sydney side after the match that they had been instructed not to associate with us at the post-match function'.[28] Rugby writer Phil Wilkins said after Sydney's 28–3 loss that 28 July 1984 was 'the day the game died of shame'.[29]

There would be many more occasions on which Alan Jones' single-mindedness offended old world rugby sensibilities. While his behaviour was selfish, it was also revolutionary. The Wallabies' new coach was on the cusp of a new era that would carry rugby towards its current professional status. Jones was not going to apologise for trying to win, especially with the prized Bledisloe Cup just one match away.

The Brisbane venue meant a triumphant homecoming. The night before the game the team shuffled in to the Albert Street cinema to watch *Indiana Jones and the Temple of Doom*, an experience that seemed to fire Alan Jones' imagination. The next day at Ballymore, the Wallabies led 12–0 after 20 minutes. But then a ghostly prophecy wrested fortune away. The All Blacks fought back to win 19–15. On Planet Alan it was all down to that bloody movie. A later radio goof-tape recorded his explanation: 'Bloody shit. Indiana fucking Jones. The reason I lost, we lost the fucking Second Test against the All Blacks was because that movie frightened the shit out of my team the night before we played. We led 12–nil and fell apart at the seams. Fucking Hawker [centre Michael Hawker] who was terrified by snakes had the worst Test I ever had 'cause ... he'd been awake all night devoured by temple snakes ... bastards.'[30]

When the Wallabies lost the next Test and the Bledisloe Cup, it was attributed to the familiar curse of the referee. Penalties and luck went against the Aussies, just beaten 25–24. Deposed captain Mark Ella did not blame Jones: 'I think the players on the field made bad options, basically, and we lost the game, not the coach, or his style or philosophy'.[31] The setback had an upside, with Ella and Jones reaching an understanding. 'We were playing too many set pieces, and I basically told Jonesy, that we, you know, when we go to Europe that we can't win playing like this'.[32] Speculation followed that Jones considered reinstating Ella as captain, but was dissuaded by fellow selectors.

A long tour of the northern hemisphere was about to begin and no one wanted to be bashed. The two preceding European tours had not gone well and now there was a chance to make history. Others had done it, but Australia had never won a Grand Slam, defeating all four British Isles opponents.

The training began on St Johns Oval at Sydney University, as intense as usual and with an additional Jones' twist. Maybe it was the Welsh in him, or that ambition to sing opera. From within the adjoining St Andrew's College chapel passing students heard the awkward strains of 'Advance Australia Fair', 'Waltzing Matilda', 'Click Go the Shears' and 'I Still Call Australia Home'. The Wallabies were undertaking choir practice.

The touring party set off with a few extra bags. Although not a registered member of the tour, after Jones threatened to pay the fare himself, Alex Evans was allowed to squeeze into a Qantas economy seat: 'I was probably the first Assistant Coach in World Rugby ... the England tour was met with a bit of opposition, the

Rugby Football Union weren't very happy about an Assistant Coach coming on board, but Alan had words—as he does.'[33]

Alan Jones was not alone in respecting Alex Evans' ability. Forward Simon Poidevin thought 'Alex Evans was a great mentor for me during that tour, probably much more than Jonesy'.[34] The brains trust of Jones and Evans, already strong, became formidable with the cooperation of the back line master, Mark Ella. '[Jones] was good at putting a game plan together. He would talk to players one on one and ask them how they thought we should play the game. He would then formulate something out of that, but if the game deviated from the plan then I would take over. He couldn't adapt. His Assistant Coach, Alex Evans, ran the forwards and I ran the backs.' Alan Jones concurred: 'Mark was captain of the back line. I just didn't interfere. He knew what he was about. My job was to give them the skills to do what they wanted to do. I didn't ever tell a back, and wouldn't today, where to stand.'[35]

With the burden of captaincy removed, however unhappily, Ella may have felt ever so slightly liberated. He made things simple for newcomers like room-mate Nick Farr-Jones, telling him: 'Mate, whether it's a good ball or a bad ball just chuck it to me. Fling it over your shoulder and I'll be there.'[36]

Jones was also liberated, given room to attend to the big picture. He activated his sleepers, informal intelligence agents recruited on earlier missions. Steve Williams remembers the plotting. 'Jones had a group of contacts from his Oxford days. They would watch the teams we played next. He did his homework and it made a big difference.' The travelling Wallabies were in effect two teams. It was as if Alan was made for this job, the art of choosing favourites now a duty. The Wednesday team to play the county sides was 'the Green Machine', with the elites saved for the big Saturday matches.

Two preliminary games before the First Test against England gave Jones a good look at his players, and his players a good look at Jones. Notes began to appear under doors specifying appointments in Jones' room. Nineteen-year-old Matthew Burke was off to an awkward start. Missing an appointment after falling asleep, he was subjected to 'a lengthy and stinging Jones tirade'.[37]

After Jones learned of his late-night carousing, Nick Farr-Jones was also summoned. 'As always Jones' room was pristine in its neatness, with everything in its place and a place for everything. The tracksuit he'd worn at training that day neatly folded over the chair, his sandshoes placed precisely beside his leather shoes at the foot of the bed, English rugby magazines—which he'd been perusing for yet more information about coming opponents—neatly opened on the study desk.'[38] Farr-Jones was also bawled out.

As it transpired, both Farr-Jones and Burke would make it into the Saturday side for their maiden Tests. At this stage Jones was not letting his heart rule. James Black, one of the touring party, was kept to the Wednesday side. Other Manly players also had trouble making it into the Saturday side. Not only did Farr-Jones replace Phillip Cox but Ross Reynolds was also dropped in favour of David Codey. A few other regulars were also dropped. Alan Jones spent time explaining his decisions, acting with unusual dispassion.

Players arriving outside Jones' door would hear him at work inside. One reason for spending a lot of time inside on this tour was probably his bad back. He later explained: 'I couldn't walk, but I didn't let them know that. The only person who knew that outside the team or outside Alex was Billy Calcraft. I was close to his family at Manly and Billy helped me to dress and lift me into bed ... they had enough to worry about, not me, and I was alright—I was still breathing.'[39]

Peter Grigg noticed that 'he sat up till the early hours of the morning watching videotapes of players and what they do and sides and how they played the game and discussed it and made notes'.[40] Music could also be heard emanating from the room. The *Turandot* opera classic 'Nessun Dorma' ('No one will sleep'), a Jones favourite, might have been his theme song. It finishes, 'Depart oh night! Set, you stars? Set, you stars! At dawn I shall win! I shall win! I shall win!'

The side that ran onto Twickenham on 3 November was beautifully prepared. Mark Ella, swooping like a kingfisher, picked up a fingertip pass from Roger Gould in orchestrated play that finished with a Simon Poidevin try. As well, improvising a planned move, Ella glided under the posts. The Poms went down 19–3.

The beaten English were generous in their praise, impressed not just with the fluid play. At the post-match press conferences Jones' fluency was noticed. Predecessor Bob Templeton thought Jones 'certainly changed the role of the coach, for up to this time the manager was supposed to represent the team to the press. Jones would have none of that, and he loved holding court, and he was good at it.'[41] Alan is still proud, British press reaction remaining on his cv. 'During the tour one British newspaper described Alan Jones as "the most approachable and articulate Rugby person to visit Britain in the last 40 years". The London *Times* sports writer stated that "Alan has the most analytical brain I have encountered in charge of a national side".'[42]

The next stop was Ireland. When the Wallabies pulled in to Dublin's Jury's Inn there was amusement at the sign 'Open 23 hours a day'. The understated Irish tended to be a more comfortable fit for the unpretentious Aussies, but less so for Alan. 'We always knew Ireland would be a bit of a mess, 'cause it was sort of a nothing game in a way. If we got over that, I felt that we could really—against these other structured sides, we could really do the job.'[43] However, not until the last 20 minutes at Lansdowne Road did the Wallabies take the lead and, eventually, the game, 16–9. It turned out to be the closest result of the series.

After Ireland it was back to Wales. While Jones was finding favour with the British press he had problems with some of his own. A traitorous Evan Whitton had written that, while Australia was winning, the team was not playing well. Whitton's later reckoning was that it was not until Alex Evans got the scrum right that the team found its rhythm. His opinion led to one cold night for the correspondent: after one of the lead-up games, tour manager 'Chilla' Wilson politely told him he was not welcome to ride with the players. Whitton believed the instruction came from Jones.

The next Test was expected to be the hardest. Welsh coalminers—with names like Jones and Evans—had a reputation akin to those New Zealand sheep farmers of being able to trample the Australian private school boys into the mud. But the Welsh pits were closing down, making it harder to mine the raw strength that made their rugby players famous. The Welsh were soon to be given a lesson in strength. While Evans was putting 'mongrel' into the minds of the forwards, Jones was putting steel into their sinews. His English contacts helped him locate a prototype 'Rhino Machine', which not only toughened muscles but reduced training injuries, because the forwards did not have to practise so much on themselves. Alan Jones explained: 'I personally paid out of my own money, someone to cart this ... and of course it was the making of us because we just had a fabulous, unyielding front'.[44]

The big moment at Cardiff Arms Park, and perhaps of the whole tour, was on 24 November. Sixty-seven thousand predominantly Welsh spectators were hushed to unaccustomed silence. In the second half, close to the Welsh line, the Wallabies unleashed 'Samson', a rehearsed move. Facing eight straining Australians, the Welsh pack went backwards. Number 8, Steve Tuynman, scored and the Wallabies went on to win 28–9.

Oddly enough, the brawl that soon broke out was not on the field. Following his intervention over a fighting incident in an earlier game, Alan Jones was now in a tangle with the hated administrators. After the Welsh Test he was cited to appear before the International Rugby Board. 'I told them to get stuffed. I'm answerable to the Australian Rugby Union, not the IRB. Many of these people are anchored in the past.'[45] The episode was the first of many that exposed the gulf between what Jones expected of others and what he allowed himself. The demand he made of players for no excuses discipline did not apply to Alan.

But only on a few occasions was there insurrection. If anyone was going to stand up to Jonesy, it was Stan Pilecki. Up the back of the bus, in the belly of the beast, the big Queensland prop was his own man, a benign incarnation of the pillaging Goth. Stan, who had done plenty of tours, saw himself as 'about Alan's age' (he was thirty-seven, six years younger than Jones). 'A lot of the younger players were afraid to say anything to Alan ... I had nothing to lose. I was a Wednesday player.'[46]

But the heavy smoker was finding Jones' training a problem. After one tough session at Swansea, he ambled from the field with the shriek of Jones still ringing in his ears, passed the coach in his green and gold tracksuit, blew a smoke ring in his face and said, 'I hope you are hoarse, you cunt, because I am fucking deaf'. Alan giggled, and the rest fell about laughing. Stan's personality could defuse an unexploded bomb.

The next time it happened, Jones was not so forgiving. Before the game against Scotland Alan Jones called aside a small group of players on the brink of exhaustion after training, instructing them to keep their boots on. When Nick Farr-Jones, a touch impetuously, objected, Alan Jones let go: 'How dare you talk to me like that! I'll be the judge of what work you can and can't do. I am the coach and my function is to decide such things ... don't you ever speak to me like that.'[47] That night Farr-Jones knocked on Jones' door seeking to apologise. He could hear Jones inside but the knocking was not answered. The young offender might have felt he was back at Newington College being disciplined by a master when writing a note of apology and slipping it under the door.

Something else that might have been slipped under Alan Jones' door at this time was a copy of an editorial that should have brought further satisfaction. In Evan Whitton's *Sydney Morning Herald* piece on 10 December 1984 there appeared an apology of another kind. Accepting the error of opposing Alan Jones as national coach the editorial said the record now 'vindicated the appointment of Alan Jones earlier this year as coach, an appointment which in certain quarters received sharp criticism'.[48]

The next stop was Edinburgh. Could they make it four out of four? At 8 o'clock on the morning of 12 December, Alan Jones says he embarked on a clandestine mission to secure crucial intelligence. There is a whiff of hyperbole in his tale of appearing at the Murrayfield ground in the near dark to lure an unsuspecting groundsman into revealing an important secret. Jones said the Scotsman explained the way the wind rose in the second half. 'And he said, oh, it comes from this side—right down the paddock this way ... So if Scotland win the toss they'll run this way, will they? Yeah fantastic—I said you do a great job here ... thanks, mate, terrific.'[49]

The Australians won the toss but in the first half were tentative, fumbling the ball and seizing no advantage. After a half-time speech by captain Andrew Slack, the mood changed. Trusting their skills the Wallabies bolted, speeding through Scots standing like gums in a pasture. Michael Lynagh, assisted by Jones' grasp of meteorology, also kicked them from everywhere. The final score, 37–12, was a record against Scotland. The Grand Slam victory was also a first for Australia.

Back in the North British hotel during the traditional post-match happy hour, deep-felt relief welled into tears. Simon Poidevin is still amazed at the scene that followed: 'When Slacky started to speak as captain and Alan Jones even didn't want him to speak for some reason and he started to speak and he started to get a bit emotional'.[50] The heavyweight prop, Topo Rodriguez, began to cry and the rest of the team followed suit. The sense of loyalty and gratitude that many rugby players direct towards Alan Jones is deeply invested in moments like these. Players such as Stan Pilecki knew they would not have done it without him: 'I would not call Alan a real close, you know, Christmas card sort of friend but I would always be indebted to Alan for what he's taught me there in life, on setting goals and achieving them'.[51]

In a post-match speech Mark Ella also acknowledged his respect for Alan Jones' contribution to the series. Ella, long conflicted about Jones, had played his best rugby ever, scoring a try in every Test. But still, the world's best player was not happy. He knew Jones could coach but that did not mean he liked him. Sitting in a freezing dressing room listening to another Jones' parable about the Rumanian gymnast Nadia Comaneci, with her mind fixed on 'getting it absolutely right', was not for Ella. An instinctive player, Mark Ella did not need to think about getting it right. And perhaps there was something else. It could never have been easy for an Aboriginal player to feel completely comfortable in a game played predominantly by middle class whites, who were not always good at concealing their prejudice. Although Alan Jones gave no overt cause for it, Mark Ella just might have believed his coach was another racist bastard.

He was not the only one to see that this tour was not as much fun as previous ones. Stan Pilecki, even more the old school rugby tourist, thought Alan Jones had taken a risk investing all in victory. 'There's more to winning than winning … when you're with Alan it's football all the way. Like you'd sit down to dinner and you'd be talking tactics about the team that you're playing next. Now you cop that for three months, it's pretty hard.'[52]

Alan Jones' idea of fun was when he was crouched at a small table with a favoured player. Ever generous, he was happy to pay the bill, and if there was a price to the players it tended to be that Alan did most of the talking. There were team trips to London shows as well, which many of the players enjoyed.

Obviously they also enjoyed winning. Despite a few whinges it had been a great tour, but it was not over. A final match against the Barbarians, players from a range of European teams, was set for 15 December. While normally a less serious match, northern hemisphere pride was on the line. A strong team, including some of France's best, was selected with an eye to matching the individual talents of the Australians. More than two months into the tour, the Wallabies were a touch ragged when they arrived back in Wales. Their 37–30 win made it an even happier Christmas.

The Grand Slam series is and always will be special to Australian rugby aficionados. The Eighth Wallabies returned from the tour of the British Isles with an enhanced international reputation. As Jones put it: 'That's what changed the face of

Australian rugby. We're now a feared force in the game wherever the game is played in the world. And I hope that we played some small role in that.'[53]

While some of the players doubted the strength of the opposition, Nick Farr-Jones was the only one rash enough to say so publicly. When Jones read his debut halfback's comment that 'the tests weren't hard enough', he was on the telephone at 6 am. 'How dare you try and belittle what was achieved over there by saying it was easy. Don't you know that if you found it was easy it was only because of the tremendous amount of work we did?'[54]

Alan Jones' belief in struggle and the unapologetic pursuit of victory had worked. He took the position that wearing the green and gold presupposed an obligation to win. He had an open suspicion that players in it for the fun were frightened of winning: 'I have never understood how people can snatch a good time out of persistent failure and defeat'.[55]

The success of 1984 would lead to further opportunities, which would bring Alan Jones wealth as well as fame. His public identity was strengthened, but beneath the surface, if better concealed, the fragile self remained. There would be more success, but pressure, too, when concerns mounted about the reach of Alan's motivation and the durability of that winning touch.

CHAPTER 8
MY TEAM

'My team', he would often say, 'my team'. Alan Jones believes the game of Rugby Union belongs more to the players than to their masters. But, obsessive and possessive, he did not seem to be able to help himself. As soon as he took over, the national side was no longer Mark Ella's team, or even Andrew Slack's team. It was Alan Jones' team—at least for three more years. By 1988, when one magnificent career came to an end, another magnificent career had begun. And when Alan Jones took on the new radio job, it was much the same. 'My staff', he would say. He still says it: 'My staff'.

Alan worked so hard and achieved so much, credit seemed a natural entitlement. So it must have been difficult for him to see his exploitative side. Nor was it easy for him to see how he could overextend himself, let alone others. In 1985, given his full head of steam, Alan was an express train bound to run out of track. But along the way there would be more wins and a new career.

Alan Jones has often said he never got anything from rugby, which is a long way from true. For a start it was rugby that gave him his chance in radio. On the road in the British Isles in 1984, Alan Jones had conducted a series of two-way interviews with Sydney radio station 2UE. Sports Director John Brennan heard a 'natural': 'Jones would make himself available wherever he was.

In his hotel or in a restaurant, he was there for us. I admired him so much. He was so fluent and had such a marvellous use of words.'[1]

Having lost star morning announcer John Laws to 2GB, 2UE was looking for a replacement. On his annual holiday at Nelson Bay, John Brennan rang someone he knew was close to Alan Jones, John Fordham. Fordham—who, ironically, later became John Laws' manager—knew Alan Jones through Ross Turnbull, whose law firm handled Fordham's business. On Brennan's behalf, Fordham asked Jones whether he was committed to his job at the Employers' Federation. Jones replied, 'Absolutely'. Fordham explained that 2UE was considering him as a replacement to Laws and asked whether he would be interested. Some 45 seconds later the answer was again, 'Absolutely'.

2UE Program Director Mark Collier arranged an audition. John Fordham brought Alan Jones to the North Sydney studio the following Saturday afternoon. According to Fordham, 'Brenno said, "Why don't you do a few editorials?" Jones nominated a couple of topics. Brenno then said, "Well here's the typist; you just need to dictate to her." Jones said, "I don't need to dictate anything. Just open the microphone." He blew them away.'

So in March 1985, Alan Jones settled in front of a microphone and began working at something he had been training for all his life. A new salary of $130 000 was sorted out[2]—petty cash by Jones' current standards, but not bad at all when Penfolds Grange could be bought for $32 a bottle.

According to Garry Brack, the Employers' Federation was sorry to see him go, although others did wonder. While Alan Jones was good at the media work, when sensitive negotiations were on around the bargaining table he did not seem so much in his element. Chris McArdle, then with the Labour Council, remembers Alan Jones blundering during negotiations in a Storeman and Packers industrial dispute. Alan Jones, he says, agreed to an ambit demand of a $24 industry allowance, which shocked the people on the other side of the table as well as Garry

Brack. McArdle says Jones and Brack were then heard in the next room, Jones shouting at Brack: 'Don't you tell me to get fucked'. Garry Brack recalls there was a difference between himself and Alan Jones about the amount, but disagrees with Greg McArdle's broader account of negotiations. He also recalls that Jones was 'effective at every level'.

Ever eager for a new challenge, Alan Jones, who had already successfully renominated for the Wallabies job, accepted the increased pressure. 2UE needed success too. The loss of John Laws meant the station had slipped from first to sixth ranking in the 9 am to noon slot. Alan Jones would not be allowed as much time off. It would be a steep learning curve, too, but already Alan was sprinting. On his second day he conducted a courteous interview with Prime Minister Bob Hawke. After his third day he went to Hong Kong to manage the Rugby 7s. Mark Collier remembers that as well as a difficult first outside broadcast, he addressed a luncheon at the Foreign Correspondents' Club, receiving a standing ovation. After his rugby team won they again transmitted the shows from Hong Kong, and were back in Sydney within a week.

It was not an altogether brilliant start. While Alan is a savant with words he is anything but adept at managing technology. His panel operators would be tested to the extreme, and some of his earlier broadcasts are probably better forgotten. On the upside the objectives he then expressed were worthy of faithful adherence.

Alan Jones came into the race to challenge John Laws, believing that 'Complex questions need to be addressed ... I don't accept the view there are dreary housewives out there with no dimension to their lives ... I prefer to think of my responsibility on air rather than power'.[3] The former teacher spoke up for intelligent and polite radio that reached for ordinary people. 'My old man's one of them ... My having been to Oxford doesn't exclude me from these people.'[4] Even in those first months as he stumbled on air, it was obvious he had something. Alan Jones' ability to distil complex issues was useful in dissecting the big stories of the day. His enthusiasm for all manner of subjects was infectious.

Archives from that time reveal a more personable Alan Jones. Some who have known him since then thought there was also more acuity in his command of language. At a clipped pace, as if on fast forward, Alan spoke with greater warmth and humour. This was again evident when, in August, he appeared as a guest on ABC TV's *Clive James at Home*. Slim shouldered, greying and with teeth that must have been subjected to later orthodontics, Jones was ribbed by James about his well-known affectation of tugging at his collar and pouting like an otter coming up for air. Alan took it well, happily responding to the request to do his ghost Melbourne Cup call. Water glass positioned like a microphone, he asked, 'Which Cup?' The last furlong of 1961 was settled on, a swift mental adjustment made and Jones was away with his steeds. James laughed alongside him as Alan crossed the winning post: 'I can't pick it, yes I can, Lord Fury has won the Melbourne Cup'.[5]

Getting serious, he used the iconic race to argue that Australia was becoming conditioned to a form of socialist handicapping. 'The Melbourne Cup is a symbol of Australian life. We put too much weight on the favourite and cheer when someone beats it.'[6]

In October 1985, the Rostrum Association made Alan Jones its Communicator of the Year, although not all the public response was favourable. Jones was only three weeks into his new radio job when the furore broke over the decision by Mark Ella, who was only 25 and about halfway through his potential playing career, to quit. In a *Sunday Telegraph* story on 7 April, he explained why: 'With Alan, it is all down to him, and I just don't enjoy my rugby that way'. Accepting Jones did know his rugby, Ella explained he was not the main cause of retirement: 'not by a long shot, but it is true I would be giving more consideration to staying on in the game I love if anyone but Alan Jones were the national coach'.[7]

Fortunately, considering the new demands on Jones, it was not going to be as hectic a rugby year. Equally as fortunate, there were plenty of options for replacing the number 10. Alan Jones needed a regular goal kicker so the spot was perfect for Michael Lynagh. There were some easy tryout games midyear against Canada, which gave Lynagh plenty of kicking practice, and also gave Jones the opportunity to cap his good and loyal friends from the Manly days, James Black and Bill Calcraft.

The real test came with a single match against the All Blacks to be played in Auckland, the only time in 1985 when the Wallabies packed their passports. Again, James Black got a chance, Alan Jones selecting him as centre. The Wallabies were eager to redeem the one point loss of the year before, but on 29 June the team again lost by a point, 10–9. James Black scored a good try, which put Australia in the lead, but towards the end, against the run of play, New Zealand crossed and took the Bledisloe once more. Jones blamed himself—after a fashion: 'My stupid little dimwits all assumed they'd kick for touch, do the typical All Black stuff. Well of course while we're drawing breath and taking a breather they've gone whack. I couldn't believe it. We didn't face up. A terrible, terrible mistake.'[8] But there was compensation. Eighteen years on Alan Jones would still say the try by James Black was one of the best ever scored by the Wallabies against the All Blacks.[9]

In Sydney it was back to work. Alan Jones expanded his staff at 2UE. In addition to John Brennan's helping hand, an assistant producer, Geraldine Russell, was hired. Alan Jones also took on his own private secretary, Susie Yabsley. As Susie Clatworthy, the former personal secretary to Malcolm Fraser, she came to know Alan Jones well, as did her husband, Liberal politician Michael Yabsley. Susie Yabsley attended essentially to rugby work, which Alan Jones' outside income continued to underwrite.

The rugby support team was also expanded. Manly-based physiotherapist Greg Craig would work on injuries until midnight and receive a 5 am phone call from Alan Jones wanting to know the results. The new physio saw in Jones a man totally in love with his work. Craig admired the professional standards Jones set. Despite all his other commitments in 1985, Alan continued to coach athletics two mornings a week, arriving at the Narrabeen Fitness Centre by 6 am for sprint work before rushing off to 2UE.[10]

Susie Yabsley, working from a small office in her Darlinghurst home, was also left both breathless and admiring: 'He is so demanding and through those demands you give of your best, you really do and if you don't, if you fail him in any way, if you don't please him it's a personal failure. There will be a flash of temper when he can see inefficiency and working with him, you should give of your best because he gives 110% all the time. He is the most extraordinary person in the world. There is nothing wrong with it—excellence is something we should all be striving for and he is always cut off at the knee.'[11]

It was hard for Alan to feel detached about his footballers. He became personally engaged in their lives, inviting them home, to the movies and to dinner parties with friends. The busy rugby coach appeared to use them to fill the remaining empty spaces in his life. While some of the encounters were probably romantic from Jones' point of view, as likely as not the players did not see it that way. As best I can tell, if the relationships were ever sexual, they were probably more psychosexual. At the end of the night Alan Jones might embrace them and tell them what wonderful young men they were, but fell short of planting a big kiss on their lips.

His passionate, emotional connection with the rugby world had a likely virtue. Alan Jones was not only prepared to devote an unusual amount of time to the sport, he could also channel repressed energy and concentrate searing power upon his charges. Inevitably some would wilt. Nick Farr-Jones had a confident and purposeful playing style that often put him at odds with Alan Jones during the winter months. In the off-season he got on better with Jones, except when he brought his girlfriend along. As it happened the girlfriend also had a Jones connection. Angela Benness is the sister of another Jones favourite, Chris Benness (King's class of 1973). She was not alone in feeling uncomfortable. Alan Jones treated many of the wives and girlfriends with ill-concealed hostility.

Alan Jones legitimised his close relationships with his athletes by casting himself as a life coach. He married the objective of winning on the field to winning in life. He spoke of the permissive sixties as an era that gave people an excuse for failure. He would say that to win with dignity and style was an objective equally applied to people's lives and the national endeavour.

One of his Manly players thought of him as a 'human self-help book'. Plenty were lent more than a hand. Bill Campbell, a medical practitioner, had expressed to Alan Jones an interest in doing postgraduate study at a university like Oxford. Jones used his connections to get Campbell an interview. Campbell, working at the time at the Doomadgee Aboriginal Community, flew to Sydney and won a Kobe Steel scholarship. The large Japanese corporation, which fielded a rugby team, had forged a connection with Oxford, creating a Rhodes Scholarship type program that assisted footballers, among others.

In hundreds of other ways Jones lent a hand, using his influence to fast-track a birth certificate, sort out a job interview, arrange a short holiday, intervene in a minor court matter and organise loans, often reaching into his own pocket. He did not seem to ask anything in return. Players like Bill Campbell were grateful.

The Christmas holidays were still lonely times, but now more often than not he travelled to England where he had an increasing circle of friends and a new rugby routine. For over a century, on the second Tuesday of December Oxford played its big match against Cambridge, which soon involved Alan Jones. Jones' network of British mates expanded, too. Beyond the rugby connections there were plenty of others, including author Lord Jeffrey Archer and his wife Mary. The hospitable British were happy to invite the Australian coach along to jolly dinner parties, although at times some of the less deferential wondered aloud about how to get a word in. Another Alan expression, which does not always work so well for him, is that 'it is not who is at the table, it is who is doing the talking'.

On Australia Day 1986, a major incident occurred that would later occupy a great deal of Alan's airtime. The Norfolk pines along the Manly foreshore must have quivered when a prominent local businesswoman, Megan Kalajzich, was shot twice in the head that evening. With his strong Manly connections, Jones shared the shocking loss of the cheerful hostess at 'K's Snapper Inn'. When Megan's husband, Andrew Kalajzich, was eventually arrested and charged with organising the murder, it was an even bigger shock. The proprietor of the Manly Pacific Hotel was not well known to Jones, but close to some of Jones' Manly friends. In time the murder would figure heavily in Alan's career, the broadcaster adopting the Kalajzich case as a major cause.

But that came later. In 1986 Alan's mind was fixed on the Wallabies' tough eight-Test schedule, including three matches against New Zealand in New Zealand. Not since 1949 had an Australian side beaten the All Blacks on their own turf. Alan Jones planned not just to bring the Bledisloe home, but to do so without recording a loss. Before the Test season began in July, though, fate threatened to step in the way of this best-laid plan. Following a series of anti-apartheid demonstrations the International Rugby Board imposed sanctions effectively banning competition with South Africa's Springboks. When an unofficial New Zealand Cavaliers team toured South Africa, 31 senior All Blacks received a two-Test ban.

And then an offer arrived that, if accepted, would mean Alan Jones would not be available anyway. Rugby mates recall Alan saying the next game was likely to be his last, as he had a political seat sewn up. They say he joked to them about what ambassadorial posts they would like when he became prime minister. The federal seat of Wentworth was again vacant. Alan Jones agreed to have a go. This time, his raised profile and rugby triumphs as much as assured preselection. He would be up against an understated, media-shy banker, Dr John Hewson.

At the eleventh hour Jones, the prospective PM, withdrew. Soon after he said that considering Australia was facing a 'crisis of ideas', he could better serve the nation staying in radio: 'I have an opportunity to emancipate people from the constraints that exist in their daily lives about just finding out what's going on. I think that's infinitely more important in the moment than sitting on the back bench and asking one question every three weeks.'[12]

There was another reason that is easier to swallow. By the time the Wentworth deal emerged, Alan Jones had a new boss. In March 1986, Kerry Packer acquired 2UE from the Lamb family's Broadcast Investments, for between $20 and $39 million.[13] Packer was expanding his media empire; 2UE would integrate with 3AK, 6PM and regional stations to form CBC, the Consolidated Broadcasting Corporation network. This meant Alan Jones' news commentaries could be syndicated to a wider audience.

Kerry Packer made a practice of getting to know the employees who interested him. Although Alan had not always been kind in the past, Big Kerry became a powerful force in his life. The two sports-loving conservatives hit it off. Packer, it is said, used his media connections to have the Sky racing service connected to Jones' home. And there was the new salary. Alan Jones' political backers had a suspicion that the Wentworth bid proved useful leverage. Alan Jones later told an audience at a North Sydney fundraising lunch: 'Mr Packer summonsed me and said without being too, sort of, vulgar about it: you're employed here and this is what I'm going to offer you … and I have to say it was a very attractive proposition. I said to Mr Packer you must understand it will take me all of five seconds to consider this proposal. And I don't apologise for that. Later the Liberal Party poured their fury on me and one senior official said to me: you'll pay for this, to which I replied: well at least I will have something to pay for it with.'[14]

The doubling of his salary did mean he could pay for a bigger house. His personal assistant Susie Yabsley was sent looking. Alan was attracted to the warehouse style living adopted by a near neighbour to the Yabsleys. Theatrical agent Harry Miller, who would become another force in Jones' life, had converted a factory warehouse at Woolloomooloo. But Jones preferred the other side of the CBD, around Chippendale. Susie Yabsley found a former clothing factory in O'Connell Street, near the main drag in Newtown, which was bought for $350 000.

With its four bedrooms, rooftop garden and view of the St Stephen's spire that reminded him of Oxford, Alan Jones was able to resume something of the campus life he loved. Habitually using the royal 'we', he explained: 'We've expanded from a small terrace in Chippendale ... on the lower level there is separate accommodation which sleeps up to eight friends—often offshore sporting visitors, regularly in town for big matches—as well as an office'.[15] O'Connell Street, his home for the next 15 years, was like Alan Jones' own boarding house. Over the years visitors would occasionally be startled by the sight of some other house guest wrapped in a towel, emerging from the bathroom.

Things were going well. Alan even managed to deliver on a dream of one of those young men he had coached back in the boarding school days. Bill Abram (King's class of 1975) always said his friendship with Alan Jones had made rugby tougher rather than easier. But there was a substantial reward at the end. When the team photograph was taken for the rugby Test against Italy, Bill Abram stood proud in his gold jersey. Though sticking to the bench he became the only player from Alan Jones' 1974 team to make it into the Wallabies.

The 1 June game, easily won, saw the return of Andrew Slack as captain, Alan Jones having coaxed him out of retirement. In the next, more difficult game against the French, Michael Lynagh got more kicking practice. The free-running French scored more tries, but Lynagh added 23 points on his own. Jones had predicted the in-form French would become flustered and ill disciplined under pressure, giving away penalties.[16]

Two more Tests at home in July against Argentina helped Jones further settle a combination. Australian mainframe prop Topo Rodriguez had played for the other side three years earlier. His new side won and won again. The Wallabies were getting back to their 1984 form. The next stop was the big one, New Zealand. Television reporter George Negus was brought in to 2UE to keep Alan Jones' chair warm.[17]

New Zealand was forced to pick a younger side because of the Cavaliers ban, but the Baby Blacks, in Wellington, would be no pushover. Simon Poidevin sweated as Alan Jones and Alex Evans lifted the pace of training. 'We had this incredibly intense, hard workout on the day we arrived in New Zealand and that set the standard for the rest of the tour and Alan drove the side extremely hard for the first ten days ... he was clearly on a mission, Alex Evans was on a mission. The team was on a mission—that we knew this was a great prize.'[18]

The 9 August game ended in another one point victory, 13–12, this time to Australia. Nick Farr-Jones, who would become the player of the tour, had virtually made the difference on his own. It was a good result but not enough to lift the team into the winning stride Alan Jones wanted. By the time of the next Test in Dunedin, the All Blacks would be released from the Test ban.

When the Wallabies arrived at Carisbrook on the nation's misty southern tip, Alan Jones was at his splenetic worst. On a few occasions television cameras have captured the Jones tantrums. This time, at a training session, the intruder was a TVNZ film crew. 'Look, you blokes know nothing about courtesy. I have constantly ... is that on or off?' Lips curled, hands on hips, strutting, Alan Jones lurched in and out of camera range, hissing goose-like for them to leave. 'Well would you turn it off please?' In the background members of the Australian squad tried to look the other way. 'Well this practice is not going on. This is absurd. And what television network are you with? Well I'll be having something to say tonight to your editors as well.'

For the Second Test, the mood was not right—on either side. The All Blacks were at full strength but struggling to resettle a split camp. Even on a good day Dunedin is intimidating for the Australians—but at least on this day the Wallabies stared down the All Blacks' pre-match haka with more than usual confidence.

Again the win was by a point. Again it was 13–12, but the victory was New Zealand's. Australia was unlucky; a refereeing decision had hurt them. Alan Jones was bleating. Losing with grace is not one of his strengths. Unlike many of his athletes, slumped with their heads in their hands, their perfectionist coach had little emotional reserve to call on when the inevitable losses occurred.

He made few friends in that miserable dressing room. One exchange, much disputed later, would cast a long shadow. Nick Farr-Jones sought to calm his coach: 'Alan, there's nothing we can do about it now, let's let it lie and we'll get 'em next time'.[19] More than a few present heard Alan Jones then utter some fateful words: 'Anyway, don't worry, men, you played without a fullback today'. Fullback David Campese missed the comment as he was in the shower at the time. Soon after, he felt the full force of Jones' displeasure at a meeting in the coach's room. When the slur went public, even the New Zealanders were offended. Alan Jones, then and now, denied he made the comment: 'I've no idea where that came from. I don't operate that way ... but somehow or other I singled Campo out and this thing ran and of course it becomes part of popular myth—didn't happen.'[20]

Alan Jones is programmed to deny more than defeat. The answer to the setback was to work harder. Morning training was brought forward from 10 am to 8 am. The Wallabies stepped up an already extensive training schedule. Jones borrowed a scrum machine from The King's School, and again had it carted around New Zealand at his own expense. A planned skiing trip was abandoned.

The hairshirt was on, and soon there was further cause for displeasure. Alan Jones spoke critically in front of the team about 'some people' drinking with the opposition coach.[21] 'Some people' appeared to be Simon Poidevin and Nick Farr-Jones. Much to the credit of the game, there is a measure that matters beyond the score. The two Australians had embraced the wider rugby fraternity, catching up with New Zealand coach Brian Lochore, a friend from an earlier European tour. Simon Poidevin, who has frequently and decently defended Alan Jones, says: 'We've all got our weaknesses and I thought that was a weakness on the part of Alan. You know Brian Lochore is one of the world's loveliest people ... and Jonesy took umbrage. We thought that was pretty ordinary. And Nick feels that and I still feel that. Alan had different viewpoints. He got us at the next town and gave it to us—both barrels.'[22] Again, Alan Jones denied the incident.

He was happy to make it clear that this ANZAC tour had delivered his team into enemy territory. There was another skirmish with the New Zealand media when the Australian coach complained that a Thames Valley hotel room was not big enough to swing a cat in. The Kiwi papers had a feast of headlines, quoting the innkeeper: 'There isn't a room in the world big enough for your mouth, Jones'. But the rooms were, indeed, small. The big second rower Bill Campbell famously observed that his legs could sleep one night, and his head and shoulders the next.

There might have been some method in the Jones approach. While making more enemies with every headline, he was gathering his troops together for the task ahead. Alan Jones' instinct in the face of the enemy is to form a huddle. He seems to gain strength from generating a collective sense of enmity. Nick Farr-Jones, whose doubts about Alan Jones were growing, could also see a plus: 'Jonesy was just absolutely so desperate to win the series that he did create an Us and Them and very much a herd mentality for the team. It's arguable that it worked. You know we were unbelievably motivated for that Third Test. Nothing was going to stop us. You know, in retrospect the way Alan went about the business in the last two weeks, you know, win at all costs, well, perhaps it's justifiable.'[23]

Even so, Farr-Jones still had misgivings, particularly about Jones' defensive strategy, enough to assemble 'the relevant players in my room to discuss the way we would do it come game day, confident that Alan wouldn't recognise the difference anyway'.[24]

On 6 September at Eden Park in Auckland, they squared off again. David Campese, back on the wing, scored one of his miracle tries and Australia would not be stopped, winning easily, 22–9. Alan Jones would later say at that moment he entered heaven. The Bledisloe win in New Zealand was a bigger prize than the Grand Slam. But even in the portals of heaven there was grumbling. The mood in the Wallabies' dressing room was impossible to spoil, but a few onlookers thought Jonesy tried, by criticising his captain for wearing an All Black jersey. Andrew Slack, who had followed the custom of swapping jerseys with the opponents' captain when they left the field, thought it 'no big deal'. Years on he found himself agreeing with Jones, reflecting when he looks at the photograph: 'Bugger, I wish I had not swapped it'.

Alan Jones should have been on top of the world. He described the win as 'bigger than *Quo Vadis*'. But it is hard to give Alan all the credit he feels he deserves. At the time he complained about a lack of gratitude from Australian rugby officials. 'We beat New Zealand in New Zealand and didn't even get lunch'.[25]

The Wallabies, inclined in victory to suppress reservations about their coach, had clearly and irrevocably returned from New Zealand a less happy camp, although Alan insisted otherwise: 'We're mates, inextricably locked together. That loyalty and mateship can move mountains. At Eden Park we won because we're mates—that's an ingredient in success.'[26]

From this moment atop the rugby world the slide began. Part of the problem was Alan Jones' denial that there was a problem. After the New Zealand tour, players began to cast a more critical eye at their coach. Simon Poidevin felt that between 1984 and 1986, Alan Jones was respected more than liked, and now that respect was running out.[27]

According to Jones, 'I can't control what other people say'.[28] But he can try. When disquiet about his behaviour continued to be aired, most particularly his alleged comment about David Campese, Jones' answer was to get Campese on air, in a joint venture denial. Campese later wrote: '... when we got back to Sydney, [Jones] rang me up and said he wanted me to go on his radio show to confirm it hadn't happened. What the hell do you do in circumstances like that—tell your national coach to get lost? So tamely and regrettably, I went along with the charade because I had no choice. I would probably never have played for Australia again if I had taken the guy to task in public.'[29]

Another source of unease was Alan Jones' position on South Africa. From 1985 the Australian Wallabies coach became a high profile defender of the South African government. At the time South Africa was proactive in putting its case to the Australian media. Alan Jones became a kind of informal ambassador, debating radio rival Mike Carlton on the Channel 9 *Midday* show, and later Archbishop Tutu, also on Channel 9. In October, Alan Jones was part of an Australian Rugby Union delegation to discuss a proposed tour with Sports Minister John Brown and Foreign Affairs Minister Bill Hayden. According to a later report: 'Hayden appeared sympathetic, though the meeting was more memorable for the repartee flashing between the two brilliant opposed wits of Hayden and Jones'.[30]

The ultra divisive apartheid debate was bound to make enemies beyond the rugby community. Alan Jones later told ABC interviewer Caroline Jones: 'You come on fairly strong born of conviction and that conviction leads to animosity against you and I get slogans daubed on my wall and phone calls of hatred and so and I suppose I've made the bed and I have to lie in it'.[31]

Alan constantly asked why it was okay to send tennis players, surfers, golfers and motor racing drivers to South Africa, but not cricketers and footballers. He pointed to the double standard of Australia playing cricket against Pakistan, a military dictatorship. He judged the Hawke Government's position on sanctions to be 'intellectually shabby'. It was a new favourite expression, which could have been applied to his own position. Alan Jones was selective in his advocacy. The many reasons the international community shunned an unsustainable pariah state, for its violations of human rights, and the impact of racial discrimination on sport, were not given equal weight.

At the same time, Alan Jones threw more support behind the closest thing Australia had to a dictator. Even back in The King's School days, Jones was noted for his fascination with Queensland Premier Sir Joh Bjelke-Petersen. 'I think I've had the same sort of upbringing. He didn't have anything and I can identify with that.'[32] Again, Alan could not see the wrong beyond the right. He does appear to have trouble integrating opposites. He maintained his belief in Bjelke-Petersen well after his administration was exposed for cronyism and corruption. 'I agreed with what Sir Joh was doing in my home state in terms of creating wealth and jobs.'[33]

In 1986, Sir Joh's Queensland Nationals were riding high, just short of a fall. They were governing alone, having abandoned the Liberal alliance and crossing swords with federal Liberals. Joh was no fan of Federal Opposition Leader John Howard, who had taken the leadership from Andrew Peacock in 1985.

With a federal election to be fought in July 1987, John Howard looked pale alongside an increasingly popular Prime Minister Bob Hawke. Towards the end of 1986 there was suspicion that Andrew Peacock was counting heads and contemplating a challenge to recover his old job. In December, reports of a new conservative alliance between Sir Joh and Peacock began to appear. Although Bjelke-Petersen was anathema to the Liberal leadership, some of whom openly declared him to be corrupt, Alan Jones hopped on the 'Joh for Prime Minister' caravan. Jones was in constant contact with and thought to be advising Sir Joh, who believed his fellow Queenslander would make a great deputy prime minister.

As Alan's year closed there was jumping between the Sir Joh and apartheid bandwagons. The South African government was selectively handing visas to those who could help rebuild the government's image. Politicians, sporting identities and media figures were taken on orchestrated tours. In December, Alan Jones also visited South Africa on a trip that encompassed a series of lectures and a visit to Soweto. He then moved on to England to guest coach the Oxford team for the annual Cambridge encounter. Oxford won 15–10, their second victory after a five-year run of losses.

When Alan Jones returned to Australia and the morning microphone, he found he had yet another boss. In January 1987, after two hours' negotiation, Alan Bond bought Channel 9, the CBC network and the television cricket rights for $1 billion. In addition to his on air shift, Jones was asked to write speeches for Bond. He was preparing enough of his own, as by now requests for speaking engagements were arriving daily. Many of the commitments he undertook were well rewarded. Others, particularly for sport or charity, he did for no fee. Susie Yabsley knew well his habit of saying yes too often. He clearly needed a manager.

A well-tailored solution seemed to come their way when she went to work for Harry Miller's Speakers Bureau. Harry Miller had taken on Alan Jones as a speaker. Now Jones took on Miller as an agent. New Zealand-born Harold Maurice Miller had a bigger name in Sydney than many of his clients. After serving ten months of a three-year gaol sentence for fraudulent misappropriation of $728 000,[34] he was now returned to Sydney's merciful embrace.

Miller and Jones seemed good for each other. Alan's income swelled and, in that his agent got 20 per cent, so did Harry's. A 2UE colleague who, unlike Jones, read the fine print said, 'The contract Jones has with Harry is unbelievable. Harry doesn't even have to get out of bed in the morning to make money off Jones. Any deal, whether Harry has helped negotiate it or not, Harry gets a cut.' Another said that even if a freebie box of wine was delivered to the studios, the requisite number of bottles were allocated for Harry.

Nineteen eighty-seven was going to be another busy year. Alan Jones was back on air, back banging the South Africa drum and back in support of Sir Joh's push for Canberra. Interviewed for the Channel 9 *Sunday* program in March, John Howard said he thought Sir Joh would make a very poor prime minister: 'I don't think he has a clear idea of what he wants to do for Australia. He has just a grab bag of cliches. He has no clear vision.'[35]

Although Alan Jones' professed support for the shift John Howard represented away from the 'warm inner glow' Liberal policies Alan Jones abhorred, he was not a supporter of Howard, according to radio colleagues at the time. Certainly Alan's support for Joh did his later friend's brittle leadership no favours. Although the wheels were bound to fall off, the Sir Joh push was destabilising for John Howard. Increasingly reluctant to explain exactly where he stood in the Joh campaign, when pressed by ABC interviewer Paul Murphy, Jones admitted: 'there would be a lot of worse people to occupy the Lodge'.[36]

Alan Jones was already at full strap before his most demanding rugby season started. The Wallabies began training in January for the inaugural World Cup, which Australia and New Zealand would co-host. The world's biggest rugby knockout competition would then be followed by the Bledisloe and a tour to Argentina. Preparing the team would not be easy, and not just because Jones was already so busy. For the World Cup, the Wallabies encountered an odd home ground disadvantage, considering the distractions of work commitments, girlfriends, wives, and even their coach.

In April, Alan Jones corralled his squad at the Camperdown Travelodge, not far from his home. Without the momentum and excitement of touring, and locked away in a suburban motel, rapport further weakened. Alan demanded 110 per cent commitment from his players, while happily dividing his attention between his own commitments. The players, used to a pattern of morning training and afternoon rests, did not like the new routine of waiting around for the coach. Captain Andrew Slack, a 33-Test veteran, found it was impossible to accede to Alan's wish and pretend they were on tour, especially as 'Alan, I think, did lay down one law for some and not for the others, the others being him'.[37]

There was more trouble with Nick Farr-Jones who, against Alan Jones' orders, sneaked into his law offices early one morning. Farr-Jones felt the sting of the double standard when Jones found out and from his own workplace, 2UE, chastised him via telephone. The coach later explained that his 2UE commitment made it difficult: 'I was under contract in broadcasting terms, root and branch, I was becoming the linchpin of the place, the revenue base. Ratings were important.'[38]

His position was confusing and contradictory. Alan Jones said he would never put his work ahead of his team; he said the morning training program was not the routine, and he said, 'I chose to train in the afternoon because that was when the games were going to be played'.[39] His denial that there was destabilisation and disenchantment meant this time the huddle formed with Alan on the outside. Training in the grounds of Trinity Grammar School, Jones found his voice as well as words he was not allowed to use on morning radio. A troubled teacher, unable to cover the ears of an attentive class, walked to the sideline and asked fullback Roger Gould whether he could ask the coach to tone it down. Gould, considering the request for a moment, replied: 'Nothing would give me more pleasure'.

Despite the problems, with its Grand Slam and Bledisloe victories, Australia entered the World Cup as a favourite. In the first match in Brisbane against Korea, Australia won easily. It was the debut match of perhaps Alan Jones' most famous favourite. A new young Adonis, Brian Smith, scored 17 of Australia's 65 points. He also won Alan Jones' heart.

The 20-year-old former Brisbane State High student was a good-looking young man with a reputation that was yet to be moulded. And Smith, Queensland's second choice halfback, was a willing subject, the utility player falling under Jones' spell. Like Alan at that age, young Brian was prepared to train and train until he dropped. At the time Alan Jones said of him: 'This young man is one of the most gifted players in the world. Every so often you find diamonds and you have to polish them up.'[40]

The next match, in Sydney against England, saw the debut of another perceived favourite and Brian Smith mate, Troy Coker. Australia had another good win. The Sydney matches were played at Concord Oval, which had been controversially renovated by Chief Executive Ken Elphick under Ross Turnbull's watch at a cost of $13.5 million.

The Concord matches were not well attended. The atmospherics were not right with the public, the administrators or the players. Fullback Roger Gould, a popular, easygoing presence for years, got sick of the drinking bans and the generally maudlin mood. 'I spoke to some of the players and they said that Alan's coaching style had changed, not his tactics, but his approach to the team. He'd become dictatorial ... it was a very unhappy environment, to the point where I basically finished my rugby quite unhappy with the whole scene.'[41] Gould packed his bags and flew back to Brisbane.

The team followed him to Brisbane to play an easy Test against the US. Then, back at Concord, there was another against Japan. The games provided an opportunity for Alan to give Brian Smith more Test experience. A week later there was a tougher quarter-final against Ireland. Nick Farr-Jones was flattened and again Brian Smith ran on. The Wallabies won 33–15, setting the stage for an important semi-final against France which, if they won, would see Australia through to the finals.

On 13 June a disappointing crowd of 17 768 turned up to see one of the great games. Australian fans were thrilled by the free-running rugby, right up till the last two minutes. With the score at 24–24, the French raided the Australian line, most of their team handling before fullback Serge Blanco crossed. As in Dunedin, the referee missed an infringement. As in Dunedin, there was despair in the Australian dressing room. And again Jones had trouble processing the loss. Australian winger Peter Grigg, blamed for a defensive lapse, put it this way: 'I think he blamed Tom Lawton at one stage. I think he blamed Campese, I think he blamed everybody ... and we blamed him.'[42]

Not according to Alan: 'I don't whinge when I lose—nobody hears me make excuses'.[43] Australia, a host nation, was now out of contention for the first World Cup. The best they could do was run third, in a play-off in New Zealand. Alan Jones did not want to be there. Running third was never on his agenda.

On 18 June, three minutes into the game, flanker David Codey was sent off, the first Australian player to be dismissed during a Test. When Wales beat the wilting Wallabies 22–21, Jones' mood fell fouler than the acrid air of Rotorua. Alan was again embroiled in a trans-Tasman squabble. He called the judiciary hearing into Codey's dismissal a 'farce'. A local official was described as 'an objectionable turd'.[44] The 'objectionable turd', Dick Littlejohn, who was party to a running feud with the Australians, was also referred to as 'Dick Littledick'. Alan does have a way with words.

Back at 2UE on 3 July, the eve of the federal election, he skirmished with Prime Minister Bob Hawke over his issue de jour: South Africa. According to another present at the studio, it was an otherwise friendly encounter that still evokes amusement. When Alan Jones became forceful, the Prime Minister would politely and soothingly reply, after a time leaning forward and stroking Alan's arm to reinforce his point. It seemed to work. The more Bob stroked, the more Alan purred. Media minders were quick to make notes. The benefit of being in the studio is broadly understood, but the stroking trick was brand new, one to be added to an expanding repertoire of techniques useful to the serious business of managing Alan Jones.

Jones' stand on South Africa was now more of an issue for his players. In the preceding month he had talked to some of them about a tour to South Africa. Nick Farr-Jones, one of five players called to Jones' room in Rotorua, says he was told a tour was going to happen. 'Significantly he never asked them if they wanted to go but just assumed they were as keen as he was. It would be one way, Jones said, for them to prove they really were a far better team than they had shown in the World Cup. He would essay to make it happen and get back to them.'[45]

Alan Jones' friend the former Australian cricketer Bruce Francis had done some work for the South African Rugby Board, approaching Wallabies such as Andrew Slack. A Kim Hughes led rebel Australian cricket team had already controversially toured. Now an all expenses paid visit, underwritten by South African Yellow Pages, which in return received substantial tax relief from the South African government, was on offer to rugby players. This appealed to those who wondered how it was that other elite athletes were becoming wealthy while they raised money for administrators.

Stories abounded at the time of secret slush funds being used to keep players in the supposed amateur game. Ken Elphick, New South Wales CEO, later claimed he paid hundreds of thousands of dollars in secret commissions to players and others to help promote the game.[46]

July ended badly for Alan. The Hawke Labor Government was re-elected and the Wallabies lost their third straight Test playing New Zealand in Sydney. Four days after the Bledisloe loss, an interview by Janise Beaumont was published in the Sydney *Sun*. Beaumont, later to join Jones' staff, was told: 'I hope the first thing we are when our losses come along is honest. And not recriminatory. We don't say, Campo, if you had done so and so ... we don't find fault; don't nail people up against a wall.'[47]

Team morale declined further. Alan Jones' selection of a new captain, David Codey, widened the fissure with Nick Farr-Jones, then New South Wales captain. Nick Farr-Jones understood Alan Jones had opposed Nick's promotion, telling New South Wales coach Paul Dalton: 'Of the fifteen players in the New South Wales team Farr-Jones would have been only his thirteenth choice as captain'. He understood Jones warned that Farr-Jones was 'quite heavily mixed up in religion'.[48]

Nick Farr-Jones was one of the players conflicted and nervous about the proposed South Africa tour, but prepared to stand by the team view, which was presumed to be pro tour. In August Andrew Slack and new Wallaby captain David Codey flew to South Africa. Codey also believed his coach had sanctioned the project: 'I was still very much of the belief that Jones was right behind us'.[49]

At this stage Alan Jones was seen to back-pedal. His ally, Ross Turnbull, had taken the time to count the numbers. Turnbull saw that if it went to a vote the Australian Rugby Union would ban for life participants in an unofficial tour. 'I had to tell that to Alan, who in fact had to tell the team'.[50] Alan Jones' conviction that it was wrong to boycott South Africa and wrong to remain obedient to rules you don't respect did not extend to any show of personal defiance or sacrifice.

The flip-flop came at further cost to team relations, as Jones agrees: 'I think they were disappointed in me that as a person who'd been with them through thick and thin. And I stood outside that. I wanted to confront the issue. I wanted to discuss this with the ARU and I was counting up numbers on the ARU and my persuasive powers, what I could do. I thought I could give it a go, but then it got out of hand.'[51]

Alan Jones' ever-rising profile made it difficult to contain differences. When Mark Ella was back in print claiming Jones had bogged the team down in predictable play, Jones' next captain, Simon Poidevin, fired back: 'The players have a huge loyalty to Alan Jones. To read week after week that every problem is due to Alan Jones starts to become tiring after a while. It has gone on too long. Enough is enough.'[52]

The bickering went national when Jones was featured on *60 Minutes*, the coach defending himself against the 'losers yapping at [him] now'.[53] 'Someone this morning said it has been one of the most persistent and ruthless attacks on an individual that I've witnessed in Australia for a long time.'[54] Interviewed by Jana Wendt, Alan Jones, wearing a pink shirt and powder blue jacket, looked tanned and fit. Jones again advanced his Melbourne Cup analogy of Australia handicapping winners. When Jana Wendt queried: 'Aren't more things in life more complicated?', Alan Jones replied: 'Not to me they're not'.

Next came the October–November tour to South America. As the squad boarded the plane, Alan Jones held to his view that there was harmony, even as the 'bitter and twisted' club members settled in their seats. Every sport has them. Disharmony is common. Some players have to be left out. The South American tour would see the club's bitter and twisted ranks swell.

It should have been a happy trip. South America, with its nightlife and spectacular scenery, had a lot to offer. Maybe Jones actually believed they were a team. And maybe, as with the schoolboys' tour to England in 1972, he was beginning to believe he really was a miracle coach who could do without the talent. On the transpolar crossing Alan was like Icarus flying too close to the sun. 'Alas Smith and Jones', might have been muttered as the team decamped in Buenos Aires. The habit of loving some players and dividing others was better contained in his first years as the Wallabies' coach. But by the end of 1987, control was as much as abandoned.

Brian Smith was well liked by his team mates and admired in particular for his athleticism and dedication to training. He was skilful too but, as with many gifted players, had the bad luck to be competing for spots when greater genius, in the form of Michael Lynagh and Nick Farr-Jones, was on tap.

Alan Jones' hold over Brian Smith and his compulsion to push the young player's cause was met with widening disapproval. The two were constantly seen together. Players and officials had to sit sweating on the bus after a training session while Alan collected balls for Brian, who was getting in some extra kicking practice. Even spectators became aware of the cosy relationship. A tour bus of Australian fans noticed how Alan Jones preferred to dine with Brian Smith rather than take his place at the team table. At a table in a Mendoza restaurant, they saw Alan staring 'goggle eyed' at Brian, the coach 'never drawing breath'.

It became clear that Alan was intent on selecting his protégé into the Test side. Brian Smith's chances were strengthened when Nick Farr-Jones suffered a medial ligament strain. Ricky Stuart, who went on to fame as a Rugby League halfback and coach, flew in from Australia while Nick Farr-Jones was undergoing intensive physiotherapy. John Bain, an Australian selector, had preferred Stuart to Smith. Now, as one of the travelling band of supporters, he had no say in team selection.

Physiotherapist Greg Craig and Farr-Jones worked to get the knee right for the First Test. When Craig heard from journalists that the coach had ruled Farr-Jones out of further play, he confronted Jones and there was an argument. Greg Craig had seen sustained effort repair the damage to an extent where the stocky halfback won a team three-kilometre run by half a lap. A week before the Test, Craig declared Farr-Jones fit. It made no difference. Alan Jones had decided: Brian Smith was the first choice halfback, with Nick Farr-Jones in reserve. Heads were shaking all through the camp. Team discipline was also fractured: veteran players partied at the discos, with one seen tucking into the Jack Daniels before breakfast.

At the Valez Sarsfield Stadium in Buenos Aires on 31 October, the Wallabies wobbled, managing only a 19–19 draw. The following midweek game against Rosario offered Farr-Jones an opportunity to get his position back. But by now Jones' blind spot for Smith was chronic. Farr-Jones at half played a powerful game but, according to Alan, fullback Brian Smith was pure inspiration. Alan Jones was moved to deliver a dressing room sonnet. It was, in a way, a declaration of love. It had happened before. Alan had often embarrassed players on whom he had a crush. 'Brian Smith, many players have played as well for Australia at fullback as you did today, but none have played better.'[55]

Treatment was forthcoming. A telephone call from Ross Turnbull and some local lobbying persuaded Alan Jones to leave Brian Smith out of the next Test. One insider says he was told: 'If you don't put Nick Farr-Jones in and drop Brian Smith there will be a riot'. But Alan Jones was not done. Like others before him Troy Coker, a mate of Brian Smith and thereby cast into the Jones' camp, felt his status among peers subsequently diminish. It caused another stir when, despite the physiotherapist's contrary advice and a Jones rule that unfit players would not be approved, Alan Jones selected Troy Coker. Greg Craig again argued with Alan Jones that the coach should stick to his own rule and rest Coker, but Jones wanted him on the field. The matter was decided by neither the coach nor the physiotherapist but by the knee, which gave way during training.

During the next Test in Buenos Aires, Australia seemed to do better. Ian Williams, playing in his first Test series, scored an exceptional try and Australia led 13–3 at half-time. But again Argentina kicked their way back, winning 27–19. Alan Jones' fifth straight Test loss was a bleak contrast to the five big wins of his Grand Slam tour. The sacrifices were worth it while the

Wallabies were winning, but became all the more painful as the losses mounted.

According to the coach, however, it was not all bad: 'We played brilliant football in Argentina. Some of the provincial football was the best we ever played and some of the training, the best we've ever done. But you know there were always forces marshalled against me because of the kind of person I was. I was very outspoken and upfront and front door.'[56] Alan had a fair point. His 'my team' approach had mixed outcomes. It took attention away from the players and it relieved them of pressure. It meant more good publicity in the good times, but more bad publicity when fortunes faded.

As it turned out the losing streak persisted. Alan Jones' rugby season might have ended when the last Test was played in November; coach and players, often sick of the sight of one another by this time of the year, are usually keen to separate over the Christmas break. But not Jonesy. His season extended into December when he coached Oxford in the annual varsity game.

To do so he had to be invited. A long-established custom saw the team elect the captain, and the captain choose the coach. In 1987 the captain was Bill Calcraft, an old Manly mate. Bill Campbell, another Wallaby assisted to Oxford by Alan Jones, was also in the team. Oxford was the clear favourite. It is no small event. On 8 December 50 000 people turned up at Twickenham, almost as many as came to see Jones' Wallabies in 1984. Cambridge won 15–10.

Nineteen eighty-seven had drifted a long way from 1984. The Bowring Bowl was added to the World Cup, Bledisloe and Argentina losses, with Alan Jones now battling to keep both treasured coaching positions. Just before Christmas, Mark Ella, a Bob Dwyer supporter, said in a 2KY radio interview that Alan Jones was on the way out: '... he's having more and more arguments with the players ... Brian Smith and Troy Coker are certainly very good players but nowhere near the standard of, say, Nick Farr-Jones and Steve Cutler, yet he pushes those guys to the forefront.'[57]

A day later Simon Poidevin, in an awkward position as his club coach was Bob Dwyer, again defended Alan Jones: 'It's easy to blame Alan Jones, he opens himself up to attack. He goes about his work in a fairly ruthless manner.'[58] The 47-Test veteran pointed out that consideration should also be given to circumstances beyond the coach—like the tough competition, the tensions over South Africa and increasing demands on amateur players.

Alan Jones renominated for the Wallabies position. The vote was set for 26 February 1988. A week before the vote, a poll conducted by two rugby writers, Peter Jenkins and James (Jim) Tucker, indicated only ten of the 31-member squad wanted Jones back. David Campese, the most famous Wallaby of the day, later admitted he was one of the disgruntled outsiders. Campese had even telephoned rugby officials to speak against Jones: 'I rang up a couple of people and said that I knew a number of players who would no longer play for the Wallabies if Alan Jones remained as coach'.[59] Campese now regrets his action, and has long since reconciled with Alan Jones, whose life coaching skills helped Campese into a career after football, the world's leading try scorer buying into a chain of sports stores. 'He talked about trying to get a Canterbury franchise or get my own label out and that was in '86. Looking back now, you know, he was right.'[60]

Andrew Slack, the man Jones still calls 'my captain', sees the glass half full. 'I feel some sort of sense of loyalty and gratitude. But he does things that can drive you and others nuts. But at the end of the day, if his worst enemy was in strife, then Jones would help him out. That's why I stick by him.' Roger Gould, driven nuts to the point of walking out of the World Cup, still says Alan Jones was the best coach he ever had. Another player says the same, but sums up the mixed feelings by explaining that Alan Jones was also the worst coach he ever had.

Nick Farr-Jones, whose rugby career improved after the Jones era, has remained openly critical, but was among the many to turn up to the 20-year reunion of the Grand Slam squad in 2004. Farr-Jones, who had resisted Alan Jones' control, felt that in his heart Alan was not a 'rugby man'.

Largely because of team dissension, Alan Jones missed out on reappointment—but only by one vote. Four years at the helm was not a bad run. And as Jones' own publicity records, the proof endures in black and white. According to the 2GB website biography, 'He is the most successful Australian Rugby Coach ever'.[61] His Wallabies achieved 89 victories from 102 matches. Of 30 Tests, twenty-three were won and four were lost only by a point.

At the end of 1987, Alan Jones would have been wise to step aside, to recontest the coveted job after a sensible interval. But Alan was like a Melbourne Cup favourite who had applied his own handicap. Alan's strength was his weakness. His narcissistic confidence invited high achievement, but it also pushed him to overreach himself.

Good teachers and coaches show their charges how to do it and then stand back, but the constitution of this clever man did not allow this approach. He had to hang on, and in doing so, betrayed another purpose. Alan Jones was coaching rugby not just for the sake of developing fine young men and a winning culture for themselves and the nation. Alan wanted to be around young men. He wanted excuses that would involve him in their lives. Sensitivity about homosexuality in the aggressively male rugby world gave new cause to deny an interior motive, the Wallabies years adding a further layer of concealment of the inner self.

So a golden era of Australian rugby came and went, in part due to one man's fascination with beefy thighs. It was, in the end, painful for Alan Jones, but overall immensely worthwhile. Australia forgives its sporting icons, even the homosexual ones. That Bledisloe Cup victory in 1986, in particular, was like a 'get out of gaol free' card. It would come in handy in the years ahead.

CHAPTER 9
WATERSHED

WE ALL HAVE OUR BAD YEARS. The sacking of Alan Jones as Wallabies coach meant 1988 started badly and it ended even worse. After arriving for his regular London sojourn in December, there was an incident so shattering, a ripple of fear that Alan might commit suicide reached all the way to Sydney. Friends rushed to his side.

On 26 January there was a good moment, when, in the Australia Day honours list, Alan Jones was awarded an Order of Australia for his services to rugby. It was ironic that, soon after, the Australian Rugby Football Union declared his services no longer desirable. What might have made it harder was the naming of Bob Dwyer, his rival beaten in 1984, as his replacement. Alan Jones' archrival may well have ended up profiting from the earlier loss of his job. He was able to return to a more professional outfit thanks to the higher standard set during Jones' stewardship.

Resuming another career as a newspaper columnist, Alan Jones showed a dignified public face. 'It would never be my intention to detract from the legitimacy of Bob Dwyer's claim to the job, or to deny him and his team the unity and cohesive national support to which they are entitled and which regrettably, we were denied ... Let us now forgive the acrimony generated by a few (you can't forget it) and join in the collective hope that 1988 will be a beneficial year for Australian Rugby and those entrusted with its safekeeping.'[1]

But Alan never got over getting the punt from rugby. A year later he severed all official ties, resigning his New South Wales executive position and developing the same poisonous regard for the forces that unseated him as he had for the jealous Liberals who had kept him from parliament. Alan was hurt by the way so many of his boys turned against him. After David Campese's book was published Jones spoke of his disappointment with people who had 'shared a slice of history with me'.[2] Charlie Jones was also wounded. 'My father rang up in tears after my sacking. He'd been reading on the front page of the Brisbane *Sun* that David Codey, whom I'd made captain for one Test, said that the Wallabies were a rabble under me at the end. That borders on the unacceptable.'[3]

Meanwhile his media career moved forward, not just with the *Sun Herald* column, but also a better timeslot on 2UE. Since his start in 1985, Alan Jones' ratings had steadily risen. At the end of 1987, when his station lured John Laws back from 2GB and into the 9 am to noon shift, Alan was asked to move to the earlier timeslot. The breakfast shift, where a chunk of the daily news agenda is set, would extend both his audience and influence. Usually, the downside is the hours, but less so for a man who never let the sun reach his blanket while he was under it. Alan Jones had been reading the papers before dawn for decades. Now it would be his well-paid duty.

Nigel Milan, the new general manager of 2UE, oversaw the move. 'The number one breakfast jocks at the time were Michael Carlton and Doug Mulray, the Bollinger Left if you like. Alan obviously had a very different perspective on the world. You know you looked for a unique selling point in commercial radio, something very different. He had enormous energy, obviously great intellect and I thought he was worth a go.'[4]

A powerhouse at this time of the day, Alan Jones was again uniquely suited. As a colleague put it: 'Part of his appeal is that he is always so upbeat and full of energy. That's what you want in a breakfast host. He also gives people a sense of empowerment—that they are listened to and can have a voice. He also allows them to say things that are not always acceptable, lets them be a bit sexist or racist or whatever.'

So from March 1988, Alan Jones would rise at 2.30 am and make his way from Newtown to North Sydney. It was already well known around 2UE that Jones' buoyant on air persona stood in contrast to the fiend who materialised once the microphone was switched off. Alan, continuing to struggle with the technicalities of radio, became unpopular with some of the panel operators, one of whom said: 'He is very unprofessional as a broadcaster. He just refuses to abide by formats. At one stage he just refused to stop talking at the top of the clock, so he would come crashing in over the news ... for someone who is constantly telling other people about the need for discipline, he is very undisciplined.'

Conscious of his power in the industry, very few radio colleagues are prepared to put a name to their commentary. One of the technical staff to quit said: 'He's basically a school bully. Not a day goes by when he doesn't shout at someone. I just hated the way he treated people, drove them to tears, etc, really terrible stuff. He's a twisted, warped individual. I can't imagine what happened to him as a child but it must have been horrendous. He never admits he is wrong. He never says sorry.'

The breakfast shift started at 5.30 am with the same theme Alan Jones had used for the morning shift. Having first trialled the Mills Brothers' 'The Jones Boy', Alan dropped it after an interview with singer Laura Branigan, having taken a fancy to her disco hit 'Gloria' instead. He had showed off the tune and his eclectic taste during the 1987 *60 Minutes* profile. Flouncing into frame, Alan seemed unconscious of the camp undertones. 'Gloria' would become one of his pet Sydney nicknames.

At the radio studio where Alan Jones' captivation with the good-looking younger men could not be missed, there was a general, though not exclusive, presumption that he was homosexual. As one observer noted: 'He has this enormous need to feel loved and accepted because he finds his homosexuality unacceptable and thinks others do too. This need for acceptance drives much of what he does.'

Co-workers noticed Alan avoided dealing with the subject of homosexuality if it emerged in the news. There was embarrassment when talkback callers had to be dumped. Rugby types were still ringing in and asking what had happened with James Black in the back seat in 1983. The subjects of his phantom relationships, James Black and now Brian Smith, were also subjects of sledging. Some of the main sledgers came from that old Matraville High cabal, the Randwick hooker Eddie Jones, another Jones to take a prominent place in both rugby history and Alan's hit list.

Within Jones' inner circle there was fervent denial that Alan was in any way homosexual. His friend Ross Turnbull, defence counsel-like, was frequently brought to his feet when the familiar slurs were cast. In 1988 Turnbull was one of about 40 mostly rugby people to assemble in a private room at the Wentworth Hotel to pay tribute to Alan. There have been many such occasions over the years. Alan developed a routine whereby he'd move around a table, clasping the shoulders of individuals and giving a brief testimonial to their character and achievements: 'Australia can never be grateful enough for the hard work and sacrifice ...', etc. On this occasion, a rare and remarkable hesitation is remembered. When he reached James Black, Alan Jones stood silently for a moment, his voice breaking as he finally said: 'This fine young man has shared with me a dreadful experience ... there has been terrible innuendo ... terrible innuendo ... but we have to go on with our lives'.

To close friends Alan expressed a wish for a woman in his life. He did so publicly as well. In a 1985 interview, he said his dad had just about given up on him. 'I've had some disappointments there and don't talk about that ... (laughs) What I really want is a wealthy heiress so I can stop all this working.'[5] In the *60 Minutes* profile he told Jana Wendt that he moved too fast for a long-term relationship.

In 1988, for her *The Search for Meaning* program, the gentle interrogatory style of Caroline Jones prised out more. Alan Jones seemed eager to address the question, confessing to the failure of his private life:[6]

> I've been unsuccessful in relationships. I suppose that's a function of this so-called success ... I think relationships require time and that's where there is a contradiction in what I am about because I call for commitment and discipline and all that and you have to have that if you're going to succeed in a relationship, commitment and time. On the other hand I have given commitment to two relationships in my life which through circumstances that neither of us could prevent, uh, failed, and I would have liked them to have succeeded and the legacy is still there. You still share the same love but it's incapable of being fulfilled and that is difficult, I think, but at the same time I take the view that every aspect of your life can't be fulfilling, I don't think. You've got to be grateful for the moments that you get, I think. I've had a lot of pleasure and a lot of enjoyment and a lot of satisfaction ... I must say in one that I won't talk but which will be with me for some time, not deliberately. One thing most extraordinary set of circumstances occurred and I had taken a job in another place and I thought in doing that we were going to be able to sort of move together into that employment and something happened which kept us apart and as a result you've got to say to yourself do I stop here because I've got to sort of keep going and I did keep going. It might have been the wrong decision to make at the time ... I don't know, how do you know?

Although the detail of gender was missing, Alan did seem to be talking about female companions. One was likely to have been Madonna Schacht, in that Alan told people they were lovers. As much as she had wished it otherwise, Madonna explained this was not so: 'Never at any time in my relationship with Alan did he express heterosexual yearnings or reveal any feelings that would be likely to lead to a fuller expression of a sexual relationship. We have always been—just good friends.'[7]

The blurring of the lines between acquaintance, friend and lover can be confusing for more than the odd athlete forced to cope with a love-struck Jones. This lonely man had a way of jumbling the personal, in other words assuming closeness that is not always reciprocated. Alan Jones can enter into impassioned support for someone he has just met, as if they were lifelong friends.

Even back then, the idea that Alan Jones was a 'relationship person' was of interest to Sydney's canny media advisors. In the months leading up to the March 1988 election in New South Wales, Alan Jones' good relationship with a bright young Nick Greiner had been helpful to the New South Wales Liberals. Both in favour of reducing public debt and increasing public accountability, Alan Jones and Nick Greiner appeared to be on the same wavelength. The new Liberal Party media machine was doing some pioneering work in the now practised art of manipulating talk radio. It established a network of fax machines in the homes of loyal supporters. Briefing notes and questions were sent out, suggesting new ways to attack Labor's position on topics such as gun control. The supporters would then ring broadcasters like Alan Jones, and push a prescribed line under the guise of free speech.

A lacklustre Labor leader, Barrie Unsworth was no match for Nick Greiner and his revived party. On 19 March, after 12 years in the wilderness, the Liberals were back in power. The new government showed its respect for Alan by anointing him to the board of the Sydney Cricket Ground Trust. The post is a Sydney equivalent to a box seat at the Vatican. It would be important for the Trust and Jones, placing him on holy ground and in the company of Sydney's elite. Prominent lawyer John Marsden, who had touted for the job, was thwarted, as he explained, when 'the Minister for Sport, Roland Smith, dug his heels in. There was no way he was appointing a homosexual to the Trust.'[8]

Premier Nick Greiner continued to be interviewed in the feature 7.15 am timeslot, but as his term progressed so did Alan

Jones' habit of talking over him. Alan seemed to like Nick more than he liked his government, stocked as it was with moderates such as Ted Pickering and John Hannaford.

The more interesting political relationship forged at this time was from within the other camp. Two weeks after the election, Labor appointed a new Opposition leader, the Member for Maroubra, Robert John Carr. The 40 year old was, like the Ella brothers, a product of Matraville High and, like the Ellas, Carr's regard for Alan Jones over the years veered between extremes of appreciation and rancour. Through the next decade and a half Jones and Carr would flirt and tiff like teenagers, each an important barometer of the other's success.

In the beginning, it was not just the Liberals who thought Bob Carr as colourless as predecessor Barrie Unsworth. Some in the Labor Party saw Carr as a stopgap choice. New South Wales Labor Party General Secretary Stephen Loosley had more faith, recognising in the former ABC reporter a natural broadcaster's voice and an ability to use it. Loosley saw this as a tremendous attribute, knowing that 'Barrie Unsworth had suffered electorally because Nick Greiner had used talkback more effectively'. A courtship was encouraged. Bob Carr's advisor at this time, Malcolm McGregor, was in a position to further the relationship. Like Alan Jones he had managed rugby touring teams and shared a friendship with Ross Turnbull. McGregor knew that Jones had 'an enormous ego and could be courted'.

Alan Jones, perhaps looking for leverage and by various accounts genuinely impressed, began to give Bob Carr airtime. A turning point was a Bicentennial dinner for visiting British Prime Minister Margaret Thatcher. Bob Carr, assisted by speechwriter Graham Freudenberg, made a speech that Margaret Thatcher singled out for praise 'while barely mentioning Greiner's contribution'.[9] Alan Jones, with his Churchillian love of a fine phrase, played excerpts on air and referred to Bob Carr's 'eloquence' in his newspaper column.[10]

Alan Jones' mate north of the border, Sir Joh Bjelke-Petersen, was not doing so well. The push for Canberra had proved calamitous, and by now the Fitzgerald corruption inquiry had revealed enough of a mess to render him unelectable in his own state. Bjelke-Petersen resigned after being sacked as National Party leader.

One Queenslander who did make it south, for a time at least, was Alan's dad. In his eighties, Charlie Jones was in need of constant attention after a series of strokes. He tried to settle in Sydney, where some of Alan's friends came to know and like the stooped and humble man. But the alien inner urban environment was plainly unsuitable. 'I'd leave Dad to go to work with the radio tuned to 2KY for the horse races, but one day I came home and he was sitting in the chair crying. He told me he might as well be dead as be here, because he had no friends.'[11] Charlie Jones, who did not want to go into a nursing home, returned to Brisbane. Alan paid $500 a week for a housekeeper to look after him.

At Newtown, Alan Jones was soon in need of his own housekeeper. His spare rooms were made available to many friends, particularly footballers. By putting Troy Coker up in Sydney and arranging for orthopaedic surgeon Merv Cross to repair his weakened knees, Jones effectively saved Coker's rugby career.

Brian Smith was another guest at the Newtown premises which, to visitors entering the gallery stairwells, was like a shrine. They could not miss the walls covered with framed newspaper articles and pictures of Alan alongside famous people and favoured athletes. A particular talking point was a framed portrait spotted at Alan's bedside, featuring Smith. 'There used to be this amazing picture. It was taken in a changing room with lots of people but somehow the light just showed up the two of them.'

Alan Jones had also been helping some of his old players with further education. His 1987 winger, Ian Williams, like Bill Campbell before him, won a Kobe Steel scholarship to Oxford. With their respectable undergraduate credentials it was comparatively easy to assist these two Wallabies and Alan Jones wanted to do more, but getting in others who did not have the marks was a taller order. So he got together with mates such as

Ross Turnbull and stockbroker Rene Rivkin, and started a new scholarship scheme. Each put in about $30 000 and, as a result, Brian Smith and Troy Coker were on their way to Oxford. Some jealous onlookers did not regard the stipend as a serious scholarship as no real application process or selection criteria appeared to be used.

The Dons run Oxford's autonomous colleges to their own rather than university rules. Entry was achieved by going through the colleges, Alan Jones finding a good connection in a flexible admissions tutor. Entry standards were not so exacting for diploma courses, such as the one Alan Jones had done in the 1970s. Smith and Coker sat for a Graduate Diploma of Social Studies.

Relief from academic pressurers meant there was plenty of time for rugby. The footballers lived more comfortably off campus in a well-appointed terrace house. Smith was seen arriving at football training in a bright red BMW, which team mates understood had been supplied by Alan. Smith and Coker were part of what was again an Oxford side with a heavy Anzac lacing. Ian Williams was on one wing, with future Wallaby Rob Egerton on the other. In addition, there was David Kirk, the New Zealand World Cup winning captain, who had diplomatically conceded leadership to an Englishman, the multiple Oxford blue Rupert Vessey.

Having been asked before, Alan Jones anticipated being invited to guest coach Oxford again for the big December encounter with Cambridge. He was, in a sense, uninvited instead. The 1987 experience, when Oxford played percentage football and lost, had not met with complete favour. Rupert Vessey, along with some team mates, decided Alan Jones was not needed. Vessey rang Jones and gave him the news.

Alan Jones' radio year was a lot better than his rugby year. His 2UE audience had jumped from 7.3 per cent to a remarkable 14.3 per cent share. Alan Jones was now the highest rating AM announcer, but still behind FM broadcaster Doug Mulray, who reached a different, younger audience. When his radio shift came to an end in December Jones played 'Wish Me Luck As You

Wave Me Goodbye'. Despite the setback at Oxford, Alan Jones stuck with his plan to head to England. He was keen to catch up with mates such as Brian Smith and the Irish international Brendan Mullin. But first Alan headed for Queensland.

By this time pulling in around $1 million a year, the broadcaster had further expanded his property portfolio to include a villa at Mike Gore's famous gated Gold Coast resort. Alan is still remembered for an awkward appearance in a television commercial, in which he is perched precariously on a li-lo, promoting Sanctuary Cove. He rented out the $767 505 villa for one dollar a week, making it available to friends. As one commented: 'His is an uncomplicated generosity. All he would ask is that you keep it clean.'

On Saturday 3 December, Alan Jones was guest speaker at a private function at Sanctuary Cove hosted by Ross Turnbull. The next day he travelled to Brisbane where he caught a plane for London. He arrived behind schedule at Heathrow airport at 8.15 am on Monday 6 December. Alan Jones later said: 'The plane was delayed at all stops and I was dog tired when I finally got to the flat on Monday morning. I had a cup of coffee and I couldn't go to sleep.'[12]

Long before and since this occasion members of Alan Jones' staff presumed he waited for these moments to 'have his fun'. He knew the beats in Sydney and Brisbane, because he had been seen there and had commented on the rent boys as he drove past them with friends. But Sydney and Brisbane were risky. As one colleague said, 'I don't think he allows himself to play in Sydney. I think that's why the London incident happened. He had it all bottled up inside until he just had to act, let himself go.'

The flat Jones turned up at in St James Street, Mayfair belonged to his friend Rene Rivkin. After dumping his luggage, he headed out again. 'I thought I'll go for a walk which is what people usually do when they come to London. I'd been walking for about 35 minutes. I just had light clothes on and it was very cold. I had this virtuous feeling that I was working the muck [of the flight] off me.'[13] The six block walk from Mayfair took him to Piccadilly Circus, where he crossed into familiar territory, the West End theatre district. He later explained he was going to have a look at the posters for a Jeffrey Archer play, *Beyond Reasonable Doubt*. This is where his public account of what happened came to an end.

In the same area around Soho there was a gay beat with its own 'wall', known locally as 'the meat rack', a place where cruising men could pick up young male prostitutes. In Margaret Thatcher's Britain, the police had been urged to be more vigilant about 'cottaging', the liaising of homosexuals in public toilets. To the cops, protection of underage males was seen as legitimate work, but there were mixed views about the legitimacy of targeting homosexuals. So it was not always popular work with the young police who were usually assigned to this area.

To make it more interesting, the West End branch had begun an informal competition: because the occasional judge or politician was caught in their net, who paid for drinks at the end of the week rested on whose catch was the biggest. Later that day the word went breathlessly around the station that one team had caught Australia's future prime minister. Two plain-clothes officers had been watching the underground public toilet at Broadwick Street from the roof and a nearby corner. They had seen a man in an aqua coloured Lacoste sweater enter the toilet and became suspicious when he stayed inside for a longer than usual period.

Alan Jones was arrested and taken to the Mayfair station where he was charged with 'outraging public decency' and 'committing an indecent act'. One charge appeared to refer to alleged public masturbation, and the other to an alleged attempt at picking up an officer by, to use the colloquial term, 'flag waving'. It is only fair to point out that prosecuting authorities were ultimately unprepared to present any evidence to support the charges.

Meanwhile at London's Lensbury Club, the Oxford rugby team gathered before the big game. They were watching a video, *Action Jackson*, when a call came through from a Mr Alan Jones seeking to speak to Mr Brian Smith. Smith made an excuse and hurried to his friend's side. According to another friend, Alan was 'shot to pieces'. He did not attend the Twickenham match, in which Brian Smith starred, scoring two tries. Oxford won 27–7, the largest victory margin since 1909.[14]

Yet another friend later said by Alan Jones to have provided 'immeasurable' assistance was the man whose new play had drawn Jones to Soho. Alan Jones came to know Lord Jeffrey Archer through the author's book promotion tours. It is easy to see how they would have got on as there are remarkable similarities. Both came from poor backgrounds. Both had strong-willed mothers who urged them towards superior schooling. Both became teachers and inspirational sporting coaches. Archer and Jones did similar education courses at Oxford. The fellow fabulists had populist followings; they stood for parliament, in Archer's case successfully, and gave a considerable amount of their time and money to charity. And there was something else. One year earlier Jeffrey Archer had been before a London court as the result of a sex scandal. He sued a British newspaper, which had alleged Lord Archer had slept with and later bribed a prostitute in an effort to secure her silence.

Although evidence was later to overturn the finding, Jeffrey Archer won the libel action. The same high order advocacy used by Archer was now made available to Jones. Archer, and now Jones' solicitor Lord Victor Mishcon, litigation consultant at UK legal firm Mishcon de Reya, were not figures to be commonly found in a lowly magistrate's court. A barrister, Stephen Reading, was also assigned.

It was dawn on a Tuesday when the story broke in Australia. First glimpses are commonly fleeting and newsrooms had only sketchy details of a high profile Australian arrested on a morals charge. Alerted by bureau chief John Highfield, ABC London correspondent Peter Cave was concerned not just about identifying the right person, but the right Alan Jones. (Another prominent Australian sports identity is the racing driver and 1980 Formula One champion, Alan Jones.)

When Peter Cave found Alan's address he hurried to the Mayfair flat and knocked on the door. Although he thought he heard someone inside, the door stayed shut. Given the circumstances, the no-nonsense ex-serviceman doorman, who had seen Alan Jones enter, became worried that he might have harmed himself. So he knocked again, and then used his keys to open the door to reveal an ashen Jones. Cave, recognising the former rugby coach, introduced himself and asked whether he wished to comment. Jones declined and closed the door.

On 7 December, when Lord Mishcon's shining Bentley approached the Marlborough Street Magistrate's Court, there was bedlam. A mass of journalists had assembled for what the presiding magistrate described as a minor matter. When Australian television reporter Richard Carleton appeared by coincidence on the scene, he was mobbed by colleagues who knew only of an Australian media figure being charged and presumed he was the story rather than the storyteller. Richard and his wife Sharon, unable to dissuade fellow reptiles, took refuge in a nearby print shop.

The concern about suicide was more keenly felt a world away at 2UE. Alan Jones' broadcasting colleague, John Laws, telephoned to offer comfort. Laws recalls Jones was so distressed he spoke about wanting to jump out the window. Station boss Nigel Milan was worried. John Brennan was put on the case, strings began to be pulled and, in the busy pre-Christmas period, airline seats found. Passengers were offloaded as Brennan, John Fordham and Ross Turnbull found space on that afternoon's QF1 to London.

Another 2UE colleague, Phillip Adams, shared a concern that, in a homophobic nation, the scandal could mean that Alan Jones' 'commercial career was over'. Phillip Adams was one of many to send Alan Jones a telegram of support. He joshed about 'British spunk', an attempt to soften if not laugh off the matter. Adams was offended not by Jones' alleged conduct, but by the idea that police could treat homosexuality as a crime.

Stephen Loosley conveyed his good wishes through Jones' 2UE producer, John Stanley. Malcolm McGregor urged Bob Carr to 'extend the hand in his hour of need and he will never forget you'. The Opposition leader sent a personal note, quoting Richard Nixon, telling him that his contribution to public life would sustain him through the difficult time.[15]

Advertiser John Singleton sent a fax: 'Mate don't let the bastards get you. Kick heads, fight, but don't you ever give up.'[16] Brisbane-based Robert Jones, now virtually out of touch with his brother, was buoyed by the strength of the support. 'If we take the London episode—I was quite surprised by the number of phone calls that I got from people in England saying don't worry one little bit. It was just endless, people just ringing.'[17]

Considering the crowd out front at Marlborough Street, Alan Jones was hustled into the court through an alternative entrance. Before the case was heard the Crown withdrew the more serious charge, leaving the charge of committing an indecent act. This charge, to which Alan Jones pleaded not guilty and which attracted only a small fine, was to be held over until January. He left the court via a front entrance and was photographed by the assembled media. Barrister Stephen Reading told them: 'Mr Jones is a man of good character. He is completely innocent of the charge against him. It will be opposed vigorously.'[18]

Under siege from a range of media, and with the location of the Rivkin flat now known, Alan Jones needed somewhere else to stay. John Fordham got straight on to Terry Holmes, managing director of the Ritz. Fordham, who held a public relations account with the hotel, persuaded a reluctant Holmes to make a room available. Holmes was told Alan could prove to be a valuable customer, so a room was found and the advice validated.[19]

Fordham and Jones' other mates also went to work on damage control. Back in Australia the *Daily Mirror*'s front page story on Tuesday had included a photo of Alan and a bold headline: 'ALAN JONES ARREST "OUTRAGING PUBLIC DECENCY" CHARGE'.[20] On Wednesday, with the blow softened, the *Daily Mirror*'s headline declared: 'ALAN JONES: I'LL STAY AND FIGHT CHARGE. HE'S NOT GUILTY SAYS LAWYER'.[21] On Thursday, again on the front page, it was 'MY STORY: "I'm not immoral ... I'm not indecent"'.[22] The accompanying photograph pictured Alan and supporters at a lunch at the Ritz: Brendan Mullin from Alan Jones' 1987 Oxford team, Brian Smith, Ross Turnbull, John Fordham and John Brennan. Although the 'Alan Jones Arrest' newspaper banners did not join the many others he had framed and mounted in his Newtown home, the photograph of Alan and friends, with scotch in hand, would find pride of place.

The article carried endorsements from Michael and Susie Yabsley, *Good Morning Australia* host Kerri-Anne Kennerley, and Wallaby Steve Cutler. Others to publicly support Alan were Liberals Kerry Chikarovski and John Spender, and media colleagues George Negus, Geraldine Doogue and Steve Liebmann. At this stage Alan Bond was in control of the former Packer empire but a link to the old regime was maintained through Channel 9 boss Sam Chisholm. Both Chisholm and Packer were also there for Alan.

Alan Jones was interviewed via satellite on Channel 9's *A Current Affair*. An emotional Alan explained he had no choice but to abide by his lawyer's instructions and limit his responses. 'I've got nothing to hide. I am proudly a moral person and a decent person and I have maintained that morality and decency right throughout my life.'[23] Alan Jones promised that in time all would be explained.

Back in Australia there was a gradation of whispering. Within Alan's old school and rugby circles there were plenty of 'I told you so' telephone calls. In the King's diaspora parents who had taken opposing positions on Alan Jones either ducked for cover or openly crowed. One woman who had long suffered for her suspicions within her mothers' group began to gather newspaper cuttings into a scrapbook.

Meanwhile in London, the lawyers also gathered to contest the second charge of committing an indecent act. Alan Jones' story to friends, and presumably counsel, was that he had been standing at the sink in the lavatory with his pants unzipped, but had not been masturbating. He said that having had a bit to drink on the flight he had a full bladder, but as can be the case with older men, he was having trouble getting the urine to flow. So he had gone to the sink to wash his hands, hoping that the hand motion and flow of water would help.

It did not matter. Before Christmas, the Crown decided to drop this charge as well. Alan Jones was free of all but decade after decade of fervent speculation about what caused him to be charged in that London dunny, and how and why he got off. On the upper floors of the Ritz Hotel there was considerable relief. Jonesy wanted to party, booking rooms for Brian Smith, Troy Coker and another friend, Sue Havers. Presents were handed out and the aqua Lacoste sweater, which had been stuffed in a bin, was souvenired.

After Christmas dinner, Alan Jones flew back to Australia. A Harley Street doctor had advised rest. He headed first for Sanctuary Cove where he caught up with Madonna Schacht. 'He was keen that I fly to Sydney to attend some functions with him. In the aftermath of all the negative publicity, Alan felt the need to appear in public with some female company.'[24] The relief that flowed from the dropping of the charges did not stop him worrying about how the public and others would greet him. Alan Jones' self-belief could not accommodate shame. Back in Sydney he was reluctant to show his face. John Fordham had to push him out the door.

Fordham encouraged Jones along to a big cricket testimonial where Dennis Lillee, Rod Marsh and dozens of sporting luminaries made him feel welcome. Underlying much of the show of support was concern that a man should suffer so pointlessly. It was a case at least one supporter was keen to make when Alan arrived to thank him. At Phillip Adams' Darlinghurst home, his then 2UE colleague seized the opportunity to tell Alan Jones what many people felt, that he would not be judged harshly because he was gay. Adams remembers Jones replying: 'But it did not happen'. Adams persisted, explaining that his support was unconditional and telling Jones that people who were offended by homosexuality could 'get fucked'.

The meeting with Bob Carr took the form of a thank-you dinner at an Italian restaurant at Lavender Bay. Bob Carr's advisor, Malcolm McGregor, went along and was not entirely surprised that a 'genuinely conservative' Bob Carr got on with Alan Jones. 'It was a funny night and Jones was at his charming best ... I told Carr that Jones was a relationship bloke and this kind of loyalty only starts when you are in trouble. That paid off big time.'[25] McGregor was buying when the stocks were low. He said that following the dinner Jones prompted them to send him briefing notes.

2UE General Manager Nigel Milan had also experienced a troubled Christmas break. Although promising Alan Jones that his job was safe he had reasonable concerns about how the audience might react. 'When he came back from London he went back on air with a lot of expectation—he handled himself, I have to say, extraordinarily well ... I think he came out of it a stronger man.'[26]

When Jones returned to the microphone on 16 January 1989, the month-old story about the London dunny was still alive and kicking. Alan Jones said he was deeply grateful for the thousands of messages. 'It's only in adversity that you learn of the great reservoir of goodwill that exists among thousands of Australians.'[27] He read a prepared statement: 'Let me say that on this show and in my life, I've always articulated the adherence to certain values and standards and to levels of honesty and openness which I believe we all ought to try to embrace. I have not betrayed those standards. I am and always was innocent of the charges levelled against me. What I can say to you is limited by the fact that I have retained leading English lawyers who have instructed me not to comment on the matter.'[28]

Alan Jones' lawyers won the remaining costs in the order of £70 and by the end of January the case was closed as far as the courts were concerned. Now presumably free of legal constraint, Alan was not heard to open up as promised about what had happened. But rumour, as well as nature, abhors a vacuum. Conspiracy theories began to do the rounds. Most had it that Alan's high-powered pals had pulled strings. Perhaps from within his support base three further theories began circulating. The first was that jealous rugby figures set him up. The second was that he was a victim of a plot organised by an anti-apartheid movement and, thirdly, the Australian Labor Party wanted to kill off any chance he had of becoming prime minister. In all three scenarios, the London police had somehow been aware that three hours after arriving in London, Alan Jones would be in a Soho lavatory. What is most likely is that the Director of Public Prosecutions came to a pragmatic judgement that the low scale of the offence and the high order of opposition meant the fight was not worth it.

Having won the legal battle, there was still more to do in the court of public opinion. Those jealous colleagues in the media had so far been extremely kind to Alan. Instead of going in for the kill in the way Jones does, the Sydney media had been gentle. The tabloids are normally aggressive in their coverage of such stories. That considered, it is hard to think of anyone who got a better deal than Alan Jones. The reporting was unusually limited to the barest facts about what was delivered in court and a range of positive commentary. There was no further digging into London or his past. Among the favours extended to Alan was some obvious soft-pedalling.

In June 1989 *New Idea* ran a story under the headline 'Alan Jones: a future PM?' It hung on the improbable peg of Alan's ambition to run the country. His friendship with Benazir Bhutto was recounted, but the main purpose of the interview was to resecure the mask. The reporter told us: 'Alan is a loner. Although there is now a woman in his life … At 45 [he was 48] he has never married and he sees this as a big gap in his life.' It quoted Jones: 'A lot of people have gaps in their life and that's mine. I have been privileged in many ways and I don't think it is fair to complain about my lot. I once worried about never becoming a father, but not anymore. I don't believe you should worry about what you've missed out on. There is a woman in my life but it is a personal thing. She is a professional woman and we are very close but she isn't always here.'[29]

A later, unattributed piece in the magazine *Ita* described the then 49-year-old Jones as in his early forties, and pushed the same line: 'His friends say he would like to have a wife. Sometimes older women listeners on Radio 2UE, where he hosts the top-rating breakfast talkback show, ring him on the open line to tell him he is doing too much, that he needs someone to look after him. He agrees. He talks quite openly about his failed romances and laughs it off, but in a serious moment admits: My main flaw in relationships is that I'm emotionally overpowering. Then he quotes a line from a John Donne sonnet—"Whatever dies was not mixed equally." I'm conscious of the fact that I don't have anyone to share my life with—a person with whom I can talk.'[30]

At the time, Harry Miller, who routinely vetted interview requests, would ask, 'Are there going to be any questions about London?' If you wanted the interview you conceded, as journalist Lenore Nicklin later confessed: 'Okay, Harry, no questions about London dunnies'.[31]

But even the cleverest PR doctor could not kill the ghost of London. Following the episode the tortured, homophobic, closet homosexual 'Gloria' began to make regular appearances on the rival Doug Mulray show. Comedian Dave Gibson has a repertoire of clever impersonations, one of them a creditable Jones. One morning, rushing from Mulray's farm to reach the studio by 6 am, the pair heard Alan Jones on the car radio begin his program at 5.30 with his signature tune, 'Gloria'. The tortured homophobic homosexual Jones character got a name, which Gibson later dropped when Andrew Denton took over the program and 'Gloria' became Alan. The characterisation was more affectionate than cruel but even so the mocking evoked in Alan Jones a fury not felt since the 'pansy' jeers back at Oakey.

At the National Convention Centre in Canberra in August 1989, one of many awkward moments occurred. At a taping of ABC TV's *Hypothetical*, 'Beggar Thy Neighbour', Alan Jones did a double-take when asked by Geoffrey Robertson: 'What's the first thing to do if you get arrested in a foreign country?' There was laughter in the audience at Jones' dropped jaw and his rarely seen state of being lost for words.

The toilet episode was indeed a watershed for Alan Jones. On top of all the other evidence that might have led people to suspect Alan was homosexual, the London incident was going to strengthen if not confirm suspicion. An opportunity arose for him to admit his homosexuality. The generally sympathetic response made it is easier for him to be himself. There was no need to confess to wrongdoing. It is not, nor should it be, a crime to be homosexual. It is not a sin to have your penis out in a public toilet. But having easily defeated the criminal charges, Alan Jones sought to defeat common sense as well, by asking the rest of the world to join him in his denial.

The incident also advanced the prospect of a more tolerant Jones. Certainly Alan thought so. 'Whatever experiences you have in life somehow changes you, doesn't it? You don't know quite how at the time, but it changes you. Perhaps I'll have a greater appreciation of the traumas that others face and the difficulties that they have to overcome and if that's the case I'll be a better person.'[32]

In a *Good Weekend* profile nine years later, Jones reiterated: 'I've never said this before ... I often think about it ... and of course it's fair to say it created significant anguish at times ... but I spent most of my life being the victor. And that was one period of my life when I was the victim. I think it's influenced a lot of my attitudes towards a lot of people. I see things from a different standpoint. It's a silly thing to say but I think in many ways I'm most probably I hope, a better person.'[33]

Despite Nigel Milan's and Phillip Adams' fears that Alan Jones' audience might desert him, the opposite occurred. The ratings increased. Alan was building an audience he had long been able to charm. What had worked for the mums and many of the dads at Ironside, Brisbane Grammar and King's was working its magic in Sydney. Alan Jones appealed mainly to an older generation. A condition of signing on is believing him. While some of his older listeners perceived him to be homosexual and were unconcerned, Alan Jones could reasonably presume that others, perhaps the majority, would be as intolerant as they were of other divisive and provocative public issues: 'Congratulations, Alan, on your exposure of the perpetrators of crime in this country. Australia has the wrong gene pool. Multiculturalism doesn't work. These Muslims and Asians are not my equal. Anyone who covets a rear end is not my equal.'[34]

The promise of a better person, a more humane and compassionate Alan, seemed to last no longer than one of his fitful slumbers.

PART 2
THE MYTH

CHAPTER 10
FROM PEDAGOGUE TO DEMAGOGUE

ALAN JONES' MOTTO MIGHT BE drawn from German philosopher Friedrich Nietzsche, who said: 'What does not destroy me makes me stronger'. Jones' ability to survive a range of near-death experiences might have led him to suspect he was indestructible and, perhaps, beyond sanction.

Over the next decade Jones' power accelerated as he grew in a medium that was itself developing. Bob Carr was fascinated with talk radio, referring to it as an 'electronic democracy'.[1] John Howard would also favour the medium, explaining, 'I think you get more out of this type of exchange than just about any other kind of media contact between a member of parliament and a journalist'.[2]

At its best, talk radio can have premiers and prime ministers answering directly to the electorate, giving ordinary Australians an improved sense of participation and belonging. Alan Jones believed politicians should listen to the people and saw his program as an ideal medium. A favourite form of praise he directs at politicians is that he or she is a 'good listener'. 'Radio has become the pulse of the city and if you want to understand the public you have to go to talkback radio'.[3]

An admirable feature of Alan Jones' approach to radio is his attitude that he is there to do more than earn squillions. He uses his skills and influence as a social and political weapon. His power is wielded on behalf of wealthy mates, but also the weak. Alan Jones goes further than anyone I know in the media to help people with serious problems, as well as those whose storm water drains are blocked or who are struggling with their wheelie bin.

While other announcers adapted to the existing formula, Alan Jones adapted talk radio to himself. As such, although it has been tried, the *Alan Jones Show* is impossible to copy. He dislikes comparisons, loathing the 'shock-jock' pejorative, and even the milder description of 'breakfast announcer'. Alan Jones does more than play music and read traffic reports. He also sees 'talkback' as an unfair term, as until 2005 the microphone was shared with listeners for less than a quarter of his time on air. Alan has been critical of commentators whose only qualification for public debate is a microphone. He was right in seeing himself as better qualified than many of his peers. Having coached the Wallabies and written speeches for a prime minister, Alan Jones' breadth and intellect meant that in substance he towered over rivals.

'I don't tell people what to think. I ask them what they think.'[4] He is not the only dogmatic radio host. The medium favours lively opinion. The audience relies on commentators to interpret as well as impart the news. Alan Jones was happy to service this need and be forthright with it. As a member of Jones' team, Ross Geddes, put it, 'He does people's thinking for them'.[5]

'When I started on radio I was told nobody would understand what you are talking about and I would say that's why I'm talking about it.'[6] While competitors took care to avoid the abstract and the boring, Alan took on any subject, confident of his ability to make sense and keep people listening.

2UE General Manager Nigel Milan was one of many colleagues to respect the pedagogue, seeing Alan Jones' teaching background as important: 'I mean we live in times of great change, particularly a lot of the older population are quite nervous about what they see happening around them. I think Jones has taken the big issues—things like globalisation—and broken it down to bite-sized pieces and I think that role as an educator has taken him into the confidence of the heart of Sydney.'[7]

Although he had some tutoring from experienced broadcasters such as John Brennan, Alan's was never the mellifluous voice born to the turntable and microphone. Unlike other less successful broadcasters, Alan Jones has never acquired an exquisite sense of timing, which melds the components of a program in the way a conductor leads an orchestra. But after five years, his technical clumsiness and shrill delivery mattered more to work colleagues than to an audience increasingly impressed by his communication skills. So confident was he of his powers of persuasion, Alan Jones was happy to push a contrary and sometimes unpopular view. A 2UE colleague observed: 'He's become really good at being able to deny things, or believe in whatever he is telling himself'.

These communication skills had been grafted on to radio and journalism rather than crafted in. Alan Jones has never had a journalist's grounding in identifying fact and essaying balance. He has never come with a reverse gear. The absence of neutral, as well, seemed less of a concern in a medium that favours certainty. While this was a more critical weakness, again his audience rarely complained. Alan Jones compensates to a degree through his reliance on village voice feedback. Another favourite saying is 'my listeners are my best researchers'. While he breaks many rules journalists are trained to observe, he also breaks a lot of stories experienced journalists miss.

Just as there were many positive features to the Alan–talk radio alliance, there were also negatives. Radio has its own structural weaknesses, the pressure of immediacy settling awkwardly on a poor research base. There are not the resources to undertake extensive inquiries, let alone check the provenance of every caller. There is a kind of reverse index of certainty that anchors firm opinion to fragile evidence. As was seen in the

Greiner campaign of 1988, the formula can easily be manipulated.

Although his team would expand, in 1989 Alan Jones had three people to help with a busy program. The amount of information covered meant they were forever scrambling. The combination of hard opinion and soft research would land Jones and 2UE in a lot of trouble. As a 2UE colleague observed, 'His worst quality is his lack of judgement. If he has four people in the room and has to pick one he always picks the worst one. He is very easily influenced by pressure groups. He gets four letters and says it is a torrent. He goes on air on the flimsiest of evidence.'

While newspapers are content with one or two editorials, Alan Jones' opinion threads through the entire program like one long editorial. The format, established in 1987, has largely stayed its course. Alan Jones would come on air at 5.30 am and deliver a daily news summary prepared by one of his producers. After the hourly news bulletins he presented a more formal editorial, which was either written for him, prepared in sketch form or was his own work. He had an early talkback segment, a prerecorded segment called 'It Happened Today', a report from a UK correspondent and a sports report. During one of the news broadcasts he would prerecord editorials for broadcast on some of the stations syndicated to 2UE.

Sydney listeners could tune their morning to it. At 2GB, as at 2UE, he does his main editorial after the 7 am news. The feature interview is scheduled for the slot when the biggest audience is listening, approximately 7.15 am. There are more news and traffic bulletins, more interviews and a finance report. Between 8 and 8.30 am he has his more entertainment-based interviews and the US report. All through the morning there is a sprinkling of jokes and community bulletin board announcements. The last half-hour before 9 am has more talkback. A half-hour version of the program's highlights was later packaged for broadcast the following morning between 5 and 5.30 am. In 2005 his 2GB program extended to 10 am, doubling the talkback component.

While journalists might spend days on a single story, Alan Jones deals with dozens of stories in a single day. Having to cover so much territory, with so little opportunity to filter the facts, has not impaired his confidence and righteousness. There are very few corrections and apologies. Over the years, Alan Jones on his own has occupied more space on the defamation list of the New South Wales Supreme Court than entire broadcasting and publishing organisations.

From the beginning of his radio career he was critical of Australia's defamation laws, seeing them as 'intimidating and inhibiting'.[8] He also accepted that an impulsive medium allowed him to 'go over the top' sometimes. When asked whether he had ever regretted saying something on air, Alan Jones told Maggie Tabberer: 'Oh well, I suppose the lawyers would think I should have ... the answer to that is yes. I think you should avoid being personal ... you are there and you are saying things all the time and you don't have time to have a committee meeting ... sometimes I am sure I have said things that might have hurt people or were inaccurate.'[9]

In this respect Alan Jones was a nightmare for bosses and production staff. 'Ah the defamation half-hour. That's the first half-hour of the show,' one colleague explained: '... the producers provide him with a list of all the events of the last 24 hours and he adlibs around them. The amount he adlibs is dictated by how tired he is. When he didn't get much sleep the night before, that's when he would say whatever came into his head. He never ever took the opportunity to consult with our inhouse lawyers on any possible dangerous legal matter. There's a cowboy element to it. He's convinced himself he's doing the right thing so he just goes ahead and says it.'

A frustrated executive went further: 'He just cannot admit he has made a mistake. To manage him you would have to work out how to provide him with a door, the theory being that no matter what the problem is, Jones has a way of walking out on the problem. He would defame people ... And the station would have to pick up the tab for those defamation payouts. It is not that he doesn't think the law applies to him. He honestly believes in what he is saying at the time. I think it stems from the "closet" attitude.'

Alan Jones has a contract, standard for many broadcasters, indemnifying him against 'all loss, cost, damage and expense' suffered as a result of litigation. This covered his first major action, heard in 1989, which flowed from an October 1986 interview with NRMA President James Milner. During the interview, one of Milner's fellow candidates for re-election, David Parker, was defamed. It was alleged in court that Jones said Parker was 'disastrously unsuitable' and would waste NRMA money if elected. Parker led evidence to show that before the broadcast, directors of the NRMA gave Jones a transcript of a mock interview, which Jones closely followed, doing most of the talking. The court noted that Jones' words 'formed 174 out of the 244 lines of the transcript'.[10]

Alan Jones' interviewing style evolved in keeping with his approach to dialogue. Journalists are taught to avoid asking questions that attract a yes/no response. Jones takes the opposite approach, stating a proposition and inviting a single-word reply. He is happy to take over the discussion if the interviewee is not up to the pace. Alan Jones is not so much at home in the witness box, in that the witness can't control the dialogue. The answers matter and so does logic. David Parker was awarded damages in excess of $70 000. 2UE appealed, secured a retrial, and such is the agonisingly slow timetable of the defamation system, almost two decades later, in 2003, the matter was still unresolved when David Parker died.

Alan Jones' regular appearances before the defamation court do not seem to have deterred him. It may be that he believes in standing up for his stories and subjects or, as one colleague thought, it may be that he does not care. 'He's not interested in abiding by the law, contempt, defamation, etc ... If he thinks that it will make him look good in the eyes of the audience he will go ahead regardless. He knows that the radio station will pay up.'

It is true that the station mostly covers the bill, but the costs of attenuated litigation are not measured in monetary terms alone.

The process can be wearing and Alan Jones can find the experiences stressful. One month after the David Parker case Alan Jones was in hospital after chest pains forced upon him an unusual break. He was taken to the cardiac unit of the Royal Prince Alfred Hospital where it was found he was suffering from a virus rather than a heart ailment. Doctors advised rest and he was off work for two days. Ian Wallace, the station manager, said the pains were a result of 'overwork and a lot of stress. The guy works 20 hours out of 24, seven days a week. He's a workaholic.'[11]

While the campaigns he undertook carried a cost there was also a benefit. The *Alan Jones Show* needed forward momentum. Argument and controversy are the meat and drink of such a show, which turn into a feast if the issue is ongoing. Midway through 1989, Alan Jones picked up the Andrew Kalajzich case. Its elements—wealth, murder and intrigue—came with a human-interest guarantee. Since the murder of Megan Kalajzich in 1986, Alan Jones had paid little attention to the prosecution of her husband Andrew. His on air commentary had thus far condemned the multimillionaire 'King of Manly', who in 1988 was found guilty of commissioning the murder of his wife.

In May 1989 Andrew Kalajzich's appeal to the Supreme Court failed. Retaining a fighting fund in the order of $100 million, Kalajzich employed his former hotel manager, Merrill Barker, to work full time on a campaign to overturn the conviction. Merrill Barker's team wanted maximum media exposure and discussed approaching Harry Miller. Barker worked from the city office of Kalajzich's accountant, John Thomas, who also managed some of Alan Jones' financial affairs.

In June 1989, partly in response to Jones' criticism, Andrew Kalajzich wrote a letter pleading his innocence and complaining that his own lawyers had let him down. He told Alan Jones: 'Due to legal advice I did not speak with the media and I have paid the penalty'. Kalajzich also pointed out their mutual friend in John Thomas.

According to Merrill Barker, midway through 1989, Barker, Jones, Thomas and Andrew's brother Tony Kalajzich met and discussed the case. Alan Jones made a suggestion. He recommended they employ a young man, Tim Barton, who had done research for Jones.[12] Like Alan Jones before him, Tim Barton was a slim, artistic youth from a bush background who built himself into a competitive athlete. Alan Jones had known him since the early 1970s when he coached Barton in athletics at The King's School. After leaving King's, Barton studied law, qualified as a solicitor in 1986 and was looking for a home for his skills beyond the occasionally oppressive cloisters of the legal industry.

Alan Jones advised Merrill Barker that Tim Barton's research could have the mutual benefit of assisting Kalajzich and informing Jones. When Jones and Kalajzich later met at Parklea Gaol, Tim Barton came along. In July 1989, the Kalajzich team accepted Alan Jones' suggestion and put Tim Barton on the payroll. Barton was to receive approximately $50 000 per annum plus expenses.

In that same month Alan Jones swung to Kalajzich's support. Although I did not know it at the time, our paths had crossed over the Andrew Kalajzich case. Similarly intrigued and harbouring some doubts about the conviction, I had also made my way to Parklea Gaol. It always was a puzzling murder. The triggerman, Bill Vandenberg, inept and faint-hearted, seemed an unlikely assassin. His suicide in gaol in May 1989 raised more questions about why a multimillionaire who had everything but an apparent motive would arrange so clumsily to have his wife murdered. But you need more than suspicion to take on a serious investigation. Without fresh evidence, only the vain and foolhardy think they know better than the courts. When such evidence proved unforthcoming, I set the Kalajzich file aside, at the very time Alan Jones ploughed ahead. In doing so, I am unaware of any single clue, objective fact or chain of logic that led him to reverse his former opinion and move to the view that Kalajzich was a worthy cause.

Alan Jones might also have been motivated by a desire to prosecute, on air, a big case that would demonstrate his capacity to extend the talk radio horizon and prove that he was more than a shock jock. He began to cite cases such as Lindy Chamberlain's as evidence of the fallibility of the justice system. Perhaps hidden, Morse code-like, was a signal that his own London experience had parallels.

The appointment of Tim Barton to the Kalajzich team marked the beginning of a five-year on air campaign to clear the convicted murderer. Only the faintest of Chinese walls separated Alan Jones from a conflict of interest, and to his partiality there was no partition. Tim Barton would now supply Jones with information paid for by Kalajzich in order to help Kalajzich. Jones did not disclose to his listeners that the information he relied upon was funded by Kalajzich. Nor did his employer know of the arrangement. The hours of prime time radio devoted to clearing Kalajzich would be worth a fortune.

Unusually free of sporting commitments in this period, Alan Jones had more time for radio. He seemed to wish it otherwise, but hopes of returning to the Wallabies further diminished when, in 1989, Ross Turnbull's long run as chairman of the New South Wales Rugby Union came to an end. Under Turnbull's watch the disastrous Concord Oval scheme left debts of around $20 million. As Peter FitzSimons wrote: 'Even though Turnbull had loaned the Union a million dollars of his own money to see the NSWRU out of the muck, it had not saved his reputation when it came to rugby administration'.[13]

The new administration was no more impressed with Ross Turnbull than with Alan Jones, who now abandoned his 1988 pledge to keep a dignified silence about the performance of successor Bob Dwyer. In June, Dwyer's Wallabies narrowly lost a home Test against the British Isles and were again beaten by New Zealand. An Alan Jones' *Sun Herald* column listed Bob Dwyer's errors, conspicuous among them a failure to select Brian Smith. At this stage Brian Smith was still at Oxford. Unable to crack a spot in the Australian team, he achieved a rare honour of becoming a dual international. In 1989, Brian Smith was made an honorary Irishman when he was controversially selected into the Irish national team.

At different ends of the earth, at 2UE and Oxford, witnesses observed Alan Jones exercising a measure of remote control, the fax machine working overtime. A broadcasting studio is one of those places where it pays to hold your tongue as well as your temper, as there are live microphones about. Recordings of many a temper tantrum live on. 'We still can't send a bloody fax at 2UE. It's unbelievable. Every other bastard in Sydney can send a fax except 2UE. Christ, it's unreal. Anyone would think sending a fax machine was like putting a man on the moon. Jesus Christ I mean there are 11 year olds sending faxes around the country but two days in a row we can't get a fax right ... Mate, I send faxes every day to Oxford and London and I have schoolkids send them back to me.'[14] A long-suffering 2UE colleague noticed that Alan Jones' informal coaching extended to informal tutoring of his protégé. 'He would fax his assignments to Alan and Jones would fill them out and fax them back and Brian would rewrite them.'

In 1989 Brian Smith was elected captain of the Oxford rugby team. This was good news for Alan Jones' coaching aspirations, as it as much as guaranteed no repetition of the 1988 dumping. An Australian bloc of support for Alan Jones had expanded. As well as international Troy Coker, Morgan Jones, a handy front rower and brother Bob's son, was also now at Oxford, thanks to Uncle Alan. Queensland fly half Kent Bray and former Warringah second rower and Rothmans Medal winner James Fewtrell were further benefactors.

James Fewtrell and others refer to the funding organised by Alan Jones as the Britcorp Scholarship. Britcorp Finance was the company established by accountant John Thomas and used for the offshore arbitrage trading of his major client, Andrew Kalajzich. Alan Jones, another of Thomas's high profile clients, also had access to the trustee entity. Jones evidently instructed the accountant to make the payments through Britcorp. When asked in gaol whether he had also contributed to the Britcorp scholarships, Andrew Kalajzich said he had no knowledge of the scheme.

The brash behaviour of some of the Australians and the long shadow of Alan Jones had further cooled relations at Oxford. Foreign takeovers of sports like rugby and rowing long strained goodwill at the university, sometimes making even the foreigners uncomfortable. New Zealander David Kirk, conscious of the sensitivities, had yielded the captaincy to an Englishman in the preceding year. Now he wrote to Brian Smith cautioning him about the need for diplomacy. Smith told Kirk to take his 'nose out from where it wasn't wanted'.[15]

Towards the end of 1989, the prospect of Alan Jones returning to coaching further improved. Beyond the Oxford gig, Alan was reported to be in negotiations with the North Sydney Bears. It would have been a big step; switching codes would cut off all possibility of a return to Rugby Union, the Bears being a Rugby League team.

Meanwhile, the potential for a vacancy at the Wallabies also improved. Alan Jones' nemesis, Bob Dwyer, was struggling. In November the Wallabies played two Tests in France, winning one and losing one. On air Jones described Dwyer's record as 'abysmal'. He was reported as claiming that Bob Dwyer was squandering talent and performing even worse than he had done in his first term as coach.[16]

In the same month, the researcher recommended by Jones, Tim Barton, and a former police officer turned private detective, Duncan McNab, took off on a world trip in search of evidence to help Kalajzich. The witnesses they approached included a Canadian ballistics expert and a New York fortune-teller. Alan Jones was in touch with Andrew Kalajzich at the time, warning him of the importance of keeping an independent eye on the legal team and their fees. The new team had wanted to release Barton, but Jones successfully implored Kalajzich to keep him on.

When the radio year ended in December, Alan Jones also headed for the northern hemisphere, arriving in London to continue his coaching of Oxford in person. Some of the players wondered why this should be necessary. Brian Smith already had substantial coaching support in, among others, a later World

Cup winning coach, Clive Woodward. But the Oxford captain is all-powerful and Smith wanted Jones.

After his arrival, one of the players remembers a series of 'ponderous speeches'. They did not do the trick. On 12 December Oxford failed to find its rhythm. As *The Times* of London reported: 'They [Oxford] had trailed throughout yet, at 13–18, stood poised to seize the initiative with a scrum on the Cambridge line when Jones, their Australian prop [and Alan's nephew] went in with boot raised at a ruck which had ended. He was penalized.'[17] Cambridge went on to score and win the match. Oxford's controversial and unexpected loss drew more negative attention to the Aussies.

A subsequent episode was even more damaging to Alan Jones' relationship with his favourite university as well as any reputation he might have had for selfless conduct. A week after the game, the team began the process of selecting their captain for the following season. Considerable prestige is attached to the role. There are sponsored international tours and the captain selects the coach.

Alan Jones wanted Troy Coker, and with a strong voting bloc of seven sponsored players (five Australians and two members of the United States Eagles rugby team), he looked like getting his way. He might have too, but for a dilemma facing one scholarship holder, James Fewtrell. The lofty young Australian, grateful to Alan Jones for a life-changing experience, was enjoying his time at Oxford. He understood the Britcorp Scholarship came with no strings attached. He further understood the other scholarship holders were pushing for Troy Coker.

James Fewtrell's problem was that he saw Irish flanker Mark Egan as a better candidate. When Jones telephoned, telling him to vote for Coker, Fewtrell explained his position. He recalls being told to vote for Coker or his scholarship would be withdrawn. The other scholarship holders applied further pressure, claiming their allowances were also at risk. Seeking advice from his father, Fewtrell was told to vote for the best man.

Despite the Alan Jones' voting bloc, Mark Egan was comfortably elected. When James Fewtrell next checked at an ATM, he found Alan Jones apparently true to his word. His allowance had not come through. When he explained what had happened to the Dean of St Anne's College, there was a firm telephone call put through to Alan Jones. Fewtrell's scholarship was restored and Jones' term as guest coach at Oxford came to an end. Within the tight-knit rugby world those who doubted the strength of Jones' altruism exchanged knowing glances. The affair supported suspicion of self-interest among those who wondered whether Alan's idea of strength of character meant obedience to Alan's will.

Alan Jones often talks in glowing terms of the fine young men he has helped develop into good and decent Australians. Although Fewtrell did not please, his stand qualifies him for higher praise. When James Fewtrell, now a communications manager at Canon Australia, told his story he insisted upon acknowledging his gratitude for Jones' help with his Oxford education.[18]

In 1990 Alan Jones' credit in the rugby world slipped a further notch. Not that he saw it that way. When he was asked to contribute to an official program for the 1990 French Tests, a series of exchanges between the publisher and Jones' solicitors followed. The sticking point was how Jones would be introduced. Alan's counsel argued for 'Australia's most successful coach'. No agreement was reached and the article was scrapped.[19]

Away from his football family, Alan Jones was incomplete. At the dinner table, friends had their ears bashed about the failings of the incumbent coach. So relentless and remorseless was the Jones rant, one diner remembers getting up to take Panadol. An *Ita* profile was more sympathetic: '... when he talks about football you can hear the frustration in his voice. You know he believes that he could do better. And he probably could. But like so many successful Australians he has his fair share of knockers; and the mediocre who control so much of our country cannot understand or appreciate such an entrepreneurial thinker.'[20]

Bob Dwyer, on notice with the selectors, was reappointed Wallabies' coach. The two-year contract meant Alan Jones had no hope of recontesting the following year's Rugby World Cup. Speculation that he might switch codes intensified. While the North Sydney Bears' vacancy had closed, a new one with the Balmain Tigers was about to open. *Sydney Morning Herald* reporter Roy Masters asked: 'Would you consider the Balmain coaching position if offered it?' Alan Jones replied: 'My philosophy in life is that you don't close doors on anything and if one is asked something it is always churlish not to give an appropriate consideration. It's very hypothetical. I haven't been asked.'[21]

The appointment had a lot of appeal to Alan Jones' biggest fan at 2UE, program director John Brennan, who was also one of Balmain's biggest fans. An extra benefit was the connection of Jones to the common man's code, Rugby League. The additional exposure had the potential to extend an audience that was already growing. So too were station profits and Alan's income.

By now Harry Miller had negotiated a cut of advertising revenue. The bigger the audience, the more sponsors were prepared to pay Alan Jones to boost their products. Like other announcers, Alan got a percentage of the 'live' reads, which advertisers often feel worth the additional standard 20 per cent premium because of the implied endorsement. In 1990 Alan received $50 per read. When 2UE sent him his fortnightly cheque of around $30 000, 20 per cent had already been deducted for Miller.

The advertising deals exposed another structural weakness. Alan Jones did not have time to do the due diligence on every product he promoted. He would tell his staff how much it annoyed him to advertise untruths, which is exactly what occurred. In the early months of 1990, the investment company Estate Mortgages was quietly going broke. In order to lure further investors, the company embarked on a noisy $6 million advertising campaign. The *Alan Jones Show*, with its high proportion of self-funded retirees, delivered a valuable target audience. Estate Mortgages ran advertisements promising guaranteed returns of 18 per cent.

Alan Jones plugged Estate Mortgages investments almost to the day the Victorian Corporate Affairs Commission declared a moratorium, freezing investments.[22] The company was found to owe banks around $170 million. Jones' listeners were among those caught. Alan Jones, who claimed he too had been stung, was embarrassed. 'I investigated it. I even minuted all the details I was told. I was constantly assured there was nothing wrong. There's a limit to what you can find out.' At least one listener was angry, telling Alan on air: 'The power you have on radio, myself and my friends have invested in Estate Mortgages. We accepted your credibility and we are going to go down the tube.'[23] The Estate Mortgages saga would be repeated 17 years later with the collapse of Fincorp, which Alan Jones also endorsed, describing it as 'a great Australian company'. Returns of 11.75 per cent were spruiked. Seven thousand eight hundred mostly retired investors lost over $200 million. This time Alan Jones blamed the Australian Securities and Investment Commission, dismissing the corporate regulator as 'not worth two bob'.

The same weakness in professional discipline proved a problem in relation to legal as well as financial matters. In his program on 9 July Alan Jones spoke of an ex police officer, John Killen, being tried on a charge of conspiracy to pervert the course of justice. The next day he also interviewed a former member of the drug squad, Paul Kenny, about matters to be canvassed during the trial. The following day, because of potential prejudice to the case, the jury was discharged and the trial aborted. When contempt charges against Alan Jones and 2UE were eventually heard, the court found: 'At the time of committing the contempts, 2UE had no systematic procedures in operation designed to minimise the risk of contempts being committed by either their own employees in the course of the broadcasts or persons being interviewed during such broadcasts'.[24]

Despite his claims of thoroughness, Alan Jones could be extremely sloppy. One of the most famous examples of cavalier negligence emerged in a newspaper column in August 1990. Following Iraq's invasion of Kuwait, Alan Jones wrote of the world running out of oil, quoting an alleged US report: 'The American response to cheap oil has been increased demand, higher crude and product imports and shrinking domestic production. Even if America started now with a crash program, massive investment and big scale federal incentives, it would take 10 years to rebuild the human skill pool, remanufacture or mobilise the machinery and execute the work to bring our now total reliance on the Middle East back to manageable proportions.'[25]

There is irony in the story of how he was caught. A Manly dentist, Alan Marel, had learned to read Alan Jones with a critical eye. Marel, having been taught English by Jones at The King's School, was one of the circle of doubters who knew the story of Jones castigating a boy for following crib notes that Jones was also supposed to have used.

You might say it was karma when Marel pondered over a phrase in Jones' column: 'gas-guzzling inefficiency'. It did not sound like Australian terminology, and he thought he had read it before. He walked to a shelf and pulled out a book, *The Negotiator*, by Frederick Forsyth. On page 15 he found the same 'gas-guzzling' reference, and soon after an account of the US report. The lines he read were identical to those in the *Sun Herald*. A primary sin of journalism is to fudge a source. The offence is aggravated when the source turns out to be drawn from a work of fiction.

Alan Marel, no fan of Alan Jones but no hater either, wrote a letter to the *Sun Herald*. When, weeks later, there was still no reply, Marel informed the ABC TV program *Media Watch*. On 27 August Stuart Littlemore's lead segment was the crib from Frederick Forsyth. Littlemore began speaking of the classic problem of the 'quasi journalist, who works in the medium but is not bound by the disciplines and collegiate standards'. As he

Alan Jones' trade unionist father Charlie (centre) was a proud supporter during his son's failed bid as Liberal candidate for the New South Wales seat of Earlwood in 1978. (ABC Document Archives)

Alan Jones' judgement was found wanting when he dressed in Greek costume to woo voters. A senior Liberal heard 'lead balloons landing all over the place'. (Newspix/Will Burgess)

'You've worn the green and gold and that makes you special', said Alan Jones. He was proud to wear his nation's colours when appointed Wallabies coach in 1984. (Fairfaxphotos/Ian Cugley)

Alan Jones and the Wallabies undertook choir practise before the Grand Slam tour in 1984. Maybe it was the Welsh in him or his ambition to sing opera. (Newspix)

Without a script or notes at his audition behind the 2UE mircrophone in 1985, Alan Jones 'blew them away'. (Newspix/Steve Brennan)

The 1986 Bledisloe Cup victory in New Zealand was a crowning achievement. Peter Grigg and a shirtless Nick Farr-Jones flank their coach. (Newspix)

But there were soon costs to team relations. By 1987, Alan Jones lost the support of star winger David Campese, among others, and by 1988 his prized coaching position. (Newspix/Philip Brown)

Worse was to follow. Jones' arrest in a London public toilet in December 1988 was so shattering there was concern back at 2UE that he might commit suicide. He is seen here on his way to Marlborough Street Court. (Newspix/John Hartigan)

Friends rushed to his side. From left: Brendan Mullin, Brian Smith, Ross Turnbull, John Fordham and John Brennan. (Newspix)

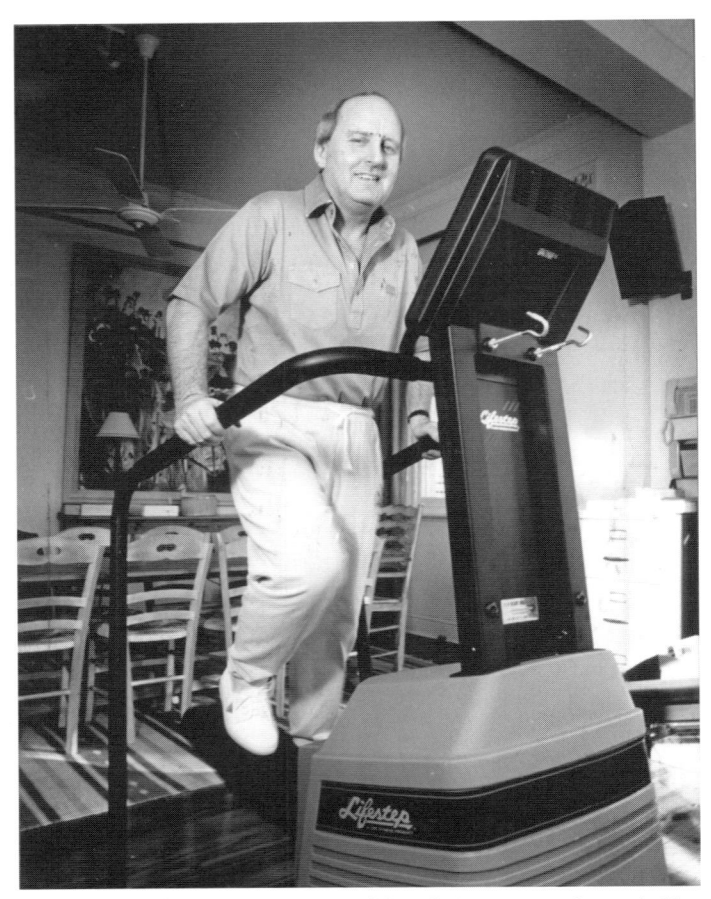

What does not kill me makes me stronger. After all charges were dropped, Alan was on the front foot improving his fitness, building his audience and accepting a new coaching position with the Balmain Tigers. (Newspix/Iain Gillespie)

The Jones Midas touch was reversed in rugby league. Alan Jones had long treated his football teams as family, but at Balmain the 'family' became dysfunctional. (Newspix/Barry McKinnon)

Various attempts were made to settle a toxic rivalry between Alan Jones and radio colleague John Laws. All failed. Laws would chide Jones in writing: '…you are starting to give megalomania a bad name.' (Newspix/Michael Perini)

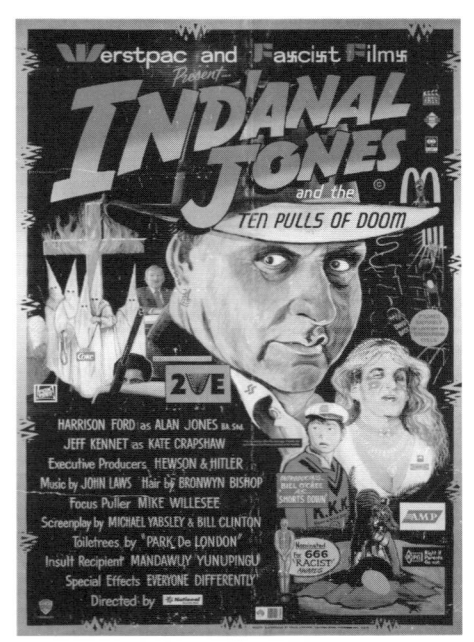

In 1993, following a public debate about comments made by Alan Jones on aboriginal issues, this poster appeared on King Street Newtown (near his home), outside 2UE and along Oxford Street, Sydney's gay beat.
(Private collection)

Alan Jones' radio success did not translate to television. Network Ten's *Alan Jones Live* ran for 13 weeks. His first guest, Federal MP Bronwyn Bishop, was described by one critic as an 'unforgivable choice'. (Newspix/Bob Barker)

would do on later occasions in court, the lawyer and media critic comprehensively unstitched Alan Jones.

The next day Harry Miller was again in damage control mode, telling the media it was all 'just a lot of gobbledegook'.[26] Fairfax staff, probably unaware that the error had already been pointed out to management, began a petition to have Alan Jones dismissed. The Jones dictum 'my listeners are my best researchers' was looking a little ragged when he blamed a member of his audience he later determined to be 'eccentric', and read on air a prepared statement:[27] 'I'll accept that I was deceived and was wrong'. He argued that plenty of journalists are similarly fooled, citing Murdoch Press's publication of the fake Hitler diaries.

On 31 August, four days after the *Media Watch* report, the *Sun Herald* announced that the Alan Jones column would cease. The separation from the Sundays proved temporary. A few years later, another one-page column, 'To the Point', began to appear in the rival *Sunday Telegraph*.

2UE colleagues, impressed by Alan Jones' intelligence, could not understand why he would plagiarise. Like his manager, Alan Jones was unrepentant, seeing any small measure of discredit overwhelmed by his many good deeds. 'While someone was belittling me on television I at least can rest in the knowledge that along with John Singleton, the Prime Minister, Normie Rowe, Judy Stone and some of Australia's greatest athletes, I was helping raise one million dollars for Special Olympians at Sydney's Sheraton Hotel'.[28] At the same time he was also assisting Nyngan flood victims. In the same month as the *Media Watch* flogging, the Variety Club thanked Alan Jones for helping raise $150 000.

With Jones the number one drawcard of Harry M Miller's Speakers Bureau, the mail was full of invitations. Miller said that if Jones gave up all his other work there would be enough speaking engagements to keep his star busy seven days a week. On top of his 2UE income Alan received about $250 000 a year for the oratorical overtime.

There was occasional controversy about some engagements, such as his $45 000 fee to give a dozen motivational speeches to New South Wales prison officers. Having been arranged by Alan's friend and Corrective Services Minister, Michael Yabsley, assurances were sought in parliament that Jones was not being bribed.[29] But the charity and sporting events were undertaken for free, Alan sometimes covering his own travel expenses and making his own donations.

At the microphone Alan Jones was often at his best, rising to the occasion no matter how tired he might have been. Although audience reactions tended to be mixed, those who liked him were seriously impressed. Alan worked from minimal notes, appearing to extemporise most of what he said. When one enraptured listener asked for his secret, the speaker explained: 'I have to tell you I had no idea what I was going to do ... and I never think about what I'm going to say until I get there. That may be a good or bad thing. However, I usually seem to manage, somehow.'[30]

Alan Jones was becoming more comfortable addressing a large audience than speaking one on one. His drivers and minders were taught to shield him from unscheduled confrontations as the crowd assembled. He seemed to prefer a routine that delivered him a touch late. Up on his feet before the hush he was in his element, poised to deliver in the favoured James Joyce stream of consciousness style. Like many regular speakers, Alan's addresses generally followed the same pattern, with adjustments made to suit the occasion. One journalist, describing him as a master of the art, requested a tip on how he did it: '... the generous Jones asked me if I thought Shirley Bassey changed her act every night because she didn't want to bore people. As I was wondering what on earth he meant, Jones gave me a pearl of wisdom: "Change the audience, don't change the act".'[31]

While the applause was stimulating, and Alan Jones had the support of people to research and even write for him, the constant stream of requests amplified fatigue. 'Even though it's apparent that Alan is worn out, pressured and in need of rest, his mates ask him to coach football teams or speak at fund raising dinners. He sighs. The difficulty is that sometimes people whom you most expect to understand how complicated it is, are often the very ones who make it infinitely more difficult.'[32] There was a similar lament in the *Sunday Telegraph*: 'Yes I do get tired, he says, rubbing his eyes. It's been a very difficult year in so many ways. I've chopped a lot back but I find it hard to say no to people. There are just so many good causes.'[33]

Jones felt the media was not just unappreciative but spiteful because he was not in the journalists' 'club'. 'There is a lot of jealousy in all of this which is very sad. It's sad that some people live their lives resenting the fact that others might have done well. You see the perception is that I've sort of got things in too much of a hurry. I mean I worked for a Prime Minister and I coached a First Grade Rugby Union side without ever having coached a second grade, third grade or fourth grade. We won a premiership in our first attempt and then I coached Australia and I had never coached any other representative side. And we won. Then I came into radio and I'd never been in radio before and I beat people that had been in radio forever.'[34]

At the end of 1990, Alan was walloped again by a story that did not make the news. He later recounted that in November, while driving across the Sydney Harbour Bridge, he had a premonition his 84-year-old dad was going to die. 'Alan asked his secretary to book him on the next flight to Brisbane. At home, packing for an extended stay, he rang his father's doctor. He won't get a telegram from the Queen but he's fine, the doctor told him. There's no reason to hurry home. But Alan says, at 4 pm the nursing sister rang to say my father had just died.'[35]

As Charlie might have said himself, there was a 'good turnout' at the Redcliffe funeral. Friends such as Veronica Fordham flew up from Sydney. Cousin Les Thompson said when Alan spoke he excused himself, explaining that this important occasion would be one of the rare ones when he would refer to notes. Robert Jones, who had risen through the ranks as an educator, was matter-of-fact, just like his dad, going off in his suit afterwards to help organise a GPS athletics meet. His younger brother hopped back on a plane heading south, returning to the microphone, where he would keep the memory of Charlie alive for many years to come.

At least there was now a new football family to welcome him. Throughout the year negotiations had continued with the Balmain Rugby League Club, which was about to replace its coach. Alan Jones said that, as at Manly, the initiative for his move began with players, such as League international Steven (Steve) Roach and Rugby Union convert James Grant. A meeting then followed with club officials at Jones' home, where Alan accepted the coaching appointment for no fee.

A range of pictures from the notably friendly coverage showed Alan looking happy. Photographed in a tracksuit on a walking machine, he said, 'I think you should sweat every day. It's fantastic. I used to go to the gym every day, but now I run on this machine at home. It measures things like calorie loss and it's quite tough.'[36] The move seemed a way of bringing his life back into balance, as well as extending his populist reach.

Alan was again quickly on the front foot. At the 1990 Rawards, the commercial radio industry voted Alan Jones 'Australian Talk Personality of the Year'. The last surveys of 1990 showed the ratings had again improved, although Doug Mulray on 2MMM still had more listeners. But Alan Jones' expanding demographic, the weakness of competition for his older audience, and his own unique abilities meant the gap was closing. The Forsyth saga and the Estate Mortgages debacle had inflicted no harm where it mattered. And Alan Jones was in credit with more than his own audience. His many acts of charity advanced goodwill, as well as a sense of indebtedness. Serious weaknesses in the medium and in Alan Jones were of little concern to devotees, and of considerable interest to those who could make use of a clever and amoral pamphleteer. Despite Alan's now more conspicuous flaws, the steady rise of the demagogue was sustained.

CHAPTER 11
DICTATORS AND TIGERS

'DICTATORS RIDE TO AND FRO upon tigers which they dare not dismount and the tigers are getting hungry': Alan Jones loves to quote fellow orator and light sleeper Winston Churchill. The Balmain Tigers Rugby League captain, Benny Elias, will never forget the first speech he heard Alan Jones make when he joined the club. As at Manly nearly ten years earlier, the assembled footballers were mesmerised. Elias recalls Jones evoking a different Churchillian phrase: 'Our greatest glory is not in never failing but in rising after every fall'. Elias says big Steve 'Blocker' Roach turned to him and whispered, 'Who did this bloke Churchill play for?'

Balmain was a new and different world for Alan and around Tigertown they were equally excited. The inner city Balmain Rugby League Club was losing its battler status to people who drove Renaults rather than Holdens, and rolled a different kind of tobacco. Alan Jones, who used to drive a Renault but now preferred BMWs, was ready for the social and cultural eclipse. As the suburbs evolved so too had the codes. Rugby Union was surrendering its amateur pretences. The reinvented Jonesy said he liked the professionalism of Rugby League and that its people were 'fair dinkum'.[1] 'Yes I've made a break with a lifetime of rugby. I suppose in the back of my mind I think that community will disown me now because you're considered a deserter. But you just have to get on with it.'[2]

Although the amateur Rugby Union code was moving towards the professional status of Rugby League, there were ongoing sensitivities. To the outsider the two codes may appear indistinguishable, but to individual devotees they are as different as Tooheys Draught and Pinot Noir. The variations in the way the games are played count less than the class barrier, the Union boys coming frequently from the private school system, while League historically had its constituency in workingmen's suburbs, such as the Balmain of old.

In February 1990, Alan Jones told the media the bridges were burned. 'I was banned by Joe French, the president of the Australian Rugby Union. So there is no love lost between French and me. He knows I think he shouldn't be running Australian Rugby.'[3] Alan Jones said the Rugby Union had even barred him from talking to schoolboy players.

Alan Jones' mentor John Brennan saw synergy in the deal that would be good for his club and his creation, corralling the 'Struggle Street' support base to 2UE. The station wanted to make the former private school teacher more accessible. This was one secret that helped explain the success of 2UE's biggest star, John Laws. Although the friend of the truckie and country music fan lived a life King Croesus might have envied, Lawsy had the touch of someone who still liked a good yarn with his mates. John Brennan and 2UE also saw synergy in programming their stars back to back. Laws' established audience brought listeners to Jones, while Jones' growing audience improved Laws' lead. At this time John Laws retained top billing. After 40 years on radio, the man who made Toyota Australian was a broadcasting legend.

John Laws shared the 2UE morning with Alan Jones but not much else. While in public they appeared, at first, to get on, privately they abhorred one another. Laws thought Jones' banter was forced. There was something about the way he laughed too loudly and was so convinced of what he said that got under

Laws' skin. The bigger Alan got, the more phoniness Laws seemed to see, Alan Jones' growing success becoming an affront to John Laws' professional pride.

And while Laws smelled a phoney, Jones jealously eyed a rival. His interminable need for an enemy was satisfied as conveniently close as a studio away. The most rancid media rivalries do tend to be inhouse. But even when their mutual animosity went public, 2UE saw synergy; the station profited from the free publicity.

There was a similar advantage for Balmain. Alan Jones' defection made good copy and, true to form, there would be plenty more. Like Manly nearly a decade earlier, the Tigers were talented bridesmaids. Balmain was constantly faltering after making the finals and, under coach Warren Ryan, the Grand Finals in 1988 and 1989. In 1990, when Alan Jones was approached, Balmain had again made the cut and again failed. Warren Ryan's parting comment that 'the lemon had been squeezed' offended some of the players. Alan Jones' response—'Balmain are sick and tired of coming second'—proved equally provocative.[4] The comment revealed an underestimation of the task ahead. Alan Jones would be held to his words. Rugby League is a tough game to play, let alone win. Jonesy would end up conceding, 'Rugby League is like an All Blacks Test every weekend'.[5]

When he turned up for the summer coaching sessions, whispers inevitably followed. There was banter around Balmain about pillow biting and shirt lifting. The scurrilous jokes began to circulate: 'Balmain have bought two locks, one for the scrum and one for the dressing room door'. 'The players are told to pack their groin in ice when they come off the field because Alan likes a cold one after the game.' But the club had done its homework and was relieved to have cleared Alan Jones of suspected homosexuality. A member of the Rugby Union executive, Ron Meagher, confirmed that a Tigers man had telephoned him to ask about Alan Jones' credentials and about the rumours of his 'sexual behaviour'. Meagher told the inquirer that in his view the rumours had no substance.

As at Manly, Alan Jones inherited a strong team. Although the Tigers' favourite son, Wayne Pearce, had just retired there was still a solid core of internationals, including Gary Freeman, Benny Elias, Paul Sironen, Garry Jack and Steve 'Blocker' Roach. Steve Roach thought Alan Jones gave renewed vigour to players on the downward slope of their careers: 'He had all these sayings. You are never as bad as you were yesterday. When you turn the corner, the road becomes a highway.'

Alan Jones said he was keen to give senior players more responsibility and, as he had done at Manly, call on expertise where he needed it. Wayne Pearce was supposed to help with coaching and so too was Queensland and Balmain legend Arthur Beetson. It did not seem to work in the way it had done with Alex Evans. While Pearce helped out from time to time, Beetson got sick of sitting in the grandstand and after a few sessions no longer turned up. Alan Jones seemed to prefer the partnership of newly appointed assistant coach Ken Shine, a new Alan acolyte.

Jonesy was at least as keen for new approaches as old advice. Darren Clark, a 400 metres Commonwealth Games gold medallist who had never played senior league, was recruited. He became a regular at the Newtown premises, and another to sing Alan's praises: 'He has provided me with enormous amounts of advice and support. He is a friend and a mentor. He helped me with both my training and my personal speaking. He's a really kind person with a big heart. He's like Superman actually—he just likes to help people. But sometimes that can be difficult for him because he can't save the world.'[6]

Alan Jones also lured Brian Smith back from Oxford, Ireland and Rugby Union, persuading him to have a go at Rugby League. The switch caused bitterness with the Irish Rugby Union. They had gone out on a limb to accommodate Smith, who now walked out on them. At Balmain, where the Smith–Jones stories had done the rounds, there was also disquiet.

Steve 'Blocker' Roach, who took a positive view of Alan Jones, was instead elevated and amused by his coach's enthusiasm. He remembered Jones saying of Smith and Clark: 'Think of it, the best kicker in any code and the fastest white man in the world, in the one team. The scoreboard attendant will have trouble keeping up.'

Although Alan Jones saw coaching as a hobby and had accepted he should lessen his public speaking load, he had bitten off a lot. His typical day in 1991 started at 2.30 am. The broadcaster/coach relied on a single alarm clock to wake him, trusting his capacity to resist fatigue when the rest of Sydney was in its deepest sleep. Jones, always tired when he woke, felt it was part of the discipline he required from others to splash hot water on his face and make a start. He would look through material such as press releases faxed through to him during the night and then drive the empty streets from Newtown across the Harbour Bridge to the 2UE studios, arriving at about 3.30 am. There he read the papers, barely looking up when the rest of the staff gathered.

As in his dairy farm days there was a pre-breakfast morning tea before the 5 am meeting with his production staff. By now most of Alan's editorials were typed. He sometimes pulled material from the newspapers, and as is still the case subjecting the copy to the barest rearrangement. There would also be notes in dot point form, prepared by staff the previous day, that Alan Jones converted to what sounded like original and extemporised commentary. Other 'editorials', supplied by politicians and publicists, were written for him and frequently read verbatim.

Breakfast during the 7 am news was Weet-Bix and milk. Preparing it was the job of the switch operators, one of whom said, 'It has to be heated up for one and a quarter minutes exactly in the microwave. He can tell if it hasn't been done correctly (god knows how) and he just screams. He has a total meltdown.'

Alan Jones' mood was at its worst early in the day. 'When he is yelling at you he never makes eye contact. He'll look at the floor or past you but never at you.' A bleary-eyed work experience teenager who failed to refold the morning newspaper to its original condition copped a similar withering blast. Legend has it that one producer, infuriated by Alan Jones' foul mood, had retaliated by pissing in his tea. (When contacted and asked for confirmation, the ex producer, while liking the idea of pissing in Jones' tea, insisted it had never happened.)

When the show finished at 9 am, Alan Jones had already done a full day's work. Breakfast radio requires intense concentration. Live interviews are stressful. There are quotas of advertisements that must be run. Even the business of remaining cheerful is draining. But his day was far from over. After he signed off, Alan gathered staff for a post-program conference. His nervous system still racing, leg bouncing up and down, he plotted through a 'hit list' of duties and then, as often as not, it was back to the microphone.

Alan Jones was required to prerecord commercials and also commentary for edited versions of his programs, such as a highlights package for Brisbane's 4BC. In addition, various regional stations purchased cut-down versions, with Jones recording local advertisements.

He was not at his best handling this part of the job. On air he makes much of his own bush roots and professes a view to politicians and his audience that the person in the bush needs more help than the person in the city. Along with the humble rural past, Alan Jones takes pride in his command of language and capacity for personal discipline. But as already observed, off air he can be a very different person. Many broadcasters adopt a different voice when the microphone is switched on. Many of them are also able to adjust their personality. Radio staff were now well used to the multiple faces and voices of Alan Jones.

Within the underground library of goof-tapes are out-takes from the regional prerecords from this period. One excerpt begins with a panel operator recording the tape identification: 'Prerecording for the bush'. Alan Jones follows as if talking to himself: 'What's the point of having this thing here? Is that alright? Fuck, I don't think I'm going to do that again. Dear me. Now what are we supposed to do? Who are these people from 2NZ. Where's 2NZ?' The panel operator replies, 'It's at Inverell'.

Alan Jones then switches to his on air voice and begins to read, but fumbles: 'Gee these fucking scripts ... Go again', returning to his broadcast voice. 'Howard J Finlen Jewellers in Byron Street Inverell ...'

He pauses and interjects, the tone of his voice soaring into rage: 'There's no fucking way I can make this 45 seconds ... I'm not fucking interested in really begging the bloody 2RG or someone to take the breakfast program. I feel like telling these people to get fucked. I don't care, you know. Who are they, some tin-pot town? What do they pay, $50, you know, to keep someone in a job?' A discussion follows between Jones and the panel operator, who explains that Harry Miller wants to push the program to the country. Alan Jones acknowledges that country people are always asking why they can't hear him.

The anger still evident, he carries on. 'Anyway do this. This is real chunder bucket stuff. Isn't that shit? Shove it up your arse, I feel like saying to them. I couldn't give a fuck, if they want to have it they can go and rape themselves ...' etc. He takes a breath and adjusts the warmth level in his voice: 'So over to you, thank you for the opportunity to listen to me. I look forward to hearing from you.' In an instant the bitterness returns: 'Fuck the lot of you'.

While Alan Jones was struggling with the recordings for 2NZ and elsewhere, his more celebrated colleague was broadcasting just a few glass panels away. 'Hello, world', John Laws famously began his morning program. On the same goof-tape Alan Jones can be heard scorning Laws' 'El Presidente' theme.

Their wall-to-wall jealousy became an industry talking point in 1991 when 2UE moved to new premises just up the Pacific Highway at Gore Hill. While inspecting the building, Nigel Milan found Harry Miller on hands and knees with a tape measure, checking the size of Jones' and Laws' offices. 'It's absolutely true ... Harry M Miller came in to measure the office space and make sure [Alan] got the same size office as Laws'.[7]

Measuring the respective egos was more difficult. Salary was a sore point. While Jones' Sydney audience of around 165 000 was larger than Laws' Sydney audience, 2UE paid Laws far more, an estimated $3 million per year. Although Jones' program was also the station's biggest money earner, Alan's 2UE salary at the time was estimated at around one-tenth of Laws' take.[8]

What made the essential difference and might have accentuated Alan Jones' jealousy was the fact that the golden tonsils travelled further. John Laws' show was syndicated nationally to 30 outlets, which meant his total audience was far larger, over a million listeners. This made John Laws more bankable for advertisers and sponsors, which is the main explanation for his greater wealth. Laws the walking billboard was an endorsement king, reaping rewards from a great many supplementary sponsorship deals. In contrast, Alan Jones had only a few small music deals, a royalty arrangement with EMI, and a deal with Sony which earned him over $1 every time a copy of *Alan Jones Nostalgic Memories* was sold.

One reason it was harder to market Alan was the breakfast slot itself. Syndicating a breakfast program is more difficult with so much attention directed at traffic jams on the Harbour Bridge and whether the ferries are running on time. Alan getting worked up about the filthy state of Sydney's trains did not wash with 4BC listeners.

But his fumbling with the controls was, according to technical staff, another problem. 'Jones doesn't know what makes things sound smooth on air. That makes life very tough for the panel operator. He is three times harder to work for than Laws because Laws understands how radio works.'

So while Alan Jones had the most important shift, at the time of the day when most radios were tuned in, John Laws was more valuable, not just to the bean counters but to important studio guests. When politicians and publishers were pushing a new policy or author, they looked for the program with the biggest audience. It did not make sense to have two guest appearances on the one station, so competition for high profile interviewees became another bone to fight over.

At this stage John Laws had the bigger bite, partly because of his relationship with a rising star, Paul Keating. While the antique clock collector and the antique car collector did not seem to have much in common, as the then Treasurer explained: 'Forget the press gallery in Canberra. If you educate John Laws you educate Australia.'[9] Back in 1986, Paul Keating's infamous proclamation that Australia was in danger of becoming a 'banana republic' was unbeatable free publicity when delivered on the John Laws program.

Although they see little of one another these days, when Laws' ratings were booming, Paul and John were the best of mates. The mutual benefit was that the politician's messages went unfiltered by journalists. Over time politicians would more often choose the talkback studio for major announcements. This increased their control over the message they wanted to deliver, the set-up opportunity more often preferred to the old free-for-all press conference. While other media missed out on the prospect of more thorough questioning, talk radio got a boost: station logos were on display in TV news bulletins and in newspaper photographs and their stars given greater profile. The strength of Laws' and Jones' political pull was also good for their own business: the more influence and reach they had, the greater their sponsorships and bank balances.

Although John Laws had the upper hand at hauling in the heavyweights, Alan Jones was learning and gaining ground. This was something he also needed to do out on the training pitch. Balmain players were surprised when they realised Jones seemed unaware of even the basics. In Rugby League the player numbering system works in the opposite direction to Union. Balmain's halfback Gary Freeman was asked, 'What's number one, the prop or what?'[10] The big forward, Paul Sironen, later wrote: 'There were times when I shook my head at his concepts because they had no place in Rugby League. Yet, as we tried to absorb his "new" ideas aimed at revolutionising the game Alan would stand before us at the team meeting and implore such things as "run at space, not face". It was almost like being in his radio studio as he read the slogan for a commercial.'[11] His basic strategy of intensifying fitness and skills training was not going to work so well in League, where professional players already worked to optimum standards.

There was a physical shock in store for Alan, too. With the summer heat yet to fade at Leichhardt Oval where Balmain was playing a trial match, the 50 year old experienced severe tingling sensations in his left arm. 'My arm feels like ten broken arms', he told reporters, putting the problem down to an injury from his own playing days.[12] The day did not get any better, with Balmain losing to North Sydney 16–6.

On 24 February Alan Jones was admitted to St Vincent's Hospital. 'JONES EMERGENCY OPERATION' ran the headline.[13] For months Alan Jones had been taking painkillers and Valium to counter persistent pain. 'I've been trying to avoid an operation by seeing every quack on earth, but three weeks ago I was pointed to some neurosurgeons at St Vincent's and I was admitted on Sunday night.'[14] A neck problem put Alan Jones out of action for two weeks; mate Ken Shine took over.

When the serious competition began, Alan was still recovering. The first result must have intensified the pain, with one game producing two losses. Halfback Gary Freeman was sent off seven minutes before half-time and Balmain went down to Canterbury Bankstown 26–16. Against Cronulla in round two, with Brian Smith on the interchange bench, Balmain lost 44–4. Alan Jones said, 'We were humiliated and I must accept responsibility'.[15] Six games into the season the best Balmain could manage was a 12–all draw against Newcastle, in Brian Smith's first game.

The Alan Jones' cost–benefit equation often saw quick success as compensation for the trouble, but so far at Balmain they only got the trouble. On 14 April, after a 12–9 loss against Illawarra and a noisy complaint about referee Chris Ward, the new Balmain coach was fined $10 000.

Frustration mounted. The switch from the disciplined, defensive game of former coach Warren Ryan to a free-flowing attacking game was too dramatic for some. The Tigers' fullback, Garry Jack, in his eleventh season with the club, thought Alan

Jones' approach was uniform and predictable: 'I let him know I did not embrace his coaching style and I've been on the outer ever since'.[16] Gary 'Kiwi' Freeman, after a similar experience with Alan Jones, spent half the 1991 season in reserve grade.[17]

April was not a good month, bringing separation from a fan of both Rugby League and Alan Jones: Kerry Packer. Packer had bought back his electronic media holdings from Alan Bond for $200 million, one-fifth of what he had sold them to Bond for some three years earlier,[18] but a change to broadcasting regulations meant a proprietor could not control licences for both radio and television stations in the same market. To keep Channel 9, Kerry Packer had to unload 2UE.

There was only one Alan Bond in Kerry Packer's lifetime, and perhaps only one Kerry Packer in the fortunes of the Lamb family. The Lambs, having sold to Kerry Packer in 1986 for more than $20 million, were now able to buy the network back for $3–5 million. Alan Jones might have felt he had not as much in common with the new Methodist owners, but his connection with Kerry Packer was not entirely severed, in that Alan Jones would be asked to do editorials for Channel 9's *Wide World of Sports*.

His new boss, John Conde, the son-in-law of Broadcast Investments chairman Stewart Lamb, was executive chairman of Lyndeal, the company the Lamb family used to purchase 2UE. The urbane, Harvard MBA did not seem a soul mate. Elected to a range of boards, John Conde was more likely to hear Alan Jones and John Laws on air as he made his way to BHP, Pymble Ladies College or the Australian Olympic Committee, than he was to pass them in the corridor. Not that it mattered much. Jones, like his 9–12 stablemate, were laws unto themselves, as Conde would later painfully realise.

John Conde delegated the job of maintaining discipline to program director John Brennan. It was now obvious at 2UE that Alan Jones' heavy workload was a burden for more than Alan Jones. 'Brenno' was the next best thing the station had to a straitjacket. He saw as part of his role the containment of 'artistic temperament'.[19] Colleagues at 2UE worried that Alan Jones' tantrums and John Brennan's high blood pressure were a dangerous duo. One staffer was worried for both Brennan and Jones when a particularly noisy screaming match broke out soon after Alan came off air. Brenno suffered a brief collapse, which was a problem for the station as well. 'The only one who had a bit of control was Brenno and you could absolutely tell when Brenno was on holiday because Jones would go feral.'

Although Alan Jones had an executive producer, he took principal control of the content of the program. As a team member explained: 'It is Jones who makes the decisions about what goes to air. The best his producers can do is apply a little gentle persuasion when his judgements verge on the bizarre and embarrassing.'

There was one segment, 'On This Day', which was scripted and prepackaged (and turned into a book). It was sent to eight stations, including one that was part of Jones' own history, 4AK in Toowoomba. Alan Jones would disingenuously claim it was the only segment he did not write. The prerecordings make up more of the goof-tapes: 'I'll go in three ... oh shit I've got to launch a book at eleven o'clock ... The birth dates today include children's author Beatrix Potter, born in 1866, famed Aboriginal artist Albert Namatjira, born in 1902 and Australian singer Peter Doyle. Who the fuck's Peter Doyle? (laughs) ... oh shit this is written ... oh fuck me dead, look at the fucking time will you, it's two hours since we came off air ... when you're ... oh I'm not doing this today. When do they want it? Tell them to piss off. I haven't got time to do all this shit now.'[20]

Alan Jones left 2UE between 10 and 11 am. A chauffeur, who would often catch a taxi to 2UE to take over at the wheel, was now added to his personal staff. Alan often favoured young footballers for the role, and in 1991 the Balmain player Will Robinson settled into the driver's seat of the BMW. While others assigned to graveyard shifts treated themselves to a morning nap, Alan Jones seemed to see his capacity to get by on little sleep— along with Margaret Thatcher and Winston Churchill—as proof of his greater powers. 'Sleep makes you tired. It's habit forming. The more sleep you get the more your body craves. Sleep makes your mind slower.'[21]

The chauffeur would usually drive first to Newtown, weaving through the narrow lanes and graffiti-stained walls bearing messages such as 'Fuck Authority' and 'Land Rights for All—Except the Rich'. When Alan Jones made his way upstairs the chauffeur carried on, attending to domestic duties like watering the pot plants on the upstairs terrace. A housekeeper attended to other duties, such as making the beds, doing the laundry and laying out Alan's clothes. In those days the employees were mostly female.

When he arrived at Newtown, Alan got straight to work with his personal assistant who had let herself in at 8 am. In 1991 Jones' Girl Friday was Jane Scott. Louise Langdon, who had replaced Susie Yabsley and was formerly devoted to Alan, had moved on. Fed up with Jones' tantrums, it is said Langdon got up, slammed the door and never returned.

Jane Scott had worked previously for magazine editor Ita Buttrose, another friend of Alan Jones and Harry Miller. Scott followed the routine of handing Jones a folder with the required duties filled in. As one insider put it, 'The job was basically to organise Alan's life. He would not know what he had on the next day until he got a briefing from his PA.' Telephone messages were typed on blue paper and clipped into a folder'.

If his day went well there would be a quiet lunch with a friend, but mostly the middle of the day was filled with more work. Alan Jones did get a little rest in the car on the way to his next engagement. Often he would also let his hair down a bit and talk to the chauffeurs, in whom much has been confided over the years.

Midafternoon it was back to the home office where an 'arvo tea' routine was undertaken, which linked him to his mum and Acland. 'Every afternoon around 3.30 business stops at Alan Jones' office so he and his staff can enjoy afternoon tea. It's the full kind of afternoon tea—nineteenth century tea set with all the floral embossed stuff, Alan explains, thin cups and something wonderful to eat, like freshly made pikelets and jam. Alan says it's his way of keeping in touch with something civilized in a world that's becoming increasingly uncivilized.'[22]

One Newtown employee said Alan Jones would occasionally take a rest in the afternoon but, anxious to preserve the mystique, told colleagues that if someone rang, 'we were never to say he was sleeping'. Even so, the naps had to be brief. At 5 pm five days a week there was football training which, although Alan Jones claimed was relaxation, had its own pressures considering the Tigers were still down the bottom of the table.

In the months leading up to May 1991, Alan Jones and the people of New South Wales spared some attention for a different league table. Capitalising on his popularity, Nick Greiner had called the state election one year early. But the man formerly dismissed as stopgap Opposition leader, Bob Carr, was also building popularity. Another morning person comfortable with words, Carr was lifting his profile and continuing to interest Alan Jones.

While Alan's politics drifted further to the right, he was still a man swayed more by personalities. In his book *Australian Answers*, Gerard Henderson viewed Alan Jones at this time as neither to the left nor within the ranks of the rigidly conservative: 'He is not against the monarchy but favours what he terms a republican system of government because he supports the United States process whereby political leaders face direct elections. He welcomes Asian investment in Australia and believes we should readily welcome those who want to become Australians and work hard. He is also sympathetic to the plight of refugees.'[23]

Bob Carr, similarly undoctrinaire and considered by many to be more to the right than Alan Jones' old boss, Malcolm Fraser, was now regularly couriering speeches to Belford Productions on Sundays. Bob Carr's staff knew that their boss and Alan Jones were close on education policy in particular: 'Bob would do a speech on something like the 3 Rs, something he knew would interest Alan, and send it over with a handwritten note. He knew how to pick the right issues, and he knew how to stroke Jones' ego.' Even so, Liberal Premier Nick Greiner was still a clear favourite. Labor needed a big swing and 13 new seats to win government.

It did not take long into the counting on 25 May to see Nick Greiner had taken a buffeting. Labor won 47 of the 50 seats needed to govern. Nick Greiner held on, with the balance of power in the hands of four independent MPs. The following month, the Independent Commission Against Corruption announced it would investigate a job offer made by Nick Greiner to one of his ministers, Terry Metherell, who resigned just before the election. Greiner was accused of improperly offering an inducement for the sake of political advantage. Under pressure from the independents, he also resigned (and was later cleared by ICAC). Whatever was going around Macquarie Street must have been catching. Alan Jones' closest friend in government, Michael Yabsley, quit as well, in protest over Nick Greiner's departure.

On 24 June, with the dust yet to settle, Greiner and Yabsley joined Jones for dinner at Alan's new favourite venue, the Park Hyatt. Though impromptu, it was an important and memorable gathering. Alan Jones, a people person, saw in an instant the passing of individuals at the core of what was left of his loyalty to the New South Wales Liberals. Too many of those left behind were still in Jones' bad books. The new Premier, John Fahey, not one to go out of his way to court shock jocks, was not so favoured. In searching for explanations for why and where Alan Jones places his favour, it is often wise to look in the opposite direction, at who he is against. The Fahey Government would not get a good run from Alan Jones, which was more good news for Bob Carr.

Liberal Attorney-General Peter Collins had a particularly rough trot. His story is telling of the high price of maintaining a friendship with Alan Jones. Back in 1979, Collins and Jones were closer. Indeed, when he was working for Deputy Leader Bruce McDonald, Alan Jones helped Peter Collins when his wife had a problem with the police over unpaid parking fines. Alan Jones has his own firm interpretation of the obligations inherent in personal loyalty.

Soon after the election Jones was again in trouble with the courts, when an on air comment he made was seen to interfere with the murder trial of underworld figure Tom Domican. Alan Jones was rebuked rather than once again being charged with contempt of court. But the 1990 contempt charge in relation to the trial of ex police officer John Killen proceeded following a recommendation from New South Wales Solicitor-General Keith Mason QC. In his biography *The Bear Pit*, Peter Collins wrote of his predicament: 'The Premier phoned me at home during breakfast asking whether I was prosecuting Jones for contempt of court. I told him I was acting on the advice of the Solicitor-General. Jones was beside himself. We had known each other for over fifteen years and always been on good terms. All I could do was point out that there was no personal malice in my action but that the Solicitor-General's advice left no alternative but to proceed with the contempt case against him. My relationship with Alan Jones, personal and political, was never to recover.'[24]

A year later, Alan Jones and 2UE were found guilty of contempt. Alan Jones was again unhappy when his producer, Ron Sneddon, entered a contrary guilty plea and gave divergent evidence. 2UE was forced to pay a $77 000 fine. Alan Jones was never to forgive Ron Sneddon or Peter Collins.[25] He had expected the protection of his colleagues and his party. Alan did not seem to understand that this kind of manoeuvring could be interpreted as attempting to pervert the course of justice. He clearly shared the notorious confusion of his friend Sir Joh Bjelke-Petersen about the importance of separating executive and judicial powers.

Another clue to his attitude emerged when Alan Jones appeared as guest speaker at a rally organised by friends of Sir Joh Bjelke-Petersen on the Gold Coast. The dinner at the Royal Pines Resort was to help Sir Joh with legal fees to fight a perjury trial about to be heard in the Queensland Supreme Court. Prior to the occasion, Queensland Police Commissioner Sir Terence Lewis, who had operated under Sir Joh's watch, was found guilty of corruption. When Terence Lewis's predecessor, Ray Whitrod, went public, blaming Sir Joh for the rot that had developed, Alan Jones turned on him during his lauding of Sir Joh: 'This man can go public and say Joh was to blame. It's an unworthy comment. Isn't it strange how we are regaled in the Queensland press with the latest salivation about the Fitzgerald Inquiry but the Cook Inquiry into trade union corruption was consigned to the back pages?'[26]

Alan Jones had no need to wait for the verdict on Bjelke-Petersen. He had already made up his mind about his friend's innocence: 'What we have is an old man, strong of will, proud of disposition, loyal in sentiment, broken by a relentless, unequal, personal campaign against him'.[27]

Back on the football oval in Sydney, Alan Jones also saw a conspiracy of fate: 'It's no secret I have found the attitudes towards referees a very difficult thing for teams, clubs and organisations to overcome. We have had a rough trot with referees along the way and while I'm sure everyone else has, they have cost us dearly. You have to bite your tongue and in a professional game that's difficult. The truth can be obscured and that's difficult. The system must be changed.'[28]

After a first win in round nine, the Tigers had found some form, but not enough to kick ahead. Brian Smith, now mostly in Gary Freeman's halfback spot, was playing well. While he did bring to Balmain a new golden boot, when he returned from completing an exam at Oxford, there was muttering around the dressing room that if Gary Freeman was not brought back there would be a lynching. At a fancy dress party thrown by the club, Alan Jones came dressed as Dick Tracey. The Tigers might have wished for Mandrake. Tigers' fans watched as the losses mounted and listened to rhetoric that was sounding increasingly hollow.

This was the time Alan got stuck with his most famous nickname, the 'Parrot'. No matter how many times he subsequently suggested to newspaper editors that they unstick it, it just seemed to suit as an aging Alan Jones even took on a more physically psittacine profile. The author was 'HG' of Roy and HG fame. Greig Pickhaver had joined John Doyle to form a popular call team on the ABC's 2JJJ, developing a cult following happy to popularise a series of nicknames. A tank of a forward, Glenn Lazarus, became the 'Brick With Eyes'. Balmain's captain, Benny Elias, was none too happy with his 'Back Door Bennie'.

As Greig Pickhaver explained, the 'Parrot' emerged more organically, in keeping with the code's custom of naming its celebrities after animals. The commentator Rex Mossop was the 'Moose' and new commentator Graham Hughes was the 'Trout'. Greig, or HG, happened on the name not so much because of Alan Jones' habit of reading others' words but because his repetitious 'it's a disgrace' sounded like the screech of a trained parrot.

Although players like Brian Smith had impressed with his toughness, at season's end there was still a view that Gary Freeman should have been first choice halfback. The experiment with Darren Clark had not gone so well either. The difference between running at a finishing line and 13 hostile opponents was extreme. Having failed to accelerate beyond reserve grade, Clark retired from League at the end of 1991.

Balmain finished the year with eight wins, which put them in twelfth place, well outside the finals reached the year before. But their early-rising coach had not lost heart: 'They say that sometimes the darkest hour is the one before the dawn. I believe there is a new dawning for the Balmain Rugby League side and we have every reason to be confident and optimistic about 1992.'[29]

For all that, if Alan Jones' mission at Balmain was to stick it up those ungrateful rugger buggers, it was not going well. Jones persisted with a line that Australian Rugby Union was ungrateful for his and Alex Evans' contribution. But Alan Jones was not missed and he seemed to know it. Australian Rugby was doing just fine. Bob Dwyer's Wallabies, under captain Nick Farr-Jones, ended their 1991 season with a magnificent victory in the second World Cup.

The end of 1991 did contain one important win for Alan Jones, though. A three-year campaign to get movement on the Andrew Kalajzich case brought a result. Midway through 1991, Tim Barton, who had worked as a researcher for Andrew Kalajzich, was employed directly by Alan Jones. By then the multimillionaire's fortune was severely depleted. Jones' and Kalajzich's accountant, John Thomas, who had power of attorney while Kalajzich was incarcerated, had blown millions in international arbitrage deals, trading through Britcorp Finance. JR Thomas departed JR Thomas and Company with debts of around $29 million, at the time Sydney's largest known non-corporate bankruptcy.[30]

In the meantime Kalajzich's legal team, assisted by Barton, put together a dossier which they claimed 'revealed new facts and raised matters which were not before the jury at the trial'. The Jones–Kalajzich researcher, harbouring doubts about the integrity of police evidence, believed Kalajzich was innocent. The young lawyer's input was crucial to Jones' understanding of the case. Alan Jones later admitted he had done no research himself, instead relying on Tim Barton.

For two weeks in 1991, Alan Jones used this research to argue there was serious doubt about Kalajzich's guilt. He said the case should be reopened to look into 'why things that should have been presented at the Kalajzich trial weren't'. There was also energetic behind-the-scenes lobbying of local politicians such as Brad Hazzard and Attorney-General Peter Collins. Alan Jones sent material to Bob Carr as well, which, according to a staff member, went straight in the bin.

In December 1991, the Fahey Government agreed to a Supreme Court review of the case. Justice Michael Grove was assigned to conduct an inquiry pursuant to section 475 of the Crimes Act. The clause allowed for the examination of new evidence that had come to light following a conviction. In 1992 Justice Grove would open the Kalajzich file and begin picking through the 1200-page dossier, including the supplementary 4000 pages of documents, in an attempt to locate the promised new evidence.

For Alan Jones, 1992 opened with a second chance to prove himself a Rugby League coach. The story of the biggest ever defection from Rugby Union was now old news, which meant some pressure was relieved. The team still had a strong stock of talent and the major sponsor, the electronics company Philips, had stuck by Balmain. There had been time for the players to adjust to Jones' attacking style. Alan Jones retained most of his players, although he did agree to release an unhappy Gary Freeman.

The New Zealand halfback managed to revive his career with a switch to Eastern Suburbs. Freeman believed he had lost his position in the inner sanctum as soon as Brian Smith arrived. 'I felt like Jones had, in the end, just used me.'[31]

Gary Freeman's Balmain replacement, Brian Smith, was also to prosper in 1992, playing well enough to be selected into the Sydney City side. This time the Tigers were off to a better start, winning some good matches. But bad luck stalked them, too. Among others, Brian Smith became unavailable when his collarbone was broken in the City–Country match. Some of the first round losses were by the narrowest of margins. And there was more trouble with a senior player. In an away game against St George, behind 17–2, the coach boldly replaced stalwart Garry Jack. Alan Jones later said, 'He gave me a mouthful as he left the field, which I chose to ignore and we won the game 22–17'.[32]

In the photographs taken at the time you can see the tension tearing at Jones and empathise with the lot of the coach. It is worth remembering that all this suffering was being endured on a handshake no-fee arrangement. Alan Jones had indeed chosen an unusual way to relax. Not that he needed the money. In May 1992, the law firm Allen, Allen and Hemsley negotiated a new four-and-a-half-year contract with 2UE that brought Alan Jones closer to John Laws' tax bracket. Alan would be paid $5 750 000, approximately $1.3 million a year.

Jones was also making up ground on Laws in the race to haul in the big studio guests. Following his December 1991 succession to prime minister, Paul Keating chose Jones instead of Laws for the first major interview about his 'One Nation' address. When Alan Jones then pushed to get John Hewson to fight back on the feature 7.15 am interview, he was astonished when the Opposition leader chose instead to go jogging. So Alan Jones wrote to John Hewson counselling him about lifting his game if he was to beat Paul Keating in the upcoming 1993 election. 'John Hewson doesn't have the same understanding of the media that Keating does. And he has to develop that if he is going to properly use it at election time.'[33]

John Laws joined the tug-of-war, his competition with Alan Jones undisguised: 'On the line from Canberra we have the allegedly impossible to talk to, never able to be found Dr John Hewson. Good morning.' Hewson, playing along, commented in reply that he had no idea why people thought he was difficult to pin down.[34] At the end of the interview Laws, in offering Hewson a regular slot, seemed to goad Jones: 'This is the most listened to talk radio program in the country ... feed us another [story] next week and another one the week after that and if the Government wants to argue, they must have the opportunity to do so of course ...'[35] John Hewson replied, 'Okay, John, every week I will call you up and we'll do it ... I'll cut my jogging for you.'[36]

As the Rugby League year progressed, Alan Jones' and Balmain's fortunes improved enough for them to have a chance of making the finals. But just before the finals were decided a headline appeared in the *Daily Telegraph*: 'JONES SACKED'.[37] It is often the lot of coaches and broadcasters to learn about their sackings through the media. Rugby League writer Ray Chesterton reported that the Balmain committee of ten was opposed to Alan Jones by at least seven votes to three: 'Factions at Balmain have not been happy with the playing style and want a more conventional approach next season'.[38]

On 30 August the last round match against North Sydney was played to a 14–14 draw. The result did not propel Balmain into the finals but it did give Alan Jones room to save his job. Although Ray Chesterton, by firing a warning blank, might have helped, Alan Jones was in no mood for gratitude. He told the assembled media, 'Mr Chesterton got it wrong'. *Sydney Morning Herald* journalist Roy Masters then engaged in what was described as a 'spiky exchange' with Alan Jones.[39] Masters, writing of the episode, said Jones had been saved by an eleventh-hour campaign, quoting a Balmain insider: 'The directors say Jones has divided the club. They reckon he treats them like second-class citizens.'[40]

In the same week Garry Jack, having played his 229th and last game for the Tigers, let go at Alan Jones before heading for England: 'We were virtually going on the field and feeling our way. We didn't know where to attack once we got in an attacking position and were placed under pressure. Off the field everything was far from harmonious. The JIC [Jones Inner Circle], despite denials, was alive and well. It was clear from the outset that Jones played favourites and there was a handful of players who could do nothing wrong in his eyes. One senior player in the JIC constantly whinged to me that "this bloke can't coach", but for reasons best known to him, continued to back Jones to coach again in 1993.'[41]

At the beginning of the season Alan Jones had said that if he ran ninth he should not continue as coach. They had finished equal tenth. On the positive side, Balmain was one of the best attacking teams, but defensive discipline and handling skills had weakened as splits in team unity widened. It was an old story brought back to life. One faction detested him while others remained devoted. Alan Jones won undying loyalty from players like Steve Roach who, now retiring, was encouraged into commentary work at 2KY and Channel 9. 'Of course you can do it', Jonesy told him.

While Alan Jones' ability to coach Rugby League was still in question, his capacity to attract profile and players was assured. One little coup promised to enhance the club's fading forward power. Newspapers speculated that Alan Jones' contacts and Kerry Packer's money were likely to lure the tough but brittle Mark Geyer to Balmain. Home ground attendances were also up

15 per cent. The cross-promotion might have been working. Alan Jones' radio audience was also now well in front of John Laws' Sydney figures.

By the end of the League season, Justice Michael Grove had completed his examination of the 1200-page submission that promised to reveal new evidence demonstrating Andrew Kalajzich's innocence. On 18 September Judge Grove dismissed the application to reopen the case, saying, 'Nowhere have I located a succinct expression scheduling these new facts and matters. I regret to observe that much of the submission is couched in language that is more sensational than revelatory.'[42] Grove saw some of the claims as farcical and pulled up just short of calling the entire submission fantasy.

Alan Jones, never one to be in awe of headmasters, members of parliament, referees or judges, let fly. At 7.50 am on 21 September he began a regular segment in which he devoted around six minutes of prime airtime to an attack on the Grove verdict. He related Andrew Kalajzich to other victims of Australian injustice—Lindy Chamberlain, Tim Anderson, Alexander McLeod-Lindsey and Ziggy Pohl. The next day he spoke of a briefcase belonging to Kalajzich, the combination lock of which he said was changed after it had been taken into police custody. The numbers, allegedly altered to correspond with Kalajzich's birthday, unfairly helped to incriminate him.

The following segment attacked a decision by the Crown to indemnify a witness, George Canellis, and pay him $25 000. Alan Jones would summarise the evidence in every repeated broadcast. He spoke of ballistics evidence that Canadian expert Tim Barton helped locate, which challenged findings of New South Wales Police that the bullet markings matched those of the recovered weapon.

On 13 October Alan Jones persisted with the theme that the evidence 'doesn't add up', asking the question: 'Did Justice Grove perhaps fail to understand intellectually the subtlety of some of the argument before him?' The next day Alan Jones moved to poetry, reciting his own version of John Donne: 'No man is an island entire of itself ... any man's death diminishes me because I'm involved in mankind and therefore never tend to know for whom the bell tolls, it tolls for me'.

On 15 October it was back to murder, mystery and intrigue. Like a Jeffrey Archer novel, the Kalajzich story, as told by Jones, was formed on a complicated and unlikely series of plots. Alan Jones questioned 'the dubious behaviour of police', suggesting evidence had been tampered with. On 20 October he charged them with incompetence. On 21 October he accused them of planting evidence and spoke of 'a Chinese doctor whose wife just happened to own a townhouse in Burwood, next door to that of a senior policeman involved in the Kalajzich investigation'.

Alan Jones again stretched a long Lindy Chamberlain bow: 'And just as uncontrollable prejudices convicted Lindy Chamberlain before she even went to court, prejudices in favour of dingoes against disturbing the tranquillity of Ayers Rock, against the name of the child, against Seventh Day Adventists, just as all these helped convict Lindy Chamberlain, so too did prejudice conspire against Andrew Kalajzich. After all, how could the son of an immigrant from Yugoslavia who started with a fish shop end up with a magnificent hotel right on beautiful Manly Beach?'[43]

Two days later, Alan Jones applied the political squeeze to newly appointed Attorney-General John Hannaford, the man he blamed for the failure of his own political career: 'We're all threatened if those institutions to which we abdicate so much individual power are allowed to treat even one of us unfairly, the New South Wales system of justice presided over by an Attorney-General who says today, well there's no chance of this being reopened again. Surely it can't be allowed to arrogantly disregard, Mr Hannaford, a 1200-page submission of the depth and substance of what I've seen?'[44]

Alan Jones was taken with the size of the brief, as if the larger the bulk of paper, the stronger the case. But for all those pages, and all those stories of briefcase combinations and prejudice against a fish shop owner, Alan Jones provided nothing that Justice Grove had not already considered. He did not link his expositions to construct an argument that clearly and logically challenged the court verdict. He linked instead allegations of police corruption and incompetence with improbable hypotheses of alternative and mysterious motives. Worst of all, Alan Jones did not attend to the compelling contrasting evidence that convicted Andrew Kalajzich. He ignored a fundamental responsibility to balance the story.

Listeners busily hurrying their kids to school or queuing at the Harbour Bridge tollbooths would have had trouble evaluating the credibility of his argument, but no trouble at all recognising the conviction and anger in Alan Jones' voice. It is unlikely Alan wrote all or even most of what he read. Even so, in his public statements there was nothing but certainty about his belief that the verdict was unsound.

Between 21 September and 22 October Alan Jones delivered 14 pro Kalajzich editorials. These were supported with letters to a range of political figures in which Alan Jones claimed, 'I have no brief from Mr Kalajzich. I have not discussed this material with him. I simply do not accept that this is an "open and shut" murder case as characterised by the crown.'[45] In December 1992, the Friends of Andrew Kalajzich team presented a petition to the Governor of New South Wales calling for yet another review.

By now Alan Jones was due for a rest. The Stafford Hotel in London would be a welcome respite from the 2.30 am alarm clock, an overweened sports public and the bray of debate. Breakfast announcers have a high attrition rate. It is a tough way of life, and no one made it tougher for himself than Alan Jones, who had cause to believe that the strict discipline of this routine would carry into the rest of the day. This was far from true. In his coaching and broadcasting, as seen in his treatment of the Andrew Kalajzich case, ill discipline remained a constant flaw.

If along the way doubts had emerged about the wisdom of the Kalajzich campaign, they were not expressed. It does not do to admit mistakes. There was enough power in the *Alan Jones Show* to triumph over inconvenient truth. Alan Jones was indeed riding a tiger. The tiger he dared not dismount was his own program.

CHAPTER 12
RUNS ON THE BOARD

'IT'S ALL ABOUT RUNS ON THE BOARD', Alan Jones would admonish former students who might not have met his expectations about this measure of achievement. In his radio job there is no doubt Alan Jones was hurrying the scorekeeper. He was at the beginning of a long period of breakfast radio dominance which, within 12 years, would see him accumulate an amazing century of survey wins.

The ascent of his popularity was commensurate with the ascent of his power. Alan Jones takes the view that it is a senseless waste of opportunity to have muscle and not use it. In the early 1990s his attacks on the big end of town, most particularly the giant insurance company AMP and the banking group Westpac, indicated a willingness to use his influence for the benefit of his Struggle Street constituency.

In 1992 Alan Jones began to give the AMP Society a hard time. He had concerns about AMP executive salary increases and loans to directors as well as a 'disregard for the views of its two million-odd salary holders'.[1] Alan Jones also got stuck into AMP over the sale of a substantial shareholding in the Australian biscuit company Arnotts to the US-owned Campbell Soup company. He was also critical of a suspected 'nexus' between AMP and Westpac. Alan Jones picked up on anger from people in the bush who had been stung over the bank's notorious foreign currency loans. But with Alan now well practised in camouflaging self-interest as virtue, it is wise to look beyond a claimed higher purpose for other agendas.

The AMP–Westpac campaign coincided with an attack by Kerry Packer and his chief lieutenant, Al Dunlap, who were fighting to gain control of a resistant Westpac board. There was more. Alan Jones said he was a 'former AMP policy holder' who 'doesn't have a lot of faith in insurance policies'.[2] However, before his campaign against AMP began, Jones signed up with Cigna Life Insurance to endorse income protection and disability insurance.

AMP Managing Director Ian Salmon, like many before and since, came to dread the regular beatings. At a later Annual General Meeting his board defended Salmon following 'unwarranted personal attacks in the media'.[3] The insurer's performance in New South Wales noticeably dipped. AMP policyholders were very much in Jones' self-funded retiree demographic. In 1993 the insurance company's chief actuary, Kerry Roberts, said, 'it was amazing how much influence a certain radio celebrity on 2UE had wielded among mum and dad investors'.[4]

An attempt to broker a rapprochement was made, and Salmon was advised to go on air. As the *Australian Financial Review* later reported, 'Jones' first question was about Salmon's home loan and Salmon's retort was "I don't know what planet you're coming from".'[5] AMP Chairman Ian Burgess was unhappy with his managing director's performance. Ian Salmon agreed the interview had not gone well, citing in his favour the away game disadvantage: 'you have to face the fact that when you do an interview with these guys they own the station'.[6] Salmon left AMP the following year.

In the interim the insurance giant tried a different strategy, with better results. They signed up John Laws. In March 1993, AMP did a deal with Laws to 'live read' a series of commercials. Alan Jones said he had not been asked to do them and would not do so had he been asked.[7]

The many apparently worthy campaigns Alan Jones undertook had the further benefit of, in a sense, buying him insurance. Alan was given room to speak his mind about more sensitive public issues, such as indigenous affairs. Aboriginal land rights was a hot topic at this time, especially after the High Court's 1992 Mabo decision recognising the special relationship indigenous Australians have with the land. Leading an active reform agenda was Federal Minister for Aboriginal Affairs Robert Tickner. The former Aboriginal legal rights lawyer and Alan Jones were never going to be a good fit. Tickner says he tried to take the debate up with Jones, but 'everything I stood for he opposed. Attempts at dialogue were doomed to failure.' Tickner saw one interview, when he felt he got the upper hand, as a turning point. He was never invited on a Jones program again. The attacks continued, Jones, he recalls, later referring to him as 'the most reviled person in Australian public life'.

At the beginning of 1993, The International Year of the Indigenous Person, the National Australia Day Council chose Yothu Yindi musician Mandawuy Yunupingu as Australian of the Year. Alan Jones challenged the selection criteria, calling the decision 'ridiculous'.[8] 'To promote people because of their colour or their history rather than their merit is an intolerable form of racism, which givers of such awards say they are opposing. Others call it tokenism.'[9]

A month of media debate drew more attention to Alan's program. He did not back off, either on air or in his response to the press. 'They throw names at you ... they call you a racist ... but that's just designed to intimidate you and frighten you. I won't be. I won't be muzzled.'[10]

And he wasn't. In February, Alan Jones turned his attack on the National Australia Day Council, which made the award, doubting their credentials to mirror the views of ordinary Australians. Alan Jones' former 2UE colleague and then current Chair of the Council, Phillip Adams, responded with an open letter in the *Australian*: 'I'm well aware that talkback radio is the realm of bombast, that your performance will probably bring in the bikkies. But that's hardly an excuse. To paraphrase Our Lord, what does it profit a man if he increaseth his ratings at the cost of his immortal soul?'[11]

The punch-up continued, with Aboriginal spokesperson Charles Perkins swinging a few in a live debate: 'A lot of your comments are very racist, Alan, and you've got to learn to control yourself, mate, because you're getting very redneck and right out of order. What you've got to realise is that the Aboriginal people and the white people are trying to work something out in this country and they want to do it in a proper way, they don't want to be incited by people like you with your remarks. You've sat on your white bum at 2UE in Sydney all your life and you wouldn't know what goes on out there.'[12]

Considering the talkback responses, Alan Jones' position on Aboriginal affairs was met with the general approval of listeners who heard a man not frightened to speak his mind. Sitting in the studio Alan Jones could sound insensitive and inflammatory, and when he thought the microphone was turned off, he was even more so: 'I'm so pissed off and sick of this country, and fucking Aborigines …'[13]

But landing an accusation of racism on him was difficult, considering the direct support Alan gave to Aborigines. 'Last year there was a New South Wales Aboriginal league championship here in Sydney. At the eleventh hour a team of Aboriginal boys approached me. Would I buy the jerseys? Would I buy the tracksuits? Would I pay for the hotel accommodation? They had no money. Of course I said yes.'[14] Alan Jones later accepted a seat on the board of the National Aboriginal Sports Corporation Australia (NASCA), helping out by again putting his hand in his own pocket.

While Jones' contribution was on his own practical terms, and again there was the prospect that the largesse bought insurance, he could and would point to some genuine runs on the board. He could also point to strong personal connections with Aboriginal sportsmen. One of them, Rugby League player Darrell Trindall, would become very close.

At the beginning of the Rugby League season in 1993, Alan Jones showed he was not going to shrink from the disappointments of 1991 and 1992. He still had a strong team, Balmain fielding four players in the New South Wales State of Origin side, including new favourite Jacin Sinclair. Jones also did a bit of quiet lobbying at the New South Wales Rugby League, pushing to be considered as Blues coach. Giving him points for confidence, the League politely declined.

The Balmain team of 1993, unlike many others Alan Jones had coached, was to prove weaker than the sum of its parts. Alan still put tremendous effort into coaching, players like Benny Elias, saying, 'he would not even stop to take a call from the Prime Minister'. But when the players took to the field they appeared clueless, the opposition easily predicting the play. The now departed Garry Jack said the Tigers 'had been using the same tap moves for 15 months'.[15] Not until the seventh round, on Anzac Day, did Balmain manage a win.

One problem might have been the same one that had surfaced with the Wallabies in 1987. Alan Jones was a deeply lonely man who could not help using the team as a family substitute. After the loss of his parents there were few people in his life to love him unreservedly. Alan told columnist Mike Gibson, 'It's tough out there on Struggle Street. I'm a bit of a causes person and I like to give as much time as I can to those who deserve a helping hand. But sometimes it's at your own expense. The phone rings here at work all week, but not so often at the weekend when I've got a day off from the football and I'm home on my own.'[16]

Alan's 2UE colleagues saw much the same. He hated being alone—so much so that one Easter Monday, a public holiday when they had a rare opportunity to sleep in, he organised for the team to come over for breakfast. A 2UE worker recalled: 'It was sort of sad because no one wanted to go but felt they had no other choice. So we had breakfast and chatted a bit. Then he said he had to go off to work as he always did when he had enough. He is a total workaholic. Even on a day off he can't stand not working on something.' People who did telephone Alan during his vacant moments were surprised at how touched and grateful he was for the call.

Footballers sometimes took late-night calls from Alan asking them to come around as he was in need of company. The new favourite, Jacin Sinclair, was soon regularly by Alan's side. As with Brian Smith there is no suggestion of a physical relationship. As he had done with Brian Smith, Jones treated him like something in between an object of romantic longing and a prodigal son. Tigers' jaws dropped when Alan proclaimed young Jacin as 'the next Reg Gasnier'.

Although Jacin Sinclair was talented, he was not as committed a trainer as the displaced Brian Smith. If Sinclair pulled up during a workout, he would be excused with an expression that goaded the crouching Tigers: 'Never flog a thoroughbred', Alan would say as Jacin took a rest. Stalwart Paul Sironen thought that the players Jones was soft on took advantage of him. 'Unfortunately, such incidents eroded the senior blokes' respect for Alan.'[17]

Brian Smith was now more distant. Fellow players put the problem down to him making more of his own decisions and spending more time with his girlfriend. Jacin Sinclair also had a girlfriend but, like an earlier Brian Smith, was amenable to making space for Alan Jones in his life, and was appreciative of Jones' generosity. A genuine refugee from Struggle Street, young Jacin was taken under Jonesy's wing. He would be another to nominate Alan as a godfather to his children.

The team was indeed like a family, and an expensive one at that. Favourites were reported as receiving 'unlimited petrol, free stays in city hotels, holidays at Sanctuary Cove and cash handouts ... during the Jones era'.[18] Roy Masters quoted a Balmain source as estimating that 'He has spent $200 000 out of his own pocket helping players set up their homes, businesses and appearing in court for them'.[19] The coaching job was financially draining for a further reason. According to another report, Alan Jones 'knocked back $300 000 in public speaking engagements and promotional activities because of his commitment to Rugby League'.[20]

That there might have been more to this 'commitment' was widely presumed but rarely given voice. At the ten-year reunion of the 1983 Manly rugby team, there was an embarrassing moment when a drunken guest yelled during Jones' speech: 'Alan, are you gay or what?' Alan Jones attempted a dignified reply but, according to sympathetic onlookers, had trouble recovering his composure.

In response to the puff-piece profiles of Alan that maintained the line that all would be well if only the right woman came along, on 2JJJ Roy and HG began a campaign to find Alan a wife. Having picked up on Alan Jones' often quoted comment about being very close to Benazir Bhutto, Roy and HG began to ask their listeners if they could think of the perfect woman for Alan.

At this time there was also a more explicit outing, this one in response to Alan Jones' views on another beset minority, Aboriginal Australians. Posters looking like movie advertisements began to appear along Sydney's gay boulevard, Oxford Street, depicting Alan Jones with cocked hat and curled lip, under the headline 'Ind'anal Jones and the Ten Pulls of Doom'. Jones' hardline views were anathema to some gay men. His adherence to traditional family values was also seen as hypocritical. The poster made the link, referring to 'insult recipient—Mandawuy Yunupingu' and picturing hooded members of the Ku Klux Klan assembled behind a leering Jones. Back at 2UE, Alan appeared indifferent, telling staff that 'people always say that about bachelors'. It may, however, have been a show as at home in Newtown personal staff saw him collapse into a funk when all the smirking went public.

The Rugby League season progressed with a few more wins, but at least as many losses. The strength of Alan Jones' determination to win was offset by the weakness of his emotional control. He could not help treating Balmain like a social club. Players were rewarded with a visit to Kerry Packer's showpiece farm, 'Ellerston', in the Upper Hunter Valley. Alan Jones knew the way not just because he was close to the Packers, but also because it happened to be up the road from another hallowed haunt, the

White family's 'Belltrees'. 'Ellerston', with its air-conditioned stables, 160 polo ponies, manmade lake, guesthouses, tennis courts, Olympic-size swimming pool and so on, was an eye-opener for his players. So too for Alan Jones, who would send his new personal assistant on a scouting mission for his own rural retreat.

In 1993 Jill Newcombe took over from Jane Scott. Alan also now had a new producer, Niamh Kenny, who would prove of immense value. Kenny was bright, straight talking and industrious. She loved the buzz of the job and there was enough Irish in her to stand up to Jones. Niamh began to write a swathe of Alan's programs, quickly getting the knack of his language. At the pace they both worked, meltdown would be inevitable. But even with this close proximity to Jones, it was impossible to know him well. Jonesy was still short of close confidants in his life, and there were so many secrets. When the 'cash for comment' scandal broke years later, employees working closely with Alan were surprised at how little they knew.

In the early 1990s, following partial deregulation of the telecommunications industry, Optus became the nation's second telephone service provider. In April 1993 Harry Miller began working on a deal, playing the rivals off against one another. In a file note Miller recorded: 'We both agreed that it would be nice if we could do it for Telecom because it was so Australian'. He also noted 'how loyal I felt to Optus'.[21]

Alan Jones' economic philosophies are in frequent internal opposition. He believes in protecting Australian business and commerce and he believes in competition. The preferred Telecom deal appealed to the nationalist Jones, while the Optus deal appealed to the pro-choice and anti-monopoly Jones. Having taken advice from an advertising agency, Optus had decided to bid for the services of Alan Jones and John Laws. Between them, Optus and Telecom had an estimated war chest of $150 million to spend on marketing. Optus carved off $100 000 per year for Alan Jones, their main rationale for buying him being to keep him out of the hands of Telecom. In April 1993 Optus also signed a similar deal with John Laws.

In the same month, as required by a separate 2UE commitment, Alan Jones was doing live read advertisements for Optus. 'Have you ever stopped to think exactly what Optus can do for your business? It seems there's no end to what they can and will do for you.'[22] As already explained, advertisers are prepared to pay a premium for live reads because the reader, by personalising and enhancing the copy, appears to genuinely endorse the product. At this time 2UE charged $800 for a 30-second live read on Alan Jones' program, compared to $480 for a prerecorded 30-second advertisement.

2UE management saw that Jones had a particular gift for them, as did the advertisers. Jones' old teaching techniques, the messages repeatedly beaten home, seemed to work. As one of the 2UE sales staff put it, 'Advertisers love Jones because he gets results ... they can see the difference at the cash register'.

Under the guise of editorial opinion, which is not supposed to be for sale, it soon became clear which side Alan Jones was on. 'Telecom's muddying the waters for 101 reasons and it's becoming a very ... unsavoury war ... Optus has fired the latest shot with some legitimacy, accusing Telecom of trying to maximise public confusion.'[23] Again as editorial comment, but indistinguishable from the live advertisements, Alan Jones mirrored the Optus 'Dial One' campaign. 'Put "One" before your number. If I'm dialling Brisbane I dial "One" 07.'[24]

On 5 May Harry Miller wrote to 2UE Chairman John Conde informing him of a commercial relationship with Optus 'which involves Alan doing some paid consultancy work for them and of course he will do whatever live reads are necessary to be done for the station. Optus are aware that any charges by 2UE for commercials are of course a matter between them and 2UE and their arrangements with Alan for his consultancy and promotional services are separate.'[25]

Quarantining his station and his stars from a damaging and deceitful conflict of interest was a challenge for John Conde. Telecom and Optus were engaged in a high stakes battle for market share, which was about to intensify with the introduction of pay TV. There was the risk that his stars could favour their sponsors with free time and use the airwaves to attack the opposition. There was a risk his employees could double-dip, cheat the station of revenue and deny the opportunity of revenue from rivals. There was the further issue of the integrity of his stars and his station. How would it look if it could be shown his broadcasters were, unknown to the listeners, pretending to maintain editorial objectivity while accepting payments to advance a particular argument or, worse, to attack competitors?

The Optus deal, still hidden from listeners, was a serious management issue for both John Brennan and John Conde. But when the program manager finally heard his star had done the deal, Brennan was untroubled, believing Alan Jones' pro-Optus stance reflected 'unmistakeable personal opinion'.[26] This was also Alan Jones' position. He later argued that the commercial arrangement with Optus in no way influenced his 'genuine opinion that Telstra [as it came to be known] is an oppressive entity, which has been exploitive of the Australian people'.[27]

While Harry Miller had argued the deal was 'separate' from Alan Jones' 2UE work, what John Conde did not know was that the contract had a performance clause, which meant Alan Jones would receive additional revenue 'based on how many subscribers they hook in'.[28] So quarantining the consultancy arrangement from 2UE was more difficult than even Conde realised.

The telecommunications war was now a common staple of Alan Jones' editorials. A 2UE colleague said Jones would read as if it was his own 'almost everything' Optus sent him. 'See, there's tremendous featherbedding in Telecom, enormous. I mean when Telecom get into a spot of bother that's the way they go about it, spend money ... Telecom of course will try to muddy the waters as Optus gains a foothold in the telecommunications market ... it's a very simple story: Telecom are trying to muddy the waters. All it's saying is that Optus don't want the local market ... Optus is saying well try us. Dial "One" before all the numbers. Try us and you dial "One" now.'[29]

Two days later, again as an editorial: 'They say they can do it better, they can do it more cheaply, try us if you dial "One" now, and it'll be charged under the Optus system ... Telecom, bureaucratically driven and heavily overmanned, have been found by the Trade Practices Commission to be guilty of misleading advertising, the ads incorrectly quote Optus prices—now you can't get much worse than that, can you? If you can't fight fairly don't fight at all ... Their only answer to the challenge posed by Optus seems to be to spend money and hope they can confuse the debate ... now I know we advertise here for Optus but this war between Telecom and Optus has got out of hand.'[30]

There was more, including an advertorial interview with Bob Mansfield: 'He's the head of Optus and he's already right on top of the issue'. Q: 'How much has Optus spent in Australia at a time when investment is pretty crook?' A: 'Over one billion dollars, Alan.' Q: 'And how many jobs?' A: 'Twenty-two hundred people.'[31]

While Alan Jones was benefiting from the competition, the 2UE share began to weaken. After Optus signed contracts with Jones and Laws, John Conde noticed Optus spending less on station advertising. Conde had another problem too: Jones was not keeping up with his 'live read' quotas.

Alan Jones' new contract and salary package obliged him to read 'up to 30 per program'. Alan's admirable enthusiasm for the stuff in between the ads—the program content—had long been a worry for the commercial schedulers. If he got worked up interviewing the Prime Minister it would be a strain getting him to stop for the news, let alone an advertisement for Paradise Markets. 2UE made a fortune from Alan Jones' program, but they lost money too. As Harry Miller explained to Alan Jones: 'the situation is that where there is a scheduled number of reads during your program for the specific commercial breaks, if you don't do the read, then 2UE is entitled to deduct $50 per "dropped" read'.[32]

While Alan Jones was lifting Optus subscriptions and revenue, the Philips-sponsored Balmain Tigers slipped further down the table. Of all Winfield Cup teams, Balmain had the highest number of penalties awarded against it. St George coach Brian Smith (a different Brian Smith) was quoted as saying Balmain was the most undisciplined side in the competition.[33]

The losing margins were often small, although in the third last round, playing away against eventual premiers Brisbane, the Tigers were belted 50–0. Alan's brother Robert, now running a catering business, happened to be at the ANZ Stadium, which put him in the company of his brother for the first time in years. Robert walked over to watch the Tigers warm up. 'I said to the lass that was working there, I said I'll just go and say hello and I said, how are you going? He [Alan] sort of looked at me with glazed eyes—his mind was just fixed on those Balmain fellows—didn't realise, didn't sort of recognise—he was completely mesmerised.'[34] Robert Jones suggested no criticism in not being recognised by his famous brother. He was not so much offended as struck by Alan's total concentration on the job at hand.

The 1993 Rugby League season turned out to be his worst for Balmain. Alan's own dictum that 'you can't deny the scoreboard' had come back to haunt him. In 22 matches there were only six wins, and in one, the points were taken away because of a mistake in the use of replacements.

In 1993 Balmain finished twelfth. Back at Manly a decade earlier he had said, 'Losers can look in their pockets and find a thousand reasons for not winning. Our pockets will always be empty.' In 1993 there were more excuses than pockets—bad luck, bad referees, persistent injuries, not enough time to develop new players, a hostile media and all that inhouse disloyalty. He wrote: 'It is very difficult to work in an environment where stories are circulated and statements are made which can only be damaging to the fabric of the club and the morale of the side. I would be less than honest if I said it didn't happen. I would be less than honest if I said that it wasn't destabilising.'[35]

While the preceding season's end had coincided with a blow to his campaign to assist convicted murderer Andrew Kalajzich, this time there was better news. Alan Jones had kept the pressure up on air and in his newspaper column. In October 1993 the top-rating broadcaster was invited to be guest speaker at a fundraiser at the Dalmacija Social Club at Terrey Hills, a function well attended by influential supporters, including local politicians.

The following month the New South Wales Liberal government announced Justice John Slattery would head another inquiry into the Kalajzich conviction. Twelve months earlier, Attorney-General John Hannaford had ruled out an inquiry. While no new evidence had emerged in the meantime, there was some genuine concern that the questions Alan Jones raised about the integrity of the ballistics evidence justified reinvestigation. The earlier section 475 inquiry rejected the arguments Alan Jones and the Kalajzich team had promoted, but John Hannaford agreed to again use the clause declaring 'there were questions arising as to Mr Kalajzich's guilt'.[36]

In reporting the development, the *Sydney Morning Herald* noted that the inquiry had been approved 'on exactly the same information that was dismissed with strong criticism by a Supreme Court judge twelve months ago'.[37] The *Herald*'s reporter, Sandra Harvey, was criticised by Jones for failing to disclose an interest in the case. Harvey was the co-author of *My Husband, My Killer*, according to Alan Jones a 'scurrilous book which, as the title suggests, roundly condemns Kalajzich'.[38] Alan Jones thought the public was 'entitled to know that'. It was apparently not so important for them to know that Andrew Kalajzich had paid for the research Alan Jones relied upon. While many of Alan Jones' listeners had signed a petition calling for the case to be reopened, Andrew Kalajzich's biggest friend was unquestionably Alan Jones. As one politician put it, he had 'nagged like a dentist's drill'.

Alan Jones had not given up on Kalajzich, and despite his earlier promise that a poor result should disqualify him, he was not giving up on Balmain. A tenacious Alan reapplied for the coaching position, offering a business plan to the board to help the financially embattled club. When it was knocked back, Alan Jones resigned.

In the club's 1993 *Annual Report* there was an unusually long account by Alan Jones of his term at Balmain, which tried to explain in words what he could not deliver in deeds. It reads like the reports he had given in school magazines in the 1960s and 1970s: 'In sport as in life, one must look forward not backward'. There was also praise for the newly beloved: 'Jacin Sinclair opened for us with a remarkable try—one of the many occasions on which he served notice of his extraordinary and often unacknowledged gifts'—and more.[39]

As a Rugby Union coach, Alan Jones claimed a higher purpose to his endeavours. He said greater satisfaction than winning was found in the development of those fine young men who would go on to succeed as stockbrokers and merchant bankers. In 1993, he again spoke of the game being more than the score: 'We've had some triumphs ... we might have kept a few people out of gaol, dragged a few people up out of the gutter along the way.'[40]

Balmain Club President George Stone agreed: 'Because he took a great interest in the welfare and personal development of players, we have some young men who will be not only better players, but will be better people and enjoy better lives due to the influence of Alan Jones'.[41] But no matter what he said about the importance of being an inspirational force in the lives of young men, the Tigers and Alan were finished. Balmain needed a coach more than it needed a social worker. As one of the players put it, football teams are like families—and Alan Jones had made this one dysfunctional.

Alan Jones' dictatorial approach to the Tigers failed because he had none of the experience he was able to bring to Rugby Union. His attitude to improving fitness and skills was of limited use when the fitness and skills were already there. His motivational techniques did not work when the same speech was heard the fourth and fifth time. And at Balmain, Alan Jones' agenda of seeking the company of young men was even more apparent.

Interestingly, in League the proposition that Alan Jones was homosexual did not bring on the same defensiveness as it did in

Union. The Union boys appeared more self-conscious about any latent homosexuality contributing to dressing room humidity. In contrast, League players were more open about their nakedness and not so inhibited when ogled. Some of it might have been a form of flirting, but mostly it was for the sake of amusement. One player took to dropping his pants and asking Alan to examine his bum.

Paul Sironen has written of how far regard for Alan Jones had sunk: 'I can well recall the day we were sitting about in a circle as he gave a pep talk at training and Benny [Elias] started pulling faces behind his back. Well, I started sniggering, which caused a chain reaction and the other guys broke up. When it became a straight out symphony of laughter Jonesy lost it and he shouted at different blokes.'[42]

Getting the boot from Balmain did not mean a separation from Rugby League, however. A major blow to Alan Jones' pride was softened with the announcement that he would become General Manager of Football Operations at the South Sydney Rugby League club. Balmain's famous rival worked out an arrangement that capitalised on the positives. Souths could profit from the sponsorship and exposure Alan Jones delivered without so clearly having to put up with his coaching. Not that Alan completely lost the whistle. As part of the deal Souths picked up his disciple, Ken Shine, who would take over the coaching from local hero Bob McCarthy in 1994. Later Jacin Sinclair also transferred to Souths. The new Tigers coach, Wayne Pearce, was circumspect about the reasons for his release: 'I just want to leave it that he failed to meet his commitments at the club. I don't want to say any more because it wouldn't be in Jacin's interests to do so.'[43]

While Balmain had dropped to number 12 in the League during Jones' three years with the club, the now ex coach had risen to number one in radio. When he started in the mid 1980s, Alan Jones had about 5 per cent of the market. By the end of 1993 almost 21 per cent of the available listening audience at breakfast was tuning in. While Alan Jones wanted a more sophisticated and qualitative accounting of his contribution to football, in radio the simpler 'runs on the board' measure seemed to do. The ratings system drew on a sample of listeners who made note of their listening in a radio diary. The information was extrapolated to estimate audience share (percentage) and reach (numbers). This standard industry measure, although not exact, was good enough to show Alan Jones with a clear lead, approximately 200 000 Sydneysiders tuning in at any one time during the morning. Again what counted was the numbers. Again it mattered less if what they were told was flawed, dishonest, secretly paid for, malicious or just plain wrong.

Alan Jones' increasing audience share seemed to have an intimidating effect on politicians in particular. The numbers taking notice of Alan could have been five or ten times the numbers supporting an individual MP. It was an easy enough leap for some of them to share Alan's view that his opinion was public opinion. But the processes that brought measure and discipline to the behaviour of politicians did not apply to Alan. Although he was becoming more powerful than many of the state ministers he scorned, the talkback host's power came without commensurate responsibility. Furthermore, Alan Belford Jones was not someone who could be voted out of office.

CHAPTER 13
THE GODFATHER

ANY AMBITION TO HAVE CHILDREN of his own now in the past, Alan Jones is literally godfather to reportedly 'dozens' of children, the children of friends, mostly from the sporting community. But through the 1990s in Sydney, Alan Jones became a godfather in another sense.

Australia's largest urban jungle has its own survival rules. A dominant ethos accommodates a kind of 'dingo' principle, which accords respect to Australia's most cunning and ruthless survivors. Getting on in business, paying your mortgage, dealing with officials and competitors is tough everywhere, and certainly tough enough in Sydney for people to look for an edge. Perhaps the greater density of the jungle leads to a view that easier paths through the strangling systems are more necessary. Or perhaps the law of all cities is, the larger you are the less room there is for standards.

An essential service of the *Alan Jones Show* was the provision of such shortcuts. Pensioners who had lost a beloved pet or plutocrats whose wealth was threatened might approach Alan. Politicians also beat a path to his door, often secretly allowing Alan Jones the right to advise and prioritise policy. Whether or not they were correct in their estimation, politicians and their minders came to see Jones as a make-or-break force. In the mid 1990s a

New South Wales and a federal election changed governments in different directions with, in each case, the Jones factor seen as influential.

The influence Jones was able to exert was less the kind fairly won by an informed and responsible broadcaster. While Alan Jones got things done because a lot of the time he was right, it was also his Godfather-like presence that frightened people into action or submission. The power to come on air and regularly beat up transgressors is hard to counter. Even his station managers did not have an answer. Alan Jones was too important to 2UE to be easily told when to pull his head in.

The lesson learned by many people was to either stay out of his way or find a means to appease him. Flattery was often a good choice. Anyone who did manage to broker a meeting with one of his minders would be greeted by Alan with an offer of tea. Sitting resplendent in silk tie and matching handkerchief, he would receive pleas for forgiveness or retribution. In a curious way, paying this kind of respect seemed to strengthen the chance of support. To feed Alan Jones' narcissism was to nourish the worth of the cause.

In matters of business, justice and politics, 1994 was a busy year for Godfather Jones, his first as a true multimedia personality. As well as being number one in Sydney radio, Jones had a well-read newspaper column and now a television deal. In November 1993 Harry Miller had negotiated with Network Ten for Alan Jones to take over from Derryn Hinch. Miller saw Jones' future in television. Hinch saw his replacement as 'a despicable man ... [with] a lot of lead in his saddlebag'.[1]

Australian television current affairs shows are often fashioned after their American counterparts. This one would copy the CNN *Larry King Live* show, with Alan Jones taking live questions from a national audience. Harry Miller had bargained for a two-year contract estimated to be worth $200 000 a year.[2] Ironically, Miller's deal would introduce Jones to a rival for his management role. Years after he introduced Jones to the new medium, Executive Producer Grant Vandenberg would take over some of Miller's minding duties.

As he had shown with Balmain and Rugby League, Alan Jones had the courage to tackle something new, and again the challenge appeared to refresh him. After the summer break a trimmer and younger looking Alan emerged. He put the change down to a diet of steamed vegetables and grilled fish, though there was speculation that cosmetic surgery had been of assistance as well.

Alan Jones believed his success on radio would carry to the new medium and a wider national audience. He believed that he was in better contact with ordinary people and the issues that really mattered: 'Outside [the media] the people with the most views and the most relevant views and who are consistently ignored by the media, except for a couple of letters to the editor, are the public. The public have views that may well be contradictory to the so-called experts. We'll be hearing their own views.'[3] Alan Jones did not count himself among the hated 'experts', even though in Sydney there was no more influential opinion-shaper: 'Plurality of choice absolutely confounds and confuses people. Life's not all that straightforward out there and in that complicated world ... in a sense you're making their minds up; you're helping them to come to some sorts of conclusions.'[4]

The conventional promotional push by Channel 10 put Alan Jones under the spotlight of the tribal enemy, the out-of-touch mainstream media. He was unhappy with some of the coverage he got. 'Later, asking a nice story be written from this interview, Jones explains that none have ever penned a nice word about him. A look through newspaper clippings proves that assertion wrong—he received high praise in the *Australian* and the *Sunday Telegraph* last year—but he apparently remembers bad things better.'[5] Very capable of dishing it out, Alan's thin skin was well known to colleagues at 2UE, as was his thirst for feeling underappreciated: 'He is not happy unless he's unhappy. He has to have something to whinge about. I have seen memos sent to him congratulating him on his ratings success then he'll walk out half an hour later complaining bitterly that not a single person has congratulated him on the ratings.'

Up against *Sale of the Century*, *Home and Away* and the ABC *News*, *Alan Jones Live* began at 7 pm on Monday 31 January with a stern to-camera editorial. Although counselled otherwise, he insisted on having his pal Bronwyn Bishop as his maiden guest. Bishop was asked about her leadership ambitions. The Melbourne *Age* reviewer called the questions 'excruciatingly tame'.[6] The *Sydney Morning Herald* saw the choice of opening guest as 'impossible to forgive'.[7] Alan, Bronwyn-like, ticked off the first caller, June of Moore Park, who failed to ask a question. Politician Carmen Lawrence was the next guest and then there was a prerecorded story of a 95-year-old man whose driving licence had been confiscated for speeding. The Melbourne reviewer thought the debut program 'just lousy'.[8]

New current affairs shows have difficulty swiftly establishing credibility and identity. It was always a gamble, with Ten needing ratings of around 15, an audience more cheaply and easily bought with an American sitcom. Of all the capital cities, Melbourne seemed to have the biggest problem with Jones. It was not the first time they sniffed at a host imposed from the north, but in Alan Jones' case there was a particular repugnance for the ex-'thugby' coach. The early Melbourne ratings went down to 7 and levelled out between 9 and 10.[9] But as television bosses tend to do, Carmel Travers claimed she was thrilled: 'There's a long way to go. Jones, I think, is one of the most interesting new talents to come on television in about ten years. Jones is sensational. He has surpassed all of my and other people's expectations. I think he's remarkable. Quite remarkable.'[10]

Stuart Littlemore agreed, but he thought Alan Jones 'remarkably awful'. The ABC's *Media Watch* reviewed two months of programs, focusing on Alan Jones' position on the Telecom–Optus competition. The *Media Watch* inquisitors looked back further to Jones' radio treatment of the telecommunications debate, calling it a 'case study of blatant bias'.[11] At this stage *Media Watch* knew no more than the public about Alan Jones' secret deal with Optus. Littlemore thought Jones was 'bashing Telecom for nothing'. The revelation that broadcasters' opinions were being secretly purchased would be left to later *Media Watch* programs.

In early 1994 *Alan Jones Live* paid a lot of attention to Optus and Telecom. In one program, Jones rehashed interviews with 'casualties of Telecom', business people who believed they had been bugged by the telephone company, shown weeks earlier on Channel 9 and the ABC. Heavily made up, wearing a grey suit and with his hair thinning and grey, Jones proclaimed a grim suspicion that he too was being spied upon: 'Filming part of tonight's story Telecom rang Channel 10 and offered to do an interview on one of the cases you'll see shortly. Funny that, from our understanding Telecom had never been told about the story. Did they get their information from a bugged call as well?'[12]

He interviewed Opposition Communications spokesperson Richard Alston, although 'interview' is an inefficient description. Among a fully loaded six-gun of questions aimed at Telecom was: 'Senator Alston, are they corporate thugs?' Alan Jones went on to invite calls from people who were having problems with Telecom.[13]

One month later the autocue rolled on more indignation: 'You don't need a Harvard degree to know that a monopoly over any essential service is a licence to print money. Telecom's monopoly over local telephone calls has led to profits that would make Joe Average go weak at the knees. Its half-yearly profits, Telecom's, are reported to be about one billion "B" for billion dollars. The eighties were supposed to be the decade of greed but the nineties, recession or no recession, as far as Telecom is concerned don't seem to be shaping up as anything different.'[14] There was much more along these lines.

The cooperative nature of current affairs usually applies checks and balances as staff debate the merit of content. Those who worked for Jones found he was more attentive to his own counsel. 'If something came in from Optus he would say, take a look at this stuff and see if there's anything in it. I think he really convinced himself they were his opinions.'

Alan Jones Live lasted thirteen weeks, a short run even in the high-risk world of television current affairs. The rejection was not confined to Melbourne: 'It continued to rate dismally in Brisbane, Adelaide and Perth—a complete washout on network terms ... last week averaging 221,000 viewers in Sydney, its fourth-best performance. But the decision to quit became inevitable three weeks ago when the audience dropped to an average 173,900.'[15] The *Daily Telegraph* pointed out that Derryn Hinch had been axed on 301 000 viewers.[16]

On Friday 29 April *Alan Jones Live* was replaced with an episode of *Are You Being Served?*. Alan Jones later complained that Channel 10 bureaucrats did not protect him as bravely as did their counterparts at 2UE. 'In television it was different. Everybody rang—and all sorts of people—all trying to shut me up. I think people [at Channel 10] got a bit uncomfortable about it.'[17]

The bigger problem, which he chose to ignore, was his poor adaptation from radio to television. Although both are electronic media, the differences are extreme. The brighter light that television shone on Alan Jones highlighted weaknesses radio listeners were more likely to miss. The passion and fluency that carried him far at 2UE was harder to believe on the box. And when not believed, Alan Jones looks silly and sounds boring. Alan's certitude and appetite for simplification can be irritating for people who want the facts and the right to make up their own mind. Under the all-seeing studio lights Alan's lack of range in humour, warmth, understatement and irony wept through the makeup.

The experience was a serious challenge to both the notion that Alan Jones was in better touch with the public than most, and the idea that his charm would carry. The episode highlighted the reality of Alan's limited appeal, not just in the television market but in radio as well. His entire 2UE audience was one-quarter of the audience watching *60 Minutes*. As rival current affairs presenter Peter Luck commented, 'the bottom line is a huge radio audience is only a couple of ratings points on television'.[18]

Despite the cancellation and the cruel reviews, Alan Jones retained some prospects as a television presenter. The Nine Network, which had used his editorials on *Wide World of Sports*, was considering making more use of him. Also, with pay television now on the horizon, his contract with Optus kept alive the prospect of a similar *Alan Jones Live* show.

On 2UE Jones kept up his championing of Optus and continued to give time to the many problems his listeners had with Telecom. 2UE management was unaware of the performance bonus payments Jones would receive if Optus improved its market share in Sydney. In 1994, as its share rose by approximately 10 per cent, these additional cheques started to arrive.

Considering the stakes and considering what they were paying Jones, Optus was hardly buying impartiality. Between the corporate and political bunkers, there is a fair bit of interchange, so it is not surprising that political advisors took a similar line with Alan Jones. They knew Jones hated to sit on the fence and that courtship takes many forms.

Nineteen ninety-four was that crucial pre-election year in New South Wales when both sides did their best to be nice to the public and the shock jocks. Opposition Leader Bob Carr was going well. When, seemingly out of the blue, he telephoned Jones on air to have his two bob's worth, Jones was pleased. Although insiders presumed the calls to have been stage-managed, to outsiders Bob Carr could have been just another listener.

On the other hand, the New South Wales Liberals were struggling. Attorney-General John Hannaford got on air, but just before the 7.30 newsbreak. By the time Alan Jones asked a few hostile questions there was not enough time to have a proper say before the throw to the news. After a few such muggings a 2UE staff member took to ringing John Hannaford to offer fair warning.

The source of the animosity appeared to be Alan Jones' belief that John Hannaford's vote in 1979 had stymied his political career. Privately, Alan Jones referred to John Hannaford as 'that double crossing miserable bastard'.[19] Peace talks over lunch at Darcy's restaurant were brokered. Hannaford says the first mistake he made was to deny he had ever been involved in any preselection vote. An irritated Alan Jones reminded him of North Sydney. Hannaford, only then remembering he had been drafted in as a late replacement for Lyenko Urbanchich, made his fatal mistake. He told Jones, 'I don't remember you as a candidate.' Jones froze. The lunch came to an abrupt end. Hannaford realised later he'd committed a sin worse than having voted against Jones. He'd forgotten who Jones was.'[20]

Others seen to have opposed Alan Jones, such as faction leader Ted Pickering and Health Minister Ron Phillips, received similar treatment. After Pickering became leader of the government in the Upper House, the attacks were more harmful to the government. Winning Jones' approval was a game politicians on both sides played with varying degrees of enthusiasm. 'Alan Jones demands tribute', said one Liberal who came to the reluctant position that courtship was the preferable option.

And Alan Jones was not totally anti-New South Wales Liberal, just anti those who did not pay tribute. While other commentators saw danger in taking sides, recognising that a formal endorsement of one side compromised objectivity, Jones did not care. One Liberal to have got the tick was another former King's student, Jeremy Kinross. The Sydney barrister was preselected to the safe seat of Gordon in 1992 with the help of a Jones endorsement complete with 2UE letterhead.

One New South Wales minister from this period confessed that both Alan Jones and John Laws had insinuated their presence into the Cabinet room: 'A lot of time was spent considering their views and trying to predict what their reaction to decisions would be. We were appalled when somebody used their views to support their case, but we cynically did exactly the same when it benefited us.'[21]

One issue that was difficult for the New South Wales government in the lead-up to the 1995 election was the tender process for the lucrative and controversial Sydney casino licence. The development of a legal casino in Sydney had bedevilled a range of governments. In a pre-election year, Premier John Fahey did his best to keep the subject clear of politics, managing the process through the establishment of an independent Casino Control Authority.

The final contenders were the Leighton Holdings–Showboat consortium up against Kerry Packer's Darling Harbour Casino consortium. When Leighton won, 'Jones railed at the outcome, insisting the process was flawed and that the Packer bid was by far the better of the two. He also lashed out at the Fahey Government.'[22] Bob Carr joined the attack, raising questions in parliament about Mafia connections to Leighton's US partner, Showboat. After a probity check, the Leighton consortium got a further nod. In the ensuing debate Bob Carr said his information about Mafia connections had not come from the Packer consortium, but that his office might have spoken to them.[23] Alan Jones also denied the presence of Packer in the background: 'Do you actually think people can give me running orders?' he barked. 'I don't do anyone's bidding.'[24]

The smell of fear about crime, often in the air as an election approaches, was redolent at this time. In May 1994, following pressure from the independent MP John Hatton, the Fahey Government agreed to a police corruption inquiry. Alan Jones disapproved. He thought coming down on cops for bashing a few drug dealers was going too far. Some of the advice he received about policing seemed to come from some of the cops under pressure to change their ways. Jones shared their argument that confronting reform would make crime worse.

In discounting the evidence that corruption ran dangerously deep, Alan was at least consistent. He opposed the Wood Royal Commission in the same way he had opposed Queensland's Fitzgerald Inquiry. In his *Sunday Telegraph* column under the heading, 'THE DANGERS OF UNCHECKED POWERS', he wrote: 'The question is whether a drawn out and expensive royal commission could be any more effective in dealing with police corruption than those mechanisms which are already in place to deal with it'.[25]

As both sides ramped up their law and order agenda, the president of the New South Wales Bar Association, Ian Barker QC, made the routine call for restraint, accusing 'Mr Fahey and the Opposition Leader, Mr Carr, of embracing "Alan Jones driven" law and order philosophies'.[26] Alan Jones' position on law and order is consistently baffling. While he believed expensive monitoring of integrity was a restraint to effective policing, he campaigned that no cost was too great in re-examining the Kalajzich conviction—largely because he did not trust the police case.

In November 1994, the 'free Kalajzich' campaign suffered a blow when a story emerged that a key witness had been offered over a million dollars by Kalajzich to change his story. Alan Jones, responding on air to the development, might not have had his head around Tim Barton's briefing notes, identifying the figure as $100 million.[27] Even this new evidence did not shake his belief, though; Alan Jones smelled another cook-up. 'I simply say what I've said many times in the past, many of us can be wrong, I don't understand. Kalajzich had no reason to want to kill his wife and the explanations I've seen offered to the murder remain to me, to put it mildly, absurd.'[28]

One week later the story broke that Alan Jones was relying on information from the Kalajzich camp: 'the Friends of Andrew Kalajzich group had used broadcaster Alan Jones in their campaign to overturn the millionaire's murder conviction'.[29] Alan Jones responded on air: '... the fact is I know of no such group, and I've never had discussions with anybody associated with the Kalajzich defence in relationship to anything I've said on air other than to authenticate information'.[30] Alan Jones must have overlooked his direct communication with Kalajzich and his billing as guest speaker at a Kalajzich supporters' dinner in November 1993.

The *Telegraph Mirror* report connected Alan Jones to the Kalajzich camp through researcher Tim Barton, describing him as 'the head of Kalajzich's support group'. Alan Jones dissembled: 'I mean that's laughable. Mr Barton has never been the head of any support group. He was previously a legal researcher on the Kalajzich case but since 1992 Mr Barton has been a member of my staff.'[31] Jones did not tell his listeners that he had recommended Kalajzich employ Barton, and further urged Kalajzich to keep Barton on the payroll, which, in short, underwrote the information Jones relied upon. 'The wire service story clearly implies that I was a mouthpiece for somebody. Such a comment I don't think even by my critics could be taken seriously—that I was a mouthpiece for somebody.'[32]

Feeling the brunt of Jones' attack on the police case was the man in charge of the Kalajzich inquiry, Detective Inspector Bob Inkster. Years later, after the detective had rounded up Lebanese crime gangs, Alan Jones would reverse his position on Inkster and proclaim him a hero.

Another case indicative of Jones' bizarre approach to picking sides was the Keith Waite matter, which occupied talkback space at this same time. Alan Jones hammered Attorney-General John Hannaford when it was revealed that a young woman had been awarded $40 000 in victim's compensation even though her complaint of indecent assault against Waite was dismissed and the woman was charged with public mischief. Keith Waite's arrest in 1998 was the beginning of a five-year nightmare, he believed, as a consequence of inept police work. He believes to this day he should never have been committed for trial as he had provided convincing evidence to Detective Tim Priest, which refuted a further complaint by the woman.

In 1990 the Independent Commission Against Corruption investigated an allegation that Priest and another officer had solicited a $1500 bribe. No finding of corruption was made against Priest and he later resigned, asserting that the decision was unrelated to the corruption claims, that he had done nothing wrong and was worn out. In 1994 he rejoined the NSW Police. Seven years on Alan Jones would hail the troubled officer as another hero.

It was not just logic that was all over the place. Alan Jones' respect for language was also at odds with the way he expressed himself. He often talked of playing the ball and not the man, believing criticism should be constructive and impersonal. Earlier in the year he told an interviewer, 'I don't think people put up with being insulted. I've never done that.'[33]

Five months later, Sydney hosted the Women's World Basketball Championships. China's Zheng Haixia, like some of Jones' rugby line-out specialists, had been selected for her height. 'Oh, it's the most grotesque thing I've ever seen in sport is that Chinese woman ... six ... was she a woman? Six feet nine. I mean the Chinese are knee high to a grasshopper at the best of times, and this great big beast ... of a heifer, six feet nine. And they call it sport. And all she does is stand and put her hands up when they throw the ball to her. And these other women are jumping, and then she whacks a basket and then lumbers away up court. God I hope they don't beat anybody. China. You know they walloped us because this heifer put her hands up in the air and sort of kept on catching the balls. Dreadful. Not my idea of sport.'[34]

When attention was drawn to his comments in other media he sought to make amends. 'I want to say to anyone who was offended, that the offence is legitimate. I certainly apologise. And I apologise to the lady and I'd be happy to do that.'[35] It wasn't long before repentance ran out, though. Alan Jones later referred to ACTU President Jennie George as 'the only woman in Australia who could turn a glass of milk into yoghurt by staring at it',[36] and likened the appearance of Labor's Martin Ferguson to 'a rat looking through a broom'.[37]

It may well be that one Jones does not know what the other Jones just said. He is heard on occasions disowning his own words and admonishing others for derogatory comments milder than his own. The character shifts were also evident when he walked from the studio into different environments, such as the South Sydney dressing room. There, players noticed that among the sweaty footy players, Alan's blokey persona moved into hyperdrive. He could outbutch and outswear the lot of them. When Alan joined Souths supremo George Piggins in the downstairs bar, Piggins warned him that some of the rough, tough locals might give him trouble because of his right wing views. According to Piggins, Alan defiantly replied, 'I'll have a go, y'know'.[38]

In 1994 Souths had a reasonable year, finishing ninth in what turned out to be the last year of the 16-team competition. As he had done at Balmain, as Souths' General Manager of Football Operations, Alan Jones did a lot more than attend to football. Again he embraced the role of unofficial social worker. At this time, perhaps the strongest and strangest of his many alliances with footballers formed. Big Al and Little Tricky are indeed an odd couple.

Classically, the bond was formed in adversity. When Darrell Trindall (or Tricky, as he was known) was picked on the wing and Craig Field moved into his halfback spot, Tricky skipped training. Soon after, Jones and Trindall had the first of many intense discussions: 'He just took me aside and said just listen, mate, you know you got a chance here to make something out of your life. I've seen where you come from. You're an Aboriginal kid and your parents have died, and this is your one ticket, and if you put your head down and your bum up, you can make something out of your life.'[39] According to Darrell Trindall, after that initial encounter they would speak every day.

Tricky proved a handful. In September an apprehended violence order was taken out against him by a girlfriend's father. Soon after, Trindall and another footballer were reported as having 'knocked out three men in a Sydney football stadium lift'.[40] The more celebrated incident in the trifecta occurred at The Edge nightclub in Coogee. After some heckling a fight erupted in the toilet. When it died down someone noticed what looked like a 'piece of calamari' on the floor. It was the top half of Trindall's ear. The *Sun Herald*'s Danny Weidler reported quick thinking by Sydney City halfback Nathan Wood, who had the piece of ear transferred to an ice-filled glass. Trindall, intoxicated and bleeding, was ushered into a cab and Jones was summoned on a mobile phone.

The story has entered football folklore. The players, barely coherent in the taxi, were struck with wonder by Jones' calmly recounted advice. 'Geez, he's a fucking doctor too' they concurred as the taxi driver changed direction and headed for the Masonic Hospital at Ashfield. Alan Jones picked up the phone again and called microsurgeon Dr Bruce Sheldon. Within hours the undigested portion of ear was successfully reunited with its other half.

A recuperating Darrell Trindall was contrite when visited by Alan Jones. 'He said, mate, this is probably the third or fourth time that I've come and helped you out, mate. Every time you get on the drink, you know, you done yourself harm, got into trouble, you know. If it happens again I'm going to wipe my hands on ya, and I give him my word there, give him me handshake and looked him in the eye. I said, mate, I'll get off the drink and I know every time I get on the drink that's when I cause you trouble so I give him me word. We had a shake on it and I never touched a drink for three years after that.'[41]

Alan Jones' defence of Darrell Trindall was not confined to off-field violence. Tricky was a regular before the Rugby League judiciary, where Alan proved equally impassioned. In 1995 Judiciary Chairman Alan Sullivan QC was moved to chastise Souths' football manager for 'unacceptable' behaviour when Alan Jones' shouting interrupted a hearing that led to Darrell Trindall's suspension.

Competing for the top favourite spot was Jacin Sinclair. While the former State of Origin player's football career appeared to stall, Alan Jones was helpful in other ways. In August the *Sun Herald* reported: 'Radio spruiker and Rabbitoh team manager Alan Jones picked up a $255 000 Putney home yesterday on behalf of South's handsome, dark haired centre Jacin Sinclair'.[42]

Trindall and Sinclair were two of many footballers helped by Jones. Julian O'Neill, another in perpetual trouble with the bottle, was given aid and comfort. So too was Craig Field and the big centre, Terry Hill. After Hill was charged with assault occasioning bodily harm, there was public debate about whether he should be allowed to participate in a Kangaroo tour of Britain. Alan Jones, on air, took Terry Hill's side. It made grim listening for the man, half Hill's size, who had been severely beaten when he tried to help Hill's female partner after he saw her being dragged by the hair outside the Woollahra Hotel.

Here was another contradiction. 'It's not a question of throwing the book at them. We should throw the whole damn library.'[43] Alan Jones' on air position about taking a tough line on violent offenders, attacking street hoodlums and the bleeding hearts who get in the way, was in contrast to his stance on footballers. Over the years, Tricky Trindall would get multiple second chances. No heart bled more profusely than Alan's when he argued that social and environmental factors, as well as the scourge of booze, had to be considered when his boys were involved.

At South Sydney Alan Jones' advocacy of particular players again put him at odds with other members, who thought Alan either had his own agenda or was being used. But this potential for instability was offset by the assistance Jones brought not just to players but to the club. In the mid 1990s, the famous Rabbitohs were on the run from bankruptcy. Jones has said he put his own money into Souths. He also used his connections to help with sponsorship. According to George Piggins, in 1994 Alan Jones brokered a meeting with Kerry Packer, which began with an attempt to persuade him to merge his club with Sydney City and ended with Packer writing Souths a cheque for $750 000.[44]

AMP, having not long weathered an attack by Jones, organised a loan to refurbish club headquarters. George Piggins explained: 'With the help and guidance of Alan Jones, we borrowed $6 million from AMP.'[45] Although AMP Chairman Ian Burgess did claim 'it had something to do with placating Jones', Burgess also said the insurance company wanted to help Struggle Street. When the *Sydney Morning Herald* later made a link between Jones' attacks on the insurance company and the loan, Alan Jones sued the *Herald* and won. Jones told reporters: 'The *Herald* had no hesitation in going ahead with the story even though my lawyers warned them that that story was incorrect'.[46] The verdict is under appeal.

Alan Jones' backing of Souths would become even more important in the months ahead, when a challenge led by Rupert Murdoch's News Limited threatened not just the future of the club, but the administration of Rugby League. On April Fool's Day 1995, the Murdoch organisation launched a brazen raid on the game of Rugby League. It set out to hijack the competition, offering huge sums to the big name players, as well as clubs such as Canberra and Brisbane, to abandon the Australian Rugby League and embrace a new 'Superleague'.

There was not much doubt about which side Alan Jones would take in what proved to be a bitter and divisive civil war. Kerry Packer's Nine Network had a free-to-air contract with the Australian Rugby League and an option of pay television rights until the year 2000. The Packers were also allied to Optus, with the Nine Network parent, Publishing and Broadcasting Limited (PBL), holding 5 per cent of Optus Vision, and PBL's James Packer sitting on the Optus Vision Board. Optus Vision's mortal enemy was Foxtel, a consortium formed between part publicly owned Telecom and News Limited.

Central to the success of each venture was ownership of a major sport. The world pay television experience indicated subscribers would first of all commit to the $25 a month fee if their lounge room could be transformed into their favourite sports stadium, akin to Alan's own description of the space in front of his television set, 'The Alan Jones Stand'. Furthermore, if hooked into pay television subscription by a major sport, there were ongoing prospects of selling further services.

It is not often Kerry Packer is made to look small. Early in 1995, in a move that caused throats to dry at Rugby League and Packer headquarters, Rupert Murdoch showed off his international might by buying the international rights, declaring his capture of the game in the United Kingdom and New Zealand. But the battle was far from won. Alan Jones was merciless in his attack on Superleague and Rupert Murdoch, the conflict becoming the most mentioned issue on Jones' radio program during 1995.[47] News Limited executives, superconscious of the damage to their own populist audience, were stung by his attacks. The ones who remembered going in to bat for Jones during his London public toilet episode of December 1988 began to shake their heads about an apparent lack of gratitude.

Alan Jones' position was that he was representing neither the Packers nor the ARL, but the principles of sport. The game was, after all, the property of the people. But here was another contradiction. In the same year when the same market forces were brought to bear on the game of Rugby Union, Alan took the opposite line. While Alan Jones backed the existing Rugby League administrators, he was scathing about their Rugby Union counterparts, this time backing the rebels, one of the leaders being Alan's old mate Ross Turnbull. In addition Packer's PBL had put substantial seed money into the breakaway World Rugby Corporation.

As Peter FitzSimons explained in his book *The Rugby War*, 'Ross Turnbull, for one, was gratified by this support from his long-time friend, but not at all surprised, for he had already talked to him quite a lot on the subject. Turnbull knew that Jones personally supported the WRC proposal, as he had long been a proponent of the modernisation of international rugby union. But there was an added bonus. "He wanted ... to be the next coach".'[48]

At this time Alan Jones was at a radio peak, his morning ratings having climbed to an outstanding 22 per cent share. This made him easily the station's biggest earner. As a 2UE executive put it, 'Jones brings in more money than anyone else in radio'. There was the best part of two years to run on the existing contract and John Conde was not about to let go of the horn of plenty. The slow process of negotiation got underway in the latter months of 1994, John Conde offering a better deal to Alan Jones and attempting to shore up some management difficulties.

A problem persisted with Alan Jones' handling of commercials. John Conde had written: 'While I can appreciate that there will be some days when a particular interview or piece of programme material will cause the commercial content to be moved, I do not understand why commercials cannot be broadcast pretty much as scheduled'.[49] John Conde also billed Alan Jones for the cost of a missed advertisement. 'Up until now I have tried to turn a blind eye to the mentions of John Serafino, Park Hyatt, the Hyatt at Sanctuary Cove, Boyded Holden at Lakemba, and others ... The advertisement you broadcast for your former football team member's Mazda on Tuesday has been the trigger for my current action.'[50]

The new contract offered an incentive to Alan Jones to do what he was already paid to do. Unusual by industry standards was a proposed 'Schedule Adherence Bonus'. If all the advertisements were read within the half-hour specified, and within four minutes of the time specified, Alan Jones would be paid an additional $1500 a day.

There was also some sorting out to do with the Optus contract, due to expire at the end of March 1995. Alan Jones' listeners and 2UE management were still unaware of key details. A further problem for John Conde was that Optus revenue to the station had slowed and Telecom was knocking on the door. 'For your confidential information, we are in receipt of a very considerable advertising expenditure proposal from Telecom and I would like to know what impediments there may be, if any, to our considering such advertising for any "live read" presentations in your program.'[51]

Conde spoke in the memo about having 'no desire nor intention to cause any problem with personal credibility', no doubt aware of the position Alan Jones had taken on air—that Telecom was akin to the devil. Not that Alan was opposed to doing a deal with the devil. In 1995 Harry Miller again negotiated with Telecom, who appeared only too keen, a Miller file note recording that the Telecom–News Limited entity Foxtel 'are very keen to have Alan Jones even though he has been "slagging" Rupert Murdoch'.[52] One witness recalls a Telecom executive proposing that Alan 'do to Optus what you do to us'.

Harry Miller was in a win–win situation, the competition for his boy driving up the asking price. Furthermore, in the Telecom camp there was also now a friendly face, Channel 9 boss Sam Chisholm having moved on to become boss of Rupert Murdoch's pay TV operations in the UK. Harry Miller told Alan Jones: 'My current state of mind is that if we want to get out of the Optus contract because the Pay TV/Telecom thing may materialise ... You and I ... should hold fire until we hear from Sam Chisholm and then punt ... if we can't lock up Telecom.'[53]

Despite what he said on air about Optus, Alan Jones had problems with his existing deal. He had already written a note that, in Harry Miller's words, had 'bitten my ear off about this', Jones telling Miller: 'In many ways Optus have been very disappointing. For example as part of "an agreement" with me through Bob Mansfield, they were to provide 5 jobs for South Sydney. You will remember that discussion. That hasn't happened ...'[54] As ever Alan was using his connections to do favours for his boys, chasing phones and jobs through Optus and, via the 2UE airwaves, sorting out freebies with electrical suppliers, and including the use of cars, which according to others at South Sydney were promptly given a thrashing.

The sweetener that would keep Alan Jones at Optus was not just a five-fold boost in dollars but the prospect of a pay TV program. Here Optus was being cute. They knew Alan Jones was smarting over the canning of the Channel 10 program, and that he wanted it revived. Foxtel would end up developing such a program for John Laws, so Alan Jones knew it could be done. He expressed keenness to an equally enthusiastic Harry Miller, and appeared to get young James Packer onside. But in the engine room of Optus the pay TV deal was mostly talk. According to one executive, 'as far as Optus was concerned the idea of a Jones TV program was not a priority at all. There was no vehicle—no channel—to put an Alan Jones show on. It was just window dressing.' What Optus really wanted, beyond keeping Alan Jones away from Telecom, was his salesmanship and radio program. The new deal on offer comprised another incentive bonus of $20 'per Optus Vision customer signed up'.[55]

Come 1995, the Labor and Liberal parties, like Optus and Telecom, were also battling for Alan's help in advancing market share. Although the Fahey Government might have been riding high, having secured the 2000 Olympics for Sydney, they were not campaigning or polling well. In contrast, Labor was on a roll, Bob Carr boldly and imaginatively stretching the promises.

As a former Liberal contender, Alan Jones' buttressing of Bob Carr was a worry to some of his conservative mates. But Alan made no apologies. He told them he did not believe the Fahey Government deserved his support. Alan Jones argued that it was impossible for Premier Fahey to achieve change because he could not escape the 'boring' advice from his bureaucrats.

The other view was that the Fahey Government had escaped too much of Alan's advice. They were to pay for their sin with Alan taking every opportunity to bash them and the Fred Many case was a shock jock's dream. The convicted rapist was due for release just weeks before the 25 March election. Alan Jones and other media would not accept that John Fahey could do nothing to prevent a rapist's return to the streets. But Fahey was stuck, not just by boring advice from bureaucrats, but by the law. Fred Many had committed a horrible crime, but he had also served his sentence. John Fahey tried to distance himself from the 'mongrel' Many, but defending due process before Alan Jones proved a waste of time. Alan Jones wanted the law changed, one interview ending with a directive: 'I trust you do something in the next 24 hours'.[56]

It wasn't just John Fahey who was bashed. The Fred Many case was at the heart of what would turn into a Jones jihad on Fahey's amiable federal compatriot, Senator Amanda Vanstone who, in a parade of portfolios, could do no right by Alan Jones. As Federal Opposition justice spokesperson at the time, Amanda Vanstone defended the rule of law when interviewed by Jones about Fred Many, arguing that it is meant to be protective as well as punitive. When Jones took no notice the exchange became heated, Vanstone telling him: 'You know, you and I could be anywhere, overseas, in a public place and never know what you could be charged with'.[57] The line went frosty. The comment was an obvious reference to Alan Jones' London public toilet experience. The interview was terminated and it would take a very long time for Vanstone to be forgiven, a time during which Jones' commentary became vicious and personal: 'Senator Vanstone has no place in public administration in this country and should be run out of government'.[58] 'And you've heard me on Senator Amanda Vanstone who's a disaster.'[59] 'What an awful woman she is.'[60]

On 25 March Labor, polling well in the marginal electorates, took government and the 'unelectable' Bob Carr became the second most powerful person in the nation. The Liberals had suffered from a small margin and a second term dogged by scandal. One minister had a sexual harassment complaint against him upheld. Another member was convicted of making death threats over the telephone. For all that, there are plenty in the Liberal Party who still blame Alan Jones for the loss.

Two weeks later John Fahey was dropped and a leftie Liberal, even more disliked by Alan Jones, was made Opposition leader. Peter Collins thought he was at last on a winner when Bob Carr had to renege on a promise to abolish tolls on two new Sydney motorways. When Peter Collins was finally invited into the 2UE studio, he was one of many open-mouthed when Alan Jones turned the attack, accusing him of not properly costing Labor's promises. 'I was stunned. I'll bet even Bob Carr could not believe his ears when Jones in effect blamed me for Labor's reckless promise to abolish tolls on the new motorways we had built in the previous two terms.'[61]

Another political bête noire at this time was Prime Minister Paul Keating, who would face his own election in a further 12 months. The catfight between John Laws and Alan Jones to get the big interviews had now swung Laws' way. Jones' sympathy for Bob Carr was balanced by a distrust of his federal counterpart.

Alan Jones believed the Keating Government was guilty of gross economic mismanagement, accusing Keating of hiding his failure behind a 'sickening confidence trick'. So developed another clash of narcissists. In 1994 Paul Keating began to refuse requests to be interviewed on Jones' program. Alan Jones was reported as saying he had 'asked a million times' and the Prime Minister had said, 'You are too fucking difficult'.[62] An annoyed Greg Turnbull, Paul Keating's press secretary, explained the boycott 'might have had something to do with his being a pamphleteer for the Liberal Party'.[63]

John Laws relished his advantage as 2UE employees relished the entertainment. They happily snitched as the big stars bitched. Some of the spy stories found their way into the intelligence holdings of Harry Miller, who noted: 'One of the insiders says the Jones–Laws conflict now makes the Grand Canyon look like a small crack'. Miller went on to list a series of his client's grievances: 'Laws was absolutely outrageous about Bronwyn Bishop ... PR still has "John Laws leads 2UE to the top" ... Australis is paying John Laws $5,000 per month to give free plugs ... We are unaware that there has been any reprimand for the last slagging that Laws gave Jones on air.'[64]

On air John Laws coaxed the Prime Minister to go where politicians are usually too fearful to tread, making public his criticism of Alan Jones. Paul Keating responded: 'You know he's got a good rating programme, even though it's basically middle of the road fascism'.[65] When Alan Jones is publicly attacked he often assumes a dignified silence, preferring to let emissaries speak on his behalf. His number one caller, Stephanie Millar, a former air hostess from Kirribilli, weighed in: 'that very nasty little interview yesterday obviously took place between two very little men'. So did Harry Miller, who thought Keating 'wasn't game' to go on Jones' program.[66]

Laws kept it up: '... if we have reached a stage where a broadcaster of a metropolitan radio station is better equipped to run a country than the man who is running the country then we have a big problem'.[67] 2UE was thrilled. John Brennan told the

Sydney Morning Herald: 'They are provocative. They do flaunt themselves. They remind me of professional wrestlers at times.'[68]

At this stage Alan Jones' good friend Kerry Packer was also bluing with Paul Keating over media ownership rules. On the Monday following the state election, according to media commentators, Packer unleashed an attack dog. If Jones is known outside Sydney it is likely to be because of his morning editorials on Channel 9's *Today* show. Alan Jones often says, 'If you are going to get a dog, get an Alsatian'. Now the Parrot appeared to metamorphose as Packer's Alsatian in his maiden *Today* show editorial broadcast on 27 March 1995.

Like the Channel 10 television experience, the segment was never a winner with either production staff or the public. But the network would stick with Alan Jones irrespective of bleeding ratings, from the start rejecting any proposition that the Packers directed editorial content: 'Kerry respects Jones' intellectualism and would never dream of telling him what to say'.[69]

The deal meant Miller and Jones shared up to $500 000 a year from Nine. This was also the figure agreed to when Alan Jones signed his new contract with Optus. In May, while he was enjoying a brief respite in London, an amended contract was faxed and delivered to Room 6 of the Stafford Hotel. It specified Alan Jones was not obliged to 'cover for Optus Vision, Optus or PBL' if this was to 'prejudice his integrity as an experienced radio commentator'. But he was expected to use 'his best endeavours to assist the Optus Group in remedying public attitudes arising from any such event'.[70]

Back in Sydney, the old routine of Optus faxing scripts or 'talking points' to Jones' home/office continued. Optus personnel also visited the Jones bunker and as one soon learned: 'The purpose of the visits [was] to discuss scripting ideas but when you got there you didn't converse with Jones, you simply listened. It was a pointless exercise.'

Earlier reservations about the Optus arrangements were laid to rest, Alan Jones expressing on air his ongoing faith: 'Pay TV is about three things I think and three things only, sport, movies and current affairs and as I understand it the new starter on the blocks so to speak has got the sport side of it sewn up and that may well be the single most powerful inducement to buy pay TV'.[71] He 'interviewed' Geoffrey Cousins, a director of PBL and CEO of Optus Vision. 'So in a sense you've got a healthy menu along with Rugby League with the opposition Foxtel fighting for a menu. Even Foxtel acknowledge that you're in front on the menu, don't they?' Cousins: 'Indeed they did'.[72]

The following year, after *Sun Herald* columnist Alex Mitchell, suspicious about continued pro-Optus campaigning, rang to ask what deal they had with Alan Jones, he reported: 'An Optus Communications spokeswoman denied that Jones had any financial or contractual arrangements with the company'.[73]

The additional income from Optus, and the television deals, helped Alan Jones pay for a new acquisition that would have bowled over his dear old dad. While not exactly the Packers' 'Ellerston', Charlie would have worshipped 'The Church'. In 1995 his son bought the property near Jamberoo, two hours to the south of Sydney, for $615 000. The four-bedroom retreat was snuggled in eye-catching dairy country. Three years later, Alan invested a further $300 000 on adjoining land, expanding the holding to 26 hectares. He told staff he needed a space to relax, distant from the pressures of the Belford Productions home/office. Jamberoo would become a getaway not just for Alan but for lots of mates from his various constellations of school, work, politics and football.

In June, having a place to retreat to proved handy. After 18 months of trawling through the Kalajzich case, Justice Slattery handed in yet another report, which again found Andrew Kalajzich guilty. Despite Alan Jones' counter-proclamations, the millionaire hotelier did have motives to kill his wife. For example, he had been conducting an affair with his secretary. A divorce threatened not just the family's reputation but his hold on his empire. Beyond the evidence from people such as the confessed killer, there was an exhibit room stacked with convincing corroboration.

Some evidence advanced by the Kalajzich defence to cast doubt on the conviction was also shown to be deceitful. There was talk that one of the expert witnesses could be charged, and Jones' role investigated. This might have been why Alan Jones shut up after the finding. He did not expound as he had done after the similar Grove verdict.

The seven-year saga was a miserable experience for investigating police. Bob Inkster, the dogged chief detective/superintendent, would have been the main culprit if Jones' interpretation was believed. As the deputy Crown prosecutor put it: 'Some 27 police and civilian witnesses would have had to be involved in nine separate conspiracies and then lied on oath at the inquiry to support the conspiracy allegations in the petition'.[74]

Inkster was 'wild': 'The comments Jones made offended me, my friends and family. It was blatantly obvious to anyone who took an interest in the Kalajzich investigation and conviction that no conspiracy to frame him for the murder of his wife—for whatever reason—could possibly succeed unless I was personally involved ... People like Jones never spent one second in court listening to the evidence.'[75] Kevin Woods, a fellow investigator, wondered whether the inquiry budget might have been better used 'assisting drought stricken farmers and on our health and education systems'.[76]

Alan Jones' irresponsible campaigning had cost the New South Wales taxpayer over $5 million. His poor understanding of what constitutes fact meant that even the Kalajzich family suffered. As John Slattery QC noted, the inquiries had exacerbated their pain, with Andrew Kalajzich himself of the view that the Slattery inquiry had been 'a disaster'.

Alan Jones did not apologise to his listeners, to the taxpayers, or the police. When, years later, he praised Bob Inkster on air as an 'old style copper', there was no explaining his reversal.[77] Furthermore, not at this or any other time did he tell the truth about the commercial arrangement with Kalajzich.[78] The New South Wales government made no complaint. No embarrassment appeared to attach itself to either Alan Jones or 2UE.

By August 1995 Harry Miller and Alan Jones' new legal team at Freehill Hollingdale and Page had sorted out the final details of the new 2UE contract. Alan Jones retained the standard clause that '2UE indemnifies and saves harmless each of the Company against all loss, cost, damage and expense suffered or likely to be suffered'. He also won the right to 'retain lawyers of his choosing'.

The contract would keep Alan Jones at 2UE until 2001. Chairman John Conde fulfilled his promise of a 'dollar adjustment', 2UE paying $100 000 to Jones as a sign-on fee. In a note to his client, Harry Miller explained: '[Conde] asked me about the sign on fee and I told him that one of the reasons to do this ... was his opportunity to show you that 2UE really cared'.[79] Jones would be further paid $1.4 million each year with additional bonuses if ratings targets were achieved.

The *Sunday Telegraph* reported the deal was signed on 14 September with John Conde anxious to beat off a rumoured approach from rival talk station 2GB: 'An immense offer from John Singleton's camp' could well have spurred Conde on to make sure 2UE did not lose Jones. Conde says, 'I have no sure knowledge [of an offer] but it wouldn't surprise me'.[80] If not at this stage, John Singleton and 2GB would embark on a quiet and persistent courtship of the ratings leader.

While Alan Jones would later proudly transfer his allegiance to John Singleton, for the moment he was staying with 2UE out of loyalty. He spoke of his appreciation of the support he received from management: 'A lot of people don't understand that the nature of my program apparently provokes antipathetic attitudes. They never come to me they go to the chairman, who without exception rings me immediately. People always know they can't divide and rule.'[81] This account did not ring true around the corridors of 2UE. After the multimillion dollar contract was signed, Alan Jones' familiar complaints about an underappreciative management intensified if anything.

At the same time Jones' new contract was sealed, so too, it appeared, was the fate of his Rugby League team, South Sydney.

In August the new 20-team competition round was completed, with Souths finishing third last. Jones' Rabbitohs had had plenty of glory, but most of it well before he showed up at the club. While there was a continued impassioned support base, not a lot of it actually turned up at the matches. Although Alan's advocacy had been helpful, problems with management and budgets persisted. Alan Jones' connections attracted money, but critics argued that he spent more than he brought in. When Alan wanted his way, he was hard to refuse. If he pushed for the purchase of a particular player the club believed they could not afford, Jones would say he would find the money. As one prominent Souths person put it: 'Alan was extremely generous. He must have lost money looking after Souths. The trouble was he needed autonomy, which meant when he wasn't there to control things, everything fell apart.'

One of Souths' most famous sons, former captain Nathan Gibbs, a medical practitioner, acted as the club doctor until the end of 1995. Gibbs, a life member of Souths, left the club, it is understood, because of difficulties over Jones' selections. When Alan Jones countermanded the doctor's judgement about whether a footballer should or should not play, Nathan Gibbs must have wondered why he was there. As one departing Rabbitoh put it: 'Alan Jones was in charge of everything, but his management skills were hopeless'.

Alan Jones' judgement was further called into question when he recommended for the position of chief executive officer the exiled Kevin Humphreys. His colleagues at Souths shook their heads. Humphreys, the boss of the League in the dark ages of the early 1980s, had been charged and convicted of defrauding the Balmain Rugby League Club.

As the Rugby League civil war dragged on, the Murdoch press, substantially through the *Daily Telegraph*, was giving Alan Jones both barrels. News Limited had argued the game was being underutilised by Channel 9, which screened only a few games, and poorly managed by the ARL. The Murdoch reporters were as scathing of the management of clubs such as South

Sydney as Alan Jones was of News, which cancelled Jones' *Sunday Telegraph* column.

Before Jones could drag himself away for another holiday at the end of another brutal year, there was one more blue to settle. In December 1995 he was enlisted to the support of another maligned millionaire, bookmaker Robbie Waterhouse, who was a friend. Robbie's wife Gai, also a friend, has trained many of Alan's horses over the years. Robbie Waterhouse had been warned off racecourses after it was demonstrated that he had prior knowledge of the notorious Fine Cotton ring-in affair back in 1984 (in which a white blaze was painted on a horse to give it the appearance of a different horse). Now, a committee of the Australian Jockey Club (AJC) was to hear an appeal against the lifetime ban. The bookie was advised not to testify, leaving it to others like Gai and Alan to speak on his behalf.

Alan Jones' evidence was entertaining and colourful, if ultimately unhelpful to his friend. Again, he used his power over language to reverse the conventional flow in which facts shape arguments. Again, the episode raised doubts about the worth of proving Alan wrong. In the box, questioned by AJC counsel Bob Stitt QC, Alan Jones scoffed at the idea that someone as knowledgeable about racing as Robbie Waterhouse would engage in the clumsy Fine Cotton scam. He fulminated about murderers and rapists getting lesser sentences. He drew again on the Lindy Chamberlain saga as proof that courts are fallible. He portrayed Waterhouse as a scapegoat and the victim of racing administrators' jealousy of his success. He accused police of responding to orders to 'go out and get' Robbie.[82]

Alan Jones, not used to being challenged, confronted some sensible questions from Bob Stitt, who calmly exposed the emptiness behind the eloquence. When asked whether he properly understood the case, whether he had read the findings of the previous tribunal hearings, Alan Jones said: 'No, I went to the butcher, not to the block ... Surprisingly, Mr Stitt, and this might not sit comfortably with you, I actually trust and believe Mr Waterhouse. Stitt: So the total extent of your knowledge of

Mr Waterhouse's involvement is what he has told you, is that so? Jones: Well I think Mr Waterhouse would have a greater knowledge of his involvement than anyone else, wouldn't that be true?'[83]

Some of the questions made Alan Jones look silly enough for laughter to begin to leak from the public gallery. The hearing did not go well for the bookmaker, and the broadcaster did not seem to forget the humiliation. In later broadcasts, when Stitt was not facing him across the room, Jones said: 'The man who appeared for the AJC against the Waterhouses on almost every occasion is a bloke named Stitt ... Bob Stitt QC, or as he is known in the legal world and outside, Rhyming Slang QC. We know what Stitt rhymes with. You can understand why he's called that, and that's what he is, Stitt by name and rhyming slang by nature.'[84]

There was more, enough for Bob Stitt to sue. He was later awarded $50 000 plus costs. However, he lost his retainer as counsel for the Thoroughbred Racing Board, the *Sun Herald* reporting: 'The widespread perception is that Stitt's removal is designed to win the on-air approval of shock-jock Alan Jones when the hearing resumes'.[85] Alan Jones would also put AJC Chairman Bob Charley on his hit list.

Well on top of the list at this time was that silver-tongued opponent, Prime Minister Paul Keating. It is worth pointing out that Alan Jones was not the only one disenchanted with the Member for Blaxland. When, on 27 January 1996, Paul Keating announced an election for March, the polls counted Labor, then 13 years in government, as eight per cent behind the Coalition. Alan Jones' contrasting approval for Leader John Howard had moved some distance from the time Jones gave aid and comfort to the bumblebee challenger, Sir Joh Bjelke-Petersen. Jones' support for Howard, while perhaps a degree opportunistic, did appear genuine. Here was one of many occasions when mainstream media commentators were out of touch with the polls and the people. Paul Keating maintained an enchanted following in the Canberra press gallery while John Howard continued to be dismissed as a perpetual loser. In 1989 speculating about reviving his political career after being beaten by Andrew Peacock for a second time, Howard had described himself as 'Lazarus with a triple bypass'.[86]

Alan Jones was not the only media barracker for John Howard, but there was none more strident. At a Liberal Party fundraiser in February he told the audience: 'the interests of the nation are more important than the objectivity of Alan Jones'.[87] New South Wales Liberals might have wished for some of that Jones-style objectivity a year earlier.

Alan Jones later admitted to personally campaigning for Liberal and National candidates, Dana Vale and De-Anne Kelly,[88] although Jones' campaigning in Hughes may have been motivated as much by antipathy for the incumbent Robert Tickner as support for Dana Vale.[89]

On 2 March the Coalition won well with a five per cent swing. New Prime Minister John Howard's first major interview was on the *Alan Jones Show*. The two election results in the space of a year that saw Bob Carr and John Howard rise to power were also an enormous boost for Alan Jones' reputation. Alan got it right both times, backing changes of government in different directions. Furthermore he had shown faith in two men who had earlier been dismissed as losers, and who went on to record terms. In an age when television appeal seemed to mean everything, Alan Jones, at the peak of his own popularity on radio, appeared to be well ahead of the even bigger game of getting inside the public mind. In Alan Jones' entire career nothing would do more for his mystique than those ratings of 22 per cent and the ascension of Howard and Carr. In Sydney, in particular, the Jones factor was talked up even further.

What was of interest to researchers in the major parties was the way the election results reflected a shifting political paradigm. The old left/right divide was adjusting. Alan Jones had a strong following in electorates, mostly in Sydney's west, that were changing character. It was easy to see a communion between Jones' battlers driving Holdens but dreaming about Mercedes, and mortgage belt voters. Working class voters were building bigger houses and taking out bigger loans. Troubled by deregulation, threatened by interest rates and issues such as migration, they were shifting allegiance. With Jones' loyal listeners seen to be settling in the crosshairs of this movement, both sides drew closer to him.

Alan Jones had also peaked at a time when politicians were gaining confidence in their capacity to manage and even control the media. The major parties were no different to Optus and Telecom in the way they looked at the media as a giant advertising agency. The following years saw propaganda develop as a growth industry. The propagandists even gave themselves the softer name of 'spin doctors'. Governments and corporations doubled, trebled and quintupled their public relations staff. As with the corporations, governments accorded a higher value to those who could be bought.

These converging forces elevated Alan Jones' political as well as public standing. Although a broadcaster rather than an elected representative, he became a quasi politician, and not just any politician. Godfather-like, he formed his own power base, the Lord Protector presiding over a kind of Ministry of Alan Jones.

In New South Wales, Alan Jones and John Laws were already thought of as the 21st and 22nd members of Cabinet. Now those in Opposition more often sought Jones' patronage, while those in power more readily attended to his demands. In a sense he was like a traffic cop in the middle of a policy traffic jam. Neither side could move forward without Alan's green light. He was able to cleverly play one side off against the other: if one proved defiant, the other would quickly seize the advantage. Politicians saw no upside in doing a Keating and fighting him; ironically, opposition came instead from the few in the media to notice what Alan Jones was up to.

So, as with the Kalajzich case, and like a Godfather, Alan Jones had the power to bury deeply his losses and profit in excess from his wins. While it was likely that Bob Carr and John Howard would have won irrespective of the support of Alan

Jones, both leaders accepted a debt of gratitude. And Alan would certainly not forget that he was owed. In the years to come, when the prime minister's office was slow to answer a request, Alan could be heard to bellow at staff: 'Get John Howard on the phone and remind him who put him there'.

CHAPTER 14
PICK AND STICK

KERRY PACKER WAS ONE, OF COURSE. So too is James Packer, who has referred to Alan Jones as being 'like an aunt to me'. He is fond of Liberal mates Michael Yabsley, Tony Abbott and Bronwyn Bishop. He is still close to the Whites of 'Belltrees'. Tennis player John Alexander is an old mate and Mark Philippoussis is one of the newer recipients of Jonesy's text messages. There are his rugger buddies: Ross Turnbull, Terry Curley and Simon Poidevin. The cricketers Mark Waugh and Brett Lee are more recent favourites. From racing there are the royal Waterhouses and the breeder–businessman John Messara, said to be his best friend.

He had a curious soul mate in his fellow sponsor of athletes and mentor of young men, Rene Rivkin. Business leaders such as Patrick Stevedores' Chris Corrigan and Qantas chief Geoff Dixon get a good run on his program. His agent, Harry Miller, was another nominee, although socially they did not see a lot of one another, the relationship probably being more businesslike than personal. There are more. He calls his close circle the 'pick and stick' club. It is an expression he might have borrowed during his time at Balmain, even though you could not say the Tigers' slogan, 'Smile and Stick', had worked so well for him.

On radio, in close conversation with James Packer, the expression was part of a projectile vomit of praise. Packer:

'You're a proud Australian, a unique Australian, and we need more Australians like you'. Jones: 'Thank you, James, catch up soon, we pick and stick'. Packer: 'We pick and stick'.[1] Of Liberal powerbroker Michael Kroger, Alan Jones said: 'We talk all the time. He's a very good supporter. We pick and stick. We're in the pick and stick club. We're mates and we've got a little circle of friends and we stick with one another.'[2]

Alan's friends are a sustaining presence in his life. He would tell those he believed were close to him that the power of friendship is always greater than the forces of opposition. He would say: 'We're all loyal, terribly loyal, very loyal. No way you would divide us. But that wins wars. Loyalty.'[3]

However the idea of loyalty as a noble bonding agent only goes so far. It sits nicely with images of diggers in the trenches and footy players reaching for that something extra. Loyalty, however, can also have its roots in blind allegiance and the basest self-interest. Gang rapists stick together. Crooked cops form close covens. Loyalty is a wonderful thing, but not when it stands as a barrier to reason.

Besides, Alan Jones' idea of what constitutes loyalty has its limits. His pool of friendship is a tidal one, regularly refreshed by new and exciting talent. Swimmer Brett Hawke is a recent favourite and Grant Hackett shares ownership with Jones of the racehorse Freestyle.[4] In the mid 1990s it was Chris Fydler and Scott Miller. When Scott Miller shared ownership of a horse with Alan he was fleet and fair, a *Cleo* magazine Bachelor of the Year and a world-class athlete. Alan Jones then described him as the most remarkable Australian swimmer since Dawn Fraser. Scott Miller, who would encounter the odd spot of bother, was another to receive emotional and financial support.

Because a lot of these relationships had a use-by date, it is hard to put all of them in the 'pick and stick' club. And when money was involved there was a worry, one that Alan Jones seemed to share, that the friendship just might be for hire. On different occasions Alan Jones has expressed concern about friends seeming to want him for what he could do for them, more than wanting him for himself.

For similar reasons it is hard to put members of his staff in the 'pick and stick' club. Here, loyalty also has a way of running out. His executive producer, Paul Christenson, has stayed with him since 1990, panel operator Ross Geddes is still there, and a producer, Lyndall Sutton, has largely stayed the course. But the majority came and went. According to one report, 'in ten years Jones had 19 researchers/telephonists (or assistant producers, as they call themselves). Several left with stress related illness.'[5]

It is fair to say that even among these casualties there is often residual goodwill. Alan Jones was cruel and abusive, but many can also remember being moved by acts of kindness. Producer Niamh Kenny was one such witness to a kind of bipolar boss. Kenny—who baled out in 1996 and later returned only to bale out again[6]—has never forgotten the good side of Alan, despite cataclysmic disagreements. The sponsors too, and through the late 1990s there would be many more of them, were not exactly permanent fixtures. Alan Jones' loyalty to Optus, allegedly ideologically based, would last only as long as they kept paying him that $500 000 a year.

Serving politicians, with a similar desire to secure Alan's blessing, don't really fit into 'pick and stick' either. Alan Jones frequently asked Bob Carr to join him for a weekend at Jamberoo, and was none too pleased when the Premier continued to decline. With John Howard he did better. They were, after all, politically closer, but within the PM's office efforts were made to keep Jones from making policy as opposed to thinking he was making policy.

A great many politicians lining up for a chance to be on his program knew Alan Jones had a deep need to be needed. They understood by now that the force field of his power formed around personalities more than politics and policies. It was easier to win Alan with a show of tribute than with a good idea. He does not have a lot of time to listen and, although claiming to be well researched, not a lot of time to read. The key to getting him onside was bound up not only in bundles of cash but also in payments of courtesy, respect and friendship. Despite his constant claim that he was no one's mouthpiece, it was increasingly understood, by media operatives in particular, that Alan Jones could not just be bought and his beliefs retuned, but that it need not cost a fortune.

There is one more group within the 'pick and stick' club that can't be overlooked, and that is Alan's radio audience. His listeners are treated with the same variations of admiration, ambivalence and outright contempt that are common dynamics of extended families. One staff member puts it this way: 'He can't communicate. He has no empathy. He is contemptuous of people on Struggle Street. He hates average people. He says to us, "How am I supposed to help everyone? These people!" He is not naturally warm. It is a big act.'

And another says, 'He really does care ... He would go out of his way to help. I think his heart is in the right place ... People think he is amazing because he takes an interest.' A protean Alan loves them too. His gift of sounding as though he believes melds with a talent for making morning radio personal. According to another fellow traveller: 'They find it comforting to hear him. He seems so strong, it makes them feel safe. It's his strength and reassurance. Almost like they are listening to Daddy.'

Through the 1990s, 2UE had the oldest radio audience in Sydney. It was a demographic not well catered for, and Alan Jones captured double the figures of his closest competitor for these older listeners: 50 per cent of his audience was over the age of 65; almost 60 per cent were over 55; 80 per cent were over 40.[7] Here was another important secret of Alan's success. While the rest of the industry turned its attention to the Coca-Cola generation, Alan Jones had huge sway with the aging demographic. Surveys showed his listeners as predominantly lower middle class retirees from Sydney's south and southwest, and more likely female. It may have been that, like Alan, many were also lonely. They had picked him back in the 1980s and now they stuck to him. They loved him, loved him, loved him and he loved and hated them in return.

One of the reasons they loved him was the way he stood up for them and got things done. Alan was their barking dog, baying before the might of institutions such as Westpac and AMP. Banking issues had long got a good run on Jones' program, Alan giving his attention to the constant closure of bank branches, particularly in the bush. He was generally in agreement with his listeners about the bastardry of banks, complaining that their fees were a modern form of 'highway robbery'.

Ironically, this made him valuable to these organisations. The banks, well capable of paying for premium media advice, knew that if they could not completely control the media, they could have a hand in setting the agenda. Implicit in the endorsement agreements offered to the likes of Alan Jones, John Laws and others was the assumption that the mouthpiece would not bite the hand that fed it.

'Mouthpiece' was the precise word used by the State Bank of New South Wales when, in 1996, it hired Alan Jones. At the end of May, the bank's head of marketing, Lorna Davis, wrote to Harry Miller stating that in principle they were interested in working with Jones: 'His understanding of how a large percentage of the public thinks is well known and his ability to explain complex concepts simply, is extraordinary'.[8] Davis went on to propose Jones be used for live reads, for interviews with experts, charity work in collaboration with the bank, staff training and bank presentations. In later internal correspondence, another executive wrote to Lorna Davis indicating the bank might also have intended to use Jones for damage control: 'If Alan Jones is to be used as a "mouthpiece" for State Bank ... it may be appropriate to also have him undertake some of the more "public" elements proposed in the arrangements ... I think we could run the risk, if we give Alan Jones too much exposure internally, of him being seen as a hired gun rather than as an objective commentator who can, when we need him, put the bank's position forward'.[9] This and a range of correspondence from other sponsors would become important evidence at a later Australian Broadcasting Authority inquiry.

Harry Miller used a familiar bargaining chip, in this case an offer from FAI, telling the bank 'even though it hasn't been signed yet Alan was very vigorous in promoting the State Bank's cause in the last two days and again this morning'.[10] A fee of $300 000 per year for two years was agreed, the arrangement imposing a tax on Jones' objectivity, at least with the State Bank. Clause 2 of the contract did not prevent him bashing other banks, but it required him to confer with the State Bank if an 'event occurred' that might harm the goodwill of the bank, and not to make any 'public utterance' on the subject until he had done so.

In 1996 a longstanding contract with Sony Entertainment was also renegotiated with Alan Jones' royalties advanced to $1.50 per copy sold of recordings such as *Alan Jones Presents Musical Memories from the Fifties*. In subsequent radio and *Today* show editorials, Alan Jones took a strong position in support of the local music industry when the government proposed allowing cheap imported CDs into Australia, arguing that prices of local product would not fall. Alan Jones centred his attack less on federal politicians overseeing the policy than on 'those morons in Treasury'.[11]

Nineteen ninety-six was another busy year. Between July and August, 2UE turned its schedules inside out to accommodate the Atlanta Olympics. It turned out to be a stressful experience, more so perhaps for the production staff than for Alan Jones himself.

Jones broadcast live from Atlanta with a small support group, working difficult days. They had to chase hard to stay on top of the results, let alone broadcast three and a half hours of live radio from the other side of the world. Their apartment block, the Peachtree Loft, with bare floors, exposed and noisy concrete pipes, and no room service, was no treat to come back to after a 12-hour day.

Alan Jones' enthusiasm for sport and his ability to convey the moment made an impact on his hard-pressed colleagues: 'He was amazing during the Olympics. He would research all the stuff and retain it. He'd then spew it out and make it sound 100 per cent.' But it still wasn't fun and Alan might have been a tad unhappy too.

His colleagues saw how he wasn't noticed in the United States. When he travelled to England his rugby credentials gave him some profile, but in Atlanta they did not count for much. This did nothing for his mood. The name 'Alan Jones' did not galvanise publicists in the way it did in Australia. Alan's appointment book was too often empty when he could have been dining with other famous people. Production staff had trouble getting celebrity interviewees. When US gymnast Mary Lou Retton won gold, numerous calls were put in without a single reply.

It was also a disappointing Olympics for Alan Jones' then favourite, Scott Miller. Miller had every right to be proud of the bronze he won in the medley relay and his silver in the 100 metres butterfly, though his good chance of taking gold had been unhappily torpedoed by the Russian, Denis Pankratov, who controversially captured the world record after swimming 85 per cent of the race underwater.

As the Olympics wound down, Alan Jones' tantrums escalated and his notorious mood swings turned monsoonal. 'He was impossible to deal with', said one colleague. On the phone back to 2UE, Alan Jones told the program director that 'everyone was useless over there'. When she returned from Atlanta Niamh Kenny is remembered for abusing management for allowing Jones' ego to run out of the stadium. Dissatisfied with their response, she resigned.

Many of Alan Jones' fellow workers believe he is tougher on women. According to one: 'He tells [...] women how to dress. They must look feminine ... He believes women are stupid and should not be given equal status to men.' Another said: 'He did have girls in tears quite often'. And a third: 'He hates women like you wouldn't believe. He was so appalling to his female staff. It was shocking.'

When preparing a profile of Alan Jones that drew on a similar period, journalist David Leser got identical responses. He wrote of Jones screaming at women: '"Don't you know who I am?" ... "I am Alan Jones ..." "I am not shouting", he was heard shouting. "Aren't you aware of my profile? Get out, get out ..." "We have all worked very hard for him", said one former staffer, and showed him the kind of loyalty he demands. But his loyalty to his staff can be very lacking. Says another: "Alan seems to have a problem with women. He treats us like we have no business being in the workforce. His language is gutter level".'[12]

Alan Jones maintains to this day that he does not swear in front of women, an assertion that must cause teeth to grind in that revolving door of departing female employees. Months after Niamh Kenny resigned, Alan Jones' personal assistant, Jill Newcombe, also left, after suffering a nervous breakdown. Housekeeper, Barbara Roughsedge was another casualty. A motherly regard for Jones over time turned into something very different; Roughsedge was not able to cope with the three different mood swings in a single hour. Friends say it took her two years to get over an acrimonious separation. When Jones was confronted about his treatment of these women, he would not make eye contact or apologise. Some felt his bad behaviour and complaints about trivial matters were part of a deliberate strategy to move them on. It was as if their time had passed, the crush was over and they were made more and more aware that Alan did not want them anymore.

Jill Newcombe's replacement, Micki Braithwaite, had worked at New South Wales Rugby League headquarters as personal assistant to Chief Executive Officer John Quayle. Although there were more high tension moments, she became an efficient and loyal gatekeeper until moving on to a job with Channel 9 a decade later.

Barbara Roughsedge was replaced with the first of a range of male butlers. Alan must have felt it was at last safe to overrule earlier advice. Black, and expressly camp, the new butler made quite an impression when receiving the hats and coats of arriving guests.

Beyond the butler at the door, Alan Belford Jones also now appreciated the comfort of a sleek black Mercedes-Benz in his garage. Mercedes-Benz is another sponsor to value Alan Jones' live reads and access to an aspirational Struggle Street market. According to David Leser's article: 'Mercedes-Benz reportedly not only provides him with a complimentary car but also offered to send someone to his home to wash it for him'.[13] As well as regularly upgrading cars Jones also changed his drivers. Paul Armour from Strathfield Hire Cars was a regular, but a lot of the chauffeur work still went to footballers he was keen to help. Jacin Sinclair became a semi-permanent driver, as did South Sydney footballer Grant McWhirter. McWhirter, another to witness Jones' generous and miserly spirit, was one more to walk after one too many complaints.

Nineteen ninety-six proved to be another troubling year for their club, South Sydney. The Rabbitohs slipped further down the ladder, finishing second last. In the parallel battle for control of Rugby League, the Australian Rugby League loyalist clubs such as Souths had started the season with a win when a trade practices ruling went against News Limited. Some of Justice Burchett's criticisms of News Limited senior personnel had stung, the judge seeming to share Alan Jones' view that Rupert Murdoch headed an expensive and misguided wrecking crew. But News Limited appealed and in October 1996 was relieved by an important recovery, the Full Bench of the Federal Court overturning Burchett's ruling. This meant that the following year the competition would split into two camps, with ill feeling between Jones and News persisting as the fortunes of Souths continued to fade.

October 1996 also saw an extension of Alan Jones' endorsement portfolio with Harry Miller pulling off another deal, this time with the Australian fruit juice company Sunraysia. A contract worth between $10 000 and $20 000 a year was drawn up, with an incentive clause for additional payments if case sales in his broadcast areas exceeded 10 per cent of the monthly average. The contract stated that 'Belford shall ensure that Alan Jones will use his best endeavours where possible on 2UE to endorse the Sunraysia products ... These endorsements will be in addition to the live reads currently undertaken as part of the normal Sunraysia advertising relationship with 2UE.'[14]

As with the Sony deal, the Sunraysia deal was accompanied by a Jones campaign opposing foreign competition. Alan Jones attacked Primary Industry Minister and ex-King's student John Anderson over import policy. Jones was now being paid to do the bullying he used to do for free. 'John Anderson, you're a joke, an absolute joke.'[15] 'John Anderson, I mean, he's got the use-by date on him. He's got the stamp right across his forehead ... I'm sorry—the bloke's got rocks in his head ...'[16] 'He's an absolute joke that John Anderson! That is what he is saying. Raising exports rather than import protection...'[17]

John Anderson attempted to answer his critic point by point, explaining that protecting low value Valencia oranges worth $70 a tonne did not make as much sense as encouraging a higher value export product worth $400 a tonne.[18] It did not convince Jones, who saw that Anderson had made an 'absolute mess of the Primary Industry portfolio' and 'will take bureaucratic advice and nothing else'.[19]

Throughout the campaigning Alan Jones failed to disclose his Sunraysia deal or the tax benefits afforded his own fruit-growing enterprise. Alan Jones had an interest in a vineyard that supplied fruit to a New South Wales winery.

In his defence of Australian enterprise and his business allies, Alan Jones was consistent. While he was attacking Anderson he was defending the Packers, interviewing James Packer on 2UE about how cross-media rules restricted PBL's growth. Packer: 'Well the one thing that you have to recognise in Australia, Alan, is that we have the highest level of any major industrialised country of foreign ownership in our media. The highest.' Jones: 'Foreign ownership in anything, never mind the media, in anything'. Packer: 'Absolutely, absolutely. I mean we've got 90 per cent of our newspapers, we've got Channel 10, you've got pay television. All of those assets are controlled by foreigners.' Jones: 'And yet you haven't read one headline about that in all of this debate. There hasn't been one headline about that. The only headlines are about Packer and Fairfax ... It's a poor show, though, when it comes to pass that an Australian who is successful, who wanted to expand his Australian business, suddenly finds himself the subject of a whole deal of opposition when, in fact, foreign ownership seems to attract no attention at all.' Packer: 'Absolutely. For an Australian company, wanting to use Australian capital to buy an Australian asset that is presently controlled by foreigners, we think that the government should be encouraging more and more companies to do that.' Jones: 'Yep. I have no difficulty with that argument. Good to talk to you.'[20]

Later that year a political ally with a similar belief in protectionism made her maiden speech in the national parliament. One Nation's Pauline Hanson, who hailed from Alan Jones' home country of southeast Queensland, became another favourite with Alan and his audience. Pauline Hanson's 10 September speech, making clear her dislike of economists, Aboriginal land rights, Asian immigration and multiculturalism, read like a transcribed summary of the *Alan Jones Show*. Alan Jones has also demonstrated plenty of form in his support for other homespun, simple-message, straight-talking politicians such as Sir Joh Bjelke-Petersen, Bob Katter and Ernie Bridge. As he frequently complains: 'Common sense is regrettably uncommon'.

Alan Jones conducted a poll on his program, finding 98.48 per cent of respondents in favour of Pauline Hanson's views. The poll, and Hanson's apparent harmony with Alan's audience, were further persuasive of his argument that he spoke for the silent majority. A day before the speech a listener told Alan Jones: 'I think you are the greatest thing representing us, and if the people of New South Wales want anything done, it's no use going to anyone else. It's Alan Jones, mate, believe me and I appreciate what you are doing for the people.'[21]

A day after the speech another said: 'For over 20 years I've felt unrepresented in parliament. And every night I've said a prayer saying, please God when I wake up let me be a non-English speaking or black lesbian unmarried mother. And every morning

I wake up I am still a 70-year-old Anglo-Saxon who worked all her life. My husband and I paid our house off, we never had a bean of a handout from the government and hallelujah along comes Pauline ... and I say thank God ... I feel at last I have someone speaking for me in parliament.'[22]

Alan Jones was clever and cowardly in riding the Hanson wave without getting too wet. He claimed he was supporting free speech rather than Pauline Hanson. As he told his listeners, 'Some people only believe in democracy when it suits them'. Alan's expansiveness about free speech did not extend to political groups such as the Greens, who were unrelentingly disparaged. Nor did his argument for moderating the vilification of Pauline Hanson curb his own language in his attacks on politicians such as Tasmanian Greens Senator Bob Brown, who was also elected to federal parliament in 1996.

The emergence of Pauline Hanson as a political force did draw attention to weaknesses within media and politics in attending to the interests of Australians who felt left out of public debate. But once Pauline Hanson made it on stage, the mainstream media paid attention, on the one hand ridiculing, on the other, monitoring talkback responses. Politicians such as Bob Carr, who had helped legitimise the populist forum, were now paying a price. In her early months the Member for Oxley and her One Nation party gained enough momentum for the major parties to worry and take measures to neutralise her. This created some difficulties within Alan Jones' sometimes complex network of loyalties. The senior Liberal invested with the task of riding shotgun on Hanson, Employment Services Minister Tony Abbott, was an Alan Jones' confidant—close enough for their disagreements over Hanson to largely play out in private.

This was not the case with Bob Carr. Pauline Hanson was a first major spike in what had been a warmer relationship. The conservative, intellectual Carr had no time for Hanson, seeing her policy platform as divisive, simplistic and illogical. According to staff, he was exasperated when Alan Jones and others continued to give her oxygen. Jones' line, in turn, was that

Hanson existed because of the 'bumbling' of leaders like Fraser, Hawke and Keating.

After the summer break at the end of 1996, the contracts continued to roll in. The timing of one deal is deserving of the closest scrutiny. Soon after he came back on air in 1997, Alan Jones raised queries about the Walker Corporation's sudden withdrawal from sale of the Woolloomooloo Finger Wharf apartments. The Walker and Multiplex consortium proposed a range of luxury waterfront apartments, some selling for $3 million, as well as a hotel, restaurant and marina development. Alan Jones said: 'It leaves open the suspicion expressed by one buyer that the rush of purchasers may have made the developers think they were offering the apartments too cheaply'.[23]

In March, Harry Miller spoke to Lang Walker about Alan Jones helping out with the public image of the big-end-of-town developer. Jones would be required to do live reads bought separately through an advertising agency, which would be interspersed with 'off the cuff comments about Walker and specific projects'.[24] What was suspicious about the deal was the prospect that the developers wanted Alan Jones' silence as well as his approval. According to a Miller file note, Walker's was 'anxious to prevent an "anti-development" campaign'.[25] A day after the meeting the developer offered either a straight fee of $200 000 a year for three years, or one tied to the share price.

Jones' later claim that his opinions were quarantined from commercial influence did not sit well with a deal in which payments were tied to the share price. Belford Productions was offered a $200 000 bonus if the shares reached $3.50.[26] Harry Miller did some quick projections, concluding: 'the bottom line is if all these share prices happen Alan Jones would get a fee of $1,750,000'.[27]

Another big deal—which would become another big deal—was agreed soon after. Through the early 1990s Alan Jones was flying free around Australia courtesy of the second major carrier, Ansett.[28] In April, Harry Miller was in negotiation with competitor Qantas. Miller said that 'Alan would rather form a permanent relationship with Qantas than Ansett'.[29] Qantas first proposed $100 000 cash a year and $100 000 contra—that is, services such as airfares to that value. This was helpful to Jones who was frequently using his connections to obtain flights for needy travellers. The athlete Dean Capobianco, at this stage staying in Alan Jones' house, had already been helped in this way by Qantas.[30]

There was a bit of argy-bargy, and in the end Qantas agreed to a two-year deal whereby they would pay Jones $100 000 a year, plus $50 000 contra and two first class Sydney–London return tickets for Jones every year. Harry Miller's conventional 20 per cent cut gave him $20 000 of the retainer and $10 000 of the contra.[31] In return Alan Jones accepted an obligation that involved regular on air editorial comments on topics proposed by Qantas. Public Affairs Manager Bernard Shirley and Qantas boss Geoff Dixon would liaise with Alan Jones and keep him up to date with developments.

While Alan retained the right to consider what was 'appropriate', Qantas trusted he would accept their word and do the right thing. In the following years, as was later revealed, Jones would take up the cudgels for Qantas over deregulation and Sydney's proposed second airport.[32] The arm's length arrangement struck through Belford Productions allowed Alan Jones to argue later that, despite his listeners' lack of awareness of his commercial arrangements, these beliefs were sincerely held, and uninfluenced by all that money and the personal briefings. There was a further shield in the form of Harry Miller himself. Jones believed it was Miller's job to be on top of the detail of the contractual obligations, freeing him from the burden of fully understanding his own contract.

Not that any of it was true. There was plenty of evidence to show Alan Jones kept up with what was required of him. Two months into the Qantas contract he wrote to Miller after he was asked to launch a duty-free range at the international airport: 'What are my contractual obligations. Ideally shouldn't all these things go through your office in order to "filter them" first.'[33]

A memo he wrote to Harry Miller one month later demonstrated his awareness of the share price deal with the Walker Corporation: 'Harry, please get back to me on two issues. The share price. Who in our office is monitoring that? The Piano Factory and the Wharf. I need to discuss both with you.' Jones also spoke of being 'jacked off about the stuff in relation to the coffee business'.[34]

This was a reference to another Miller deal. Jones and 2UE were hawking 'Alan Jones breakfast blend' coffee. Harry Miller had worked out that on a worse case scenario if 100 000 of his listeners bought four packets a year, they would share $140 000, but the arrangement had led to a few problems. For seven years Alan Jones had also given live endorsements of Vittoria Coffee. Suppliers Cantarella Brothers were annoyed, complaining to 2UE about Jones' counter-loyalty and cancelling their $150 000 advertising contract with 2UE.[35]

The Australian Food Council also took issue with claims being made about the coffee. Alan Jones told listeners: 'I'm proud to have put my name to what I believe is the best coffee in Australia. The Alan Jones Breakfast Club Special Selection, with its full rich aroma and great taste is a better brew by far. I mean, how many other coffees made in Australia are wood-roasted? The answer is none! This special process makes for a better cup of coffee; and because there's less acidity and less caffeine, it's better for you!'[36]

The Food Council responded: 'There appear to be a number of inaccurate and misleading claims in the promotion. Specifically it is claimed that wood roasting of the coffee beans not only lowers the caffeine and acid content but actually "gets rid of" all the caffeine. We are unaware of any technical or scientific basis for such a claim.'[37] Despite his personal endorsement and giving the impression he was closely involved with the product, Alan Jones expected this sort of detail to be managed by the people who were decaffeinating their 20 per cent. Accordingly, Jones got Miller to take it up with his sponsor.

Miller had also sweetened the deal with the increasingly

prosperous Walker Corporation. Jones' agent thought that an increase in the retainer plus 'a serious carrot—a windfall, shares, apartment or whatever to notch the deal up to $1,000,000' would do it.[38] As part of an improved deal, Jones was offered a cut-price luxury apartment at the Woolloomooloo wharf. A Miller office file note reported a conversation with Geoff Davey from Walker Corporation: 'He also said that the correct value of the discount should have been $187,500 but that it had been rounded up by HMM on behalf of AJ to $190,000. AJ received a "free" $2,500 discount on his apartment through HMM negotiations. As Geoff Davey said "That's Harry for you".'[39]

Alan Jones was later reported as paying $1.49 million for the apartment, which overlooked Woolloomooloo Bay.[40] He could certainly afford it. Deal upon deal meant Alan Jones was pulling in more than he could easily keep an eye on. At 2UE his prime time live reads were now charged out at $1100 for 30 seconds. Beyond a bonus for reading them as scheduled, he received 50 per cent of the payments for the prerecorded reads.

The butler, chauffeured Mercedes and luxury properties did not stop Alan Jones talking constantly on air about humble beginnings and never taking a holiday. The drift from Struggle Street was more a puzzle to his staff, who wondered at his attacks on others for losing touch when Alan himself 'never put petrol in his car or bought a pint of milk'. When the electronic funds transfer system was introduced, Alan Jones scoffed at briefing notes about EFTPOS, declaring 'nobody would have a clue what that means'.

The property portfolio further expanded. The native Queenslander acquired two units in the Lloyd Williams Crown Towers development at Surfers Paradise, one for $332 000, the other $620 000. Jones' Queensland properties were made available to friends in need.

As he had done with Jacin Sinclair, he also applied a helping hand to his protégés' own investments. The *Daily Telegraph* reported that swimmer Scott Miller purchased a 'plush $590 000 Manly home ... with the guidance of his friend broadcaster, Alan

Jones'.[41] Scott Miller, a keen punter, would also share ownership in a racehorse, For a Lark, with Alan Jones and James Packer.[42] As also happened with Jacin Sinclair, Scott Miller's athletics career was going backwards. There was a series of bad news stories for Jones' protégé. Scott Miller had tested positive for marijuana use and then, following a nightclub scuffle, was expelled from the Australian Institute of Sport (AIS).[43] Institute Director John Boultbee, investigating the story after it hit the press, discovered Miller had also missed a series of training sessions.

Boultbee, who had given Miller his place partly as a result of urging by Jones, felt he had no choice but to let the swimmer go. An enraged Alan Jones let John Boultbee have it on air and over the telephone: 'It was a tirade. He was very abusive. He did not want to hear my reasons, which were not related to the fight but the non-attendance at training. Jones threatened: "We will get you for this". There was no acknowledgement of Miller's fault in the matter. When I tried to explain the facts he just ignored me.'

When factoring deals with Alan Jones media executives should by now have been clever enough to figure that one way to please him was to ensure you did not displease his boys. When Scott Miller lost his $25 000 scholarship with the AIS, another more lucrative deal was arranged with Westfield. In the run-up to the Sydney 2000 Olympics, the shopping giant entered a range of generous sponsorship agreements with promising athletes.

At the same time, Westfield had a less than easy relationship with Alan Jones. Jones had broadcast false claims that Westfield, controlled by the Jewish Lowy family, had banned the playing of carols before Christmas. Jones was also aware of problems with at least one Westfield franchisee. After a series of on air attacks, Alan Jones and a Westfield representative met to try to settle their differences.

Although the circumstances may not be connected, Westfield agreed to a $100 000 sponsorship deal with Scott Miller. There is some likelihood that the company might have considered swimmers such as Kieren Perkins a better bet. Alan Jones also arranged for Scott Miller to switch management away from Graeme McNeice to Alan Jones' manager, Harry Miller. As it turned out, Scott Miller did not make the 2000 Olympics squad.

At least one of Alan Jones' staff formed a dim view of his mentorship of some of these athletes: 'He thought he was helping them but he was really controlling them, controlling them through money. He'd take away their hunger to win. He would send around chauffeured cars and pick them up to take them to first nights.'

Alan Jones had not completely given up on plans for a sporting comeback of his own. In August 1997, an opportunity, however slight, appeared to present itself when the Wallabies took a thrashing in South Africa. A humiliating 61–22 loss led to coach Greg Smith's resignation. Former rugby official Ross Turnbull pushed the case for his mate's return to his world-favourite job. 'Turnbull made a public (some would say ridiculous) call for the reappointment of Jones to a joint coaching position with Rod Macqueen'.[44] When John O'Neill was asked by the media about a prospective return of Alan Jones to the Wallabies, the ARU boss dismissed the suggestion with words to the effect that they wanted to look forward rather than backward.

After Rod Macqueen won the job solo, Alan Jones had this to say on air: 'John O'Neill, the boss of the ARU, is a failed banker. If he keeps running Australian Rugby the way he is, then he's equally going to destroy the lifeblood of the game, club football. And wherever you go, that's exactly what supporters of the game are saying. Now the appointment of Rod Macqueen as the Australian coach has given a fresh face to the game at a national level. What it now needs is a fresh face administratively. The players deserve better than to be run by ego-trippers like John O'Neill.'[45]

O'Neill, who had formerly headed the State Bank, was on a different occasion praised by Alan Jones as a 'successful banker'. The broadcaster waxed but mostly waned on O'Neill, in private castigating him as a show pony with 'no feel for the real traditions of the game'.[46] On 14 occasions Alan Jones assailed John O'Neill on air. The Australian Rugby Union boss issued defamation proceedings; 2UE later settled, paying O'Neill a reported $50 000.

The end of 1997 saw Alan Jones in busy housemaster mode. Swimmers Scott Miller and Chris Fydler were staying at the Newtown address. Fydler, described by Jones as 'a wonderful young man from the bush', was seen as another battler whose swimming career was waiting to be rescued.

By now Jacin Sinclair had moved on to Sydney City where he finished the season as a reserve for reserve grade. Sinclair was genuinely fond and appreciative of Alan Jones, telling a reporter: 'Jonesy cares about me. He's not worried about anything but me doing well. He says I can ring him whenever I want and he's the godfather for two of my kids. If you're feeling down he always makes you feel good. He'd do anything for anyone but all he cops is a bagging and I've had plenty of stinks over the years because of it.'[47] Sinclair was another to pay for the friendship. The last gasp of a once promising career saw 25-year-old Jacin suspended after spear tackling a player who allegedly made derogatory comments about Jones.[48]

Rugby League player Julian O'Neill also kept Alan Jones busy. In 1997, after being sacked from three clubs, O'Neill was given another chance at Souths. One of a series of sticky episodes was O'Neill's removal from a casino after he urinated at a gaming table. Jones, according to O'Neill, '... deserves a medal for what he has done for me. His door is always open if I have a problem and he always has something positive to say.'[49] As one prominent Souths player put it: 'If your life was well organised, if you went home to your wife and kids and were not one of the weaker characters, you were less likely to get on with Alan'.[50]

The 1997 Rugby League season had been another disappointing one, the Rabbitohs again finishing second last, playing on the ARL side of a split competition. On 19 December, a meeting between the competing gamekeepers promised peace. It did not help the mood at Souths. A condition of an arrangement that saw the warring parties merge was the elimination of four clubs by the year 2000. The poor performance of the once mighty Rabbitohs was a threat now not just to the support base, but to Souths' very survival. After a win in the first round of 1998, the Rabbitohs lost thirteen of the next fourteen games. Club morale sank lower. While the two factions united under the National Rugby League banner, South Sydney was a house divided by internal politicking.

Jones had stood aside as Football Operations Manager, but he was still influential and close to the president, George Piggins. Depending on your position, Jones' presence was greeted with appreciation or derision. The latter was the case when, following pilferage from players' lockers, Jones advised he had applied secret invisible powder that would identify the culprit. In February 1998, there was a similar occurrence at 2UE; this time Sherlock Jones attracted more attention.

When a carton of his special aloe vera tissues went missing along with a telephone, Alan Jones posted a memo: 'There are thieves in the building. This note is to serve notice that I am in possession of a powder which is invisible on surfaces. However once touched it leaves indelible stains for up to five days. So now I'm going to play my game!! It will be left on certain books, pens, phones, staplers, coffee cups, etc. Please feel free to steal these from my office at your risk.'[51]

One employee, out of mischief, had pinched the tissues and, through absent-mindedness, another forgot to return the telephone they'd borrowed. His response was another example of how Alan Jones' exclusive universe and the limits to his emotional intelligence isolate him from the common sense he reveres. It also further isolated him from any goodwill that remained at 2UE. Someone scrawled 'Up Yours' on his note and the next day another memo appeared, signed 'The Thief', declaring that 'special gloves' would defeat the special powder. It was later discovered that Alan Jones even installed secret cameras in his office to expose future delinquency in the affair that the Sydney press gleefully dubbed 'Tissuegate'.

Soon after, Alan Jones showed a very different face, one that supports former Wallaby captain Andrew Slack's view that Alan Jones would help his worst enemy. In early 1998, when another former Wallaby, Ricky Stuart, was stricken with viral encephalitis, Alan Jones rang Kerry Packer and arranged a private jet to transport Stuart from Canberra, where he played Rugby League. Jones was helping not just a Superleague rebel, but the man making the request, John Fordham. 'Fordo', a former member of the 'pick and stick' club, was now on the outer as manager of Jones' key rival in radio, John Laws. (A glutton for punishment, Fordham later also took on management of Jones' rugby rival, Bob Dwyer.)

John Fordham appreciated the help; his hands were full at the time running damage control for John Laws. In March 1998, the ABC's *Media Watch* began the long process of prising open the 2UE stars' Aladdin's cave of sponsorship deals. John Laws was the target, presenter Richard Ackland identifying Laws' contracts with 'people like Qantas, Foxtel, Toyota, and the Home Loan outfit, RAMS. Each of them pay him anything up to a five figure amount every month to broadcast endorsements, embellishments and ad-lib flattery.'[52]

At this stage the attention of *Media Watch* was not on Alan Jones. But at the same time there was an embarrassing outing of Jones, ironically on his own network. Following an appearance by celebrity criminal Mark 'Chopper' Read on another ABC show, there was a chorus of criticism about the public broadcaster allowing an intoxicated Read to defend a life of antisocial behaviour. Alan Jones joined in and on 20 March 1998 was asked to appear on Nine's *Midday* show. Viewers were invited to call in. Both the presenter, Kerri-Anne Kennerley, and her guest, Alan Jones, looked as if they were suddenly stricken by salmonella when 'Chopper' Read himself got on the line, telling Alan Jones: 'People who throw stones better make sure they don't live in glass houses ... I never got arrested in a public toilet in London'.[53]

While the *Midday* appearance caused titters at 2UE, the *Media Watch* repercussions were more serious. 2UE boss John

Conde should not have needed an ABC program to alert him to the on air behaviour of his broadcasters. That his station was being milked was bad enough, but the prospect of damaging publicity and trouble from the regulators also loomed. It is a breach of the broadcasting code to misrepresent material, to present advertisements as news and withhold relevant information from listeners. Worse, it is a breach of the law to extort money from sponsors in order to allay negative commentary. Conde later told of speaking to Alan Jones about his concerns at this time. The discussion had no apparent impact on the deals, which continued to roll in.

In April publishing company HarperCollins offered a monthly retainer of $10 000 plus a bonus of $1 for every endorsed book sold in New South Wales.[54] Alan Jones liked the idea a lot better than he liked hawking coffee. Requests to suggest on air that the prime minister enjoy a cup of Alan Jones Breakfast Blend Coffee had not gone down well. 'Harry, I don't say this very often about matters involving my programme but I think this is an excellent idea. In the first place I think there is tremendous virtue in promoting the notion of literacy and reading and I'd like from them, rather than tax my mind, a few dot points about all of that.'[55]

One of the first authors nominated for promotion was a Jones mate, Jeffrey Archer. The deal was agreed and Jones' touch in the publishing world was soon renowned. If he told his listeners to buy a book, a great many dutifully did. The very promise of a Jones' endorsement became an important factor in the commissioning of a book.

News of his touch in clearing a path for the big property developers was also getting around. Towards the middle of 1998, following the Walker deal, Walsh Bay Finance approached Harry Miller. The building giants Mirvac and Transfield had formed a consortium to redevelop another sensitive stretch of Sydney waterfront, the heritage listed Walsh Bay wharves. As with the Walker deal, Alan Jones' value to the partnership was not clear. Walsh Bay Finance was prepared to pay Jones $200 000 a year 'in order to assist with the development of key media relationships and the general promotion of Walsh Bay and its scheme for redevelopment'.[56] Suspicion again arose that what the developer wanted most was for Alan Jones to avoid laying into them.

On air the day after Walsh Bay confirmed its $200 000 fee, Alan Jones commented on a *Daily Telegraph* article by Piers Akerman that rejected criticism of the development: 'I have to confess to yet again, agreeing with Piers Akerman, which doesn't bother me, I think he's a highly intelligent man who writes beautifully, writing in the *Tele* today, writing about the development of Walsh Bay. Something which I regret to say I've stumbled upon ...'[57]

The following month, when the project still awaited government approval, he thought Walsh Bay a 'fantastic proposal', being strangled by red tape: 'Mirvac and Transfield ... they've put forward this fantastic proposal. Now it is unbelievable. Trust me ... I'm telling you this proposal is fantastic ... Now Craig Knowles, the Premier and Ron Dyer are going to have to shake up a few bureaucrats if the government lets this magnificent proposal slip.'[58]

At this time, with the three-month-old *Media Watch* segment still ringing in his ears, John Conde wrote a memo to staff headed 'Personal Endorsement Agreements'. It asked them to come clean about arrangements he should know about. 'I cannot stress highly enough the potential damage to the integrity and reputation of 2UE should it be perceived that the content of 2UE broadcasts may be dictated by the marketing imperatives of third parties ... 2UE would be greatly concerned, however, if it transpired that an announcer was receiving remuneration direct from a third party to embellish ... advertisements booked with 2UE.'[59]

The memo found a few marks. Harry Miller, offended, replied on Alan Jones' behalf: 'I received a scatter gun fax addressed to "All On-Air Broadcasters" ... without being facetious, I am certain such a notice board circular would not be directed to Alan Jones who (one would assume) as being the Station's top rating Broadcaster, would have had a personal letter addressed to him directly. Having said that, I wish to place on the record that any activities by Alan Jones would come under the existing arrangements and practices between the station and Belford Productions. No doubt if you have some matters that you wish to discuss arising from that contract, I would be grateful if you would advise me directly. Yours sincerely, Harry M. Miller.'[60]

Conde reminded Miller that the Belford Productions contract with 2UE included 'an obligation to observe the policies of the station'.[61] Conde went on to explain that he had already discussed the issue with Jones. A similar discussion with John Laws would later be disputed. Soon after the July memo was circulated, Laws said he and Conde met in a 2UE corridor. When the subject of the memo was raised, Laws claimed Conde said, 'This doesn't necessarily apply to you' and, gesturing towards Jones' office, added something like, 'it's more for you know who'.[62] Conde later denied giving Laws implied consent to carry on as before. Indeed, he denied the conversation ever occurred.

John Laws and Alan Jones were disinclined to see fault in their own behaviour, but were happy to see each other brought to book. Their testy relationship was not helped by an interview Laws conducted at this time with another broadcaster Jones loathed, Andrew Denton. Denton's own radio program regularly spoofed Alan Jones, comedian Dave Gibson enthusing so much about Jones' love of 'The Poo' (tennis player Mark Philippoussis) that Gibson and Denton were left rolling on the floor.

On 11 August, the following exchange occurred on John Laws' Foxtel interview program. Denton: '... how much of this do you edit by the way?' Laws: 'Not much'. Denton: 'You'll edit this bit. I want to run a competition to get Jonesy laid, nothing to do with his sexuality. It's to do with, we know the type. Very stressed out people, very tense people who are very angry about a lot of things and who just, sometimes you just need a good root to calm yourself down and I think that's what Alan needs, I really do.'[63] The segment was not edited, no doubt lifting Laws and Denton a notch higher on Jones' black list.

Months after his July memo, John Conde was not aware of the full extent of Jones' and Laws' endorsement agreements. He knew they had the right to work outside 2UE and was respectful of commercial privacy considerations. Although he later came to the view Alan Jones was 'equivocal', he had read Jones' response at the time 'as assuring me he had no such arrangements'.[64] Conde understood the Optus relationship was still somehow clinically separated from Jones' work at 2UE. Beyond a raft of others, he did not know about the Qantas and the State Bank deals, nor the new Mirvac–Transfield contract.

On 21 August Jones told his listeners that Bob Carr would that day be announcing the go-ahead for the developer's Walsh Bay proposal. Jones interviewed the Premier and told his listeners: 'I've looked at this in detail, and I think it is a magnificent, integrated embellishment of what is a forlorn but significantly historic area'.[65] Following a protest rally a few days later Alan Jones again applauded the project.

The perception that Alan Jones' power extended to rearranging the Sydney skyline put him in a curious position with his client the State Bank. In 1998 the bank, purchased by the Colonial Group of companies, was going through a restructure which saw it emerge as the Colonial State Bank. Alan Jones had earlier given Colonial trouble over their purchase of a piece of land considered by many to be Sydney's finest. Number 1 Macquarie Street, on Bennelong Point, is the nearest neighbour to the world famous Sydney Opera House. In the mid 1990s, after a ten-year battle, Colonial and Hong Kong and Shanghai Hotels built the infamous 'Toaster', a box of luxury apartments, shops and restaurants a short stroll from Circular Quay.

At the time, Alan Jones joined a clamour of protest, describing the development as a 'monstrosity' that would make a 'mess' of the Quay.[66] Jones did not like the exclusiveness of a property more available to wealthy foreigners than ordinary Australians. He did not like it blocking the view of the Opera House, opting for a rival project proposing a taller, wineglass-shaped building. Early in 1997, Alan Jones still maintained his criticism of Colonial's role at East Circular Quay.

On 19 September 1998, Alan Jones' contract with the restructured Colonial State Bank was due for renewal. Belford Productions and the Colonial State Bank agreed to a new contract defining 'certain services' Alan Jones was expected to fulfil. He was to act 'with professional skill as an advocate for and a consultant to Colonial State Bank with a view to promoting, enhancing and improving the reputation, image and goodwill of Colonial State Bank and its products and services'. The 1996 clause, which gave the bank forewarning of any potential adverse public utterances, was retained. Jones also got a rise. His new annual fee of $433 000 boosted his and Harry's annual take by $83 000.

The bank also negotiated for as much time with a busy Jones as he could manage so they could understand the way he operated on air. They would deny that the purpose of the meetings and the briefing notes was for the sake of securing favourable mentions. The bank also rejected any suggestion that a further purpose was to buy Alan Jones' silence. Their need to talk to Jones before a potential bad news story was, they claimed, for the sake of informing him. Soon after the lunch to celebrate the new contract, the bank sent Jones a press release about an education day. Alan Jones introduced the item: 'Here is a good story ...'[67] Over the period of the new contract there would be more good stories.

At the same time as the bank deal renewal was due, so too was the Optus contract. In the preceding months Harry Miller wrote to Optus telling them Alan Jones had been doing a good job savaging the competition. 'Alan says it's vital that you listen in the morning as he is doing a really heavy piece about Greyhound Coaches suing Telstra. They are launching (and asking other companies to join them) a class action against Telstra over backdated telephone bills.'[68]

Since his last Optus contract there had been a change of guard. Former newspaper editors Chris Anderson and Max Suich were, respectively, new CEO and director of marketing. There had been a change in the camp of the enemy too: a still part-publicly owned

Telecom was renamed Telstra. Chris Anderson sent a handwritten note to Alan Jones after a landmark ratings win: 'Dear Alan, Thanks for your continued push for competition—and lower prices—in telecommunications. It is a big one—and one (if they have the sense) that could be a big winner for the government. Congratulations too on 50 in a row! You're amazing! Regards, Chris Anderson.'[69]

There were more faxes to Anderson and Suich, making them aware of Jones' work 'exposing the Telstra atrocities'.[70] But Optus was not entirely happy with the bang they were getting for their ten thousand bucks a week, and Alan Jones was still waiting for his pay TV program. Internal Optus correspondence complained: 'No evidence that AJ is using our prompts to embellish the scripts. What is unclear is whether AJ sees his role as one which promotes and delivers a pro-Optus stance on major issues (ie local call resale), in which case he will say he is delivering (ie i/v with Alston on competition and the local call market ...) or whether he is prepared to "stretch" our advertising dollar by editorialising.'[71]

Optus felt it should be getting two or three mentions a week. Harry Miller thought they were doing just fine. 'I assume you are aware of Alan's huge burst yesterday in regard to local telephone calls and the disgraceful situation that exists with Telstra. His advocacy was extremely powerful yesterday.'[72] Suich replied in a conciliatory tone, assuring Miller that Jones' 'advocacy' was appreciated and asking: 'Finally our scripts sent for possible use on Friday were not used. If there's a problem with the tone I'll discuss with Alan when we lunch shortly.'[73]

Max Suich got a little annoyed with Harry Miller's hustle. 'What about a little give? We're committing $2.25 million to your client. I have disobeyed the CEO's instructions to agree to no more than our last contract price; your client's contract is extremely open yet your phone seems to be emerging as some sort of deal breaker. What's going on?'[74] Sponsorship Manager Alexandra Lutyens was put on the case. The next day Harry Miller sent a gushing fax: 'You are a stylish and intelligent woman and I believe your communication today was quite fantastic. Congratulations ... I am indeed looking forward to meeting you in the near future. Regards, Harry M Miller. PS Alan Jones also read your reply and thinks you are a pretty special person.'[75]

Lutyens sent Jones more talking points, which did appear to lure the Parrot back onto the perch. 'Dear Alexandra, Thank you for your note on July 21 about Optus Update. What an excellent idea. I gave it a real bash the other day. Please make contact with Micki to see how this applies to my mobile. Over to you. I hope the publicity helped. Don't be afraid to be in touch at any time. With best wishes, yours sincerely Alan Jones.'[76]

On 18 September the new deal with Optus was struck: Belford Productions would receive $500 000 per annum plus CPI increases in the second and third years. The contract would run to 31 December 2001. The incentive payments were deleted. Alan Jones pushed Optus on a range of further occasions, using Optus talking points. Again his listeners could have readily mistaken the commentary for editorial opinion. Optus had indeed stretched its advertising dollar.

It was also another busy political period. The strings tying Alan Jones to his political mates were much the same as those connecting him to his corporate ventriloquists. The New South Wales Labor government, wary of offence, was forewarning Alan Jones of new policy. The government had also overruled another recommendation that Alan Jones be charged with contempt of court. After an August broadcast in which Jones spoke about the trial of gangster Neddy Smith, the trial judge claimed that Alan Jones' comments transgressed 'all the principles of reporting court matters'.[77]

Jones pushed the interests of another mate, Dr Marlene Goldsmith, to fill a Liberal Senate vacancy. The more favoured candidate, Marise Payne, a small 'l' former senior advisor to Liberals such as Ted Pickering and John Fahey, was disliked. On 14 March 1997 Jones wrote to Goldsmith: 'Dear Marlene, Thank you for your note. How is the pre-selection going? Can I help in any way by giving one or two people a stab or a lift? If in need ring Georgina ... and she will take down anything you need. With best wishes. Alan Jones.'[78]

Marlene Goldsmith replied two days later: 'Dear Alan, How do I thank you for your generosity and kindness? I regard your good opinion—coming as it does from one of Sydney's most incisive intellects—as something to be treasured in its own right, quite apart from your considerable media clout ... However regarding your generous offer of assistance, it would be improper of me to ask you to assist me. Warmest regards, Dr Marlene Goldsmith.'[79]

Alan Jones helped anyway. On air the next day he said of his preferred candidate: 'Marlene Goldsmith [has] ... a very clear view of social issues ... and a bit of scholarship which enables her to understand them'. And of graduate in law and arts, Marise Payne: 'This is a woman who on a range of fronts has criticised John Howard ... She also supports Australia becoming a Republic which she is entitled to do, but how could the Liberal Party consider choosing someone who publicly has criticised her leader?'[80]

Alan Jones continued to observe his protected species approach to 'pick and stick' mates. When former King's student John Sharp, then Federal Transport Minister, was forced to repay over $8740 worth of travel allowance, the story ran on the front page of the papers. On the same day Sharp came on 2UE, and Jones introduced his friend with the words: 'I should say at the outset that I organised the interview with Mr Sharp yesterday morning. Since then there has been a story raised about Mr Sharp's TA allowance and Mr Sharp has elected not to speak on that matter. That is entirely right. He will speak when he sees fit.'[81] So the story of the day was ignored and rorting by maritime workers given a workout instead. Later that day John Sharp resigned.

The 1998 Maritime Union of Australia (MUA) dispute was a new catalyst for the cooling of the romance between Alan Jones and Premier Bob Carr. Between January and April, trouble spread from berth 5 at Melbourne's Webb Dock, with maritime workers locked out by Patrick Stevedores and police unable to contain the violence.

Alan Jones, who was both courted by and well disposed toward elements of the union movement, this time backed the federal government and executive chairman Chris Corrigan of Patrick Stevedores. Patrick and its lawyers were in close contact with Jones. Patrick's union-busting chief wanted police to take a tougher line with the picketers, many of whom were women and children. Jones joined the call when the dispute spread to Sydney. On 2UE he urged the police to get tough. He was heard publicly wishing for the return of 'one hundred Roger Rogersons'. (Rogerson, Australia's most notorious police officer, known for being tough as well as crooked, was by now vanquished by a decade-long anti-police corruption purge.)

One who had taken to dropping in on Jones was the new police commissioner, Peter Ryan, who in August 1996 took over a job that a then sympathetic Jones said was more difficult than governing Papua New Guinea. Having arrived from the United Kingdom and wary of his new environment, Peter Ryan listened to advice from Alan Jones and, like other senior police, attended to Jones' many requests. But the MUA dispute seemed to trigger a change in attitude towards a previously accommodating police commissioner. Alan Jones laid into Peter Ryan, calling him useless for not taking more forceful action. Ryan, having sought advice, ordered his officers to keep the peace rather than enforce a court injunction by breaching the pickets. 'Jones' attacks on me continued on and on. He was constantly pushing Patrick's point. It was always Patrick's that were mentioned. I thought this was going well beyond reasonable interest and comment on the matter. He was saying, "For God's sake, Commissioner, get down there and get blood on your hands". I rang him and, on air, asked him, "Whose blood, Alan, women's and children's?"'[82]

Alan Jones' anger can be intimidating to interviewees who might mistake it as born of personal conviction. Bob Carr appeared to understand otherwise. He generally agreed to debate

Alan Jones, even when the broadcaster was at his frothing worst. At 7.19 am on 3 June 1998, Bob Carr and Alan Jones had their first major public barney. Jones introduced the interview with a warning to Carr that he was not listening to the electorate. Jones had earlier criticised Carr for moving the governor out of Government House. He saw this and the rise of Pauline Hanson as consequences of arrogant politicians pursuing an agenda without consultation with the people.

As with Peter Ryan, he told Bob Carr off for not getting tough on the waterfront protesters: 'An injunction was issued by the Supreme Court against picketing at Botany Bay and you, the Premier of the state, did not lift a finger to support the injunction'.

Carr: 'Alan, the government received advice from no less than the Crown Solicitor about the Supreme Court decision on April 15th ... He said the injunction was civil in nature, the injunction simply has nothing to say to police officers, this is the Crown Solicitor, Alan.'

Jones: 'You shouldn't need an injunction, the Crimes Act makes what was happening at Botany a crime ... they were in breach of the law and you wouldn't uphold it'. Jones and Carr talked over the top of one another for minutes more with Jones concluding: 'You were gutless, Premier, in the face of the Maritime Union. You're frightened of them.' It went on for more minutes before Jones switched to Hanson: 'Do you understand that Pauline Hanson factor that people are just sick of politicians doing it their way and not the way that the electorate perceives it should be done, do you understand that?'

The ground shifted. Jones was used to doing the attacking, with victims swinging like limp punching bags. Carr swung back and Jones might have got a tiny fright. Carr: 'Alan, I think it's deplorable that you are supporting Pauline Hanson. I'd like to explain to you the damage that she is doing to this country. That she is doing to our exports, that she is doing to the sale of Australian services throughout the world and Australian products throughout the world.' Jones: 'Who said I was supporting Pauline Hanson?' Carr: 'Well you've been going at it nonstop'.[83]

It was never quite the same after that. You are not supposed to debate Alan and win. The timing is also important. The interview followed a succession of disagreements and occurred nine months out from a new election. A day before the interview Alan Jones wrote a confidential letter to Opposition Leader Peter Collins, signalling a possible preparedness to release him from the freezer. For some time Collins had been trying to get Jones to see him. A meeting was brokered by Harry Miller and on 26 May 1998 Peter Collins and Alan Jones finally sat down together.

According to Collins, Jones did most of the talking, criticising the Opposition for not having policies. He even criticised the Opposition leader for not taking notes during the meeting. Peter Collins says he told Alan Jones he was taking in what was being said and to prove it would send him a summarised account of the meeting.

Collins' letter to Alan Jones was something of a white flag, revealing more than Peter Collins' surrender. It documented the pre-election issues that mattered as far as Alan Jones was concerned, as well as the broadcaster's observations about the calibre of Collins' team. Significantly, he regarded Kerry Chikarovski as 'non existent'. Alan Jones' views on back-to-basics policing and his disappointment with Commissioner Ryan over the MUA fracas was also evident. The Collins–Jones manifesto is reproduced in full in the endnotes because it offers a rare opportunity to reveal the degree of Alan Jones' politicking, and the preparedness of politicians to defer to the broadcaster.[84]

On 2 June Jones wrote back: 'Dear Peter, I said I'd mark you out of 10. It's certainly worth 8. Better typing would have given you a 9!! I'm happy to discuss the detail of any of these further if that is necessary. I won't go into further print here. With best wishes, Alan Jones.[85]

Clearly Jones was not shy about articulating and prioritising policy and he expected his advice to be followed. There is little doubt that neither Collins nor Jones had an honest regard for one another, but both seemed prepared, and in Collins' case eager, to exploit a working relationship. Alan Jones may have given consideration to supporting Peter Collins more for the sake of obtaining greater leverage over a recalcitrant Bob Carr. If so, the strategy was short-lived.

Jones' attention was soon turned to a bigger show. On 31 August 1998 John Howard sniffed the wind and called an early election. The campaign preceding the 3 October poll would be short and intense, with Alan Jones praising the government and damning Labor. 'The Rehame study found that during the campaign Jones mentioned the coalition tax package 32 times, and not one comment was negative (59 per cent were neutral, 41 per cent positive). By comparison he mentioned the ALP tax package 22 times, and not one comment was positive (45 per cent were neutral, 55 per cent negative). Also, Jones did four interviews with John Howard, and only one with Kim Beazley, during which he said Beazley was a liar.'[86] Following John Howard's second victory, Alan Jones' mate Michael Kroger said on the ABC's *Lateline* that Jones had played a 'pivotal role in delivering the Liberals' message to marginal seats'.[87]

The most vocal critic of Jones' partisanship was not so much Labor as Laws. Jones' 2UE colleague gave an interview to the *Daily Telegraph* saying that he would never reveal how he voted and thought that commentators who did 'become a whore, you're just used then. You're Lord Haw Haw of an election battle ... or Tokyo Rose.'[88] Their boss, John Conde, tried to hose the flames but did not stop John Laws going on Channel 9's *A Current Affair* to repeat his attack. Alan Jones defended his support of John Howard, pointing out '... that he was entitled to his opinion, and entitled to air it, and that, after all, was why his program was called The Alan Jones Show'.[89]

To a correspondent, Alan Jones cited his popularity as further justification: '... one commentator ... for reasons that only he could understand, suggested that my coverage wasn't "objective". I have to say that the conclusions that I reached were consistent with the conclusions that were reached by most editorial writers in the country. You don't have time in radio to be on anyone's side. You have got to be on the side of the truth. And at the end of the day, the public will decide whether you are "pushing barrows". My ratings would suggest that the public have already made their decision on that. This program continued to rate during the election and after, far in excess of any other program on Sydney radio.'[90]

In November 1998 the Howard Government made Alan Jones deputy chairman of the Australian Institute of Sport. By now Jones had been a member of the Sydney Cricket Ground Trust for ten years. One member said in that time he had, from a green beginning, evolved into a brilliant and deft lobbyist; indeed a 'perfect board member'. Jones was also an effective member of the New South Wales Institute of Sport so had readily earned his place within the ranks of those hated sports officials. The Opposition spokesman on sport, Kate Lundy, said the appointment to the Australian Institute of Sport was 'more than curious given his political affiliations. Could it be said that Mr Jones is being appointed as some kind of special thank you for his clear support for the Coalition during the last election?'[91] A story later emerged that the government had intended only to offer him a directorship but a clerical error meant the wrong message was sent; the error was detected only after Alan Jones had received the papers at his Newtown address and duly signed them.[92]

In December, with a state election due the following March, any faint prospect that Alan Jones might support Peter Collins in the way he supported John Howard was dashed. The New South Wales Liberals have developed a habit of dumping leaders. A challenge was hatched, the hatchers observing the convention of seeking Alan's sanction before proceeding. Jones has admitted receiving a telephone call, which he says indicated 'someone in the Liberal Party had taken leave of their senses'.[93] On 4 December 1998 it was Peter Collins' turn. And who replaced him? The person Jones had referred to in his manifesto as 'non existent': Kerry Chikarovski. In the foreword to Chikarovski's later autobiography, Jones takes a different position: 'I pointed out to my caller that I knew Kerry Chikarovski well and regarded her as a talented female politician who would do a good job'.[94]

Alan Jones' treatment of politicians such as Peter Collins and John Hannaford had recently been given close attention in a profile of Alan Jones, much quoted in this book. 'Who's Afraid of Alan Jones?' was the cover story of *Good Weekend* magazine on 14 November. Throughout 1998, David Leser made over 200 telephone calls in compiling the Walkley Award-winning report. It was the most comprehensive study of Alan Jones undertaken by the press, insightful and revealing for more than its many factual expositions. Leser had worried the tripe out of Alan Jones. He learned people had been asked by Jones to withhold cooperation. Jones also threatened defamation action, before agreeing to Harry Miller's recommendation that he be interviewed.

Alan Jones hated the report, telling a correspondent: 'Be assured, they're not interested in a good story! They scoured the gutters in the hope that they would find whatever they could.'[95] One of the many details David Leser uncovered might have been of interest to Alan Jones' boss, John Conde. At this stage, while Jones was still resisting coming clean on his endorsement agreements, Leser exposed the Colonial deal. 'Simon Morgan, spokesman for Colonial Limited (formerly Colonial Mutual), was happy to confirm that the company employed Jones to do live reads, give motivational speeches to staff and address regional meetings in NSW. Morgan insists, though, that the money—estimated to be about $200 000 a year—was never designed to buy his favour.'[96]

Harry Miller told David Leser: 'Alan gets no side kicks. He doesn't get paid for live reads or anything. He does the reads as long as they don't conflict with his beliefs. [There are] no deals with restaurants or truckloads of electronic equipment delivered to his house. He tells it like it is. That's why people listen to him.'[97]

These people, the most important members of Alan's fan base, had not been told of the many secret deals arranged by Miller. It is the way it goes with Alan. It is hard to have an equal relationship. An implicit condition of sticking is allowing domination and extending trust. If you shared a certain specialness, entry to 'pick and stick' was easier, but still came without a lifetime guarantee. According to some former friends, Alan was capable of biting anyone but a Packer. So membership was not for everyone. These awkward conditions of entry have never suited the majority. As has been pointed out many times, Alan's 20 per cent audience share meant 80 per cent weren't buying.

One old friend, noticing over the years how the faces changed at Alan's Christmas parties, said he thought the former friends could fill the Sydney Cricket Ground while the current friends gathered in the members' dining room. He took to renaming Alan's constellation the 'pick and flick' club.

CHAPTER 15
A VERITABLE TSUNAMI

'I'VE HAD A MILLION LETTERS about this ... there's correspondence everywhere ...' In 1999, Alan Jones sent 7578 letters.[1] An exasperated Jones often lamented the burden of answering what he says was an average of 70 letters a day. The figure is likely an exaggeration. If true, he was receiving 25 000 letters a year, and as Alan Jones' employees know, Alan insists every letter gets a reply. In his responses, and on air, Alan Jones refers to the deluge as 'a veritable tsunami'. He is not one to reveal how much of it is of his own making. To track the correspondence is to observe an industry at work, an industry that also sustains Alan Incorporated.

This chapter, for the most part, examines that industry up to and beyond the time another massive wave broke, in the form of the Australian Broadcasting Authority—or 'cash for comment'—commercial radio inquiry. There is a good reason to do so. In order to explain the power of Alan Jones, it is necessary to reach beyond the microphone. Although Alan Jones does have a large audience, it has never been large enough to explain his sway. The often-quoted listening audience of 500 000 is an accumulated tally. The ratings through the morning are calculated in 15-minute segments, and the numbers averaged out over a week. Although an estimated average cumulative audience of 500 000 listen at different times for eight minutes or more, this number reduces to 300 000 listening at any one time. While syndication and *Today* show viewers add to the tally, it is hard to see the numbers supporting a proposition, sometimes put, that Alan Jones is worth up to three per cent of the Coalition vote in New South Wales.

The best way to explain how his unquestionable power extends beyond the mandate of his audience is to look at his activism, and his letter writing in particular. When Alan Jones comes off air he continues his wrestle with decision makers, at high-powered meetings, in boardrooms, at the speaker's podium and, most of all, poised before a dictaphone. Even if the figures are massaged, Alan Jones must still be Australia's most prolific correspondent. And while Jones says he is lobbying for Struggle Street, there is a bulk of evidence to show he lobbies also for powerful mates, and—most particularly, if indirectly—for himself.

But it would be wrong to see his obsession as strictly power related. There is a personal element too. Alan Jones is moved when a writer slips a little piece of their soul into the envelope. His fondness for personal correspondence can be traced to those treasured tomes he received from his mother as a teenager at boarding school. When he taught school and coached rugby, Alan Jones was also known for the notes penned late at night and pushed under doors. He has always liked the courtesy and manners of correspondence. Evident still is his special fondness for handwritten notes, and a teacher's regard for an elegant hand. For all that, his own is an appalling hand, his signature scrawled in a circular flourish that looks like a small gas explosion. Considering the nature of many of the letters, it is an apt way to close.

Alan Jones does not write all the letters he sends out, and he types virtually none of them. He likes his workers to be multiskilled, and a common duty is attending to the mail. He tells his worker bees: 'We have no titles, just tasks'. Taskmaster Alan reads many of his replies into a dictaphone, to be typed and turned around as soon as possible. This explains the at times atrocious spelling—for example, 'reched' for 'wretched', or 'rort iron' for 'wrought iron'.

He does not have the time to thoroughly read all that he signs, and if an error is later drawn to his attention, he is not pleased. Alan Jones acknowledges the arrangement to some correspondents, joking about never making spelling errors and always having the advantage of being able to blame the typist. Many of the more complicated communiqués are researched, written and typed by other staff members. His niece, Tonia, has done a powerful amount of the typing.

Handling Alan Jones' correspondence can be a full time job. Michael Darby was one of many Jones' letter writers. Darby, the son of former Liberal MP Douglas Darby, is referred to earlier in the book as assisting Jones during his 1978 Earlwood campaign. In May 1998, Michael Darby took a job with Alan Jones, staying until August 2001, when they too fell out. The clash of fiery particles had inevitability written all over it. Darby—like Jones, proud, loquacious and opinionated—took the job as a step along the way to his own career before a microphone. When he came to believe his employer was obstructing his path, Darby became another to wheel through the departure gate.

One comment by Jones, uncovered among the tsunami of correspondence, says a lot about the role he sets himself: 'If only government did its job properly there would be less for me to do.' Alan Jones' system of dealing with mail looks like a throwback to his days in Prime Minister Malcolm Fraser's office. He has resumed the old procedures for dealing with mail, as if he is still there.

Alan Jones is 'proud of the private and public contributions I have made to advancing the concerns and well being of my listeners and many worthy causes'.[2] As he says, he attends to real people's real concerns. Some of Alan Jones' responses—for example, to a person who has had problems with a builder—might contain two or more pages of detailed advice. He can be impressively sensitive when he tries to persuade someone who is obsessed by a misfortune that sometimes it is better to let go and move on. He will take up someone's case over a rail fine and write not one, but a marching battalion of letters. His help is often genuine, and is genuinely appreciated.

Most of the incoming letters praise him. Doing justice to the scope of this appreciation is difficult, as most say much the same: 'Alan, this note is to thank-you for all your care and assistance in trying to help the people in need'; 'Thanks to yourself and your highly efficient staff my son has now commenced with …'; '… there must be a lot more people who feels like us out there because I've heard so many people talk about the help you have given them over the years'.

Alan Jones has come to see this link to the public as a valuable source of unfiltered information. Beyond picking up good leads and breaking good stories, he often tells writers to call in and raise a matter on the open line, or says 'don't be surprised if I mention this on air'. As his listeners know, Alan Jones is sometimes true to his word. He also puts questions raised by his listeners to their leaders.

When he is questioned about why he keeps up the production line, Alan Jones says, 'These people are the backbone of the show … Each of these individuals deserves a positive and, where possible, helpful response.'[3] But there is also much in Alan Jones' approach to his mail to raise suspicion about whether we see pure altruism at work. According to one inside observer: 'It services his loneliness. The people who write to Jones show him the unconditional love that is otherwise missing from his life. He wants to be everybody's guardian angel. It makes him feel like god.'

Alan Jones' massive correspondence files show him stepping well beyond his role as a broadcaster. The mail does provide program content, but one person's rail fine and another person's septic tank problem are not the stuff of great radio. His employees bear a heavy burden of handling matters that have nothing to do with radio. 'People think he is amazing because he takes an interest and would get us to follow up, which was a total pain in the arse. You would never do it anywhere else.' And another: 'One night we were there till midnight trying to sort out a problem for one guy. And all I could think of was what a loser he was. Alan has chosen to support some very strange causes and people.'

A willingness to work beyond his salary should be praiseworthy. What is curious is the way Alan Jones himself bellyaches. Having accepted the burden, he then bewails the public treating him like an unpaid politician or ombudsman. 'I just wish some of my listeners could see the correspondence that comes across my desk. I am not the Prime Minister, the Premier, the Ombudsman or anybody else!'[4] A constant refrain is why am I doing this, and why is my effort not better appreciated? 'I get a million and one letters here. I have to answer them. I'm answering yours at 3 o'clock on Sunday afternoon when most sensible people are having a break.'[5] 'It is 11 o'clock at night and this is the 100th letter.' 'Sometimes, I have to confess, I wonder why I bother.'[6] '... there's only one of me [he lies] ... sometimes I think I am going around the bend.'[7] Michael Darby, one of those of disappearing faith, says: 'He does not care at all about the pain that his listeners feel, and he is in fact personally antagonised by the fact that they approach him'.[8]

As members of his staff know, Alan Jones generates unnecessary work. A computer illiterate, he has avoided the efficiency of electronic correspondence. 'There is so much paper, he must cut down forests every day', said one of his e-authors. 'I would print off the email and type a reply. If he approved, the reply was ticked and sent. If he scrawled a cross on the draft, Jones would dictate an alternative reply, which would be then retyped and checked again before the send button was finally pressed.' Alan Jones' support workers are obliged to plot through barely legible correspondence and retype it before Alan sees it.

He also generates unnecessary mail. He replies to Christmas cards. He replies to press releases. He replies to letters from people who don't identify themselves. One whole file of correspondence is designated 'To the householder'. He replies to advertising brochures and form letters from publicists. He replies to letters that expressly say no reply is necessary or even wanted. He will write a thank you to a thank you card and get a letter saying, 'I did not expect to get a thank you for my thank you'. And he will write again. Alan loves to write.

Whereas others see wisdom in binning vexatious correspondence, the argument that it is better to avoid encouraging cranks does not hold with Alan: 'I take the view that such people still have rights, and that personal idiosyncrasies should not exclude individuals from help'.[9] So the racial vilifiers get their say and receive a courteous response, which, unsurprisingly, attracts another letter.

It is clear a great deal of his mail comes from older Australians. Alan Jones shows his respect: 'a man of your age deserves my full attention'. The handwritten notes received, particularly from important people, are treasured because he knows they are originals. They represent a personal commitment and connection to the sender. Alan Jones hates receiving letters he suspects are written by functionaries.

Constantly looming through this mess of paper is his hated enemy, the bureaucrat. An easy target, Jones works at delivering blame and an occasional eviction. He says of them, 'nothing frightens the bureaucracy more than the thought of a new idea'. This criticism seems to ignore the shambles of Jones' own bureaucratic systems, and the contradiction of using his own functionaries to deal with the bulk of his mail. The Belford Productions boss condemns politicians and bureaucrats who don't jump to attention when these letters arrive, and then complains about not having the time to deal with the detail of his listeners' many problems.

Jones hates form letters. Admirably, individual communications receive unique and personalised responses. But there is form, none the less, in routine phraseology: 'I know you understand' is an example of common curtness. When he has little to say, and that is a lot of the time, he will rebound some of the content: 'You have advised me about a problem with tarpaulins ... many people would agree with your view that ...', 'You make a valid point when you say ... you go on to describe ...', 'Leave it with me ... we'll keep at it.'

A pet hate is when people don't identify themselves by their first or, as he puts it, Christian name. He actually uses the word 'hate', replying 'I hate people who don't sign with their Christian name.' Even worse are those who can't spell his name. The hundreds of correspondents who seek his help in finding a job are off to a bad start if they misspell, commonly offending by use of the double 'l'. He is peeved when loyal listeners have not worked out by now that he is a one 'l' Alan. A writer who addressed correspondence to 'Mrs Alanna Jones' brought Jones' dictaphone to melting point.

The former teacher does not take kindly to the occasional corrections offered by attentive listeners. 'This is getting a bit tiresome. With respect I don't need a grammar lesson!'[10] He is offended when chided for singing along with the music: 'What a wet blanket!'[11] Another curiosity is the constancy of his pronunciation errors: 'chic' is pronounced as 'kick', canapes to rhyme with 'shapes', 'Mojave' with a hard 'j'. As one listener pointed out, 'Don José' was pronounced as 'Don Hose'.[12] Former teaching colleagues put the mispronunciations down to Alan being a poor listener.

When he is chided for the blueness of his humour he generally offers a mea culpa: '... Actually on reflection, I think the jokes were a bit over the odds ... What seems funny at that hour of the day may, upon reflection, not be funny at all.'[13] His apologies don't seem to change the tone of the jokes, which are selected by production staff and read in a way that suggests Alan does not know what is coming. However blue, or lame, he laughs and then tells his audience for the umpteenth time, 'my mother used to say never laugh at your own jokes'.

There are plenty of letters to show his system also works: employers write to say thanks for finding staff, job seekers write to thank him for getting them into paid employment, people are grateful for mentions of local fetes and open days. The general impression is that most correspondents find comfort in the personal contact and appreciate being treated as individuals.

The most common target of the Jones tsunami is the political community. In March 1999 an election was due in New South Wales. After 14 years on air, the trick of courting Alan Jones with handwritten notes was well known. His spat with Bob Carr over Pauline Hanson and the Maritime Union was in the past. Bob would put more effort into media management as an election neared.

Peter Collins' courting of Alan Jones had proved useless when the party dumped him for Kerry Chikarovski, which further helped Bob's cause with Alan. At this stage, even though she tried, Alan was not buying a Chika-led government. Kerry Chikarovski had no time to build confidence, let alone policies. Before the polls, her approval rating sank to 25 per cent beside Carr's 58 per cent. Chikarovski had attacked Peter Ryan's management of policing, which would have pleased Alan, but she ran counter to Jones' advice about the 'folly' of electricity privatisation.

On 27 March 1999 Labor won nine new seats and Bob Carr improved his primary vote, if only by one per cent. In the immediate aftermath, Alan Jones wrote a congratulatory letter, in doing so referring to an *Age* newspaper article by author and speechwriter Bob Ellis:[14]

> My Dear Premier ['Premier' crossed out and 'Bob' overwritten by hand]
>
> I have no doubt that you read the piece in the Melbourne Age ... 'A New Labor Star is Born'. That's you! Written by this bloke Bob Ellis. I don't know whether he's a mate of yours! However, it is in many ways a most generous piece! ... He can write this bloke. I liked the bit which said, 'He ran and amazingly won a campaign of no big promises standing on his record, not criticizing the Opposition. That took some doing. He stood on the table last Friday night, and thanked his staff in remarkable, tired, unconfident, self-effacing speech. There were

lines on his face and a searing of his spirit, a cathartic gathering of inner exhaustions. He looked and felt like Chifley, or Dunstan, a Labor hero ...'

You have to be careful. You need a rest. There's a beautiful spot at Jamberoo! But then I've told you that before. If you're too stupid to take advantage of it, then even Premiers can't be helped!

With best wishes.

Alan Jones was not one of those English teachers who disapproved of the exclamation mark. It litters dictated correspondence, on this occasion almost half his sentences ending with the 'dog's dick' of punctuation anatomy.

The next day Alan Jones received a handwritten note from Bob Carr, attaching a report articulating his manifesto for the new term. Jones replied, calling, as he often does, for a meeting of minds: '... congratulations on the thinking work that you do. I think we need some time to talk about what we collectively see are the big issues facing the State. Why don't we have an uninterrupted lunch at some point down the track. Congratulations on the good work that you do.'[15]

Alan Jones often passes on to the premier his listeners' problems, from difficulties claiming 'Scratchie' winnings to the pestilence of the New South Wales government's land tax. 'I take this opportunity of mentioning that Land Tax remains a genuine concern for many of my listeners. The issue was very badly handled by the Opposition [in] the election campaign, so I know you will not be encouraged to interpret your excellent poll result as a specific endorsement of the Government's Land Tax policies.'[16]

Alan Jones sent so many letters he often lost track of his own demands. The Jones machine wrote repeatedly to Carr about 'offensive material produced by the band Regurgitator'. He told the Premier: 'Recent tragic events in the USA reinforce the suspicion of links between hostility generated material and hostile behaviour. If you decide to campaign against such material, then you can depend upon my support.'[17]

When Carr's office wrote back about his Regurgitator grumble, Jones asked Michael Darby to match the letter with other correspondence and find out what he was complaining about.[18]

Jones also offered advice to Carr's staff, making clear his disappointment that even Bob Carr's name found its way into bureaucratic letters.[19] In August 1999, he wrote to Carr's advisor, Wendy George, about the state government's shared opposition to the proposed second airport site. Jones gave her some free advice suggesting Bob Carr get stuck into Canberra over Badgery's Creek.[20]

Alan Jones' support for New South Wales Labor called for bravery at times, in the face of disapproval from conservative fans. When, during these short-lived love fests, anti-Carr listeners wanted more aggression, Jones explained: 'Re Bob Carr. Don't worry I've had a few slanging matches with him'.[21] When one complained about him going soft on Carr's broken promises, and failing to give Chikarovski a better run, Jones replied: 'I receive hundreds of letters. A low priority of response is given to those where I am obliged to look up the postcode because the author has not included it. A lower priority of response is given to letters where I don't know whether I am writing to a lady or a gentleman and where the Christian name of the writer is absent or illegible ... You appear to express disappointment in my failure to endorse the NSW Opposition Leader. I am a broadcaster, and I try to give credit where it is due. The NSW Opposition, quite simply, did not earn my support.'[22]

While Alan Jones had formerly written Kerry Chikarovski off as 'non existent', by the time the election rolled around, there had been a partial eclipse of opinion. Alan Jones began to tell writers that 'Kerry Chikarovski has made a fist of a very difficult situation. I think she's an excellent prospect in the long term.'[23] 'I think Kerry Chikarovski is improving. She's had an absolutely impossible job. I am confident that one day she'll make it. However it's damned tough!'[24]

A pattern was now established. When Bob routinely tired of massaging Alan, the Opposition stepped up to provide relief. As

Carr had done in opposition, Chikarovski installed a party line to Belford Productions, which would be kept busy over the next few years. The more cynical in her party saw that one of Chikarovski's few attributes was her ability to win over Jones. Throughout her term, she hunted for issues that would give her traction with Alan, and make ground on the government. The 2000 Olympics offered hope. There were plenty of problems getting the biggest show in town on the road and, besides, Alan Jones had come to detest Olympics Minister Michael Knight.

Jones missed few opportunities to flay the Olympic organisers. Ticket sales were a mess, but within the Olympics administration there was a belief that the bigger problem was Michael Knight's failure to give Alan Jones a prestigious post as 'the voice of the games'. One insider said Michael Knight stood up to pressure even from Bob Carr to appease the broadcaster. Knight is alleged to have pushed a case in Cabinet that the rest of them follow suit.

Jones wrote to Knight, forwarding a listener's complaint: 'Michael, we are bloody joking. I've a good mind to go berserk about this on air.'[25] And he did, slanging Knight on 2UE as a 'bully boy' and 'henchman'.[26] Jones allegedly threatened that Knight would not still be minister when the Olympics rolled around, but the Minister stood firm. An insider heard him declare, 'I won't deal with him. I won't give him a thing.'

In contrast, Jones' relationship with Kerry Chikarovski warmed. 'Thank you for your note. Kerry, what you're suggesting to me makes eminent good sense. Leave it with me and we'll see if we can find some time to talk.'[27] He took it upon himself to direct Liberal policy: 'Thank you for your note about the issues paper ... One piece of advice to you. Every issues paper that is released must be virtually known by the leader off by heart ... I'll try to be back in touch when I've made some sense of it all. Thanks for sending it to me.'[28]

Alan Jones passed on feedback from a 65-year-old female listener who thought Chika's voice a bit dull and difficult for the hard of hearing, and was rewarded with a handwritten reply:

'Dear Alan, Thank you for forwarding the note from one of your listeners. I'll certainly accept the criticism in the spirit with which it was offered—constructively. I'm trying to work out how I can sound more lively at 6:30 am, as I believe that's when the problem is worst. Any suggestions? Kind regards, Kerry.'[29]

The more the goodwill flowed from her fountain pen, the more effusive was Alan: 'Dear Kerry, Thank you for your note. It was kind of you to write back. Totally unnecessary. And in your own handwriting! Kerry I do understand the difficulties that you face. And I must say I think you're working like a Trojan to try and turn the show around. Believe me, and I wouldn't say this were it not the case, I think you're doing outstandingly better than you were six months ago. And I think that's starting to appear. You're sounding more confident. The nervousness has gone out of the presentation. You're getting a few issues that you can grapple with.'[30]

He went on, citing his own success as a model for inspiration: 'It's the age old axiom offered by the farmer—after the drought comes the rain; at the end of the long road, there's always a turning; the darkest hour is often just before the dawn. These sound like clichés but they help to remind us that there is hope and opportunity if we stick with it. You can do it. Keep at it. With best wishes, Alan Jones.'[31]

'Thank you for your unbelievable hand written note. You are remarkable.'[32] This one is from Alan Jones to Labor's Faye Lo Po. The Minister for Community Services challenged the Opposition leader when it came to obsequiousness, wearing down nib and knee in her crawling to Alan. When two full pages of tidy and detailed copperplate arrived, Alan gave her top marks. 'You must have been a schoolteacher in another calling!'[33]

As Alan Jones explained to Peter Collins in his 1998 manifesto, Lo Po did have a luckless portfolio. Picking up the pieces of broken families is often thankless work. Faye Lo Po was also Minister for the Ageing and Disability Services, putting her close to Alan Jones' audience, which included an exhausted band of carers. When Alan Jones advocated on behalf of these deserving people his letters were invariably marked 'For the attention of the Minister', Jones expecting nothing less. So when another letter arrived from Lo Po's office bearing the computer-generated signature of her private secretary, Alan Jones was displeased, telling Michael Darby that he did not want to attack Faye Lo Po but that they needed to be vigilant in pursuing bureaucrats who pose as ministers.[34]

Maybe it was stark terror that caused the fountain pen to shake when Lo Po realised what had occurred. An obliging member of Jones' staff retyped her handwritten note, which was not quite as legible as normal: 'Dear Alan, You can imagine my horror yesterday when I discovered that the Minister's office, that you were criticising, was mine ... I would hate to think that you believed that your correspondence or indeed anyone's correspondence was being ignored by me or any of my staff.'[35] They were swiftly reconciled. Further down the track, when Minister Lo Po was shunted by one child protection scandal too many, Alan Jones lamented her departure on air, calling her a 'saint' and citing the personalised correspondence as a reason for his high opinion.[36]

Faye Lo Po was one of many politicians Alan Jones believed was educated in the art of turning around correspondence. Then Deputy Premier Andrew Refshauge also got a High Distinction. Michael Darby is proud of his and Jones' work. 'Ministers, state and federal, could see that Jones was capable with his resources of dealing with a complaint on the same day. And because we would make it clear to the ministerial staff, you've been sitting on something for 3 months. We've handled it in 24 hours thence over a period of time there was noticeable improvement in the performance of state and federal ministers.'[37]

The minister with the biggest file of Alan Jones' letters might have wondered at the end of the day whether it was worth it. In 1999, Carl Scully received 84 letters from Jones.[38] But as the 2003 election approached Jones gave Scully a bashing despite his eagerness to please, and told his listeners the minister would go.

The Transport Minister had another tough portfolio, with at least as many innate problems as Community Services. Alan

Jones expected micromanagement of the first order. When a listener complained to Jones about a train carriage door failing to open, Alan wrote his 'what a shambles, leave it with me' reply, promising to 'drop a note to Carl Scully', which soon followed: 'Dear Carl ... this is the kind of stuff you can do without. How the hell does this happen? Can you rattle some cages and shake a few people to some common sense?'[39]

On this occasion Carl Scully replied with four pages of detail, attending to a parade of listeners' problems. The minister pointed out the carriages were locked in keeping with the Nightsafe program, which concentrated passengers in safer carriages.[40] Alan Jones was delighted. Michael Darby drafted a reply. 'I note your status as Minister who is willing to work on weekends—dealing with the concerns of my listeners on many issues. I commend your willingness to acknowledge and correct errors.' The letter finished with a recommendation from Jones that a bus port be constructed above Strathfield Railway Station.[41]

There were good results. On 31 May Hayden Blessie, a young South African in Australia on holiday, suffered a serious eye injury when a rock was thrown at the train he was travelling in. Alan Jones would not let go. He wrote letter after letter urging the government to do something for the Blessie family: 'I am absolutely, utterly, totally and incomprehensively [sic] disgusted with the way in which this poor woman and her innocent child/son have been treated ... Carl, I am getting angry about this. This is nearly a ten past seven story.'[42]

As a gesture of goodwill, Carl Scully agreed to contribute to medical expenses and provide a free travel pass. Scully personally telephoned the Blessie family, which in Jones' book is as good as it gets. Alan Jones saw the Blessie case as an example of how his intervention sharpened communication: 'The Hayden Blessie case demonstrated how hard it is for an individual to catch the attention of the decision makers, and how much the situation can improve when their attention is finally captured'.[43]

By the end of the year Carl and Alan were great mates. While resting at Jamberoo, the broadcaster received a handwritten

Christmas card: 'Dear Alan, It must be very satisfying for you at the end of what has surely been a really tough year to be on top of the ratings (yet again!). Your strong support is much appreciated. I hope you have a good break, a great Christmas and I look forward to seeing you back on deck in the New Year. Warmest regards, Carl.'[44]

Alan Jones can point to many further examples to show how his intervention assists a functioning democracy. Ministers like Carl Scully had no chance of convincing Alan Jones that the arrangement was also dysfunctional. Jones was neither qualified nor informed enough to set the agenda and priorities for not one but dozens of portfolios. Jones wanted a dynamic and accountable government, which somehow denied process. Appeasing Jones meant Scully and others would waste a lot of time. Although he acknowledges some of his representations lacked merit, Jones appeared to believe the great majority were worthy.

As Scully later discovered it was basically a losing game. Resisting the temptation to assist an unworthy cause for the sake of appeasing Alan Jones was all the more difficult as Jones became more powerful. The problem Scully could never overcome with Jones was not over the failing rail system but rather hire cars.

Mr Struggle Street is a big customer of Sydney's limousine services. A constant driver was Paul Amour, the proprietor of Strathfield Hire Cars. Driving Alan Jones around, Armour had plenty of opportunity to get in his client's ear about his problems with state deregulation of the hire car industry. Armour felt the changes had cost him tens of thousands of dollars. He believed he was owed compensation. The New South Wales Transport Department saw things differently. The dispute between the parties was already eight years old when Jones wrote to Scully: 'It's no secret that Paul Armour has been a driver for me for more years than I can imagine. I've always found him to be unfailingly decent and uncompromisingly honest.'[45]

Alan Jones had not just taken up Paul Armour's claim but Armour's side. In doing so he backed his own wobbly processes against the government, showing once again that his plan of attack was less for the sake of ensuring efficiency as for achieving a prescribed result. In this case Scully at first acquiesced, supporting the waiving of a $40 000 debt, but then writing to say before doing so that his department needed to check probity concerns with the Independent Commission Against Corruption. ICAC found there was an issue, and the matter dragged on for more years.

Carl Scully's chief bureaucrat at the time, Director General of Transport Michael Deegan, had been Michael Knight's chief of staff during the Olympics. Deegan, who resisted pressure to pay the compensation package, became another target. As sometimes occurs when there is a stalemate, an independent review was commissioned. It agreed with Deegan's position.

On 26 February, before the release of the finding, Michael Deegan made a file note: 'Phone call from Scully last night. Very distressed about threats from Jones in a conversation the two had Wednesday night (prior to him calling me). Scully indicated that Jones had said unless Scully did three things then Scully would not only not become Premier, he would be lucky to be Minister for picking up leaves and paper (or words to that effect). One of three things Scully had to do was sack the Director General of Transport on March 3, 2003 or Jones would get rid of him.'[46]

The day after the release of the report, two weeks out from the 2003 election, Alan Jones told 2UE listeners: 'Carl Scully goes into this election as an agent of corporate theft. There's nothing more to this than theft ... he's got the whole hire car crisis and crisis it is ... the assets of the small businessman, the hire car owner are diminished and devalued. This is theft. There has been no compensation. Talk of compensation but there has been no compensation ...'[47]

Alan had turned a fifth order issue into a first order, career-threatening pre-election scandal. It was a tough time for Scully, also battling with the aftermath of the Waterfall train crash. Following the 2003 election, Carl Scully was removed from

Transport. Michael Deegan was also sacked from the department, the father of three pitched onto Struggle Street. After being considered for the director general position in Scully's new housing portfolio, Deegan was told the appointment would be too difficult because Scully was so scared of Jones. Michael Deegan, one of a range of public servants to suffer because of Alan Jones, wrote to ICAC: 'Threats to Ministers and senior public servants that they will be axed unless certain commentators get their way is having a serious negative impact on the NSW public sector'.[48]

Another New South Wales minister to step up to the correspondence plate, and another with cause to question the merits of doing so, was Craig Knowles. Like Scully, Knowles, the Urban Affairs and Planning Minister, was touted as a favoured successor to Bob Carr. Early correspondence again showed Alan Jones as an intermediary in representing listeners' concerns about blocked sewage pipes, white ant infestations and the like. Craig Knowles' office gave priority to these representations and Alan Jones was pleased. Jones: 'Thank you for the interest and the detail ... If only your Government had people similarly concerned with detail, then some of the problems confronting us might not have arisen. Keep at it. You're doing an excellent job. Thank you for the courtesy of your note ... Alan Jones.'[49]

Once ministers and departments were so engaged, Alan Jones was extended power that made him more fixer than facilitator. A no-win situation for ministers sometimes arose when Alan Jones' demands could not be met. The big loser for Knowles was a tender process for a waste treatment contract with, again, a Jones crony in the background. Entrepreneur John Messara was chairman of a gaming enterprise, Stargames, alongside another Alan Jones mate, Deputy Chairman Neil Gamble. Alan Jones co-owned, with Neil Gamble and Mrs Ann Messara, the racehorse Mr Freeze.[50] Alan's shared interest in racing brought him closer to the Messaras, owners of the Arrowfield stud in the Hunter Valley.

In 1998 another Messara company, Kolback, was bidding for a new waste treatment plant. The Kolback tender proposed the plant be established at Ardlethan, northwest of Wagga Wagga. Kolback's main competitor was a French company, Collex. Jones did not disclose his relationship with Messara when he wrote to Knowles during the summer break: 'My dear Minister, I am writing this letter to you on Christmas Eve because I believe it concerns a matter of critical public policy. Indeed Craig, I am writing it on the day when, you would be aware, Peter Mandleson has resigned from the Blair Government in Britain over the failure of public policy being executed in a proper way.'[51]

Jones said the Kolback proposal was obviously superior. He rubbished the opponents not just because they were foreign: 'Here is a French proposal which seems to break all the basic rules. More than that, they have had court cases against them in France, as I understand it, alleging payoffs to councils. My further understanding is that some of their senior executives and directors have been jailed.' The letter threatened: 'Craig, here's the rub—your department has been hopelessly uncooperative towards Ardlethan. If I were on air, I would have something to say about this.'[52]

Jones had also gone over Knowles' head: 'Craig, I spoke to Bob Carr verbally about this matter. I am writing to you to confirm the seriousness of it. I repeat what I said at the beginning. With an election coming up, the whole process of this would not pass public muster. You owe it to yourself to make sure that whoever is responsible for this nonsense is booted out. The process needs to be objective and capable of withstanding public scrutiny. At the moment it is neither. I am contactable should you need to talk to me. Yours sincerely, Alan Jones.'[53]

As with the hire car issue, the process dragged on for years. Collex was finally awarded the tender in November 2003, after the government overrode opposition from the Land and Environment Court. At that time Craig Knowles, then health minister, was copping it over trouble at Campbelltown Hospital, another issue raised on Jones' program. It was left to Carr to weather another Jones jihad. In a telephone interview Jones listed the government's woes, his first question more a comment:

'Premier, a dreadful week by any standards of democracy'. Carr: 'You're wrong about a great many things you've just catalogued and I'd really like an opportunity to reply'.[54]

For the next 15 minutes the pair squabbled. Bob Carr tried to explain the rationale for the government's acceptance of the Collex transfer station at Clyde, and the overturning of the Land and Environment Court recommendation. Alan Jones took the opposite tack from his usual argument that governments should not be captive of the courts. Carr explained this was not a criminal matter and that the Collex project represented a lesser burden on the taxpayer. There was little chance of the audience following either argument as Alan Jones talked over the answers. Jones: 'Well I can't allow you to tell lies to my listeners'. Carr: '… you're not allowing me to say anything …'[55]

The New South Wales Premier's thermostatically controlled composure started to waver before Alan Jones' rapid-fired interjections: '… rubbish … hang on, hang on … that's not true …' Carr: '… well, Alan, if you want to rant and not hear what I've got to say you could have done it without inviting me on the program …'[56]

Alan Jones' skill with words does not make him a good interviewer. If he did have an argument to defeat Bob Carr the audience heard neither it nor the Premier's point of view. And at no stage did he or Carr raise the issue of Jones' well-known relationship with the other bidder, John Messara.

Jones did not accept he had threatened Craig Knowles. Nor did he see a conflict of interest in the failure to disclose his relationship. In correspondence with Anne Davies he explained that he did not want politicians to make a decision on the basis of his relationship with the individual concerned.[57]

The letter was in response to inquiries by Davies, a *Sydney Morning Herald* reporter. In 2000 she made a series of Freedom of Information requests of government departments, seeking examples of Jones' correspondence. When Alan Jones was notified about the request he told the premier's office that he had no difficulty with releasing the correspondence as all he was trying to do was assist battlers.[58]

The 200 documents Anne Davies retrieved were part of the same tsunami examined in this chapter. Having scrutinised the letters, Davies put eleven written questions to Jones. His nine-page response opened with a salvo telling her he was unimpressed by the snide nature of her questions.[59] But he accepted the opportunity to put his case, which he saw as glowing in contrast to the *Herald*'s 'witch-hunt'. Jones said that 'in contradistinction' he was proud of the public and private contributions he had made to his listeners and worthy causes.[60] The way Alan Jones saw it, he was helping needy people, forcing discipline on shoddy parliamentary procedures for handling mail and having some success doing so. In no way was he abusing power in advocating either for himself or close mates.

One such mate was another frequent correspondent. Alan Jones does not conceal his friendship with the Federal Member for Warringah, Tony Abbott, or his belief in Abbott's leadership qualities.[61] Given his Sydney audience and the nature of their grievances, Jones has more dialogue with state politicians, but federal politicians like Abbott copped the tsunami too. While he was generally kinder to the Coalition, there were also broadsides, and again a sense that what mattered most was the status of the personal relationship.

Abbott has a mutual high regard for Alan Jones and is grateful for his assistance in showing Abbott's good side. When, in 1999, Abbott wrote to Jones to thank him for assisting with a fundraising venture, he spoke about the importance of politicians looking more approachable and staying in touch with everyday Australians. Following the typescript is a handwritten jotting: 'I really enjoyed our lunch the other day—thank you for all your friendship'.[62] Two weeks later the Minister for Employment Services' gratitude had not run out: 'Thanks very much for treating me to a splendid lunch the other week. As always it was a pleasure and an inspiration to catch up ... We did not get a chance at lunch to discuss the Sharples matter. Basically, this is a mess but I'm only too happy to take you through it, if you wish.'[63]

The Sharples matter was a test of mateship. Terry Sharples alleged that Tony Abbott promised financial support for a court action against One Nation's Pauline Hanson, who also benefited from Jones' support. Jones wrote to Abbott apologising for having to express his 'alarm': 'I have to say I am concerned about the treatment of Pauline Hanson. We are either a free society or we're not. And we are certainly free to offer views that might be in disagreement with those of others. And I have no difficulty with many of the things Pauline Hanson says ... Tony I need some assurance from you ...'[64]

The assurances must have satisfied Jones, and the mates continued to look after one another. Abbott's office supplied Jones with the favoured 'dot points' that the broadcaster cleverly translated into extemporised editorials. In turn, Alan Jones received direct access to the Minister, who listened patiently to Alan's monologues. The Minister also gave Alan Jones a say in the running of his office, which was not always up to scratch.

When Jones received a form letter from a member of Abbott's staff, acknowledging a representation from a listener, the Minister was admonished: 'This stupid letter from your office is typical of the stuff that comes out of Canberra. It's obviously in response to a letter you have never sighted. It's absolutely meaningless. It borders on the insulting.'[65]

Abbott replied, explaining his preferred system of swiftly acknowledging correspondence, but apologising anyway: 'As I hope you know, any letter from you receives my immediate personal attention'.[66] Jones then lectured the Minister about how it should be done: 'You do as I try to do—keep abreast everyday with the correspondence. I make sure that I spend some time checking everything that comes across my desk. There is a stack of it! I would like to swap notes! ... There are no shortcuts to the dreaded correspondence scourge!'[67]

Many of Alan Jones' representations to the Minister were about listeners seeking employment. Tony Abbott was of the view that his own staff in the newly formed Job Network had a lot to learn from Alan Jones: 'It's not altogether surprising that Australia's finest salesman, broadcasting to hundreds of thousands of people, can find potential employees while Job Network members (pitching their message to Centrelink clients) have more difficulty. I'm not flattering you unduly to say that you have rather more ability to "sell" the job than the average Job Network staffer and that many of the listeners have more "get up and go" than the average person in the Centrelink queue.'[68]

At this time Abbott had instructed his staff to intervene on behalf of a Jones correspondent. 'Dear Tony,' Jones wrote back, 'Thank you as always for your answer and the personal nature of the answer. I wish there were other people in the Ministry who could follow the same example. You are a mile in front of them!'[69] When Abbott picked up the phone and spoke directly to a listener, Jones was over the moon. 'You're brilliant. Let's be honest! I know of no other Minister who actually rings people up.'[70]

When Philip Ruddock was Minister for Immigration and Multicultural Affairs, he too received the veritable tsunami, which coincided with an alleged deluge of asylum seekers cum illegal immigrants. Alan Jones was a strong supporter of the government's tough approach to maintaining control of its immigration program and keeping out the undeserving. Alan Jones' many representations on behalf of a range of potential citizens keen to fast-track bureaucratic processes is therefore surprising.

Philip Ruddock had a powerful authority to apply ministerial discretion to applications. Although Alan Jones could not have had the time and resources to be certain of the merits of claims, he repeatedly lobbied for them anyway: 'Philip, I repeat what I said before. When are we going to come to the realisation that we're not dealing with shonks or fakes ...'[71] On the same matter soon after: 'When can we get some resolution on this? I don't want to go public about it which would be embarrassing to everybody. I trust you understand.'[72] Philip Ruddock replied saying he had decided to intervene and grant a visa.[73]

Again Jones' representations were given priority. On behalf of his correspondents he managed to have visas issued and stop a deportation. He lobbied to have a separate individual deported. He lobbied for visas for spouses. He acted as a kind of unpaid and unlicensed immigration agent. Certain of the propriety of his own conduct, Alan Jones was less sure about that of others. Writing to Philip Ruddock about migration agents, he asked: 'If the task is to assist potential immigrants in lobbying on their behalf with officials of the Immigration Department how would someone with a name like Nailin Wang or Wee How Fam or Subendra Vimalarajah—how would these people be proficient in the kind of needs of a potential immigrant?'[74]

For the Minister's courage, courtesy and industry, for his toughness to others and kindness to Jones, Philip Ruddock also got top marks:[75]

> Dear Philip,
> I can't but write to you following your many excellent representations of worthy causes. No praise can be too heightened for your wonderful efforts in stripping away the bureaucracy and the insensibility from so much Government does. I am so immensely grateful for your efforts in taking the concerns I've raised with you with seriousness, compassion and effectiveness.
> You can be very proud of your remarkable successes. I deal with Government every day of my life. I write to more Ministers, I suppose, than anyone in the country. I have to say your efforts, in your difficult portfolio, are as good as it gets.
> Many thanks, Philip. Congratulations, on behalf of so many 'battlers', for your outstanding work.
> With best wishes,
> Alan Jones.

Treasurer Peter Costello also received bags of letters. Although Jones appeared to favour Sydneysider Abbott to succeed the Sydneysider John Howard, at this stage Melburnian Peter Costello got high marks. Treasury issues tending to be more complicated, and small print never his long suit, Alan Jones asked others to fill in the details. When a listener queried a section of the Goods and Services Act, Jones told Michael Darby to draft a letter to Costello expressing alarm and concern.[76]

Alan Jones was not so pleased with the responses to his tsunami from then Health Minister Michael Wooldridge. He maintained his dim view of Finance Minister John Fahey (who had transferred to federal politics). National Party ministers were a barren lot, exasperatingly unreceptive to common sense. Tim Fischer was as uncooperative as his successor, John Anderson, of whom Alan Jones said, 'More people listen to Yellow Taxis than to his message'.[77] According to Jones, then Deputy Mark Vaile was also a 'dud'. But easily the most loathed Coalition member was Amanda Vanstone, who on air had bravely reminded Alan Jones of his personal stake in a fair and decent justice system.

It became particularly tough when she took on disability services, an area of special interest to Alan Jones: '... she is the worst person who has ever held that portfolio'.[78] Jones blamed Vanstone again and again for problems that were often the responsibility of the state government. 'I've said over and over again, the administration of that whole social security area by Amanda Vanstone is a disgrace and don't be surprised if it doesn't become a big issue at the next election.'[79]

Alan Jones made little secret of his campaign to have her sacked. 'I spoke off air to the Prime Minister yesterday about this farcical issue of caring.'[80] 'Will John Howard get rid of this woman before she single-handedly gets rid of the Howard Government? I will try and speak with the Prime Minister's office today.'[81] 'Maybe someone is starting to get the message or maybe someone is aware of the fact that the Prime Minister is not happy with the way this portfolio is being administered'.[82]

Jones even invited Opposition politicians to have a go. Wayne Swan claimed Amanda Vanstone's performance was embarrassing the Prime Minister.[83] Former union leader Jennie George joined in a public kicking. George: 'Good morning, Alan'. Jones: 'What a joke'. George: 'Oh it's a joke. It's just ridiculous ...' Jones' nastiness towards Vanstone was at times personal: '... and they have got to be confronted by a tart like Senator Vanstone ... what sort of a woman is this? Is she a woman?'[84]

The broadcaster takes the view that being tough on politicians has the virtue of keeping them on their toes. His opinions do cover a lot of bases, and sometimes slip mysteriously into reverse. After the minister who 'could not run a pigsty' took over immigration, Jones told listeners, 'Amanda Vanstone is doing a good job in this portfolio'.[85] There was more praise to follow.

Never too shy to snitch to the boss about unsatisfactory performances of his ministers, Alan Jones has directed many complaints to John Howard. The Prime Minister, as you might expect, is also at the top of Alan Jones' mailing list. In 1998 Jones was frank in his determination to educate the PM and his staff on how correspondence should be handled: 'I have a suggestion for the Department of the Prime Minister and Cabinet. When replying to correspondence addressed to the Prime Minister it is a good idea to begin with a frank statement along these lines: "because of the volume of correspondence, the Prime Minister has not had an opportunity to read your helpful letter. However I am aware of the Prime Minister's views on the matter you have raised".'[86] Jones was pleased when the PM appeared to follow his advice expressing satisfaction when, in what he saw as a result of this prompting, John Howard began to crack the whip.[87]

Alan Jones expressed to the PM his litany of pet hates about impersonal and rubber-stamped correspondence. When John Howard wrote to Alan Jones proposing he sponsor the nomination of Professor Geoffrey Blainey to the Companion level of the Order of Australia, the letter came addressed to 'Dear Mr Jones'. A displeased Alan Jones complained to staff of receiving a letter not personally penned by Howard then in the same breath instructed them to construct a reply.[88]

When the PM's performance continued to falter, Jones remonstrated: 'Please take this matter seriously, as I am obliged to tell you that the Howard Ministry lags far behind the NSW Government in responding to correspondence. My dealing with the Queensland Government, on a smaller scale, also reflects ministerial enthusiasm in swift handling of correspondence, an enthusiasm which does not prevail among your Ministers.'[89]

Alan Jones went on to bag Ministers Michael Wooldridge, Darryl Williams and Amanda Vanstone, and to praise Tony Abbott. 'I mention these matters, Prime Minister, because if responses to a prominent broadcaster are so disappointing, then responses to the general public are likely to be no better. One reason for the Carr Government's success at the polls has been the willingness of Ministers to take seriously the vital question of response time.'[90] Five days later, Jones again faxed his complaints about Howard's ministers, and added their parliamentary staff to his hit list, complaining that Young Liberals on the staff were devoting their time to jockeying for winnable seats rather than serving constituents' interests.[91]

John Howard's reaction was to appoint one of these younger Liberals to personally take charge of Alan Jones' demands. Anthony Roberts, who did go on to win the state seat of Lane Cove, became Alan Jones' troubleshooter in the PM's office, known unofficially as the 'Minister for Alan Jones'. He became another of many employed to attend to the multitude of requests from the broadcaster.

Roberts and the PM's senior advisor, Anthony Benscher, also gave personal briefings, Benscher penning a handwritten note after one get-together: 'Thanks so much for a lovely evening last Wednesday. Your hospitality was overwhelming ... we should contrive that practise every 6–8 weeks or so, your program permitting. I felt we achieved a great deal. With thanks, Anthony Benscher.'[92]

It is hard to imagine there was not some gagging in the PM's office about the demands of the failed member for Earlwood, who sometimes wrote twice in one day. They could not have been unaware of Alan Jones' boastful and imperious behaviour. Radio station employees are embarrassed when they are instructed to inform the nation's leader that Alan Jones will soon be ready to see him.

John Howard does, if politely, resist being pushed around by Alan Jones. In September 1999 Jones received a two-page typewritten letter, which began in the PM's hand: 'Dear Alan ... I have always admired the passion with which you advocate your views. However, in some cases, your views and those of the Government may differ. I understand such differences will not usually be to your liking. However, sometimes we will have to agree to disagree.'[93] After promising to get Anthony Roberts to redouble his efforts, John Howard went on to explain why he was refusing a representation by Jones to grant a New Zealand doctor, Alan Evans, a Medicare provider number: 'Alan, I understand that will disappoint you. Please be assured that I do appreciate your raising issues of importance, as I regard your efforts as a valuable resource to ensure our policies deliver outcomes focussed on the needs and aspirations of mainstream Australia. From time to time however, we will disagree. Please continue to correspond with my office. Anthony Roberts will be in touch following our weightier consideration ...'[94]

Alan Jones advocated on behalf of the New Zealand doctor, having been persuaded of the merits of the case by Dr Stanley Stylis, the founder of the Sydney Sleep Clinic, who had offered employment to Dr Evans. When the government examined the issue again and stuck to its position, Alan Jones was not content to accept the umpire's verdict. Jones did not see he had succeeded in ensuring efficiency, but that he had failed in not achieving the intended outcome. Alan Jones' belief that he was right and John Howard's advisors wrong was unshaken telling them he still regarded Dr Evans treatment by the bureaucracy as reprehensible.[95]

It is hard to think of many Australians who have done as much to devalue the office of public service as Alan Jones. Attacks on people with little opportunity to fight back occur almost daily. Defending bureaucratic process seems hopeless. One minister who was having trouble convincing Jones that a listener had not given him the full facts was driven to improperly reveal a confidential file. To the distress of many a public servant, the Jones bias too often infects their bosses. When, late on a Sunday night, a 2UE employee tried to line up an interview with a rear admiral, she was told by a navy public relations officer that it was too late to get the admiral on air for the following morning.

After the interview was obtained by other means, Alan Jones went on the hunt for the scalp of a bureaucrat. He wrote to the Prime Minister, copying his letter to the Defence Minister, naming the offending public relations officer. 'I write in relation to this bloke who presumably is a public servant. Your Government should know that these sorts of people are very difficult to deal with and, in my view, have limited worth ... can you believe the impertinence of this fellow who told me that my request for an interview should have been made on Friday! ... Could you please let me know what the Government's attitude is to people like this. In my position, we're only trying to assist the public and the cause ... I'd be interested in your response.'[96] The prime minister's office politely declined Alan Jones' invitation to a lynching. David Ritchie, a senior advisor, replied, telling Jones: 'The Prime Minister was concerned to learn of the difficulties you describe in your letter'.[97]

Jones also went on the hunt for a highway patrol officer who booked him for speeding. Jones wrote to New South Wales Police Minister Paul Whelan: 'Paul, this is policing of the very worst kind. This bloke, by his irresponsibility and his refusal even to be concerned as to what he'd done, disqualifies himself from any entitlement to be handling the public ... Needless to say, I expect something to be done. I am sick and tired of defending the police force when it's peopled by yahoos like this.'[98] Jones paid the fine. The officer kept his job. But as explained in a later chapter, after Paul Whelan crossed Alan Jones over a different issue, he was replaced as police minister.

The powerful broadcaster wrote similarly to other powerbrokers. In June 1999 his 'pick and stick' pal James Packer received a letter of complaint about a Channel 9 employee. Brendon Julian, a cricketer and Perth-based presenter, was deemed guilty of disrespect. The offence arose when Alan was hosting a function for the returning Australian team. Jones complained to James Packer that Brendon Julian had acted like a boofhead and a yahoo, not showing him enough respect. He finished by telling James Packer that perhaps a 'galah' like Brendon Julian should not be a presenter on Channel 9.[99] Brendon Julian held on to his television career.

Antipathetic, sympathetic: as a fellow King's teacher once observed, to Alan Jones a boy was either brilliant, brilliant or a no-hoper. To an infatuated Alan, the South Sydney Rugby League player Darrell Trindall was the former. In May 1999 the League judiciary cited Trindall following an alleged high tackle on a Newcastle player. Jones' boy, who had five previous suspensions, was given seven weeks. To Jones, the sentence was the gravest of charges.

Alan Jones claims his only rationale for selecting subject matter is its newsworthiness. In his prime time spot on 31 May Jones devoted nine angry minutes to this minor sports story. The broadcaster might have been Atticus Finch in an Alabama courthouse defending Tom Robinson, so impassioned was his plea. 'I want to say something this morning, with some alacrity I might add, about the issue of Darrell Trindall.'[100] Jones did not agree Trindall's tackle was dangerous. Alan Jones attacked judiciary panellist Jim Hall, calling him one-eyed. He implied the panel was biased against Souths, even though two members, Hall and Rabbitoh's legend Bob McCarthy, had played for the club.

Jones also got stuck into Newcastle coach Warren Ryan, claiming he had called Trindall, as Jones put it, 'a black c___'. Jones alleged Ryan 'told the official that Trindall was a criminal off the field, and urged this official to get him and do something about it'. The 11-page editorial read on air was stapled to a letter written to the chairman of the Newcastle club, Michael Hill.

Jones told Hill that in defence of a poor and decent person, he was obliged to pursue the matter.[101]

Alan Jones' argument that the tackle was not high was not supported by video evidence. Darrell Trindall lost his appeal. The four members of the New South Wales Rugby League judiciary, accused of selective vision, sued Alan Jones. The blindness of Jones' own position became evident before the defamation court, when no contest was offered. 2UE settled and an apology was made.

Darrell Trindall was also forgiven for off-field misbehaviour. Other correspondence shows Alan Jones assisting with bills, and pushing business and career opportunities his way while problems with violence, alcohol and the law persisted. Alan Jones' allies, such as Souths' boss George Piggins, saw the upside: 'Despite having stubbed his toes more times than he should have, he's one of the quiet success stories of the game. He has invested wisely and well.'[102] Piggins saw Trindall living in his own home, and with investments to help him in a life beyond football. As the argument goes, without Alan Jones' intervention he could have been in a cell or worse. Other lesser fans at Souths wondered if the 'quiet success story' was not playing Jones off a break.

After Trindall's 1999 suspension, there was worse news for Souths. In October, the club with the most successful premiership record was eliminated from the National Rugby League. 'On Rugby League, Rupert, you are wrong', Jones told a baying crowd at the Save South Sydney ball. The boardroom assault on the spirit of the game so offended supporters, as many as 30 000 had gathered in the city of Sydney to voice their protest. News Limited, held largely responsible by supporters and Jones, reported the rally in the *Daily Telegraph* on page 44.

Rupert Murdoch's Superleague venture cost News Limited as much as $700 million and now there was further loss of goodwill as the story dragged on. A solution was critical, with an obvious option being the merger of Souths with one of the existing teams. Alan Jones publicly supported a popular view within the club that Souths should continue to compete, as it had done for 90 years, in a stand-alone fashion. He took a public set against Souths' board members who demonstrated disunity, attacking one of them for 'breaking bread with Cronulla'.[103] He was further critical of those who, in their manoeuvring for a solution, appeared to go behind the back of Chairman George Piggins.

Souths' appeal against the Federal Court verdict was set for July 2001. Although they mounted a worthy case, there was no grand cause for confidence. Some 'realists' thought the verdict would go against them. Souths supporter and Alan Jones' rival Andrew Denton, as well as ex-cricketer Michael Whitney, had taken the initiative and secured funding from Network Seven owner Kerry Stokes to help with the legal battle. Looking for a way through the impasse, Andrew Denton also met twice with News Limited chief John Hartigan.

Openly critical of Denton, disunity and deal making, you can only wonder what was in Alan Jones' mind when he organised his own meeting. Unbeknown to a great many Souths supporters, and apparently to George Piggins himself, John Hartigan turned up at Alan Jones' home in mid April 2001. A small and influential group of Souths stalwarts listened alongside John Hartigan to Alan Jones speak up for a merger with one of the Superleague clubs, Canberra. They were told the merged club could be something like the Southern Rabbitohs, they could be headquartered in Canberra but play some of their games in Sydney. The lime green jersey of Canberra could be adjusted to something closer to the green and red of Souths. Alan Jones took charge of the pitch, with John Hartigan nodding in agreement. Alan Jones told those assembled: 'George [Piggins] has got to realise we can't win every round. We should get together. It is better to have a bit of something rather than a lot of nothing.'

To Rabbitoh loyalists, a proposed merger with a Superleague club was a marriage made in hell. When South Sydney chose to reject all ideas of a merger, Jones appeared to quietly disown the Canberra deal.

Against the expectations of many within the Souths camp, the red and greens won their appeal, and readmission to the

Another football career, this time at South Sydney, brought Alan Jones into contact with a new favourite, Darrell 'Tricky' Trindall. (Newspix/Grant Turner)

Olympic swimmer Scott Miller is one of many athletes assisted and given accommodation by Alan Jones. (Newspix/Gregg Porteous)

While some staff remained loyal, others wilted before Jones' notorious temper. Radio producer Niamh Kenny resigned following the Atlanta Olympics only to rejoin and resign once more. (Newspix/Frank Violi)

Alan Jones, who places great store on personal loyalty, supported John Howard's rise to Prime Minister as well as his friend Ross Turnbull whose fortunes declined following his troubled stewardship of the Australian Rugby Union. (Newspix/Anthony Moran)

Important to each other's careers, Alan Jones and New South Wales Premier Bob Carr flirted and tiffed like teenagers. While spin-master Carr generally got the better of Jones, Carr's apprentices floundered. (Newspix/Rohan Kelly)

During a 'no-speakies' period with Bob Carr, Alan Jones became an enthusiastic supporter of New South Wales Opposition leader Kerry Chikarovski despite having earlier regarded her as 'non existent'. (Newspix/Dan Peled)

Australia's richest man, Kerry Packer, was a charter member of Jones' 'Pick and Stick' club. Here Alan accompanies Kerry and his wife Ros to a function for US President George Bush. (Fairfaxphotos/Andrew Taylor)

Other members of the 'Pick and Stick' club were manager Harry M Miller and friend Veronica Fordham. (Newspix/Mossop)

**Office of
Professor David Flint
Chairman**

**Australian
Broadcasting
Authority**

Level 15 Darling Park
201 Sussex St
Sydney
PO Box Q500
Queen Victoria Building
NSW 1230
Phone (02) 9334 7700
Fax (02) 9334 7799
E-mail info@aba.gov.au
DX 13012 Market St Sydney

11 June, 1999

Mr Alan Jones
2UE
PO Box 954
St Leonards
NSW 2065

Dear Alan,

Thank you for your letter of 2 June. Alan, you have an extraordinary ability of capturing and enunciating the opinions of the majority on so many issues.

This of course annoys those who have a different agenda. I suspect it is extremely irritating to them that you do it so well.

Hence in parts of the media and our academic institutions reference to your programme is greeted in the way I suggested. Which, I am sure, does not concern you greatly.

Keep up your considerable contribution to the widening of our national debates.

*Sincerely
David*

David Flint

Recycled Australian Paper

Alan Jones sends and receives what he calls a 'tsunami' of correspondence. This is the famous fan letter from ABA chairman David Flint. (Private collection)

Alan Jones was often made to look silly inside the 'cash for comment' hearing room. But outside, where he faced the court of public opinion, Jones was a textbook study in media management. (Newspix/Mark Evans)

Alan Jones joined dissident police officer Tim Priest (right) and academic Richard Basham(left) in a campaign that led to the demise of Police Commissioner Peter Ryan and Police Minister Paul Whelan. According to one politician, Alan Jones stopped dead police reform. (Newspix/Chris Hyde)

Nicknamed 'The Parrot', Alan Jones appeared to grow into his psittacine profile. The *Sydney Morning Herald's* Alan Moir depicted him (top) with John Howard and David Flint, and (bottom) with New South Wales Labor Minister Michael Costa. (Alan Moir/*Sydney Morning Herald*)

Alan Jones has many faces, at least one of them exceedingly generous. He is seen here at a 2003 charity fundraiser for the Waddell and Koroneos families, victims of a tragic fire. (Newspix/Noel Kessel)

A godfather many times over, Alan is devoted to Hunter Taylor, who is known to some at 2GB as 'the heir'. Hunter is the son of Alan's niece, Tonia Taylor. (Newspix/Lannon Harley)

competition. Alan Jones is credited as an important force in the ultimate survival of the club. Those who saw him drift into the camp of the enemy and give support to a dreaded merger are content to keep him onside.

It has not been easy. When George Piggins was deposed as chairman in 2003, Jones was furious with the people who opposed Piggins and came between him and his dressing room. Alan Jones attacked the new administration on air and threatened the new board with a swingeing chain of correspondence: 'Unless I hear from you, by way of immediate response to this communication, I think it's in the best interests of South Sydney if all its supporters and members learn, in the public place of the awful mess that you have already made of the place and are in the process of making'.[104]

Souths' temporary absence from the competition was another problem for the prodigal Trindall. Alan Jones was able to help once more, by using his influence to get the aging athlete a run with the Canterbury Bulldogs. There was more trouble. Not long into his contract, Tricky Trindall was released from the club after a fight with a team mate and an alleged assault on a female receptionist. Alan continued to blame alcohol rather than Darrell, or the shortcomings of his own mentorship.[105]

Alan Jones also advocated for his other particular favourite, Jacin Sinclair. In 1999, when Sinclair was playing in the feeder First Division competition, Alan Jones wrote to manager Wayne Beavis asking for help.[106] Jones seemed to be aware that his own involvement in the lives of these athletes was not always to their benefit. He told Beavis that Sinclair should not be disadvantaged because Alan Jones was godfather to his kids.[107]

Despite the defection to Rugby League and the many setbacks in a quest to return to Rugby Union, Alan Jones kept alive the dream of being again asked to coach a national side. He wrote to a friend in Ireland saying he would seriously consider relocating to Ireland to coach the national side.[108]

Nineteen ninety-nine was a Rugby World Cup year and the Wallabies were on their own quest to win back the Webb Ellis trophy, lost to South Africa in 1995. A bitter Jones maintained his swipes at officials. He told Communications Manager Strath Gordon: '... you're part of the bureaucracy! There are plenty of you! ... Quite frankly, the treatment of clubs and provinces in the modern day organization of the game leaves a lot to be desired.'[109] In a letter to an old rugby mate he repeated his defamation of rugby boss John O'Neill, declaring that he had made an absolute mess of the State Bank and was doing the same to Australian Rugby.[110]

Not wanting instability and bad publicity at a time when greater attention was being focused on the game, the beleaguered Union adopted the familiar containment policy. Coach Rod Macqueen invited Alan Jones into the dressing room to address his team during the build-up period.

When the Wallabies fought their way through to face France in the final, Alan Jones' friends joked that he had become the Tricolour's number one fan. After Australia's 35–12 win, captain John Eales' speech, forgiving French spite, was replete with the grace absent in Alan Jones. Nineteen ninety-nine turned out to be a great year for Australian rugby. John O'Neill must have got something right.

The next World Cup, staged in Australia, saw a replay. Ross Turnbull again argued that Alan Jones should be brought back to rescue the team. Alan Jones' hatred for the new Wallabies coach, Eddie Jones, eclipsed his feelings for John O'Neill. Eddie Jones was one of the Matraville cabal at Randwick, known for his on-field sledging of Alan Jones favourite Brian Smith. Of his namesake and successor, Alan Jones wrote in a widely circulated email, '... he's a dunce, a dope, a fool, a pig and a classic case of a bloke promoted once too often'. Alan Jones attributed Eddie Jones' success at the Brumbies to Rod Kafer. 'He was the eyes and ears of the team ... I often think you're better off not being coached than badly coached.'[111]

When Australia last staged a Rugby World Cup, Alan Jones' Wallabies finished fourth. Under Eddie Jones in 2003, the Wallabies found form and fought their way to the final, where they lost to England. The supposedly clueless Eddie Jones, whose coaching career would, with some urging from Alan Jones, also reach its use-by date, had on this occasion shown some class. As for mess-maker John O'Neill, under his administration turnover had lifted from $9 million in 1995 to $72 million in 2003.

Alan Jones did not hold himself to account for his earlier position that the game was a shambles and John O'Neill was the problem. In a post-World Cup editorial, which acknowledged O'Neill's success, Alan Jones made a virtue of his attacks: 'We have all had our arguments with John O'Neill. I have had them as well. But that's why he's successful. You can have an argument with him. He's got a view. He gets things done. He puts people offside. That's the nature of successful people.'[112]

John O'Neill shared with Olympics Minister Michael Knight a single-mindedness that does not win popularity contests. They shared similar experiences in their dealings with a single-minded Alan Jones. One major difference was that Michael Knight would not be forgiven.

Before the 2000 Olympic Games, Alan Jones also predicted there would be 'structured chaos'. Below Knight in Jones' bad books was events organiser Ric Birch and SOCOG chief John Coates. The trio appeared to share a view that the success of the Games mattered more than what Alan Jones said. In Jones' good books were former AOC Secretary General Phil Coles and SOCOG Chairman Sandy Hollway. When Knight lost confidence in his chairman over ticketing problems and began to snipe, Jones sided with Hollway, a respectful correspondent. Jones wrote to Hollway suggesting personalities such as Don Burke be used to promote ticket sales: '... that's better than listening to that dreadful Michael Knight leer his way onto the public screen'. He went further, suggesting the games be popularised by identifying them with such figures as Tony Lockett, Laurie Daley and, guess who, Darrell Trindall.[113]

Jones joined a media attack on the proposition that marching bands be imported. The events organiser was lashed on 2UE: 'No one would have any faith that he would know how to organise an opening ceremony ... Ric Birch ... give him the birch ... You should never have been given this job.'[114] The 'fiasco', as he called it, ended up costing SOCOG an additional million dollars when the original plan was junked. As author Harry Gordon put it: 'The double back-down over a fairly trivial issue, driven mainly by shock-jocks, cost SOCOG more credibility and good-will than it could afford.'[115]

When, in an effort to mollify him, Alan Jones received a late invitation to an event showcasing the Stadium Australia suites, the broadcaster declined: 'I'm not into all that business about "rubbing shoulders" with notables! I am happy to enjoy the track and field in more modest circumstances.'[116]

After the Sydney Olympics and the opening and closing ceremonies proved to be anything but a shambles, Ric Birch wrote that Alan Jones had repeatedly tried to have him removed.[117] Alan has a different story, again seeing his attacks as virtuous: 'There has been a lot of criticism along the way of Ric Birch. I was among those critics, but I'm delighted to say that he delivered. I'm not one of those people who sits hoping for others to fail, and I think those people who were critical, were critical in the hope that Ric Birch would do justice to Australia on this important occasion.'[118]

In politics, business and sport the lesson in handling Alan Jones was now largely understood. If you could swallow it, avoid the problem in the first place with a show of courtship and respect. And if you could not avoid a thrashing, push your message through rivals such as Mike Carlton and John Laws.

The most common opposition to Alan Jones occurs through other media, often media completely beyond the orbit of Alan's audience. At the top of Alan Jones' media hit list in the lead-up to the Olympics was the Fairfax Press. He despised David Leser's 1998 profile, and he bridled at persistent references to the Parrot. Alan Jones was as certain of the villainy of Fairfax as he was of his own virtue: 'Where are we going to be able to achieve any standards of honesty in journalism ... I don't know when society has been worse. The Fairfax Press are out of control ... what a battle. Thank God we've got the energy for it.'[119]

His relationship with the *Herald*'s major competitor, the *Daily Telegraph*, was more complicated. Alan Jones' listeners were more likely *Tele* readers, and Alan often quarried material from the paper for his program. A tag team relationship between the *Tele* and Jones increased the potency of both parties. The Superleague fallout had been damaging. Alan Jones' attacks left blood trails through the pages of the *Tele*. Remembering their earlier support over the London episode, there were mutterings around News Limited to the effect that 'getting into bed with Alan Jones was like getting into bed with a cobra'.

But neither side saw an interest in maintaining the feud, News adopting the familiar containment strategy. In 1999 *Daily Telegraph* editor Col Allan wrote to Alan Jones and an awkward peace was brokered. On air Jones was again an enthusiast: 'There's a lift-out in today's *Daily Telegraph* about Manly Beach in 1912. Given that most people have given up buying the *Sydney Morning Herald* ... it's not worth reading until it dedicates itself to the truth—and finds itself incapable, on many instances of doing that. So have a look at your *Daily Telegraph* ... fantastic stuff.'[120] Alan Jones was not reading an advertisement.

He also resumed a respectful relationship with the *Tele*'s chief columnist, Piers Akerman. There was much that united the conservative commentators, but one issue to put them in opposite corners was media policy. Both were heavyweight bother boys, Alan weighing in for Packer, and Piers for Murdoch. When Alan Jones argued for a limiting of competition in the new digital television market, Akerman responded in print with an opinion piece headlined: 'YOU'RE WRONG ALAN'. Piers Akerman argued that Jones' position served to profit the Packers: 'Indeed his remarks might have been seen as an echo of those held by his close friend James Packer'.[121]

It was a gloved assault from the bare-knuckle columnist. Akerman also showed respect, calling Jones 'the undisputed king of breakfast radio'. Alan Jones was equally keen to avoid offence. He first sought intelligence to reinforce his original argument but, unsure of his reply, passed the material to a researcher with an attached memo saying that he had drafted a letter to Akerman but that he was unhappy with it. Jones explained that he had further information from Andrew Robb regarding digital television and that he wanted the information included in a response that was gentle, but he also managed to point out that Piers Akerman's criticism equally applied to Piers Akerman.[122]

With the help of the Liberal Party's Andrew Robb, and his own wordsmith, Alan Jones set out to impress and beguile. Identifying a common enemy might have helped. Alan Jones argued that to continue a predictable Packer versus Murdoch debate would be sterile, insulting to their intellects and very ABC.[123]

Alan Jones was careful to quarantine his responses to newspaper criticism. When his friend New South Wales Liberal politician and former King's student Jeremy Kinross was similarly offended by an Akerman article, Jones advised that he had made it a matter of conspicuous personal policy never to respond to comment of any kind made about him in the newspapers. He thought that overall they tended to even themselves out and that by focussing on the negatives wider attention is drawn to articles that the bulk of Sydney people had not read. He finished: 'Please discuss this with me before you go any further.'[124]

Alan Jones' position on the ABC is also complicated. In correspondence to listeners, and often on air, he adopts the Akerman line that the public broadcaster is leftist and unaccountable. But there is a soft spot too. In his youth, particularly in the bush, Jones was alive to the benefits of the ABC regional service, which kept him in touch with diverse interests such as horseracing and opera. Occasionally on air he promotes and praises individual programs. Generally, he is a fan of the television series *Australian Story*, although he was less keen on the August 2000 episode about the battle to save South Sydney, in which Andrew Denton featured prominently and Alan Jones was barely seen. When a tape of the program was sent to Belford Productions, the ABC was told Jones tossed it straight in the bin.

Alan Jones often pretends he pays no attention to programs that displease. To those around him it is clear the opposite is true, with Alan sometimes inadvertently detailing knowledge of content he alleges not to have seen. The ABC's *Media Watch*, which features Alan Jones in its opening titles, is at the bottom of his barrel: 'I find the Media Watch performance quite repulsive! The world can do without these knockers. That's what's wrong with this country.'[125]

At the beginning of 1999, his revulsion was moderated by *Media Watch*'s unstitching of his rival, John Laws. In February, John Laws interviewed Tony Aveling from the Australian Bankers' Association, giving the banks a good run. His position contrasted so markedly to a former position, *Media Watch* went on the prowl and discovered a deal between the bankers and Laws. Later in the year John Laws' contract with the Australian Bankers' Association was leaked to *Media Watch*, which continued to untangle the secret deals. A series of reports between May and July forced a different ABA, the Australian Broadcasting Authority, to examine the propriety of the arrangements.

The ABA would use its powers to consider potential breaches of 2UE's licence conditions, which saw Alan Jones dragged into the net. The ABA said: 'After further allegations appeared in the media concerning financial arrangements between 2UE's breakfast program presenter, Alan Jones and commercial interests, the Authority announced that it would be widening the scope [of] its inquiry to include 2UE broadcasters other than John Laws'.[126] In replying to correspondents who commiserated with him about being roped in, Alan Jones was at first unfussed, assuring them he had not made comment for money or changed his mind for money. He told them he resented his name being dragged into the controversy.[127]

At 2UE there were mounting ructions. Chairman John Conde was still having trouble getting his stars to confess their commercial arrangements. Four days after the ABA announced its inquiry 2UE's company secretary issued a memo about 'on air promotion of third parties'. Belford Productions was directed to 'supply within seven (7) days a list of all Promotional Contracts to which you, or any company with which you are associated, is a party'.[128] Alan Jones did not comply within the specified timeframe. John Laws was equally reluctant. The theory around the station at the time was that if a sacrifice was called for, Laws rather than Jones would go, as Alan Jones was worth more to the station.

Laws fought back on air, making his feelings about Jones known. Alan Jones did not respond in kind but in private was less circumspect, telling one anti-Laws correspondent that he agreed with the criticism of Laws and that he hoped the truth would find its mark. He went on to say that jealousy is a terrible thing and that Laws was worried about the inquiry. Alan Jones believed a further difficulty for him was that News Ltd now loathed him because of the Super League drama and that the *Sydney Morning Herald* was always opposed.[129]

At this stage Alan Jones insisted he was not worried, although to his staff he exhibited more caution. Two weeks after the Australian Broadcasting Authority announced the inquiry, Alan Jones distributed a memo to his broadcast staff on the subject of 'Confidentiality'. He asked that stuff not be left lying around and that confidential material be properly handled. '... How does anyone imagine the A.B.C. have got hold of certain documents in relation to John Laws. It can only be from sloppy handling of confidential material ...'[130]

While Alan was worried about enemies at the ABC, he had reason to see a friend in the ABA. Chairman David Flint is a member of the Liberal Party and as National Convenor for Australians for a Constitutional Monarchy shared a further allegiance. A referendum on the question of Australia becoming a republic was due in November. Alan Jones launched the 'No' case in New South Wales Parliament, warning the public not to trust the news media 'who agree with the last person they had lunch with'.[131]

Alan Jones had another reason to believe David Flint was on his side. Flint was already a declared fan of Jones and talkback radio, and a declared enemy of *Media Watch*. In a speech two years earlier the chairman told the Communication and Media Law Association: 'Although *Media Watch* frequently attacks ... and lambasts Mr Alan Jones ... these programs give generous opportunities to other people's views, opposing views. When did we last hear this on *Media Watch*?'[132] At the time, David Flint sent Alan Jones a copy of the speech, referring to then *Media Watch* host Stuart Littlemore as 'the ABC's resident media critic'.

Alan Jones replied: 'I'm just acknowledging it prior to reading. However your reference to that ogre on the ABC most probably gives him a notoriety to which he certainly isn't entitled. David, his career is best summed up by saying that he is a failed broadcaster. The ABC, at taxpayers' expense has room for such people. In the world of spending your own money, the bloke wouldn't be able to find a job. And thanks for demonstrating a rare understanding of the democracy of talkback radio. Keep at it, David. I think they are on the run, otherwise they wouldn't be so defensive in their behaviour.'[133]

Another groundhog day occurred on 25 May 1999. Following the first of the *Media Watch* 'cash for comment' reports, David Flint addressed the Sydney Institute. Again he quibbled about elitist snubbing of Jones: 'Now if you say you listened to Alan Jones in some circles you will be greeted with at least polite silence, and more likely outraged disapproval'.[134] Again Flint sent Jones a copy, and again Jones replied: 'David, you must be moving in the circles of the media! They just hate people who've had success or who can attract an audience far greater than their own. I must say things as I see them and work very hard at putting my ideas together. The fact that we seem to have some success is most probably the biggest problem I have! However, we keep at it. Sometimes I wonder why. Thank you for writing to me.'[135]

Using Australian Broadcasting Authority letterhead, the chairman responded with a now famous letter: 'Alan, you have an extraordinary ability of capturing and enunciating the opinions of the majority on so many issues. This of course annoys those who have a different agenda. I suspect it is extremely irritating to them that you do it so well. Hence in parts of the media and our academic institutions reference to your program is greeted in the way I suggested. Which, I am sure, does not concern you greatly. Keep up your considerable contribution to the widening of our national debates. Sincerely David.'[136]

The following week Alan Jones wrote back: 'Dear David, Thank you for your kind and generous note. I do understand what you're saying. Mind you, much of all this is informed by jealousy. Some of these people thought that they were going to "call the shots" for years to come. They've had the rug pulled from under them. It's absolutely essential that we don't give them any more breathing space! I don't frighten easily! I really appreciated the fact that you'd taken the trouble to write.'[137] Prime Minister John Howard was known for similar beliefs. Howard's supporters saw his success as an expression of the failure of an elitist media which had constantly opposed him and was now resentful.

Three weeks after Alan Jones' reply to David Flint, the ABA formally began its 'cash for comment' inquiry. A cultural ally of his own chief regulator, unaccountable to his own employer, in a position to lecture his prime minister, Alan Jones had cause to feel his power would protect him. The broadcaster who often champions tougher regulations works within an industry that has minimal oversight. The broadcast industry, with its own aversion to Big Brother scrutiny, likes to think its best regulator is its public.

Alan Jones probably felt safe here too, with good cause to believe his public was happy with his work. They listened in large numbers and frequently expressed their gratitude for his many good deeds. And then there are those 7578 letters he sent out. Attention to his tsunami of correspondence positioned Alan Jones at the spearhead of a constituency which empowered him beyond the strength of his own words. When Jones applied leverage, additional force was delivered by the weight of his audience, the mighty voice of democracy appropriated as his own. The increasing thousands of letters received each year became more ammunition in the arsenal of a demagogue and fuel in the furnace of the narcissist.

The tsunami reveals only the occasional challenge. When one listener identified an inconsistency in his position on welfare for single mothers, Alan was angered, attacking the writer as 'ungenerous and unworthy'.[138] When the correspondent wrote again, pointing out that his abusive response failed to confront the logic of her argument, Jones fell back on righteousness: 'You must realise that I have on my left approximately 65 letters which I've just answered and on my right another 65 which have to be answered and I look forward, enthusiastically, you can imagine, to tomorrow's mail!!!'[139] It seems the critical mass of correspondence is its own argument. All those letters made him more right.

The exchange of correspondence with David Flint revealed more righteousness. Alan and David believed themselves in better touch than elitist media with the ideals of ordinary Australians. The integrity of this relationship was now to face a sterner test than either David Flint or Alan Jones could have anticipated.

CHAPTER 16
MONEY FOR NOTHING

'THE CURIOUS THING MR JONES is this: that you seem to be saying that what you have done you weren't obliged to do, and what you were obliged to do, you didn't do.'[1] It took these few well-chosen words from Australian Broadcasting Authority counsel Julian Burnside QC to remove another Alan Jones disguise. Jones' stand before the 'cash for comment' inquiry was that he had unwisely failed to comprehend the detail of his contracts, but that at no stage had his opinions been influenced by the millions of dollars he received.

Before giving evidence, Alan Jones told his listeners: 'The only spin that Jones puts on anything that he does on this program is Alan Jones' spin. Let me tell my listeners what they most probably already know—I've never been paid to say anything, no one's ever asked me to say anything in return for money. And certainly no one has ever prevented me from saying something, and it's not the way I operate.'[2]

Over five decades and four careers, Alan Jones survived a range of crises: the departure from King's, the loss of a New South Wales Parliament seat long held by the Liberals, sacked as a winning Wallabies coach and arrest in a public toilet. Now came a public trial with the potential to wreck his radio career and even produce criminal charges. But despite the folly of his argument and the finding going against him, Alan Jones was to triumph over this crisis as well, the experience highlighting the weakness of media regulations and the contrasting strength of owning the stage.

The public hearings began on 19 October 1999. Alan Jones seemed to genuinely welcome them. He seemed to genuinely believe that he would, in 'contradistinction' to his colleague John Laws, appear erudite and principled. Considering the Authority Chairman's flattering correspondence to Jones, it is possible Flint thought likewise.

Although the Australian Broadcasting Authority avoided the 'c' word, the issue was corruption. If broadcasters were receiving secret commissions to boost sponsors or bash up competitors, they were in potential breach of the law. However, the ABA is not a crime-fighting agency but a regulator of broadcasting codes of practice. The potential breaches of codes of practice related to clauses calling for the promotion of 'accuracy and fairness in news and current affairs programs', ensuring that 'viewpoints are not misrepresented' and that advertisements 'not be presented as news programs or other programs'.[3]

Before the inquiry began it was obvious the target would be 2UE rather than its stars, existing legislation putting the station rather than Laws and Jones in the frame for possible breaches of licence conditions. And there were further limits to sanctioning the stars: 'Neither the Codes nor the conditions imposed on licensees under the Act specifically address commercial arrangements entered into by presenters'.[4]

On the opening day, panel members were obliged to declare any contact they might have had with the parties concerned before the inquiry. Chairman David Flint explained that he had normal industry contact with 2UE Chairman John Conde. He painted a picture of insignificant contact with Alan Jones, saying they had once been introduced and that a month earlier, Alan Jones launched a book containing a chapter by David Flint. 'Apart from saying good morning to Mr Jones and his reply to me, there was no contact and no discussion.'[5] The Chairman did not publicly declare his private view that the 2UE breakfast broadcaster was a pen pal and soul mate. The 'stream of correspondence',[6] as he later described the letters between himself and Jones, which were a clear challenge to his independence, went unmentioned at this time.

But his objectivity was in question anyway. David Flint stood prominently alongside Alan Jones as a pro monarchist in the biggest public issue of this time, the republican debate. Professor Flint had also attended James Packer's October wedding at a time when the ABA was investigating the Packer family's stake in the Fairfax group.

Soon after the public hearings began the matter was settled by an astonishing own goal by David Flint. The ABA Chairman and Convenor for Australians for a Constitutional Monarchy left observers open-mouthed when he went on John Laws' show to defend an attack by former Prime Minister Bob Hawke and to promote the 'No' vote. When he went against the advice of his own Authority and did it again, allowing himself to be interviewed by another broadcaster under investigation, Howard Sattler, David Flint was unsavable. On 8 November David Flint got to his feet and announced that in order to avoid the distraction, destabilisation and delay of a proposed Federal Court challenge, he would stand down, even though he was confident he had done no wrong. Deputy Michael Gordon Smith took over.

At this stage John Laws was still more centre stage. Laws had been the focus of the *Media Watch* reports and he appeared to have more endorsement agreements than Jones. By now the ABA had identified only three Jones deals—Optus, Qantas and the Colonial State Bank—while Laws had similar deals with Optus, Qantas and the Australian Bankers' Association, as well as six other agreements. Alan Jones had not complied with 2UE's directive to supply details of all his contracts by the end of July. According to his boss, John Conde, it was not until 3 September that he learned of four further agreements with Walsh Bay, Walker Corporation, HarperCollins and Sunraysia.

Early media reports of the hearings concentrated on tensions between John Laws and John Conde. A *Bulletin* story by John Lyons, pre-empting Laws' evidence, revealed the controversial 1998 corridor episode, in which Conde allegedly indicated he was more worried about Jones. Conde immediately issued a press release disputing Laws' account. In the witness box soon after, Lawsy confessed to feeling he had been hung out to dry: 'With the greatest respect Mr Burnside, this to you is purely academic, but this to me is a 46 year career. If it is possible I would like to continue to be loyal to John Conde, but could I answer it by saying I feel let down.'[7]

By the first week of November, the tenth floor hearing room of the Australian Industrial Relations Commission in William Street was the best theatre in town. The retinue of silks from the A-list of the bar—Bret Walker SC for Jones, Jeffrey Hilton SC for Laws, Julian Burnside QC for the ABA, Tom Hughes QC for 2UE—took up seats alongside the A-list of the media. John Lyons of the *Bulletin*, Mark Day from News Limited and David Marr for the Fairfax group were just some of the journalists battling for elbow room in the 'cash for comment' colosseum.

Despite having already done a full day's work, when Alan Jones arrived to give evidence on 9 November he looked fresh and, if anything, eager to perform. In an immaculate steel grey, double-breasted suit and pale blue shirt with green and yellow silk tie and hanky, he was described by various media as 'cocky', 'confident', 'articulate', 'pre-emptive', 'relaxed' and 'jaunty'. Bret Walker, the King's School dux of 1972, had already worked hard for his client, pinning the ABA down in advance to the detailed particulars of allegations, narrowing the opportunity for later attack. Alan Jones did not enter the box until the early afternoon, following the completion of John Laws' evidence. Bret Walker started by taking his client through the easier part, the recounting of his prepared statement.

Alan Jones described his radio show as a news program. He accepted the requirement of the Broadcasting Code that advertisements should not be presented as news. According to

Alan, 'The only rationale behind anything that I do on-air is whether or not it is newsworthy; whether or not it is of interest to my listeners'.[8]

Alan Jones was certain he had not breached the code. Bret Walker asked him whether his contractor, Qantas, had proposed he broadcast his 'Open Skies' editorial. Alan Jones explained the editorial was entirely his own initiative. When Bret Walker asked about the clause in the Qantas contract whereby Jones agreed to regular editorial comment on 'topics proposed by Qantas', Alan Jones said he had not read it: 'I acknowledge that is not an excuse. I signed it, so I'm responsible for it.'[9]

Alan is used to sympathetic audiences, but there are moments when he misjudges the crowd. He will say at a business lunch, 'It is good to see so many men have brought their wives along', to be greeted by a groan from a room scattered with businesswomen. One attendee remembers a younger Jones, after a similar gaffe, being pelted with bread rolls.

At the ABA he was before as tough a crowd as he could find. The more he spoke the more they turned against him. Even Jones' major concession that he was remiss in not reading his contracts did not go down well. Alan, who still claims he reads everything that comes across his desk, was confessing to ill discipline he did not tolerate in others. And he was not plausible. Documents recovered from Harry Miller's files revealed a sometimes detailed understanding of his arrangements. Of the clause in the Colonial State Bank contract guarding against comment that would adversely reflect upon the bank, Jones said he was only now aware of it. Walker: 'How carefully did you read this agreement before you signed it?' Jones: 'Well not as carefully as I should have'.[10]

The other problem for Jones was his boasting. Where others saw dishonesty, Jones saw virtue. Where others saw corruption, Jones saw saintliness. He argued that the half-million dollars paid by Optus was more to secure an option for a pay TV program rather than to buy access to his radio show. He boasted about his support for Optus, seeing it as pioneering a push for competition in the telecommunications industry. Jones said he also 'led that charge' against the Circular Quay eyesore, the Toaster, despite it being a Colonial Bank investment.

Neither could he contain his hyperbole. When he spoke of assisting the bank's profile in regional Australia, the boy from southeast Queensland said: 'I think they knew that I was from the bush. My family came from Western Queensland, and there was a big problem facing all banks in that, for economic reasons under this notion of rationalism, bank branches were closing in large numbers in the bush.'[11]

When he left the witness box after two hours on that Tuesday afternoon, he ran into a tangle of reporters and microphones in the lift and on the street outside. Alan Jones would have known the public arena was, perhaps, a more important forum. While he had faced other challenges to ethical conduct, such as the Frederick Forsyth plagiarism affair, this inquiry posed a more serious risk to his public reputation.

If Alan Jones expected a favourable review of his first day's evidence, he would have been disappointed. The coverage, while not exactly hostile, was, at the least, cynical. At 10 am on 10 November, Bret Walker began Alan Jones' second day by admonishing the ABC, SBS and the *Australian* for 'shoddy' coverage. Bret Walker identified errors of fact, putting journalists on notice and asking for greater care to be taken. He then resumed his questioning.

Jones was again relaxed, articulate and proud of his work, explaining how he was solely responsible for the content, balance and integrity of his show: '... nothing on my program derives from my contractual arrangements which exist outside my program'.[12] When the subject of enhancing live reads was raised, Jones did not quite say he had learned to believe what he wanted to believe. 'As it says in Alice in Wonderland, I suppose, words mean what you want them to mean.'[13] For his failure to understand the fine print of his contracts, Jones did not blame his manager, Harry Miller. 'He does all the detail. I though am responsible for it. So any faults, they are not his, they are mine.'[14] (Outside the witness box, however, Jones seemed to have a very different view, calling Miller a 'cunt', and blaming him for much of the predicament.) He told a broadcasting colleague that he was aware that some of his contracts had been appallingly drafted. While avoiding going into detail he said he had to take responsibility, but 'I'm sure you can read between the lines'.[15]

While John Laws' agent, John Fordham, was called as a witness, Harry Miller escaped a grilling. How Miller avoided questioning clearly involved some tap dancing. Harry Miller was overseas at the times the ABA sought to call him. His absence enhanced a view that Miller abandoned Jones. Another possibility is that Alan Jones did not want his voluble manager anywhere near the witness box.

It was midmorning when Bret Walker SC finished questioning Jones and Julian Burnside QC got to his feet. Burnside had been drafted in from Melbourne, the ABA presumably feeling they were better off with an outsider. Being able to tactically withdraw to Melbourne when it was all over also meant Burnside would have had fewer concerns about making enemies.

Burnside, like Walker and all good barristers, is a professional advocate who accepts all comers. Although described as a 'political agnostic', the libertarian Melburnian appeared every bit the ideological opposite of Jones and Flint. The silver-haired silk became, with the women in particular, a media favourite.

It is tempting to see Sydney v Melbourne in Jones v Burnside. As the cross-examination wore on, the hot flashes of Jones meeting the cool reserve of Burnside was like lava hitting the sea. Julian Burnside was neither rude nor aggressive. He gave Alan Jones no cause to complain of brutal badgering. He gave no members of the public gallery opportunity to sympathise with the witness. He did, however, give Jones a terrible hiding, which was not forgotten. In subsequent years Julian Burnside's high profile role in assisting asylum seekers brought forth scorn in radio commentary, Jones referring to the human rights advocate as a 'bleeding heart'.

The cross-examination began gently, with Burnside showing sympathy as Jones struggled with his spectacles to read the evidence placed before him. Burnside: 'You've been up since 2 o'clock'. Jones: 'If I get into trouble I'll give you a shout'.[16] In most two-way dialogue Jones has control. This time Burnside took charge, checking Jones' verbosity and confining him to the question: 'Step by step, step by step, if you don't mind'.[17]

The ABA had not been able to purchase most of the broadcast transcripts they wanted. Given the unscripted nature of the medium, radio archives are not comprehensive. A lot of what had been said on air over six years was now lost in space. The inquiry having been rushed upon them, there was not much time to get on top of the rest of the paper trail either. The ABA had not, for example, collected all available documents from Harry Miller. But Julian Burnside still had plenty. And his evidence was well organised. Having compiled an electronic database, the lawyer wore out the search key, methodically matching the sponsors' documentation with Alan Jones' on air commentary.

Alan Jones, dismissive of any 'inquiry into memos', maintained he should be judged by what was said on air rather than what a contract said. Burnside began to produce examples of Jones doing what he said he was not doing. Quickly aware of the Burnside pattern of taking him through the memos and then producing the evidence of what was broadcast, Jones began to snip. 'I've got an easy answer to that Mr Burnside although it might not be satisfactory to you'.[18]

A low point for Alan Jones was his 'dog ate my homework' defence of his promotion of an Optus mobile phone as newsworthy comment. Alongside one another, the Optus briefing read much the same as Alan Jones' one-minute editorial. 'I've had so many calls about mobile phones ... Well Optus have got a new Freestyle pack ... So that's Optus Freestyle. Sounds interesting. Go into any Optus mobile outlet or ring 13 39 99 to find your nearest Optus World ...'[19]

As he dug his heels in, insisting that telling people to 'Freestyle it with Optus. Ask for the Freestyle Pack. 13 39 99' amounted to reporting news, there were more hoots from the gallery. Jones spluttered, 'Well it is interesting, isn't it Mr Burnside. It is interesting, and we have got a few laughs from the gallery ...'[20]

Alan Jones' credibility was also in doubt when he claimed that despite his manager's negotiations with Telecom/Telstra, he would never sign a contract with the hated competitor. Burnside: 'You wouldn't?' Jones: 'No'. Burnside: 'You wouldn't?' Jones: 'Never'. Burnside: 'Never. Never, is that right?' Jones: 'Never ...'[21] Later, panel member Kerry Henderson pressed further: 'Mr Jones am I correct in my understanding that what you have said, you would not be prepared to do live reads for Telstra or Telecom, as they then were?' Alan Jones replied, 'That's correct. That's correct.'[22]

There were more scoffs and chuckles from the gallery when Jones argued that his attacks on Telstra were not for the sake of boosting Optus. As the afternoon wore on his performance frayed. Fidgeting in his chair and whipping his spectacles on and off, there were also signs that his command of language was becoming strained. He began to reach too far, grabbing for words such as 'synonymity' and that new favourite, 'contradistinction'.

Before the day wound up, Burnside asked Jones for his response to the *Media Watch* program in July. The witness professed detached dignity, explaining he did not see or read about it. 'Those sorts of things are very difficult matters. I just have a policy I don't discuss ... on air matters relating to other broadcasters.'[23] Julian Burnside went on to ask whether John Conde or anyone else in management at 2UE had asked questions about his sponsorship agreements. Although Belford Productions had received a directive to provide a list of promotional contracts on 19 July, Jones replied, 'No'. Burnside asked, 'How many have you got now?' Jones: 'Well I don't know that. I think seven. But look I shouldn't answer because I don't know.'[24]

Alan Jones was back in the witness box the next morning. It was 11 November, Armistice Day, with no sign of a ceasefire in sight. At the beginning, Julian Burnside had trouble shutting the broadcaster up. Now the opposite was the case, the lawyer's questions meeting with lengthening pauses. Burnside: 'I think I see the problem. You're looking for a hidden trap. And there isn't one, there isn't one.' Jones: 'You're wily. We learn.'[25]

Nineteen minutes into the session, Alan Jones' temper let go: 'What are we on about, Mr Burnside? Let me just say something ... with respect—with respect—with respect, I mean there does come a time when one is entitled to become just a little impatient because if there is an attempt here to challenge my veracity then I must defend myself ...' Burnside: 'All I was driving at, Mr Jones, and I'm sorry if you feel defensive this morning, all I was driving at ...' Jones: 'I'm not defensive this morning. When one's integrity is challenged, Mr Burnside, you too would be defensive.' Bret Walker intervened in an effort to shield and settle Jones. Burnside carried on: 'Let's take it step by step, if we can. I'll warn you if I'm setting a trap, all right?' Jones: 'Oh yes. Next you'll be telling me the sun comes up in the west.'[26]

The next challenge to Alan Jones' spin was a touch sly. Julian Burnside turned to a memo criticising an Optus briefing note. Jones had complained that even with his education he could not understand it. Burnside: 'In the third paragraph, you say: "I have got three university degrees"; is that the fact?' Jones: 'Well, I've—did I say that? I don't think one of them's a degree, but close to that, yes.'[27]

The broadcaster was again unsettled as he listened to evidence such as his broadcast of the pro-Qantas 'Open Skies' editorial, and continued to deny the self-evident. For Qantas alone the ABA identified '30 "free" editorial-style mentions, on top of his embellished live reads.'[28] When the session finished and Alan Jones left the hearing room, Anne Davies of the *Sydney Morning Herald* asked him to reveal his additional contracts. Alan Jones snarled, 'I would if it was any of your business'.[29] Day three had been even worse for Jones. That night the ABC's *7.30 Report* described his run in the witness box as 'disastrous'.

John Brennan, the man with direct responsibility for enforcing compliance, had an even worse time. The 2UE program director was a forlorn figure when he slunk from Burnside's questioning. 'Brenno' put his hands up in minutes, conceding his terror at the prospect of questioning 'megastars' about outside deals. When Julian Burnside asked whether 'all hell would break loose' if he asked how much Optus was paying Mr Jones, Brennan replied, 'You could say that'.[30] By the end of a crippling experience, and the end of the month, the commercial radio veteran would announce his resignation from 2UE.

John Conde, a former member of the St James Ethics Centre, similarly departed the witness box leaving the impression he exercised little real control over the ethical conduct of his station and its stars. The 2UE chairman said, 'I wish I had been, I think in summary less trusting, more vigilant and more vigorous'.[31] He also said he felt 'betrayed' by John Laws and 'disappointed' by Mr Jones. Questioned about Jones' additional contracts, Conde was the first to identify them. Burnside: 'Doing your best what are their names?' Conde: 'The names are Walsh Bay, HarperCollins, Sunraysia and Walker Corporation'.[32] John Conde said he had asked Alan Jones to terminate all the deals, with the possible exception of Sunraysia.

Sydney Morning Herald reporters were quickly on the hunt. The next morning the newspaper reported Alan Jones' broadcast from Walker Corporation's Broadway Shopping Centre when it opened in 1998. The *Herald* also reported how, before the March state election, the Carr Government approved the Walsh Bay development after 15 years of argument.[33] Two days later, the man who started all this, Richard Ackland, revealed: '2UE breakfast broadcaster Alan Jones is believed to have been paid between $60,000 and $80,000 for favourable on-air treatment of the contentious Walsh Bay project'. Ackland, scouring the *Media Watch* files, found a range of endorsements from Jones, which were broadcast prior to and on approval of the development.[34]

The next day Anne Davies reported Walker Corporation was paying Alan Jones $30 000 a month. Davies also reported the developer 'was recently revealed as the company which had offered a $2.5 million lifeline to Alan Jones' beloved South Sydney Leagues Club'.[35] On air that morning Alan Jones, furious after reading the broadsheet's report, described the *Herald* coverage as 'disreputable', accusing the newspaper of being at the centre of a 'relentless campaign'.[36] He denied he had an endorsement agreement with Walker Corporation, describing himself as a consultant instead.

On the same day, the ABA declared it was actively investigating the four new sponsorship deals and had subpoenaed documents from Walker and Walsh Bay. It was also considering calling representatives from the companies and recalling Alan Jones.

The next day David Mann, the corporate public relations manager for the Mirvac Group, which oversaw the Walsh Bay development, was briefly in the box. His evidence was damning of Jones. Mann made it clear that their agreement was motivated by concerns about negative coverage. He said in response to the potential for bad press, Alan Jones and others were lobbied and Jones was asked 'to minimise the negative publicity and impact of that publicity'.[37]

Then Alan Jones was back in the hot seat. Burnside confronted Jones' proposition that he was merely a consultant, pointing out that three of the four clauses in the Walker agreement specified on air obligations. Alan Jones denied its thrust was about what he did on air: 'My commitment to Walker away from the radio station is quite significant ... I mean obviously the language of the contract doesn't capture what I understood my obligations off-air were'. Jones explained he was often flying off to view and launch their projects: 'I am perceived as being able to handle myself in front of a microphone, to command ideas and present them as Walker would want them presented ...'[38]

Alan then got himself into a little trouble before the ABA microphone. In seeking to find a clause in the contract that favoured his argument, he read the wrong section. The gallery again laughed. Jones bristled: 'I wasn't aware that this was a sort of comedy hour'.[39] When the questions about what he did understand his obligations to be persisted, Jones blustered:

'Chairman, heavens. I have worked very hard for my people off air. Can I just say—I didn't want to get to this point—but I am not just Alan Jones a broadcaster. I'd like to think I am Alan Jones a former senior advisor to a prime minister, who knows something about the political process; I think I am Alan Jones, a public speaker who has some capacity to handle ideas, which might be beneficial in the corporate sense. I am significantly in demand for work, which combines all of those things.'[40]

Chairman Michael Gordon Smith was now incredulous: 'The point I think that Mr Burnside has made to you is: how can you seriously expect us to take it that in signing this contract you did not believe yourself to be making any commitment about on-air behaviour?'[41] Jones responded by saying Walker Corporation had no problem with his service to them.

It was now Burnside's turn to be exasperated, asking Jones to explain how it was that he did what he wasn't obliged to do and did not do what he was obliged to do. Alan said the problem was the wording of his contract rather than anything said on air. He was then asked how this stand squared with his share price agreement with Walker, which provided a secret incentive to Jones to push the developer's interests. Alan Jones said he had put the share price issue out of his mind: 'I didn't start imagining that I was going to be some overnight sensation, that with live reads the share price would go through the roof'.[42]

Julian Burnside produced another of those telltale documents, the one in which Alan Jones wrote to Harry Miller pointing out Walker's share price had risen, finishing with the words: 'Let's face it, they wouldn't be in the public place without moi! Tell me what you think?'[43] Burnside: 'Do you suggest that you did not have in mind the terms of the agreement when you wrote that memo?' Jones: 'Well Mr Burnside, I think you can gather by the exclamation marks and the peculiar language I was jesting'.[44]

Julian Burnside asked whether it was just coincidence that on the day after he signed a $200 000 a year deal, Alan Jones made 'long and favourable' on air comments about the Walsh Bay proposal. The witness replied: 'Yes, and let me just explain why.

I've told this Tribunal persistently that for anything to be the subject of news or opinion by me, it must be newsworthy. It must be of interest, and it must have relevance to the concerns of my people.'[45] In Alan Jones' universe, if Alan says it is newsworthy, it is newsworthy. It seemed that what mattered were not the objective facts, but what was in his mindset. And if Alan could not see conflict of interest, it was unlikely listeners in his universe would recognise it either. But Court One of the Australian Industrial Relations Commission was a different place.

When he left the hearing room after his encore performance, the *Daily Telegraph*'s Mark Day asked: 'Do you believe your credibility has suffered through this whole process?' Alan Jones replied: 'Your credibility never suffers when you tell the truth'.[46] While the performance in the box drew poor reviews, outside the court Alan Jones was a textbook study in media management. Errol Simper of the *Australian* was another observer: 'Jones found himself again—bailed up outside the lifts by a microphone/camera-wielding media scrum. Jones politely answered each and every question, some of which were bluntly hostile. He found within himself a smiling precision, bordering on the punctilious.'[47]

There were only 100 seats in Court One. Millions would be watching the news that night. What mattered was not just what was in Alan Jones' mind, but what he could put in the minds of others. Alan was acculturated into a world where the facts matter less than what is believed. Over and over in the years to come he would continue to chant, mantra-like: 'everyone knows Alan Jones' opinions are not for hire'.

Writing up his observations, Mark Day described Alan Jones as 'affable, smiling and utterly composed' when explaining to reporters that the inquiry was probably a good thing, in that it cleared the air and would in all likelihood initiate helpful industry reforms.[48] Alan held to a well-prepared defensive line, conceding a weakness in not telling his listeners, having suggested from the start a register disclosing such arrangements. Behind that defensive line his listeners joined the huddle. When the ratings results were announced in December, Alan Jones won his 62nd straight survey. The audience was down by 0.3 to 17.7 per cent, the smallest drop at 2UE.[49] By February 2000, he was still on top with 17.5 per cent. By March he lifted to 18.9 per cent.[50]

Alan Jones' cachet also held with the politicians. Within two weeks of giving his ABA evidence, Jones was the host of a $500 a plate Liberal Party fundraiser. Two days after the ABA report was handed down Alan Jones interviewed Prime Minister John Howard. A federal election was due in 2001 so the government was going to need its friends. An interview with Bob Carr followed the next day, even though, in his case, an election was three years off. The New South Wales Government, although increasingly uncomfortable with Alan Jones, had made its bed and was forced to lie in it. Besides, when the now routine pre-election barneys came upon them, Bob Carr probably felt that if he had to play Jones' game, he could do so and win.

Julian Burnside was unsurprised: 'It was apparent during the hearing that the people who were worried about this were not the same people who listened to Mr Jones and Mr Laws. Their audiences were substantially uninterested in what was going on in the hearing. So it doesn't surprise me in the least that they didn't lose their audience and if they didn't lose their audience they didn't lose their power.'[51]

One listener, writing to the *Sydney Morning Herald*, expressed a possibly typical audience reaction: 'His program is interesting, entertaining and informative and I do not give a hoot if he is getting paid by other people outside 2UE'.[52] As a radio colleague said at the time: 'Jones will continue on. He has nothing else in his life. He is a lonely man. His audience is his family and because it is such an intimate relationship, family members always put disagreements aside and are willing to forgive infidelities.'

By the end of the inquiry the focus had swung from John Laws to Alan Jones. In his closing submission, Julian Burnside was critical of John Laws, identifying a higher number of alleged breaches of the broadcasting code. But in the witness box, Laws made no pretence of being anything other than a salesman.

Julian Burnside identified a lesser number of occasi[?] Alan Jones allegedly presented advertising as news and w[?] knowledge of a commercial relationship. But Burnside app[?] to be more critical of Jones because of scepticism about [?] different defence, which strained for the high moral groun[?]. According to Burnside: 'The net effect of the evidence—and I d[?] not mean to trivialise it—in Mr Jones' part of the case seems to be that he signed without looking, they [sponsors] paid without listening; he spoke without knowing and they heard without complaining. It is simply difficult to accept.'[53]

In his defence of Alan Jones, Bret Walker was every bit as tough as his colleague from the south. Walker complained that the Burnside style of cross-examination had 'oppressed' his client by provoking laughter in the gallery. Burnside's charm made him suitable for 'a future in broadcasting', but Walker reminded the tribunal that this was serious, and the tribunal should not be thinking about making findings that went beyond its powers. Alan Jones' brightest English student chose his words so that there could be no mistake the ABA understood that a finding against Alan Jones' credibility would be fought through the courts.[54] Bret Walker rejected the proposition that codes of practice had been breached and that Alan Jones had been misleading, and said that it was 'impertinent' to suggest that money had influenced Jones' opinions.[55]

The ABA did not agree. It found a causal link between the existence of an agreement and Jones' on air conduct. Alan Jones' insistently asserted the problem was the words in the contracts rather than the words that went to air. 'There is not one single word which suggests that I or anybody else, if paid money, would give the payer the comment that they wanted.'[56]

Again the ABA panel disagreed, identifying 40 breaches by Jones. On 31 occasions Jones had misled his audience by failing to disclose a commercial relationship. On nine identifiable occasions he broadcast advertisements as news. The panel found 2UE breached the Broadcasting Act on five occasions and identified 90 breaches of codes of conduct. It recommended,

tty much as Alan Jones had done at the start, disclosure of off
and on air commercial agreements. A recommendation that
the station licensee undergo a training program to assist in
understanding their obligations was a further birching with a
feather.

After the February 2000 release of the ABA report, Alan Jones
spent 15 minutes on air stating his position. He asked his
listeners what an inquiry into other sections of the media might
reveal, stated the ABA had not found instances where his
contracts had changed his views but conceded again that 'the
failure to disclose was a mistake'.[57]

It could have been much worse. Alan Jones was not asked
about Sunraysia, Sony, Warner Brothers and the coffee deals.
There was not the time. Alan Jones' Channel 9 broadcasts were
not thoroughly investigated. On the *Today* show he had
editorialised about matters of interest to sponsors such as Qantas,
Optus and Sunraysia. To his considerable chagrin, Channel 9
production staff, worried about hostile viewer feedback as well as
the integrity of their show, pulled at least one editorial. Regular
appearances on *Today* by *Bulletin* correspondent John Lyons,
painting an unflattering portrait of Jones at the ABA, further
poisoned a difficult relationship with his television colleagues.

There was also a limit to the questions the ABA could ask.
The inquiry was into 2UE rather than Alan Jones. What
intrigued many observers was that a serious inquiry should be
investigating 'cash for no comment' as well as 'cash for
comment'. If Jones was paid to lay off, and the evidence
regarding Walsh Bay suggested that was a motivation, the
circumstance was not something 2UE would reasonably know
about. As far as the Walker deal is concerned, there remains
curiosity about why the property developer was prepared to pay
so much for so little. No transcription service on earth can
provide what is not said. When favourable opinion is purchased
it is logical to presume silence might be part of the deal.

The prospect of a criminal charge being brought was raised in
the press. 'If someone ceases publishing material for money,

that's extortion under the act.'[58] The New South Wales director of the Department of Public Prosecutions (DPP) had announced a preparedness to look into the matter. Nick Cowdery QC thought a charge might be relevant if it could be proved Alan Jones had received 'hush money'. But nothing was forwarded to the DPP from the ABA or the NSW Police, so nothing was done. There were, however, costs to Alan Jones. The loss of the majority of his endorsement agreements hurt his bank balance. Optus cancelled its sponsorship deal 18 months early.

There did seem to be miscommunication between Alan Jones and Harry Miller about a requirement to publish contractual arrangements. Two weeks after the ABA report was released, Miller wrote a curious letter to Jones: 'I had a meeting with David Mann who wants me to keep everything going along nicely, but obviously it would suit them at this time, to cease current arrangements (so it would fit in with your requirements of there being nothing on the 2UE website). He would then like to look at a new structure, later down the road, as the building proposal comes forward at Walsh Bay towards the end of this year.'[59] Alan Jones replied: 'Dear Harry, Re: Contracts/Mirvac I don't understand your note of February 23. If I have a contract with Mirvac, it must appear on the website. If I don't have a contract, it won't.'[60]

Syndication of his program through the Sky Radio network suffered. At the beginning of 2000, a range of regional stations in New South Wales and Queensland changed ownership and cancelled existing arrangements. Jones' program, in one-hour and half-hour cut-down versions, now broadcast to only eight regional centres.

Brendan Sheedy, the general manager of Sky Radio, wrote to Miller: 'With the fallout from last year's ABA inquiry now behind us, we are having another sales drive to bring more stations on line. The stations running the program are very pleased and are achieving great results.'[61] Harry Miller passed on the ratings information to Alan Jones with a comment: 'Brendan Sheedy is a fool'.[62] Alan Jones seemed to agree, telling Miller that he too read the ratings. He found it depressing that such excellent results could not be sold.[63]

While the accountants and sales staff had good cause to want to keep their star, it was evident that after 15 years, Jones was sick of 2UE and 2UE was sick of Jones. Since the Tissuegate episode of 1998, goodwill had deteriorated. As if in magic powder, the writing was on the wall. The inquiry had not just sapped morale but also buckled 2UE's winning poise. One employee commented: 'There are a lot of people who have nothing to do with this and have been hurt, ethically sound people who have been tainted with the same brush. It is as if there is one world for them and one world for us.' Not that it mattered too much to Alan. While the likes of David Flint, John Conde and John Brennan would pay a price for their loyalty, Jones would, as ever, sail forward.

Alan Jones' temper tantrums, his way of playing favourites and his power to have staff sacked because of personal dislikes meant goodwill was fast wearing out anyway. 'He had favourites particularly among the younger males in the newsroom. If you weren't in the in-crowd it could be unpleasant. There was always the fear that if you got offside with him you'd be out the door.' In keeping with the experience of other workplaces, the outer circle grew larger than the inner circle.

Chairman John Conde wasn't the only one who could not talk to him. There was no one who could warn him about behaviour that might harm the reputation of the station or made him look like a prat. The great communicator's difficulties communicating with colleagues extended to on air staff other than John Laws. On the first day of the ABA hearing sports editor Ray Hadley and Alan Jones were reported as screaming at one another about perceived undue influence. 'I've had plenty of fights with Alan Jones—the only difference this time is I gave a bit better than I normally do,' Hadley told the *Sydney Morning Herald*. 'Normally I get lectured. This time I gave a lecture.'[64] A pragmatist in his dealings with Jones, Hadley would later share a career trajectory, joining forces with Alan at another station.

Broadcaster Mike Carlton's relationship moved in the opposite direction. Carlton's entrenched dislike of Jones had its origin in another shouting match. When the drive time host learned that Jones had recommended 2UE listeners switch to the ABC to listen to the cricket, Carlton was ropeable. He threw Jones' office door open and bellowed at him. Alan Jones ordered Mike Carlton to 'get out of my office this minute'. Carlton shouted back, 'Not before I have called you an unprofessional cunt', and slammed the door.

As far as Alan Jones is concerned the feeling is mutual. He complained to John Brennan that his drive time colleague had four people to produce a simple program. He thought the afternoon team was resting on its laurels, 'whatever are left'.[65] He went on to say he was not confident about the good health of the station, which had been significantly damaged by 'appallingly temperamental outbursts'.[66]

The switch of focus throughout the course of the inquiry from John Laws to Alan Jones was more perplexing to Jones than it was to some colleagues. 'No one knew Alan Jones was involved. This came as a surprise to us ... common sense dictates you don't do it ... it's appalling to use your employer's facilities to work for a third party. Laws is different. Everyone knows he is a walking advertisement.'

Alan Jones' high self-regard made it difficult for him to accept blame. Writing to Geoff Davey of Walker Corporation after his second outing in the witness box, he complained about the whole inquiry going off the rails.[67] His position to other correspondents was that John Laws should have been slotted, but the *Sydney Morning Herald* in particular had turned proceedings into a vendetta against him.

The day after he left the box, Alan Jones wrote to a public relations associate putting his position that the inquiry began because someone had been paid to change their mind and their opinion and that he had been roped in because the media saw a chance to get his scalp. 'They have been at it for a long time.'[68]

A sounder explanation for the greater hostility toward Alan Jones is to be found in his greater hypocrisy. The evidence before the ABA challenged Alan Jones' stance as a champion of Struggle Street. While Jones constantly pretended to be out there battling for the little man, he was receiving back pocket deals from the biggest of the big. While Laws was the salesman, Jones was more the con man. While Optus and company were the ventriloquists, Jones was more the dummy.

Alan Jones had been demonstrably caught cheating. It is hard to imagine a journalist enduring similar disgrace. It is even harder to imagine the politicians and bureaucrats that Alan Jones castigates daily surviving a tenth of the findings against him. But Alan Jones is unstoppable. Those who liked him liked him more, and those who were already sceptical liked him less. The divide deepened. Journalist David Marr saw the episode as evidence that Sydney had no shame. Other commentators throughout Australia were sure the same deals could not have gone down in other capital cities. Alan Jones was Sydney and Sydney was Jonestown: brazen, extrovert, smug and amoral.

CHAPTER 17
THE EMPEROR'S NEW CLOTHES

KEEPING UP WITH ALAN JONES is difficult. The seven lives—or is it nine?—he leads all at once can't be comprehensively documented. While Alan goes on, this book has to end. So this chapter will pause at only some of the many barbecue stoppers along the road beyond the 'cash for comment' affair, focusing primarily on the issue that originally brought Jones to notice, the one that, in my view, demonstrates his influence at its most destructive. Having survived the Australian Broadcasting Authority, Alan Jones was now able to exercise control over a far more powerful regulator, effectively evicting the New South Wales Police Commissioner and Police Minister, and seriously impeding police reform.

Although his credibility had been stripped bare before the ABA, Alan Jones' commercial value increased. After the drama passed he moved upwards, to a palatial office suite at another radio station, where, with his arrival, profits also climbed. Jones getting sick of 2UE and 2UE getting sick of Jones was good news for at least one Sydneysider. John Singleton's rival 2GB was ready to kill for the ratings champion. The flagship station of the Macquarie Network had been leaking audience figures badly since its glory days of the 1960s and 1970s. When he bought the station in 1996, John Singleton was keen to bring the audience back. But by 2001, 2GB held only a 3.8 per cent share of available listeners, compared to 2UE's 12.7 per cent share.[1]

John Brennan had long referred to his discovery, Alan Jones, as the Moses of the airwaves. 'Brenno' figured the devoted would follow Alan anywhere. 'Singo' had a similar view and was keen to capture Jones when his 2UE contract ran out at the end of 2001, although the opposite might have seemed the case during the 'cash for comment' affair, when John Singleton attempted to capitalise on his competitor's embarrassment. Following Alan Jones' first horror stretch in the box, Macquarie ran full-page advertisements showing an unflattering picture of Jones with his tongue out and a banner that read: 'Why pay double for all this trouble?' Above the picture was a taunt: 'Alan Jones: The opinions which I express are always my own'. It was a plea to advertisers to come across. 'Whatever 2UE charge 2GB/2CH will charge half ... Plus No live read fees. No endorsements. No rorts. No kickbacks.'[2]

Later, John Singleton threatened to sue 2UE if new industry restrictions resulting from 2UE's bad behaviour damaged 2GB's interests. He wanted 2UE expelled from the Federation of Australian Broadcasters.[3] He also argued that 2UE should be stripped of its role as official Olympics broadcaster.[4] But privately, John Singleton yearned for a slice of the trouble. Alan Jones had properly explained to all comers that under the terms of his 2UE agreement, he was not free to discuss a new deal until the contract expired. Despite the opportunistic sniping, Singo and Jonesy got on well. John Singleton was another who offered support during the London episode. They both loved their horses, sometimes running into one another at racing or charity dos. An understanding had developed that when the time was right, they might have a serious talk.

There was also some courting by post. In August 1997, when Alan Jones' amazing constitution had succumbed to illness, John Singleton faxed him at home: 'Have a selfish day/week/month, whatever. Let me know if you need/want anything. Singo.'[5]

In the following month, after another note, Alan Jones wrote back. At the time, the multimillionaire Singleton had been busted in his Bentley barrelling along at 50 kilometres over the speed limit. A good driving record and a lenient magistrate helped him hang on to his licence, which led to some minor fussing in the media. Alan Jones passed on his congratulations for the way Singleton handled that 'nonsense' pointing out that he made no mention of it and that Singo was the best.[6]

Singo scratched Jonesy's back too. When one of his own broadcasters had a shot at Alan on air, Singleton sent a note to the announcer, which was copied to Jones: 'Fax Peter Hand, 2GB. Alan Jones is a long-term and loyal personal friend of mine. Please read the attached. There will be NO repetition of any such personal attacks on Alan by you or anyone else ... I require your written acceptance of this before you go on air tonight.'[7]

In November 1998, executive Bill Currie, from Singleton's Macquarie Radio network, sent a fax congratulating Alan Jones on another ratings win. Jones wrote back thanking his competitor for his generosity pointing out what a funny world it was when it took a rival to acknowledge his success. He said he did not know of anyone else in the industry achieving a 20 rating and that he had achieved it on almost 40 occasions. His explanation was the familiar one, that the media 'absolutely loathes me'.[8]

There were more congratulatory notes from 2GB after more 2UE ratings wins. Alan Jones' opponent at breakfast was another outspoken Packer employee, the former ALP heavyweight Graham Richardson. In the Olympics year, when Richardson was Olympics village mayor, a job Jones might have felt better qualified for, Alan passed on his best to 'Richo' further conveying his suggestion that Richardson get rid of the 'dead wood' in the set up, starting with Michael Knight. He complained again about Ric Birch, advising Richardson to distance himself.[9]

As described earlier, Alan Jones managed a U-turn on Ric Birch when the Olympics opening and closing ceremonies drew rave reviews. Somewhat more mysteriously, he would, over time, do the same with Peter Ryan. After Ryan became New South Wales Police

Commissioner in 1996 they got on well. Although the Maritime Union dispute spoiled relations, they had since healed. Alan Jones makes many representations to the police and Peter Ryan became used to doing his best, personally attending to complaints by Jones about listeners being stalked, traffic incidents and the like.

Alan Jones' original sympathetic view, that Peter Ryan had one of the world's toughest jobs, was close to the mark. The public has never been told the full truth about the extent of the necessity for police reform. For decades politicians had avoided confronting a reform agenda that would be unnerving and destabilising, in that ultimately the spotlight had to fall on themselves. The anarchy of the 1980s, when systemic corruption had been exposed, showing police engaged in serious crime such as drug trafficking, armed robbery and even murder, meant reform was, at last, unavoidable.

It was going to be difficult, the burden of decades of neglect falling on the shoulders of one generation. And reform was not just about corruption. New skill sets were needed to meet new threats. Reform meant getting rid of the crooks while keeping up experience, morale and skills development. Managing trouble-free change was always going to be beyond Peter Ryan. It was probably beyond anyone. But doing nothing was no longer an option. In the period when Peter Ryan and Alan Jones discussed getting together for tete-a-tetes, they appeared to agree that the Wood Royal Commission reform recommendations had reached too far.

At this stage Ryan was still considered to be one of Bob Carr's political assets. His matinee idol visage had begun to displace many of the ugly stories about corruption and scandal which dominated earlier media coverage. The well-spoken and courteous British bobby went over well with some of Alan Jones' older listeners. One wrote to Alan describing Ryan as 'the police officer to whom manners mattered'.[10] Alan Jones passed the note on to Peter Ryan: 'Dear Peter, I just thought I would send you a beautiful letter. We only ever hear from the crook people. This ought to have a frame around it. It's a wonderful tribute to you and a very gracious endorsement.'[11]

Later Alan Jones began a vicious campaign to run Peter Ryan out of town. Ryan never understood why. My own best explanation is threefold. First, it was a case of Jones joining an Opposition scalp hunting exercise in the prelude to the 2003 election. This also enjoined Jones in a bizarre alliance of haters who, for their own reasons, had it in for Ryan. Lastly, controlling the commissioner meant that, effectively, he controlled the police.

One thing is for certain, Alan Jones' professed reason for going after Peter Ryan—the mismanagement of policing at Cabramatta—was never true; it was another U-turn. Just before the issue caught fire, Alan Jones wrote to Deputy Commissioner Ken Moroney expressing satisfaction with police initiatives: 'Congratulations to Commander Horton and all other Police involved in combating the drug problem in the Cabramatta area.'[12]

Despite Alan Jones' then positive view, Cabramatta, often described as Australia's heroin capital, had serious problems. So did many other communities, but at Cabramatta they were more conspicuous. Commuters observed drug deals going down openly while police appeared to stand helplessly on the sidelines. At this time Local Area Commander Peter Horton was having troubles with more than crime. As in much of the police force, officers at Cabramatta seemed afflicted by a permanent personality disorder. Horton was fighting to suppress a civil war within his own command.

The rebel leader of a band of dissidents was Michael Patrick Timothy Priest. He is the same Detective Constable Tim Priest who popped up in an earlier chapter in the Keith Waite case. Having rejoined the New South Wales Police in 1994, Priest was later posted to Cabramatta and in 1997 promoted to sergeant. But his troubles did not go away. He fell into dispute with Commander Horton, engaging in a bout of spiteful name-calling.

In Priest's view, a vengeful Horton, who oversaw Priest's transfer out of Cabramatta, had stabbed him in the back. Tim Priest thought 'other people have been scheduled under the mental health act for less'.[13] Sergeant Priest believed Commander Horton was against him because 'I refused to accept that the drug situation at Cabramatta could not be won by the Police'. According to the officer, a 15-member 'boys' club' at Cabramatta opposed effective policing.[14]

The opposing view was that Tim Priest was more a problem than a solution at Cabramatta. According to one of the 'boys' club' members, 'Priest just wanted to get out there and bang heads. But he did not do his other duties.' There is not much use arresting criminals if you can't properly secure convictions and, as his record shows, Tim Priest was weak on the follow-through. His complaints also distracted attention from his personal difficulties. According to an opponent, Priest had 'turned a personal vendetta into a crime issue'.

At this stage, as his letter to Deputy Commissioner Moroney showed, Alan Jones was happy with Commander Horton's stewardship of Cabramatta. And besides, there was much else on his mind. Another change of ownership was on the horizon at 2UE. The slaughter before the ABA might have increased the willingness of the Lamb family to sell 2UE. Back in 1998, the Southern Cross Network had shown an interest. Two years later, John Conde told its managing director, Tony Bell, an offer might be accepted.[15]

The fighting between Alan Jones and John Laws was not helpful to 2UE at such an awkward time, so on 28 November a get-together was arranged. The perfect conciliator was John Laws' agent and Alan Jones' old mate, John Fordham, who over the years was occasionally called upon to broker peace.

In a rear courtyard at Fordham's home, the multimillion-dollar men enjoyed some excellent wine, drawn from the wine writer's personal cellar. Alan Jones may have liked it a little too much, as it appeared to loosen his lips. According to half a dozen people present, Alan spoke enthusiastically about ABA Chairman David Flint. Laws and Fordham recall Jones saying, 'If it wasn't for David Flint god knows where we would be. In fact I was so determined to have David Flint re-elected that I personally went to Kirribilli House and instructed John Howard to reappoint David Flint or he would not have the support of Alan Jones in the forthcoming election.' Such an encounter, denied by the PM and described by Jones as 'fanciful and ludicrous', appears more likely an example of Jones seizing an opportunity to remind Laws of his Sydney supremacy. Laws and Fordham recall that when Jones walked off to take a mobile telephone call about another footballer fracas, they turned to each other, exclaiming, 'I can't believe he just said that'.

After the Christmas break Alan Jones did get a new employer, though it was not yet John Singleton. One year after the ABA report was handed down, Southern Cross, based in Melbourne, bought 2UE, 4BC and the Sky network for $90 million. Tony Bell said he believed Alan Jones and John Laws were 'worth every cent'.[16] Alan Jones, perhaps offended that he was not properly consulted, and unappreciative of being traded like one of his own horses, did not take to the situation.

The change of ownership occurred two years out from the state election. By now the smouldering Cabramatta issue had caught fire. Foolishly, the volatile command had been downgraded in 1999. In 2000 Peter Horton was replaced with a new commander who was also soon replaced. In 2001, as the smoke continued to rise, Peter Ryan threw one of his best troubleshooters, Assistant Commissioner Clive Small, into the flames.

Clive Small is better at catching crooks than making friends. His 1989 reinvestigation of the notorious Harry Blackburn affair had not endeared him to all his superiors, in that he demonstrated fellow officers' incompetence as well as proving Blackburn could not have committed a series of rapes. In 1992, Small's career prospects improved when he led the backpacker serial killing task force which locked up Ivan Milat. He did not do so well when he sat down with Tim Priest and cohorts to hear their concerns.

Clive Small says a proposition was later put to him that if he came onside, with Alan Jones' help he could become commissioner. Small says he rejected the proposal, as well as Priest's 'back to the 1980s' ideas. This did not help his popularity. The more troubleshooter Small saw Priest as troublemaker, the more the Assistant Commissioner became a new focus of the sergeant's angst.

Meanwhile the streets of Cabramatta were turning into a political battleground. An Upper House inquiry into Cabramatta had been called in 2000. In February 2001 Tim Priest, its star witness, presented dramatic testimony. Senior police were ignoring gang warfare, which threatened to tear the city apart. Priest said Asian gangs were recruiting members from local schools. 'We are not breaking up the continual cycle of recruitment of gang members from Cabramatta High School and the other schools in the area. These gangs drive down there in their cars, they get out, they show their fancy jewellery to kids; they show wads of money, fast cars, easy women ... They are actually going directly to the schools to recruit these kids.'[17]

He got a big run. Daily journalism provides few opportunities for thorough analysis. The outspoken sergeant—received as one of those sacred purveyors of truth, the whistleblower—was good for easy copy. It did not seem to matter that his evidence was weak on detail; for example, the school recruitment story turned out to be nonsense, with Tim Priest later falsely alleging he had actually identified Canley Vale rather than Cabramatta High. Even so, there was no denying Cabramatta had problems. Priest's complaints caught the imagination of the media and the support of many cops. Although the sergeant was not universally respected, his grumbles about bad bosses and aggressive oversight resonated with other police who felt marginalised by the reform era. A divide was deepening between newer 'academic' police and the older street-wise cops. Getting the right skills mix was going to take time.

On 25 February, two days after Tim Priest's evidence, Alan Jones spoke with the officer by telephone. Jones was introduced to Priest via the detective's father, 'Rusty' Priest, the New South Wales Returned Services League president who was often interviewed on Jones' program. The conversation was followed up with a meeting that obviously made a striking enough impression on Alan Jones to bring on an amnesic state with respect to his previous position on Cabramatta. In the months and years to come, Alan Jones celebrated Tim Priest as a hero and martyr.

The day after their first conversation, Alan Jones declared: 'Sydney today is what New York city was ten years ago ... high school students are being recruited in the playground by drug gangs'.[18] He began to editorialise about a law and order breakdown in New South Wales, his secular sermons blaring like a thousand sirens: 'The police service is in crisis, there are no police ... Something needs to be done about the increasing lawlessness in society.'[19]

It is easy to overestimate the ability of individuals to bring down crime rates. Australia was not the only Western country struggling with the same trouble. At first Peter Ryan escaped direct attack. The official position was more that he was being misled. After Premier Bob Carr accepted the police had 'dropped the ball' on Cabramatta, Ryan was increasingly besieged. Ryan could see an alternative explanation for Priest's stand. An Internal Affairs finding had gone against Priest for 'failing to follow brief handling procedures resulting in the dismissal of criminal proceedings'.[20] But Ryan was snookered: 'If Ryan were to reveal this ... doubtless Priest would complain to the media that the move was exactly the kind of cover-up tactic he was trying to expose'.[21]

The question of an alternative motive escaped Alan Jones and other media. Some journalists raised Priest's credibility by describing him as a former Special Air Services soldier. In an early draft of his book *To Protect and to Serve*, a similar claim was made: '... maybe it was the years he spent in the SAS where he was taught that "who dares wins".' These accounts of SAS service were wrong. Priest had left the army as a military police corporal in 1982. While the SAS was annoyed about the proposition that he was one of their sacred band, they did not publicly complain out of respect for his father, 'Rusty' Priest.[22]

Attempts to set other matters straight also fell on deaf ears. Cabramatta High School teacher John Steinmetz felt Priest and Jones unfairly tarnished the school he saw as a safe haven. Steinmetz, who had seen nothing of drug dealing or gun running at the school, wrote to Jones: '... the suburb of Cabramatta is not a pretty place. I don't know what the solution is. I just know that my colleagues and I, and the students with whom we work, are trying to do the best we can. Having someone take cheap potshots at us without giving the benefit of the facts, is depressing and dispiriting. Our students deserve better than this.'[23]

Alan Jones not only denied this other side of the story a run, he ticked Steinmetz off: 'Would you like me to indicate to you the number of people who have spoken to me about having "guns at their head". I am dictating this to you at 10.35 pm on Wednesday, 11 July. I have 15 minutes ago, spoken to one such person. What sort of program do you think we run? I am sick and tired of the apologists for all of this. I don't care who you teach and where you teach. I am saying, take off your rose coloured glasses and see it as it is.'[24]

Tim Priest's ragged command of the facts might have been one reason the detective's performances on the *Alan Jones Show* were limited. At this stage Alan more often drafted in Priest's mate, another 'expert' witness, Sydney University-based Dr Richard Basham. Basham, who described himself as a 'psychological anthropologist', was introduced on 2UE as a professor and a criminologist.

What was not declared was Richard Basham's own animus towards Peter Ryan. The angry American, who had been an advisor to the New South Wales Police, had fallen out with the British bobby. Basham had also given evidence to the Upper House inquiry and assisted with a submission to the parliamentary inquiry under the heading 'My Life as a Gang Member'. In this submission Basham had rewritten the evidence given at the inquiry by an alleged Caucasian member of a Vietnamese gang. The kid, with the pseudonym 'James' (or was it Basham?), argued for the creation of a task force made up of cops like Tim Priest. Basham, who had reconstituted the statement, concluded: 'But there has to be someone who is trusted—and who knows what's happening—there all the time to watch over the task force. He can't be a cop.'[25]

It did seem a bit like Richard Basham was looking for another job. He was lifting his profile at the time, providing briefing material for Alan's editorials and being regularly interviewed on the program, the academic adding 'scholarship' to the slagging. Of Peter Ryan he said: 'He doesn't have support—he's irrelevant. Nobody is taking responsibility for being in charge.'[26] 'The Government's approach to this and the Police Service approach to this is absolutely bankrupt.'[27] 'Peter Ryan is beyond hope ... it really shows the guy is not living in the real world. I've described it as an Alice in Wonderland situation or Mad Hatter's tea party ... Ryan himself is so internally preoccupied. He's kind of a navel gazer and he's completely concerned with himself and his own image.'[28] Of Police Minister Paul Whelan, Basham said: 'He really has just been a waste of space.'[29]

Cabramatta Chamber of Commerce president and political aspirant Ross Treyvaud was another regular Alan Jones guest, as was a reputable former assistant commissioner sidelined by Peter Ryan, Geoff Schuberg. Together with Priest and Basham the commentators became known as the gang of four. Richard Basham's star witness, the street kid 'James', had been delivered to the public via a Cabramatta local known alternatively as Peter Collis and Peter Starr. Collis/Starr was later charged with aggravated indecent assault of a minor after allegedly sexually molesting a ten-year-old boy.[30] While 'James' was concerned that Starr's interest in him might have been sexual, he had agreed to become involved because Starr pretended to be a police officer.[31]

The 'James' allegations turned the Cabramatta fracas into a national scandal when he was featured in a Channel 9 *60 Minutes* program in July 2001. The young man spoke of trashing a shop, carrying weapons such as knives and a machete, and selling 'dozens' of guns. There were many sensational claims, one of them being that handguns and heroin were sold at school.

The next morning on the Jones program the claims were repeated. 'James' said gang members killed for the fun of it, gangs wearing school uniforms trafficked firearms, and he personally had sold 10 to 12 guns. Unwittingly, the semi-literate drug addicted teenager became a pawn in a power struggle. 'James' was being used. He later spoke to Peter Bodor QC about being tricked into becoming involved with the media and having his words misconstrued. While the boy had considerable knowledge of criminal activity, it transpired he was not a member of a Vietnamese gang; he had not trashed the shop, witnessed a murder, sold guns or chased a teacher with a machete.[32]

The broadcasts assisted the rise of moral panic. Jones' listeners, most of whom had probably never been near Cabramatta, began to see new reasons to add another lock to the door. Amazingly, at one point Basham and Jones seemed to be proposing Sergeant Priest for the position of Commissioner. Jones: 'A reaction I've had to Detective Sergeant Priest is overwhelming. People are admiring of his courage.' Basham: 'Let me tell you they should be. Tim is a thoroughly decent guy. Actually we should be considering him as the next ...' Jones: 'Yes, yes'. Basham: 'He's someone who has done the hard yards. He's been out on the street. He knows what he is talking about.' Jones: 'Speaks Vietnamese ...'[33]

A constant argument pushed on the Jones program was that the Wood Royal Commission anti-corruption measures were counterproductive to practical, effective policing. Jones: 'Anti-corruption policies are impeding the hard yards of long term criminal investigation ...'[34] Beyond relying on intelligence from his fellow haters, Alan Jones proclaimed, as usual, a mandate from the strength of material coming his way: 'Some of the emails I have received from serving and retired police have made me sick in the stomach'.[35] 'I have been inundated by correspondence.'[36] 'The fax machine has been in meltdown.'[37]

Jones attacked Police Minister Whelan for telling lies, telling lies of his own in the process. His researcher Michael Darby noted on 23 April 2001 that when Jones claimed he had received hundreds and hundreds of emails about an issue, there were in fact twenty-three.[38]

A positive feature of the campaign was that more resources were thrown at Cabramatta. Another new commander, Superintendent Frank Hansen, was drafted in while Inspector Deborah Wallace was made Crime Manager. But the new efficiency that was brought to operational policing and the new order on the streets found no favour with some of the old guard opposed to Wallace. Alan Jones began to verbally beat up on a woman he had met only once, at which time, it is recalled, he looked her up and down and sneered: 'How would you go in a brawl?' On air he attacked her in a series of broadcasts: 'Deborah Wallace altered a police record, and she has since been promoted'.[39] 'Wallace's appointment should be cancelled immediately by Ryan. She may not have told the truth to the Upper House inquiry.'[40] He also called her a 'blindly ambitious' and 'ruthless' woman.[41]

The detective inspector sued. It was yet another case of Alan Jones not being able to put up about what he could not shut up about. Far from standing in the way of fighting crime, there was a strong argument to show Inspector Wallace as an important factor in a turnaround taking place at Cabramatta. The woman Alan Jones referred to as 'Miss Debbie' later received a substantial settlement from 2UE.[42] As was clear from the defamation proceedings, Alan Jones was being fed a great deal of misinformation. But, either unwilling or unable to admit he was being misled, Jones stuck by the turbulent Priest.

After giving evidence to the parliamentary inquiry, Priest had taken leave as a consequence of what he saw as harassment and intimidation from senior officers. While Tim Priest promised to resign, senior officers tried to find a happy home for him. Commissioner Ryan's personal appeal did no good. Priest played his death scene again and again: 'They will hunt me down whether it takes one week, one month, one year or several years ...'[43]

Alan Jones was finding more and more time in a crowded diary for his crime advisors. They were doing somewhat better than his new bosses. A new Southern Cross manager, David Bacon, was reportedly ordered from the studio.[44] There was already speculation in the media that Alan Jones was on his way to 2GB, because John Singleton was offering him a share in ownership. Amanda Meade reported in the *Australian*: 'But insiders say the refusal of Southern Cross to treat Jones like a king is what lies at the heart of the current standoff.'[45]

John Laws, in contrast, was back in the good books having signed up for a further five years. The détente with Alan Jones had not lasted. The two had taken different sides over Taxation Commissioner Michael Carmody, whom Jones described as a 'thug' and a 'disgrace', telling the PM to 'sack him immediately'.[46] Laws also got stuck into Jones' mate, author Lord Jeffrey Archer, describing him as a 'detestable and egotistical little bore'.[47] Archer's past had come back to bite him and Alan Jones could not help but be concerned. Archer was found to have lied during his 1987 libel case. On 19 July 2001 he was convicted of perjury and conspiracy to pervert the course of justice.[48]

When John Laws carried on joking on air about 'Polly the Parrot', Alan Jones complained about the 'pot shots' telling Laws that when he had been in trouble with the law (presumably a reference to a contempt of court charge brought against Laws after he had interviewed a juror) Jones alone stood up for him. Jones thought Laws' memory was 'short' and his sense of gratitude 'limited'.[49]

John Laws replied on the same day: 'Dear Alan, You are a very strange man. Of course I have always known you are a very strange man, it's just that I didn't know quite how strange. I am aware that my opinion of you matters very little. In fact I suspect the only opinion _of you_ that matters _to you_ is yours. How you manage to keep it elevated as you do is nothing short of amazing.'[50]

Laws denied his gratitude was limited: 'You may not like to recall an incident in the past but circumstances rather demand you do, when you were in trouble with the law and on the "brink of going to gaol", and I must say under far less seemly circumstances, I trust you recall I rang you at the Ritz Hotel. You talked of feeling like jumping out of the window. I did my best to support you. I realise I wasn't alone ...'[51]

Long John pointed to another double standard: 'It's all very well to appease your conscience by letter writing, but it is a lot better to confront the facts head on, and the facts are you have been, at times, vicious in your comments about me. You may well have been privately supportive, by privately I mean by way of letter to me, but publicly the story is very different—and that's all right because you are entitled to your point of view. Dishonesty whispers, hypocrisy shouts—you shriek! But for God's sake lay off the "Holier than Thou" attitude. It's stupid apart from anything else.'[52]

He picked up on the subject of Jones' execrable comedy. Alan had a 1950s collection of 1001 jokes that grew weaker by the week. 'Q: What do you call a knight who is afraid to fight? A: Sir Render.'[53] His colleague's forced laughter got under Laws' skin: 'You are good at laughing Alan. What a pity you have never developed the ability to be able to laugh at yourself. If you found this morning's Polly performance offensive then why didn't you just tell me? If I were to write a letter to all the people who have ever made a comment about me on radio that I didn't like I would have run out of ink 47 years ago. You must be careful, Alan, you are starting to give megalomania a bad name. Yours in haste John Laws CBE.'[54] Laws might have been alluding to a similar comment by Winston Churchill, who said of a homosexual colleague, 'he gives sodomy a bad name'.

At this time Alan Jones had come to believe he had many more sinister enemies than John Laws. A paranoid Tim Priest, who was now seen accompanied by large Pacific Islander bodyguards, appears to have persuaded Alan Jones that he was similarly at risk. When the exterior of Jones' Newtown warehouse was vandalised, there was a major froth, Jones and Priest ever keen to appropriate the Anzac spirit:[55]

> It was no ordinary vandalism, it was a clear message to me that I've struck a nerve in my efforts to rid our streets of the mongrels who presently roam them at will. But we will not frighten easily. And it's not only me, Richard Basham, Tim Priest, Geoff Schuberg, Ross Treyvaud ... and I can assure you we won't be intimidated or harassed into giving up. Imagine if the diggers of the First or Second World Wars gave up because the going got tough. It's the memory of these men and women

and the sacrifices they made that gives everybody the energy to
go on. Perhaps it was that that motivated Tim Priest to speak.
He's the son of a respected returned soldier, Rusty Priest. These
people fought to protect their citizens from the ultimate price
and we've got a fight on our hands too—the country being
taken over by forces we don't approve of. Well none of us can
afford to stop until the job has been done. The thousands of
emails, letters and faxes urge me to continue ...

Tim Priest believed Assistant Commissioner Small was out to get him. Richard Basham claimed Clive Small also threatened Alan Jones and set me on Jones' trail. Richard Basham, according to one critic, seemed at home in 'the world of rumour, innuendo and "secret" unattributable information'.[56] He began to peddle a dirt file on Clive Small, replete with sketchy and scandalous assertions.

It was not the only dirt file supposedly tucked away. At his earlier meeting with Tim Priest and Richard Basham, Clive Small recalls being questioned about a file the police were supposedly keeping on Alan Jones. The presumption was that there were further details of alleged dalliances in public toilets. Certainly more than one Sydney rumour mill churned out stories of dossiers being kept for a rainy day. As it happened, neither Peter Ryan nor Clive Small had any knowledge of any dirt file on Alan Jones. But in this fevered environment it is not hard to see the Jones camp suspecting such a file existed.[57]

Alan Jones joined the attack on Clive Small and, in doing so, in time, attracted another defamation writ. Jones might have believed the dirt peddled about Small, but he also might have feared a police officer resistant to control. By now Alan showed plenty of form in seeking favours, improperly interfering in police affairs. When his favoured son, Tricky Trindall, was again in trouble, Alan the Intimidator was straight on the phone. As a very senior officer who took his calls explained: 'Jones could exert pressure to make the knees wobble. There were many ranting calls, which could leave me trembling. We knew Jones needed to be looked after. We would get a blast otherwise. If you did not want to be blasted tomorrow morning you dealt with him. But it was hard. Jones would complain about the treatment of Trindall, and then you would get on the phone and learn Jones was defending a circumstance which caused a woman with facial injuries to be taken to hospital.'

While there was no likelihood a Jones dunny dirt file existed, Alan Jones did have a secret life to protect. One example is a dalliance that occurred in his Newtown warehouse just before the place was vandalised. It was 5.30 pm on Monday 3 September when Marcus Schmidt arrived for his first appointment with Alan Jones. The story of what transpired is revealing of a corner of Alan's life usually kept well hidden. Jones often proclaims his contact with younger males is altruistic. He proclaims himself an enabler, a facilitator and catalyst for bringing out the best in them. The brief encounter with Marcus Schmidt advances cause for doubt about whether this is always the only motivation. Marcus Schmidt was 26 years old when he wrote to Alan Jones explaining he had a distant family connection. Jones' father had been a friend of Schmidt's grandfather back at Acland. In Alan's time, Schmidt's father was a good middle distance runner.

Thirty-four years Jones' junior and looking even younger, Schmidt enclosed a picture of himself posing seductively barechested. The photograph, taken at an Oxford Street studio, is of a good-looking unmistakably gay man. Marcus Schmidt, like many of his age, was adrift in search of a career. In time he planned to study law, but for now he hoped the contact with Jones might help him open doors. Schmidt is unabashed about his sexuality. Relationships with older, wealthy gay males helped him towards an appreciation of what he called his 'sexual capital'. He knew the older men desired him in the main for his youth and beauty and saw it as fair he be commensurately rewarded. Marcus Schmidt, living at times a hand-to-mouth existence, was pragmatic about being paid for sex.

Having received the letter and photograph, Alan Jones wrote back on 8 August 2001 telling Marcus that his father had been a magnificent athlete, wondering whether the young man had inherited any of his father's genes, and inviting him for a cup of tea.[58]

When he arrived for the meeting early in September he found Alan Jones awkward and unsettled. 'We sat on separate sofas and he asked questions about my family and I about his. He spoke about his career and said, "It's all bullshit, isn't it?" I laughed and agreed. After a while he seemed to become bored and turned on the television and switched to the swimming.'[59]

Marcus Schmidt says he took command, starting to flirt, telling Alan Jones about his pectoral implants. Jones turned off the television and, according to young Schmidt, began to flirt back, lowering the blind, embracing him, kissing him and fondling his chest. Schmidt then withdrew, partly because he had another appointment and partly because he did not want to give too much without being sure he would get something in return. Alan Jones asked Marcus Schmidt to supply him with a list of career options.

After that first encounter the young man says Alan Jones 'began to call me constantly. I mean every day constantly. He told me that he had no one else to chat to the way we chatted. We were free in what we talked about yet I could tell he was always a little cautious.'[60]

He sent Jones another letter enclosing a list of ambitions, which included 'Children's TV Programming', 'Pop star', 'Actor', 'Radio presenter' and 'Big Brother participant'. Schmidt says they chatted every day for the next six weeks. He says Jones wanted him to send text messages, but was careful not to text replies. From a distance, it seems that Alan Jones wanted the flush of romance. He wanted to flirt like a teenager, but was forced to be furtive about it. It did not do to be seen in public with a gay man.

Some of the dialogue is telling of the barrenness of Alan Jones' emotional life. Marcus Schmidt remembers Alan Jones wanting to speak of being in love. 'He would often tell me that he loved me, at the beginning of our relationship I had told him that I didn't love him and that I was just willing to sleep with him to get ahead which had been really blunt. I had always been blunt and forward and this he liked about me and he would tell me when we talked on the phone that I was the boss and we should talk about what I wanted to talk about and we would do what I wanted to do. This was quite a trip for me as at these times I had one of the most powerful men in Australia under my control.'[61] He says Alan Jones acknowledged the reality of the relationship, but wanted to talk of love because it made him feel better about himself.

Alan needed these small escape hatches from his frantic schedule. As 2001 wore on it got busier. A federal election was due in November. In June, Alan Jones hosted a fundraiser for his old boss's son, Larry Anthony, who was just hanging on to his dad's northern New South Wales seat of Richmond.[62] While the Coalition could again be confident of Alan Jones' continued support, once more the Labor Opposition had to consider how to manage him. There was concern about drifting allegiance in a traditional support base, demonstrated in the last poll. It was easy enough to see Jones' audience of older workers and small-business people as occupying that same shifting ground.

Federal Labor saw little chance of winning Alan Jones over. Kim Beazley had heard the stories of Jones walking the corridors at 2UE loudly proclaiming, 'Thank god for John Howard'. The Opposition leader preferred to deal with John Laws. Laws' program reached beyond Sydney to some of the Queensland electorates where Labor also needed to improve its chances. Beazley thought 'it was better to be onside with Laws and it was an easier price to pay'.[63] But advice from state colleagues was that, however awkward a price, a little flattery went a long way, every vote counted, and there was no obvious upside in fighting with Alan.

An attempt was made to get Beazley and Jones to sit down over supper. Kim and Suzie Beazley did enjoy an evening at Newtown. In person, Alan Jones was a charming host who appeared to be on common ground with the genial Opposition leader. But as soon as they said goodbye it was back to sticking the boot in.

At this same time Alan Jones and Bob Carr were going through another no-speakies period. The bashing of the Carr Government over law and order and Cabramatta was hurting. As ever in the offices of the police and government, employees were rostered on early to transcribe Alan Jones' morning editorials.

The government's wobbling on the police was good news for the Opposition. Both sides must have known the trouble was unproductive and ultimately would have to be paid for. Both sides also knew it would take years rather than months for police reform initiatives to work, and that there were more Cabramattas out there.

In October 2001, Alan Jones signalled another outrage-in-waiting: 'A truly shocking scandal is about to explode in the police force proving the past five years have been a disaster'.[64] He was referring to a Police Integrity Commission (PIC) investigation into corruption at Sydney's northern beaches command. Alan Jones and the Liberal Opposition were set to depict the waiting revelations as further proof that the government had lost control of policing and that Peter Ryan could not cope. As far back as August, Jones had tipped that 'Police Commissioner Ryan may be on the way out'.[65]

Law and order, and Peter Ryan's shaky stewardship, constituted an area where a shaky Kerry Chikarovski was finding leverage. She needed a win and the looming scandal at Manly looked promising. In politics it mattered not a whit that the former British bobby could not fairly be blamed for the decades of political cowardice and complicity that had allowed corruption to become so bad. The PIC's Manly investigation was a watershed in a sorry history of neglect. Peter Ryan initiated the inquiries. For the first time the police were prepared to make public what had formerly been kept hidden. It was a risky move: trusting the public with the truth, while commendable, could prove unwise politically. Politicians don't get much credit for incremental success. The saga of 'James', still fresh in people's minds, showed the danger of exposing scandal, no matter the provenance. Peter Ryan deserved credit for the initiatives at Manly. Instead, he was about to cop it.

So too was I. The Opposition and Alan Jones attacked my *Four Corners* program on the Manly investigations. Unconscious of the plot at hand, I had taken some wind from their sails. The words read out in parliament by Opposition police spokesman Andrew Tink, critical of my prior knowledge of the investigation, were very similar to the words Alan Jones read out on air. He was, after all, being routinely faxed material from the Opposition leader's office: 'In exchange for buying the official spin of the policing disgrace in New South Wales, Chris Masters was given exclusive access to highly confidential, secretly taped evidence of police corruption and broadcast some of it before it was tendered into evidence before the PIC'.[66]

Alan Jones' backing of Kerry Chikarovski was now almost as enthusiastic as his backing of John Howard. As the November federal election approached, of 477 political comments made by Jones, three favoured Labor.[67] As with their New South Wales colleagues, federal Labor was wary of the benefits of going on a program to be beaten up. Alan Jones preserved his dislike of Kim Beazley's press secretary, Greg Turnbull. Turnbull learned the broadcaster had tried to have him sacked: 'He thought I was the reason he could not snap his fingers and have Keating or Beazley on air'.

Greg Turnbull and Kim Beazley were both from the school of thought that said if you are going to be interviewed by Alan Jones, be sure you are in the studio looking him in the eye and making it harder for him to interrupt. After some angry exchanges relayed via a Jones staff member, an appointment was made to get Beazley into the studio one month out from the election. It became a celebrated encounter, another of those episodes that raise the question of whether beating Alan Jones is worth it. The Beazley camp felt certain the Jones camp would have been handed a barbed stick of material by the Liberal camp. When they entered the studio they were prepared for a beating. This is the way it goes. The Liberals expect much the same when they enter the studios of suspected enemy collaborators (for example, at the ABC).

Alan Jones homed in on the weakness of the Labor Party's policy platform. Kim Beazley said anyone who wanted to know what Labor believed need only look at the website. 'But now on your website those policies aren't there ... why have they been taken off the website?'[68] Beazley, uncertain of the truth of Jones' claim, was wrong-footed. 'Well, to my knowledge they are there.' Jones: 'Well I'm very sorry but they're not ...'[69] Kim Beazley's minder, Greg Turnbull, rushed into the 2UE newsroom, borrowed a vacant computer terminal, checked the website—which indeed carried the policies—printed off the pages and dropped them in front of his boss.

Beazley recovered. 'You took me by surprise ... because you said all our policies had been removed from our website. And you lied. That is a bad piece of behaviour on your part.'[70] Now Jones was wrong-footed. He tried to switch the attack, bringing Beazley's daughter into the argument, claiming the Opposition leader used an episode of his daughter being turned away from a public hospital to score a political point.

Afterwards, Kim Beazley was openly delighted that he had got one over Alan Jones. He was not so thrilled when the polls closed one month later. When the votes were counted after the 10 November election, the government's support across the nation had improved by 2 per cent. In the Sydney electorates where Alan Jones had a presence, the Labor vote was again down. While Jones probably had contributed to the result, issues such as international terrorism and border security had more clearly counted. While Beazley conceded Jones had had an effect, Labor would not have won even if there had been a way to appease Jones: 'And I would not have bought that'.

The result did appear to rattle Bob Carr. Earlier on Carr had approved of Beazley confronting Jones. Greg Turnbull remembers Bob Carr saying, 'This guy is killing us. We won't talk to him anymore. The situation is beyond repair. I don't let my people go on his show.' With a state election 16 months away, Carr might have again decided no vote was worth losing and it was better to appease Jones. On 3 and 17 October Jones and Carr did speak again off air. According to Tim Priest and Richard Basham, Alan gave Bob the rounds of the kitchen over policing, suggesting Carr open himself up to their perspective.[71] In no time flat, out Cabramatta way it was being whispered that two big heads were about to roll.

The government had one major mission in mind when Michael Costa was sent as an emissary to meet Alan Jones' chosen advisors on law and order. The mission was to keep police scandals off the front page. According to Priest and Basham, on 12 November, two days after the federal election, Michael Costa, of the unmistakable shaven head, attended to his role of official quisling, sitting down with an enemy who had been mercilessly bagging his government for months. The newly appointed member of the Legislative Council might have had a spring in his step, given his custody of an important secret. Even Police Minister Paul Whelan did not know that Michael Costa was about to take his job.

At the Newtown warehouse Alan Jones introduced Michael Costa to Tim Priest, Richard Basham and Ross Treyvaud. Jones left them to it; later, Costa and his new friends were seen enjoying a drink at the nearby Marlborough Hotel. Costa's pals were soon saying they felt they could 'work with him'. A week after the Newtown meeting the story leaked, before the appointment was formally announced. It led to a report in the *Australian*, headlined 'RUN IT BY THE SHOCK JOCK'.[72]

The New South Wales government lamely attempted to make a virtue of meeting with its critics. It was revealed that Paul Whelan had already signalled an intention to retire. Michael Costa, one of Bob Carr's action men and a former secretary of the New South Wales Labour Council, claimed to know Alan Jones from the old days when Jones was at the Employers' Federation.[73] This can't be true. Costa was a locomotive engineman with the State Rail Authority when Jones left the Employers' Federation. They were, however, correspondents, Costa being one of the many to court Jones with the keyboard.

Since Costa's extraordinary ministerial inauguration, whenever cartoonist Alan Moir drew the politician, there was a parrot perched on his shoulder. Removing the stain of parrot poo was going to be difficult. Comedians Roy and HG now wrote into their routine a skit that had 'Bob Carr' interviewing applicants for the job of police minister. '"Carr": Let me give you a hypothetical. Let's say you enter a public toilet to see Alan Jones massaging his truncheon. What do you do? "Costa": I get my truncheon out too and massage it alongside him. "Carr": You've got the job.'

Nine days after the unofficial swearing in at the Newtown bunker, Tim Priest submitted a claim for damages against the New South Wales government, citing psychological impairment as a result of his employer's negligence. His statement to the court listed disabilities such as 'feelings of anger', 'binge drinking' and 'morbid depression symptoms'.[74] The unhappy, erratic detective had told the media he would 'rather resign with dignity than endure continued persecution'.[75] Soon after, Michael Costa seconded the psychologically disturbed officer to a job as a 'special advisor to police on drugs and gang policy'. Three months later, Tim Priest quit his job in the ministry when a politician who failed to apologise to him was promoted.

Costa showed he was more than a good listener. He actually took notice of his ragged band of advisors. Soon the Police Service was again a Force. Specialist squads of detectives, abandoned because of entrenched corruption, were to be reintroduced. More police were to be put on the beat, and in order to fast-track the training process, ethics training was tossed. Costa joined in condemning Priest's perceived enemies, belittling Clive Small and calling him a 'media whore'.[76] Small was removed from his job as assistant commissioner and parked as an advisor in the Premier's Department until the election was out of the way. He was later dumped.

The old-time policy whereby all media outlets got a fair go was abandoned. Police media boss Tracey Arthur was also parked somewhere distant and a new media manager drafted in from the government. Alan Jones' producers' numbers were programmed into the new cellular phone. The media department began to favour the outlets that were more likely to treat them well. And it worked. Amazingly, those appalling scandals in 2001 proving crime was out of control and the police could not cope fell away in 2002. Miraculously, overnight, the streets were safe again. Jones' complaints about Carr Government spin were not as much of an issue when the spin favoured Jones.

Despite budgeting for sophisticated research on crime, the government had ignored it, turning instead to advice they not only disrespected, but knew to be wrong. While Alan Jones was insisting that crime was out of control, a heroin drought was starting to bite. In 2001 the tide began to turn, with crime figures in most categories falling. According to the New South Wales Bureau of Crime Statistics and Research, from January 2001 the overall level of property crime in New South Wales began to fall far below the level it was at in the mid 1990s. Alan Jones' response has been to repeatedly defame bureau chief Don Weatherburn. The episode demonstrated that when Alan Jones was on the wrong tram he now had the power to simply force the government to change the tracks.

While Jones was getting his way with the police, he was not doing so well with young Marcus Schmidt. After Schmidt had sent him a list of career options, another meeting was scheduled at O'Connell Street. Before their dinner date, Alan Jones gave him a tour of the warehouse and again embraced him. Schmidt remembers opening Jones' shirt, but resisted taking the physical relationship further. Schmidt says that before they moved to the garage Jones handed him the keys to his Mercedes-Benz, insisting Schmidt drive.

On the trip to the Dante Restaurant in Leichhardt, Alan Jones was awkward about being seen by members of the public but excited enough to risk reaching into Schmidt's trousers. This annoyed the young man who, with his hands on the wheel, was in a weak position to resist.

At the restaurant, Jones introduced Schmidt as a family friend. Jones suggested Schmidt pursue a career as a painter as he had already sold some works. Schmidt says Jones spoke philosophically of being a 'giver rather than a taker'. Schmidt thought the opposite. Alan, a practitioner of mind games, appeared to have met his match. Schmidt says he leaned across the table and interrupted Jones, telling his date, 'You're not going to get a head job out of me tonight'. According to Schmidt, his date 'stopped talking and a big grin crossed his face and he leaned towards me and said "I was hoping to give you one"'.

In the car afterwards, Alan Jones continued to fondle Marcus Schmidt. Schmidt said that in Jones' garage he struggled to break the embrace. He said Jones had him trapped, but Schmidt was, in his words, adamant that Jones 'would have to make something happen for me before I put out'.

Afterwards, there were fewer telephone calls and a new tension as well. Schmidt, out of pocket as a result of the telephoning ritual, asked to be reimbursed. On the phone Jones was angered but later sent him a $100 note with an attached letter apologising for its late arrival, explaining that given the delay he had added some interest to the $60 owed.[77] There was very little further contact. Marcus Schmidt returned to Queensland and wrote a few more letters. Alan Jones replied, encouraging him to keep up his studies and expressing 'lots of love'.[78]

Marcus Schmidt is insightful in his description of the encounter and happy to have his story told. Indeed, he has written about it in greater detail in an unpublished autobiography. His account of the flirtation with Alan Jones is revealing of Jones' repression, loneliness and fear. The encounter with Schmidt does more than challenge the proposition that Jones' attention to young men is always unselfish. Alan also pretends his tough line on public policy matters such as policing is all about keeping the system honest, whereas it can equally be concluded that self-interest may be a factor in his efforts to influence the police.

After his contract expired on 31 December 2001, Alan Jones resigned from 2UE. He severed contact with agent Harry Miller when their contract ran out on 24 January 2002. At this time the ABC's JJJ network broadcast a bloopers tape leaked from 2UE of edited highlights of Jones the profane in full fury: 'Oh shit a fucking brick and I hate doing 60 second fucking commercials. Fucking sick of this. Jesus it annoys me, these fucking people. I mean I just tell 'em I wouldn't do it. This is just bullshit, no one listens, just a fucking waste of time and money. Oh shit fucking copy. Oh shit a fucking brick. God almighty. It's just rubbish this, absolute rubbish. Oh shit, oh shit a fucking brick. Fucking sick of this. It's one thing to prop up the bloody station and you are just treated like offal. I've had a gutful for one day and I'm also sick and tired of propping up the fucking station and having to put up with them. Fucking sick of the lot of them and the whole bloody show. Just a fucking waste of time and money. I'm Alan Jones.'[79]

The damage to Jones' upright persona was inconsequential. His audience was not likely to tune to a youth network. Indeed, his status was blooming. While 2GB was opening its chequebook, Alan was rubbing shoulders with a president. During an unusually long off air break, Alan Jones acted as master of ceremonies on a speaking circuit for former United States President Bill Clinton.[80]

To help negotiate his new deal, Alan Jones took advantage of the Packer connection, using his former Channel 9 boss, Sam Chisholm, as an informal manager. According to John Singleton's biographer, Gerald Stone: 'After being told Jones was wavering over a huge cash offer he was receiving from 2UE, [Singleton] shouted into the phone. "Why can't we get rid of all these fucking advisers and let me sit down with him face to face!"'[81]

Chisholm, a director of Telstra, helped seal the deal with an offer to Jones of an equity stake in the network. Macquarie Broadcasting was reported as paying Jones a sign-on fee of $4–5 million with an annual salary of $3–5 million. The deal gave Jones 20 per cent of accrued increase in the value of Macquarie shares following his arrival. Chisholm said it was the biggest single deal done in Australian media history, the seven-year contract worth an estimated $40 million. Indeed, just three years later, when Macquarie was floated, Alan Jones accrued a paper profit of $14 million overnight.[82]

The big day nominated to announce the new deal was a triumph for Alan Jones in more than one way. February 7 was two years to the day since the ignominy of the ABA ruling. John Singleton, trumpeting his arrival, told a packed house that Alan Jones had changed the face of radio. Seventy-eight consecutive survey wins made him the 'best broadcaster in the world'. John Singleton explained that, rather than continue to try to compete, it made sense to buy the 'unbeatable foe'.[83]

Dressed in a black and white ensemble, Alan Jones, suntanned after his better than usual break, spoke of his humility in signing a licence to 'work hard'. The *Sydney Morning Herald*'s David Marr asked, 'Have you read your contract?'[84] Jones laughed, explaining the days were over when he trusted others to do that. When questioned about the JJJ bloopers tape, Alan Jones again laughed, pushing his line about not swearing in front of women. He explained that, beyond the equity deal, the biggest reason for his move was the challenge it represented. As a part owner, Alan Jones would share the risks as well as the profits.

Overnight the Macquarie Group added $56 million to its share value. 2GB rates for live reads at breakfast lifted from $400 to $1850.[85] His old employer, Southern Cross, commensurately lost $28 million in market value.[86] The group's share price fell 4.4 per cent with the ratings soon following them down. The main compensation, according to 2UE staff, was the improving mood. The departure of Alan Jones made the place poorer but happier.

At the Macquarie studios across the Bridge, Alan Jones spoke of a similarly improving mood. At lunch he told of a female colleague in tears at his arrival, overcome with happiness because the station was now competitive. When Alan Jones walked in there was a tumult of applause from sales staff. On 4 March he began broadcasting on 2GB, using his old 'Gloria' theme to signal that the change would mean more of the same. Alan Jones took the format of the show and the core of his staff with him. And, Moses-like, he also brought the majority of his listeners. Tony Abbott was his first political guest.

Alan Jones did lose some of the rusted-on older listeners: a long run of survey wins was temporarily interrupted with Alan dropping to 14.5 per cent.[87] A bigger loss was the syndicated audience. 4BC Brisbane listeners now missed out, as did his regional listeners, who were tied to Southern Cross. But the following survey saw Alan on top again. The lead-in helped lift figures through the day for the rest of the station. John Singleton, having prepared to wait for the profits to flow, found they came almost immediately. It was unquestionably an extraordinary achievement and unquestionably it was down to the extraordinary Alan Belford Jones.

Just three weeks into his new stint on air, Alan Jones ran into an unanticipated challenge to his Sydney omnipotence. The New South Wales Liberals, now one year out from the next election, did it again. Jones was happy with his mentorship of Kerry Chikarovski, believing she had improved to the point of becoming competitive. But others in the Liberal machine feared she was never going to make it. That was not their only fear. Tackling Chika was not as much of a worry as tackling Jones. By March 2002, Alan Jones was all that was stopping a challenge which would otherwise have been mounted months earlier. At a Royal Agricultural Society function, Alan Jones was told about a plan to replace Chikarovski with a fresher face.

The Member for Pittwater, John Brogden, was not to his liking. In 1996 Jones was critical of the preselection of the then 27 year old. Jones, who had never met Brogden, disapproved of off-the-rack politicians, arguing they knew nothing about the real world.[88] Brogden was later energetic in his attempts to make up lost ground with Jones.

When the succession plan was put to him at the function, the broadcaster was overheard loudly defending Kerry Chikarovski, citing as a criterion of excellence that he 'had never been better served by any Leader of the Opposition'. The Chika media team were diligent faxers to the Jones program. Jones was also overheard declaring: 'If you go ahead, John Brogden will go down in history as the second Opposition leader never to appear on my program'. The prospect that John Brogden would be frozen Peter Collins-style did cause a few sleepless nights. It took courage for Brogden to proceed with the challenge which, on 28 March, narrowly defeated Kerry Chikarovski.

But Alan Jones would not be denied with respect to the fate of Peter Ryan. In his first month on air at 2GB, Jones kept up the pressure on a wilting commissioner: 'It is clear the Police Commissioner Peter Ryan is incapable of doing the job'.[89] 'The past five years under Ryan have been an unmitigated disaster ...'[90] The new minister, Michael Costa, was also busily making Peter Ryan feel unwanted. According to the now marginalised Commissioner, Michael Costa arrived with a hit list headed up with the name of the Priest–Jones nemesis, Clive Small. 'As well as Small he wanted a number of other senior officers.'[91] Ryan says he refused to sack people because they 'might have upset Alan Jones or the Minister ...'[92] Ryan came to describe Jones as 'a menace to democracy'.[93] Costa denied the existence of a hit list.

It was only a matter of time. On 10 April Peter Ryan was summoned to the Premier's office and sacked by Bob Carr. Another telling episode had unfolded earlier that morning. Behind his new 2GB microphone, Alan was miffed: '... Premier Bob Carr has declined without reason to appear on the program this morning'.[94] The reason was Ryan. Carr, certain to be asked about Ryan by Jones, and aware of the imminent scalping, was forced to cancel. Alan Jones' response to the Bob Carr snub was to give the airspace to the Opposition leader. John Brogden had been in the Opposition leader's chair only one day when Alan Jones was forced to break his pledge.[95] It is more likely Jones wanted to belt Carr rather than boost 'Broggers', but there was one other benefit. Alan Jones secured a promise that John Brogden would seek an audience with Jones' advisors, 'Tim Priest and Geoff Schuberg etc'.[96]

Jones was one of a cheer squad trying to elevate Priest's credibility. On 9 June columnist Miranda Devine wrote of Priest: 'At 46, looking much older than the photo on his driver's licence, and still smoking too much, he is about to get a medical discharge from the police service he joined in 1981 after leaving the SAS. He had dinner with the Prime Minister last week and hopes now to escape public life ...'[97]

The politicians were not the only ones conflicted and cowed by Alan Jones. Macquarie Bank executive Nicholas Moore responded to the *Australian Financial Review* in relation to Alan Jones' criticism of the bank's acquisition of Sydney Airport: 'I don't think anyone really cares what he thinks'.[98] Moore went on to say Jones was 'famous for his impartial comments', an apparent reference to the 'cash for comment' affair.[99] Moore was wrong. His bank cared absolutely about what Alan Jones thought. It swiftly bought space in the *Australian Financial Review* and ran what was headlined a 'clarification': 'Macquarie Bank apologises unreservedly for the inference that Mr Jones' views were other than his own'.[100]

Alan Jones crowed on air. Soon after, the *Australian Financial Review* ran a big colour spread in its magazine placing Alan Jones at number one on its list of the ten most culturally powerful Australians. Philip Ruddock ran second, with John Howard fourth. Alan Jones was photographed in glossy colour, wearing a charcoal pinstriped suit with purple tie and hankie. He was looking very pleased. On air, there was unconcealed delight about his endorsement in the quality press. A cosier relationship with the Macquarie Bank developed. In 2004, when Jones' prodigal Tricky Trindall had near exhausted his pool of friends and employment prospects, the bank's property manager, Bill Moss, a friend to Jones and a range of Aboriginal causes, was able to help get him a start with a local developer.[101]

On 17 July there was a much bigger deal, the one he had said, back in 1999, would 'never, never' be done. Alan Jones signed up with the formerly evil Telstra. A key difference as far as Jones was concerned was that the contract was with his radio station rather than directly with Jones. Telstra also did a deal with the other star of the 'cash for comment' affair, John Laws. Before the first Australian Broadcasting Authority inquiry, Alan Jones criticised his then stablemate for accepting money to change his mind. The $1.2 million Telstra contract and the position Alan Jones now took on air suggested he had a similar case to answer.

Yet another ABA investigation was begun, again headed by David Flint. John Laws was found in breach of the code and Alan Jones was cleared, even though the report's fine print acknowledged: '... that prior to the commercial agreement Alan Jones made a number of on air statements critical of Telstra, especially with respect to its fees and charges. The dates for these statements are 17 April, 18 April, 22 April (twice), 23 April (twice), 26 April and 11 July 2002. From 17 July 2002 [the day the Telstra deal was executed] onwards, however, the material provided to the ABA records Jones making predominantly positive commentary, supporting Telstra's service standards, public image and credibility. It may be noted that Mr Jones' views on the privatisation of Telstra also seem to have changed over time.'[102]

It transpired that behind the Telstra deal lurked a grander plan. Telstra was still mainly government-owned. The government's plan for the full sale of Telstra had foundered. Surveys constantly revealed that a majority of Australians opposed full privatisation. The Telstra marketing plan for Alan Jones explained why Telstra was prepared to spend $1.2 million securing the Macquarie Radio agreement: 'Alan Jones is a prominent player in the media industry and hosts the highest ranking radio program in the breakfast time slot from 6am to 9am. The audience is extremely loyal to Jones and they listen to and respect his opinions and use them to influence their friends and families.'[103]

Three weeks later Alan Jones put a proposition to his listeners: 'Why couldn't we sell Telstra and guarantee a proportion of the money would go towards a comprehensive national scheme to water Australia so we don't have to run around the track every time there's appalling levels of drought ...'[104] At the time Australia was enduring another exhausting dry spell. The Moses behind the microphone saw drought as a compliance problem. To Jones, the weather was every bit as disobedient as an Ella and, like an errant footballer, needed to be brought into line. After returning from a weekend in the Hunter Valley he thundered: 'Well what are we going to do? I was in the bush, deliberately went to the bush at the weekend to check all this out. And it is extraordinary, we're not short of water, we've just got the water in the wrong place. The water is in one place, the need is in the other.'[105]

Jones spoke of the mass of water stored in the Ord system in north Western Australia and how most of it emptied into the Timor Sea. 'Four billion litres of water a day not used in the Ord system. The Clarence River, Grafton's on the Clarence, the Pioneer River, Mackay's on the Pioneer River. Bundaberg, the Burdekin River. All the rivers up there. The Daly, they can all be turned inland and used. And then you flood your river system in drought time, dam the water, flood the river system, irrigate off the rivers. Build dams. What are we doing?'[106]

Alan Jones rejected the proposition that he was trying to turn his audience as well as the rivers. In October 2002, he helped launch the Farmhand Foundation to lend a hand to the battlers in the bush. As ever, Alan was defiant and contemptuous of can't-do bureaucratic advice, rejecting conventional wisdom and research which had come to a painful recognition that European farm practices did not always work in Australia. The debate had long moved on from grand Snowy River-like schemes towards revising farming methods to match a fragile landscape. Large parts of Australia were already lost to salinity, a consequence of unwise irrigation practices.

But Alan was back in Acland in the 1950s. He has long claimed the blight of his parents was more the weather than the limits of a 154-acre block. Under Queensland crony capitalism, Country Party mates were granted water licences at minimal cost to themselves and maximum cost to the future. Alan was being true to his roots.

Alan Jones said then as he says now, we have plenty of water—why not pipe it? We can pipe gas, why can't we pipe water? When his researcher Michael Darby pointed out that gas can be transported economically because it can be compressed, Jones dismissed his argument. Through the 1990s Jones called for actuarial studies to support his proposition that the inland should be watered. The studies were done, but Alan did not like the results, which showed the cost of piping water would be greater than the resulting productivity gains.

Columnist Ross Gittins, long admired by Alan Jones, would not have pleased when he pointed out: 'If you hate farmers, be sure to give generously to the Farmhand appeal. If you want the drought problem to get worse, applaud the politicians as they hand out more taxpayers' money to drought stricken cockies. And if you want to see our farmers continuing to stuff up the Wide Brown Land—and then demanding that you and I pay to clean up the mess—nod wisely when ignorant loudmouths spout about "drought-proofing" Australia.'[107]

Never mind the facts, Alan continued to spin a tale full of sound and fury. The Farmhand appeal secured the support of some seriously successful Australians. 2GB, Channel 9, Visy Industries, Foxtel and Telstra kicked in $4.5 million with the Federal Government contributing a similar amount. Kerry Packer, Dick Pratt, Bob Mansfield, Sam Chisholm and John Singleton were Farmhand Foundation principals alongside Alan Jones.

Alan Jones' more fanciful propositions threatened more than his credibility. Somebody must have tried to rein him in. Kerry Packer corrected some of the enthusiasm, explaining, 'I don't think it is possible to drought proof it. But I think we can have a say in it, and I think it's possible for this country to be a lot better drought proofed than it is at the moment.'[108]

Alan Jones' Farmhand appeal caught the attention of the much-loathed *Media Watch*, now presented by David Marr. 'Oh dear, is Jonesy dreaming the old dream of turning the rivers around? Yes he is.'[109] Jonesy's response was to deny his words, claiming instead that it was a listener who raised the proposition of turning the rivers. He sought the support of his panel operator: 'In fact Ross is with me here, put your microphone on—Rossco, just from your point of view, you've been with me for years and years ... Have you ever heard me on this program argue the case for turning the rivers inland?' Operator: 'I can't recall you ever—' Jones: 'I can't recall ever. Exactly right. Exactly right and we were talking to the staff here this morning—never.'[110] The next day on Channel 9's *Today* program he showed how Jones' brainwashing starts with Jones: 'Those of you who've been listening to me talk about watering Australia will know you've never heard me speak about turning rivers inland.'[111]

One of Alan's talkback callers later politely pointed out he had heard Alan speak of turning the rivers inland. Jonesy was momentarily addled. He is not used to disagreement. *Media Watch* revisited the subject, replaying Jones' words: 'The Clarence River, the Burdekin, the Daly could all be turned inland'.[112] He twice made the claim on the same day. The *Media Watch* broadcast ended with David Marr declaring: 'Alan, you are, as we say in the trade, a liar. Goodnight.'[113] Bob Carr was said to have been so excited when David Marr called Alan Jones a liar that he tuned in at 5.30 the next morning to hear Jones' response. From time to time Jones had also accused the New South Wales Premier of lying.

As is often the case with a Jones campaign, there was merit. The Farmhand appeal raised over $24 million and gave temporary relief to 18 000 farming families. It also drew attention to a critical issue: water management. The downside was the extension of the misery of farmers struggling on marginal land and Jones' determination to force a Jones outcome.[114]

Five months out from a state election Jones was struggling to position himself for the result. Since 2001 he had been telling listeners Bob Carr was hopeless. Throughout 2002 he attempted to elevate a range of fifth order issues. The proposed closure of Hunters Hill High (stopped largely as a result of Jones) and the approval of a charcoal plant at Mogo were two of the many 'disgraces' blamed on Carr. 'The Carr Government is in absolute and abject disarray.'[115] 'Bob Carr, if you can't do the job, stand aside and let someone else do it.'[116] 'The Carr Government must want to be thrown out in a landslide.'[117]

When he came back on air in January 2003 there were some first order issues to confront. With the smoke of a frightening bushfire season not yet cleared, Alan Jones tackled the government on bushfire preparedness, complaining how tired he was of Carr's obsession with turning the state into a national park. The Waterfall train disaster of 31 January, which cost seven lives, signalled the end of Carl Scully's run as transport minister and dented his prospects for premier. As explained in an earlier chapter, Alan Jones was unhappy when Scully's department head, Michael Deegan, defied Jones over reforms in the hire car industry: 'Carl Scully's career is over even if Bob Carr is returned.'[118] Scully's sycophantic 'Dear Alan' letters ended up counting for little.

Jones was again riding high in the ratings, the boost at breakfast lifting the general performance of the station. His confidence was up. He described himself on air as the Lleyton Hewitt of the airwaves. Like the Wimbledon winner, he was indeed at the 'top of his profession'.[119] His first question to Bob Carr in their first interview of the year was: 'What the hell is going on?'[120] But the two-year Jones jihad had a flaw: by now Alan should have been getting a pretty good idea that Carr would be re-elected anyway.

The difficulties Jones faced in finding his own winning position brought forth a kind of schizophrenia. The Crikey website likened him to the Smeagol/Gollum split personalities in Tolkien's *The Lord of the Rings*. Smeagol: 'Well I see a story today that says that Bob Carr has declared his intention to stay in the job as Premier well into the decade ... Look, however you might look at it, Bob Carr has been an outstandingly successful leader of his party, firstly, and of the State.' Gollum: 'There are major pockets of trouble for Labor in this election ... there are aspects of public administration here which are going to cause problems for the Carr government to say nothing of him falling over the Greens seemingly at every turn'.[121]

On the eve of the 22 March election, after hammering Carr about workers' compensation, land tax and hospitals, Jones said: 'Bob Carr represents the most experienced state politician in the country. He's able, he's intelligent and I'm sure the election campaign has taught him an awful lot ... for all those reasons Mr Carr is entitled to another term in office ... Come Monday it'll have to be the latent decency and goodness of Bob Carr that must prevail.'[122] It was a very long way from the 'Bob Carr, if you can't do the job, stand aside and let someone else do it',[123] of just a few months earlier.

The latest screeching U-turn was never going to explain the result. Labor improved its vote by one per cent, winning in the fringe seats that had gone to John Howard in 2001. In Bob Carr's office they were delighted. The Premier stopped listening to Jones. However, despite growing doubts about the true reach of Alan's influence, there was no lessening of political pandering. The New South Wales government, obsessed during Bob Carr's time with media management, was not going to break the habit overnight. There were others who hoped Jones could do for them what he had done for Howard and Carr.

Ironically, not long after being re-elected, the Carr Government was run over by reality when it confronted a range of problems with hospitals and transport that no spin-doctor could ever fix. According to the Opposition, since it left government in 1995, State Rail had increased its public relations staff from one to fifteen. All that skill in tweaking perception did not help get Sydney to and from work when the wheels started to fall off the rail system. Michael Costa, the Mussolini lookalike who had moved on from the police to preside over the transport system, failed to get the trains running on time but was still given an easy go on Jones' program: 'He's a good listener, Michael Costa.'[124] 'He's a toughie.'[125] New Police Minister John Watkins and Morris Iemma, Health Minister and later successor to Bob Carr as Premier, were fellow crawlers.

As the trains were ailing, so too were the hospitals. And as usual, according to Alan, the problem was bad people rather than bad ideas or systems. A hospital crisis, similar to the police crisis, also got priority on Jones' program. He broke the story of mismanagement and neglect at Camden and Campbelltown hospitals, taking the side of a team of whistleblower nurses.

When the courage to oppose Jones could not be found, the government followed the new routine of commissioning an independent inquiry. Morris Iemma was quick to appease. Alan Jones lectured him in writing: 'Morris, there is massive "work outstanding" in this portfolio ... I do believe you should get up to speed on all this.'[126] And again: 'I really think I need to talk to you about the issue'.[127] Alan Jones won another human sacrifice with the sacking of, among others, Area Health Services General Manager Jennifer Collins.[128]

Police Commissioner Ken Moroney, now in regular contact with Alan Jones, no doubt gave some thought to the fate of his predecessor when he and Alan got together. Jones' influence with the police, always undue, was now potentially sinister. As a senior Liberal politician commented at the time, on his own, Alan Jones had stopped dead police reform. Jones' elevation of Tim Priest to hero and martyr status was as stupid as it gets. Alan continued to represent him as a saviour of policing despite the disturbed officer's difficulties holding on to a sergeant's job.

On 5 September 2003 Priest and Jones discussed on 2GB yet another commissioned inquiry, the *Bodor Report* into the 'James'/Cabramatta allegations. Both would publicly exult in the Bodor finding that 'James' had essentially done his best. But there was a great deal more in the report that should have made Jones' advisors uncomfortable. Peter Bodor QC actually said of on air comments: 'Priest's allegations relating to Bodor's review were completely false and misinformed. This reflects poorly on Priest's reliability and credibility.'[129]

Tim Priest's intelligence and advice did not appear to help Alan Jones during the Deborah Wallace defamation trial. Nor did it seem to help when Clive Small also won the first stage of his defamation action against Jones. A further case between Jones and former NSW Police Commander Lola Scott saw the judgement go to Jones, with accounts varying about who actually won and which party paid costs.

Although Alan Jones was known to complain privately about Tim Priest's incessant demands and this widening mess of litigation, the pair remained superglued. In October 2003 Priest received a bravery award, after Jones had lobbied to overturn a previous independent panel's decision. At the same time he received a 'special risk benefit' of $109 000. One year later the Liberals made use of Priest prior to the federal election, naming him chairman of the Prime Minister's Crime Advisory Group, ostensibly to fight crime in Sydney's western suburbs.[130]

Here was another example of Jones' power spinning out of control. With Alan on his side, Tim Priest persisted with his compensation demand for a reported $2.5 million. The Police Legal Department, aware of his spotty record, saw every reason to contest the claim. Police Legal became a new enemy and Jones wanted to get rid of them. He wrote to Ken Moroney, attacking Director Michael Holmes: 'My understanding is that despite the best efforts and advice from Minister Costa to you before the election to settle the matter, you have done nothing. What are we trying to achieve Ken? Are we going to drag this out to cost Priest more money and drain him financially and ultimately destroy him?' Jones threatened: 'And then, Ken, what happens if this goes to trial? I wonder can the Police Service afford this, because it will be a very public trial ...'[131]

Alan Jones maintained the pressure in further correspondence and on air, pushing the line that the claim was meritorious and Police Legal was deliberately obfuscating. The government's own advice was to the contrary. They saw that the case could easily be challenged and that the delays were largely coming from the other side.

Jones' would have no doubt seen that rather than avoiding the process all he was doing was trying to help another battler. Maybe Alan really believed in Priest, or maybe it did not matter. Triumphing in the Priest affair did more than validate his campaign to run Peter Ryan out of town. It did more than help empower those who might help Alan. A win was a wedge that secured further control over an important institution. The little skirmish over Priest was another way of showing the police and Sydney who was boss.

Despite Alan Jones' on air attacks and pressure from superiors to get him off their backs, Michael Holmes and his deputy, Bryan Doyle, stuck to what they believed was the responsible course. As the heat was turned up, Holmes moved on to a job as a magistrate. Soon after, Doyle also moved on. It seemed the way was now clear for the settlement to go ahead, and it might have too, but for broadcaster Mike Carlton getting wind of what was going on. When Carlton threatened that he and John Laws would make an issue of the secret settlement on air, the government reluctantly went back to accepting the Crown Solicitor's advice and opposed the claim.

It took years for the case to eventually settle, resolution coming on 13 April 2007, three weeks after a subsequent March state election. Although the advice recommending it be contested had not changed, former Police Minister John Watkins said: 'There was a risk of greater cost to the taxpayer if this case continued'.[132] It was reported at the time another former Police Minister, now Treasurer, Michael Costa had written an affidavit on behalf of Priest containing 'words to the effect that Mr Priest could have made the senior ranks of the police service, such as assistant commissioner or deputy commissioner, had he not been sidelined after a stint at Cabramatta'.[133]

Tim Priest has had some powerful advocates, in particular Alan Jones. The proposition that he might have made the senior ranks of policing to me seemed ludicrous. While I had not seen Priest as corrupt, I had seen a troubled, divisive and dangerously unworthy standard-bearer, undeserving of the championing by Jones and it seems, Michael Costa.

My judgement did not triumph. As it turned out, a civil action brought against the author of this book and its publisher was also finalised with an out of court commercial settlement in 2007.

CHAPTER 18
THE MISINFORMATION REVOLUTION

> Whoever can speak, speaking now to the whole nation, becomes a power, a branch of government ... the requisite thing is to have a tongue that others will listen to.
>
> THOMAS CARLYLE, 19TH CENTURY HISTORIAN

WHEN ALAN JONES RUSHES FROM the fourth estate of the media to cross the line into one of the formal estates of government, too often he meets an eager politician scurrying to cross the line in the other direction. If we could sit democracy in the stands to observe the spectacle, it is hard to imagine the majority applauding. But the majority do not see and the majority do not listen.

In 2004 Alan Jones had his 1988 Australia Day honour upgraded to Officer of the Order of Australia. When the *Australian Financial Review* magazine again examined power in Australia, Alan Jones ranked eighth, behind his friend Kerry Packer and ahead of another magnate, Frank Lowy.[1] It was not the size of his audience that delivered the standing, but the way he uses it. Alan Jones harassing and haranguing, on air and in writing, intimidates others into submitting to the belief that he really does represent public opinion.

At this time Jones also won his 100th ratings survey. It was a strong win, too. His 16.7 per cent share showed he was rebuilding his following since the 12.8 per cent low of late 2003. The August survey counted an accumulated daily audience of 455 000 Sydneysiders.

As was now apparent, the age of his audience gives him his lead. FM station Nova had more numbers tuned in but for lesser periods of time. ABC local radio also had higher numbers but for a younger age group. People rushing to work don't have a lot of time to settle in front of a radio. For the audience aged 70 plus, Jones held a massive 60.8 per cent share. The second place getter for this group was well behind at 21.9 per cent. The many retirees who follow Alan have more time to listen. Even so, when the figures are averaged out, only 175 000 people were listening at any one time.[2] The earlier May survey showed, on the basis of total listeners, Jones finishing fifth rather than first.[3]

Alan Jones has a national television audience too, estimated at a maximum of 250 000. The segment on Channel Nine's *Today* show has stayed the course despite attempts by a succession of junior executives to get rid of, or cut it back. According to those who have moved against him, what protects him is his closeness to the Packer family.

After Kerry Packer's death on Boxing Day 2005, Alan Jones was one of the few to attend the private funeral, and he was master of ceremonies at the state funeral. On air Alan Jones would sometimes say the failure of politics could be remedied if parliament was closed and Kerry was allowed to run the show. They were close to the end, and there is no doubt they had a lot in common.

Following the death, when Alan Jones contributed a eulogy of Kerry Packer to the *Australian*, he might have been speaking of himself. Jonesy cited KP's preference for private generosity and praised his friend's ability to simply argue complex theory, identifying Packer as being 'rarely seen to be keeping step with the times, but, rather marching ahead of them'.[4]

Kerry Packer's passing did not lessen support and loyalty from the Packer family. Alan Jones continued with the *Today* segment despite rivals mocking it as egocentric and out of date. Indeed there is every indication it was at this moment, when the editorial was first aired, that Network Seven broke the spell of Nine's ascendancy in news and current affairs. For years, in every market, when Alan Jones came on the *Today* show, 30 000 to 40 000 viewers turned off. Viewer feedback ran two to one against Jones. It is not hard to work out why. A humourless, hectoring Jones is not everyone's cup of breakfast tea.

Alan Jones takes a contrary view, blaming the former *Today* team for bleeding ratings and telling colleagues that his segment keeps the show going. Jones had not seen himself to blame for a similar failure back at Channel 10, when *Alan Jones Live* had its brief run. When exposed to a cross-section of the Australian public, the majority response appears to be negative. After co-host Steve Liebmann was replaced by a younger Karl Stefanovic in January 2005, Jones' appearances became more personable and his keen support for Stefanovic was noted around the station. The 'Q' rating—a qualitative assessment ranking, on a five-point scale, what viewers like and dislike—consigns Jones to the bottom order. In this survey personalities such as Magda Szubanski and Andrew Denton are in the top order, scoring in the 30s. One survey ranked Jones at minus six.

Eventually simple arithmetic told. It cost Channel Nine $500 per *Today Show* editorial to lose an audience. Soon after James Packer sold 75 per cent of the network's parent company PBL to CVA Asia Pacific, the segment was dumped. It was left to Nine's news and current affairs director, Garry Linnell, to inform Alan Jones. The last editorial was aired on 15 June 2007, Jones farewelling his audience with the words: 'I am reminded of a simple saying, which applies to work as much as it applies to life. Don't cry because it's over. Smile because it happened. See you somewhere'.[5] Alan Jones appeared to take well a significant blow. His reach beyond his Sydney audience was over. Although he and James Packer were still close, the three-quarters sell-out diminished the potency of the Packer/Jones alliance by a greater sum. While Kerry Packer had paid close attention to his television interests, son James was not so interested. Although they put a brave face on it, twenty years on Kerry Packer's original political attack dog had been at last put down.

Despite his power, Alan Jones is not a winning brand. Corporations such as Optus have seen that an association with Jones can have negative consequences. It is worth noting that Telstra also ended its sponsorship with Alan Jones and 2GB in 2005 and soon after returned to damage control mode as Jones' attacks again increased. There is the worry that a high profile association with Jones could be damaging to the broad consumer base. While Alan Jones promotes Mercedes-Benz cars on his radio program, he is not used for major nationwide promotions. Taking this qualitative rating as a guide you might wonder whether, if they did use him, more people would be getting rid of Mercedes than buying them.

As was the case back in Brisbane in the 1960s Alan's beliefs are difficult to pigeonhole. His Liberal background and support for the Federal Coalition does not necessarily make him a friend of business. While his Struggle Street credentials are underpinned on a preparedness to take on the big end of town, his relationship with the corporate sector remains tense. Nor is a personal association an absolute guarantee of immunity from attack.

When in 2005 Alan Jones took on NRMA Insurance, a member company of Insurance Australia Group (IAG), anxiety led to outright bewilderment. Jones backed the motor repair industry in its long running dispute with selected motor insurers. At the heart of the quarrel was the issue of choice. NRMA wanted more control over how and where repairs were conducted. A range of motor repairers angry at the changes rallied and lobbied. Alan was persuaded, giving NRMA Insurance a hiding over its web-based repair tendering system: 'Quite frankly the NRMA/IAG are under the hammer here and no amount of apology will get them off the hook'.[6] A personal relationship with Michael Hawker, the former Wallaby and boss of IAG, did not help the insurer with Jones taking a position he often takes with politicians—that Hawker was being misled by subordinates.

The dispute, played out constantly on 2GB, showed no mercy to IAG/NRMA and was hurtful to the tune of millions. What was bewildering to some insurance insiders was not just how damaging Alan could be, but how imbalanced and illogical were some of the attacks.

While Jones was belting NRMA he was flogging rival AAMI, which for similar reasons was also on the nose with protesting repairers. Alan read live advertising copy which promoted lack of choice as a virtue: 'If you're lucky enough to be with AAMI then the process couldn't be easier. Take your car to an AAMI customer service centre and your own personal client manager will arrange the repairs from start to finish'.[7] The dispute was unlucky for NRMA, which lost heavily, while lucky AAMI picked up business.

Members of Alan's audience persuaded to shift from NRMA are yet newer brethren. Although his ratings are down on the figures of 10 years ago, since that 100th survey win his program continued to grow in a more competitive market. By the middle of 2006, up against new FM stations and opposing John Laws between 9 am and 10 am, Alan Jones had lifted again to 17.1, while his old rival's figures faded. Alan still has plenty of ability to communicate and generate controversy enough to gather in newer listeners as his older audience dies out. His equity deal ties him to the fortunes of the station and he still has a strong lead on his nearest competitor.

And don't forget, his audience is his family. 'He seems to go out there and fight for the underdog and especially for people that are underprivileged', said one. 'I listen to Alan Jones in the morning … he's very positive', said another. A third: 'Well I think Alan is a very fair person … and he gives a voice to people that have no other means of getting to the media'.[8]

Alan Jones helps his listeners feel connected in a fast-moving, troubled world. He helps them feel they belong and matter. It is a great service to them, and in extending that service he demonstrates a rare gift. When he communicates his knowledge and enthusiasm for sport his presentation is equal to the brilliance of those grand moments such as Cathy Freeman breasting the tape. Alan accepts his responsibility to explain the arcane and confront the abstract. That he is on the right side of truth on many occasions is undeniable. It stands to reason that many of the campaigns he joins are worthwhile. Jones gets a drag racing strip built. He raises money for flood victims or a family wiped out when their house burned to the ground. He stands up for people, such as school cleaners, who find their jobs in jeopardy, and for children with special needs. Tuned in over the past few years, there were plenty of times when I understood what the fuss is about.

Listening to Alan calmly and patiently dealing with a nervous caller is impressive, but then, soon after, you hear him maniacally gibbering alongside a 'no excuses, lock 'em up for life' interviewee. '... I'm the person who's led the charge here. Nobody wanted to know about North Cronulla and now it's gathered to this'.[9] Alan Jones' treatment of the attacks on lifesavers and tensions that led to race-based riots in Sydney's south in December 2005 saw him pandering to public prejudice, and covering a lot of bases. 'What kind of grubs? This lot were Middle Eastern, we're not allowed to say it but I'm saying it.'[10] Alan at times spoke for the mob, repeating one correspondent's suggestion: 'to invite one of the biker gangs to be present in numbers at Cronulla Rail Station when these Lebanese thugs arrive ... it will be worth the price of admission to watch these cowards scurry back onto the train ... Australians old and new shouldn't have to put up with this scum.'[11] There was a rally cry for a show of strength and support at Cronulla, Jones speaking of the benefit of Pacific Islanders turning up. '... all those Samoans and Fijians they love being here. Proud to be here and they say ha ha ha you step out of line look out, and of course the cowards will always run.'[12] While he challenged the toughness of authorities such as police to get in there and protect the public he also warned against vigilante action: '... we've got to have appropriately trained authorities to do the job'.[13] The NSW Police later prepared a review, which cautioned media for inflammatory coverage. The Australian Broadcasting Authority successor, The Australian Communications and Media Authority (ACMA), also investigated, triggering greater ferocity from Alan.

In April 2007 ACMA released a finding that Alan Jones had broadcast material likely to encourage violence and vilify people of Lebanese background. As he had done after the ABA finding in 2000 Jones used his own program to attack and ridicule the report as 'unreadable rubbish', pointing out he had cautioned against violence.[14] Alan's listeners assembled at his side. As Jones explained, they were not the ones who had complained to the ACMA. The complaints, he argued, had instead followed replays of transcripts on the ABC. Alan Jones expressed his unhappiness with ACMA Chairman, Chris Chapman, in 'pick and stick' style. 'Chris Chapman has gone around this town on many occasions — to me and others — seeking references to be written for his appointment to a stack of jobs.'[15] Chapman and his board had found against Jones and 2GB on three of eight allegations. As the ABA had done seven years earlier, they looked at the objective evidence. While Jones wanted them to see the angel on one shoulder, ACMA could not ignore the devil on the other. Alan had been all over the place on the Cronulla story, in one breath soothing, in another fulminating.

The calmness and the craziness can come and go, sometimes in the space of minutes. When I listened to Alan Jones, for example, unwinding about Muslim clerics, I felt myself in the presence of an Australian fanatic. It is clear enough his audience will stick with him even though it is equally clear he can serve them poorly. With rasping insincerity Alan plays the tabloid flattery card: 'The public are not stupid'. 'My listeners are so intelligent'.[16] I have heard it many times and Jones sounds like he means it. If not for what his co-workers have to say about what comes out of his mouth when the microphone is turned off, I might believe him.

Like a jockey caught in the stirrups, his audience is dragged over his hurdles of logic and around the many U-turns. Alan tells them Bob Carr is hopeless. He then tells them to vote for Bob Carr. He then tells them Carr is again hopeless. He promotes extremist tax schemes, attacking the treasurer, and then gets him on air and flatters him.

The massive contrast between Alan Jones' professed honesty and his actual behaviour does not seem to matter. He was always good at fooling people willing to be fooled. And three to four and a half hours of radio a day for all those years become such a blur. The truth is just more ephemera. As long as he keeps talking the inconsistencies are swept along in the sheer volume of verbiage: his editorials and opinions must now number in the tens of thousands.

Alan Jones supports democracy as long as it does what it is told. He wants laws that are strict but can be adjusted like bookmakers' odds. He wants commanding decisions and he wants process and consultation. He wants strong competition as long as it isn't too strong for local competition. He speaks up for the virtues of civilised debate while using words like weedkiller to wilt his opponents. And, of course, his opinion is not for hire. As long as there is conviction in your voice, you begin to convince yourself. As Alan Jones understood from his days at Toowoomba Grammar, what matters is being someone. What matters is who is talking, not what is said.

In his talkback segments there is little disagreement or debate. Listeners agree with Alan. Alan agrees with the listeners—'You're a hundred per cent correct', 'That's a valid point', 'Well said'—as if someone is pulling the string on a talking doll. There is not just familiarity in the dialogue, but in the voices. If you listen long enough you hear the same callers. There is Stephanie, Marie, Brian, Peter, Terry and Graham, plus a succession of other regulars who share the Jones mix of bonhomie and bitterness. Monday to Friday they gather in a huddle, united in fear and confusion. When he rants and misleads, you can feel them forgiving him as they would an unworthy but much loved son.

Ever since his teaching days Alan Jones has shown himself as more a man for the executive summary. While he claims to be well researched, thoroughly reading boxes of documents delivered, for example, in relation to the Camden and Campbelltown hospitals dispute, I have my doubts. It takes days and days, if not weeks, of focused research to gain a competent understanding of such issues. It does not take a lot of figuring to conclude that Alan Jones' crowded hours leave little time for ploughing through detail. It shows in his program, which these days sails along as if on autopilot. As *Media Watch* noticed, during the selection process for a new Pope, Jones referred twice to 'Colonel' instead of 'Cardinal' Ratzinger.[17]

'Both sides of the story have to be represented.'[18] Or so he says. The notion of the Jones program as an electronic democracy is unarguably ridiculous. Alan Jones' ease with the spoken word is used to exclude rather than liberate truth. One of his editorial writers explained how, when research briefs were delivered in the favoured dot point style, Jones would read a brief and strike out any conflicting evidence. Another explained that when information was offered to help balance a Jones campaign, it was ignored. A third said he learned in time to leave out contrasting information and write what Jones wanted. Alan is fond of dismissing detail he fails to comprehend, or finds inconvenient, as 'gobbledegook'.

That overpowering certainty precludes learning. In October 2005, after Jones attacked the management of a King's Cross injecting centre, he sneered at an offer to see another point of view. 'I couldn't, in all conscience, tour something that is involved in this kind of social disaster.'[19]

His Farmhand campaign is an example of how those who seek to take advantage of his patronage overlook and excuse his weaknesses. It is one of many for which Alan assembles interviewees and facts to suit his own agenda. He is not satisfied with generating useful debate. When he persists with his push for practical, 'common sense' engineering schemes, Prime Minister Howard and Treasurer Costello politely humour him. His failure to confront the other side of the debate, which questions the commercial viability and environmental costs of these schemes, does no favours to the public, let alone the battling farmers. When he received a standing ovation from farmers at a drought crisis summit in 2005, was he a hero for standing up for them, or a charlatan for encouraging a belief that others are to blame and easier solutions are at hand? Alan believes bold people who make decisions shape history. He sees conciliation as soft and leftist. But in the end the facts conciliate the truth. While Alan may be able to deny contrasting evidence, history will not so readily look the other way.

Again, in 2005, when Alan Jones editorialised about the death of his hero, former Queensland Premier Sir Joh Bjelke-Petersen, he borrowed from an editorial written by an old boss, Doug Anthony, ignoring the mass of evidence that weighed against Sir Joh. As Alan/Doug argued, 'Bjelke-Petersen's achievements were not brought about by a leadership that tried to be all things to all people'.[20]

Alan and Joh do have a lot in common. Sir Joh's defenders have long excused the selfishness and corruption, pointing to the (doubtful) benefits secured on behalf of Queensland. Alan's defenders do much the same, forgiving the negatives for the sake of the positives. Like Sir Joh, Alan Jones is at his most appalling when he uses his power, as he did with the police, to help a poor idea win. Alan Jones' campaigning for a return to the bad days might be amusing if it wasn't taken seriously. Left to Jones and Bjelke-Petersen it is plain the crooks and cronies would still be in charge.

Although Alan Jones works hard at pulling Canberra's strings, his intervention in state politics is where he is most dangerous. The Faustian bargains struck by local politicians over the past few decades did the most to cement his power, and there is further irony when his regular pre-election scaremongering about law and order ended up biting them. Alan Jones' campaigning was not merely distracting, it was also harmful and destabilising for politicians and the police. On the government side politicians such as new Premier Morris Iemma are stymied, having understandably copied Bob Carr's approach of dealing with—and on occasions surrendering to—Jones.

While the spin master Carr generally got the better of Jones the apprentices flounder. In November 2005, Morris Iemma failed to be available for a prime time interview, because of, shock horror, having to attend a Muslim function. Jones: 'Premier, is it out of order for me to suggest that when you have an opportunity to speak to hundreds of thousands of people and someone in your office shoves you as well to a Ramadan breakfast in Lakemba that someone has their priorities upside down'. The new Premier's quavering contrition was a new peak of embarrassment: 'Oh Alan we had a bit of a traffic ah, a bit of a traffic problem, ah in ah coordinating this, my apologies'.[21] The Opposition is no better placed as policies and initiatives can't always develop without Jones' approval.

Although they know well how harmful Jones can be, like much of the media he is there to be used, and politicians figure they are mostly able to quarantine the association. People who might be troubled by Alan Jones' endorsements are not listening to him. Only rarely, such as in the case of New South Wales Minister Michael Costa, does the relationship, and its potential negative impact, reach a more critical audience. So politicians, too, often ignore the downside in bearing allegiance to Alan. Indeed, the federal Coalition, although conflicted—as I pointed out in the beginning, numbered among them are his biggest doubters—is in general constrained by the view that the media are, in the main, ungenerous. John Howard, who got a poor run from the media early in his career, seems to place a higher value on those who have backed him. The winning view appears to be, if you get him onside Alan delivers. A newer use is the shortcut he provides to that mystical ground 'public opinion'. When Bob Carr contested the 2003 election, television advertisements featured him with headphones on, as if listening to talkback. When in 2006 the Federal Coalition changed its position at the last minute on the sale of Snowy Hydro, an initiative strongly opposed by Jones, the back flip was spun as proof of a government in touch with the people.

Alan, who once worked in a prime minister's office, speaks to politicians in their own special language. At least they can read the code. When Alan Jones says Michael Costa is a 'good listener', it means Costa will do what he is told. When he complains that Commissioner Ken Moroney is losing his grip on police administration, it means Jones is worried that Jones is losing his grip. When he said 'Bob Carr is not listening to the public', it meant Bob Carr had (if temporarily) given up taking notice of Alan Jones.

As with the 2003 New South Wales election, in the 2004 federal election, the Jones factor was not so visible. Alan could take little credit for John Howard's substantial win in October 2004. His campaigning for Liberal Ross Cameron, who, pre-poll, had admitted adultery, was not able to save the member for Parramatta. In the seats to the west and southwest of Sydney where Alan Jones has his biggest audience, the trend was no different to elsewhere.

The captivation with the Jones factor in the 1990s might have been, in part, a misreading of trends. Sometimes the grey army of Jones' listeners can be confused with the mortgage belt, where the real battle was fought. The demographic under pressure to keep up mortgage payments credited the Coalition with superior economic credentials and was progressively turning conservative. As audience research shows, the younger mortgagees are not classic Alan Jones listeners.

So if his program is not reliable and impartial, if his audience is neither huge nor representative, and if his influence is understood to be often negative, why do politicians continue to deal with him? The answer has a lot to do with the talk radio medium, which has risen in influence during the Jones era. Talk radio has its limits. A poor research base, that reverse index of certainty, the rush to judgement and, most of all, a vulnerability to manipulation do not always deliver the credibility accorded talk radio by premiers and prime ministers. Many of Jones' radio colleagues see his dishonesty and activism as harmful to an industry that also has its virtues.

They deal with Alan partly because it is easier to go along with him, and partly because honesty is not what they are looking for. The media management industry that has also grown with Jones' success needs people to peddle its wares. It follows that an industry intent on control would seek out a controlling individual. Corporations with a negative image to overcome and politicians with more ambition than ability are keen to buy.

The misinformation industry is interested in his audience too. Again, influence reaches where it can. Modern market research is capable of determining not just which suburbs prefer cornflakes to muesli, it can work out what these consumers want to hear. So market research matches opinion to market share. It is not just a matter of telling people how to think, but also of knowing what they want to think. Like those columnists recruited for their access to a constituency rather than the quality of their ideas, Alan Jones has become a standard bearer for a misinformation revolution.

While public debate continues to become bogged along the increasingly trammelled left–right battlelines, the great divider helps us identify a more meaningful boundary. If governments and corporations are more confident about controlling information, and if part of the deal is ceding power to media demagogues, what really matters is an understanding of the difference between news and advertising, the subject of the 'cash for comment' inquiry.

As the Australian Broadcasting Authority showed, Alan Jones is for sale. The only thing in doubt is the price. As we have seen, Alan's admiration and aggression have been bought for large sums of money, but they have also been bought for next to nothing. It might take no more than a fawning letter, especially one delivered by a handsome envoy. What is important is a show of homage. And the game is getting sneakier. One New South Wales politician orchestrated Alan Jones' approval by keeping a staff member back late so a faxed response to Jones' demands would appear to be the product of late-night toil.

There is in all this a fear much larger than the cowering of politicians and business leaders. Prominent in the Alan Jones story is how he brings out both the bully in the media and the coward in Sydney. Perhaps it is inescapable—the more labyrinthine the city, the more diminished the community, the louder the voice of the town crier. Maybe Sydney is comfortable with Jones, or maybe it is too consumed with other matters to take him on. An objective of this book is not to do a Jones on Jones and drive him out of town, but rather, to urge the town to stand up to him.

Since the move to 2GB, Alan Jones has made changes, signalling, you would think, a new beginning, or an end game. In 2003 he took to the attic, selling a virtual warehouse full of memorabilia. The auctioneers listed 46 items, including a cricket bat autographed by, among others, Don Bradman; a photograph of himself with actor Mel Gibson; and a 1984 Wallabies jumper.

In the same year Alan Jones upgraded his rural retreat, buying a 28-hectare farm near the Southern Highlands, 'Sanford Orcas', with its guesthouses, tennis court and stables, for $2.6 million and spending an estimated $1 million improving it.[22] Jones soon renamed it 'Charlieville', in honour of his father and alter ego. In honour of his mother, the homestead is called 'Elizabeth Farm'.

He advertised the old Jamberoo property for sale as well as the Newtown warehouse at 12–18 O'Connell Street, with its two separate apartments, commercial grade coolroom and parking for five cars. His home for 15 years went on the market soon after the New South Wales election and was sold for close to $3 million. Following the earlier federal election, Alan Jones moved to a new Sydney home in the Toaster at East Circular Quay, next to the Opera House—the same apartment building that he had formerly criticised as a 'monstrosity', 'out of the reach of Australians'. He had changed his mind about Newtown too; having been of the view back in 1997 that selling it would be 'the ultimate piece of folly'.[23] Alan Jones was reported as leasing the new $3.6 million, three bedroom apartment from Westbus director Slavko Bosnjak for $4000 a week.[24] Here Alan is looked after by his butler, David, who, it is said, once worked for the royal family. While increasingly fretting about putting on weight, Alan has his meals prepared by his butler. While a good walk might help keep him trim, Alan seems now more often to avoid the footpaths, taking his favoured limousines everywhere even, it is said, across the courtyard to the Opera House. The new address does give pause for further consideration of that proposition that Alan is one with the common man.

There were also new premises at 2GB. Macquarie relocated to modern studios at Pyrmont. Alan Jones had easily the biggest office with its own boardroom table and personal bathroom. Occupying one-tenth of the total space, it became known as 'The West Wing'.[25] A pull-out bed was fitted and used more often by his infant great-nephew Hunter. Hunter's mum, Alan's niece Tonia, occupies a nearby desk. 2GB staffers report that more and more of Jones' time is devoted to Hunter, who is referred to behind Jones' back as 'the heir'.

It was as if he was clearing the decks. He makes a habit of never looking back. There was talk of plans to move to 'Charlieville' and broadcast from the farm. So maybe Alan Jones is also in some way contemplating retreat. While I can only observe from a distance I see few signs of a happier and gentler Alan. One close associate says he continues to complain of having no real friends. The biggest gap in his life remains, as he has admitted, the absence of a life partner. Jones' loneliness is evident when he crashes his way into the company of his young friends. There have been moments of embarrassment when a smitten Alan barges uninvited into the company of a fancied sportsman or pesters a rising musician.

On the subject of shame, it is hard to be sure whether Alan has too much or too little, for example, the London toilet episode indicating too much and the 'cash for comment' affair, too little. He continues to use his power to insinuate a place in younger lives. He remains generous in his help to old friends too, but there are occasions when Jones' employees are asked to find a polite way to kiss off calls from older mates seeking help, mates who have, often without explanation, fallen from favour.

As with the old young friends, the new young friends do not often see a homosexual Alan. Despite a 40-year obsessive habit of surrounding himself with young men, many still argue their good mate Jonesy was jilted by a woman or is asexual. This is hardly likely. Jonesy is one of a generation unluckily trapped by passing attitudes.

When he grew up in Acland in the 1950s it was impossible to be openly gay. For much of his life it was illegal to practise homosexuality. Not until 2003 did New South Wales lower the age of consent for homosexual sex to sixteen. He could not tell the truth in the bush, in the schoolyard, to the mothers of the boys he spent so much time with, or to the fathers of all those rugby players. It must be hard to escape feeling ashamed of being something that was, until 1984 in New South Wales, illegal. Now Alan, like many of his generation, is consigned to a life without a visible partner. The habit of secrecy and denial is ingrained. Jonesy also maintains the secret, according to those a bit closer to him, because it might not be well received by his older audience. If so, he is probably partly correct. A study undertaken on behalf of The Australia Institute by Roy Morgan Research found: 'In one of the most notable differences between Jones' audience and other Australians, 46% of his listeners believe that homosexuality is immoral, compared to 35% of all Australians.'[26]

Clearly it is a secret that does no favours, least of all to Alan Jones, constrained in a prison in part of his own making. Neither is the guise effective. Whenever there is talk of Jones, speculation about his sexuality is high on the agenda. The more he hides, the more he draws attention to himself. And the more this goes on, the more anxious he becomes about controlling those who threaten his fragile identity. Ironically, a man who relies on a perception that he stands in the middle of mainstream Australia has always lived on the margin. I sometimes wonder whether this compulsion to represent himself as the majority is related to his disguise. Meanwhile, a constant theme of his broadcasts is the decline of public and moral standards.

At the office a red-faced, apoplectic Jones continues to harass his workers. If they argue he gets redder and screams. They learn it is easier to apologise. Not long after the fury passes, a different Jones is sure to appear, offering cups of tea and charm, but his co-workers find it hard to forget the abuse. When Alan Jones laments on air the escalation of public violence, I wonder whether he ever thinks of the violence of his own words.

So who, if anyone, is capable of regulating Alan Jones? The Australian Broadcasting Authority could have found a better way to sanction Jones as well as his station. The least his dishonesty deserved was temporary suspension. But sanctions generated by Jones affect many more broadcasters than Jones. And however many pretenders there are, Alan remains an anomaly. The people best placed to regulate him are his station managers. At 2GB the likelihood of someone telling him to pull his head in grows more distant. Now that Alan is one of the bosses, his influence on the station and the newsroom is more evident, and there is no sign that he is any more accountable than he was at 2UE.

John Brennan, his handler back at 2UE and now resurrected in that role at 2GB, is credited with taking some of the shrillness out of Alan Jones. But Brennan, who admitted a lack of toughness at 2UE, is still one for pampering his stars. After another ratings win, John Brennan wrote: 'May I say congratulations on an awesome accomplishment Alan. To do it in the face of the most incessant campaign of scorn—is miraculous. Some press journalists—radio and TV commentators have vindictively hated him—plotted against him—maligned him—warped and twisted his words—falsely reported him—and set out to expressly get him. YET he goes on and obliterates the judas' who try to betray him. You are a freak. Jack Davey might have been the greatest ENTERTAINER on radio—Bob Rogers the greatest music presenter—Ray Hadley the greatest sports broadcaster—Tony Witgers the greatest disc jockey ... but you're the greatest all round broadcaster of all time. I've heard 'em all. You're a common man touched by genius. Congrats.'[27]

Standing up to Alan Jones is wearing. As in so many other of his workplaces, Jones collects people who agree with him. At all those places Jones had his fans. There is still a strong band of them but, as always, they are a minority. The difference now is how much sway that minority holds. When Alan Jones is allowed to make policy, good or bad, everyone pays whether they listen or not. Alan Jones represents a hole in democracy, his power neither explained by his support base nor matched by a measure of responsibility.

While his audience is free to listen, the politicians who bargain with him are obliged to do better. It stands to reason that if a criterion for succeeding in politics is getting on with broadcasters like Jones, we will see a lessening of standards. Privately, politicians must know that the quality of debate and the integrity of office have already suffered. Meanwhile Alan Jones continues to bully them with his tsunami of correspondence.

One member of his staff, exhausted by the madness of it all, has taken to deleting emails before Jones sees them, and sneaking wads of letters home and dumping them. It makes little difference. The madness comes in tides. On the strength of a listener's assertion or a nudge from a mate, Alan Jones begins another dizzying charge. It is not a race for the truth, it is a race for victory. Not content to report the event, Alan Jones seeks to control the outcome.

As the evidence shows, a controlling Alan can get out of control. As the evidence shows, there is a moment when that negative energy begins to bring out the worst in a place. They saw it at Brisbane Grammar and The King's School, the Wallabies and the Tigers and at 2UE. It seems to take a lot longer to see it in Jonestown.

AFTERWORD
THE CRINGE FACTOR

IT IS EASY TO ADMIRE ALAN JONES, but too often for the wrong reasons. As he did after the 'cash for comment' crisis, Alan Jones weathered the publication of this book with barely a backward glance. In October 2006, when *Jonestown* was first published, Alan Jones was in London. Jones' radio station 2GB strained credibility by declaring the journey was prearranged and had no connection to the release of the book. The way Sydney's media minders saw it, taking refuge was the only sensible course. There was no worth in giving oxygen to negative publicity and there was an excellent chance Jones' loyal audience would either not listen or not want to know. 2GB did not pay attention to the news of the book's release or the swirl of discussion surrounding it. The television network Alan Jones works for, Channel 9, similarly sidestepped the story. The master interrogator answered none of the questions raised in *Jonestown*, much debated by other media in the months to come. As was the case following the 'cash for comment' crisis, Prime Minister Howard was the first major guest when Alan Jones returned to the studio. Among the many skilful practitioners of the art of modern media management, Alan Jones has few equals.

And this book, it appears, was just another swing at him. There have been many. Alan has long held that critics are merely jealous of his influence. Criticism is effortlessly processed. It is much the same as praise. Those who love him love him because he is great and those who hate him hate him because he is great. A character of his own invention Alan tends to emerge stronger, able to reinvent himself and face a new horizon.

As expected minions and acolytes were not so quiet about *Jonestown*, contemptuous of a book so riddled with errors and outraged that such a wonderful Australian could be traduced. Privately Alan Jones said, as expected, that he had not bothered with the book. Even some who are close to him found this hard to swallow. Those outside the inner-circle, who have heard the gossip about his library being chosen by his interior decorator, joked that to the contrary, perhaps *Jonestown* is the first book he has ever read. If so there was no-sign in his on air commentary that anything in the book would alter his unerring course. Alan went on exactly as before. The unelected broadcaster continued to blame unelected, 'do nothing' bureaucrats for the country's problems, in particular the failure to spend up big on water diversion schemes.

As before, Alan ignored the barking while the caravan moved on. If life is all about winning he had triumphed again. From the prime minister down they paid tribute. With the polling indicating Alan Jones' audience as largely conservative, it made political sense, at least for John Howard.

At first it was much the same with the NSW government, which resumed its kneeling position as another election approached. There were still marginal seats out there and there was no sense in taking chances. Ministers publicly praised Jones and privately sought briefings where they endured more ritual soakings of humiliation. Alan Jones was heard boasting that Michael Costa was made Treasurer because of his influence. To another minister he was heard declaring: 'I will bury you'.

But as the March 2007 election came closer, the NSW Government began to crawl out of his way. Alan Jones' support for new opposition leader Peter Debnam became strident. The Member for Vaucluse had, Chikarovski like, come some distance with Alan. Back in 1999 Peter Debnam put himself through the routine courtship process, sending his speeches to Alan Jones. At that stage the broadcaster sniffed: 'This bloke must think I'm an MP!' A reply was then drafted chiding Debnam for 'a lack of research'.[1]

By 2007 Alan Jones had little option but to support Peter Debnam. He was not the only one in the media to notice the almost daily calamities confronting the Iemma government. Alan's proclaimed lack of objectivity when it came to the Liberal Party and his support for John Howard had to rub off at a state level. As Bob Carr put it: 'Alan is a 1000% paid-up Liberal as soon as an election approaches'.[2]

Bob Carr's successor, keen to show himself as his own man, eventually gave up on Alan Jones. Morris Iemma did one interview where he sat and listened while, as an advisor put it, 'Jones ranted' becoming more and more 'feral'. The NSW Premier then walked away. According to an insider: 'Morris Iemma does not have the same view on Jones as Bob Carr. He does not see a need to pander'. While Iemma was available to other radio stations he largely stayed away from 2GB, with other ministers following his lead. There was a noticeable lessening of enthusiasm in responses to invitations to those cosy tete-a-tetes at the Macquarie Street apartment.

Then in the final week of the election Alan Jones went missing. He does not often give in to sickness, but at that critical time laryngitis overcame him. The sore throat came on as circumstance conspired to challenge Jones' status as a kingmaker. The crown would look a little tarnished if he endorsed Debnam and Debnam failed. Not that it mattered much. Morris Iemma did go on to win. Newspapers, talk radio and Alan Jones had not turned the electorate and Alan's failure to appear would not shroud the myth.

Jones' lack of real influence was again laid bare as his audience figures rose once more. In March 2007 Alan Jones achieved a rating of 17.9, the highest since he joined 2GB.[3] The result was of particular personal interest. For most of the preceding year I had been caught up in a battle generated by this book about my motivation for writing *Jonestown*. What I was trying to do was expose the myth. The objective was never to damage his audience but rather to challenge the way he uses them.

The battle had begun in earnest nine months earlier when Alan Jones had another win — of sorts. In June 2006, his lawyer Mark O'Brien wrote to the ABC complaining I was biased and had acted selectively, pointing out that there would be no hesitation in commencing defamation proceedings against the ABC.[4] Later that month the ABC abandoned *Jonestown*, Head of ABC Enterprises Robyn Watts telling me that the letter from Alan Jones' lawyer had influenced the decision

The news came as a shock despite plenty of warning. For the best part of four years I had been sniffing trouble. The project had begun early in 2002, soon after I finished one book for the ABC and a television report on Alan Jones. The Manager of ABC Books, Stuart Neal, wanted another book and the idea stared us in the face. The Sydney broadcaster and his remarkable power base was an obvious subject. *The Alan Jones Phenomenon* was Stuart Neal's working title.

In some respects I did not like what stared at me. It would be a difficult project, forbidden territory almost, but then in my 40 years at the ABC I had been educated to take on tough subjects. I had long been told that is what the ABC is for. At the time a few colleagues challenged me about whether I was right about this, suggesting I talk to other publishers. Indeed a few publishers also made approaches, but I explained I was bound to the ABC.

In 2003, I took three months long service leave, hoping to get most of *Jonestown* written. But by the time I went back to *Four Corners* there was still more to do, so every spare corner of my life became occupied as I tried to work through Alan's crowded life. *Four Corners* is also demanding, the schedules can't be put off, so each report was given priority and all leave and weekends used up writing a story that was additionally complicated by having no clear conclusion.

By the end of 2003, when I was closer to finishing the first draft, it was obvious that within upper reaches of the ABC discomfort was growing. Anxious murmurs trickled down. 'We should not be doing this book. The ABC needs a period of stability. What is the matter with those people in News and Current Affairs? Now that we are beginning to communicate with the government they make more trouble.' 'The ABC should not be taking on a commercial rival.'

I had presumed from the beginning there would be reliable support from the ABC Legal Department. After a range of testing court matters such as 'The Moonlight State' litigation, which had dragged on for 13 years, I had developed strong allies for whom there is enduring respect. But this was going to be different. ABC Enterprises is not *Four Corners* and the old Legal Department had seen a changing of the guard. This time the principle that mattered was commercial more than editorial. The book would have to survive as a business proposition and here too questions were mounting. 'How legally justifiable is it to be looking into a person's private life from all those years ago?' 'Alan Jones is very litigious. If this goes to court how much will it cost?'

The messages became confusing. ABC lawyers thought the early draft material defensible. But an external review was considered necessary to be safe. So in April 2004, in barrister's chambers high above the city I joined a roomful of lawyers and editors to talk through a range of issues. When I left I felt further encouraged. While problems had to be ironed out, the discussion seemed in the main, positive.

Then within weeks more word sifted back, this time from other corners of the big end of town. A stockbroker friend told me he had heard at a cocktail party that according to an ABC executive, the Jones book was unpublishable. I told him he was wrong, but further inquiries suggested to me that perhaps the ill-informed person at the centre of all this was me.

Needing to understand and deal with the legal issues as I approached a second draft, I asked to see the legal report. There followed a peculiar episode where Stuart Neal and myself were allowed to read it in General Counsel Stephen Collin's office while a witness looked on. We were not allowed to take a copy away. By then I was wondering whether the word filtering down to me was not the same as the word filtering up to the executive. So I telephoned and asked for a meeting with Managing Director Russell Balding, and on 18 June 2004 I took the lift to the 14th floor.

I have never seen myself as a natural enemy of management. We can forget that managers give us the opportunity to do our work, that they have a duty to administer, and in my case, beyond the Jonathan Shier period, had been supportive. Indeed, together we had been through some bruising battles, such as 'The Moonlight State' saga.

I put my case to Russell Balding that here was another fight worth taking on. I said if we did not confront power and abuse of power by the media, who would? We spoke about the processes that apply to ABC broadcasting and comparative processes that apply to the *Alan Jones Show*. A few people had suggested I go public with my concerns that the ABC was trying to nobble my book. I told the Managing Director I was not going to do this because I was not sure of what was going on, that as an ABC employee I had no wish to embarrass the ABC, and that I did not want to advance the Jones' mystique by accentuating his aura of omnipotence.

Russell Balding gave me a good audience but he did not give much away. He conceded he had concerns about estimated legal costs and explained again that the decision to publish rested on commercial considerations. When I left I felt I was drifting towards a kind of stalemate, with my organisation uncertain about which was the lesser shame, proceeding with the book or abandoning it.

This is the way it went for the next few years. I had strong supporters in Enterprises who were proud of the book and wanted to do more than stick to publications about knitting and cricket. We worked together on the editing, completing a second draft by mid 2005.

On one occasion a query reached me suggesting the process of publication would be easier if I assigned copyright of the book to the ABC. It was an odd request. I knew there was concern that some ABC employees were taking intellectual property to outside publishers. I wondered why I was being targeted for doing the opposite. But I offered to sign such an agreement if a clause was added allowing copyright to revert to me if the ABC chose not to publish. This did not seem to be part of the plan and the proposition was not raised again.

By the end of the year, ABC lawyers completed a further detailed review. Then there was another delay when outside counsel withdrew, concerned about a conflict of interest. So a new raft of legalling was commissioned. Again discussions were positive. At one level there was keenness but at another I could not miss the intensifying coolness creeping down through the air-conditioning.

There were no more meetings with management and after a series of false starts, by early 2006 *Jonestown* seemed at last ready for publication. The latest round of legalling was almost complete and indications again were that the work was considered defensible. All that was needed to secure a comfort zone were some witness statements, which I set about obtaining. As best I can tell, in doing so, one went astray, ending up with Alan Jones and his lawyer, Mark O'Brien.

While it was hardly good news, I saw the threatening letter that followed as no bombshell. News organisations receive them every week. Even so, the flashing green light turned amber again. I learned an intended reply had not been sent and the Mark O'Brien letter had been referred upstairs. I later heard the ABC Board had taken an interest in *Jonestown* and called for a report. On 29 June 2006 the board met. Soon after it retired Robyn Watts made her telephone call to me. When I asked what the board had to do with the decision, she said she was not privy to discuss board matters, but the decision had been hers and hers alone.

It did not take long for serious doubt to be cast on this proposition. The ABC's *Media Watch* reported the following Monday that the information paper from Enterprises to the board had been generally supportive of *Jonestown*. The board had been advised the legal process was underway and written advice would confirm a preliminary view that the book was defensible. A widespread conclusion by media commentators that the short-circuiting decision had been made by the board was not denied.

More was revealed later as the result of a Freedom of Information search undertaken by Crikey correspondent Margaret Simons. It showed that back in 2004, eight days before my meeting with Russell Balding, Chief Operating Officer David Pendleton had written to Robyn Watts asking: 'is Enterprises of the view that this publication is commercially viable and do you wish to incur further legal cost on the book at this stage?' The answer as far as I was concerned must have been yes and yes, as work continued. In fact, there were eighteen more months of it. But after the detailed line-by-line legal checking had been completed and approved, faith seemed to wilt once more.

On 5 December 2005 Robyn Watts wrote to Stuart Neal asking: 'What is the status of reaching an agreement with him by which he can take the book to another publisher?' Between that time and the time Watts rang me to suggest I take the manuscript elsewhere, more money had been spent on legal advice, which again found the book defensible.

Looking back it seems the ABC's *Jonestown* had fallen victim to a combined cringe of senior management and the board. By its own admission, the ABC caved in to a threat from Alan Jones — not a great moment in the history of the national broadcaster. The submission to the board had warned of damage to the reputation of the Corporation, but this was unlikely to be a major concern to board members known for their dim view of the ABC's reputation.

For me, along with the sense of betrayal, there was a worry the episode signalled the emergence of a future model of a preferred ABC. One of the admirable features of Alan Jones' broadcasting is his fierceness. He does take on big subjects. If in doing so he were guided by a command of the facts and respect for the truth, admiration would be total. The ABC I have admired has encouraged respect for facts and truth, and enthusiasm for taking on big subjects.

What worried me, and a great many of my colleagues, was that upward referral of contentious material might be more often used to sidestep the editorial process. A significant strength of the ABC is it willingness to contest litigation on the merits of a case and not just the related expenses. The high cost of the law has made commercial settlement commonplace. If over the years the ABC had caved in to plaintiffs with bigger legal budgets, there would not be the reputation to fuss over. But if it is all about winning, as with a lot of what Alan Jones does, you wonder whether the win was worth it. The decision to dump *Jonestown* generated an immediate outbreak of interest and soon a new publisher, Allen & Unwin took over. The ABC had estimated a print run of 20 000. Within weeks Allen & Unwin ordered three times that number.

While it pained me to be at odds with my employer it dawned on me that there was no point proceeding without dedicated support. The good news was the opportunity to work with a new team, unhesitating in its courage and commitment. The fact that other publishers were also interested shed more doubt on the proposition that the ABC had withdrawn for commercial reasons. Indeed, the submission from Enterprises had predicted this, pointing out that the book would almost certainly be published elsewhere.

In the beginning I accepted the risk that in writing about Alan Jones I would be press-ganged into a culture war, cast against my will as a soldier of the Left taking on a hero of the Right. What I did not anticipate was how swiftly the spotlight would swing from Alan Belford Jones to the Australian Broadcasting Corporation. The instant the press release went out from the ABC announcing the decision not to publish, the argument started at full pitch with the usual players taking up their positions on both sides of fixed battle lines. Despite none of the commentators having read the book and being on occasions seriously ill-informed, confident and predictable positions were taken.

When the book was published they banged on just the same.

The *Sydney Morning Herald* won the right to publish extracts, selecting much of the more personal and salacious material. Many readers and commentators who read only the extracts saw what was anticipated, condemning the book as cheap and prurient. It was much as I had seen while researching the book. Eager denunciations about invasion of privacy shared space with inquests into all the juicy details, analysis swerving between tut-tut and wink-nudge.

If Alan Jones' sexuality was a secret, it was an open secret and not one a biographer could honestly ignore. Those who have read this far will hopefully accept that I am not affronted by homosexuality. But I am worried when we persist with this cringe and surrender to fear and panic. Most of us have moved on from the Acland Alan grew up in. A modern generation is not so fixed on nervously separating homosexuals and heterosexuals. Silence and denial reinforces prejudice and in Alan Jones' case, from what I can see, it continues to generate loneliness.

Besides, it was never the main story. *Jonestown* is about power more than influence, and it is about collusion between power groups, most particularly politics and media. And here we see another cringe. Alan Jones is not the only media figure to moonlight as a pretend politician. It is no surprise commentators who do much the same would shrink from debate about media excess and trespass.

To me Alan Jones is more politician than broadcaster. As he has done in all his careers, Jones shapes his own way, with little regard for understood rules and conventions. And he is not just any politician. Listening, you can hear many below the rank of a John Howard or Peter Costello accepting Alan's ordained order. While politicians generally disapprove of media figures playing politics, too often they make an exception for him. I have already said how this has a lot to do with his aggressive activism — getting him off their back and making sure they don't alienate his audience. I wonder also whether it is because they are in awe of his wealth and power. While many media people make a transition to politics, the traffic the other way is not so dense with success.

Alan Jones' ascendance highlights weaknesses in both communities. A constant justification for the meddling, that he 'gets things done', has to indicate a failure of media to expose issues, and of politics to deal with them. One consequence of the collusion is the likelihood that more often the problem that is confronted is the public relations one rather than the real one. Another is the creation of poll driven policy with the same dank taste as focus group driven programming.

In *Jonestown* there is always the risk that making Alan again the centre of attention is but a larger slice of shepherd's pie for the glutton. His workers say he is often at his most buoyant when controversy throbs around him. But too late, I have come this far and still consider the story worth telling, mainly because of that scary prospect of counterfeit Alans to come. We see signs of it already in the celebrity blogger. The nonsense that they connect ordinary people to the affairs of the nation should be challenged. Alan Jones' blarney, his flattery, his fear mongering provides an illusory attachment to a world that has passed his audience by. And his undue power disconnects the rest of us from a sense that honest debate, collective purpose and genuine participation is still achievable.

The presumption in *Jonestown* continues to be that if you take Alan on you must win, which as I have explained, was never the objective. I could hardly take exception to abuse of power while blindly crossing my own line. One difference is an acceptance that truth is not exclusive. My suspicion is that greater virtue is found in slow change rather than the urgent and dramatic reforms Jones habitually demands. It takes time for public wisdom to grow. I am content for people to make up their own minds, and take their own time.

ENDNOTES

Notes to the endnotes

1. *Identity of sources:* Perhaps unsurprisingly, many of the people spoken to during the course of researching this book were prepared to be quoted only on the condition that they not be identified by name, most being from the media industry and other circles in which Alan Jones still has significant influence. Accordingly, all quoted material that is not sourced within the text or these endnotes is attributable to personal communication—including, but not only, formal interviews and correspondence—from individuals for whom remaining unnamed was an express condition of including their contribution in this book.
2. *Personal communication:* All quotes that have named sources in the text but no endnote are a result of personal communication, including interviews, with the author and, to avoid repetition, have not been relisted in these endnotes.
3. *The use of [sic]:* There are a significant number of grammatical and other linguistic errors in the quotes from Alan Jones, both in his verbal output and, in particular, his written material. Because of the number of errors, rather than draw attention to them with the use of [sic] or a correction made in square brackets, they have been included verbatim, except in a very few instances in which to do so would hinder comprehension.

Chapter 1: Son of the Earth

1. Out-take interview, Greg Hoy and Alan Jones, *Inside Business*, ABC TV, August 2002.
2. *Alan Jones Show*, Radio 2UE, 8/9/97.
3. *Alan Jones Breakfast Show*, Radio 2GB, 25/3/02.
4. 2GB, op. cit., 13/3/03.
5. 2GB, op. cit., 12/12/03.
6. Miranda Devine, 'The making of a radio tsar', *Sun Herald*, 10/2/02.
7. 2GB, op. cit., 1/7/03.

8 Correspondence, Bank of Australasia to Deputy Curator Insolvency, Intestacy and Insanity, 30/12/13.
9 Richard Yallop, 'The silver-tongued "dictator" who talked the Wallabies to the top', *Age*, 10/6/87, n.p.
10 Titles record, Parish of Watts, No 593219.
11 Correspondence, Mary Ann Jones to the Deputy Curator of Insolvency, Intestacy and Insanity, 8/7/13.
12 Correspondence, Bank of Australasia to Deputy Curator Insolvency, Intestacy and Insanity, 5/7/13.
13 Correspondence, Bank of Australasia to Deputy Curator Insolvency, Intestacy and Insanity, 22/7/13.
14 Correspondence, Charles Brady to Deputy Curator Insolvency, Intestacy and Insanity, 8/7/13.
15 ibid.
16 Queensland Registry of Births, Deaths and Marriages.
17 Correspondence, Gary Brady to author, 13/11/06.
18 Devine, op. cit.
19 Willowburn Asylum file records for Patient 147, 25/5/27.
20 Correspondence, W Harth to the Department of Public Instruction, Brisbane, 10/8/32.
21 Gerard Henderson, *Australian Answers*, Random House, Sydney, 1990, p. 167.
22 David Leser, 'Who's afraid of Alan Jones?', *Good Weekend: The Sydney Morning Herald Magazine*, 14/11/98, pp 17–18.
23 Henderson, op. cit., pp 166–7.
24 Alan Jones, 'Give farmers a hand to break awful cycle', *Daily Telegraph*, 3/10/02.
25 2GB, 15/4/04.
26 Caroline Jones, *The Search for Meaning*, ABC Radio, 28/4/87.
27 Leser, op. cit., p. 19.
28 2GB, op. cit., 10/12/03.
29 Jim Webster, 'Alan Jones: a jack of all trades and a master of all ...', *National Times*, 15/3/85.
30 *The Search for Meaning*, op. cit.
31 ibid.
32 Henderson, op. cit., p. 166.
33 2GB, op. cit., 13/2/04.

Chapter 2: 'Big Al'

1 2GB, op. cit., 12/11/02.
2 Henderson, op. cit., p. 166.
3 2GB, op. cit., 31/1/03.
4 Devine, op. cit.
5 2GB, op. cit., 9/9/03.
6 Ex student Robert Windsor Whip, quoted in John Keeble Winn, *Still Playing the Game*, Playright Publishing, Sydney, 2000, p. 285.

7 ibid., p. 327.
8 2GB, op. cit., 25/7/02.
9 Maggie Tabberer, *Maggie ... at Home with*, Foxtel FX, 9/11/01.
10 Winn, op. cit., p. 325.
11 *The Search for Meaning*, op. cit.
12 *Toowoomba Grammar School Magazine*, 1957, n.p.
13 *The Search for Meaning*, op. cit.
14 State Liberal Party election dossier for the seat of Earlwood, 1978.
15 *Toowoomba Grammar School Magazine*, 1958, p. 7.
16 Interview, *The Rise and Rise of Australian Rugby*, ABC TV, 26/2/03.
17 *Toowoomba Grammar School Magazine*, 1960, p. 6.
18 *The Search for Meaning*, op. cit.
19 'Headmaster's report, 1957', *Toowoomba Grammar School Magazine*, 1958, p. 7.
20 *The Search for Meaning*, op. cit.
21 Winn, op. cit., p. 520.

Chapter 3: The Birthday Boy

1 Alan Jones, quoted in Mike Colman, 'More to the Jones boy than meets the eye', *Sunday Telegraph*, 4/11/90.
2 Betty Vievers, then Betty Pratt, is the aunt of international tennis player Nicole Pratt.
3 Correspondence, Madonna Schacht to author, December 2002.
4 The struggling boy was Philip Veal, known to other boys as 'Chops'. He is another to say he has never forgotten Alan Jones. On 22/7/06 he spoke to the author, telling of being kept after school at Ironside and of being 'belted, and belted and belted'. Philip Veal believes Alan Jones developed a particular animosity to him after the young student retaliated. 'I pushed him.' For many years Veal considered suing Jones.
5 Correspondence, Warwick Gould to author, 8/1/94.
6 Schacht, op. cit.
7 ibid.
8 Harry M Miller and Company, Biographical notes on Alan Jones, 1987.
9 Schacht, op. cit.
10 *Clive James at Home*, ABC TV, 12/8/85.
11 The following description of narcissistic personality disorder is quoted from 'Narcissistic personality disorder', *Diagnostic and Statistical Manual of Mental Disorders*, American Psychiatric Association, Washington, DC, 1994, p. 661.

A pervasive pattern of grandiosity (in fantasy and behaviour) [and] need for admiration, beginning by early adulthood and present in a variety of contexts, as indicated by five (or more) of the following:
- has a grandiose sense of self-importance (e.g. exaggerates achievements and talents, expects to be recognized as superior without commensurate achievements)

- is preoccupied with fantasies of unlimited success, power, brilliance, beauty, or ideal love
- believes that he or she is 'special' and unique and can only be understood by, or should associate with, other special or high status people (or institutions)
- requires excessive admiration
- has a sense of entitlement, i.e. unreasonable expectations of especially favourable treatment or automatic compliance with his or her expectations
- is interpersonally exploitive, i.e. takes advantage of others to achieve his or her ends
- lacks empathy; is unwilling to recognise or identify with the feelings and needs of others
- is often envious of others or believes that others are envious of him or her
- shows arrogant, haughty behaviours or attitudes.

Chapter 4: Riding in Cars with Boys

1 Keith Willey, *The First 100 Years: The History of Brisbane Grammar School*, Macmillan, Melbourne, 1968, p. 171.
2 Perri Atkins, *Moments of Truth: The Turning Points of 60 Prominent Australians*, New Holland, Sydney, 2002, p. 58.
3 Interview for *Four Corners*, ABC TV, 17/4/02.
4 Correspondence, Graeme Twine to author, 7/5/02.
5 The ABC broadcaster, who died of a brain tumour in 1995, had related his experiences of Alan Jones to his wife, Annette Olle, and the author.
6 *The Search for Meaning*, op. cit.
7 Correspondence, Madonna Schacht to author, 2/1/03.
8 ibid.
9 Leser, op. cit., p. 19.
10 *Brisbane Grammar School Magazine*, 1966, n.p.
11 Schacht, op. cit., December 2002.
12 Sue Williams, 'All about that Jones boy', *Daily Telegraph*, 28/8/92.
13 Schacht, op.cit., December 2002.
14 Colman, op. cit.
15 Schacht, op. cit., December 2002.
16 Jonathan Jackson, 'Alan Jones: the voice of success', *Wealth Creator*, November–December 2004, p. 24.
17 *The Search for Meaning*, op. cit.

Chapter 5: Among Kings

1 Interview, *Four Corners*, op. cit., 8/4/02.
2 Secretary of State for the Colonies, Sir George Murray, quoted in Lloyd Waddy, *The King's School 1831-1981*, David Ell Press, Sydney, p. 20.
3 Interview, *Four Corners*, op. cit., 11/4/02.

4. *Moments of Truth*, published in 2002, says he was in his mid 20s. The *Wealth Creator* profile of November 2004 says he was 25 when he was offered the job.
5. The most distinguished White, author Patrick, attended one of King's junior schools, Tudor House, but completed his secondary education in England.
6. Interview, *Four Corners*, op. cit., 8/4/02.
7. Jackson, op. cit. p. 24.
8. Interview, *Four Corners*, op. cit., 11/4/02.
9. *The King's School Magazine*, 1970, p. 67.
10. Interview, *Four Corners*, op. cit., 17/4/02.
11. Correspondence, Dugald Anthony to author, 1/5/02.
12. Interview, *Four Corners*, op. cit., 5/4/02.
13. Correspondence, Charles Milne to author, 15/8/03.
14. Interview, *Four Corners*, op. cit., 20/4/02.
15. Interview, *Four Corners*, op. cit., 8/4/02.
16. Alan Jones, as godfather to one of Antony White's children, is still close. During the 2002 drought he was heard interviewing Anto about life in the bush (2GB, 3/12/02), which was a bit different way back then when the cockies were richer than Alan.
17. Milne, op. cit.
18. *The King's School Magazine*, 1971, p. 59.
19. Interview, *Four Corners*, op. cit., 24/4/02.
20. *The King's School Magazine*, 1972.
21. Leser, op. cit., p. 19.
22. Interview, *Four Corners*, op. cit., 8/4/02.
23. ibid.
24. *The King's School Magazine*, 1973, p. 40.
25. Ian Humphreys, Unpublished valediction, 1974.
26. *The Search for Meaning*, op. cit.
27. Interview, *Four Corners*, op. cit., 1/5/02.
28. Schacht, op. cit., December 2002.
29. Leser, op. cit., p. 20.
30. Interview, *Four Corners*, op. cit., 25/4/02.
31. Humphreys, op. cit.
32. ibid.
33. Interview, *Four Corners*, op. cit., 8/4/02.
34. *The King's School Magazine*, December 1975 pp. 15–16.

Chapter 6: Citizen Jones

1. Alan Jones, 'Too much government—too many elections', *Quirindi Advocate*, 21/6/78.
2. Sally Loane, 'Jones alone', *Good Weekend: The Sydney Morning Herald Magazine*, 25/4/92.
3. 2GB op. cit., 11/11/02.
4. Interview, *Four Corners*, op. cit., 17/4/02.

5 'Airline runs into stormy weather', *North West Magazine*, 6/2/78.
6 *The King's School Magazine*, 1974, p. 42.
7 Quirindi Rugby Club minutes, 14/10/76.
8 Webster, op. cit.
9 Williams, op. cit.
10 Susan Chenery, 'Look at Alan when he's talking to you', *Australian*, 27/1/94, p. 10.
11 Alan Jones' friend, the British novelist, Jeffrey Archer, completed a similar one-year Diploma of Education course ten years earlier, although it took him three years.
12 'From England', *Quirindi Advocate*, 18/5/77.
13 *The Search for Meaning*, op. cit.
14 Correspondence, Joanna Parker, Librarian, Worcester College, to author, 26/11/02.
15 *Clive James*, op. cit.
16 Webster, op. cit.
17 Richard Coleman, 'Alan Jones and the art of winning', *Sydney Morning Herald*, 8/6/85, p. 45.
18 Jayne Newling, 'Alan Jones: a future PM?', *New Idea*, 10/6/89, p. 19.
19 *The Search for Meaning*, op. cit.
20 Correspondence, Victoria Schofield to author, 28/11/03.
21 Melba, 'By Bhutto! A pinker shade of our Jones', *Australian*, 29/3/94.
22 1978 Earlwood election dossier.
23 Alan Jones, 'The Way I See It', *Quirindi Advocate*, 25/1/78.
24 Jones, 'The Way ...', op. cit., 30/11/77.
25 Jones, 'The Way ...', op. cit., 14/12/77.
26 Jones, 'The Way ...', op. cit., 18/1/78.
27 Jones, 'The Way ...', op. cit., 16/11/77.
28 Doug Gowing also says that the interviewer was myself. I am not sure. However, it is true that I worked at the ABC's Tamworth office at this time.
29 'Candidate not wasting any time', *Sydney Morning Herald*, 24/4/78.
30 'Alan Jones wins Liberal pre-selection', *Quirindi Advocate*, 26/4/78.
31 Wayne Greer, 'Liberal candidate woos Greeks', *Daily Mirror*, 12/7/78.
32 Paul Barry, *The Rise and Rise of Kerry Packer*, Bantam/ABC Books, Sydney, 1993, p. 202.
33 Marian Wilkinson, *The Fixer*, Heinemann, Australia, 1996, p. 103.
34 Interview, *Four Corners*, op. cit., 13/4/02.
35 Coleman, op. cit., p. 45.
36 Jackson, op. cit.
37 Scott Benett, New South Wales State Election report, p. 14.
38 Peter Bowers, 'Triumph for Wran's moderate style', *Sun Herald*, 8/10/78, p. 2.
39 Peter Collins, *The Bear Pit*, Allen & Unwin, Sydney, 2000, p. 103.
40 Tabberer, op. cit.
41 Coleman, op. cit.
42 *The Search for Meaning*, op. cit.

43 Jackson, op. cit.
44 Coleman, op. cit.
45 Miller, op. cit.
46 Errol Simper, 'A challenge to keep up with Jones', *Australian*, 14/2/02.
47 Interview, *Four Corners*, op. cit., 22/1/02.
48 *The Search for Meaning*, op. cit.
49 Interview, *Four Corners*, op. cit., 17/4/02.
50 *The Search for Meaning*, op. cit.
51 Henderson, op. cit., p. 170.
52 ibid.
53 Coleman, op. cit.
54 Henderson, op. cit., p. 171.
55 Coleman, op. cit.
56 Whenever Alan Jones was questioned about the 'Life wasn't meant to be easy' phrase, he commonly attributed original authorship to Swiss-born philosopher Jean Jacques Rousseau. Jones said Rousseau's phrase was completed with the words '... but with patience it can be beautiful'. It was in fact George Bernard Shaw, who wrote in *Back to Methuselah*: 'Life is not meant to be easy my child, but take courage: it can be delightful'.
57 Jackson, op. cit., p. 25.
58 Liz Van Den Nieuwenhof, 'Struggle St gets a TV champion', *Sunday Telegraph*, 16/1/94.
59 Kate Askew and Anne Lampe, 'Wheels within wheels', *Sydney Morning Herald*, 4/1/03, p. 15.
60 Williams, op. cit.
61 Tabberer, op. cit.
62 Williams, op. cit.
63 2GB, op. cit., 20/3/03.
64 ibid., 19/3/03.
65 ibid., 22/11/02.
66 Yallop, op. cit.

Chapter 7: Wearing the Green and Gold

1 2GB, op. cit., 24/2/03.
2 I can't say with the same assurance that Manly and Australian front rower, Ollie Hall (class of 1970), was as much of a fan.
3 Interview, *The Rise ... of Australian Rugby*, op. cit.
4 Interview, *Four Corners*, op. cit., 8/4/02.
5 ibid.
6 ibid.
7 ibid.
8 Interview, *The Rise ... of Australian Rugby*, op. cit., 12/2/03.
9 Alan Jones, *Manly Rugby Club Annual Report*, 1983, pp. 23, 26, 27.
10 Interview, *The Rise ... of Australian Rugby*, op. cit., 20/3/03.
11 Peter FitzSimons, 'Mark Ella unfinished business', *Sydney Morning Herald*, 17/6/96, p. 32.

12 Interview, *The Rise ... of Australian Rugby*, op. cit., 20/3/03.
13 2GB, op. cit., 27/2/03.
14 ibid.
15 Interview, *The Rise ... of Australian Rugby*, op. cit., 26/2/03.
16 Malcolm McGregor, 'Revealed: the campaign to boot Jones out of the Rugby hot seat', *Sydney Morning Herald*, 24/2/88.
17 Interview, *Four Corners*, op. cit., 17/4/02.
18 Spiros Zavos, 'Keeping up with a Jones', *Sydney Morning Herald*, 25/4/91.
19 Interview, *The Rise ... of Australian Rugby*, op. cit., 26/2/03.
20 Jackson, op. cit., p. 26.
21 Interview, *Four Corners*, op. cit., 12/4/02.
22 Interview, *The Rise ... of Australian Rugby*, op. cit., 9/4/03.
23 Alan Jones, National Press Club address, 25/1/85.
24 Peter FitzSimons, *Nick Farr-Jones*, Random House, Sydney, 1993, p. 86.
25 *PM*, ABC Radio, 27/7/84.
26 Interview, *The Rise ... of Australian Rugby*, op. cit., 26/2/03.
27 *Australian*, 28/7/84, n.p.
28 Peter Fenton, *Sport—The Way I Speak It*, Little Hills Press, Mt Druitt, 1992, p. 59.
29 ibid., p. 59.
30 Out-take, 2UE, op. cit.
31 Interview, *The Rise ... of Australian Rugby*, op. cit., 20/3/03.
32 ibid.
33 ibid., 5/2/03.
34 ibid., 9/4/03.
35 ibid., 26/2/03.
36 FitzSimons, *Nick Farr-Jones*, op. cit., p. 103.
37 Sandra Lee, 'Jones' genius comes adrift', *Daily Telegraph*, 2/5/91, p. 39.
38 FitzSimons, *Nick Farr-Jones*, op. cit., p. 96.
39 Interview, *The Rise ... of Australian Rugby*, op. cit., 26/2/03.
40 ibid., 7/2/03.
41 Max Howell, *Tempo*, Celebrity Books, Auckland, 2000, p. 195.
42 2GB website at <www.2gb.com>.
43 Interview, *The Rise ... of Australian Rugby*, op. cit., 26/2/03.
44 ibid.
45 ibid.
46 ibid., 10/2/03.
47 FitzSimons, *Nick Farr-Jones*, op. cit., p. 112.
48 Zavos, op. cit.
49 Interview, *The Rise ... of Australian Rugby*, op. cit., 26/2/03.
50 ibid., 9/4/03.
51 ibid., 10/2/03.
52 ibid.
53 ibid., 26/2/03.
54 FitzSimons, *Nick Farr-Jones*, op. cit., pp 115–16.
55 National Press Club, op. cit.

Chapter 8: My Team

1. Richard Ackland, 'The genius of a baked potato', *Sydney Morning Herald*, 23/8/93.
2. Jackson, op. cit., p. 26.
3. David Browne, 'The coach gets ready to face the champ', *Australian Financial Review*, 12/4/85.
4. ibid.
5. Clive James., op. cit.
6. ibid.
7. Mark Ella, 'Mark Ella: why I quit', *Sunday Telegraph*, 7/4/85, p. 19.
8. Peter Jenkins, *Wallaby Gold*, Random House, Sydney, 1991, p. 285.
9. 2GB, op. cit., 16/10/03.
10. Webster, op. cit., p. 54.
11. Lee, op. cit., p. 39.
12. Michael Cordell, 'The Alan Jones gospel of rugby and politics', *Sydney Morning Herald*, 8/11/86.
13. Ean Higgins, 'Packer's plunge into Sydney radio', *Australian Financial Review*, 12/3/86.
14. Tom Burton, 'Alan Jones: why I quit Liberal race', *Sydney Morning Herald*, 30/5/90.
15. 'Alan Jones's secret world', *Sun Herald*, 16/10/88.
16. Philip Derriman, *The Rise and Rise of Australian Rugby*, ABC Books, Sydney, 2003, p. 141.
17. In a reshuffle of shifts I took over the midday shift from Steve Liebmann and, in doing so, met Alan Jones for the first time—as well as gaining some slight appreciation of the demands of talk radio.
18. Interview, *The Rise ... of Australian Rugby*, op. cit., 6/2/03.
19. FitzSimons, *Nick Farr-Jones*, op. cit., p. 133.
20. Interview, *The Rise ... of Australian Rugby*, op. cit., 26/2/03. David Campese's autobiography, *On a Wing and a Prayer*, Queen Anne Press, London, 1991, pp. 157, 158, supports Nick Farr-Jones' account.
21. FitzSimons, *Nick Farr-Jones*, op. cit., p. 136.
22. Interview, *The Rise ... of Australian Rugby*, op. cit., 9/4/03.
23. Interview, *The Rise ... of Australian Rugby*, op. cit., 12/2/03.
24. Nick Farr-Jones, *The Story of the Rugby World Cup*, Australia Post, 2003, p. 12.
25. Jenkins, op. cit., p. 287.
26. Janise Beaumont, 'Success and the Jones Boy', *Sun*, 12/11/86, p. 13.
27. Simon Poidevin, as told to Jim Webster, *For Love Not Money*, ABC Books, Sydney, 1990, p. 198.
28. 2GB, op. cit., 24/10/03.
29. David Campese, with Peter Bills, *On a Wing and a Prayer*, Queen Anne Press, London, 1991, pps 159, 160.
30. Adrian Mcgregor, 'Did Hayden Play Dirty?', *Sydney Morning Herald*, 14/6/88.
31. *The Search for Meaning*, op. cit.

ENDNOTES

32 Loane, op. cit., p. 15.
33 ibid.
34 Elisabeth Wynhausen, 'The Miller's tale', *Australian*, 15/2/00, p. 15.
35 David Barrett, *John Howard: Prime Minister*, Viking, Melbourne, 1997, p. 434.
36 *PM*, op. cit., 4/3/87.
37 Interview, *The Rise ... of Australian Rugby*, op. cit., 6/2/03.
38 Interview, *The Rise ... of Australian Rugby*, op. cit., 26/2/03.
39 ibid.
40 Yallop, op. cit.
41 Interview, *The Rise ... of Australian Rugby*, op. cit., 11/2/03.
42 Interview, *The Rise ... of Australian Rugby*, op. cit., 7/2/03.
43 Janise Beaumont, 'Success and the Jones boy', *Sun*, 12/11/86, p. 13.
44 Greg Growden, 'Jones strikes back at NZ complaint', *Sydney Morning Herald*, 24/6/87.
45 FitzSimons, *Nick-Farr Jones*, op. cit., p. 156.
46 Elphick did not name the mostly foreign players he alleged were paid so-called 'boot money'. He confirmed he had not paid senior Australian players such as Andrew Slack, Nick Farr-Jones and Michael Lynagh. In any case his evidence was not believed. In 1997 Elphick was convicted on fraud charges and sentenced to a maximum of five years gaol.
47 Janise Beaumont, 'A winner talks about losing', *Sun*, 29/6/87.
48 FitzSimons, *Nick Farr-Jones*, op. cit., pp 143–4.
49 Howell, op. cit., p. 203.
50 Interview, *The Rise ... of Australian Rugby*, op. cit., 12/2/03.
51 Interview, *The Rise ... of Australian Rugby*, op. cit., 26/2/03.
52 Peter Bills, 'Poidevin douses the fire', *Sydney Morning Herald*, 25/6/87.
53 *60 Minutes*, Channel 9, 2/8/87.
54 ibid.
55 FitzSimons, *Nick Farr-Jones*, op. cit., p. 173.
56 Interview, *The Rise ... of Australian Rugby*, op. cit., 26/2/03.
57 'Players will "sack" Jones warns Ella', *Sun Herald*, 20/12/87.
58 John Macdonald, 'Poidevin: Jones should stay', *Sydney Morning Herald*, 21/12/87.
59 Campese, op. cit., p. 162.
60 Interview, *Four Corners*, op. cit., 12/4/02.
61 2GB website, op. cit.

Chapter 9: Watershed

1 Alan Jones, 'I've paid the price', *Sun Herald*, 6/3/88, p. 109.
2 Lee, op. cit., p. 39.
3 Loane, op. cit.
4 Interview, *Four Corners*, op. cit., 8/4/02.
5 Webster, op. cit.
6 *The Search for Meaning*, op. cit.
7 Schacht, op. cit., 2/1/03.

8 John Marsden, *I Am What I Am*, Viking, Melbourne, 2004, p. 97.
9 Malcolm McGregor, 'Howard strikes vocal discord', *Australian Financial Review*, 27/11/96, p. 16.
10 Andrew West and Rachel Morris, *Bob Carr: A Self-Made Man*, HarperCollins, Sydney, 2003, p. 177.
11 Jayne Newling, 'Nobody loves me unconditionally now', *New Idea*, 8/6/91, p. 18.
12 Carolyn Beaumont, 'Jones tells of anguish', *Daily Mirror*, 8/12/88.
13 ibid.
14 David Hands, 'Smith forges the link to create Oxford's control', *The Times*, 7/12/88.
15 West and Morris, op. cit., p. 194.
16 John Fordham, 'Nothing to hide, says Jones', *Sunday Telegraph*, 11/12/88.
17 Interview, *Four Corners*, op. cit., 17/4/02.
18 'Alan Jones: I'll stay and fight charge', *Daily Mirror*, 7/12/88, p. 2.
19 Terry Holmes would go on to run the Stafford Hotel, a Jones' London sanctuary for years to follow. He was also interviewed by Alan Jones about the impact of the 2005 terrorist bombings on the people of London (2GB 13/7/05).
20 Rosie McKay, *Daily Mirror*, 6/12/88, p. 1.
21 ibid., 7/12/88.
22 ibid., 8/12/88.
23 *A Current Affair*, Channel 9, 9/12/88.
24 Schacht, op. cit., 2/1/03.
25 West and Morris, op. cit., p. 195.
26 Interview, *Four Corners*, op. cit., 8/4/02.
27 'Jones back on air', *Daily Mirror*, 16/1/89.
28 'Fine tuning', *Sydney Morning Herald*, 17/1/89.
29 Newling, op. cit., p. 18.
30 'Alan Jones ... destination unknown', *Ita*, October 1990, p. 25.
31 Lenore Nicklin, 'Jonesy: the new all-talking Tiger', *Bulletin*, 18/9/90, p. 44.
32 Heather Chapman, 'I can stand up and face the world', *Sunday Telegraph*, 15/1/89.
33 Leser, op. cit., p. 20.
34 'Brian', a talkback caller on 2GB, op. cit., 29/10/03.

Chapter 10: From Pedagogue to Demagogue

1 Mark Day, 'They're tuned in, but they're not listening', *Daily Telegraph*, 18/12/96, p. 11.
2 Neil Mitchell program, Radio 3AW, 3/12/99.
3 Chapman, op. cit.
4 2GB, op. cit., 16/5/05.
5 Sue Williams, 'Talking tough', *Daily Telegraph*, 29/8/92.
6 2GB, op. cit., 29/8/03.
7 Interview, *Four Corners*, op. cit., 8/4/02.

ENDNOTES

8 *The 7.30 Report*, ABC TV, 7/5/87.
9 Tabberer, op. cit., 9/11/01.
10 'Radio announcer must pay $70,000 damages', *Australian*, 1/9/90.
11 'Chesty Jones back on the mike', *Sydney Morning Herald*, 10/11/89.
12 Tim Barton contests this account insisting he did not work for Alan Jones prior to this appointment.
13 Peter FitzSimons, *The Rugby War*, HarperCollins, Sydney, 2003, p. 56.
14 Out-take, 2UE, op. cit.
15 David Kirk, *Black and Blue*, Hodder Moa Beckett, Auckland, 1997, p. 143.
16 Peter FitzSimons, 'It's time Jones stopped barking at the caravan', *Sydney Morning Herald*, 22/11/89, p. 70.
17 David Hands, 'Vain pursuit at Twickenham; Oxford's presents eagerly accepted', *The Times*, 13/12/89, p. [?].
18 Following Mark Egan's selection as captain ill feelings led Brian Smith and Troy Coker to drop out of the team to contest the next annual Cambridge match. This led to grumbles about poor sportsmanship and delight when, without the Australians' help, Oxford won 21–12. *The Times* reported: 'Seldom can a game have proved so powerful a vindication of one player'. It was, according to the report, Mark Egan's match. 'More than that, success ended the period of introspection through which the Oxford club has gone and the game at the University will be better for it; the measure of support for Egan was amply demonstrated when his players chaired him from the field.' David Hands, 'Dark Blue Mark of Egan', *The Times*, 12/12/90.
19 John Macdonald, 'Off the beat', *Sydney Morning Herald*, 26/5/90.
20 'Alan Jones ... destination unknown', op. cit., p. 25.
21 Roy Masters, 'Face to face with Alan Jones', *Sydney Morning Herald*, 18/8/90.
22 Bill Elgar, '$6m campaign used to lure life savings', *Sunday Telegraph*, 24/6/90.
23 ibid.
24 *AG v. 2UE and Jones*, 19/3/93.
25 Alan Jones, 'The issue is all about self-preservation', *Sun Herald*, 12/8/90.
26 'Fine Tuning', *Sydney Morning Herald*, 29/8/90.
27 Heather Chapman, 'Keeping up with Jones', in 'The Guide', supplement to the *Sydney Morning Herald*, 26/5/97, p. 5.
28 'Jonesy's standard remains high', *Sydney Morning Herald*, 30/8/90.
29 Jeni Cooper, 'Uproar over bribes claim', *Sydney Morning Herald*, 11/8/89.
30 Correspondence, Alan Jones to 2UE listener, 7/8/97.
31 Christine Hogan, 'Unaccustomed as I am ...', *Sun Herald*, 10/10/99.
32 'Alan Jones ... destination unknown', op. cit.
33 Mike Colman, 'More to the Jones boy than meets the eye', *Sunday Telegraph*, 4/11/90, p. 54.
34 Liz van den Nieuwenhof, 'Alan's coach trip', *Daily Telegraph*, 8/9/90, p. 123.

35 Newling, op. cit.
36 van den Nieuwenhof, op. cit.

Chapter 11: Dictators and Tigers

1 Masters, op. cit.
2 van den Nieuwenhof, op. cit.
3 John Hogan, 'Jones: a cup for Tigers then the title for Wales', *Australian*, 21/2/91.
4 Daniel Williams, 'I'll go for the premiership, boasts Jones', *Sydney Morning Herald*, 5/9/90.
5 Daniel Lane, 'Third time lucky', *Bulletin*, 2/3/93, p. 97.
6 Interview, *Four Corners*, op. cit., 21/11/01.
7 Interview, *Four Corners*, op. cit., 8/4/02.
8 Tim Blue and Dennis Shanahan, 'The king-makers', *Australian*, 11/5/92.
9 Phillip Adams and Lee Burton, *Talkback: Emperors of the Air*, Allen & Unwin, Sydney, 1997, p. 2.
10 Trevor McKewan, 'Jones' inner circle', *Rugby League Week*, 12/8/92, p. 5.
11 Paul Sironen and Daniel Lane, *Sirro: Tales from Tigertown*, ABC Books, Sydney, 1997, p. 143.
12 John Macdonald, 'Alan Jones in hospital to treat spinal injury', *Sydney Morning Herald*, 25/2/91.
13 Ray Chesterton, 'Jones emergency operation', *Daily Telegraph*, 26/2/91.
14 ibid.
15 *Big League Magazine*, Winfield Cup Round 2, 22–24 March 1991
16 Peter Frilingos, 'Tigers star slams Jones', *Daily Telegraph*, 2/9/92, n.p.
17 Richard Becht, 'Tiger Tiger Kiwi Rooster the Gary Freeman Story', Hodder Moa Beckett, Auckland, 1992, p. 124.
18 Barry, op. cit., p. 390.
19 Australian Broadcasting Authority, *Commercial Radio Inquiry Report* (hereafter, *ABA Inquiry*), Statement of John Patrick Brennan, 11/11/99, Exhibit 65, p. 5.
20 Out-take, 2UE, op. cit.
21 Mike Colman, 'The life and times of Alan Jones', *Sunday Telegraph*, 28/7/91, p. 110.
22 'Alan Jones ... destination unknown', op. cit.
23 Henderson, op. cit., p. 171.
24 Collins, op. cit., pps 178, 179.
25 Alan Jones and his station 2GB were convicted of contempt of court again in 2007. He had read on air a *Daily Telegraph* article that identified a juvenile witness in a murder trial. Jones, who was fined $1000, had assumed the newspaper was free to print the name. The court saw that a broadcaster of his experience should have known better.
26 *PM*, op. cit., 8/8/91.
27 ibid.
28 Warren Partland, 'The motivator', *Adelaide Advertiser*, 22/6/91.

29 Alan Jones Comments, Balmain Rugby League Club, *Annual Report*, 1991.
30 Jonathan Chancellor, 'The accountant to Sydney's famous goes bust', *Sydney Morning Herald*, 5/3/92.
31 McKewan, op. cit.
32 Frilingos, op. cit.
33 Blue and Shanahan, op. cit.
34 ibid.
35 ibid.
36 ibid.
37 Ray Chesterton, 'Jones sacked', *Daily Telegraph*, 22/8/92.
38 ibid.
39 Ian Heads, 'What a week it was down in Tigertown—but roll on the cricket season', *Sydney Morning Herald*, 3/9/92.
40 Roy Masters, 'Sponsors the key to survival in the Tigers' den', *Sydney Morning Herald*, 1/9/92, n.p.
41 Garry Jack, 'A time for change ...', *Rugby League Week*, 2/9/92, p. 5.
42 Supreme Court of New South Wales, Criminal Division, Justice Michael Grove, In the Matter of Andrew Peter Kalajzich, Direction, 18/9/92, p. 8.
43 2UE op. cit., 21/10/92.
44 2UE op. cit., 23/10/92.
45 Correspondence, Jones to various, 30/10/92.

Chapter 12: Runs on the Board

1 Sheryle Bagwell, 'AMP recruits John Laws in radio war with Alan Jones', *Australian Financial Review*, 29/4/93.
2 ibid.
3 ibid.
4 'Laws keeps up with Jones boy', *Australian*, 21/6/93.
5 Pamela Williams, 'AMP, Westpac and the Packer fear factor', *Australian Financial Review*, 22/7/99, p. 1.
6 David Leser, 'Nightmare on Struggle Street for former AMP boss', *Sydney Morning Herald*, 20/7/99.
7 Bagwell, op. cit.
8 'Why Alan Jones believes it is simply ridiculous', *Daily Telegraph*, 28/1/93.
9 2UE op. cit., 27/1/93.
10 Bruce Loudon, 'Talkback's Don Quixote', *Sunday Herald Sun*, 31/1/93, p. 35.
11 Phillip Adams, 'An open letter to Alan Jones', *Australian*, 13/2/93.
12 Margaret Keneally and Mark Jones, 'Perkins calls Jones a racist in TV clash', *Daily Telegraph*, 9/6/93. Jones had an equally low opinion of Perkins. In correspondence (30/11/98) he said he was 'sick and tired' of Charles Perkins, describing him as a 'jerk' who needed to be 'put in his place'. Correspondence [Jones to listener], 30/11/98.
13 Out-take, 2UE, op. cit.
14 Loudon, op. cit.
15 Jack, op. cit.

16 Mike Gibson, *Daily Telegraph*, 22/3/93.
17 Sironen and Lane, op. cit., p. 143.
18 'Gladys Craven', 'Why Jacin walked out on Balmain', *Sun Herald*, 27/3/94.
19 Masters, op. cit.
20 Lane, op. cit.
21 Harry M Miller and Company, File note, 20/4/93.
22 2UE, op. cit., April 93.
23 ibid., 28/5/93.
24 ibid.
25 Correspondence, Harry M Miller to John Conde, 5/5/93.
26 *ABA Inquiry*, op. cit., Brennan, op. cit., p. 17.
27 *ABA Inquiry*, op. cit., Statement of Alan Belford Jones, 9/11/99, Exhibit 62, p. 21, clause 74.
28 Miller, op. cit., File note, 20/4/93.
29 2UE op. cit., 2/6/93.
30 ibid., 4/6/93.
31 ibid., 13/7/93.
32 Correspondence, Miller to Jones, 3/8/93.
33 Phil Rothfield, 'Rothfield's roast: Jones fights to avoid axe', *Sunday Telegraph*, 18/7/93.
34 Interview, *Four Corners*, op. cit., 17/4/02.
35 Balmain Rugby League Club, *Annual Report*, 1993.
36 The Hon JP Hannaford, Ministerial Statement, *Hansard*, 16/9/93.
37 Jennifer Cooke and Sandra Harvey, 'Kalajzich case reopened despite judge's rejection', *Sydney Morning Herald*, 17/9/93.
38 2UE, op. cit., 17/9/93.
39 Balmain Rugby League Club, op. cit.
40 Tony Squires, 'Exit Alan Jones: he did it his way', *Sydney Morning Herald*, 21/7/93.
41 Balmain Rugby League Club, op. cit.
42 Sironen and Lane, op. cit., p. 144.
43 *Sydney Morning Herald*, 24/3/94.

Chapter 13: The Godfather

1 Marcus Casey, 'Keeping up with Jones', *Telegraph Mirror*, 29/1/94, p. 29.
2 Marcus Casey, 'Curtain comes down on Alan Jones show', *Telegraph*, 29/4/94, p. 4.
3 Casey, op. cit., p. 29.
4 'Now you see him', in 'The Guide', supplement to the *Sydney Morning Herald*, 31/1/94, p. 4.
5 Casey, op. cit., p. 28.
6 Ross Warneke, 'Jones needs to avoid soft and obvious targets', *Age*, 3/2/94.
7 Robin Oliver, 'Jones' first night of Bron's long sweet nothing', *Sydney Morning Herald*, 1/2/94.
8 Warneke, op. cit.

ENDNOTES 485

9 Peter Wilmoth, 'Screen test—can Carmel Travers save the Ten Network from itself?', *Age*, 6/3/94.
10 ibid.
11 *Media Watch*, ABC TV, 28/3/94.
12 *Alan Jones Live*, Channel 10, 23/2/94.
13 ibid.
14 ibid., 23/3/94.
15 Robin Oliver, 'Network silences TV's talking head', *Sydney Morning Herald*, 29/4/94.
16 Marcus Casey, 'Curtain comes down on Alan Jones show', *Daily Telegraph*, 29/4/94.
17 Chapman, 'Keeping up with Jones', op. cit.
18 Marcus Casey, 'Why it didn't work, by the experts', *Daily Telegraph*, 29/4/94.
19 Leser, 'Who's afraid of Alan Jones?', op. cit. p. 21.
20 ibid.
21 Anne Davies and David Humphries, 'Jonestown', *Sydney Morning Herald*, 20/11/99.
22 Leser, 'Who's afraid of Alan Jones?', op. cit. p. 22.
23 Linda Morris and Sonya Voumard, 'Packer still in casino running', *Sydney Morning Herald*, 11/8/94.
24 Leser, 'Who's afraid of Alan Jones?', op. cit. p. 22.
25 Alan Jones, 'To the point', *Sunday Telegraph*, 15/5/94.
26 Paolo Totaro, 'Barristers attack "primitive" law', *Sydney Morning Herald*, 24/6/94.
27 2UE, op. cit., 22/11/94.
28 ibid.
29 'Kalajzich sought Jones' aid', *Daily Telegraph Mirror*, 1/12/94.
30 2UE, op. cit., 1/12/94.
31 ibid.
32 ibid.
33 The Guide, *Sydney Morning Herald*, 'Now you see him', op. cit., p. 4.
34 2UE, op. cit., June 94.
35 'Jones replies', *Sydney Morning Herald*, 10/6/94.
36 Brad Norington, 'Soft heart, hard line', *Good Weekend: The Sydney Morning Herald Magazine*, 14/12/96.
37 Liberal Party federal election launch, 1996.
38 George Piggins, *Never Say Die*, Pan Macmillan, Sydney, 2002, p. 155.
39 Interview, *Four Corners*, op. cit., 24/4/02.
40 Danny Weidler, 'South star has ear bitten off', *Sun Herald*, 17/3/96, p. 56.
41 Interview, *Four Corners*, op. cit., 24/4/02.
42 Andrea Dixon, 'Jones does footy star's bidding', *Sun Herald*, 29/10/95.
43 2GB, op. cit., 11/3/05.
44 Piggins, op. cit., p. 116.
45 ibid., p. 121.
46 Deborah Cameron, 'Jury says Jones was defamed', *Australian*, 1/3/00.

47 Adams and Burton, op. cit., p. 215.
48 FitzSimons, *The Rugby War*, op. cit., p. 255.
49 Correspondence, Conde to Jones, 4/8/94.
50 ibid.
51 ibid., 6/2/95.
52 Miller, op. cit., File note, 6/4/95.
53 Correspondence, Miller to Jones, 17/2/95.
54 Correspondence, Jones to Miller, 7/2/95.
55 Miller, op. cit., File note, 2/5/95.
56 2UE, op. cit., 2/3/95.
57 ibid., March 95.
58 2GB, op. cit., 27/5/02.
59 ibid., 13/6/03.
60 ibid., 10/9/03.
61 Collins, op. cit., p. 254.
62 Tony Stephens and Debra Jopson, 'Big Chief Little Laws and Killer Jones: are they losing their grip?', *Sydney Morning Herald*, 12/11/94.
63 ibid.
64 Miller, op. cit., File note, 25/7/94.
65 Stephens and Jopson, op. cit.
66 ibid.
67 ibid.
68 ibid.
69 Jane Freeman, 'Jones bounces back onto the box', *Sydney Morning Herald*, 23/3/95.
70 ABA schedule 8 clause 6.2 Optus contract, Mr Jones' Agreements, p. 2.
71 2UE, op. cit., 17/8/95.
72 ibid., 21/8/95.
73 Alex Mitchell, 'Kissing cousins', *Sun Herald*, 31/3/96.
74 Jennifer Cooke, 'Doubt remains over Kalajzich case', *Sydney Morning Herald*, 3/6/95.
75 Jennifer Cooke, 'A detective goes home happy', *Sydney Morning Herald*, 2/6/95.
76 ibid.
77 2GB, op. cit., 28/11/03.
78 Jones has not changed his position on the case. In November 2002, at the launch of the book *Doubt and Conviction: The Kalajzich Inquiry*, by a cousin by marriage, Pip Kalajzich, Jones expressed an unshaken faith in Kalajzich's innocence. Anxious to understand the basis of that faith I listened hard. Jones was confident and eloquent but never once during a 15-minute unscripted performance did I hear him articulate the set of facts that underpinned this belief. (Book launch, State Library 18/11/02)
79 Miller, op. cit., File note, 22/8/95.
80 Heather Chapman, '$10 million man', *Sunday Telegraph*, 17/9/95.
81 Jane Freeman, 'Jones signs a king-sized contract with 2UE and now he's lording it over Laws', *Sydney Morning Herald*, 18/9/95.

82 Max Presnell, 'David puts the boot into Robbie', *Sydney Morning Herald*, 20/12/95.
83 'Alan Jones' lobby for Robbie paints a confusing analogy', *Sun Herald*, 24/12/95, n.p.
84 Alex Mitchell, 'Jones' furious attack on QC', *Sun Herald*, 14/9/97.
85 The Gadfly, 'Losing the thread?', *Sun Herald*, 2/8/98.
86 Peter Bowers, 'Silence in the house as Peacock goes a-hunting', *Sydney Morning Herald*, 10/5/89.
87 Gerard Henderson, 'Right, left, ravers in step', *Sydney Morning Herald*, 15/2/97.
88 ibid.
89 In April 2004 Veterans Affairs Minister Dana Vale endured public humiliation after sending a herogram to Alan Jones which read: 'Thinking of you Alan and want to assure you of our warm support, and to add our names to the long list of your friends. Stay brave and true.' The note was faxed to the wrong radio station. Correspondence, Dana Vale to Jones, 29/4/04.

Chapter 14: Pick and Stick

1 2UE, op. cit., 14/12/01.
2 David Leser, 'Just leave it to me, mate ...', *Good Weekend: The Sydney Morning Herald Magazine*, 6/12/97, p. 14.
3 ibid.
4 'Getting some thrills at Strawberry Hills', *Sunday Telegraph*, 28/11/04.
5 Elisabeth Wynhausen, 'Ratbag king of radio ga ga', *Weekend Australian*, 31/10/98, p. 23.
6 Niamh Kenny went on to produce Jones' 2GB breakfast rival, Graham Richardson. She later returned to Jones and then left again to work for archrival John Laws.
7 AC Nielsen and ABC audience research.
8 Correspondence, Lorna Davis (State Bank of New South Wales) to Miller, 31/5/96.
9 Email, Margot McKay (Head of Public Affairs) to Davis, 6/6/96.
10 Correspondence, Miller to Colonial State Bank, 29/8/96.
11 Correspondence, Jones to Denis Handlin (Sony Music), 2/6/98.
12 Leser, 'Who's afraid of Alan Jones?', op. cit.
13 ibid., pp. 16, 17.
14 Contract clause 5, Agreement between Belford Productions and Sunraysia, 14/10/96.
15 2UE, op. cit., 13/5/97.
16 ibid., 8/9/97.
17 ibid., 21/10/97.
18 2UE, op. cit., 22/6/99.
19 Correspondence, Jones to 2UE listeners, 14/7/99.
20 ibid., 12/5/97.
21 ibid., 9/9/96.

22 ibid., 11/9/96.
23 ibid., 3/2/97.
24 Correspondence, Walker Corporation to Miller, 8/4/97.
25 Miller, op. cit., File note (Irene Stone), 25/3/97.
26 Correspondence, Walker Corporation to Miller, 8/4/97.
27 Miller, op. cit., File note, 26/3/97.
28 Leser, 'Who's afraid of Alan Jones?', op. cit. p. 16.
29 Miller, op. cit., File note (Irene Stone), 1/5/97.
30 Dean Capobianco, the fourth fastest man in the world over 200 metres, was enduring an agonising and expensive battle to be reinstated after a failed drug test. Jones said of him: 'He is a young man who has done a lot for Australia and his sport, yet he has been treated like a common criminal for a year'. Roy Masters, 'In defence of Capo', *Sydney Morning Herald*, 19/2/97.
31 File note, Miller, 10/6/97.
32 The relationship with Qantas had its problems too. In attempting to use the connection to get a deal for famous British athlete turned politician Sebastian Coe, Alan Jones hit a hurdle and complained to Harry Miller: 'I asked Bernard Shirley whether or not Qantas could see their way clear to provide the fare to Sebastian gratis. Look what Shirley has done. He has to be the greatest wimp I've ever met. He's now credited my Visa card with the amount, but debited my credit account. In other words, I'm buying the ticket for Sebastian Coe. Can you believe this ... this bloke is the most miserable and mean person with requests that I've ever known. I could amplify what I mean by that.' (Correspondence, Jones to Miller, 17/3/98.) Miller, gently and with the assistance of a full throttle grovel, suggested Jones pull his head in. 'I had a long talk to Bernard Shirley and I have to tell you that he has enormous respect for you and indeed thinks that you are a special human being. He is aware (which may surprise you) of your quite extraordinary generosity on occasions both with money and time to people in need ... my view is you shouldn't do anything about it except to enjoy your excellent relationship with Qantas.' (Correspondence, Miller to Belford Productions, 18/3/98.) Alan Jones is still a regular Qantas passenger and is regularly assigned seat 1A. Jones is said to be one of the few passengers for whom Qantas will hold up a flight.
33 Correspondence, Jones to Miller, 13/7/97.
34 ibid., 11/8/97.
35 Correspondence, Cantarella Brothers to 2UE, 8/7/97.
36 2UE op. cit., live read, 25/8/97.
37 Correspondence, Australian Food Council to Jones, 8/10/97.
38 Miller, op. cit., File note (Irene Stone), 26/3/98.
39 Miller, op. cit., File note (Jane Smith), 15/5/98.
40 Spike, 'Party alert no joke', *Sydney Morning Herald*, 23/1/04.
41 Kate de Brito, Catriona Dixon and David Luff, 'Too cool for the pool', *Daily Telegraph*, 7/6/97.
42 Peter Holder and Jo Casamento, 'Miller marriage is "fabulous" ', *Daily Telegraph*, 14/2/00.

ENDNOTES

43 de Brito, Dixon and Luff, op. cit.
44 Kate Askew and Anne Lampe, 'Wheels within wheels', *Sydney Morning Herald*, 4/1/03.
45 2UE, op. cit., August 97.
46 Correspondence, Jones to 2UE listener, 17/7/99.
47 Adam Hawse, 'An outcast on his last chance', *Sunday Telegraph*, 8/3/98.
48 ibid.
49 Adam Hawse, 'My debt to Alan Jones', *Sunday Telegraph*, 8/2/98.
50 Alan Jones' positivism with Julian O'Neill did not have the intended effect. A year later another story entered Rugby League folklore after an incident at a Dubbo motel. The sibilant O'Neill was alleged to have boasted over the telephone that he had just 'shat in Schlossy's shoes'. (Danny Weidler and Greg Prichard, 'Shame on you', *Sun Herald*, 21/2/99, p. 112.) The proprietors of the Palm Motor Inn were unhappy not just with the deposit of faeces in Jeremy Schloss's shoes, but also with the general drunken behaviour by a range of Souths' players, which led to a $10 000 fine. (Steve Mascord, 'Jones lashes but then helps bad boy O'Neill', *Sydney Morning Herald*, 20/2/99, p. 53) Jones arranged treatment and alcohol counselling and, thanks significantly to his intervention, O'Neill was given another chance. 'Rabbitohs to *shout* O'Neill a tough contract', *Illawarra Mercury*, 25/2/99, p. 60.
51 Miranda Devine, 'Hanky panky brings out joker', *Daily Telegraph*, 19/2/98.
52 *Media Watch*, op. cit., 16/3/98.
53 *Midday*, Channel 9, 20/3/98.
54 Correspondence, HarperCollins to Miller, 1/4/98.
55 Correspondence, Jones to Miller, 8/4/98.
56 Correspondence, Walsh Bay Finance Pty Ltd to Miller, 1/6/98.
57 2UE, op. cit., 2/6/98.
58 ibid., 22/7/98.
59 Correspondence, Conde to 'All On-Air Broadcasters', 27/7/98.
60 Correspondence, Miller to Conde, 5/8/98.
61 Email, Conde to Miller, 6/8/98.
62 John Laws' evidence to ABA, 8/11/99.
63 John Laws, *Laws*, Foxtel, 11/8/98.
64 *ABA Inquiry*, op. cit., Statement of John C Conde, AO, 11/11/99, clause 1.14, p. 4.
65 2UE, op. cit., 21/8/98.
66 ibid., 10/4/95.
67 2UE, op. cit., 3/12/98.
68 Correspondence, Miller to Optus Communications, 13/5/98.
69 Correspondence, Chris Anderson to Jones, 19/5/98.
70 Correspondence, Jones to Chris Anderson and Max Suich, 20/5/98.
71 Correspondence, Alexandra Lutyens to Suich, 26/6/98.
72 Correspondence, Miller to Suich, 26/6/98.
73 Correspondence, Suich to Miller, 29/6/98.
74 ibid., 14/7/98.
75 Correspondence, Miller to Lutyens, 15/7/98.

76 Correspondence, Jones to Lutyens, 29/7/98.
77 'Alan Jones escapes charge', *Daily Telegraph*, 4/11/98.
78 Correspondence, Jones to Marlene Goldsmith, 14/3/97.
79 Correspondence, Goldsmith to Jones, 16/3/97.
80 2UE, op. cit., 17/3/97.
81 ibid., 24/9/97.
82 Sue Williams, *Peter Ryan: The Inside Story*, Viking, Melbourne, 2002, p. 233.
83 2UE, op. cit., 3/6/98.
84 The letter typed by Peter Collins reads as follows:

Alan Jones: 26 May, 1998.

Bob Car [sic] will be a tough opponent. He is very articulate.
A major problem for the Coalition is whether it is seen as capable of putting up an alternative Ministry.
Performance of Shadow Ministers varies:
[Jillian] Skinner [Health]—does a reasonable job.
[Stephen] O'Doherty [Education]—needs to show what he stands for.
[Michael] Photios [Transport—ex-King's student]—doing well; would talk under wet cement.
[Kerry] Chikarovski [Corrective Services]—non existent.
[Barry] O'Farrell [a former Liberal state director and the new Member for Gordon who displaced former King's student and Jones pal Jeremy Kinross]—should be given more to do. He is clever and capable. Good to use for strategy.
Development of issues:
1. Crime—The community has had enough. Police don't need degrees unless they want to be Commissioner. Need to streamline the process so police can get out on the streets. Commissioner's honeymoon is over as of the MUA dispute. Could put him on notice.
2. Electricity—No votes in it either way. Promoting privatisation of electricity could lose votes. Expect no support on this.
3. Debt—Too much obsession with debt by [Treasurer Michael] Egan. Get third party endorsement of a reasonable State debt level to employ more police, teachers etc.
4. Education—Teachers are asked to do too much these days. Go back to core curriculum. Pay them better overtime. Avoid becoming captive of Teachers Federation. Good advice from Rod West [headmaster of Trinity Grammar and ex King's School] and Lauchlan Chipman [Vice Chancellor, Central Queensland University].
5. East Circular Quay—Too many people on both sides were involved in this for anyone to now come out looking good. AJ was opposed to Quay development four years ago.
6. Cricket Ground/Stadium—Failure to use SCG Trust expertise to manage Olympic Stadium means strong competition rather than constructive partnership between venues. Must look at better coordination to attract events to appropriate venues.

7. Housing—Craig Knowles had looked very promising until this week's proposal to establish a separate Department of Aboriginal Housing. This would be a disaster.
8. DOCS—No point beating up Lo Po at the moment over daily DOCS story because she hasn't been there long enough.
9. Sorry Day—A big turn-off to the electorate who weren't around then anyway. White people were forcibly adopted out over the same time [Brennan] and there is no sorry day for them.
10. Arts—Encourage popular emerging artists like Genevieve Davis, graduate of the Talent Development Scheme. Don't pander to the classic arts.

Strategy:

Ask Shadow Ministers to list the top ten specific issues they would raise publicly [across all portfolios]. Keep updating the list of ten to provide a focussed and disciplined approach.

Form a small group to provide strategic advice which might include Michael Magnus [former advertising executive], BO'F [Barry O'Farrell] and HM [presumably Harry Miller].

85. Correspondence, Jones to Peter Collins, 2/6/98.
86. Caroline Overington, 'Talkback bias: Laws reads the riot act', *Sunday Age*, 23/10/98.
87. *Lateline*, ABC TV, 6/10/98.
88. Sue Javes, 'Feud goes public', *Daily Telegraph*, 21/10/98, p. 1.
89. Overington, op. cit.
90. Correspondence, Jones to 2UE listener, 4/6/99.
91. Malcolm Farr, 'Polly gets a cracker', *Daily Telegraph*, 26/11/98.
92. In March 2001 John Boultbee, the director of the Australian Institute of Sport, the man who had terminated Scott Miller back in 1998, and who heard as a result that Jones would 'get him', was himself terminated. According to the *Sun Herald*, Sports Minister Jackie Kelly 'baffled sports leaders with her decision last month to axe John Boultbee, the loyal and successful director of the Australian Institute of Sport for the past five years. Boultbee had no warning that he had suddenly fallen out of favour after supervising the institute's triumph at the Sydney Olympic Games.' (Fia Cumming, 'Jumping Jackie Flash now the invisible woman', *Sun Herald*, 1/4/01.) Alan Jones was one member of the selection panel. The 51-year-old Boultbee, says Jackie Kelly, had taken him to lunch, telling him: 'The government can't afford to upset Alan Jones because he provides the only good publicity we get in Sydney'. Kelly agrees that Alan Jones was a good friend to the government, but disagrees with the proposition that Jones was instrumental in Boultbee's departure.
93. Alan Jones, 'Foreword', in Kerry Chikarovski and Luis Garcia, *Chika*, Lothian, Melbourne, 2004, p. v.
94. ibid.
95. Correspondence, Jones to 2UE correspondent, 17/11/98.
96. Leser, 'Who's afraid of Alan Jones?', op. cit.
97. ibid.

Chapter 15: A Veritable Tsunami

1 Paul Sheehan, 'Sound and fury', *Sydney Morning Herald*, 9/2/02.
2 Correspondence, Jones to Anne Davies, *Sydney Morning Herald*, 21/7/00.
3 Correspondence, Jones to Davies 21/7/00.
4 2UE, op. cit., 30/8/99.
5 ibid., 1/3/99.
6 ibid., 30/8/99.
7 ibid., 1/3/99.
8 Interview, *Four Corners*, op. cit., 9/4/02.
9 Correspondence, Jones to Davies, 21/7/00.
10 Correspondence, Jones to 2UE listener, 13/4/99.
11 ibid., 6/9/99.
12 Correspondence, 2UE listener to author, May 2002.
13 Correspondence, Jones to 2UE listener, 6/3/00.
14 Correspondence, Jones to Bob Carr, 13/4/99.
15 ibid., 19/4/99.
16 ibid., 31/3/99.
17 ibid., 27/4/99.
18 Memo, Jones to Darby, 23/8/99.
19 Memo, Jones to Darby, 12/3/99.
20 Correspondence, Jones to Wendy George, 18/8/99.
21 Correspondence, Jones to 2UE listener, 21/4/99.
22 ibid., 10/4/99. When he was later criticised for Liberal sympathies, Alan Jones explained on air that his own vote at the 1999 election had gone to his then local Labor member, Andrew Refshauge. 2UE, op. cit., 17/8/01.
23 Correspondence, Jones to 2UE correspondent, 26/3/99.
24 ibid., 31/3/99.
25 Anne Davies, 'Dear Minister ...', *Sydney Morning Herald*, 5/8/00.
26 ibid.
27 Correspondence, Jones to Kerry Chikarovski, 1/2/00.
28 ibid., 13/3/00.
29 Correspondence, Chikarovski to Jones, 20/4/00.
30 Correspondence, Jones to Chikarovski, 2/5/00.
31 ibid.
32 Correspondence, Jones to Faye Lo Po, 20/8/98.
33 ibid., 11/8/99.
34 Memo, Jones to Darby, 24/2/00.
35 Correspondence, Lo Po to Jones, 14/3/00.
36 2GB, op. cit., 21/7/02.
37 Interview, *Four Corners*, op. cit., 9/4/02.
38 Davies, 'Dear Minister ...', op. cit.
39 Correspondence, Jones to Carl Scully, 25/2/99.
40 Correspondence, Scully to Jones, 7/3/99.
41 Correspondence, Jones to Scully, 10/3/99.
42 Davies, 'Dear Minister ...', op. cit.
43 Correspondence, Jones to Davies, 21/7/00.

44 Correspondence, Scully to Jones, December 1999.
45 Correspondence, Jones to Scully, 10/11/98.
46 File note, Michael Deegan, 26/2/03. Correspondence, Deegan to author, 14/2/04.
47 2GB, op. cit., 5/3/03.
48 Correspondence, Deegan to ICAC, 17/6/03.
49 Correspondence, Jones to Craig Knowles, 11/5/98.
50 Alex Mitchell, 'Why the Parrot loves the pokies', *Sun Herald*, 2/4/00.
51 Correspondence ('Personal and Confidential'), Jones to Knowles, 24/12/98.
52 ibid.
53 ibid.
54 2GB, op. cit., 21/11/03.
55 ibid.
56 ibid.
57 Correspondence, Jones to Davies, 21/7/00.
58 Correspondence, Jones to Office of the Premier, 15/3/00.
59 Correspondence, Jones to Davies, 21/7/00.
60 ibid.
61 2GB, op. cit., 22/3/05.
62 Correspondence, Tony Abbott to Jones, 22/4/99.
63 ibid., 5/5/99.
64 Correspondence, Jones to Abbott, 14/4/00.
65 ibid., 14/5/99.
66 Correspondence, Abbott to Jones, 21/5/99.
67 Correspondence, Jones to Abbott, 10/6/99.
68 Correspondence, Abbott to Jones, 24/8/99.
69 Correspondence, Jones to Abbott, 26/8/99.
70 ibid., 10/11/99.
71 2UE, op. cit., 11/3/98.
72 ibid., 27/3/98.
73 Correspondence, Philip Ruddock to Jones, 8/4/98.
74 Correspondence, Jones to Ruddock, 8/9/99.
75 ibid., 15/9/99.
76 File note, Jones to Darby, 1/4/99.
77 2GB, op. cit., 6/8/02.
78 *Today*, Channel 9, 30/9/03.
79 2GB, op. cit., 2/6/03.
80 ibid., 8/8/03.
81 ibid., 10/9/03.
82 ibid., 12/9/03.
83 ibid., 19/9/03.
84 ibid., 27/5/02.
85 ibid., 8/3/04.
86 Correspondence, Jones to the Department of Prime Minister and Cabinet, 23/11/98.
87 Memo, Jones to Darby, 18/2/99.

88 ibid., 9/3/99.
89 Correspondence, Jones to John Howard, 15/4/99.
90 ibid.
91 ibid., 20/4/99.
92 Anthony Benscher to Jones, 7/8/99.
93 Correspondence, Howard to Jones, 21/9/99.
94 ibid.
95 Correspondence, Jones to Davies, 21/7/00.
96 Correspondence, Jones to Prime Minister and Defence Minister, 13/12/99.
97 Correspondence, David Ritchie (Office of the Prime Minister) to Jones, 2/2/00.
98 Davies, 'Dear Minister ...', op. cit.
99 Correspondence, Jones to James Packer, 29/6/99.
100 2UE, op. cit., 31/5/99.
101 Correspondence, Jones to Michael Hill (Chairman, Newcastle Rugby League Club), 31/5/99. In an interview with the author (18/8/05) Warren Ryan disagrees with the proposition that he spoke to Trindall in the manner alleged by Jones.
102 Piggins, op. cit., p. 186.
103 Correspondence, Jones to 2UE listener, 1/3/00.
104 Correspondence, Jones to various members of the board of South Sydney Rugby League Club, 3/11/03.
105 There were further violent incidents involving Darrell Trindall, some of them against women. There were three apprehended violence orders placed on him. At the 2003 2GB Christmas party he was reported to have hit from behind the husband of 2GB Program Director Lou Barrett. ('Tricky situation', *Sun Herald*, 21/12/03.) Following his departure from Canterbury, a former Bulldogs sponsor, the National Telecom Group, employed Trindall and offered any club that took him an estimated $200 000 sponsorship. There were no takers. (Adam Hawse, 'We'll pay you to give Tricky a go—sponsorship with a difference for NRL', *Sunday Telegraph*, 3/11/02.)
106 Correspondence, Jones to Wayne Beavis, 7/9/99.
107 ibid.
108 Correspondence, Jones to Irish friend, 22/10/99.
109 Correspondence, Jones to Strath Gordon, 21/7/99.
110 Correspondence, Jones to rugby friend, 28/7/99.
111 Correspondence, Jones to rugby friend, 5/12/02.
112 2GB, op. cit., 27/11/03.
113 Correspondence, Jones to Sandy Holloway (Chairman, SOCOG), 31/5/99.
114 Mark Day, 'Marching to the beat of a different drum', *Daily Telegraph*, 20/9/00.
115 Harry Gordon, *The Time of Our Lives*, University of Queensland Press, St Lucia, 2003, pp. 130–1.
116 Correspondence, Jones to SOCOG, 28/2/00.
117 Ric Birch, *Master of Ceremonies*, Allen & Unwin, Sydney, 2004, p. 280.

118 2UE, op. cit., 18/9/00.
119 Correspondence, Jones to 2UE listener, 10/4/00.
120 2UE, op. cit., 22/11/99.
121 Piers Akerman, 'You're wrong Alan', *Sunday Telegraph*, 22/3/98.
122 Memo, Jones to researcher (2UE), 30/3/98.
123 Correspondence, Jones to Piers Akerman?, 14/4/98.
124 Correspondence, Jones to Jeremy Kinross, 12/3/98. Jones' power behind the Kinross throne is manifest in later communication. When Kinross' seat was threatened he faxed Jones ten pages outlining the extraordinary plot to unseat him. Jones was terse in his response, warning that in the wrong hands the correspondence would be immensely damaging. Correspondence, Jones to Kinross, 26/3/98.
125 Correspondence, Jones to listener, 1/8/00.
126 *ABA Inquiry*, op. cit., 'Background to the Hearing', p. 7.
127 Correspondence, Jones to various correspondents, 13/8/99.
128 Correspondence, Harry Dutton (2UE Company Secretary) to Jones, 19/7/99.
129 Correspondence, Jones to correspondent, October 1999.
130 Correspondence, Jones to his broadcast staff, 30/7/99.
131 Jonathan Este, 'No case to answer for the Jones boy', *Australian*, 23/9/99. Ten years earlier, Alan Jones was quoted as favouring the United States republican system of government (Henderson, *Australian Answers*, op. cit., p. 171).
132 David Flint, Address to the Communication and Media Law Association, 26/11/97.
133 Correspondence, Jones to David Flint, 3/12/97.
134 Flint, Address to the Sydney Institute, 25/5/99.
135 Correspondence, Jones to Flint, 2/6/99.
136 Correspondence, Flint to Jones, 11/6/99.
137 Correspondence, Jones to Flint, 22/6/99.
138 Correspondence, Jones to 2UE listener, 8/2/99.
139 ibid., 17/2/99.

Chapter 16: Money for Nothing

1 *ABA Inquiry*, op. cit., 17/11/99, transcript of hearing, p. 1489.
2 2UE, op. cit., October 1999, reported in Anne Davies, 'Money talks', *Sydney Morning Herald*, 23/10/99.
3 Commercial Radio Codes of Practice, clauses 2 (d) and 3.1 (a).
4 *ABA Inquiry*, op. cit., Report, p. 3.
5 *ABA Inquiry*, op. cit., 19/1/99, transcript of hearing, p. 43.
6 *The 7.30 Report*, op. cit. 27/4/04.
7 *ABA Inquiry*, op. cit., 9/11/99, transcript of hearing, p. 958.
8 ibid., p. 1018.
9 ibid.
10 ibid., p. 1025.
11 ibid., p. 1028.

12 ibid., 10/11/99, p. 1039.
13 ibid., p. 1044.
14 ibid., p. 1055.
15 Correspondence, Jones to 2UE colleague, 31/1/00.
16 *ABA Inquiry*, op. cit., 10/11/99, transcript of hearing, p. 1064.
17 ibid., p. 1069.
18 ibid., p. 1124.
19 Optus briefing note for Jones, 19/8/98. Optus Freestyle editorial, 2UE, op. cit., 21/8/98.
20 *ABA Inquiry*, op. cit., 10/11/99, transcript of hearing, p. 1138.
21 ibid., 1095.
22 ibid., 1097.
23 ibid., p. 1142.
24 ibid., p. 1142.
25 ibid., 11/11/99, p. 1168.
26 ibid., p. 1174.
27 ibid., 1178.
28 Amanda Meade, 'Once more to the breach, Mr Jones', *Australian*, 20/11/99.
29 Anne Davies, 'Jones keeps full list of sponsors close to his chest', *Sydney Morning Herald*, 12/11/99.
30 *ABA Inquiry*, op. cit., 11/11/99, transcript of hearing, p. 1235.
31 ibid., 12/11/99, p. 1332.
32 ibid., p. 1380.
33 Bernard Lagan, 'Revealed: Jones's secret deals', *Sydney Morning Herald*, 13/11/99.
34 Richard Ackland, 'How Alan Jones turned hitman for Walsh Bay deal', *Sydney Morning Herald*, 15/11/99.
35 Anne Davies, 'ABA ready to recall Jones over Walsh Bay', *Sydney Morning Herald*, 16/11/99.
36 2UE, op. cit., 16/11/99.
37 *ABA Inquiry*, op. cit., 17/11/99, transcript of hearing, p. 1473.
38 ibid., pp. 1480, 1481.
39 ibid., p. 1481.
40 ibid., p. 1487.
41 ibid., p. 1488.
42 ibid., p. 1491.
43 Correspondence, Jones to Miller, 24/2/98.
44 *ABA Inquiry*, op. cit., 17/11/99, transcript of hearing, p. 1492.
45 ibid., pp. 1494–5.
46 Mark Day, 'Reality bounds being pushed', *Daily Telegraph*, 18/11/99.
47 Errol Simper, 'Charming until proven guilty', *Australian*, 18/11/99.
48 Mark Day, 'Words his weapon', *Daily Telegraph*, 20/11/99.
49 Heather Chapman, '2UE slips but Jones still a winner', *Sydney Morning Herald*, 8/12/99.
50 Amanda Meade and Matt Price, 'Radio scandal dials a windfall', *Australian*, 29/3/00.

51 Interview, *Four Corners*, op. cit., 11/4/02.
52 Marilyn Grass, 'My friend Alan', *Sun Herald*, 20/1/00, n.p.
53 *ABA Inquiry*, op. cit., 2/12/99, transcript of hearing, p. 1718.
54 David Marr, 'Jones is Jones: credibility doubts are impertinent', *Sydney Morning Herald*, 4/12/99.
55 Mark Day, 'The listeners will judge Laws and Jones', *Daily Telegraph*, 4/12/99.
56 2UE, op. cit., 8/2/00.
57 ibid.
58 Phillip Adams, 'Ethics flushed down the drain', *Australian*, 19/2/00.
59 Correspondence, Miller to Jones, 23/2/00.
60 Correspondence, Jones to Miller, 24/2/00.
61 Correspondence, Sky Radio to Miller, 9/5/00.
62 Correspondence, Miller to Jones, 10/5/00.
63 Correspondence, Jones to Miller, 11/5/00.
64 Bernard Zuel, 'Jones and Hadley feud a winner on timing', *Sydney Morning Herald*, 21/10/99.
65 Correspondence, Jones to Brennan, 20/11/98.
66 ibid.
67 Correspondence, Jones to Geoff Davey (Walker Corporation), 22/11/99.
68 Correspondence, Jones to PR associate, 18/11/99.

Chapter 17: The Emperor's New Clothes

1 Amanda Meade, 'Will Jones follow his ego to 2GB?', *Australian*, 11/10/01.
2 Macquarie Radio Network advertisement, *Sun Herald*, 14/11/99.
3 Melba, 'Conscience nonsense', *Australian*, 11/2/00.
4 Kathryn Bice, 'Singleton turns up heat on 2UE', *Australian Financial Review*, 9/2/00.
5 Correspondence, John Singleton to Jones, 29/8/97.
6 Correspondence, Jones to Singleton, 23/9/97.
7 Correspondence, Singleton to Jones, 22/4/98.
8 Correspondence, Jones to Bill Currie (Macquarie Radio Network), 9/11/98.
9 Correspondence, Jones to Currie, 28/6/99.
10 Correspondence, 2UE listener to Jones, 21/7/99.
11 Correspondence, Jones to Peter Ryan (Police Commissioner), 23/7/99.
12 Correspondence, Jones to Ken Moroney (Deputy Police Commissioner), 17/4/00.
13 Correspondence, Sergeant Tim Priest to Police Association of New South Wales, 5/4/00.
14 ibid.
15 Mark Day, 'Bell joins the big boys', *Australian*, 29/3/01.
16 ibid.
17 Inquiry into Police Resources in Cabramatta, General Purposes No 3, p. 7, 23/2/01.

18 2UE, op. cit., 26/2/01.
19 ibid., 4/7/01.
20 Peter Bodor QC, James Investigation and *James Report*, 20/2/04, p. 5.
21 Sue Williams, *Peter Ryan*, op. cit., p. 264.
22 Unpublished draft. Tim Priest and Richard Basham. 'To Protect and to Serve', correspondence, former member of SAS to author, 27/8/02. When the Festival of Light presented Tim Priest with a Good Citizen's Award in 2001 there was a reference to his army service: 'A highlight was selection to the Special Air Services Regiment (SAS) in 1975 at 19 years of age', Reverend Charles Pass, Festival of Light press release, 24/10/01. Tim Priest blames the media for incorrect claims about membership of the Special Air Service. He says having been selected into the SAS he was unable to take the physical training course because of a football injury.
23 Correspondence, John Steinmetz (Cabramatta High School) to Jones, 10/7/01.
24 Correspondence, Jones to Steinmetz, 12/7/01. Borrowing one of his own expressions, Jones has 'more positions than the Kama Sutra'. Two years later, broadcasting with an air of innocence, Jones spoke up for a 'much maligned Cabramatta'. 2GB, op. cit., 26/9/03.
25 Statement to Inquiry into Police Resources in Cabramatta (GPSC) No 3, 10/5/01. A later inquiry undertaken by Peter Bodor QC found: 'The submission presented ... did not faithfully accord with James' tape recorded statement.' Bodor, op. cit, p. 19.
26 2UE, op. cit., 5/7/01.
27 ibid., 11/7/01.
28 ibid., 20/7/01.
29 ibid.
30 John Kidman, 'Whistleblower on abuse charge', *Sun Herald*, 20/4/03.
31 Bodor, op. cit., p. 15.
32 ibid., 4. Critical analysis of the *James Report and Investigators*, pp. 1–77.
33 2UE, op. cit., 11/7/01.
34 ibid., 14/8/01.
35 ibid., 24/7/01.
36 ibid., 28/8/01.
37 ibid., 5/10/01.
38 Correspondence, Darby to David Bacon, 16/11/01. At a 2004 law and order rally promoted by Jones with Tim Priest and Ross Treyvaud as speakers, an estimated 90 spectators turned up. When a talkback caller lamented the poor turnout, Alan Jones changed the subject.
39 2UE, op. cit., 17/7/01.
40 ibid., 17/7/01.
41 Neil Mercer, ' "Snugglepot" Jones sent scurrying', *Sydney Morning Herald*, 21/8/02.
42 ibid.
43 David Penberthy, 'Inquiry officer quits in disgust', *Daily Telegraph*, 26/7/01.
44 Sue Javes, 'Jones takes the walk of fame: there's no fury like a star scorned', *Sydney Morning Herald*, 8/2/02.

45 Meade, 'Will Jones follow his ego ...', op. cit.
46 2UE, op. cit., August 2001.
47 Anne Davies, 'The message fish and chips', *Sydney Morning Herald*, 2/8/01, p. 25.
48 Alan Jones would visit his friend, Lord Archer, in gaol. To friends he carried a tale that Archer was an innocent victim of a conspiracy.
49 Correspondence, Jones to John Laws, 6/8/01.
50 Correspondence, Laws to Jones, 6/8/01.
51 ibid.
52 ibid.
53 2GB, op. cit., 20/4/05.
54 Correspondence, Laws to Jones, op. cit.
55 2UE, op. cit., 5/9/01.
56 Sue Williams, *Peter Ryan*, op. cit., p. 328.
57 Tim Priest denies there was any discussion between Clive Small, Richard Basham and himself about Jones' dirt file. Interview with author, 1/11/05.
58 Correspondence, Jones to Marcus Schmidt, 8/8/01.
59 Marcus Schmidt, Unpublished manuscript, p. 212.
60 ibid., p. 214.
61 ibid., p. 216.
62 Anne Davies, 'Coming to the aid of the party', *Sydney Morning Herald*, 28/6/01.
63 Interview 22/4/04.
64 2UE, op. cit., 2/10/01.
65 ibid., 10/8/01.
66 ibid., 22/10/01.
67 Rehame media monitoring, quoted in Melissa Fyfe, 'When politicians take talkback too seriously', *Age*, 1/12/01.
68 2UE, op. cit., 9/10/01.
69 ibid.
70 ibid.
71 Tim Priest and Richard Basham, *To Protect and to Serve*, New Holland, Sydney, 2003, pp. 235, 236.
72 Luke McIlveen, 'Run it by the shock jock', *Australian*, 22/11/01.
73 ibid.
74 Statement of Claim, Supreme Court of New South Wales No. 20927/01, 21/11/01.
75 Penberthy, op. cit.
76 Priest and Basham, op. cit., p. 247.
77 Correspondence, Jones to Schmidt, 20/11/01.
78 ibid., 13/3/03.
79 Edited Goof tape, 2UE, op. cit., broadcast on Radion 2JJJ, January 2002.
80 On one notorious occasion it is said Alan Jones spoke for longer than the ex-president, with whom Jones is proud of an ongoing friendship. In 2004, when launching his autobiography, Clinton granted Jones the exclusive Australian radio interview.

81 Gerald Stone, *'Singo': The John Singleton Story*, HarperCollins, Sydney, 2002, p. 289.
82 Teresa Ooi, 'Jones in $14m windfall on float', *Australian*, 21/4/05.
83 2GB Press Conference, Park Hyatt Hotel, Sydney, 7/2/02, reported in Peter Holder, 'The $40m coup', *Daily Telegraph*, 8/2/02.
84 ibid.
85 Stephen Brook, 'Old habits follow radio man to rival', *Australian*, 5/3/02.
86 Paul Sheehan, 'Wherever you go there's Alan Jones—or will be', *Sydney Morning Herald*, 11/2/02.
87 Sally Jackson, 'Price eats into breakfast', *Australian*, 7/8/02.
88 Shelley Gare, 'Scant debate in a shock jock', *Australian*, 13/6/98.
89 2GB, op. cit., 25/3/02.
90 ibid., 29/3/02.
91 Sue Williams, *Peter Ryan*, op. cit., p. 312.
92 ibid.
93 Bernard Lagan, 'Copping flack', *Bulletin*, 9/7/02.
94 2GB, op. cit., 10/4/02.
95 John Brogden became embroiled in a personal scandal following a July 2006 function. The Opposition Leader, said to be in a euphoric mood after the departure of Bob Carr, had been heard making inappropriate comments. He resigned from parliament in August 2006, attempting suicide two days later.
96 2GB, op. cit., 10/4/02.
97 Miranda Devine, 'Doozey of a farewell by honest cop Priest', *Sun Herald*, 9/6/02. When a small ruckus later broke out over the claims of SAS service, Miranda Devine excused Tim Priest saying: 'The first reference to an SAS background came in an article in *The Australian* in 2001, which he says emerged from a misunderstanding'. (Miranda Devine 'Injustice rolls on — over the messenger', *Sydney Morning Herald* 23/2/06, p. 13.) Journalist Kate Legge had written that Priest had 'served with the elite Special Air Service unit', pointing out that the Army service in part 'prepared him well for the toughest combat role of his life'. (Kate Legge, 'The man who stuck his neck out', *Weekend Australian*, 27/10/01, p. 13.) According to Legge's notes, Priest told her he had served in a variety of Army units including the SAS. Kate Legge says: 'He made one other reference to the SAS in our conversation about the dangerous nature of training in the SAS, which he said resulted in a high death rate. This laid the foundation he said for "very strong mental defence for the rest of life"'. (Correspondence Kate Legge to author, 24/4/07)
98 Rear Window, *Australian Financial Review*, 26/6/02.
99 Adam Shand and Brett Clegg, 'Blue sky and a $5.6bn buzz', *Australian Financial Review*, 29–30/6/02.
100 Macquarie Bank advertisement, *Australian Financial Review*, 29–30/6/02.
101 In 2006 Darrell Trindall was given another start thanks to Bill Moss and Alan Jones, with the launch of Lime Taxis. Moss, who suffers from muscular dystrophy, headed Macquarie Bank's move into the taxi business. The wheelchair accessible taxi fleet was given government

approval, it was reported, after the last minute intervention of Alan Jones. Lime's Chief Executive, Stephen Albin, said of employing Trindall in what appeared to be an executive role: 'For him it's a great opportunity for a fresh start. I'm impressed'. (Lisa Murray, *Sydney Morning Herald*, 'New taxis flagged for July start', *Sydney Morning Herald*, 2/5/06)

102 ABA news release, 5/4/04, p. 4.
103 Peta Stratford-George, Telstra, Marketing Plan for Alan Jones (Confidential), 2/7/02, p. 1.
104 2GB, op. cit., 22/7/02.
105 ibid.
106 ibid.
107 Ross Gittins, 'Farmers who fail don't deserve pity', *Sydney Morning Herald*, 16/10/02.
108 *A Current Affair*, op. cit., 3/10/02.
109 *Media Watch*, op. cit., 7/10/02.
110 2GB, op. cit., 14/10/02.
111 *Today*, Channel 9, 15/10/02.
112 *Media Watch*, op. cit., 28/10/02.
113 ibid.
114 Farmhand's own research had discounted Alan's grand plans, but Alan was having none of it. One commissioned report dealt with an Alan Jones favourite—if Libya can build manmade rivers, why can't we? The Farmhand report identified prohibitive costs and further limits of doing a Libya: '... the scheme has a limited lifetime as it is pumping out more water from the aquifer than is going in'. (Farmhand, *Transporting Water*, June 2004, p. 98.)
115 2GB, op. cit., 2/7/02.
116 ibid., 3/7/02.
117 ibid., 8/7/02.
118 ibid., 12/3/03.
119 ibid., 26/2/03.
120 ibid., 4/2/03.
121 ibid., February 03.
122 ibid., 21/3/03.
123 ibid., 3/7/02.
124 ibid., 11/4/03.
125 ibid., 1/5/03.
126 Correspondence, Jones to Morris Iemma, 7/4/03.
127 ibid., 20/4/03.
128 The official inquiry, undertaken by Jones' former student and counsel Bret Walker SC, found a problem far more complex than Jones' good whistleblower/evil bureaucrat scenario: 'the chimera of no-fault in health care should be banished. But the equal absurdity of expecting that all adverse outcomes—or even many of them at all—are due to some hapless doctor's or nurse's fault for which they should be blamed or condemned should also be exploded. Life with all its manifold frailties and

vicissitudes and its inevitable end is not like that.' (Bret Walker SC, *Final Report of the Special Commission of Inquiry into Campbelltown and Camden Hospitals*, 30/7/04, p. 90.) A further inquiry in the Independent Commission Against Corruption concluded that, while the whistleblowers believed what they were saying, their allegations were founded on nothing more than gossip, speculation and hearsay. (ICAC *Report on investigation into allegations relating to the new South Western Sydney Area Health Service*, Executive Summary, September 2005, p. 6.)

129 Chronological Summary, Bodor Report, ref. 5/9/03, op. cit., p. 70.
130 Miranda Devine, 'A crime fighter to woo the west', *Sun Herald*, 19/9/04.
131 Correspondence, Jones to Moroney, 29/4/03.
132 Andrew Clennell, 'Costa's affidavit help for Priest', *Sydney Morning Herald*, 16/5/07.
133 ibid.

Chapter 18: The Misinformation Revolution

1 'Overt? power', *Australian Financial Review Magazine*, August 04, p. 38.
2 AC Nielsen, *Media Research No 5*, 2004.
3 AC Nielsen data, reported in Marcus Casey, 'Spinning the numbers in airwaves battle', *Daily Telegraph*, 31/5/04.
4 Alan Jones, 'A giant oak tree has crashed in the forest', *Australian*, 28/12/05, p. 10.
5 Alan Jones, *Today*, 15/6/07.
6 2GB, 14/7/05.
7 2GB, 19/7/05.
8 Interviews, *Four Corners*, op. cit., 6/5/02.
9 2GB, 8/12/05.
10 2GB, 5/12/05.
11 2GB, 7/12/05.
12 2GB, 8/12/05.
13 ibid.
14 2GB, 11/4/07.
15 ibid.
16 2GB, op. cit., 15/5/05.
17 ibid., 5/8/04.
18 ibid., 15/5/05.
19 Email. A. Jones to M. Jauncey, 13/10/05.
20 *Today*, op. cit., 3/5/05.
21 2GB, op. cit., 3/11/05.
22 '$1m later, and cashed-up Jones is all fenced in', *Sun Herald*, 18/4/04.
23 Correspondence to listener, 14/7/97.
24 'On the other hand, he likes it', *Sydney Morning Herald*, 25/10/01.
25 Sue Javes, 'How suite it is', *Sydney Morning Herald*, 17/2/03.
26 Dr Clive Hamilton, The Australia Institute, 'Preaching to the Converted', June 2006, p. 8.

27 Email, Brennan to Jones, 21/6/04. Following the publication of extracts from this book, John Brennan would write a similar letter to the *Sydney Morning Herald*. It provoked mirth from readers and, it would seem, an instruction from Jones to shut up. Brennan had compared Alan Jones as a latter-day Jesus Christ. 'He reminds me of another man some 2000 years ago who had the worst interpretations put upon His kindest actions, yet He went on; who had His words warped, twisted, falsely reported, minimised, yet He went on; was slighted, even laughed to scorn when He gave of His very best, yet He went on. And so will Alan Jones go on, despite all those who malign him. He is driven by his quest to serve the common man and he will not let us down, no matter how many stones are thrown at him. They cannot weaken his spirit or his destiny.' John Brennan, 'Spite and fear leads to this attempt at crucifixion', *Sydney Morning Herald*, 23/10/06.

Afterword: The Cringe Factor

1 Correspondence, Jones to Debnam, 23/9/99.
2 Adam Harvey, 'Bias, scandals, legal action tarnish the kingmaker's halo', *Sunday Telegraph*, 1/4/07, pp. 40/81.
3 Sue Javes, 'Election pushes Jones higher', *Sydney Morning Herald*, 28/3/07, p. 2.
4 Correspondence, Mark O'Brien to Stuart Neal, 5/6/06.

ACKNOWLEDGEMENTS

I SEEM TO HAVE A HABIT of picking projects that make new sets of enemies. The advantage is the new friends made along the way. I am grateful to ABC Books Manager, Stuart Neal, who was also an ally through occasionally difficult times. His colleague Brigitta Doyle was another smiling, steadfast presence. Editor Jo Jarrah, who came to know every last semi colon, is in my view one of the sharpest tools in the publishing shed. Jo guided me through a massive reduction process, which without question made this a better book. Somewhat unexpectedly my gratitude to the publishing world—where profit is not the only principle—has to be extended. Patrick Gallagher, Paul Donovan and Rebecca Kaiser are three of a praiseworthy team from Allen & Unwin, who welcomed me and got swiftly on with the job after the ABC withdrew.

Unsurprisingly a flock of lawyers also assisted. I am in debt to many of them, in particular to Michael Martin, Ross Duncan, Terry Tobin QC and Richard Potter.

I am also thankful to Sydney University's Professor Rod Tiffen for his reading of passages and useful advice. The same applies to the ABC's Mark Colvin. Justin Pooley and Iain Knight, who made the excellent *Rise and Rise of Australian Rugby* for ABC TV, saved some harder labour by virtue of the many detailed interviews conducted for the series, excerpts of which appear in the rugby chapters.

ABC election analyst Antony Green was a grand guide through the landscape of politics. Lisa Walsh from ABC Audience Research assisted me to an understanding of ratings data relating to the radio chapters.

My long held view that librarians deserve a special place in heaven was reinforced. There was efficient and comprehensive help from Ellen Mackie at the Quirindi Library, Bill Kitson from the Queensland Department of Natural Resources, and varied staff at the Queensland State Archive. ABC librarians Adelaide Beavis and Keryn Kelleway fielded many calls, as did the indefatigable Cathy Beale, who also performed the odd miracle catch.

I have a similar respectful view of teachers, surely some of the world's best observers and commentators. The many teachers from The Brisbane Grammar School and The King's School, who helped with information, insights and fact checking about the peculiarities of survival within Alan Jones' sphere of influence, brightened an occasionally dispiriting inquiry.

Two former students from those schools deserve special mention. Dr Phil Byth, now a Newcastle medico, spoke with courage as well as perceptiveness. Scott Walker, now professionally known as Scott Kilminster (having had his real name purloined by one of the Walker Brothers), is a talented musician who in my view could have done at least as well had he chosen a career as a writer.

Michael Darby, who worked with Alan Jones at 2UE, deserves recognition as well, if alone for being one of a rare bunch from the radio industry prepared to speak openly about widely shared concerns.

My *Four Corners* colleague Morag Ramsay made a significant contribution. Morag, the producer of the original *Four Corners* report, did extensive research particularly on the radio industry. Linda Carroll and Jo Puccini also generously assisted.

Journalists/authors David Leser, Caroline Jones and Gerard Henderson deserve more than acknowledgement. Their interviews with Alan Jones, each of them skilful and revealing, are frequently quoted.

There are many people I would like to nominate for thanks who would not thank me for doing so. The nature of this work has produced an army of secret helpers whose preference for anonymity is understood and respected.

My wife, Tanya, a psychologist and counsellor, was a professional as well as personal ally. Never has the benefit of having someone close to me to warn me when I am being an idiot been more apparent. My children, extended family and friends provided more moral support, deserving thanks alone for hearing more about Alan Jones than might have been their choice.

INDEX

AJ = Alan Jones. Page numbers followed by an 'n' refer to endnotes.

AAMI, 445
Abbott, Harold 'Bud', 97
Abbott, Tony, 302, 357–9, 363, 428
ABC, xi, 322, 374–5, 385, 462–7
  see also Four Corners; Lateline; Media Watch
ABC Radio, 442
Abernethy, CS, 5, 7
Aborigines, 256–7, 260
Abram, Geoff, 105, 106, 107–8, 112
Abram, Victor, 104
Abram, Will, 74, 103–4, 105, 106, 107, 166
Ackland, Richard, 322, 390
Acland, 4, 14, 21
Acland Primary School, 15
Action Jackson (video), 195
Adams, Phillip, 197, 200, 204, 256–7
Airport Users Association, 105
Akerman, Piers, 324, 373–4
'Alan Jones Breakfast Blend' coffee, 316, 323
Alan Jones Live (television program), 273–6, 443
Alan Jones Nostalgic Memories, 236

Alan Jones Presents Musical Memories from the Fifties, 307
Alan Jones Show (radio program), 210, 215, 222–3, 253, 270, 299, 410
Albin, Stephen, 501n
Alexander, John, 302
Allan, Col, 373
Allen, Allen and Hemsley, 248
Allen & Unwin, 467
Alston, Richard, 274
AMP Society, 254–5, 284, 306
Anderson, Chris, 327
Anderson, John, 4, 88, 311, 361
Anderson, Tim, 251
Ansett, 314–15
Anthony, Doug, 102–3, 450
Anthony, Dugald, 75, 102, 116
Anthony, Larry, 419
apartheid, 171, 172
Applause (play), 85
Archer, Lord Jeffrey, 163, 195, 196, 323, 414, 475n, 499n
Archer, Mary, 163
Ardlethan, 355
Argentina, 181–2
Armour, Paul, 310, 352
Arnotts, 254
Arthur, Tracey, 424
Askin government, 112

asylum seekers, 359
Austen, Jane, 48
The Australia Institute, 456
Australian, 272, 385, 393, 423, 442
Australian Answers (Henderson), 242
Australian Bankers' Association, 375, 382
Australian Broadcasting Authority
  begins second inquiry, 432
  'cash for comment' inquiry, ix, 306, 338, 378, 380–400, 453
  David Flint as chairman of, 375–8
  investigates AJ's comments on Cronulla riots, 447, 457
Australian Communications and Media Authority, 447
Australian Financial Review, 255, 431, 441
Australian Food Council, 316
Australian Industrial Relations Commission, 383, 393
Australian Institute of Sport, 318, 335
Australian Jockey Club, 297
Australian Labor Party, xi, 38, 125, 329–30
Australian Rugby Football Union, 178, 185, 230, 246, 286
Australian Rugby League, 285, 310
Australian Securities and Investments Commission, 223
Australian Story (television program), 374
Australians For a Constitutional Monarchy, 376
Aveling, Tony, 375

Baby Blacks, 167
Bacall, Lauren, 85
Bacon, David, 413
Badgery's Creek, 347
Bain, John, 144, 180
Balding, Russell, 464, 466
Ball, Merle, 22
Balmain Rugby League Club, 222, 228–33, 237–9, 245–50, 258, 264–8, 296
banks, 306–7
Barbarians, 155

Barker, Ian, 279
Barker, Merrill, 215, 216
Barlow, Harry, 32
Barnett, David, 123, 126
Barrett, Lou, 494n
Barton, Tim, 215–17, 219, 247, 251, 280, 481n
Basham, Dr Richard, 410–11, 412, 415–16, 423, 498n, 499n
bastardisation rituals, 72
The Bear Pit (Collins), 244
Beaumont, Janise, 19, 178
Beavis, Wayne, 369
Beazley, Kim, 334, 419, 421–2
Beazley, Suzie, 419
Beetson, Arthur, 232
Belford, Barnie, 18
Belford, Bill, 11–12
Belford, Elizabeth *see* Jones, Elizabeth (Beth) (AJ's mother)
Belford, Elizabeth (AJ's aunty), 9
Belford, Freda, 9–10, 11, 12, 17, 60
Belford, George, 22
Belford, James, 9
Belford, Keith, 36
Belford Productions
  arm's length contracts through, 315, 325, 327, 329
  asked to declare commercial arrangements, 375–6
  directed to provide list of promotional contracts, 388
  origin of name, 19
  South Sydney video sent to, 374
Belford, Richard, 9
Belford, Ted, 32
Bell, Stuart, 107
Bell, Tony, 406, 407
Belltrees (farm), 261
Benaud, Richard, 114
Benham, John, 106
Benness, Angela, 162
Benness, Christopher, 84–5, 162
Benscher, Anthony, 363
Bhutto, Benazir, 111–12, 202, 260
Birch, Ric, 371–2, 403
Birney, RJ, 115
Bishop, Bronwyn, 273, 291, 302
Bishop, Inge, 91, 96–7

INDEX 509

Bjelke-Petersen, Johannes
  AJ's support for, 171–2, 244–5, 298, 312
  becomes premier, 64
  eulogised by AJ, 450
  on homosexuality, 64
  'Joh for Prime Minister' campaign, 172, 173
  as Minister for Works and Housing, 47
  resigns after being sacked as leader, 191–2
Black, James, 135, 136, 139–42, 150, 161, 188
'blackballing', 72
Blackburn, Harry, 407
Blainey, Geoffrey, 362
Blanco, Serge, 176
Blazey, Peter, 117
Bledisloe Cup, 147–8, 164, 169–70, 182, 184
Blessie, May Hayden, 351
Blind and Deaf School, Brisbane, 11
Bodor, Peter, 411, 438, 498n
Bodor Report, 438
Bond, Alan, 173, 199, 239
Bosnjak, Slavko, 454
Boultbee, John, 318, 491n
Bowring Bowl, 182
Brack, Garry, 126–7, 135, 158–9
Bradman, Don, 454
Bradstreet, Peter, 134–5, 136, 138, 141, 142
Brady, Charles, 5, 7
Brady, Charles Junior, 7
Brady, Gary, 7
Brady, Jack, 7
Brady, Margaret, 5, 7
Brady, Mary Anne *see* Jones, Mary Anne
Braithwaite, Micki, 309
Branigan, Laura, 187
Bray, Kent, 218
Brazil, 180–1
Brennan, John
  at the ABA inquiry, 389–90
  admiration for AJ, 157–8
  approves of AJ's deal with Balmain Tigers, 230

Brennan, John cont.
  assists AJ, 161
  compares AJ to Jesus, 502–3n
  fan of Balmain Tigers, 222
  flies to London to comfort AJ, 197, 199
  given job of controlling AJ's behaviour, 239–40
  on the Laws-Jones conflict, 291–2
  pampers AJ, 457
  pays price for loyalty to AJ, 398
  receives complaints about 2UE from AJ, 399
  refers to AJ as 'Moses of the airwaves', 402
  tutors AJ in broadcasting, 211
  untroubled by AJ's support for Optus, 263
Bridge, Ernie, 312
Brisbane Grammar School, 47–66
Britcorp Finance, 218, 247
Britcorp Scholarship, 218, 220
Brogden, John, 429–30, 431, 500n
Brown, Bob, 313
Brown, John, 171
Brumbies, 370
Bryan, Richard, 52
Bulletin, 383
Burchett, Justice, 310
Burgess, Ian, 255, 284
Burke, Don, 371
Burke, Matthew, 149–50
Burnside, Julian, 380, 383, 386–9, 391–2, 394–5
Buttrose, Ita, 241
Byth, Phil, 54, 61–2, 63, 66, 89, 90

Cabramatta, 405–8, 412, 413, 423, 438, 498n
Cabramatta High School, 408, 409–10
Calcraft, Bill, 150, 161, 182
Camden hospital, 438, 449
Cameron, Jim, 119
Cameron, Ross, 452
Campbell, Dr Bill, 146, 163, 169, 182
Campbell Soup, 254
Campbelltown hospital, 438, 449

Campese, David, 144, 145–6, 168–71, 176, 183, 186
Canellis, George, 251
Cantarella Brothers, 316
Canterbury Bulldogs, 369
Capobianco, Dean, 315, 488n
Cargher, John, 51
Carleton, Richard, 197
Carleton, Sharon, 197
Carlton, Mike, 171, 186, 372, 399, 440
Carlyle, Thomas, 441
Carmody, Michael, 414
Carpenter, Inge *see* Bishop, Inge
Carr, Bob
  accepts failings of police, 409
  on air with AJ, 276, 331–2, 355–6, 394, 436
  AJ on, 435–7, 452
  AJ sends material on Kalajzich to, 247
  on AJ's political affiliations, 461
  approves Walsh Bay development, 326
  becomes premier, 290, 299
  begins to lift profile, 242–3
  cultivates AJ, 242–3
  declines AJ's invitation to visit, 304
  election campaign (2003), 451
  eloquence of, 191
  fascination with talkback radio, 209
  as leader of the opposition, 289
  listens to AJ's response to Marr, 435
  lunches with AJ, 201
  opposes Pauline Hanson, 313
  pays price for legitimising talk radio, 313
  Peter Collins on, 490n
  raises concerns about casino tender, 278
  relationship with AJ, 191, 420, 422–3
  reneges on promise to abolish tolls, 290
  resignation makes Brogden euphoric, 500n
  sacks Police Commissioner, 430

Carr, Bob *cont.*
  scant respect for AJ, ix
  sends AJ his political manifesto, 346
  sends speeches to AJ, 242–3
  sends supportive note to AJ, 197–8
  strategy of dealing with AJ, 451
  wins 1999 election, 345
Caruana, Nancy, 117
'cash for comment' scandal, 261, 375–6, 380–400
Casino Control Authority, 278
casino licence, tendering for, 278
Catchpole, Ken, 106
Cave, Peter, 196–7
CBC, 165, 173
Centrelink, 359
Cerutty, Percy, 133
Chamberlain, Lindy, 217, 251, 252
Channel 9
  AJ attempts to have employee sacked, 365–6
  AJ does editorials for, 239, 276, 292, 396
  bought from Bond by Packer, 239
  free-to-air contract with ARL, 285, 296
  gives to Farmhand Foundation, 434
  Steve Roach works for, 250
  tries to dump AJ's segment, 442–3
Channel 10, 271, 272, 275
Chapman, Chris, 447
Charley, Bob, 298
Charlieville (property), 454, 455
Chesterton, Ray, 249–50
Chifley, Ben, 14
Chikarovski, Kerry
  AJ on, 336, 347, 421, 429
  corresponds with AJ, 348–9
  as leader of the opposition, 335, 345
  Peter Collins' opinion of, 333, 490n
  replaced as opposition leader, 430
  supports AJ during London incident, 199
  tries to use law and order as an issue, 420
  tries to win over AJ, 348

INDEX

Chipman, Lauchlan, 490n
Chisholm, Sam, 199, 288, 427, 434
Christenson, Paul, 304
Chubb, Justice, 6
'The Church' (property), 293
Churchill, Sir Winston, 229, 415
Cigna Life Insurance, 255
Clark, Darren, 232, 233, 246
Clatworthy, Susan
  see Yabsley, Susan
Clinton, Bill, 427, 499n
Clive James at Home (television program), 160
Cloudland (dance venue), 36
Coates, John, 371
Codey, David, 150, 176, 178, 186
Coe, Sebastian, 488n
Coker, Troy, 175, 181–2, 192–3, 200, 218, 220, 481n
Colborne, Greg, 29–30
Coleman, Peter, 115–16, 117, 118, 119, 129
Coles, Phil, 371
Collex, 355–6
Collier, Mark, 158
Collin, Stephen, 464
Collins, Jennifer, 438
Collins, Peter
  AJ helps wife of with parking fines, 243–4
  blacklisted by AJ, 132
  defers to AJ, 333–4
  dumped as Liberal leader, 335
  lobbied by AJ in Kalajzich trial, 247
  as a moderate liberal, 119
  prosecutes AJ for contempt, 244
  reprimanded by AJ on air, 290
  secures meeting with AJ, 333
  sends letter to AJ, 490–1n
Collins, Richard, 77
Collis, Peter (aka Peter Starr), 411
Colonial Group, 326–7
Colonial Limited, 336
Colonial State Bank, 326–7, 382, 385
Comaneci, Nadia, 155
Communication and Media Law Association, 377
Concord Oval, 175, 217

Conde, John
  in the ABA inquiry, 388, 390
  asks broadcasters to declare deals, 375
  background, 239
  concern over AJ's on-air advertising, 264, 286–7
  contact with David Flint, 381
  delegates to John Brennan, 239
  denies conversation with Laws, 325
  informed of AJ's deal with Optus, 262–3
  informs AJ of prospective deal with Telstra, 287
  on Laws and AJ, 390
  learns of AJ's commercial deals, 322–3, 382
  pays price for loyalty to AJ, 398
  renegotiates contract with AJ, 295
  on the sale of 2UE, 406
  tensions between Laws and, 382–3
  tries to smooth conflict between Laws and AJ, 334
  unaware of personal endorsement deals, 325–6, 336
  writes to staff about endorsements, 324
Conrad, Joseph, 48
Consolidated Broadcasting Corporation, 165, 173
contempt of court, 482n
Cook Inquiry, 245
Coppock, Anthony, 88
Corfe, John, 27
Corrigan, Chris, 302, 331
Costa, Michael, ix, 423–4, 430, 437, 440, 451, 460
Costello, Peter, 360–1, 449
'cottaging', 195
Country Party, 102
Courier Mail, 36
Cousins, Geoffrey, 293
Covacevich, John, 49, 65
Cowdery, Nick, 397
Cowie, Russell, 55, 56–7, 59–60
Cox, Phillip, 141, 150
Craig, Greg, 161, 180, 181
Crean, Simon, 146

Crikey website, 436, 466
crime statistics, New South Wales, 425
Crittle, Peter, 131
Cronulla riots, 446–7
Cross, Merv, 192
cross-media ownership rules, 311–12
Crowley, Lyn, 143
Cuff, Tommy, 87
Curley, Terry, 302
A Current Affair (television program), 199, 334
Currie, Bill, 403
Cutler, Steve 'Skylab', 145, 182, 199
CVA Asia Pacific, 443

Daily Mirror, 198
Daily Telegraph
  AJ enthuses over, 373
  AJ praises article by Akerman in, 324
  AJ reads article from on air, 482n
  announces sacking of AJ as Balmain coach, 249
  announces Scott Miller's house purchase, 317
  on axing of AJ's television show, 275
  buries report on rally, 367
  criticises AJ, 296
  Laws criticises AJ's partisanship in, 334
Daley, Laurie, 371
Dalmacija Social Club, 266
Dalton, Paul, 178
Darby, Douglas, 340
Darby, Michael
  on AJ's attitude towards his audience, 342
  on AJ's exaggeration re emails, 412
  confirms support of Liberal Uglies for AJ, 120
  as letter-writer for AJ, 351, 361
  on piping water, 433–4
  works as AJ's assistant, 340, 347, 350, 351
Darling Downs, 14
Darvall, Cholmondeley 'Chum', 94
Davey, Geoff, 317, 399
Davey, Jack, 457

David (butler), 454
Davies, Anne, 356–7, 389, 390
Davis, Genevieve, 491n
Davis, Lorna, 306
Day, Mark, 383, 393
Debnam, Peter, 460–1
Deegan, Michael, 353–4, 436
defamation law, 213–14
Denton, Andrew, 203, 325, 368, 374, 443
Deuble, Paul, 40, 50, 54, 62–3
Devine, Miranda, 23, 430–1, 500n
Dixon, Geoff, 302, 315
Dodshon, Simon, 81
Domican, Tom, 244
Donne, John, 251–2
Doogue, Geraldine, 199
Dorney, Sean, 58
Downlands College, 29
Doyle, Brian, 440
Doyle, John, 246
drought relief, 14
Duggan, Jack, 38
Dunlap, Al, 255
Dwyer, Bob
  AJ criticises, 217, 219
  coaches Randwick Greens, 138
  coaches Wallabies, 139–40, 142–3, 185, 219, 222, 246
  Crowley votes against, 143
  John Fordham as manager of, 322
  partiality to Randwick players, 145
  sees bright future for AJ as manager, 131
  supported by Mark Ella, 141, 182
Dyer, Ron, 324
'dyking', 72

Eales, John, 370
Earlwood, seat of, 115, 116
The Edge nightclub, 282
Edinburgh, 153–4
EFTPOS, 317
Egan, Mark, 220–1, 481n
Egan, Michael, 490n
Egerton, Rob, 193
elections *see* federal elections; New South Wales state elections

INDEX

Elias, Benny, 229, 232, 246, 258, 268
Eliot, George, 48
Elizabeth Farm (house), 454
Ella, Glen, 143
Ella, Mark
   AJ takes captaincy from, 144
   attitude to discipline, 144
   attitude towards AJ, 154–5, 160
   criticises AJ's coaching, 179, 182
   decides to quit rugby, 160
   misses crucial goal, 140–1
   plays well in match against England, 151
   as Randwick captain, 138
   supports Dwyer as coach, 141
   in Wallabies' back line, 149
   on Wallabies' Test loss, 148
Ellerston (farm), 260–1
Ellis, Bob, 345
Elphick, Ken, 175, 178, 479n
Emerson, Roy, 37, 48
EMI, 236
England, 151–2
Enright, Phil, 52
Estate Mortgages, 222–3, 228
euthanasia, 130
Evans, Dr Alan, 364
Evans, Alex
   AJ on contribution of, 246
   as candidate for Wallabies' coach, 143
   gives AJ advice on rugby, 57, 138
   meets AJ at Brisbane Grammar, 64–5
   as a mentor to Poidevin, 149
   as Wallabies' assistant coach, 148–9, 151, 167

Fahey, John, 243, 247, 278, 289–90, 329, 361
FAI, 307
Fairfax Press, 372
Fancutt, Trevor, 54
Farmhand Foundation, 434–5, 449, 501n
Farr, Malcolm, 52, 53
Farr-Jones, Nick
   AJ opposes promotion of, 178
   on AJ's coaching style, 169

Farr-Jones, Nick cont.
   as captain of the Wallabies, 246
   informed of South African tour, 177
   injuries, 176, 180
   left out of Test side, 180–1
   maiden Test, 150
   Mark Ella on, 182
   not paid by Elphick, 479n
   opinion of AJ, 183
   player of tour in NZ Test, 167
   playing style, 162
   relationship with AJ, 162
   reprimanded by AJ, 146, 153, 156, 174
   as a rival of Brian Smith, 180
   seeks to calm AJ, 168
   selected by AJ for Wallabies, 145
   strategy with Mark Ella, 149
Fay, Peter, 96, 120
federal elections
   (1980), 125
   (2001), 419–22
   (2004), 452
Federation of Australian Broadcasters, 402
Fenton, Peter, 142, 147
Ferguson, Martin, 281
Festival of Light, 498n
Fewtrell, James, 218, 220–1
Fiander, Henry (Toby), 77
Field, Craig, 282, 283
Fiji, 145–6
Fine Cotton affair, 297
Finger Wharf development, 314, 316, 317
Fischer, Tim, 361
Fitzgerald Inquiry, 192, 245, 278
FitzSimons, Peter, 136, 137, 146, 217, 286
Fletcher, Ken, 37
Flint, David, 376–9, 381–2, 398, 406, 432
For a Lark (horse), 318
Fordham, John, 158, 197, 198, 199, 322, 386, 406–7
Fordham, Veronica, 227
Forsyth, Frederick, 224, 228
Four Corners (TV program), ix, xi, 421, 462

4AK, 240
4BC, 234, 407, 429
Foxtel, 285, 287, 288, 293, 434
Francis, Bruce, 177
Fraser, Malcolm, 103, 122–6, 131, 135
Freehill Hollingdale and Page, 295
Freeman, Cathy, 446
Freeman, Gary, 232, 237, 238, 239, 245, 246, 248
Freestyle (horse), 303
French, Joe, 230
French rugby team, 176
Freudenberg, Graham, 191
Fydler, Chris, 303, 320

Gabb, Ken, 116, 118
Gamble, Neil, 354
Geddes, Ross, 210, 304
Gemell, Peter, 85, 93
George, Jennie, 281, 361–2
George, Wendy, 347
Geyer, Mark, 250
Gibbs, Nathan, 296
Gibson, Dave, 203, 325
Gibson, Mel, 454
Gibson, Mike, 258
Gittins, Ross, 434
Goldsmith, Dr Marlene, 329–30
Good Weekend, 204, 336
Gordon, Andy, 27
Gordon, Harry, 372
Gordon, Ken, 18–19
Gordon, Strath, 370
Gore, Mike, 194
Gould, Mark, 39, 41, 44, 50, 51–2, 54, 66
Gould, Roger, 143, 151, 175–6, 183
Gould, Warwick, 41
Gowing, Doug, 106, 114–15
GPS rugby, 56–7
Grant, James, 228
Greater Public Schools, 26–7
Greiner, Nick, 190, 242–3
Greyhound Coaches, 327
Grigg, Peter, 150, 176
Grimm, Graham, 116–17
Grove, Michael, 247, 251, 252

Hackett, Grant, 303
Hadley, Ray, 398, 457
Hall, Jim, 366
Hall, Ollie, 476n
Halliday, Sir George, 96
Hand, Peter, 403
Hanna, Norm, 15
Hannaford, John
  on AJ in Greek national costume, 117–18
  AJ's treatment of, 336
  as Attorney-General, 252, 266, 280
  blamed by AJ for failed preselection, 120, 132
  fails to remember AJ, 276–7
  lobbied by AJ re Kalajzich case, 252
  as a moderate Liberal, 119, 191
  reprimanded by AJ re compensation, 280
  rules out inquiry into Kalajzich case, 266
Hansen, Frank, 412
Hanson, Pauline, 312–14, 332–3, 345, 358
HarperCollins, 323, 382, 390
Harrison, Adrian, 104
Harth, William, 10
Hartigan, John, 368
Harvey, Peter, 94
Harvey, Sandra, 266
Hatton, John, 278
Havers, Sue, 200
Hawke, Bob, 135, 159, 172, 177, 178, 382
Hawke, Brett, 303
Hawker, Michael, 148, 444
Hay, Nev, 37–8, 45
Hayden, Bill, 125–6, 135, 171
Hazzard, Brad, 247
Heenan, Len 'Pud', 24–5, 27, 32, 33
Henderson, Gerard, 19, 21, 125, 242
Henderson, Kerry, 388
Henry, Pauline, 105, 108
Hewson, Dr John, 164, 249
Highfield, John, 196
Hill, Michael, 366–7
Hill, Noel, 79, 106

Hill, Sinclair, 79
Hill, Terry, 283–4
Hilton, Jeffrey, 383
Hinch, Derryn, 271, 275
hire car industry, 352–3, 436
Hollway, Sandy, 371
Holmes, Michael, 439, 440
Holmes, Terry, 198, 480n
homosexuality, 64, 91, 127–8, 260, 267–8, 455–6, 468
Hong Kong and Shanghai Hotels, 326
Hopman, Harry, 37, 45, 114
Horton, Peter, 405–6, 407
hospitals, 437–8, 501–2n
Howard, John
    AJ favours Abbott as successor of, 360
    AJ gives advice to, 34
    AJ's attitude towards, 301
    AJ's support for, 419, 461
    appeasement of AJ by, 363, 460
    appoints AJ to Institute of Sport, 335
    on Bjelke-Petersen as PM, 173
    calls election (1998), 334
    changes mind on sale of Snowy Hydro, 451
    controls influence of AJ in office, 304
    criticised by Marise Payne, 330
    grows up in Earlwood, 116
    humours AJ, 449
    interviewed by AJ, 394, 459
    opinion of talkback radio, 209
    ranks fourth in list of powerful, 431
    resists AJ's influence, 364
    as rival to Bob Hawke, 172
    told by AJ to reappoint Flint, 406–7
    treatment of by media, 451
    views on media, 378
    wins 1996 election, 298–9
    writes to AJ, 362, 364
Howell, Max, 53, 55, 59, 62–3, 65
Hughes, Graham, 246
Hughes, Kim, 177
Hughes, Tom, 383

Humphreys, Ian, 83–4, 86–7, 94, 95
Humphreys, Kevin, 296
Hunt, Ralph, 102
Hutton, Drew, 49, 53
Hypothetical (television program), 203

Iemma, Morris, 437, 450–1, 461
Independent Commission Against Corruption, 243, 280, 353, 354, 502n
Ingham, Walter, 69, 73
Inkster, Bob, 280, 294
Insurance Australia Group, 444–5
International Rugby Board, 152, 164
International Year of the Indigenous Person, 256
Ireland, 151
Irish rugby team, 176
Irish Rugby Union, 232
Ironside Primary School, 38–41
Ita, 203, 221
Izatt, David, 51

Jack, Garry, 232, 238, 248, 250, 258
Jamberoo, 293, 454
James, Clive, 45, 110, 160
James, Henry, 48
'James' (street kid), 411–12, 420, 438, 498n
Jaoweir people, 9
Japanese rugby team, 176
Jenkins, Andrew, 57, 58–9
Jenkins, Peter, 183
Job Network, 359
Johnstone, Tony, 70, 81–2
Jones, Alan (racing car driver), 196
Jones, Caroline, 17, 29, 54, 109, 111, 122, 125, 171, 189
Jones, Charles Thomas (AJ's father)
    admiration for Ben Chifley, 14
    AJ on, 13
    attempts to settle in Sydney, 192
    birth, 5
    buys back father's farm, 11–12
    character, 18
    courts Elizabeth Brady, 10
    death, 227
    eldest of five children, 7

Jones, Charles Thomas (AJ's father) cont.
  financial worries, 26
  fondness for betting, 18
  lives in Acland, 4
  lives on Brady property, 8
  love of sport, 17
  moves to Brisbane, 60
  pleased about AJ's coaching appointment, 143
  pride in AJ's tennis prowess, 27
  sayings of, 18, 19
  supports AJ against criticism, 186
  works in mines, 13
Jones, Clarence Joseph (AJ's uncle), 5, 7, 13
Jones, Colleen (AJ's sister), 4, 26, 42, 66
Jones, Eddie, 188, 370–1
Jones, Elizabeth (Beth) (AJ's mother)
  AJ's tribute to, 19
  becomes ill, 60
  belief in education as a liberator, 21–2
  correspondence with AJ, 27, 66
  dresses AJ well, 15–16
  encourages AJ at school, 28
  expertise as a cook, 13
  falls ill and dies, 130
  family of, 9
  as a governess, 10
  hairbrushing ritual with AJ, 18
  lives in Acland, 4
  marries Charles Jones, 11
  moves to Brisbane, 60
  as a musician, 17
  pride in AJ's tennis prowess, 27
  as a teacher, 8–9, 10, 11
  as a tennis player, 17
  works in pharmacy, 10
  works on farm, 12
Jones, Hunter (AJ's great-nephew), 455
Jones, John Reginald (AJ's uncle), 5, 7
Jones, John Thomas (AJ's grandfather), 5–7, 8, 23
Jones, Lindsay, 35–6, 38
Jones, Mary Anne (AJ's grandmother), 5, 6, 7
Jones, Mary Elizabeth (May) (AJ's aunty), 5, 8
Jones, Morgan (AJ's nephew), 218
Jones, Robert (AJ's brother)
  on AJ's dress sense, 36
  on AJ's experience in London, 198
  on AJ's strength, 30
  birth, 11
  at father's funeral, 227
  on Fraser's kindness, 124
  on his father, 13–14
  on his mother, 9, 10–11, 12
  at Kelvin Grove Teachers' College, 35
  lives in Acland, 4
  not recognised by AJ, 265
  pleased about AJ's coaching appointment, 143
  practises tennis with AJ, 16
  relationship with AJ, 30–1, 66
  schooldays, 15, 22, 23, 24
  similarity in nature to father, 19
Jones, Tonia (AJ's niece), 340, 455
Jones, Vincent (AJ's uncle), 5, 7, 17
JR Thomas and Company, 247
Julian, Brendan, 366

Kafer, Rod, 370
Kalajzich, Andrew
  AJ denies discussions with defence group of, 279
  AJ takes up cause of, 215–19, 247, 251–3, 265–6, 280, 486n
  charged with wife's murder, 164
  conviction confirmed by inquiry, 293–4
  denies knowledge of Britcorp scholarships, 218
  has application to reopen case dismissed, 251
  inquiry into conviction of, 266
  offers bribe to key witness, 279
  writes to AJ, 215
Kalajzich, Megan, 164, 215
Kalajzich, Pip, 486n
Kalajzich, Tony, 215
Katter, Bob, 312
Keating, Paul, 125, 236–7, 249, 290–2, 298

Kelly, De-Anne, 299
Kelly, Jackie, 491n
Kelvin Grove Teachers' College, 35–6
Kennerley, Kerri-Anne, 199, 322
Kenny, Niamh, 261, 304, 308, 309, 487n
Kenny, Paul, 223
Kerr, John, 103
Killen, John, 223, 244
The King's School, Canterbury, 83, 85–6
The King's School, Sydney, 65, 68–99
Kinross, Jeremy, 277, 374, 490n, 495n
Kirk, David, 193, 219
Kirkwood, Bob, 135
Knight, Michael, 348, 353, 371, 403
Knowles, Craig, 324, 354–6, 491n
Kolback, 354–5
Korean rugby team, 175
Kroger, Michael, 303, 334
Kuhl, Max, 4, 12
Kurrle, Canon Stanley
  accompanies AJ on tour to England, 84
  on AJ as a sports coach, 78
  on AJ's appointment to King's School, 65
  on AJ's arrival at King's School, 68
  on AJ's conservatism, 72
  on AJ's position on religion, 88
  receives letter of complaint about AJ, 90–1
  sacks AJ, 96, 97, 98
  supports AJ's political ambitions, 117, 118
Kurrle, Lorna, 78
Kurrle, Winton, 73, 80
Kuwait, Iraqi invasion of, 224

Lamb family, 239, 406
Lamb, Stewart, 239
land tax, 346
Lane, David, 96
Lane, Robert, 96, 134
Langdon, Louise, 241
Larry King Live (television program), 271
Lateline (television program), 334

Laurence, Lawrie, 48
Laver, Rod, 37
Lawrence, Carmen, 273
Laws, John
  appeasement of by politicians, 277, 300
  attacks AJ's partisanship, 334
  cash for comment, 375–6, 382–3, 394
  commercial deal with Telstra, 431
  compared with AJ, 235–7
  considered guilty by AJ in ABA inquiry, 399
  corporate endorsements by, 325
  does advertisements for AMP, 255
  Fordham as manager of, 158
  found in breach of broadcasting code, 432
  interviews Andrew Denton, 325
  interviews David Flint, 382
  interviews Kim Beazley, 419
  interviews Paul Keating, 290
  John Fordham as manager of, 322
  Kenny produces for, 487n
  Media Watch begins investigation of, 322
  mutual animosity with AJ, 230–1, 235–6, 249, 291, 325, 372, 406–7, 414–15
  opposes Priest's compensation claim, 440
  ratings (2006), 445
  relationship with Keating, 237
  returns to 2UE from 2GB, 186
  rings AJ to offer comfort, 197
  rivalry with AJ, 248–9
  signs deal with Optus, 261
  on television, 288
Lawton, Tom, 176
Lazarus, Glenn, 246
Lee, Brent, 302
Legge, Kate, 500n
Leighton Holdings–Showboat consortium, 278
Lensbury Club, 195
Leser, David, 18, 92, 308, 310, 336, 372
Lewis, Sir Terence, 245

Liberal Party
  AJ hosts fundraiser for, 394
  AJ's contempt for wets in, 125
  AJ's relationship to, xi
  factions within, 119–20
  links with Australian rugby, 104
  in New South Wales, 290, 335–6, 347, 429–30
  revived under Nick Greiner, 190
  use of Tim Priest, 439
Liebmann, Steve, 199, 443, 478n
Lillee, Dennis, 200
Lime Taxis, 500–1n
Linnell, Garry, 443
Littlejohn, Dick, 177
Littlemore, Stuart, 224, 273–4, 377
Lloyd Williams Crown Towers development, 317
Lo Po, Faye, 349–50, 491n
Lochore, Brian, 168–9
Lockett, Tony, 371
Loosley, Stephen, 191, 197
Lowy family, 318
Lowy, Frank, 441
Luck, Peter, 276
Lundy, Kate, 335
'lurkies', 69
Lutyens, Alexandra, 328
Lynagh, Michael, 145, 154, 161, 166, 180, 479n
Lyndeal, 239
Lyons, John, 383, 396

Mabo decision, 256
Macquarie Bank, 431, 500–1n
Macquarie Broadcasting, 427
Macquarie Group, 428
Macquarie Network, 401–3
Macqueen, Rod, 319, 370
Magnus, Michael, 491n
Mandleson, Peter, 355
Maniaty, Tony, 35, 39
Manly Pacific Hotel, 141, 164
Manly Rugby Club, 134–42
Mann, David, 391, 397
Mansfield, Bob, 264, 288, 434
Many, Fred, 289
Marel, Alan, 224

Maritime Union of Australia, 330–1, 345
market research, 453
Marks, Dick, 143
Marr, David, 383, 400, 428, 434, 435
Marsden, John, 190
Marsh, Rod, 200
Mason, John, 115, 119, 121–2
Mason, Keith, 244
Masters, Geoff, 54
Masters, Roy, x, 222, 250, 259
Maudsley family, 10
McArdle, Chris, 158, 159
McCarthy, Bob, 268, 366
McClelland, David, 94
McDonald, Bruce, 112, 119, 243
McDonald, Ian 'Macca', 135
McGeoch, Tony, 134, 136–7, 140
McGregor, Malcolm, 191, 197, 201
McLeod-Lindsey, Alexander, 251
McMahon, Sonia, 71
McMahon, William, 102
McNab, Duncan, 219
McNiece, Graeme, 319
McPherson, Ken, 15
McWhirter, Grant, 310
Meade, Amanda, 413
Meagher, Ron, 231
Media Watch (television program)
  Ackland researches files of, 390
  AJ asked for response to, 388
  AJ on, 375
  on AJ's attempts to turn rivers around, 434–5
  on AJ's name for the new Pope, 449
  David Flint on, 376–7
  exposes AJ's plagiarism, 224
  investigates John Laws' sponsorship deals, 322, 375
  observes AJ's attitude to Telstra, 273–4
  on the publication of *Jonestown*, 465–6
Menzies Coalition Government, 47
Mercedes-Benz, 310, 444
Messara, Ann, 354
Messara, John, 302, 354–5, 356

Metherell, Terry, 119, 243
Midday (television program), 322
Milan, Nigel, 186, 197, 201, 204, 210–11, 235
Milat, Ivan, 407
Milford State School, 11
Millar, Stephanie, 291
Miller, Harry M
  ABA studies files of, 384, 387
  advises AJ to agree to interview, 336
  advises AJ to drop grievance with Qantas, 488n
  on AJ as Fraser's speechwriter, 123
  AJ writes to about Walker contract, 392
  as AJ's agent, 173, 225
  as AJ's friend, 302
  AJ's perception of regarding contracts, 385–6
  on AJ's plagiarism, 225
  on AJ's sign-on bonus, 295
  approached by State Bank, 307
  asked by AJ to sort out coffee claims, 316
  avoids questioning by ABA inquiry, 386
  becomes Scott Miller's agent, 319
  brokers deals for AJ, 261–4, 271, 287–8, 292, 310, 314–15, 323, 327, 337
  calls Sheedy a fool, 397
  ceases to be AJ's agent, 426
  considered as Liberal adviser, 491n
  denies AJ's payment for live reads, 336
  Kalajzich defence considers services of, 215
  on Keating, 291
  on the Laws-Jones conflict, 291
  lives in Woolloomooloo warehouse, 165
  measures Laws' office space, 235
  negotiates cut of AJ's advertising revenue, 222
  offended by Conde's letter to 2UE staff, 324
  organises meeting between AJ and Collins, 333

Miller, Harry M cont.
  placates Optus executives, 328–9
  sends gushing fax to Lutyens, 328–9
  speaks to Lang Walker, 314
  used as scapegoat by AJ, 315
  vets interview requests for AJ, 203
  writes to AJ about Mirvac contract, 397
Miller, Scott, 303, 308, 318–19, 320, 491n
Milne, Charles, 76, 79
Milne, Enid, 79
Milne, John, 79
Milne, Peter, 76, 101
Milner, James, 214
Mirvac, 323, 326, 391, 397
Mishcon, Lord Victor, 196, 197

Mishcon de Reya (company), 196
Mitchell, Alex, 293
Moir, Alan, 423
'The Moonlight State' litigation, 463, 464
Moore, Nicholas, 431
Morgan, Simon, 336
Moroney, Ken, 405, 438, 439, 452
Moscow Olympics, 125
Moss, Bill, 431, 500n
Mossop, Rex, 246
Mr Freeze (horse), 354
Mullin, Brendan, 194, 199
Mulray, Doug, 186, 193, 203, 228
Multiplex, 314
Murdoch, Rupert, 285–6, 287, 296, 310, 367
Murphy, Paul, 174
Murray, JL 'Legs', 44
My Husband, My Killer (Harvey), 266

narcissism, 472–3n
NASCA, 257
National Aboriginal Sports Corporation Australia, 257
National Australia Day Council, 256
National Convention Centre, 203
National Rugby League, 321, 367
National Telecom Group, 494n

Neal, Stuart, 462, 463–4, 466
The Negotiator (Forsyth), 224
Negus, George, 111–12, 166, 199
Nelson, HG, 245, 260, 424
Network Seven, 443
Network Ten, 271, 272, 275
New Idea, 111, 202
New South Wales Bureau of Crime Statistics and Research, 425
New South Wales Department of Transport, 352–3
New South Wales Employers' Federation, 126, 135, 138, 146, 158, 423
New South Wales Institute of Sport, 335
New South Wales Police Force, 446–7
New South Wales Police Legal Department, 439
New South Wales Rugby League, 257, 258
New South Wales Rugby Union, 129
New South Wales state elections
　(1991), 243
　(1999), 345
　(2003), 436–7
　(2007), 460–1
New Zealand rugby team, 147, 164, 167–70, 176–7
Newcombe, Jill, 261, 309
Newell, Harry, 48, 53
Newmarch, Walter, 89
News Limited, 285, 286, 296–7, 310, 367, 373
Newtown, 454
Nicklin Coalition Government (Qld), 47
Nicklin, Lenore, 203
Nietzsche, Friedrich, 209
Norder, Laura, 420, 498n
North Sydney Bears, 219
North Sydney, seat of, 119
Nova, 442
NRMA Insurance, 444–5

Oakey Public School, 15, 21
O'Brien, Mark, 462, 465
O'Doherty, Stephen, 490n

O'Farrell, Barry, 490n, 491n
Olle, Andrew, 53, 473n
Olle, Annette, 473n
Olympic Games
　(1980), 125
　(1996), 307
　(2000), 289, 318, 348, 371–2, 403
'On This Day' radio segment, 240
One Nation, 312, 313
O'Neill, John, 319–20, 370–1
O'Neill, Julian, 283, 320, 489n
Optus
　advertising with 2UE, 287
　AJ editorialises about on TV, 396
　AJ's mobile phone promotion, 387
　AJ's view of deal with, 384
　cancels deal with AJ, 397, 444
　contracts with AJ, 261–4, 274–6, 288–9, 292, 304, 326, 327–9, 382, 384
　contracts with John Laws, 382
　denies contract with AJ, 293
　Packer's shareholdings in, 285
Optus Vision, 285
Osbaldeston, Elizabeth, 9
Oxford University, 108–12, 163, 182, 193, 218–21

Packer, James
　AJ complains about employee to, 365–6
　AJ criticised for support of, 373
　AJ tries to get onside with, 288
　on cross-media ownership, 311–12
　David Flint attends wedding of, 382
　praises AJ, 302–3
　sells 75 per cent of PBL, 443
　shares racehorse with AJ and Scott Miller, 318
　sits on Optus Vision Board, 285
Packer, Kerry
　AJ complains about casino table to, 34
　AJ takes friends to visit, 260–1
　argues with Keating over media ownership, 292
　asked to send jet for AJ's sick friend, 322

Packer, Kerry cont.
    on Australia's water problems, 434
    bids for casino licence, 278
    called a media bully by AJ, 129
    death and funeral, 442
    doubles AJ's salary, 165
    as a Farmhand Foundation
        principal, 434
    as a friend of AJ, 302
    gives money to Rabbitohs, 284
    listed seventh in list of powerful,
        441
    pays close attention to television
        interests, 443
    puts money into World Rugby
        Corporation, 286
    rugby war with Murdoch, 285–6
    sells 2UE back to Lamb family,
        239
    support for AJ, 199
    supports Labor in NSW, 118
    tries to gain control of Westpac
        board, 255
Palm Motor Inn, 489n
Pankratov, Denis, 308
Park Hyatt Hotel, 243
Parker, David, 214
Parkinson, Michael, 5
Parklea Gaol, 216
Parry, Ross, 57, 58–9
Pass, Charles, 498n
Patrick Stevedores, 331
pay television, 285, 287–8, 292–3, 384
Payne, Marise, 330
PBL, 285, 286, 311, 443
Peacock, Andrew, 172, 299
Pearce, Jim, 117, 118
Pearce, Wayne, 232, 268
Pendleton, David, 466
Perkins, Charles, 257, 483n
Persse, Jonathan, 98
Philippousis, Mark, 302, 325
Philips (company), 248
Phillips, Ron, 277
Phillips, Tom, 19
Photios, Michael, 75, 490n
The Piano Factory, 316
Pickering, Ted, 119, 132, 191, 277,
    329

Pickhaver, Greig, 246
Piggins, George, 282, 284, 321, 367,
    368, 369
Pilecki, Stan, 152–3, 154, 155
Pohl, Ziggy, 251
Poidevin, Simon
    on AJ's coaching, 146, 167, 170
    as AJ's friend, 302
    on Alex Evans, 149
    defends AJ from criticism, 179, 183
    on post-match happy hour, 154
    reprimanded for fraternising,
        168–9
    in Wallabies team against England,
        151
Polain, John, 85, 89, 95
police corruption, 64, 245, 278–9,
    404–5, 412, 420–1
Police Integrity Commission, 420–1
Porter, Brian, 70, 79, 81–2, 87, 88,
    90, 92
Pratt, Dick, 434
Price, Leontine, 28
Priebe, Jim, 23–4
Priest, 'Rusty', 408, 409, 416
Priest, Timothy
    AJ on, 412
    AJ tries to elevate credibility of,
        430
    on AJ's meeting with Carr, 423
    alleged service with SAS, 498n,
        500n
    attends law and order rally, 498n
    brings action against Chris
        Masters, 440
    celebrated by AJ as a hero, 408,
        438
    considered a troublemaker by
        Small, 407
    Costa writes affidavit for, 440
    demands $2.5 million in
        compensation, 439–40
    denies discussion about AJ dirt file,
        499n
    as a detective at Cabramatta,
        405–6
    drinks with Michael Costa, 423
    given award by Festival of Light,
        498n

Priest, Timothy cont.
  heads Crime Advisory Group, 439
  hires bodyguards, 415
  investigated by ICAC, 280
  makes false allegations, 408–10, 438
  paranoia of, 415, 416
  promises to resign, 413
  quits job in ministry, 424
  wins bravery award after AJ's intervention, 439
propaganda, 300
Publishing and Broadcasting Limited, 285, 286, 311, 443
Puplick, CJ, 119
Pursehouse, Mal, 106

Qantas, 314–15, 326, 382, 384, 389, 396, 488n
Quayle, John, 309
Queensland, 64
Queensland State Archive, 6
Quirindi, 104–7, 112–13, 114–15

Rabbitohs *see* South Sydney Rugby League club
Rankin, Roy, 61
Ratzinger, Cardinal, 449
Rawards (1990), 228
Read, Harry, 72–3
Read, Mark 'Chopper', 322
Reading, Stephen, 196, 198
Rees, Lloyd, 38
Refshauge, Andrew, 350, 492n
Regurgitator (band), 346
Rehame study, 334
Renshaw family, 79
republican debate, 376
Retton, Mary Lou, 308
Reynolds, Ross, 134, 150
Richardson, Graham, 403, 487n
Ritchie, David, 365
Rivkin, Rene, 193, 194, 302
Roach, Steve, 228, 229, 232–3, 250
Robb, Andrew, 374
Roberts, Angus, 74
Roberts, Anthony, 363, 364
Roberts, John, 108, 112, 115
Roberts, Kerry, 255

Roberts, Lyle, 74
Roberts, Muriel, 115
Robertson, Geoffrey, 203
Robertson, Joan, 15
Robinson, Will, 240
Rodriguez, Topo, 154, 166
Rogers, Bob, 457
Rogerson, Roger, 331
A Room of One's Own (Woolf), 54
Rostrum Association, 160
Roughsedge, Barbara, 309
Rousseau, Jean Jacques, 476n
Rowe, Normie, 225
Roy & HG, 246, 260, 424
Roy Morgan Research, 456
Royal Agricultural Society, 429
Royal Commission into Police Corruption (Qld), 64
Royal Pines Resort, 244
Ruddock, Philip, 359–60, 431
Rugby League, 229–30
The Rugby War (FitzSimons), 286
Rugby World Cup, 174, 175–6, 183, 369–70
Rush, Rodney, 16, 23–4, 25, 31, 33
Russell, Geraldine, 161
Ryan, Peter
  AJ criticises, 4, 420, 430
  AJ's campaign against, 331, 403–5, 439
  AJ's disappointment with, 333
  attacked by Chikarovski, 345
  and Clive Small, 407
  criticised by Basham, 411
  has no knowledge of AJ dirt file, 416
  initiates inquiries into corruption, 420
  sacked by Carr, 430
  sidelines Geoff Schuberg, 411
  and Tim Priest, 409, 413
Ryan, Warren, 231, 238, 366, 494n

Sabine school, 10
Salmon, Ian, 255
Sanctuary Cove, 194
Sanford Orcas (property), 454
Sattler, Howard, 382
SBS, 385

Scargill, Arthur, 110
Schacht, Madonna
  on AJ's analysis of games, 45
  on AJ's first house, 60
  on AJ's lack of political activism, 63
  on AJ's relationship to his mother, 60
  on AJ's work ethic, 55
  hears story of AJ's interview, 48
  meets AJ at Sanctuary Cove, 200
  relationship with AJ, 38, 41–2, 66, 189–90
  retrieves child from Austria, 92
Schloss, Jeremy, 489n
Schmidt, Marcus, 417–19, 425–6
Schofield, Victoria, 111
Schools' Rugby Union, 87
Schuberg, Geoff, 411, 415, 430
Scotland, 153–4
Scott, Jane, 241, 261
Scott, Lola, 438
Scully, Carl, 4, 350–4, 436
Search for Meaning (radio program), 54, 189
7.30 Report (television program), 389
Sharp, John, 73, 330
Sharples, Terry, 357–8
Shaw, George Bernard, 476n
Sheahan pharmacy, 10
Sheedy, Brendan, 397
Sheldon, Bruce, 283
Shier, Jonathan, 464
Shine, Ken, 232, 238, 268
Shipstone, Graham, 39, 44
Shirley, Bernard, 315, 488n
Short, Brian, 65, 66
Shrapnel, Helen, 15
Simkin, Andy, 75, 93, 107
Simkin, Chris, 75, 77, 85, 89
Simkin family, 80
Simkin, Marie, 80
Simons, Margaret, 466
Simper, Errol, 393
Sinclair, Jacin, 258–9, 267–8, 283, 310, 320, 369
Singers of Renown, 51

Singleton, John
  caught speeding, 403
  encourages AJ during sickness, 402
  as a Farmhand Foundation principal, 434
  helps raise money for Olympics, 225
  makes job offer to AJ, 295
  on negotiations to sign AJ, 427
  offers AJ share in 2GB, 413
  offers to pay for authorised biography, xiii
  reaps profits after signing AJ, 429
  reprimands broadcaster for criticising AJ, 403
  supports AJ in London, 198
  threatens to sue 2UE, 402
  wants AJ for 2GB, 401–2
  writes to AJ, 402–3
Sironen, Paul, 232, 237, 259, 268
6PM, 165
60 Minutes (television program), 179, 188, 411
Skinner, Jillian, 490n
Sky network, 407
Sky Radio, 397
Skyways, 104–5, 112
Slack, Andrew
  on AJ as a coach, 144
  approached for South African tour, 177
  criticised by AJ for wearing All Black jersey, 170
  defends AJ, 183
  flies to South Africa, 178
  made captain by AJ, 144
  on mock test tour, 174
  not paid by Elphick, 479n
  speaks at post-match happy hour, 154
  support for AJ, 322
Slattery, John, 266, 294
Slaven, Roy, 246, 260, 424
Small, Clive, 407, 416, 424, 430, 438, 499n
Smith, Brian
  AJ books room at Ritz for, 200
  AJ on, 175, 217
  as AJ's favourite, 180–1, 182, 259

Smith, Brian cont.
  calls in AJ to coach Oxford team, 219–20
  debut match, 175
  drops out of Oxford team, 481n
  elected captain of Oxford team, 218
  eschews Kirk's advice on diplomacy, 219
  goes to AJ's assistance, 196
  innuendoes over AJ's relationship with, 188
  made honorary Irishman, 217
  at Oxford University, 193
  persuaded by AJ to try League, 232–3
  plays for Balmain Tigers, 238, 245, 259
  replaces Farr-Jones, 176
  selected for Sydney City side, 248
  sledging of by Eddie Jones, 370
  supports AJ after his arrest, 199
Smith, Brian (St George coach), 265
Smith, Greg, 319
Smith, Michael Gordon, 382, 392
Smith, Neddy, 329
Smith, Roland, 190
Sneddon, Ron, 244
Snowy Hydro scheme, 451
'socking', 72
Solomon, Peter, 120
Sony, 236, 307, 396
South Africa, 164, 171, 172, 176–7
South African Rugby Board, 177
South Sydney Rugby League club, 268, 281–5, 295–6, 310, 320–1, 366–9, 390, 489n
Southern Cross Network, 406, 407, 413, 428, 429
Spencer, Brenda, 82
Spencer, Peter, 72, 82, 91
Spender, John, 121, 199
Spicer, John, 117
spin doctors, 300
St Catherine's School, Stanthorpe, 9
St Denis Hospital, Toowoomba, 7
St George and Sutherland Leader, 118
St Joseph's Nudgee College, 56, 58
St Margaret's Anglican Girls School, 26
Stafford Hotel, 480n
Stanley, John, 197
Stannard, David, 15
Stanthorpe Public School, 10
Stargames, 354
Starr, Peter *see* Collis, Peter
State Bank of New South Wales, 306–7, 326
State Rail Authority (NSW), 423, 437
Stefanovic, Karl, 443
Steinmetz, John, 409–10
Steyne Hotel, 141
Stitt, Bob, 297–8
Stokes, Kerry, 368
Stone, George, 267
Stone, Gerald, 427
Stone, Judy, 225
Strathfield Hire Cars, 310, 352
Stromberg Carlson (horse), 18
Struggle Street, xii, 258
Stuart, Ricky, 180, 322
Stubbs, Bill, 22, 29, 32
Stylis, Dr Stanley, 364
Sugarloaf mine, 13
Suich, Max, 327, 328
Sullivan, Alan, 283
Sun (Brisbane), 186
Sun Herald, 217, 224–5, 282, 283, 293, 298
Sunday Telegraph, 72, 160, 225, 227, 272, 278, 295, 296
Sunraysia, 310–11, 382, 390, 396
Superleague, 285–6, 367–8
Sutton, Lyndall, 304
Swan, Wayne, 361
Sydney Casino, 278
Sydney Cricket Ground Trust, 190, 335
Sydney Institute, 377
Sydney Morning Herald
  on AJ and Bhutto, 111
  AJ supporter writes to, 394
  AJ's perception of, 372, 373, 376, 399
  on AJ's speechwriting, 122
  on AJ's TV debut, 273

Sydney Morning Herald cont.
  Brennan compares AJ to Jesus in, 502–3n
  examines AJ's correspondence, 356–7
  on exchange between AJ and Roy Masters, 250
  investigates cash for comment contracts, 389, 390–1
  on Kalajzich inquiry, 266
  Marr asks AJ about reading contracts, 428
  publishes extracts from *Jonestown*, 468
  sued by AJ, 284
  Whitton apologises to AJ in, 153
Sydney Sleep Clinic, 364
Szubanski, Magda, 443

Tabberer, Maggie, 213
Talbot, Don, 133
talkback radio, 190, 209, 452
Taylor, Bill, 25
telecommunications industry, 261–4
Telecom/Telstra
  AJ denies likelihood of deal with, 388
  approaches 2UE for advertising, 287, 288
  cancels deal with AJ, 444
  commercial deals with Laws and AJ, 431–2
  criticised by AJ on air, 262, 263–4, 274, 327–8
  gives to Farmhand Foundation, 434
  Miller plays off against Optus, 261
  rivalry with Optus, 262
  share in Foxtel, 285
Telstra *see* Telecom/Telstra
Templeton, Bob, 143, 144, 151
Thatcher, Margaret, 191, 195
Thomas, John, 215, 218, 247
Thompson, Les, 10, 13, 23, 24, 25, 32, 227
Thoroughbred Racing Board, 298
3AK, 165
Tickner, Robert, 256, 299
The Times, 220

Tink, Andrew, 421
Tissuegate, 321, 398
To Protect and Serve (Priest), 409, 498n
The Toaster, 326, 385, 454
Today (television program), 292, 307, 396, 435, 442–3
Toowoomba, 22
Toowoomba Grammar School, 22–34
Transfield, 323, 326
Travers, Carmel, 273
Trenet, Charles, 84
Trewin, Patricia, 43
Trewin, Steve, 62
Treyvaud, Ross, 411, 415, 423, 498n
Trindall, Darrell 'Tricky'
  AJ finds employment for, 431, 500–1n
  plays for Canterbury Bulldogs, 369
  plays for South Sydney, 282–3
  relationship with AJ, 257
  suggested as Olympic Games promoter, 371
  violent behaviour of, 282–4, 366–7, 369, 416–17, 494n
Trinity Grammar School, 175
Tucker, James (Jim), 183
Turnbull, Greg, 291, 421–2, 423
Turnbull, Malcolm, 128–9
Turnbull, Ross
  AJ meets Fordham through, 158
  flies to London to help AJ, 199
  as a friend of AJ, 128, 302
  hosts function at Sanctuary Cove, 194
  insists AJ not homosexual, 188
  leaves NSW Rugby Union under a cloud, 217
  oversees Concord Oval renovation, 175
  persuades AJ to include Farr-Jones, 181
  plays tennis with AJ, 128
  sees futility of South African tour, 178
  starts scholarship scheme with AJ, 193

Turnbull, Ross cont.
  supports AJ as Australian coach, 140, 142, 319, 370
  supports commercialisation of rugby union, 286
Tutu, Archbishop, 171
Tuynman, Steve, 152
Twine, Graeme, 53, 77
2GB
  AJ signs contract with, 427–8
  AJ's ratings at, 461
  on AJ's trip to London (2006), 459
  convicted of contempt of court, 482n
  courts AJ, 295, 401–3
  gives to Farmhand Foundation, 434
  Laws leaves, 186
  management unable to rein AJ in, 457
  new premises at Pyrmont, 455
  share value rockets, 428
2JJJ, 246, 260, 426
2KY, 182, 250
2NZ, 234–5
2UE
  AJ moves to different timeslot on, 186
  AJ resigns from, 426
  AJ worries about job with, 201
  AJ's advertising deals on, 222–3
  appeals in David Parker case, 214
  audience demographics, 305, 338–9
  bought by Packer, 165
  bought by Southern Cross, 407
  concern over personal endorsements, 324
  conducts interviews with AJ from Britain, 157–8
  investigated by the ABA, 375–6, 380–2, 395–6
  Lamb family considers selling, 406
  Laws and AJ at, 230–1
  moves to Gore Hill premises, 235
  renegotiates contract with AJ, 295
  share price weakens, 264
  Singleton threatens to sue, 402
  sold to Lamb family by Packer, 239
  tires of AJ, 398

'Uglies', 119–20
United States' rugby team, 176
Unsworth, Barrie, 190, 191
Urbanchich, Lyenko, 119, 120, 277

Vaile, Mark, 361
Vale, Dana, 299, 487n
Vandenberg, Bill, 216
Vandenberg, Grant, 272
Vanstone, Amanda, 4, 289–90, 361–2, 363
Variety Club, 225
Veal, Philip, 472n
Vessey, Rupert, 193
Victorian Corporate Affairs Commission, 223
Viethar, Col, 13
Vievers, Betty, 38, 41
violence, incitement of, 446–7
Visy Industries, 434
Vittoria Coffee, 316
Voller, Geoff, 43, 129
Voller, Opal, 43

Waite, Keith, 280, 405
Wales rugby team, 151–2, 176
Walker, Bret
  on AJ as an athletics coach, 80
  on AJ as an English teacher, 76
  as AJ's barrister at ABA inquiry, 383–6, 389, 395
  protests about AJ's sacking, 96
  sustains injury, 81
  undertakes hospital inquiry, 501–2n
Walker Corporation, 314, 316, 317, 382, 390–2, 396
Walker, Lang, 314
Walker, Scott, 80–1, 82, 89–90, 94–5
Walkley Award, 336
Wallabies
  AJ as coach of, 143–56, 161, 164, 166–70, 174–84
  AJ's hopes of returning to dashed, 217
  ARU boss rules out AJ's return to, 319
  Bob Dwyer as coach of, 219, 246
  Eddie Jones as coach of, 370–1

Wallabies cont.
   in World Cup competitions, 174, 175–6, 246, 369–71
Wallace, Deborah, 412–13, 438
Wallace, Ian, 215
Walsh Bay Finance, 323, 382, 390–3, 396–7
Walsh, Peter, 125
Ward, Chris, 238
Warner Brothers, 396
Waterfall train crash, 353, 436
Waterhouse, Gai, 297, 302
Waterhouse, Robbie, 297–8, 302
Watkins, John, 437, 440
Watts, Robyn, 462, 465, 466
Waugh, Mark, 34, 302
Weatherburn, Don, 425
Webb Ellis trophy, 369–70
Weber, Dr Rudolph, 92
Weekes, Richard, 121
Weidler, Danny, 282
Weise, Margaret, 15
Wendt, Jana, 179, 188
Wentworth, seat of, 128, 164–5
West, Michael, 75
West, Rod, 490n
West, Roderick, 71, 82, 84, 88, 93
Westfield, 318
Westpac, 254–5, 306
Whelan, Paul, 365, 411, 412, 423
White, Antony, 71, 74, 76–7, 92, 93, 103, 474n
White, Arthur, 71
White, Brian, 25, 30, 32
White, Dennis, 123–4
White, Edgar 'Bluey', 25
White family, 261, 302
White, Judy, 78, 103
White, Patrick, 474n
The Whites of Belltrees, 78
Whitlam, Gough, 102, 103

Whitney, Michael, 368
Whitrod, Ray, 245
Whittle, Ian, 50, 51, 54
Whitton, Evan, 143, 144, 151, 153
Wide World of Sports (television program), 239, 276
Wilkins, Phil, 147
Williams, Darryl, 363
Williams, Ian, 181, 192–3
Williams, Mrs (neighbour), 15
Williams, Steve, 134, 137, 138, 140, 149
Willis, Sir Eric, 115, 116
Willowburn Asylum, 6, 8
Wilson, 'Chilla', 151–2
Wilson, Harold, 109, 110
Witgers, Tony, 457
Women's World Basketball Championships, 281
Wood, Nathan, 282
Wood Royal Commission, 278, 404, 412
Woods, Kevin, 294
Woodward, Clive, 220
Wooldridge, Michael, 361, 363
Woolf, Virginia, 54
Woolooroo mine, 13
World Cup (rugby), 174, 175–6, 369–70
World Rugby Corporation, 286
Wran, Neville, 112, 116, 118, 119

Yabsley, Michael, 161, 199, 226, 243, 302
Yabsley, Susan, 161, 162, 165, 173, 199, 241
Yeend, Peter, 79
Young Liberals, 363
Yunupingu, Mandawuy, 256, 260

Zheng Haixia, 281